The Lion
CONCISE
BIBLE
HANDBOOK

Editors
David and Pat Alexander

Consulting Editors
David Field
Donald Guthrie
Gerald Hughes
Howard Marshall
Alan Millard

Outline-guide (Parts 2 and 3) by Pat Alexander

Illustrators
Mark Astle, Simon Bull, Pauline O'Boyle,
Angela Pluess, Dorothy Tucker,
Stanley Willcocks; maps by Roy Lawrence
and Lesley Passey

Published by
Lion Publishing
Icknield Way, Tring, Herts, England
ISBN 0 85648 311 7 (paperback edition)
ISBN 0 85648 312 5 (casebound edition)

Albatross Books
PO Box 320, Sutherland, NSW 2232, Australia
ISBN 0 86760 253 8 (paperback edition)
ISBN 0 86760 252 X (casebound edition)

First edition in this concise format 1980
Text from *The Lion Handbook to the Bible*
Copyright © 1973 Lion Publishing

Printed and bound in Italy
by International Publishing Enterprises

The Lion
CONCISE
BIBLE
HANDBOOK

PREFACE

The Lion Concise Bible Handbook is an informative, exciting book-by-book guide to the Bible, designed to bring out its meaning and help readers understand its content. It includes almost all the material from the main Old and New Testament sections of *The Lion Handbook to the Bible,* of which there are now one million copies in print worldwide.

The book is in three parts. The Introduction sets the scene. The second and third parts, on the Old and New Testaments, go through the Bible book by book, section by section. A heading or brief description gives the main theme. Notes on difficulties aid understanding. Drawings, maps and charts help build up a vivid and accurate picture of the setting of the passage. Brief articles by experts allow special interests to be followed up in more detail.

The emphasis of the book is on sheer information presented in a simple, helpful and visually interesting way. Many of the contributors have previously written at a technical level on subjects which they summarize here for a wide readership.

Technical questions of date and authorship have not been tackled as such. The major concern is the content and meaning of the Bible, rather than matters of introduction, and the text has been taken simply as it stands. Though positions have had to be assumed rather than argued, careful account has been taken of current scholarship, particularly findings from the Near East which help our understanding of the setting and meaning of the text.

The Editors are grateful to all those who have contributed to this book, directly or indirectly, and to those who have given help in many other ways. They are also grateful to the many people who have expressed their appreciation of the Handbook in its many languages throughout the world. It is hoped that this Concise edition will extend its ministry and usefulness still further.

CONTENTS

CONTRIBUTORS

The Rev. Dr Phillip J. Budd, Lecturer, Westminster College, Oxford and Ripon College, Cuddesdon *(The Sacrificial System, Feasts and Festivals)*

Sir Frederick Catherwood, Member of European Parliament and Chairman of Committee on External Economic Relations *(The Bible and Society)*

David J. A. Clines, Reader in Biblical Studies, Sheffield University *(The Apocrypha)*

The Rev. Arthur E. Cundall, Principal, Bible College of Victoria, Australia *(Unravelling the Chronology of the Kings)*

The Rev. David Field, Vice Principal, Oak Hill Theological College, London *(The Bible and Christian Living, The Kingdom of God and the Kingdom of Heaven)*

Dr Richard T. France, Warden of Tyndale House, Cambridge *(Jesus Christ and the Bible, The Religious Background of the New Testament)*

Canon Michael Green, Rector, St Aldate's Church, Oxford *(Early Christian Preaching)*

The Rev. Geoffrey W. Grogan, Principal, Bible Training Institute, Glasgow *(Holy Spirit in Acts)*

Dr Donald Guthrie, Vice-Principal, London Bible College *(The Letters: Introduction)*

Dr Colin J. Hemer, Lecturer in New Testament Studies, Manchester University *(The Historical and Political Background of the New Testament)*

Kenneth G. Howkins, Senior Lecturer in Religious Studies, Hertfordshire College of Higher Education *(Meeting Objections)*

The Rev. F. Derek Kidner, Formerly Warden, Tyndale House and Library for Biblical Research, Cambridge *(Poetry and Wisdom Literature: Introduction)*

I. Howard Marshall, Professor of New Testament Exegesis, University of Aberdeen *(The Gospels and Jesus Christ, The New Testament Miracles)*

Alan R. Millard, Rankin Senior Lecturer in Hebrew and Ancient Semitic Languages, University of Liverpool *(Other Creation Accounts, Flood Stories, The Old Testament and the Ancient Near East, The Cities of the Conquest, The Temples, The Threat of Assyria, Exile to Babylon)*

Dr Leon Morris, Formerly Principal, Ridley College, University of Melbourne, Australia *(The Gospels and Modern Criticism)*

The Rev. Alec Motyer, Principal, Trinity College, Bristol *(The Names of God, The Tabernacle, The Meaning of Blood Sacrifice, The Prophets: Introduction)*

Dr Harold Rowdon, Lecturer in Church History, London Bible College *(Pilate)*

The Rev. Canon John A. Simpson, Priest-in-Charge of Ridge, Hertfordshire *(The Virgin Birth)*

The Rt. Rev. John B. Taylor, Bishop of St Albans *(The Five Books: Introduction, the Historical Books: Introduction)*

Dr Gordon Wenham, Lecturer in Semitic Studies, Queen's University, Belfast *(Literary Criticism and the Old Testament, Covenants and Near Eastern Treaties)*

The Rev. John Wenham, Formerly Principal of Tyndale Hall, Bristol and Warden of Latimer House, Oxford *(The Large Numbers of the Old Testament)*

The Rev. Canon David Wheaton, Principal, Oak Hill Theological College, London *(The Accounts of the Resurrection)*

Part One
INTRODUCING THE BIBLE

JESUS CHRIST AND THE BIBLE

Richard France

As a Christian I want to follow Jesus Christ. I want to do what he said, go where he leads, follow his example, enter into the life he offers.

To do so I must read the eye-witness accounts of those who knew him. I discover that he claimed to be the revelation of God himself, the One who shows us what God is like. And I discover too that he is the culmination of centuries of God's revelation recorded in documents going back hundreds of years before his time.

So I seek the authority of Jesus; and I am led on by him to see the authority of the Bible.

Read the beginning of John's first letter.

We cannot have one without the other. Certainly Jesus revealed God to man in a way the written Old Testament alone could never have done. Ordinary people saw him, heard him, touched him, lived with him. But we were not there ourselves. Nor can we know what Jesus was like, what he said and did, by consulting the secular historians of the time. They will only tell us that a Jewish prophet called Jesus lived, preached, fell foul of the authorities and was executed. One or two may also suggest some knowledge of his resurrection. But that is as far as it goes. If we are to know the revelation Jesus gave, we must turn to the New Testament to find it.

The fact that a book is necessary to know Jesus is not something to be regretted. It is in fact what Jesus intended. One of his top priorities was the selection and training of his apostles – that inner circle of his disciples who were to preserve and pass on his teaching. The church was founded on the apostles' teaching. The New Testament is the record of what they taught. It is a collection of those books which the early church accepted as written by the apostles themselves, or by their close associates, and which therefore set out the true apostolic faith.

THE BIBLE OF JESUS

If we are to know Jesus and his teaching, then, we must turn to the New Testament, to the testimony of those he himself chose and trusted to pass on his teaching. To do so he himself sent the Holy Spirit to 'guide them into all the truth'.

See John 14:26; 15:26; 16:13-15

If we accept the authority of Jesus we may well accept the New Testament as the source of all our knowledge of him and of his teaching. But we are also bound to accept the Old Testament. For Jesus himself, the incarnate Son of God, accepted it as God's own word to man. If he is our authority, we can do no less.

Teaching about the Old Testament

Jesus said some strong things about the Old Testament:

'Think not that I have come to abolish the law and the prophets; I have come not to abolish them but to fulfil them. For truly, I say to you, till heaven and earth pass

Matthew 5:17-18

away, not an iota, not a dot, will pass from the law until all is accomplished.'

John 10:35

'Scripture cannot be broken.'

Luke 24:44

'Everything written about me in the law of Moses and the prophets and the psalms must be fulfilled.'

Mark 7:1-13

Some of his harshest condemnations were reserved for those who tried to evade the plain commands of God (set out in the Old Testament law) by means of merely human traditions, however venerable.

Appeal to the Old Testament

Examples: Matthew 12:3-4, 5, 7; 21:16; 22:32, 44

Matthew 4:4, 7, 10
Mark 15:34; Luke 23:46
quoting Psalms 22:1;
31:5

Much more impressive than occasional pronouncements of Jesus about the Old Testament is his constant appeal to it in a wide variety of different situations. In controversy with his opponents, he regularly uses a quotation from the Old Testament to settle the argument. And this was not simply in order to meet men on their own grounds. He relies no less on the authority of the Old Testament in his confrontation with the devil! Even in the final agony on the cross, it is words from the Old Testament which are on his lips.

Quotations from the Old Testament

Matthew 24; Mark 13;
Luke 21

Matthew 24:29-31: from
Isaiah 13:10; 34:4;
Daniel 7:13; Zechariah
12:12; Isaiah 27:13;
Deuteronomy 30:4;
Zechariah 2:6

It is in Jesus' teaching to his disciples, however, that he refers most frequently to the Old Testament, both by explicit quotations and by innumerable verbal echoes, so that some passages seem like a patch-work of Old Testament words and ideas. For instance, Jesus' prediction of the destruction of Jerusalem and of his own second coming is full of Old Testament language. The words of only three verses draw on no less than seven Old Testament passages.

Fulfilment of the Old Testament

Matthew 19:18-19;
22:37-40 – see
Deuteronomy 6:5;
Leviticus 19:18

Matthew 5:21-22, 27-28,
etc.

But it is not just a matter of language. The actual content of Jesus' teaching relies heavily on the Old Testament. His central ethical rules are drawn from the law of Moses. And if he differed from his contemporaries in ethical matters, it was only because he accused them of taking the Old Testament commands too lightly and superficially.

Luke 24:27

Above all, his teaching about his own role in the purposes of God depends entirely on the conviction that he must fulfil the Old Testament. His teaching after the resurrection, when 'beginning with Moses and all the prophets, he interpreted to them in all the scriptures the things concerning himself', was the climax of what he had been teaching them through the years of his ministry.

Luke 4:21; Mark
9:12-13; Luke 18:31;
Mark 14:21, 27; Luke
22:37; Matthew 26:54;
Luke 24:44-47

In a number of passages there are emphatic statements that he had come to fulfil the scriptures. But these are only the outcrops of a conviction which underlies all his teaching about his own mission. He had come 'to fulfil', and there was a divine compulsion about what was written. It *must* be fulfilled.

So the Christian is a follower of one for whom the Old Testament was the unquestionably authoritative word of God. Jesus believed its statements, endorsed its teaching, obeyed its commands, and set himself to fulfil the pattern of redemption which it laid down. It is clearly inconsistent for one who calls Jesus 'Lord' to think lightly of those scriptures which were to him the supreme revelation of God.

THE NEW TESTAMENT ENDORSES THE OLD

The rest of the New Testament, needless to say, fully

endorses Jesus' view of the Old Testament. Constant
Old Testament quotations and allusions show the same
reliance on the Old Testament teaching for the disclosure of God's character and purposes. It was God who
spoke through the prophets, declares the writer of
Hebrews. Indeed, says Paul to Timothy, 'All scripture is
inspired by God.' The Old Testament is the message of
God.

Hebrews 1:1; see too 2
Peter 1:21; 2 Timothy
3:16

Romans 3:2

It is interesting that the New Testament makes no distinction between what 'Scripture' says and what God
says. Old Testament quotations are given as what God
said, even though God was not the speaker in the Old
Testament context. Conversely, words spoken by God
in the Old Testament narrative are ascribed to 'Scripture'. Where Jesus led the way in his acceptance of the
Old Testament as the word of God, the New Testament
was content to follow. If we Christians set our own
judgement or our inherited traditions above the Old and
New Testament scriptures we part company with the
Lord and the apostles, and cut ourselves off from our
one source of knowledge of God.

Matthew 19:4-5; Acts
4:24-25; Hebrews 1:6-12

Romans 9:17; Galatians
3:8

DEALING WITH PROBLEMS

This is not to eliminate all problems in advance. The
interpretation and application of the Bible's teaching
poses many problems, and Christians may legitimately
differ in their interpretation at some points. But where
such differences occur, our aim must always be to discover, by the most careful and rigorous study of which
we are capable, what the relevant passages really mean,
whether this turns out to agree with our own previous
ideas or not. Then, having discovered the true meaning,
we must accept it as the word of God. It will not always
be easy; it may sometimes be impossible; but that is the
ideal.

We may be convinced in our minds of the Bible's
authority: we will be even more convinced when we
allow it to have its authority in our lives. We will know
for ourselves the experience of God speaking through
his written revelation to us. The Bible is God's word,
what God has said. He still speaks to us through it
today.

THE BIBLE AND CHRISTIAN LIVING

David Field

The Bible can be read as great literature, or as a history of Israel, or as a source-book of theological information. It is all of these things. But none of them does full justice to the purpose of Scripture as set out by the Bible writers themselves, or to the cumulative experience of Bible users through the centuries.

When Ezra the scribe read from the law of Moses to the returned exiles in Jerusalem, the people, we are told, not only 'understood the reading' but alternately 'wept when they heard the words of the law' and made 'great rejoicing'. And they came back the next day to build shelters for the Feast of Tabernacles, in obedience to the law's commands. The act of hearing and understanding the scriptures had aroused their emotions and stirred them to action.

Nehemiah 8

Centuries after Ezra, J. B. Phillips describes his similar experience in translating the New Testament. 'Although I did my utmost to preserve an emotional detachment', he writes, 'I found again and again that the material under my hands was strangely alive; it spoke to my condition in the most uncanny way.'

These reactions accurately reflect the vivid metaphors we find in the Bible, used by its writers to describe the impact God's word made in their own experience. It is a fire to warm and a hammer to break, water to cleanse, milk to nourish, meat to invigorate, light to guide, a sword for the fight, and a mirror to reveal. It is 'at work in you believers', 'able to build you up', 'living and active ... piercing ... discerning'.

Jeremiah 23:29; 1 Peter 2:2; Hebrews 5:13-14; Psalm 119:105; Ephesians 6:17; James 1:23-25; 1 Thessalonians 2:13; Acts 20:32; Hebrews 4:12

THE BIBLE IS RELEVANT

All this means that the reader who approaches the Bible in a purely detached way is in danger of failing to appreciate its primary purpose, which is a practical, dynamic one. Its aim is to *do something* in the life of the person who reads it, as well as to capture his aesthetic interest and supply him with historical and theological information. The huge cultural gaps which separate Bible times from our own make such a purpose all the more remarkable, but the Bible can justify its claim to contemporary relevance in two ways.

In the first place, it deals with those elements in *human nature* which are timeless. The men and women we read about in the Bible have aspirations and failings with which we easily identify, and even the heroes of Scripture are displayed in the cold light of truth. As Augustine put it, 'The sacred record, like a faithful mirror, has no flattery in its portraits.'

Then, secondly, the truths of the Bible are ever-relevant because *God himself* does not change, either in his nature or in his dealings with men. Through reading the Bible we discover fundamental truths about God, and see them demonstrated by events in the lives of his people which illuminate his character and illustrate his will for all men at all times. So it is that even events from the distant past 'were written down for *our* instruction' in order that in the present and for the future 'by the encouragement of the scriptures we might have hope'.

1 Corinthians 10:11;
Romans 15:4

THE BIBLE IS PRACTICAL

The Bible, then, retains its contemporary bite. What are the practical purposes it aims to achieve?

It points people to Jesus

The purpose of John's Gospel is clearly set out: 'Now Jesus did many other signs in the presence of the disciples, which are not written in this book; but these are written that you may believe that Jesus is the Christ, the Son of God, and that believing you may have life in his name.'

John 20:30-31

In writing with this frankly propagandist aim – to focus on Jesus Christ – the disciple was being faithful to the remarkable way in which his Master summed up the purpose of *all* Scripture. 'You search the scriptures', Jesus once replied to his critics, 'because you think that in them you have eternal life; and it is they that bear witness to *me*. If you believed Moses, you would believe me, for he wrote of *me*.'

John 5:39, 46

Not surprisingly, the listening disciples were slow to grasp the full meaning of these words. After the resurrection Jesus had to rebuke them for their dullness before showing them once again – and this time more explicitly – how, like the spokes of a wheel, the whole message of the Bible converged on himself. 'Beginning with Moses and all the prophets, he interpreted to them in all the scriptures the things concerning himself.' And Luke goes on to tell us that Jesus drew special attention to those passages from the Old Testament which spoke of his death and resurrection, as a stimulus to repentance and the basis for forgiveness of sins.

Luke 24:27

Jesus clearly believed that the main aim of the (Old Testament) scriptures was to point people to himself; which meant in practice (if we add Luke's evidence to John's), that through repentance and faith men and women should find the forgiveness and life which he had died and risen to make possible for them.

By their preaching and writing, the apostles showed that they had finally grasped Jesus' point that the Bible's main practical purpose is to draw people to himself as their Saviour. 'To him', preached Peter, 'all the prophets bear witness, that every one who believes in him receives forgiveness of sins through his name.' James pleaded with his readers to 'receive with meekness the implanted word, which is able to save your souls'. Paul reminded Timothy 'how from childhood you have been acquainted with the sacred writings which are able to instruct you for salvation through faith in Christ Jesus'.

Acts 10:43

James 1:21

2 Timothy 3:15

It builds a relationship with God

In Martin Luther's words, just as a mother goes to the cradle only to find the baby, we go to the Bible only to find Christ. It is the Bible's primary purpose to bring men to their Saviour by arousing the beginnings of faith. But this is not the only practical function it aims to fulfil. Peter and the author of the letter to the Hebrews use the analogy of birth and growth to illustrate a further purpose of Scripture. Those who have put their trust in Jesus as Saviour 'have been born anew ... through the living and abiding word of God'; but, like all new-born babes, they must 'long for the pure spiritual milk' of the word if they are to survive and grow; and once beyond

1 Peter 1:23

1 Peter 2:2

babyhood they need solid food – which is the 'meat' of God's word.

Hebrews 5:12-14

This growth process is, above all, a growing up in relationship with God. It is the Bible's function to feed the personal knowledge of the Father which the Christian 'child' enjoys. And 'enjoy' is exactly the right word, because as the believer learns more about God his delight becomes more intense. That is why Bible study should never be dull for a Christian. 'Thy words', cries out Jeremiah, 'became to me a joy and the delight of my heart; for I am called by thy name, O Lord, God of hosts.' Any personal relationship is fostered by words, and through the pages of his Bible the Christian hears God speaking to him; an experience, says the Psalmist, that is 'sweeter than honey'.

Jeremiah 15:16

Psalm 19:10

If this sounds like love-letter language we should not be surprised, because the relationship into which God invites believers is a love-relationship. His, however, is a love which makes exacting demands. The information about God and his will which the Christian receives through reading the Bible calls for a tough response that is anything but sentimental. 'If a man loves me', Jesus taught, 'he will *keep* my word, and my Father will love him, and we will come to him and make our home with him ... and the word which you hear is not mine but the Father's who sent me.'

John 14:23-24

It equips for battle

Such a stern demand is appropriate because once a man becomes a Christian he finds himself enlisted on God's side in a lifelong battle. He is called upon both to defend his faith against stiff opposition and to spread it among his friends. For both operations, offensive and defensive, his chief weapon is the Bible. It is the 'sword of the Spirit', declares Paul, with which he can combat hostile ideas and cut a straight path for God's truth into the innermost strongholds of the human will.

Ephesians 6:17

Hebrews 4:12

Jesus himself set the pattern for this very practical use of the Bible in his own ministry. Honest enquirers, like the lawyer who asked him about the greatest commandment, were impressed and attracted by his Bible-based teaching (though, as with the rich young ruler, they did not all respond to it positively). On the other hand Jesus fought off false teaching, whether the arguments of men like the Sadducees or the insidious suggestions of the arch-enemy in the desert, with the words of his Bible. Bible words do not have magical powers in themselves, but because all words express ideas, and ideas lie behind action, the word of God is a mighty weapon to influence men's convictions and conduct. Jesus fought his battles with his own words and with the words of his Bible, and he sent his disciples out to preach both.

Mark 12:28-34

Matthew 19:16-22

Matthew 22:23-33

Matthew 4:1-11

This gives the Christian all the incentive he needs to fill his mind with Bible doctrine. Without (for example) a grasp of what the Bible teaches about human nature he will soon be speechless before the claims of twentieth-century humanity. If he is vague about the meaning of Christ's death and resurrection, he cannot hope to introduce others to Jesus as their Saviour. Hence the insistence of the later books of the New Testament that anyone who aims to serve Christ faithfully must make it his aim to know and conserve God's truth. 'Guard the truth that has been entrusted to you by the Holy Spirit', writes Paul to Timothy, 'and what you have heard from me before many witnesses entrust to

faithful men who will be able to teach others also.'
It guides conduct

In his earlier letter to Timothy, Paul had already drawn attention to the importance of maintaining right standards of conduct alongside right beliefs. To 'wage the good warfare' involves 'holding faith *and a good conscience*'. The one cannot be made a substitute for the other; indeed, any failure in right conduct inevitably brings about a downfall in right beliefs. 'By rejecting conscience, certain persons have made shipwreck of their faith'. This is a major Bible theme. In the Old Testament, farmer Amos, with rustic bluntness, flays those who attempt to keep up a religious façade without matching conduct; and James, his outspoken New Testament counterpart, exposes those who are 'hearers of the word' but not 'doers' of it. Jesus makes the same point in his parable of the two builders.

The same pressures which threaten to muddle his faith can seduce the Christian into moral laxity; but the Bible, which provides his main line of defence against false teaching, is also an effective weapon against moral temptations. It sets out, by example as well as by direct command, the differences between right and wrong, so that the man who measures his conduct by Bible standards gains from it both 'reproof' when he is in the wrong and 'correction' to set him back on a right course. The Bible becomes his bastion against moral powerlessness, too, by reminding him constantly of the divine power that is available to overcome his weakness ('for God is at work in you, both to *will* and to *work* for his good pleasure'). The man who knows and claims the Bible's promises is empowered to live a kind of life which would otherwise be completely beyond his grasp.

The moral commands of the Bible are presented more as main guiding principles and ideals than as a set of meticulously detailed regulations for daily living. They reach behind right actions to right motives, and their application may differ from person to person according to circumstances. Goodness is defined as that which pleases God, so the Christian with a clear conscience is the one who is totally absorbed with pleasing him. And, as we have already seen, it is the Bible's function to feed and foster such a relationship.

THE BIBLE IS FOR ORDINARY PEOPLE

The Bible is not written in a secret spiritual code which must be cracked if its message is to be understood. Provided it is read sensibly (see the section 'Understanding the Bible'), it is clear enough for the simplest Christian to live by, as well as being profound enough to exercise the mind of the brightest scholar for a lifetime. The decisive qualifications for profitable Bible study are spiritual rather than intellectual.

Among the qualities which the Bible itself suggests, the following are particularly prominent:
A will to obey

'Whoever has the will to do the will of God', said Jesus, 'shall know whether my teaching comes from him.' This is a fundamental requirement, if the teaching of the Bible is going to make its full impact on any reader's life. It has been well said that 'the Bible is never mastered by the reader who refuses its mastery of him'.
Concentration

Words calling for sustained effort ('search', 'meditate', 'examine') are used in the Bible to describe the way the

---

Margin references:

2 Timothy 1:14; 2:2

1 Timothy 1:18-19

James 1:22
Matthew 7:24-27

2 Timothy 3:16

Philippians 2:13

See Romans 14
Hebrews 13:21

John 7:17

scriptures must be read for maximum benefit. *'Concentrate* on winning God's approval, on being a *workman* with nothing to be ashamed of, and who knows how to use the word of truth to the best advantage.'

2 Timothy 2:15, Phillips

Patience

Hebrews 6:12

It is 'through faith and patience' that the Bible's promises are to be obtained. Patient conviction that God's word is to be trusted will bring the believer through times of perplexity.

See Hebrews 11:17-19

Persistence

Luke 8:18

Jesus' promise and warning, 'To him who has will more be given, and from him who has not, even what he thinks that he has will be taken away', was made in the context of hearing the word of God. To the persistent seeker the Bible yields more and more of its riches.

Submission to the Holy Spirit

When Jesus met his disciples after the resurrection 'he opened their minds to understand the scriptures', by relating what they read in their Bibles to what was happening around them. It is through the prompting of the Holy Spirit that the Bible reader gains the mind of Christ, which enables him to apply teaching given centuries ago to contemporary life.

Luke 24:45

It would be impossible to better Paul's summary of the practical and devotional potential of the Bible: 'Your mind has been familiar with the holy scriptures, which can open the mind to the salvation which comes through believing on Christ Jesus. All scripture is inspired by God and is useful for teaching the faith and correcting error, for re-setting the direction of a man's life and training him in good living. The scriptures are the comprehensive equipment of the man of God, and fit him fully for all branches of his work.'

See 1 Corinthians 2:9-16

2 Timothy 3:15-17, Phillips

UNDERSTANDING THE BIBLE

Often the meaning of a Bible passage is plain and obvious. When it is not, the following points may help in its understanding and application today.

Setting
When and where was the book or passage written?

Purpose
Why was it written?

Form
How, or in what form, was it written?

Context
What is the book as a whole about?

Words
What is the meaning of individual words?

History/Biography
Old Testament historical books, Gospels and Acts in the New Testament
• What was the historical background to the passage? (See historical charts and maps.) eg Ezra 1:1; Luke 2:1-2; 3:1-2
• What actually happened? Who were the people involved? eg Nehemiah 1
• Where did it happen? eg Isaiah 36
• Often material was selected to make a point: is there one stated or implied? eg Judges 6:1,7,8

Law
Exodus, Leviticus, Deuteronomy, Numbers
• Is the passage:
moral law, matters of behaviour? eg Exodus 20
social, state law? eg Leviticus 25:13f
domestic law, matters of hygiene? eg Leviticus 12
religious law, worship, sacrifice? eg Leviticus 1-7
blessings and curses? (See article on Covenants in Part Two.) eg Deuteronomy 28

Stage One

1

UNDERSTAND
What does the passage actually say?

Stage Two

2

EXPLAIN
What does the passage mean?

What did the passage mean to its original readers?

What is the main point or teaching of the passage?

Stage Three

3

APPLY
What does the passage mean today?

What is an equivalent situation today to that of the original readers?

Does the passage have some specific teaching about God, man, the world, the church . . . ?

• What was the main aim of the law at the time?
eg Leviticus 20:22-26
• Was it superseded in the New Testament? If so, what was the principle involved?
eg Hebrews 9

Poetry
Job, Psalms, Song of Solomon, prophets, etc.
• Is it a drama with characters, as in a play?
eg Job
• Or poetry, expressing one person's feelings which we can share?
eg Psalms 29, 42, 68
• Is it highly symbolical? Is the language from the worship or history of Israel? If so, what is referred to?
eg Psalms 77, 78, 79
• Is there a historical setting which will help us understand the poem? Or was it written for use in Israel's worship?
eg Judges 4-5 ; Psalms 134, 136
• Is there repetition or contrast for poetic effect? (See Introduction to Poetry and Wisdom Literature, Part Two.)
eg Psalm 67 ; Proverbs 10:11

'Wise sayings'
Proverbs, Ecclesiastes
• Is it a proverb or saying which stands alone, or is there a common theme?
eg Proverbs 8; 23:13-14
• Is it a witty comment on life? Or a statement of what happens as a general rule? Or expressing the situation of man without God?
eg Proverbs 10:1-4 ; 25:25
Ecclesiastes 1:2-11

Prophecy
Old Testament prophets, Revelation
• What was the historical background? (See historical charts, and notes on each book.)
eg Daniel 1:1
• Is it written in poetic form? (See on Poetry above.)
eg Isaiah 36:22-29
• Is the language highly symbolical? If so, what is the imagery taken from?
(See notes in Parts Two and Three.)
eg Daniel 7; Revelation 6
• What was the original purpose of the prophecy in its time?

• What is the universal principle involved?
eg Isaiah 30:1-5
• Are there specific claims to its fulfilment in the New Testament?
eg Isaiah 53; Acts 8

Parable
Gospels, Old Testament historical and prophetic books
• Was the parable told to answer a question or illustrate a point?
eg Luke 10:25-37
2 Samuel 12:1-5
• What was the main point?
eg Luke 10:36-37
• Are the details given meaning in the passage itself? Or are they just part of the story-telling?
eg Mark 4:1-20; Luke 14:15-24

Letter
New Testament letters
• What was the purpose of the letter? Who wrote it? To whom? (See notes on letters in Part Three.)
eg 1 John 4:13
1 Corinthians 1:1-2
• What is the argument or theme of the book as a whole? How does the passage fit into this?
eg Galatians 1:6

How does it compare with other, perhaps clearer, Bible passages?

If it was written to meet particular needs at the time, what is the general principle?

Is there an example to follow, or a warning, or a promise?

Is there any action to be taken in the light of the passage?

Does it lead to prayer or praise? Can we make the writer's words or expression of feeling our own?

THE BIBLE AND SOCIETY

Sir Frederick Catherwood

God created the universe. He sustains it. He cares for the whole of mankind and has given us in the Bible a guide-book by which to live.

The Bible tells us how to conduct ourselves in relation to God and to our fellow men. And since God is timeless, the wisdom of the Bible is timeless too.

The Bible is not only relevant to individuals, it is relevant to society. Christianity is not just for private behaviour and public worship. It is a world system which competes with other world systems. It argues on more than equal terms with Marxism, Existentialism, Nationalism, Capitalism. Each of these systems is based on its own particular view of human behaviour, and all have their own standards of morals. The Christian believes that since the Christian teaching is true, it will be more useful and more relevant than that of any other system. The Bible offers to twentieth-century man the very things he cries out for.

THE BIBLE ANSWERS FUNDAMENTAL HUMAN NEEDS

If there is no God, there can be no divine law. If there is no divine law men must try to agree among themselves what is right and what is wrong. But if they disagree, who is to have the last word? So classes and nations fight it out, and conflict escalates as external authority is removed.

Deuteronomy 6:24

The Bible declares that there is an external morality given by God for the good of all mankind. Rulers and ruled alike are answerable to him. His standards are binding on all men.

A basis for science

Other philosophies are said to depend on science. But science itself is based on Christian teaching. It was belief in a God of order, a God of reason, a God of unchanging decrees, which led to the development of the scientific method in the 17th century. When science forsakes this basis it loses its way. Some people have made a god of it. Many are now rejecting it altogether. Its hope lies in a return to its Christian basis.

A realistic view of man

Evil is all too apparent in our world. Education does not eradicate it, nor does an improved environment. Revolution and change of government all too often mean simply exchanging one set of evils for another. The Bible

Genesis 3; Jeremiah 17:9; Matthew 15:18-19

explains why. Evil is not simply external, it is deep inside man himself. The initial disobedience to the Creator has left human nature with a permanent, in-born bias to evil. Neither reason nor force will change this. The Bible also teaches that God provides all men with certain common benefits – conscience, the recognition of right and wrong, and certain institutions (family, state, church) which encourage good and discourage evil.

Humanity restored

The all-pervasive rationalism of our own century, infiltrating our whole culture and philosophy, has reduced man to an animal, condemned to a meaningless existence terminated by death. But men cry out against this. They feel there is something outside the box of time and space in which they find themselves. And they grope instinctively after the Christian truth that man is not just body, he is soul and spirit too. He is not just a passing atom of an overwhelming universe, but is of eternal significance.

Genesis 1:26-31; Psalm 8:3-8

THE BIBLE AND THE SOCIAL ORDER

The Bible's relevance is not confined to broad generalities. It enables us to understand and evaluate ourselves and the world we live in. It provides us with a world-view – a philosophy to live by. But it speaks also to practical situations, to the way we run our lives and order our society.

Much of the Bible's teaching goes back to the way we are made; it goes back to creation itself. The same basic principles were backed up in Old Testament law and, in the New Testament, reinforced by Jesus himself.

Hebrews 9

The Old Testament ceremonial law came to an end at the crucifixion, its purpose fulfilled. The civil law applied directly only to Israel as a nation and cannot be lifted out of its context, though many of the principles it embodies are still highly relevant to modern society. But the moral law of the Old Testament retains eternal validity. Men may be forced to change their laws but God does not change his. This moral law includes the ten commandments. Christ came to fulfil the moral law, not to destroy it. He pointed out its full implications in the Sermon on the Mount and elsewhere. Not only was the act of adultery wrong, but even a lustful look. The moral law had been covered with casuistry and hypocrisy. Christ ripped away the cover and put men's obligations to their fellow men on full view.

Exodus 20 Matthew 5:17-48

Not only is the Christian moral law valid for all time, it applies to all men. Though they may find the standards high, most people believe in right and wrong, truth and falsehood. The Christian law has wide support – and for good reason.

A law that protects the weak

The large mass of the world's population is open to exploitation of one kind or another. The Christian moral law is a bulwark against this, whenever men can be taught to respect it. It protects the weak against the strong, the poor against the rich, the women and children, fatherless and widows against those who would neglect and exploit them.

The intention of the Old Testament law on usury, for example, was to make a man use his good fortune to help tide his less fortunate neighbour over a bad patch until he could again become self-sufficient. The law protected farmers living near subsistence level who needed something to carry them over from one harvest to the next, especially if the harvest had been bad. Without some such law the rich could hold the poor to ransom. They could charge such a rate of interest that the poor farmer would have to sell his land to pay it. It was certainly not a prohibition on lending money at a rate of interest which can be earned by the recipient. Lending of unused savings is vital to economic development.

Deuteronomy 23:19-20

Most people agree that the moral law protects the weak. The trades unionist suspects that in competitive capitalism the weak go to the wall. The working man takes naturally to a creed which aims to help the weak.

Leviticus 25

Similarly, the principle of the Law of Jubilee was that the rich should not be allowed to accumulate all property rights. Every fifty years there was a redistribution of land back to the original owners.

The concept of law and order

Romans 13:1-7

The Christian law protects society against chaos. The civil power, Paul tells the Romans, is ordained by God to uphold good and suppress evil.

Exodus 21-22

When it comes to crime and punishment, the penalties laid down in the Old Testament for offences against the person are more severe than for offences against property. People matter more than things – an ideal we are often in danger of forgetting today.

Crime demands just punishment. But the criminal must be treated with compassion. So the Christian stands between the 'hard' line on punishment and the 'soft'. The Old Testament laws endeavoured to ensure that punishment was no greater than the offence, and in any case was less than private retribution. Christ himself said to the woman caught in adultery – for which the punishment was death – 'Go, and do not sin again.'

John 8:11

At the other extreme, the Christian is not at liberty to base his view of crime and punishment on the pre-supposition that all crime is just another kind of sickness, and just as capable of cure. The Bible sees crime as a moral act for which the criminal is responsible, which sickness is not. The Christian's concern for the reform of the criminal should never make him either deny the offence or fail to protect society against the offender. But once the sentence has been paid, the criminal is entitled to society's help to become a good citizen.

One danger of treating all crime as sickness is that it makes the criminal a second-class citizen. A judge's sentence is normally limited by the nature of the offence, but a doctor can detain until he decides a patient is cured. And if an objective moral standard is thrown over, what is to stop the majority in society – or even a minority in power – from putting away in a mental institution those who do not see eye to eye with them until they are 'cured'? It has been done.

Support for the family

The Christian law protects the basic institution of society – the family. The Bible has a great deal to say about the concept of the family, and the Christian ideal differs markedly from some current concepts.

Matthew 19:5-6

The idea of permanence is basic to Christian marriage. This gives security to both partners and children. Relationships can be far freer within a secure framework than when partners or children have to take into account the possible collapse of the whole basic structure. The strains arising from insecurity can often precipitate collapse. Whole new areas of jealousy and friction arise.

The Bible nowhere allows divorce on the grounds of incompatibility. There are some incompatibilities in every marriage. But the Bible sets marriage in a wider context. It is not just a romantic attachment between two individuals to the exclusion of the world at large. The wider family on both sides is involved. So too is society. The wider family protects husband and wife, as well as children, from the stresses and strains of today's tiny nuclear family, where all contact with uncles, aunts, cousins and even grandparents is limited to a weekly long-distance phone-call.

The Christian ideal is marriage between one man and one woman – a factor which has greatly raised the status of women in the world. Anyone inclined to question the advisability of monogamy should read of the troubles of Jacob, David and others who took more than one wife. The husband is to cherish his wife. He has no absolute rights over her. But he is, none the less, the head of the family, the final arbiter.

Ephesians 5:21-33

Strictly speaking, the Bible regards pre-marital sex as a contradiction in terms. Living together in physical union *is* marriage. The two partners become one flesh. But it cannot stop there. Marriage is social as well as physical. It involves leaving parents. It involves other people – society generally. The marriage ceremony gives recognition to this. The one ground of divorce seemingly allowed by Christ is the adultery of one or other partner with a third person.

Genesis 2:24;
1 Corinthians 6:16

Matthew 19:1-9

Sex, as seen in the Bible, is part and parcel of a wider relationship. It should be the expression of a lasting respect and self-sacrificing love. Within that relationship it increases the love and respect. Outside it, it seems to have the opposite effect. And the woman, because of her greater dependence, is usually the loser.

2 Samuel 13

Promiscuity has always been with us. No one knows what society would be like if everyone acted on the advice of those who openly advocate it. Even so, the majority of mankind do not find this view practicable or desirable. The Christian view of marriage on the other hand is both practical and a good deal happier than any alternative.

THE OFFER OF NEW LIFE

These are simply illustrations of the Bible's relevance to present-day society, to modern man. They are based primarily on creation and a law which is true to man and society as they really are.

But the Bible does not limit itself to God's law for humanity. It recognizes that man is unable either to keep these laws, or to make reparation for his offences against a holy God. So the law is intended not simply to regulate conduct in an imperfect world, but to show up our imperfections and so lead us to Christ.

Romans 3:9-26

For Christ, by his death, has served sentence for our sin, and offers forgiveness and a new life to all men. To Christians of all generations for two thousand years and of all nations and races, this is the supreme reality. They know forgiveness. They know fellowship with God through prayer and worship. They know the presence of the Holy Spirit who changes their lives. They know that God's laws are good and true. For them the Bible is not just a realistic book about human nature. They have put it to the test and found it true.

MEETING OBJECTIONS

Kenneth Howkins

Much of the Bible is in the form of history. It is not however *mere* history. If that is all we see, we miss the point. It is history from one point of view, history with an aim. Stories are recorded not simply because they happened, but because they reveal something of God and his activity in the world. So it is sometimes called a 'history of salvation'.

HISTORY WITH A DIFFERENCE

This alters the perspective. The secular historian may be amazed that an ancient Hebrew nomad, Abraham, occupies more than thirteen chapters, while a powerful despot, Omri, is dealt with summarily in less than a dozen verses. Archaeological records do not even mention Abraham, though his story fits well into what is known of his times; but Omri was known far and wide to later generations. In the Bible, Abraham was the founder of Israel, a man chosen by God, a man of faith, the recipient of God's promises, and a man of profound significance to both Jew and Christian; but Omri founded the city of Samaria and was an evil man. Thus he is dismissed from the story. As God's revelation of himself unfolded, and as his work of salvation continued, men and events in history assumed different proportions.

Discrepancies

It is easy to find historical problems in the Bible. But patient research has gradually solved many of them. Apparent discrepancies between different parts of the Bible are sometimes due simply to the lack of detail given, and we should not too hastily pounce on contradictions. For example, in both Acts and Galatians there are references to Paul's visits to Jerusalem. It is difficult to fit the two together, and to know which visits in the two books correspond. But Acts is clearly not intended to give a complete account of Paul's activities, and he may well have visited Jerusalem on other occasions which are not recorded.

Again, there may be apparent discrepancies between the biblical version of a story and the version in other ancient records. It is strange that those who wish to discredit the reliability of the Bible sometimes seem to have such strong faith in the reliability of other ancient records! So first we need to be sure that the other record is in fact reliable and, second, we need to remember how little total evidence we have from the ancient past. The debate on the book of Daniel illustrates this. It is no longer possible just to dismiss Darius as 'unhistorical'. There are problems: but there are also possible solutions.

Problems with numbers

A difficulty arises on various occasions in connection with numbers in the Bible. Here we find that the manuscripts themselves may vary in the figures they give. It must be remembered that letters of the alphabet in both Hebrew (at least after the exile) and Greek served also

as numerals. Because of the similarities of certain letters, errors in copying could easily creep in. Also different methods of reckoning were employed. A year may
be reckoned by the sun, or by the reign of a king.
Inclusive reckoning was also used. For example, midday
on Sunday until midday on the following Sunday could
be called eight days, rather than seven, as eight days
were involved, even though the first and the last were
incomplete. Again, there are problems, but some progress can be made with them.

Myth

An objection frequently heard today is that it is being
unduly literalistic to discuss whether or not the Bible
history is true. We are told that what matters is not
whether a certain event happened, but what it means.
This is the opposite extreme to the views that it is *mere*
history; the claim is that the stories are not history but
'myth' – a term used in varying ways, and notoriously
hard to define exactly. It does not imply that the story
is completely untrue, but that it is not literally true. The
term is brought in whenever there is anything supernatural or different from the ordinary course of nature.

Now the first question to consider is whether the biblical writers intended their words to be taken as history
or as myth. It is clear that the accounts of miracles in
the Bible are written just as factually as the accounts of
other events. The second question, therefore, is whether
we can accept them as history, or whether we must
treat them as myth and 'demythologize' them, that is,
assume that the miracle did not actually occur as a
miraculous event, but that some spiritual truth is
enshrined in the story in symbolic form.

The basis for this line of argument is that the Bible
was written in an unscientific age, when people thought
of 'a three-decker universe', with a God who kept on
interfering; but that now, in our enlightened scientific
age, we know that their view of the world was quite
wrong. Miracles are supposed to fit in with the
unscientific views of the ancients, but not with our own
scientific views. It is claimed that we now know that the
world operates in accordance with laws, and so we do
not need to bring God in to explain things.

Now this view of science is already out of date. Science, or rather scientists, no longer hold such a rigid
view of the laws of nature. The laws are descriptions of
what is observed to happen normally. If a law does not
account for all that happens, then it has to be modified.
Science, as such, does not rule out miracles, though
some scientists may reject them.

We have been considering the subject of history. The
question of whether miracles happened or not is a question of history and not of science. History deals with
what happened, and then tries to find explanations. Science takes the knowledge of what happened and tries to
systematize that knowledge.

THE QUESTION OF MIRACLES

The biggest miracle in the Bible is the resurrection of
Jesus from the dead. Some would say that the universe
is such that a resurrection could not take place, and
they would base this assertion on 'science'. But in view
of the historical evidence for the resurrection, it would
be more scientific to ask what light is thrown on the
nature of the universe by the occurrence of such a
resurrection. In other words, science does not disprove

the resurrection: the resurrection is one of the facts which science must take into account. And what is said of the resurrection may be said of other miracles.

Of course there are objections here which must be faced. If miracles were always taking place, there would be no order in the universe, and without the regularity of nature we should not know where we were. Moreover, if God were always intervening to get us out of difficulties or dangers, we should never learn to become responsible people. But the Bible does not give us a miracle on every page. It covers about two thousand years of history, but most of the miracles are clustered round a few persons and events:

Moses and the beginning of the nation of Israel;

Elijah and Elisha and the emergence of a line of prophets who called the nation back to their covenant-agreement with God;

Jesus and the final revelation of God and his salvation, followed by the apostles and the founding of the Christian church.

Thus most of the miracles occur in these three separate periods. They must be seen in perspective.

Complementary accounts

In science it is not always possible to find one theory which accounts for and describes every aspect of an event. It is sometimes necessary to have two or more theories, not as alternatives, but held together. Light can be described in terms both of waves and of particles. Neither description alone is sufficient; both are needed. There can be a number of different levels of explanation.

Now when a scientist investigates a 'miracle', he may, or may not, be able to offer a 'natural' explanation. This is the function of science. The account of the crossing of the Red Sea in the Bible refers to a strong wind. That is the natural explanation. But the same account also ascribes the event to God. There are two levels of description. Both are true. One answers the question of *how*, the other the question of *why*. To say that God did it is to give the ultimate cause and to give meaning to it. The description given by science (where one is possible) explains *how* God did it.

In the Bible miracles are not as sharply divided from other events as they tend to be in our thinking. The ordinary events of nature, as well as the extraordinary, are ascribed to God. God is seen as active in all nature, and not only in miracles; they are simply his unusual ways of working.

Religious and historical truth

On the philosophical level another objection is raised against taking the miracle stories as historically true. We are told that there are two categories which must be kept absolutely apart. Thus the objectors would want to say that it is a 'religiously' true statement that God raised Jesus from the dead, and this has a spiritual meaning; but that on the level of history, Jesus died and remained dead and buried. We are told that to say the body of Jesus actually lived again is 'to confuse the categories'. But what are those categories, and where do they come from? They exist solely in the mind of the man who invented them. They can be neither proved nor disproved. But there is something more important still. If we start off by accepting these categories, then we start off by saying that Jesus did not rise from the dead, in the ordinary sense of those words. No matter how strong the historical evidence for the resurrection, we shall never accept it. We shall simply look for some other explanation.

This philosophical objection is really the same as the so-called scientific objection that miracles just do not occur in this world or universe. In both cases the objection is simply assumed to be valid, without proof, and before the evidence has even been considered. Indeed, all 'evidence' is automatically discounted. This is a fine example of question-begging: it assumes the answer before it starts. To such objectors we simply put the question: what sort of evidence would you require to be convinced that miracles did occur?

Creation stories

A similar problem arises at the very beginning of the Bible, in the creation stories. Some dismiss these as myth in the sense of old wives' tales. Others call them myth, meaning to say that they contain truth, even though they are not literally and historically true. If this is the case, in what sense are they true? What is the real point of the stories?

Objections to the creation stories are made in the name of science. So it may be surprising to find how little there is which impinges on the realm of science. It is boldly shown that God is the Creator of all – the universe, man, and everything else. But it is not shown how God did it. If God made man from the dust of the earth, that tells us something about the nature of man, the creature, as compared with God, the Creator. We are mere dust, and live only because God has made us live. Therefore, apart from God, our lives have no meaning. But how did God make man from dust? That is a scientific question, and so we turn to science, not the Bible, for an answer, or a suggested answer. We shall not be satisfied with a theory which does less than justice to the biblical view of the nature of man, but at the same time we need to be sure that we really have grasped the biblical view, and not just read our own ideas into it.

THE VALIDITY OF THE OLD TESTAMENT

Some people reject the Old Testament, partly or wholly, as being non-Christian, or sub-Christian. This is no new idea. In the first place, the Christian's view of the Old Testament must be Christ's view of it. It is quite clear that he accepted its authority and its validity. The question is whether Christ and Christianity have presented a new and truer view of God which invalidates the Old Testament picture.

In certain respects the Old Testament *is* now invalidated. Sacrifices are no longer necessary, as Christ himself has offered the final sacrifice, once for all. The rest of the Jewish ceremonial law is similarly superseded. But that does not mean that those Old Testament rituals should now be completely ignored. They reveal something permanently true about the nature of God and man's relationship with him. The teaching is the same, but the practical outworking is different, because of Christ. God is still holy.

The parts of the Old Testament which cause greatest offence are those which depict God as a God of anger, who orders his servants to act in judgement for him. This, it is said, is a primitive view of God, and quite different from the New Testament picture, which proclaims that God is love. But there is no fundamental opposition between the Old and New Testaments. There is much about the love and forgiveness of God in the Old Testament, and much about his righteous anger and judgement in the New. Indeed some of the strongest words are found on the lips of Jesus himself. Those who reject the Old Testament picture are compelled to reject also parts of the New. The whole idea of God's righteousness, anger against evil, and judgement is not pleasant, especially in a permissive age. But this does not make it any less true. (See Parts Two and Three for notes on particular moral difficulties.)

MEN OR MACHINES?

A final objection to a Christian view of the Bible is that it bypasses human thought, and makes men into machines. It is said that on this view the writers mechanically wrote what God said, and the readers do not need to think, because every bit of truth is presented on a plate. But this objection reveals a radical misunderstanding. Although the Bible's claim for itself is that God did directly speak through men, and that he so controlled them that they said what he wanted them to say, it is clear also that the men concerned used their own minds in the process. Their own personalities come through in the different styles of writing and their different approaches. (See article 'The Bible is Different'.)

Clearly also the Christian must use his own mind to receive the word of God. He must read carefully, compare one passage with another and use all the aids he can. Besides this he needs to seek the help of the Holy Spirit, through whom Scripture was written, to illuminate its meaning. As with the writers of Scripture, so with its readers, the mind and whole being needs to be dedicated to God. It is one of the remarkable features of the Bible that it contains enough to occupy the greatest intellects for a lifetime, and yet the simplest soul can read and understand, and in reading with an obedient heart find God himself.

MODERN ENGLISH TRANSLATIONS OF THE BIBLE

The **Authorized,** or **King James' Version** of the Bible was translated over 350 years ago. The **Revised Version** in the last century kept the same language but made revisions in the light of increased knowledge of the original Hebrew and Greek texts. In the 20th century there have been a number of new translations concerned not only to reflect an accurate text but also current English usage. Their main differences are:

1. Some are revisions (e.g. **The Revised Standard Version**), some wholly new translations from the original languages (e.g. **New English Bible, Jerusalem Bible, Good News Bible**).

2. Some use 'literary' language, including formal or academic words (e.g. **New English Bible, Jerusalem Bible**). Others use colloquial English (e.g. **The Living Bible**), or 'common' English (**Good News Bible**), the language common to both written and spoken English.

3. Some translations are concerned to keep the idiom and general force and meaning of the original; others to keep as closely as possible to the original words and sentence structure.

4. Some keep the literary forms of the original when possible, e.g. by printing poetry as such.

5. Some translations are produced by one man, others by a group.

6. Some translations are made to conserve particular theological or linguistic traditions.

The main 20th-century English translations

1903
R.T. Weymouth, *The New Testament in Modern Speech*
A classical scholar's translation of the New Testament into dignified modern English.

1913 and 1924
James Moffatt, *A New Translation of the Bible*.
A free, vigorous, idiomatic translation which takes some liberties with the text.

1927
E.J. Goodspeed, *The Complete Bible: an American Translation*
A very readable version appreciated both in the United States and elsewhere.

1944 and 1949
Ronald Knox, *The Holy Bible*
A Roman Catholic translation based on the Latin Vulgate.

1946 and 1952
The Revised Standard Version (The Common Bible)
Revision of the American Standard Version of 1901, which was in turn a revision of the Authorized/King James' Version. Translated by a committee of 32 scholars, with the aim of producing a version which would retain the good qualities of the Authorized/King James' Version but take full account of modern scholarship.

1950 and 1960
The New World Translation
Produced by the Jehovah's Witnesses, emphasizing their interpretation of particular texts.

1955
H.J. Schonfield, *The Authentic New Testament*
A translation by a distinguished Jewish scholar, emphasizing the Jewish background of the New Testament.

1958
The Amplified Bible
A version giving alternative words to suggest different possible meanings; produced by 12 editors in California.

1958
J.B. Phillips, *The New Testament in Modern English*
A fresh, vigorous, free translation of the New Testament; revised 1972.

1959
The Holy Bible: The Berkeley Version in Modern English
The New Testament is the work of a single scholar, the Old Testament the work of a team of 20, in the USA: a conservative revision concerned for accuracy.

1961 and 1970
The New English Bible
A completely new translation by panels of scholars taking into account the most accurate and up-to-date linguistic, textual and historical findings; sponsored by the main British churches and Bible Societies.

1966
The Jerusalem Bible
Based on the textual studies of the Roman Catholic School of Biblical Studies, Jerusalem, this is a clear, accurate, scholarly translation.

1966 and 1976
Good News Bible
A completely new, fresh, straight-forward translation in 'common' or non-academic English; produced by the American Bible Society.

1971
Kenneth Taylor, *The Living Bible*
A colloquial, conservative American paraphrase designed for family reading and to help ordinary people understand the Bible.

1974 and 1979
New International Version
A new translation by an internation-al, interdenominational team of evangelical scholars.

FIRST ENGLISH TRANSLATIONS

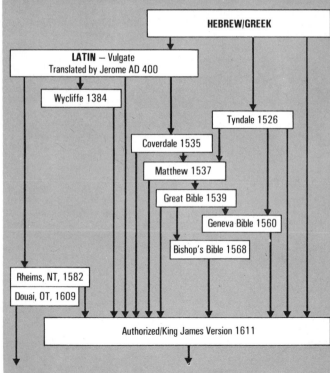

Part Two
OLD TESTAMENT

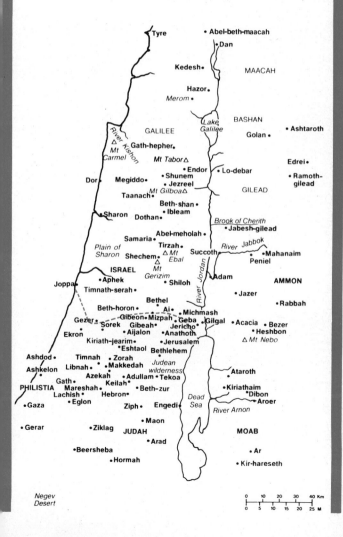

Tyre
Abel-beth-maacah
Dan
Kedesh
MAACAH
Hazor
Merom
BASHAN
Lake Galilee
GALILEE
Golan
Ashtaroth
River Kishon
Mt Carmel
Gath-hepher
Mt Tabor
Endor
Lo-debar
Edrei
Dor
Megiddo
Shunem
Jezreel
Ramoth-gilead
Taanach
Mt Gilboa
GILEAD
Beth-shan
Sharon
Dothan
Ibleam
Brook of Cherith
Jabesh-gilead
Abel-meholah
Samaria
Tirzah
River Jabbok
Plain of Sharon
Shechem
Mt Ebal
Succoth
Mahanaim
Mt Gerizim
Peniel
ISRAEL
Aphek
Shiloh
River Jordan
Joppa
Timnath-serah
Adam
AMMON
Bethel
Jazer
Ai
Rabbah
Beth-horon
Michmash
Gezer
Gibeon
Mizpah
Geba
Gilgal
Acacia
Bezer
Sorek
Gibeah
Jericho
Heshbon
Ekron
Aijalon
Anathoth
Mt Nebo
Kiriath-jearim
Jerusalem
Eshtaol
Bethlehem
Ashdod
Timnah
Zorah
Ashkelon
Libnah
Makkedah
Judean wilderness
Gath
Azekah
Adullam
Tekoa
Ataroth
Mareshah
Keilah
Beth-zur
Kiriathaim
Lachish
Hebron
Dibon
PHILISTIA
Eglon
Ziph
Engedi
Aroer
Gaza
Dead Sea
River Arnon
Gerar
Ziklag
Maon
JUDAH
MOAB
Arad
Beersheba
Ar
Hormah
Kir-hareseth

Negev Desert

0 10 20 30 40 Km
0 5 10 15 20 25 M

OLD TESTAMENT HISTORY AT A GLANCE

	2000BC	1900	1800	1700

Genesis

Israel's northern neighbours

| | | | Hittite Empire founded | |
| Ur's influence curtailed by invaders | | | Law-code of Hammurabi of Babylon | |

Israel

Abraham ●   Isaac ●   Jacob ●

Abram leaves Ur   Joseph ●

Israel's southern neighbour – Egypt

2134-1786 Middle kingdom 2nd great age of Egyptian culture			1710-1570 Hyksos rule in Egypt

2000BC	1900	1800	1700

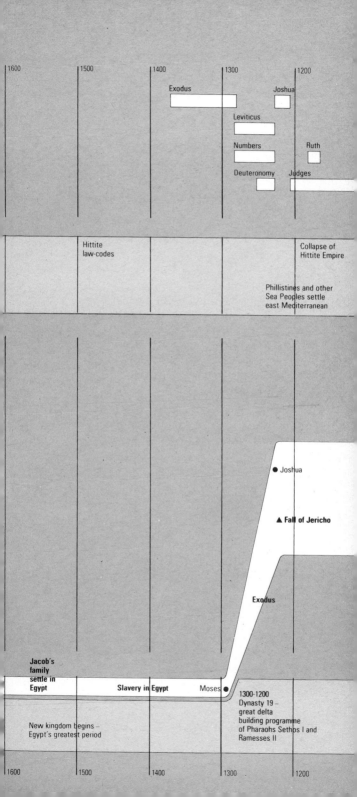

1600	1500	1400	1300	1200

Exodus

Joshua

Leviticus

Numbers

Ruth

Deuteronomy

Judges

Hittite
law-codes

Collapse of
Hittite Empire

Phillistines and other
Sea Peoples settle
east Mediterranean

● Joshua

▲ Fall of Jericho

Exodus

Jacob's
family
settle in
Egypt

Slavery in Egypt

Moses ●

1300-1200
Dynasty 19 –
great delta
building programme
of Pharaohs Sethos I and
Ramesses II

New kingdom begins –
Egypt's greatest period

1600	1500	1400	1300	1200

	1200	1100	1000	900

Joshua

Leviticus

1 Chronicles   2 Chronicles

Numbers   Ruth   1 Samuel   2 Samuel

Poetry and wisdom (Psalms, Proverbs

Deuteronomy   Judges   1 Kings

Israel's northern neighbours

Collapse of
Hittite Empire

Damascus rises
to power

Philistines and
other Sea Peoples settle
east Mediterranean

Golden Age
of Tyre
(Phoenicia)

Israel (Northern

🐂 Ahab

● Elijah and
Elisha

Israel

● Gideon   🐂 David   🐂 Jeroboam I

● Joshua   ● Solomon   🐂 Omri

● Samuel

▲ Fall of Jericho

🐂 Saul

▲ 1st
temple
built

🐂 Rehoboam

Israel's
Golden
Age

🐂 Asa

● Samson

🐂 Jehoshaphat

Exodus

Judah (Southern

Israel's southern neighbour – Egypt

✗ Pharaoh
Sheshonq I
invades
Palestine

	1200	1100	1000	900

800	700	600	500	400BC

Songs of Solomon, Ecclesiastes)

Esther   Nehemiah

The Prophets (See Prophets chart)

2 Kings

Ezra

✂ Damascus falls to
Tiglath-pileser III
of Assyria

Fall of ✂
Nineveh

Rise of
Babylon

✂ Cyrus king
of Persia
overthrows
Babylon

👑 Xerxes (Ahasuerus)
king in Persia with
Esther as queen

Rise of
Assyria

● Ezekiel

Kingdom)

▲ Ezra
returns
from exile

Fall of ✂
**Samaria to
Assyria**

Jeroboam II 👑

▲ 2nd batch
of captives
exiled

**Daniel
taken to
Babylon** ▲

▲ 1st batch
of captives
exiled

**Zerubbabel
and main
party of
exiles return** ▲

👑 Uzziah

● Jeremiah

Josiah's ▲
reformation

▲ **Nehemiah's
return to
Jerusalem**

● Isaiah

👑 Hezekiah

▲ **Jerusalem
destroyed**

▲ **2nd temple
completed**

▲ **Assyrians
besiege
Jerusalem**

▲ **Jerusalem
falls to
Nebuchadnezzar II**

Kingdom)

Egyptian power
abroad begins
to weaken

✂ Babylonians
defeat Necho
at Carchemish

800	700	600	500	400BC

THE 'FIVE BOOKS'

The name 'Pentateuch' is given to the first five books of the Bible. It comes from two Greek words meaning 'five scrolls'. But it is better to think of the Pentateuch as one book divided into five sections, rather than as five books rolled into one. In this way justice is done not only to its Hebrew origin, where it was called the 'Torah' (Law) or the 'Five fifths of Moses', but also to its own inherent unity.

That does not mean to say that the Pentateuch consists of an extended piece of narrative writing in strict chronological order. It is immediately obvious to the reader that it contains a wide variety of literary material – narratives, laws, ritual instructions, sermons, genealogies, poetry – which have been drawn together from different sources. It does mean, however, that the material has been carefully constructed within a narrative framework, with a clear purpose in mind and with recognizable objectives on the part of the author or editor.

THE FRAMEWORK

The framework of the Pentateuch consists of the story of God's people from the call of Abraham to the death of Moses. It spans a period of over 600 years, i.e. from about 1900 BC to about 1250 BC, though it is notoriously difficult to be sure of dates at this early stage of Israel's history. The story is in two sections. The first is dominated by the four generations of the patriarchs – Abraham, Isaac, Jacob and Joseph (Genesis 12-50); the second by the majestic figure of Moses (Exodus-Deuteronomy). It is preceded by a prologue (Genesis 1-11), consisting of ancient records and traditions, which serve not only to introduce the main themes of the narrative but also to relate them to God's purposes in the world of fallen men, of divided nations and of a created order which was originally good. It is best to look first at the main themes of the books as a whole, and then examine the significance of these introductory chapters.

FOUR IMPORTANT THEMES

Election

The Old Testament was written for the people of Israel – the people who looked back to Jacob (=Israel) as their common ancestor and to Abraham as the founder of their nation. Christians, too, look to Abraham as the father of all those who depend in faith on God rather than on anything they can do for themselves (see Romans 4:16). We therefore read the story of Abraham's call by God to become the ancestor of God's chosen people, not simply as an event in the distant past, but as something of present-day significance to us.

The idea of 'election' – God's special choosing of individuals – carries with it two subsidiary features: promise and responsibility. Genesis 12-22 is interspersed with words of promise spoken by God to Abraham. Abraham is promised descendants as countless as the stars of heaven. He is given the land of Canaan as his children's inheritance. He is promised a great name in days to come. And the Lord's special favour was to be shown not only to Abraham and his family but to all men through him.

So God's promises to Abraham were not just for the selfish enjoyment of a chosen few. They were to be used responsibly so that others might share in the benefits. Right at the heart of God's choice of Israel it is made plain that God has a missionary purpose. Israel's history must be read as the long story of her attempts to fulfil her responsibilities – with some successes, but with many conspicuous failures.

Covenant

To the modern mind a 'covenant' is simply a matter of legal documents and sealing-wax. But to the Hebrew mind it covered all human relationships. It was the bond which united people in mutual obligations, whether through a marriage contract, a commercial enterprise or a verbal under-taking. It was natural that man's relationship to God should have been expressed in covenant terms.

These covenant terms are used to describe three separate occasions in the Pentateuch:
— God's promises to Noah that he would never again send a flood upon the earth (Genesis 9:9).
— God's promises to Abraham (Genesis 15:18; 17:4).
— The Sinai covenant established with Moses and summarized in the 'book of the covenant' (Exodus 24:7).

Though covenants were made between equals, the religious use of the term always referred to a relationship between a greater and a lesser partner. The form of the covenant between God and Israel in Exodus and Deuteronomy has been helpfully illuminated by recent discoveries of Hittite suzerainty-treaties made between a king and his vassal. They consisted of a historical introduction, a list of stipulations, curses and blessings invoked on the parties, a solemn oath and a religious ceremony to ratify the covenant. Most of these features can be found in the Old Testament pattern of covenants. (See article 'Covenants and Near Eastern Treaties'.)

More important than the form of the covenant, however, was its theological significance.

It was based on the initiative of God. He acted in mercy and with sovereignty. He made an unconditional promise never to judge mankind with another flood (Genesis 9:11). He chose Abraham and his descendants to be the channels of his mercy to a fallen world. He cemented this election by committing himself to the Israelite nation with the words, 'I will take you for my people, and I will be your God' (Exodus 6:7).

It implied a new revelation of God. He appeared to Abraham as his shield (Genesis 15:1) and as God Almighty ('El Shaddai', Genesis 17:1). He appeared to Moses as 'Yahweh' ('I am who I am', Exodus 3:14), and later on as 'Yahweh your God, who brought you out of the land of Egypt' (Exodus 20:2). (See article 'The Names of God'.)

It made moral and ritual demands upon the people. The stipulations of the covenant included both these features. Ritual was represented by the rite of circumcision given to Abraham (Genesis 17:10), by the keeping of the sabbath, the day of rest (Exodus 20:8ff.) and by all the detailed requirements relating to worship and sacrifice found in the Pentateuch. At the same time the ethical requirements were spelt out in the Ten Commandments and other laws. Though at first sight these two demands seem strangely unrelated, they do in fact meet in the idea of God's holiness. A holy God requires his people to reflect his character both in worship and in behaviour.

Law

The idea of law is central to the Pentateuch and, as we have seen, it gave its name to the book as a whole. At its simplest, it covered the Ten Commandments (Exodus 20; Deuteronomy 5) but associated with these were various collections of laws which have been classified as:
— the book of the covenant (Exodus 21-23);
— the holiness code (Leviticus 17-26);
— the law of Deuteronomy (Deuteronomy 12-26).

Comparisons have been made with other ancient Near Eastern law-codes, especially the Code of Hammurabi, and many similarities noted. This illustrates the fact that Israel was a part of Eastern Mediterranean culture and shared in the ideas and experience of her neighbours. But what is so significant is not so much the similarities as the differences which made Israel's laws distinctive. These may be summarized as:
— their uncompromising monotheism (everything is related to the one God);
— their remarkable concern for the under-privileged: slaves, strangers, women, orphans;
— their community spirit, based on the covenant relationship shared by all Israel with the Lord.

It has also been pointed out that the laws in the Old Testament may be classified as either 'apodictic' in form ('thou shalt ...' or 'thou shalt not ...') or 'casuistic' ('when a man ..., he shall ...'). As most ancient law-codes consisted of the casuistic type, it may be that the apodictic was a peculiarly Israelite form, in which case the Decalogue (the Ten Commandments) was unique to Israel.

Some Christians have mistakenly seen Jesus' teaching in the Sermon on the Mount as a rejection of the

Jewish law in favour of his new law of love. But Jesus' criticisms were in fact directed not at the laws, but at the way the rabbis had interpreted them. ('You have heard that it was said' was the traditional rabbinic formula for introducing their interpretation.) He was uncovering the inner motivation behind the commandments, which interpreters had failed to appreciate.

Some too have criticized the Ten Commandments for being negative. But they follow a positive assertion: 'I am the Lord your God ...' Those who have experienced deliverance by the hand of God, and who live under his sovereignty, must show it by distinctive behaviour. The Ten Commandments therefore began as God's charter for his liberated people. They consisted not of generalities but of specific commands for specific situations: worship, work, home life, marriage, respect for life and property, elementary justice and the personal realm of the will. To all these areas of human experience God had a word that was explicit and inescapable. Christ did not destroy it: he fulfilled and enlarged it.

The same cannot be said of the ceremonial and ritual laws which occupy much of Leviticus and other parts of the Pentateuch. The purpose of these laws was not only to provide guidance for the day-to-day running of the Israelite community, but to teach how a holy God was to be worshipped by a holy people. So, in addition to regulations for worship (festivals, sacrifices, etc.), detailed guidance was given for the preservation of ritual purity. The Israelite people had to be kept free of contamination from outside sources, especially the corrupting influence of Canaanite religion. They must approach God with a due sense of his moral and ritual distinctiveness.

These regulations no longer apply to the Christian church, though the underlying principles still have much to teach. And the elaborate sacrificial system has found its fulfilment in the one sacrifice of Christ – the perfect Lamb of God – through whom sins are forgiven and atonement is made for all men for ever (see Hebrews 10:1-18).

Exodus

The fourth major theme found in the Pentateuch, and recurring throughout the Bible, is the exodus from Egypt, described in Exodus 1-12. To the Jew this was the great saving act of God to which all later generations looked back with thankfulness. It was a miraculous intervention by God in response to the cries of his enslaved people (Exodus 3:7). It was essentially God's act - 'with mighty hand and outstretched arm'. It was a great victory over the gods of Egypt which demonstrated his total supremacy. It was a moment in history recalled every year in the Feast of the Passover. Later generations were frequently reminded that they were once members of a slave community whom the Lord had mercifully redeemed from bondage. They were encouraged to remember the past and warned of the danger of forgetting what God had done for them (e.g. Deuteronomy 6:12).

As a historical event the exodus was definitive. The fact that God had done it once meant that he could do it again. When Israel was in exile in Babylon the nation looked for a second exodus (Isaiah 51:9-11). And when Christ came, his work of deliverance was described in the language of the exodus (e.g. Luke 9:31).

These, then, are the four themes which are never far below the surface of the Pentateuch. They are the constant preoccupation of these five books. The only other theme – which recurs with depressing regularity – is the persistent sinfulness of the people of Israel. They were slow to accept Moses as their deliverer. They grumbled about the hardships of the journey. They even hankered after the old life in Egypt (suitably glamorized, Numbers 11:5). They were daunted by the prospect of moving into the land of Canaan. And they wandered for 40 years in the wilderness of indecision. Not even Moses was immune, and he was punished by not being allowed to lead the people into their promised land. But sin was no new problem. To discover why, we must turn to the introductory chapters of Genesis.

THE PROLOGUE

The early chapters of Genesis were once regarded by some Christians as an embarrassment. But the old science-versus-faith controversies are increasingly a thing of the past. In fact, these chapters are now reckoned to be among the foremost theological statements the Bible contains. Once men were released from trying to defend them as scientific documents they were able to listen to what the text was actually saying.

The form of this message has often been described as 'myth'. But this is a misleading term, even when 'myth' is understood in the technical sense of a 'religious text designed to account for a custom, institution or other phenomenon'. It is also misleading because it is thought to be unhistorical and untrue. But in fact these early chapters of Genesis *are* historical, in that they bear witness to events which actually took place. The world was created; man and woman were made in God's image; the fall did take place in time. The problem is the degree of symbolism used in describing these events. On this, opinions will continue to vary considerably.

It is to these chapters that we turn for biblical guidance on the fundamental questions concerning God, man and the world. At every stage God is present. He is not simply presupposed; he is constantly and actively at work. This world is his world. Human history is the outworking of his plan. He is totally responsible for the world and all that is in it. All men are his creation, made 'in his image' – with spiritual capacities for goodness, worship and fellowship with him. There is no place whatsoever for other gods. Genesis 1 is all-embracing: sun, moon and stars are his handiwork, with duties to perform in his ordered universe; even the sea-monsters (the *tanninim* of ancient mythology) were created by him (Genesis 1:21).

Man is the climax of creation, superior to all else but subordinate to his Creator. Only when man aspires above his station and wants to be like God does he fall to a lowlier position in which all his relationships are soured. Sex, from being a good, companionable, shame-free relationship, becomes secretive, lustful, anomalous. Child-bearing is painful and hazardous. The noble art of husbandry becomes a drudgery. Even the ground is affected, and instead of producing food plentifully it has to be coaxed and sweated over. There is nothing that sin has not blighted. Its taint reaches out to family life, where religion turns to rivalry, brotherly love becomes murder, and justice degenerates into blood-lust (Genesis 4).

God's response to sin is, consistently, a blend of judgement and mercy. From the provision of skins for Adam and Eve, and the guarding of the way to the tree of life, to the confusion of tongues at Babel, God tempers justice with salvation. Beyond the immediate punishment of casting Adam out from the garden of Eden or Cain from human society, beyond the destruction of the flood and the scattering of the nations, there was always God's ultimate intention for man's well-being and blessing. Thus in a world of disorder and corruption, it was totally in keeping with God's nature that he should call out one man, Abraham, and through him his descendants the Jews, to be the channel of grace and revelation to all mankind.

It is this story which the Pentateuch tells.

GENESIS

The book of Genesis is an epic, a drama on a grand scale. It begins at the very beginning. God made the world, a world that was good. He made man, the apex of all creation.

The 'prologue' (chapters 1-11) provides us with a general history of man over some thousands of years. We see God's good creation progressively soured as a result of man's sin in overreaching himself in trying to become like God. Then everything is swept away in the great flood. A new beginning is made – only to end in the folly of Babel and the division and dispersion of the nations.

In chapter 12 the emphasis shifts. From the history of man in general we focus down to the story of a single individual, Abraham, and his descendants. God will not destroy his creation. Instead he begins to work, through one man of his choice, and one nation of his choice, for the renewing of the world. Genesis takes the story on through Isaac and Jacob to the death of Joseph in Egypt. And still the story of God's great purpose for mankind is scarcely begun. It continues on through the pages of Scripture to the very last words of the book of Revelation.

1 - 2:4 CREATION

The great drama of the beginning of all things starts with God. The language is simple but vivid. It evokes the wonder and richness of creation from formlessness to teeming life.

But it is more than poetic. It tells us what we need to know in order to understand ourselves and the world around us:
— The origin of the world and of life was no accident. There is a Creator: God.
— God made everything there is.
— All that God made was good.
— The high point of all God's creative acts was the making of man.
— Mankind is distinguished from all other creatures in two respects: he alone is made in God's own likeness; and he is given charge over all the rest.
— God's six 'days' of creative activity followed by a 'day' of rest, sets the pattern for man's working life.

Creation is described as taking place in six days. There are eight acts of creation, each introduced by the words 'and God said ...'
DAY 1
Light and darkness/day and night
DAY 2
Earth's atmosphere (the firmament)
DAY 3
Dry land and seas separated
Plants and trees
DAY 4
Sun, moon and stars: seasons, days, years
DAY 5
Sea creatures and birds
DAY 6
Land animals
Man
DAY 7
Creation completed, God rests

The events are described from the standpoint of an observer seeing the development of creation around him. The order is not necessarily chronological (a modern idea!). Light and darkness, for example, are described before the sun, moon and stars. The account is one which we can all understand – from the simplest peasant to scientifically educated 20th-century man.

This is not a treatise on geology, biology, or any other science. We are not told when creation took place. Nor are we given details as to how God brought the earth and life into being – nor how long it all took. The 'days' are taken by some to be periods of time. Others think that this pattern of seven days is simply the most vivid means of expressing the creative energy and satisfaction of God, the orderliness and simple majesty of the way he created all things.

The 'image' or 'likeness' of God (1:27): of all creation, only man (including both man and woman) is described as being made in God's likeness. However it is understood, the phrase sets man apart from the animals. It establishes him in a special relationship with God. God gives man control over the newly-made world and all its creatures. The 'likeness' is so basic to man's structure that the Fall did not destroy it. Sin has certainly spoiled and blurred it, but man remains a reasoning, moral, creative creature. He is still intended to be in control of his environment. To make him no more than animal is to make him less than man in God's likeness.

2:5 - 3:24 MAN: TESTING AND DOWNFALL

2:5-25 Focus on man
This second description of creation is not simply a duplicate of the first. It is written from a different point of view – this time focussing on man. It also uses a different name for God. In the first account it was *Elohim*, God the Creator, the great and lofty One who inhabits eternity. Now it is *Yahweh* (Jehovah) *Elohim*, God in relation to his people (see article 'The Names of God'). The two accounts

A 7th-century BC clay tablet inscribed with a part of the Babylonian account of the creation.

may represent two different traditions or sources. But that is no reason for trying to make them contradict each other. Nor should this be an excuse to try to carve up Genesis to fit a theory – about the evolution of religion or anything else.

OTHER CREATION ACCOUNTS
Alan Millard

Creation stories belonging to other ancient peoples have given currency to the view that Genesis contains merely another version, adapted to suit Hebrew beliefs. Genesis 1 and 2 consist of a general account of the creation of the heavens and the earth, followed by a more detailed description of the making of man. Stories of cosmic and of human creation, either separately or as unities, are numerous, and many have several points in common: pre-existent deity; creation by divine command; man the ultimate creature; man formed from the earth as a pot is made; man in some way a reflection of deity. Almost all polytheistic faiths possess family-trees of their gods which can figure in creation stories. A primal pair or even a single self-created and self-propagating god heads the divine family, all of whose members represent or control natural elements and forces.

For some peoples, the physical universe or a basic element such as water or earth always existed, and the gods arose from it. For others it was the handiwork of a god or gods. These are simple concepts based on observation and elementary logic. For example, man as 'dust' is easily deduced from the cycle of death and decay.

However, common ideas need not share a common origin; it is misleading to reduce differing stories from all over the world to their common factors in order to claim that they do. A single source for all, or large numbers, of different stories is improbable.

Ancient Near Eastern stories

Nevertheless, it is quite in order to set Genesis beside other accounts from the world of the Old Testament. When we do so, we find that few of the ancient creation stories share more than one or two basic concepts – such as the separation of heaven and earth, and the creation of man from clay. The Babylonian literature, however, affords some striking resemblances. In the century since one was first translated into English, the Babylonian accounts have been cited as the ultimate source of the Hebrew's beliefs. Recently, the recovery of more texts and the reassessment of those long known have shown that many of the accepted similarities are in fact illusory.

The famous *Babylonian Genesis*, usually linked with the Hebrew creation story, is one of several, and was neither the oldest nor the most popular. Written late in the 2nd millennium BC to honour Marduk, god of Babylon, who is its hero, it begins with a watery mother-figure, Tiamat, from whom the gods are born. (The name is related to the Hebrew word for 'the deep' through the pre-historic linguistic connections between Babylonian and Hebrew.) She is killed by Marduk in a battle with her children whose noise had angered her, and her corpse is formed into the world. Man is made to relieve the gods of the toil of keeping the earth in order.

There are clear indications that this story was made up from older ones, and earlier compositions have been found which contain some of these features. Only one theme recurs often, the relief of the gods from their labour by the making of man with a divine ingredient. The battle of the gods in the Babylonian Genesis has no Old Testament equivalent, despite attempts by many scholars to discover underlying references to it in the text of Genesis 1:2 and other passages which speak of God's power over the waters.

An epic of early man

One Babylonian poem, the *Atrakhasis Epic*, bears further comparison with Genesis. This is concerned with the infancy of man and the beginning of society, and hints at the order of the world without describing its creation. It starts with the minor gods working to irrigate the land, then rebelling at their lot, from which they are relieved by the creation of man who is to do the work instead. Man is a satisfactory substitute until his noise causes disturbance and leads to his destruction in the flood (see Flood Stories).

In outline, *Atrakhasis* (known from copies made about 1600 BC) has some similarity to parts of Genesis 2-8. Man is made from clay and a divine part ('breath' in Genesis, the flesh and blood of a god in *Atrakhasis*): man's task is to keep the earth in order (arduous labour in *Atrakhasis*, control of a paradise in Genesis); man is eventually destroyed by flood, all except one family. On the other hand, *Atrakhasis* has man toiling from the first, has no single 'Adam', no separate making of woman, no Eden, and no Fall – in fact no moral teaching at all. The sense is rather that this is how man's lot came to be, and he should accept it.

A Sumerian version names five important cities in the time before the flood, and they link with separately preserved lists of pre-flood kings whose ages far exceeded those of the patriarchs in Genesis 5. Babylonian writers looked upon the flood as a major interruption in their country's history. In their over-all coverage, therefore Genesis and the tradition represented by *Atrakhasis* look back to the same events. Some of the themes in the Babylonian story – in particular, man's place as a substitute worker – can be traced in a Sumerian poem, *Enki and Ninmakh*, written before 2,000 BC. These factual similarities only serve to emphasize the wide difference in moral and spiritual outlook between the Hebrew Genesis and its closest counterparts. There is no need to argue that Genesis was derived from the others, as critics of the Bible have hastened to do. The differences of standpoint and content are in fact so marked that they serve to highlight the divine inspiration of Genesis rather than undermine it.

God creates man. (The Hebrew word translated 'Adam' means 'man'.) He plants a garden in Eden in the east, where man is to live. But man is not made for a solitary, self-sufficient existence. Neither birds nor animals provide the kind of companionship he needs. So God creates woman, a new being, yet sharing man's own essential nature.

The pattern of chapter 1 shows the principle of one day's rest in seven. The account of chapter 2 sets the pattern for human marriage.

The two trees: the phrase 'good and evil' may well be a Hebrew idiom standing for the full range of moral knowledge represented by the two extremes. To eat of the tree of the knowledge of good and evil will therefore make man like God. The tree of life, inaccessible to man once he had sinned, appears again in the last book of the Bible. It stands beside the river in the city of the new Jerusalem, where God and his people once more live together – and its leaves are for 'the healing of the nations' (Revelation 22:2). True life is ultimately dependent on the presence of God.

3 Man disobeys God
The serpent questions what God has said, then calls God a liar. The woman has to set the enticing fruit, the desire to have knowledge like God himself, against God's plain command. The decision is deliberate, and fatal. Man has disobeyed God, rejected his authority, chosen to go his own way and become a 'god' himself.

The result is inevitable. A holy God cannot live with sin. The serpent is sentenced first (verse 14 does not mean that he had legs before). The woman is to experience suffering – in childbirth, the most fundamental human process. She is to know what it means for her husband to 'rule' over her. From now on Adam's work is to be sweat and toil.

Because of sin, access to the tree of life is now denied them. They are to leave the garden, and there is no return. Spiritual death, being cut off from God, is immediate. Physical death follows in the course of time. God's warning was true. Yet he continues to care for them, and clothes them before they go.

**4 THE FIRST FAMILY –
AND THE FIRST MURDER**
Adam and Eve, after their expulsion

from the garden, have two sons: Cain, the farmer, and Abel, the shepherd. In due course each brings his offering to God. Abel's is accepted, but not Cain's. It was not *what* Abel offered, but his faith, which made his gift acceptable (Hebrews 11:4). Cain's bitter resentment shows a very different spirit.

Cain kills Abel – it is a short step from rebellion to bloodshed – and God condemns him to a nomadic life, but provides protection against death. Verses 17-24 list some of Cain's descendants, and show the beginnings of civilized life. Enoch builds the first city. His successors learn to play and enjoy music – also to forge iron and bronze. If good things flourish, so do evil. Lamech takes two wives, and boasts to them of the murder he has committed, outdoing Cain.

The last two verses give a glimmer of hope. Seth is born to Adam and Eve, and men begin 'to call upon the name of the Lord'.

Cain's wife: verse 17 and verses 14-15 give the impression of an earth already, to some extent, populated. The simplest way of accounting for this is to assume other, unnamed children of Adam and Eve. Others would argue from the fact that the word *adam* = man, or mankind, that a race was created, not a single pair. But however we resolve the problem we must never cut across the basic teaching of other scriptures, that one man's disobedience plunged the whole human race into sin, subjecting us all to death (see for example Romans 5:12ff.).

5 FROM ADAM TO NOAH
Family-trees (genealogies) similar to this one are often given in the Bible attesting a line of descent. Many of them are selective, sometimes in order to give a pattern of a certain number of names (e.g. Matthew 1). So we cannot work out the length of the whole period simply by adding up all the figures given.

The life-span of these men is remarkable. It ranges from 777 years for Lamech to Methuselah's 969 years (apart from Enoch, whom God 'took' at 365). Many races have traditions of exceptionally long life amongst their early forebears. But none of the various attempted explanations has so far proved satisfactory.

FLOOD STORIES

Alan Millard

Memories of a great flood or floods are worldwide. As one would expect, they have such common features as escape by boat, animals taken aboard, and grounding on a high peak. Only Babylonia has given us a story so close to Genesis that the question of borrowing or of direct influence is seriously considered.

For a century this story has been known from the *Epic of Gilgamesh*, Tablet 11. Its theme is that man cannot hope for immortality, the only one who gained it being the Babylonian Noah. It was taken into the Gilgamesh series from an older work the *Atrakhasis Epic* (see 'Other Creation Accounts'). Here it forms part of a longer account of man's history from his creation, as in Genesis.

Babylonian account

After the first men were made, it relates, the noise of their many children was so great that the god of the earth could not sleep. His schemes for reducing man's noise were thwarted when the pious Atrakhasis won the help of the god whose creature man was. Finally, the gods decided upon a catastrophic flood, all swearing to keep the plan secret. Again, Atrakhasis was warned, the god instructing him in a dream to build a boat, take on board his family and animals, and explain his action to his fellow men as a punishment inflicted upon him which would bring benefit to them. When all were aboard, the storm broke, and all mankind was swept away.

The gods themselves were also affected. With man destroyed, they lost the food and drink supplied in sacrificial offerings, and sat miserably in heaven until the seven days tempest had ended. Then Atrakhasis sent out birds to learn whether the land was habitable again (an episode preserved only in the *Gilgamesh* version), and offered sacrifice on the mountain where his boat had come to rest. Eagerly, the gods gathered 'like flies', smelling the savour of the offering, swearing not to cause such destruction again. The mother-goddess swore by a necklace of blue stones. But the god whose sleep had been disturbed was not yet appeased, and after the unfairness of indiscriminate punishment had been discussed, a system was set up in which some women avoided childbirth by entering religious orders, while others lost infants through disease, thus limiting the population. (The terms used make it clear that this was an explanation of the social system of the author's time.)

A question of theology

The flood story in Babylonia is also known from a Sumerian text telling virtually the same tale, though more briefly, and many Sumerian compositions refer to the distant days of the flood or before.

The Genesis flood story has a recognizable background in Mesopotamia, and the numerous similarities suggest it is a record of the same event as the Babylonian. But its moral and theological content are obviously very different. God's revelation consists not only in the telling of the facts but also in their interpretation.

Each of the ten records follows the same formula:
When A had lived x years he became the father of B. He lived after the birth of B y years and had other sons and daughters. Thus all his days were z years, and he died.

The sombre note of the final phrase 'and he died' is varied only in the case of Enoch, the man who 'walked with God'. For him God had other plans. Noah, the last of the ten, in his turn also 'walked with God' (6:9). And in his case, too, God intervened to save him from death.

6 - 9 THE GREAT FLOOD
6 - 9:17 The rescue, and God's promise to Noah
Flood-stories have been handed down in many languages from most parts of the world. The Babylonian (Sumerian, and particularly Akkadian) accounts have considerable similarity with the story recorded here. This is not surprising, if both reflect memories of an actual event in the same general area. There is no need to assume the writer of Genesis must have drawn on the Babylonian stories for his information. Indeed, the crudeness of these (with their many bickering, capricious gods) makes this unlikely.
Extent and date of the flood: if we take the terms used in Genesis 7:19ff. in their modern sense, the flood must have been universal. But biblical writers use similar phrases in contexts where it is clear they are not speaking of the whole world as we understand it (Genesis 41:56-57; Acts 2:5). Taking the description at the very least, the flood covered a vast area, the 'whole world' of man's early history as recounted in Genesis 2ff.

Its universality as far as human life is concerned depends on when it actually happened, and we can do no more than guess at the date. The list of nations descended from Noah's sons (Genesis 10) makes it clear that the flood must have occurred very early indeed. It was certainly long before the various South Mesopotamian floods of which traces have been found in the course of excavation.
The ark: the Hebrew word means 'box' or 'chest'. It is used elsewhere only for the watertight 'basket' in which the baby Moses floated on the Nile – an interesting parallel.

The ark is vast, designed to float, not sail – and there were no launching problems! An 18-inch cubit gives the measurements as 450 x 76 x 45 feet or 137 x 23 x 14 metres.
The covenant (6-18): an important and recurring theme in Scripture. God establishes his covenant (agreement) successively with Noah, with Abraham, with the nation of Israel (through Moses), and with David. Each covenant grows progressively richer in promise, until the coming of Christ ushers in the 'new covenant'.

In every instance God takes the initiative – this is no agreement between equal parties. God draws up the terms. He makes them known. And he alone guarantees their keeping. Men enjoy the blessings of the covenant in so far as they obey God's commands.

See article 'Covenants and Near Eastern Treaties'.
9:18-29 Noah's drunkenness
Even a completely fresh start does not change man – as this shameful little story makes plain. Ham dishonours his drunken father, and Noah curses him through his descendants. The Canaanites – descended from Ham through Canaan – did indeed become subject to Shem's descendants, the Israelites.

10 - 11 FROM NOAH TO THE CALL OF ABRA(HA)M
10 The families of Noah's three sons
The genealogy is arranged in the following pattern:
Heading (1)
Japheth's descendants (2-4)
Extra detail on Javan (5a)
Summary (5b)

Ham's descendants (6-7, 13-18a)
Extra detail on Nimrod (8-12)
and Canaan (18b-19)
Summary (20)

Shem's descendants (22-29a)
Extra detail on Shem (21)
and Joktan (29b-30)
Summary (31)
Summary to the whole list (32)

Shem's family comes last, as these are the nations around which the next stage of the narrative develops.
11:1-9 Babel
In Shinar, kingdom of Nimrod the hunter (10:10), men get together on a great building project – a city and a tower with its top in the heavens.

NATIONS DESCENDED FROM NOAH'S SONS

Ashkenaz
Gomer
Meshech
Togarmah
Javan
Tubal
Lud
Aram
Caphtor
Asshur
Madai
Kittim
Put
Canaan
Lubim
Lehabim
Shinar
Elam
Mizraim
Dedan
Cush

■ JAPHETH: Indo–European peoples
▲ SHEM: Semitic peoples
● HAM: African peoples

God looks down at this co-operative effort of man trying to make himself god-like, and sees it as the beginning of worse rebellion against him. So he divides men by language barriers, and scatters them abroad – the very thing they were trying to insure against. And the great tower remains unfinished.

The tower of Babel was in all likelihood a multi-storeyed temple-tower, or ziggurat, similar to those developed in Babylonia in the early 3rd millennium BC.

11:10-32 Shem to Abraham
Here again the list of names is selective, probably abbreviating the total length of time involved. Noah's ancestors were considerably longer-lived than Terah's, and the age of parenthood is now much younger.

When Terah's name is reached the list becomes more detailed. This is the family we are to concentrate on. Terah's three sons are named, and their home-town given as Ur of the Chaldeans. After the death of Haran, Terah sets out for Canaan, with his grandson Lot and his son Abram and childless daughter-in-law Sarai. En route, however, they settle at Harran. Terah dies, and the stage is set for the story of Abraham (the new name records God's promise to make this man the father of many nations, 17:5).

12 - 25:18 ABRAHAM: A NEW START
12:1-9 God's call, and the journey to Canaan
12:1 records God's call and promise

The partially reconstructed ziggurat or temple-tower at Ur shows how the Tower of Babel may have been built, with stairways leading from one level to the next.

ABRAHAM'S JOURNEYS

Caspian Sea

Harran

River Tigris

River Euphrates

Mediterranean Sea

BABYLONIA

Babylon

SUMER

EGYPT

Ur

Persian Gulf

to one man, Abram, and his obedient response. Yet the consequences of this simple beginning were to spread like ripples on a pond. As a direct result a new nation is born. And in course of time the whole world reaps the benefits.

'So Abram went ... ' He had already left Ur, a prosperous city with security and a high standard of living. Now he sets out on the second stage of the journey, with Sarai, his childless wife, and his nephew Lot.

At Shechem, in the midst of Canaanite country, God speaks again. 'This land' is to be the heritage of Abram's descendants. Yet the journey continues, down towards the Negev, a dry region of some 4,500 sq. miles, stretching south from Beersheba to the Sinai highlands. Here there is pasturage for nomadic flocks and herds.

12:10-20 Famine
Hunger drives Abram into Egypt. Under stress of fear and insecurity he adopts a pretence which puts God's whole plan at risk. God intervenes with plagues, and Abram is ignominiously deported.

Sarai's age: it seems surprising to find Sarai, at 65, described as 'very beautiful' (12:14). Presumably, since it is said that she lived to 127, her sixties would be equivalent to our thirties or forties.

13 The parting with Lot
Increasing flocks and herds precipitate the last break in family ties. Lot, generously given the choice by his uncle, selects the fertile pasturage of the Jordan Valley.

14 War of the kings, and the meeting with Melchizedek
In Abram's day, although a semi-nomadic existence was common, there was also settled life in villages and walled 'cities'. These were ruled over by local 'sheiks', who in turn were often vassals of more powerful kings.

Chedorlaomer of Elam (1): the overlords of the Dead Sea towns came from distant Elam and Babylonia. Trade-routes made for easy travel and communications between the land of Abram's birth and Canaan. The Elamites had considerable power in Babylonia. Ur was amongst the cities they conquered and sacked at this time.

Amorites (7): Abram's allies belonged to a tribe sharing the land with the Canaanites. They had good reason to support Abram, since their own people had been victims of the attack. Speed of pursuit and a surprise attack gave Abram victory.

Melchizedek (18): this is the only appearance of the rather mysterious king/priest of Salem (probably Jerusalem). Melchizedek's authority (the 'tithe' was God's portion, so by giving Melchizedek a tenth of everything Abram recognized him as God's representative), his lack of any named ancestors and descendants (extremely important for any man claiming kingship or priesthood), and his dual role as priest and king, led later writers to see in him a fore-shadowing of the Messiah (see Psalm 110:4; Hebrews 7:1-10).

15 The covenant confirmed
Archaeology has shown that customs recorded here and in later chapters reflect the known social and cultural patterns of north Mesopotamia in the 2nd millennium BC.

The heir: it was not uncommon practice at the time for childless couples to adopt an heir, sometimes, as here, a slave. The adoption contract might contain a proviso that if a natural son was born he would take precedence as the legal heir.

Verse 6: 'And he believed the Lord; and he reckoned it to him as righteousness.' One of the most significant verses of Scripture, and in the circumstances a response of remarkable faith. Galatians 3:6ff. teaches that, as in Abram's case, our standing before God is entirely dependent on faith. We cannot win a place in heaven by good deeds – neither did he.

The covenant ritual: a typical procedure for the confirmation of a treaty (see Jeremiah 34:18). By killing and dividing the animals the parties to the treaty made it clear that the penalty for breaking the agreement was death. Here, significantly, it is only God who puts himself on oath by passing between the pieces. Darkness, smoke and fire mark the presence of God, as at Sinai (see Exodus 19:18; Hebrews 12:18).

Four hundred years (15:13) ... the fourth generation (15:16): the word 'generation' may also mean 'lifetime', and the lifetime of Abram was well over a century.

Verse 16b: New English Bible 'for the Amorites will not be ripe for punishment till then.' This helps us understand the orders to destroy the Canaanite nations at the conquest. It was a matter of justice. God gave them more than four centuries to show a change of heart. By Joshua's time they had reached the point of no return. As with Sodom and Gomorrah, judgement could no longer be delayed.

16 A son by a slave-girl
The childless Sarai falls back on custom in giving her slave-girl to Abram. This provision could be written into the marriage contract. The resulting child would become the wife's. But human emotions in such a situation are complex, and the unhappy sequel is not surprising.

17 New names and a covenant sign
God's fifth affirmation of his covenant with Abram is marked by the giving of new names – Abram becomes 'Abraham'; Sarai becomes 'Sarah' – and the physical sign of circumcision. Twenty-four years after the departure from Harran the time of the promised son's arrival is announced.

Circumcision: this was no new rite. In the nations around it marked admission to adult status in the tribe. But for Israel it was the outward sign of a relationship: God was to be their God; they were to be his people. It was a mark of ownership, and a reminder of the covenant 'between me and you and your descendants after you' (17:7). Some stress the medical grounds for the practice and the choice of the eighth day, despite the dangers.

18 Three visitors, and Abraham's prayer for Sodom
Abraham welcomed a stranger and, all unknowingly, took the Lord himself into his home. The lavish welcome and provision (despite the inconvenience of the visitors' arrival during the midday siesta) are typical of hospitality amongst nomadic desert people even today. The 'morsel of bread' offered to the guests turns out to be a meal of fresh cakes, curds and milk, and the best veal. The words 'Is anything too hard for the Lord?' reveal the visitor's true identity, and Sarah's incredulous laughter changes to fear.

Abraham's prayer gives an insight into the quality of his relationship with God. No wonder 2 Chronicles 20:7 describes him as God's 'friend' In the event, Sodom could not produce even ten good men, but we have seen something of the lengths to which God's mercy goes.

19 The destruction of Sodom and Gomorrah: Lot's rescue
The New English Bible makes the meaning of verse 5 plain. The 'knowledge' desired is through homosexual relations. Every man in the city is implicated – not one supports Lot's protest against the infringement of the most sacred laws of hospitality (not to say humanity).

The destruction: it is known from archaeology that the area was emptied of settled occupation after about 1900 BC. This catastrophe – probably caused by an earthquake and explosion of gases – may be the reason. The shallow southern waters of the Dead Sea now cover the cities. Nothing could save the cities from God's judgement, yet for Lot's sake he spares Zoar and delays the cataclysm till Lot is safe. 'I can do nothing until you are there' (19:22). Even so Lot's wife drags behind, stopping to look, and dies. Local tradition calls salty crags by the Dead Sea after her still.

Moab and Ammon (37-38): both

tribes were to prove a constant snare to Israel (see Numbers 25, and the frequent denunciations of the prophets).

20 Abraham and King Abimelech
A repetition of the same sin under similarly testing circumstances does not make this a duplicate of 12:10-20. Abraham is not the only man to be put to shame twice before those he considered to have 'no fear of God' to guide their actions. (On Abimelech, see 26:1.)

21:1-21 Isaac is born: Hagar and Ishmael leave
Twenty-five years have elapsed between the promise and its fulfilment. Isaac's elderly parents have reason to be overjoyed at his birth. Sarah's demand that Hagar and Ishmael should be sent away ran counter to custom. Abraham needs a word from God before he is willing to agree. Galatians 4:22ff. shows why the rift was inevitable.

The child (14): Ishmael was by now in fact about 16. Isaac would have been two or three years old by the time he was weaned.

21:22-34 A dispute over wells
Wells were precious to the herdsmen in the dry climate of southern Palestine, and disputes about ownership not infrequent (see 26:17ff.). Monthly rainfall in the area drops from 4 inches/100mm in January to nothing at all in the four summer months.

22 The supreme test
Abraham's previous experience of God would certainly not have led him to suppose child-sacrifice would please him. Nor was this general practice in Abraham's time. In addition, God had specifically promised descendants through Isaac, and he was not yet married. It can only be, as Hebrews 11:19 says, that such was Abraham's faith in God's word, he believed him able to raise the boy to life again. This is implied in Abraham's 'we will come back to you' (verse 5). The parallel between Abraham's sacrifice and the greater sacrifice of God's own Son is striking – yet the lesson Hebrews draws from this chapter is one of faith.

The land of Moriah (2): Abraham's offering took place on one of the hills on which Jerusalem now stands (possibly the temple hill itself – see 2 Chronicles 3:1). The journey of about 50 miles took him three days.

23 The death and burial of Sarah
These Hittites may have been early migrants from the Hittite Empire in

This statue of a ram standing upright beside a tree comes from Ur, 2500 BC.

Turkey (founded about 1800 BC). The whole transaction conforms in detail to known Hittite law (the mention of the trees, the weighing of the silver by current standards, and the proclamation in the presence of witnesses at the city gate). Family-tombs, often caves or cut from rock, were also customary. The traditional site of the burial-cave at Hebron is today covered by a mosque.

24 A wife for Isaac
This is one of the loveliest and most beautifully told stories in the Old Testament. It reflects the traditional Eastern arranged marriage. The steward's gifts in verse 53 seal the betrothal. It is a fitting conclusion that God, who has so clearly guided at every stage, should set his seal on the marriage in the deep love of Isaac for Rebekah.

25:1-11 Abraham's last days
Keturah's sons became the ancestors of a number of north Arabian peoples. Isaac remained his father's sole heir, and on Abraham's death the blessing of God became his.

25:12-18 Ishmael's descendants
'Havilah to Shur' – the tribes occupied Sinai and north-west Arabia.

25:19 - 26:35 ISAAC'S UNHAPPY HOUSEHOLD

Once again the line is continued by the direct action of God. After 20 years' waiting Esau and Jacob are born.

The birthright (25:31): as firstborn son Esau would succeed Isaac as head of the family, and inherit a double share of the estate. When he sells his birthright he forfeits all title to the blessing which goes with it.

There is no commendation of Jacob's cool calculation – but Scripture openly censures Esau's attitude. He was 'worldly minded' (Hebrews 12:16-17) – 'he sold his birthright for a single meal'. 'Thus Esau showed how little he valued his birthright' (25:34, New English Bible).

Abimelech, the Philistine king (26:1): the name is probably a family or throne-name. this is therefore likely to have been a later king than the one Abraham encountered (20-21). The Philistines (one of the trading Sea Peoples, many of whom settled the east Mediterranean coastlands), who gave their name to Palestine, invaded the area in force in the 12th century BC. The group met by the patriarchs would have been amongst earlier settlements of Aegean traders.

27 - 35 DECEIT AND SHARP PRACTICE: JACOB'S EXILE AND RETURN

27 The blessing

Not one of the family comes out well in this story. Isaac's plan goes against what God revealed before the boys were born (25:23). Esau, in agreeing to the plan, is breaking his oath (25:33). Jacob and Rebekah, although in the right, make no reference to God, but cheat and lie to achieve their ends.

Isaac relies completely on his senses, each of which lets him down – even the sense of taste on which he prided himself. When his ears tell him the truth, he will not listen. The blessing is Jacob's, as God always intended – but at a heavy price. Esau

is ready to do murder. The relationship between Isaac and Rebekah is spoilt. And Rebekah will never again see her favourite son. Jacob, the home-lover, goes into exile.

28 The fugitive

Isaac's parting blessing recognizes Jacob as heir to God's promise.

Paddan-aram, or Aram-naharaim, 'land of the two rivers' (2): Rebekah's homeland, Paddan-aram, lay between the upper Euphrates and Habur rivers. The Aramaeans later penetrated south and east, settling in Syria and Mesopotamia.

Bethel , 'house of God' (19): Jacob reaches Bethel, 60 miles north of Beersheba, as darkness falls. In this desolate spot, at a moment of unutterable loneliness, God stands beside Jacob. He repeats to this unpromising man the promise made to Abraham and Isaac. And he adds his personal guarantee of company and protection, with the assurance of eventual safe return.

The 'ladder' is in fact a stairway (perhaps like that of the ziggurat), since angels are going up and down it (compare Jesus' words to Nathanael in John 1:51).

The 'pillar' – not very large – consecrated by the oil is set up to commemorate the vision.

29 - 31 The years with Laban: Jacob meets his match

These three chapters cover the 20 years of Jacob's exile: 14 years' service for his two wives, 6 for flocks of his own. The years hold little joy for Jacob, who meets a crooked dealer after his own kind in his uncle Laban. The deceit over Leah leads to an intolerable home life. The unloved wife hopes with each new son to win her husband's affection. Rachel, lovely and loved, is embittered by continuing childlessness. And Jacob finds himself traded between the two. Small wonder the law later forbade a man to marry his wife's sister during the wife's lifetime.

29:14: 'Surely you are my bone and my flesh!' The implication may be that Laban is adopting Jacob as his son – particularly as no son of his own is mentioned at this time. Marriage to a sister by adoption was quite customary.

29:18: Jacob offers service in place of the usual marriage gift. Laban is not slow to exploit the generosity of the offer. The gift of a slave-girl to his daughter (verse 24) may have been part of the dowry.

29:26: the custom Laban refers to is not otherwise known.

29:28: after the week's festivities Rachel was given to Jacob, on condition he served another seven years for her.

30:3: this reflects the same custom as Sarah observed (16:1-2).

30:14: mandrakes were thought to induce fertility – which makes Leah's subsequent pregnancy ironic.

30:37ff.: Jacob thought the sight of the rods during gestation would affect the unborn lambs. In fact he owed his flocks to the overruling of God, and to the practice of selective breeding which the dream revealed.

31:14: Leah and Rachel were entitled to part of the wealth their marriage-gifts brought Laban.

31:19: Rachel acted, so she thought, in Jacob's interest. The possession of household gods would support the legality of his claim to an inheritance.

31:44: the non-aggression pact made by Laban and Jacob has many contemporary parallels. The covenant meal seals it.

JACOB'S JOURNEY AND RETURN

32 God meets Jacob
Although Esau has settled in Seir in the far south, the meeting between the two brothers is inevitable. The news that Esau is coming at speed, and with a force, strikes terror into Jacob. This time, though, he plans *and* prays.

Alone, and sleepless, Jacob's lifetime struggle against God culminates in this strange wrestling-bout. At the end of it, Jacob is crippled, but a new man. The next altar he erects will be, not to the God of his fathers, but to 'God, the God of Israel' ('El Elohe Israel', 33:20).

33 Jacob meets Esau
Esau's welcome to the brother who had wronged him is so amazingly generous that Jesus may have had him in mind when he told the story of the prodigal son (see Luke 15:20). Jacob's gift, and Esau's acceptance of it, seal the reconciliation.

Verse 14: Jacob has no intention of going to Seir, as the next stage of the journey shows. Even now he cannot be straight-forward about it.

34 Dinah and Shechem: rape and massacre
The city of Shechem has a long and important history. Jacob's stay there cost him dear and the treacherous vengeance of Simeon and Levi was not forgotten (see 49:5ff.).

35 The return to Bethel: Benjamin is born: Rachel and Isaac die
This chapter rounds off the section of Genesis centring on Jacob. Foreign gods are put aside. God reaffirms his covenant with Israel. Rachel dies near Bethlehem (Ephrath) giving birth to the last of Jacob's 12 sons. Esau and Jacob come face to face again at the death of the aged Isaac.

36 ESAU AND HIS DESCENDANTS
Once again, before starting a new stage in the story, we catch up on the other branch of the family.

Seir/Edom (8): the valley between the Dead Sea and the Red Sea (Gulf of Aqaba) and the mountainous area on either side. The king's highway, an important trade route, ran down the eastern plateau. In later days there was little love lost between Edom and Israel.

37 - 50 JOSEPH, THE FAMINE AND THE MIGRATION TO EGYPT
37 Joseph sold into Egypt
The final section of Genesis, centring on Joseph, now begins.

Joseph's special robe (3): Joseph's brothers saw this as a sign that Isaac intended to pass them by and make Joseph his heir (see 48:21-22 and 49:22ff.).

Verse 24: the pit, here mercifully dry, was intended for water storage.

Ishmaelite and Midianite merchants (28): both these groups of desert-dwellers were descended from Abraham. The names are interchangeable (compare verses 28 and 36; Judges 8:24). The use of alternative names is a characteristic feature of Near Eastern writing. The 'balm' of Gilead (an area roughly east of the Jordan and north of the Jabbok) was famous, and the spice-trade an important one from earliest times. Spices had many uses – in food preparation and the manufacture of incense and cosmetics. The trade-route from Damascus to the coast ran past Dothan.

Verse 28: despite the way the verse reads, and the New English Bible's interpretation, verse 27 and 45:4 make it far more likely that Joseph was sold by his brothers. Reuben's absence is not improbable – there were flocks to be seen to. Neither this, nor the matter of Ishmaelite and Midianite merchants, makes it necessary to see the story as a combination of two different traditions.

Officer (36): the word is usually translated 'eunuch', as in the New English Bible, but it may also have the more general meaning of 'court official', which is more likely here in view of Potiphar's marriage.

38 Judah's sons

This none-too-creditable story is probably included because it forms part of the family-tree of the (later) royal house, from which the Messiah himself was descended (Matthew 1:3; Luke 3:33).

Verses 8-10: if a man died childless, his brother was duty bound to raise heirs to him by his widow (set out as the Levirate law, Deuteronomy 25:5).

39 Joseph accused and imprisoned

The account of Joseph's life in Egypt given in chapters 39-50 fits perfectly into the background of Egypt under the Semitic Hyksos pharaohs. They ruled from about 1710-1570 BC, from a capital (Avaris) in the eastern part of the Nile delta. Goshen was also somewhere in this region.

The Egyptian *Tale of Two Brothers* narrates similar incidents to those in this chapter – underlining the unfortunate fact that such things do happen.

40 The dreams of the butler and baker

The story brings out the significance of dreams and their interpretation at this time. Egyptian sages had dream-manuals to help them make their interpretation. Joseph, by contrast, depends completely on God to make the meaning clear.

The butler (1): Pharaoh's cup-bearer, an important official (compare Nehemiah 2:1).

41 Pharaoh's dream and Joseph's promotion

Two years later Pharaoh himself has a dream which defeats his magicians and wise men, despite all their training and a whole library of reference books. When the cup-bearer at last remembers Joseph, he not only proves able to explain God's message, but comes up with a clear-cut plan of action.

Verse 14: Egyptian custom dictates that Joseph must be shaven and dressed in linen for an appearance at court.

Verses 40-43: Joseph's investiture follows Egyptian tradition – the ring (his badge of authority), fine linen (court dress) and a gold chain or collar in reward for his services. Horses and chariots had helped the Hyksos pharaohs to gain ascendancy in Egypt. After 13 years as a slave, Joseph becomes Pharaoh's vizier.

Verse 45: On (Heliopolis, 10 miles north-east of Cairo) was the centre of Egyptian sun-worship.

Verse 54: severe famine was not unknown in Egypt. But it was rare for famine to hit Egypt and Palestine simultaneously.

Statuette of an Egyptian high official from the time of Joseph.

42 - 45 Famine, and family reunion

These chapters give a moving account of Joseph's meeting, testing and eventual reunion with his brothers. Behind his apparent harshness lies complete and generous forgiveness of the wrong done him, and a deep understanding of the way God controls human destiny (45:5ff.). Under each new stress the brothers show a genuine change of attitude from the old days. Twenty years have not obliterated their sense of guilt (42:21-22). They will not behave towards the new favourite (Benjamin) as they did towards the old.

43:32: the Egyptians probably considered that the presence of foreigners at the table defiled their food. For the same reason, later, Jews would not eat with Gentiles.

44:2, 5: Joseph may have used his silver cup for divination (interpreting events by the movement of drops of oil on water). Or the steward may be implying the impossibility of escaping detection by his wise and powerful master.

45:10: in times of famine nomads from Palestine are known to have been allowed pasturage in the eastern delta.

46 - 47 Israel settles in Egypt

Jacob's household numbers 70 on entry to Egypt (the 66 of 46:26 excludes Jacob, and Joseph and his two sons were there already). With all the wives and servants the company would be much larger.

46:34: the Egyptian dislike of the nomadic shepherds is probably no different from the feelings of most settled people towards wandering gypsies. Here the dislike serves a useful purpose in keeping the family as an isolated unit. Otherwise the group's identity might quickly have been lost.

47:16-19: Under Joseph's economic policy Pharaoh gains ownership of the land, and the people become his tenants. Only the priests keep their estate.

48 - 49 Jacob's blessing

The blessing of Joseph's sons was an act of faith (Hebrews 11:21). How simply Jacob's hands cross over to convey God's blessing to the younger son. What a contrast to the story in chapter 27. Joseph enjoys a double inheritance through Ephraim and Manasseh.

Jacob's dying blessing focusses on the distant future, when the descendants of these twelve will occupy the promised land.

Verse 4: the outrage recorded in 35:22 costs Reuben his birthright as firstborn son.

Verses 5-7: Jacob's judgement of Simeon's and Levi's conduct at Shechem (34:13ff.) is clear. Both tribes were to be scattered, but Levi's as the nation's priesthood.

Verse 10: from Judah came the royal line of Israel, from which the Messiah would eventually be born.

Verse 13: although near enough to acquire wealth from maritime trade, Zebulun's territory did not stretch to the sea.

Verse 19: such raids are recorded on the 9th-century Moabite Stone.

Measuring grain for taxation purposes; from the Tomb of Menna, west Thebes, about 1400 BC.

50 The death of Jacob to the death of Joseph – the end of the beginning

Jacob joins Leah in the family tomb at Hebron – the last member of the family to be buried in Canaan for more than 400 years. The huge canvas of Genesis, begun with the great strokes of creation and pulsating life in Eden, continued through destruction, promise, and the birth of a new nation in Canaan, is finished with the death of Joseph in Egypt.

Verses 2-3: it was normal to employ professional embalmers – but perhaps Joseph wanted to avoid religious entanglements. Two centuries later the normal embalming period was 70 days. The mourning observed for Jacob was only two days shorter than that for a pharaoh.

Verse 22: Joseph's life-span of 110 years was the Egyptian ideal, a token of God's blessing. His dying request sums up the faith of a lifetime.

Verse 26: the coffin would be of wood, with a painted head.

EXODUS

The book of Exodus is the story of the birth of Israel as a nation. It is an epic dominated by the central figure of Moses. It was he who led the people out from Egypt, the 'exodus' which gives the book its name. Through him God gave the law. The book falls into two main parts:
1. Israel's escape from slavery in Egypt (chapters 1-19).
2. The giving of the law and construction of the tabernacle at Sinai (chapters 20-40).

An ancient Egyptian tomb-painting shows the process of making bricks and building.

1 - 12:36 ISRAEL IN EGYPT; MOSES, GOD'S LIBERATOR
1 The scene is set
Nearly 300 years have elapsed since the death of Joseph, and the end of Genesis. Jacob's people have been in Egypt some 370 years. Their old privileged status is gone. Now they are a slave nation under a new pharaoh, of a dynasty which has long forgotten Egypt's debt to Joseph (see Genesis 41).

Things have changed in Egypt. The power of the Hyksos pharaohs has been broken and the Upper and Lower kingdoms once again united. The nation is at the height of her military power, ruled from Thebes and Memphis by a new dynasty of pharaohs. But with the accession of Sethos I (probably the 'new king' of 1:8) attention once again focusses on the fertile delta region. A great building programme is begun, including a

new residence for Pharaoh. It is named after Sethos' successor, Ramesses II (who was mainly responsible for building it), 'the House of Ramesses', 'Raamses' (1:11). And there is a large, ready-made, economic labour-force resident in the area – the Israelites.

The existence of such a large (see 12:37) alien group in his borderlands has for some time made Pharaoh uneasy. Here is his chance to ensure they keep out of mischief. The people are organized into gangs, under taskmasters, to dig out mud and make the bricks for building the new cities.

But no matter how hard they are worked the population explosion continues. Pharaoh decides to tackle the problem in more direct ways (15-22), only to be defeated by the midwives' faith.
2 Moses, prince and refugee
So now all Hebrew boy-babies are to be cast into the Nile. That is Pharaoh's decree. But the water which drowns can also be used to float a watertight basket (the same Hebrew word as Noah's 'ark') – and Moses' life is saved by his mother's resourceful action.

Moses was 40 when he tried to strike his first blow for freedom (2:11-12), which ended in disaster. A further 40 years passed before the events of chapter 3 (Acts 7:23 and Exodus 7:7).

Pharaoh's daughter would probably be a daughter by one of his concubines, not a princess of blood-royal. She would have taken Moses back to the harem where he would be brought up with others, learning to read and write the Egyptian hieroglyphic and 'cursive' scripts and gaining expertise in various skills and sports (see Acts 7:22). It was not unknown for foreigners to be brought up in this way, and trained for responsible posts in the army, priesthood or civil service.

Midian (15): the Midianites were descendants of Abraham through his second wife, Keturah. They were desert-dwellers, so Moses could scarcely have had better preparation for the wilderness journeys with Israel than these years of nomadic life.

3 - 4 The burning bush: God calls and equips his man

Moses is actually at Sinai (Horeb), the very place where he will later receive the law, when God's call comes. God has a stupendous commission for Moses – he is to be God's messenger to Pharaoh, and lead his people to freedom – but the missionary is most reluctant. He raises one objection after another, and each is countered by God:

— **3:11:** 'I am not up to the job.' But 'I will be with you', says God.
— **3:13:** 'How am I to explain to people who you are?' God reveals himself as the God of their ancestors, and God of the present: 'I am.'
— **4:1:** 'The people won't believe me.' God gives him three signs with which to convince them.
— **4:10:** 'I am no speaker.' God made him; he will enable him to speak.
— **4:13:** 'Please send someone else.' This God will not do, but he will allow him Aaron as spokesman.

Mt Horeb (3:1): the precise location is uncertain, but long tradition identifies it with Jebel Musa (7,363 feet) at the southern tip of the Sinai peninsula.

The spoil from Egypt (3:21f.): see 11:2-3; 12:35-36. It was from this that the tabernacle was furnished (35:20ff.).

4:19: Pharaoh's death was recorded in 2:23.

Aaron (4:14): three years older than Moses (7:7), presumably born before Pharaoh's edict. Miriam would have been older than both.

Circumcision (4:24-26): Moses failed to circumcise his son – and God cannot overlook disobedience, even in one he has chosen. Zipporah puts the matter right and Moses' life is spared.

5 - 6:13 The first round goes to Pharaoh

The first request to Pharaoh merely aggravates the situation. The people turn against their 'deliverer'. Moses in his frustration turns once again to God.

The request (5:1): this seems less than the whole truth; but it is in the nature of a test-case. Israel had to leave Egypt in order to sacrifice because the nature of their sacrifice was offensive to the Egyptians (8:26). Pharaoh's reaction reveals his implacable hostility, already predicted by God (3:19).

Access to Pharaoh: Ramesses II is known to have made himself available even to ordinary petitioners (compare 5:15ff.). Moses, brought up in the harem, had a special claim to Pharaoh's attention.

A man of uncircumcised lips (6:12): New English Bible 'a halting speaker'.

6:14-27 The family-tree of Moses and Aaron

As so often in Scripture, the list is selective. Moses and Aaron are shown to have descended from Jacob through the line of Levi. The list covers the period of Israel's stay in Egypt.

6:28 - 10:29 The contest with Pharaoh: the nine plagues

Pharaoh has heard and rejected Moses' request. He has shown the sort of man he is: 'Who is the Lord ...? I do not know the Lord, and moreover I will not let Israel go' (5:2).

Now God begins a series of judgements to teach Pharaoh and his people who the Lord is, and to show them the extent of his power over all creation (7:5, 17; 8:10, 22; 9:14). Nine times God acts, and Pharaoh, his magicians and all the gods of Egypt are powerless to reverse his judgements. The magicians may counterfeit, but they cannot countermand.

1. The Nile – heart of the nation's economy and worship – turns to blood, its polluted waters killing the fish (7:14-24).

2. Seven days later, frogs, driven from the river banks by the rotting fish, seek shelter in the houses (7:25 - 8:15).

3 and 4. First gnats and then flies, breeding amongst the carcases of fish and frogs, plague the land (8:16-32).

5 and 6. Disease strikes the cattle,

The eighth plague was a swarm of locusts.

THE NAMES OF GOD

J. A. Motyer

THE WORDS AND THE NAME

Two Hebrew words are translated 'God':

El 'The Deity', God in the power and distinctiveness of his divine nature.

Elohim Plural in form signifying not 'gods' but the One who completely possesses all the divine attributes.

There is also a third word used for God:

Adon Describes God as 'Sovereign' or 'Lord', pointing to his divine authority and executive rule.

In distinction from these nouns, there is also the personal name Yahweh. To avoid using this divine name itself (out of supposed reverence) a word meaning 'Lord' was substituted in public reading. English Bibles unfortunately perpetuate the same scruple, representing Yahweh by 'Lord', or, when it is used in connection with Adonai (a form of Adon), as 'Lord God'. Much is lost in Bible reading if we forget to look beyond the substitute word to the personal, intimate name of God himself.

By telling his people his name, God intended to reveal to them his inmost character. As a word, Yahweh is related to the Hebrew verb 'to be'. This verb goes beyond 'to exist'; it means rather 'to be actively present'. Yahweh (Exodus 3:13-16) is the God actively present with his people – but the moment he chose to make this known was when they, as doomed slaves, needed to be redeemed.

In other words, the idea of 'active presence' tells us that God is with us but not what sort of God he is. In choosing the time of the exodus to reveal the meaning of his name, he identifies himself as the God who saves his people and overthrows his adversaries.

The holiness of God lies at the root of his self-revelation as Yahweh (Exodus 3:5). This works out in the holy redemption and holy wrath of the Passover (Exodus 12).

The Old Testament's understanding of the character which the name reveals is well seen in passages such as Exodus 34:6ff.; Psalms 103; 111; 146; Micah 7:18-19.

THE PROGRESS OF REVELATION

The name Yahweh appears in the Bible from the earliest times (Genesis 4:1) and in such ways as to imply that men both knew and used it (e.g. Genesis 4:26; 14:22). How then can God say to Moses (Exodus 6:2-3) that 'by my name the Lord I did not make myself known to them' (i.e. to Abraham, etc.)?

Specialist Old Testament study has long answered this question by saying that we have differing traditions of the early history of the people of God: one tradition in which the divine name was known from the earliest times, and another – contradictory – tradition that it was first revealed to Moses.

Influential as this theory has proved, it is neither inescapable nor necessary. 'To know' in the Old Testament goes beyond the mere possession of information, to the active enjoyment of fellowship with the person known. For instance, the sons of Eli certainly knew the name as a divine 'label' but they 'had no regard for (literally, 'did not know') the Lord' (1 Samuel 2:12; compare 3:7; Exodus 33:12-13). So Exodus 6:2-3 is telling us that what had hitherto possessed only the significance of a 'label', a way of addressing God, now became significant as a statement of the character possessed by the God who was so named – that he is the holy Redeemer and Judge, ever present with his people.

This view of the meaning of Exodus 6:2-3 is borne out by the evidence of Genesis. If Abraham had been asked 'Who is Yahweh?' he would undoubtedly have replied

'God Almighty' or one of the other titles of God used by the patriarchs:

El Shadday: Shadday probably means 'mountain', used symbolically of changelessness and enduring strength, contrasted to the helplessness of man. See for instance Genesis 17:1f.; 28:3f.; 35:11; 43:14; 48:3; 49:25.

El Elyon: 'God Most High', Genesis 14:18.

El Roi: 'God of Seeing', Genesis 16:13.

El Olam: 'The Everlasting God', Genesis 21:33.

El Bethel: 'God of Bethel', Genesis 31:13.

El Elohe Yisrael: 'God, the God of Israel', Genesis 33:20.

So when Yahweh is said to be 'the God of your fathers' in Exodus 3 (verses 6, 13, 15, 16), all this richness of meaning is added to the revelation of the holy Redeemer.

'WHO IS A GOD LIKE THEE?'
God in himself
Some attributes of God so express the heart of his divine nature that they are used as titles:

The Holy One: The most centrally important title of all: see Joshua 24:19; Isaiah 5:16; 10:17; Habakkuk 1:12.

The Holy One of Israel: A variation used especially by Isaiah, e.g. Isaiah 1:4.

The God 'whose name is jealous': shows his passionate love for his people: see Exodus 34:14.

The Lord of Hosts: is often repeated and points to the 'hosts' of potentialities and powers in the divine nature, conveying something very much like 'omnipotent'. See, for instance, Jeremiah 32:18b-23.

Furthermore, he is the *true, living* (Jeremiah 10:10) *high* (Micah 6:6) and *rewarding* (Jeremiah 51:56) God.

God of all the world
Such a God cannot be confined to one people. He is:

Creator: Isaiah 40:28.
Judge: Genesis 18:25.
King: Jeremiah 10:7.
God of all flesh: Numbers 16:22; Jeremiah 32:27.

The God of Israel
He is the God who specially reveals himself to one people:

The Angel of the Lord: Without diminishing his deity, he accommodates himself to speak to man: Genesis 16:7f.; Judges 13:16f., etc.

The God of the Hebrews: Exodus 5:3.

The God of Israel: Joshua 24:2. He is also, as if to stress the grace and condescension involved, **the God of Jacob:** (Psalm 81:4), in holiness (Isaiah 1:4) and power (Psalm 132:2).

The God of the individual
Within his chosen people, he is the God of the individual: 'my beloved' (Isaiah 5:1), 'the God of my salvation' (Psalm 18:46). The richness of personal awareness of God in the Old Testament is hardly better seen than through the wealth of metaphors for the God who was known and loved in daily life:

Rock: A title stemming from Exodus 17:1-7. See especially Deuteronomy 32.
Shepherd: Psalm 23:1.
Shield, stronghold: Psalm 18:2.
Light: Psalm 27:1.
Strength: Psalm 28:7.
Refuge: Psalm 37:39.
Sun: Psalm 84:11.
Father: Psalm 89:26; Isaiah 63:16.
Mother-bird: Psalm 91:4; compare Isaiah 31:5.
Help: Psalm 115:9.
Shade: Psalm 121:5.
Portion: Psalm 142:5.
Song: Isaiah 12:2.
Redeemer: Isaiah 41:14.
Warrior: Isaiah 42:13.
Potter: Isaiah 45:9.
Husband: Isaiah 54:5.
Fountain: Jeremiah 2:13.
Dew: Hosea 14:5.
Lion, leopard, bear: Hosea 13:7-8.

and skin infection breaks out on man and beast, carried by the frogs and insects (9:1-12).

7. Hail and thunderstorms ruin the flax and barley crops – but not wheat and spelt, which have not yet grown. And those Egyptians who take note of God's warning remain safe (9:13-35).

8. The wind blows in a plague of locusts from Ethiopia which strip the country bare of greenstuff (10:1-20).

9. For three days the light of the sun is blotted out by 'thick darkness' (probably a khamsin duststorm) (10:21-29).

The plagues probably occurred over a period of about a year. In each case God chose to use natural disorders to confound Pharaoh and the gods of Egypt (12:12). He caused the 'Nile-god' to bring ruin, not prosperity; the frogs to bring disease instead of fruit-fulness; and the power of Re, the sun-god, was blotted out. The whole sequence of events follows a logical pattern which could have started with unusually high flooding of the Nile, bringing down red earth and microcosms which polluted the water. But however it happened, this was no mere 'chance' – God was demonstrating his absolute control. He distinguished between his people and the Egyptians. He controlled the extent and the areas affected by each plague. He announced the timing of each, and could call a halt at any time in answer to prayer.

The hardness of Pharaoh's heart: several times in these chapters God is said to have hardened Pharaoh's heart and made him obstinate (4:21;

Pharaoh Ramesses II.

10:1, 20, 27). But this was not done against Pharaoh's will. Rather, where God *could* have softened Pharaoh's heart (as he did Paul's) he simply let him be. God gave him up (see Romans 1; 9:17) – let him be what he himself wanted, let him have his own way – so that in the end God's power would be plain for all to see.

11 - 12:36 The death of the firstborn, and the Passover Preliminaries are over: God's warning of 4:22-23 is about to be realized. This is the end of the road for Pharaoh and his people. But for Israel it is the beginning. This is a day to remember down the ages: when God dealt death to the first-born of Egypt, but spared and freed his own people. A new feast is insti-tuted, and a new (religious) year begun. The Passover lamb or kid speaks of God's protection and pro-vision for his people – Israel is his firstborn. The bitter herbs remind them of all their suffering in Egypt. The flat unleavened bread recalls the haste of their departure (no time to use yeast and wait for the bread to rise). Even so, they do not go empty-handed. The years of slavery are in some measure paid for by the clothes and jewellery heaped upon them by the Egyptians, now only too anxious to see them go.

12:37 - 19:25 OUT OF EGYPT: ON TO SINAI

12:37 - 13:21 The journey begins; instructions about the Passover, Unleavened Bread and the firstborn Just as God foretold (Genesis 15:13-14), after four centuries in a foreign land (from the 18th century BC to about 1300 or 1290 BC) Israel is free. The journey to the border begins. But first there are further instructions about how the Passover is to be cele-brated, who may join in, and where it is to take place. The events are to be further commemorated in two ways:

— For a seven-day period after Passover the people are to eat unleavened bread as a reminder of the hasty departure from Egypt.
— As Israel's freedom has been purchased by the death of the firstborn of Egypt, the nation's firstborn belong in a special sense to God and are to be 'bought back' from him.

600,000 men (12:37): counting the women and children this would amount to a total of some two million people – a high (though not necessarily impossible) figure which presents some problems. Subsequent chapters make it plain that their number was certainly too great for the wilderness to support – hence God's special provision of manna. They were also at times short of water, although they no doubt learnt to manage on very little, and their encampments would have been spread out to take advantage of several watercourses at each halt in the journey.

Joseph's bones (13:19): see Genesis 50:24-25.

14 Pursuit and disaster

Hemmed in between sea and mountains, with water before them and Pharaoh's forces at their backs, the people of Israel meet their first big test of faith – and they panic. As God drives back the waters so that they can cross in safety, and as he sends the wall of water rushing down upon Pharaoh's forces, Israel learns the truth of Moses' words: 'The Lord will fight for you, and you have only to be still' (14:14).

15:1-21 Moses' triumph-song

If ever a victory deserves to be recorded for posterity this one does. Moses leads the people in a great paean of triumph: God has saved Israel; he has destroyed their enemy. Miriam and all the women take up the refrain, and dance for joy. The song is a fine example of ancient Semitic poetry (see 'Poetry and Wisdom Literature', introduction).

15:22 - 17:7 The grumbling begins, but God provides

It is not long before the complaints start. There were plenty of fish to eat in Egypt, and fruit and vegetables – and no shortage of water. But in the desert the people are soon thirsty and hungry – and mutinous. God's method of provision is designed to teach them obedience, and daily dependence upon him.

Quails (16:13): twice a year the common quail's migration route takes it across the region where the Israelites were at this time. Exhausted by the journey, the birds were easy to catch.

Omer (16:16): a bowl holding about 4 pints/2¼ litres.

Manna (16:31): various natural phenomena have been identified with the description given here, but none fits exactly. This substance was Israel's staple food for 40 years, ceasing abruptly when they entered Canaan.

Water from the rock (17:6): Sinai limestone is known to retain moisture. This incident, and the names Massah and Meribah, became a byword for rebelliousness (see Hebrews 3:7ff).

OUT OF EGYPT – THE DESERT WANDERINGS

Mediterranean Sea

CANAAN

River Jordan

Jericho

Mt Nebo

Hebron

MOAB

Spies sent into Canaan

Raamses

Pithom

Succoth

Bitter Lakes

Heliopolis

'Reed Sea' crossing

Kadesh-barnea

EDOM

EGYPT

Wilderness of Paran

Ezion-geber

River Nile

Sinai

Gulf of Suez

Striking of rock

Rephidim

Mt Sinai

Quails and manna

Ten Commandments given to Moses

Gulf of Aqaba

Red Sea

━━ Probable route of the exodus

--- Route of spies

This imposing mountain, Jebel Musa, is generally held to be Mount Sinai, where God gave the Law to his people.

The route of the exodus. This is not absolutely certain. They did not take the direct coastal route (13:17) because they were unready to encounter the Philistine forces. Instead they journeyed south to Succoth, turned north before crossing the sea, and then south again down the west of the Sinai peninsula. The 'Red Sea', or 'sea of reeds', can refer to the Bitter Lakes region or to the Gulf of Suez. The actual crossing probably took place somewhere between Qantara (30 miles south of Port Said) and just north of Suez – over the papyrus marshes.

17:8-16 Battle with the Amalekites

Joshua (Moses' successor) leads a picked force against this nomadic tribe descended from Esau. But it is God who gives the victory, through Moses' intercession.

18 Jethro's advice

The burden of leadership is heavy, and Jethro's practical suggestion for reorganization and delegation is a sound one. Jethro, although a non-Israelite, is reckoned a godly man. He is welcomed and his advice taken. In religious matters, however, he learns from Moses (8-11), not vice-versa as some suggest. It is not clear when Zipporah returned home – perhaps soon after the incident recorded in 4:24-26.

19 The camp at Sinai

As God promised (3:12), Moses brings God's people to him at Mt Sinai, where he will establish his covenant with the nation. Thunder, fire, earthquake and lightning herald God's presence and demonstrate his power (20:20 explains why; compare Elijah's experience in the same place – 1 Kings 19:8ff. – and the contrast drawn in Hebrews 12:18-25). The Lord God, holy, awesome, unapproachable, speaks.

20 - 40 GOD'S LAW FOR ISRAEL; THE SETTING UP OF THE TABERNACLE

20:1-21 The Ten Commandments
This summary and climax of God's covenant-agreement with his people sets out a basic ethical norm applicable to all men in all ages (since they are in fact the 'Maker's instructions'). The first four commands concern men's relationship to God, the remaining six their relationship to one another. Hence Jesus' two-clause summary of the law in Matthew 22:37-40.

The commandments show God's concern for the whole of life. He sets out standards governing family relationships, regard for human life, sex, property, speech and thought. God made us: he alone can show us how we are designed to behave.

Written on stone tablets, preserved in the ark of the covenant, the ten 'words' were the basis of Israel's law. In form they follow the standard pattern of Near Eastern treaties current in the 13th century BC, particularly those between vassals and their overlords (see 'Covenants and Near Eastern Treaties'):

— Title: identifying the author of the covenant (2a).
— Historical prologue: describing past relations of the two parties (2b).
— Obligations imposed on the vassal (3-17), accompanied by 'blessings' (e.g. 6,12b) and 'cursings' (5,7b).

20:22 - 23:33 God's law-code for Israel
This section, known as 'the book of the covenant', is the oldest record we have of Jewish law. It consists of 'judgements' – i.e. case-laws – and 'statues', straight-forward commands. Although similar in form to other ancient law-codes of Western Asia, the Jewish code has several distinctive features:

— The whole code rests on the authority of God, not of a king.
— There is no division between civil and religious law. Most oriental codes deal with legal matters only: morals and religion belong elsewhere. In the Bible legal, moral and religious laws are inseparable, showing God's concern for life as a whole.
— There is one law for all, whatever a man's status. Regulations protecting the weak and helpless (slaves, orphans, widows, foreigners) are particularly striking.
— A high view of human life is demonstrated by fixed, limited penalties – one crime, one punishment.

The legislation looks forward to the settled agricultural life of Canaan – Israel's rebelliousness had not yet condemned her to 40 years in the Sinai peninsula. The section may be summarized as follows:
— General instructions about worship (20:22-26)
— Civil laws (21:1 - 23:13) the rights of slaves (21:1-11) manslaughter and injury to human life (21:12-32) injury, theft and damage to property (21:33 - 22:15) social and religious obligations (22:16-31) justice and human rights (23:1-13)
— Laws for the three main feasts – Unleavened Bread, Firstfruits and Harvest (23:14-19)
— God's undertakings for his obedient people (23:20-33)

These regulations fill out in detail the summary of 20:1-17.

24 The covenant is ratified
The people's assent to the covenant is formally sealed by a special sacrifice, and by the covenant meal eaten by their representatives in the presence of God. The blood sprinkled on the people and on the altar unites the two parties to the agreement. In effect, each is swearing to keep it on pain of death.

Nadab and Abihu (1): two of Aaron's sons who later died after committing sacrilege (Leviticus 10:1-2).

They saw the God of Israel (9-11): having a meal with someone is the essence of fellowship in the Near East. Here the writer gropes for words to describe the indescribable communion which followed the sacrifice and fulfilled the covenant.

Hur (14): obviously a man of standing in Israel. He and Aaron held up Moses' hands in prayer during the battle with Amalek (17:12).

Forty days and nights (18): certain numbers have special significance in the Bible. The round number '40' occurs at almost every new stage in Israel's history: e.g. at the flood, the time of the spies in Canaan, Elijah's journey to Horeb, Jesus' time in the wilderness, and the time between his resurrection and ascension.

25 - 27 Instructions for making and furnishing the tabernacle
God has brought the nation out of Egypt. He has set out the terms of his covenant and they have been agreed. Now, as a visible sign that these are his people with whom he will always be present, he gives Moses instructions to build a special tent for him. He is to have a home

A reconstruction of the tabernacle at the Bible Museum, Amsterdam.

THE TABERNACLE

J.A. Motyer

The people of God were encamped at Mt Sinai. Every day they gazed with trembling at the cloud covering the mountain (Exodus 19:16-20), for it signified God's coming down to speak with them. But during their stay, at Moses' instruction, they provided materials for the construction of the very complex tent which has come to be called the tabernacle. On the day when it was finally completed and erected, as they watched, 'the cloud covered the tent of meeting, and the glory of the Lord filled the tabernacle' (Exodus 40:34). The Lord in his glory had actually come to dwell amongst his people. This is the supreme significance of the tabernacle.

Sinai

The law had been given at Mt Sinai. But there was more to it than that. The ceremony described in Exodus 24 places the law-giving in its correct context. It included the following elements:

— The altar with its twelve pillars (verse 4) stands for the bringing of the whole people of God into his presence (for there were twelve tribes of Israel). This truth is represented in stone: the relationship is a permanent one.

— Dashing half the blood of sacrifice (verse 6) against the altar signifies that it is by means of shed blood that the people can come into the presence of God. Sin inevitably means death, being cut off from God. But when the death penalty has been satisfied, the people can be brought to God and established permanently in his presence.

— Next, Moses goes through the law of God, the pattern of obedience which God requires from his blood-bought people (verse 7).

— The people commit themselves to a life of obedience, and Moses sprinkles the remainder

of the blood over them (verse 8) – identifying them with the sacrifice made on their behalf both initially and for the failures and sins of everyday life.

So Mt Sinai stands for the fulfilment of one half of the covenant promise of Exodus 6:7: 'I will take you for my people'. God has brought them to himself, and in the shed blood has provided a way for them to live and walk with him.

The indwelling God

But what about the other half of the covenant promise? God had also said 'and I will be your God' (Exodus 6:7). By taking up residence amongst them, pitching his tent in the midst of their tents, the Lord makes this second sort of identification with his people. He is indeed their God. The tabernacle represents the completion and climax of God's redemption of his people. Everything he had done was for this final purpose, 'that I might dwell among them' (Exodus 29:43-46).

There is great emphasis on this fact of God's indwelling throughout the tabernacle narrative. It is stressed in two specific ways. First there is a whole series of verses with this as their topic (e.g. 25:8, 22; 29:42ff.; 40:34-38). It was God's intention that his people should always carry with them the values learnt at Mt Sinai. There God dwelt among them and they saw the visible manifestation of his presence. But God was not just providing a memory to cling to. He is determined to live amongst his people, to travel with them. The tabernacle represents something even more intense than the experience at Sinai (compare 24:18 with 40:35). They are not left with the diminishing glow of a receding experience. Instead, by living among them, God will himself guarantee the unabated reality of his personal presence.

The story of the tabernacle is interrupted and marred by the incident of the golden calf (Exodus

32-34). On the one side of this act of rebellion lie the details of the plan for the tabernacle (Exodus 25-31), and on the other side the details of the execution of that plan, point by point (Exodus 35-40). Why are we taken through the process of construction in such detail? Why is the summary statement of 40:16ff. not sufficient? Why must each separate moment of the work be dwelt upon? It is surely to emphasize this great truth: that not even the most audacious acts of human wilfulness and rebellion can deflect the Lord from his chosen purpose to dwell among his people. He has set his hand to it along lines dictated by his own will, and nothing can deter him. Man may impatiently rebel, but God will patiently continue.

God-centred religion

The general truth expressed by the tabernacle, then, is that the Lord determined to live among his people and the will of God – what he wants – equally governs the whole plan of the great tent and its construction. From 25:10 onwards the description moves from the inside to the outside: first the furnishings, the ark, table and lampstand (25:10-40), then the tent-covering (26:1-37), then beyond it to the altar and the court (27:1-19). It is an ordered story, but on reflection the order is striking and unexpected. One might reasonably have expected that the 'building' would come first and then the things it housed. But this would have been to start from the visible, and the whole tabernacle exists as the necessary 'wrapping' for the invisible God when he comes down to be with his people. God and his nature determines all, not man and his needs.

In this way the tabernacle sums up a basic biblical truth about religion: it must conform to the will and nature of God. Much in the Bible exists to expose man's tendency to make religion suit his own pleasure, or (as might be said) match what he finds 'helpful'. But if religion does not match the will of God it is ultimately futile (see, for example, Isaiah 29:13).

The ark of the covenant

At the very centre of this whole divinely-dictated religion was the ark. Everything pointed to it. Three matching entrances (26:31, 32, 36, 37; 27:16, 17) led to it – for the purpose of entering the court of the tabernacle was to enter the presence of God himself. Along the path leading to the ark lay the altar of burnt-offering (27:1-8), the altar of incense (30:1-6), and the mercy-seat where the blood of sacrifice was finally sprinkled (25:17ff.; Leviticus 16:14) – showing that it was only by sacrifice, prayer and the effectiveness of the shed blood that man could come to God.

Inside the ark were the tablets of the law – the supreme verbal statement of God's holiness (25:16); at one and the same time the reason why God dwelt alone (for none can match his holiness), and why by means of blood a sinner might enter his presence (for the blood speaks of life laid down in payment for sin).

The whole structure of the tabernacle, therefore, speaks clear and splendid truths. It provides a visible summary of the central affirmations of the Bible: that God indwells his people (see 1 Corinthians 3:16; Ephesians 2:19-22); that he intends his people to worship him according to his will and not their own whim (see Mark 7:6-13); and that only by means of sacrifice and shed blood can sinners ever come to live with the Holy One (see Ephesians 2:11-18; Hebrews 10:19-25).

amongst them like their own homes. He will guide and accompany them wherever they go – and they will know that he is no local deity whose power is limited to Sinai. Portable, prefabricated tent-shrines similar to the tabernacle were constructed in Egypt even earlier than this. Here, although the description is detailed, some practical points are missing – it is not a complete workman's blue-print. The roof of the tent, for example, may have been flat or raised with a ridge-pole. The frame-work of the actual tent was hung with linked curtains of linen, over which was a layer of goatskin, topped by two weather-proof cover-ings (of rams' skins dyed red, and of sealskin or porpoiseskin).

Many of the materials used were brought by the Israelites from Egypt (11:2-3) and willingly given, so that God's tent might be as worthy of him as they could make it. Before the days of banks it was practical to convert wealth into jewellery, which could be worn and carried round easily. Wood is scarce in the Sinai desert, but the acacia is one of the few trees which grow there. Their own herds provided skins, and the sealskins came from the Red Sea.

The peoples of the ancient Near East were skilled in spinning, weav-ing and using natural dyes (scarlet from the cochineal insect; purple, for the wealthy, from the murex shell-fish). Fine embroidery was also pro-duced. Precious and semi-precious stones were rounded, polished and engraved (as those for Aaron). Gold and silver were beaten and worked into elaborate designs. All these skills God called into play for the construc-tion of his tabernacle.

28 - 30 The priests and their duties

If God's tent is to be a place of beauty and splendour, his priest must also be fittingly robed. His garments, as the New English Bible puts it, are intended 'to give him dignity and honour' (28:2) – not on his own account, but as befits the One he serves and represents. The precious stones engraved with the names of the twelve tribes point to his other function, as representative of his people, making atonement for their sin.

Urim and Thummim (28:30): two objects which stood for 'yes' and 'no'. Just how they were used to discover God's will is not known.

A model of the high priest shows the blue robe fringed with bells and pomegranates; the shorter tunic (ephod) tied with a girdle; and the breastplate with its 12 precious stones, 1 for each of the 12 tribes. He holds an almond branch.

The bells on the hem of Aaron's robe (28:33-34): perhaps to ensure he does not enter God's presence unannounced.

The consecration: everything about this elaborate ceremonial points to the 'otherness' of God. He will be with his people, but there can be no familiarity. He is to be approached only in the ways he lays down. Sin disqualifies all men from entering God's presence. The priests and every item of equipment must be spe-cially set apart for his service. So Aaron and his sons must be cleansed, robed and their sins expiated by sac-rifice before they may take office. The living God is no impotent image to be worshipped as man thinks fit. He lays down the only terms on which it is possible for him to take up residence with his people.

31:1-11 God chooses his craftsmen

When God selects individuals for a particular job he also equips them to do it. Verse 3 is one of the earliest references to the work of the Holy Spirit.

31:12-18 Sabbath law

The way the sabbath is kept is an index of the nation's spiritual health. Obedience in this is a test of their obedience to God in other ways too.

32 The worship of the golden calf, and its aftermath

Only six weeks after making their solemn covenant-pledge with God the people are clamouring for a replica of the old gods of Egypt. And God's high priest not only makes the bull-calf, but identifies it with God. Death is the penalty for those who break covenant – but Moses' selfless intercession prevents Israel's extermination. The broken tablets dramatically proclaim the broken covenant. Such sin cannot go unpunished: Moses' own tribe, the Levites, mete out God's judgement.

Aaron's gold bull was modelled on one of the old Egyptian gods. This apis bull, in bronze, was found at Ashkelon in Israel.

33 Moses prays again, and sees God's glory

God will not go back on his promise, but Israel has forfeited his presence. And without that, the promised land is nothing. Again Moses pleads for the people at a time of crisis. God's answer encourages him to press a personal plea for a revelation of God in all his splendour.

34 The covenant is renewed

The tablets are engraved afresh in token of God's renewal of the covenant. This particular selection of laws is influenced by Israel's recent idol-worship, also by the coming temptations of Canaanite religion. Israel's firstborn belong to God, but are 'bought back' from him – there is to be no child-sacrifice as in Canaan. They must not forget sabbath law in the coming busy seasons of sowing and harvest. The firstfruits are to be brought to God, since it is he who makes the land fruitful. Israel is not to resort to the Canaanite practice of boiling a kid in its mother's milk to increase fertility.

Moses' long communion with God shows in his face when he returns to the people: he begins to reflect something of God's own glory (see 2 Corinthians 3:18).

35 - 40 The setting up of the tabernacle

These chapters record how the instructions given in chapters 25-31 are carried out to the letter. The craftsmen set to work, the people pour in their gifts, and the tabernacle, its fittings and the priests' robes are all completed exactly as God has laid down. When the work is finished, God gives Moses his instructions for setting up and arranging the tabernacle, and for its consecration. Aaron and his sons are anointed for service. When all is done, God signifies his satisfaction. The cloud, the visible token of his presence, rests on the tabernacle, and the place is filled with his glory. For 300 years, until it is replaced by the temple in Solomon's day, the tabernacle will remain the focal centre of the nation's worship.

LEVITICUS

Leviticus is essentially a rule-book – the book of laws given by God to his people through Moses at Sinai. The laws cover ritual and worship and many aspects of life – but all seen in relation to him. The book takes its name from the fact that it was the Levitical priests (Aaron and his sons and descendants, helped in the practical work of the tabernacle by the rest of the Levites) who administered the laws. But the book is not for the priests alone. God intended all his people to know and keep his law. Again and again Moses is told to 'speak to the people of Israel'.

To many modern readers it may seem a strange book, perhaps even a repulsive one with all its blood-sacrifices. Some see it as reflecting only an odd set of ancient taboos. Yet take it away and whole areas of Scripture become inexplicable. Without the message of Leviticus the key event of all time, the death of Jesus Christ, is an enigma. The ritual and the rules were never simply an end in themselves. As the sacrifices were performed day after day, year after year, as the Day of Atonement came and went, Israel was constantly reminded of the sin which cut them off from God's presence. They had broken covenant with God by disobeying his laws and were under sentence of death. But God in his mercy showed them that he would accept a substitute – the death of an animal, perfect and blameless, instead of the offender. God was holy – a moral holiness unknown in the gods of the nations around. He demanded holiness in his people. The laws on ritual purity hammered this home in practical everyday experience.

Yet the book has value apart from its vital role in God's message of salvation. The laws in Leviticus show God working in harmony with his own natural laws for the good of his people. Although Israel had to obey the laws in blind trust (when they chose to do so at all), we can see how those laws were actually working for the nation's health and well-being. Because we know more today about the sources of infection and pollution, about quarantine and isolation, hygiene and preventive medicine, we can watch Israel's obedience actually fulfilling God's promise to take away their sickness (Exodus 23:25). And this not by magic, but by the natural working of principles we now, at least in part, can understand.

Many of the laws which seem strangest to us fall into place, too, when we look at them in relation to the contemporary religions of Egypt and Canaan. Against this dark back-cloth the morality and religion of Israel shines like a star. Only God himself can account for it.

1 - 7 THE SACRIFICES
Priests and people are given instructions about five different offerings:
1. The burnt-offering (chapter 1 and 6:8-13): the only one in which the whole animal was burnt; a token of dedication.
2. The cereal- or meal-offering (chapter 2 and 6:14-18); often an

This small stone incense altar with four 'horns' was found at Megiddo in Israel.

accompaniment to burnt- and peace-offerings.

3. The peace-offering (chapter 3 and 7:11-36): re-establishing fellowship between the offerer and God; or it could be a thank-offering.

4. The sin-offering (4:1 - 5:13 and 6:24-30): made in order to obtain forgiveness. The relationship between this and the guilt-offering is not clear. Generally speaking the sin-offering seems to have referred to offences against God, and the guilt-offering to social offences. (But even sin against others is seen as sin against God, as 6:2 plainly states.)

5. The guilt- or trespass-offering (5:14-6:7 and 7:1-10). There was a standard pattern of ritual. The worshipper brought his offering (a physically perfect animal from his herd or flock, or, in the case of a poor man, doves or pigeons) to the forecourt of the tabernacle. He laid his hand on it, implying that it represented him, and slaughtered it. (If it was a public offering the priest did this.) The priest took the basin of blood and spattered it against the altar. He burnt a specified part with certain portions of fat (or the entire animal in the case of the burnt-offering). The remainder was then eaten by the priests, or by the priests and their families, or (in the case of the peace-offering) by priests and worshippers together.

Sacrifice of some sort was almost universal practice amongst ancient peoples, and Israel's sacrifices have some similarities with those of her neighbours. Nonetheless, certain features are unique:

— Israel's absolute monotheism – belief in the one true God – and the ritual as a direct revelation from him.

— The emphasis on ethics and morality, stemming from God's own absolute moral holiness; sin as a bar to communion; the need for repentance and atonement; the insistence on obedience to God's law (moral as well as ceremonial).

— The complete absence (and prohibition) of associated practices in other religions; no magic or sorcery.

— The high tone of the sacrificial system: no frenzy, or prostitution, orgies, fertility rites, human sacrifice, etc.

THE SACRIFICIAL SYSTEM
Philip Budd

The offering of sacrifice was a regular feature in ancient Near Eastern religion. Israel appears to have shared many of the techniques and conceptions of sacrifice of her neighbours, but her own observances were set firmly in the framework of God's revelation at Sinai. The procedures set out in Leviticus presuppose a sanctuary, an altar, and an officiating priesthood, though the historical use and development of these rituals remains obscure.

Burnt-offering (Leviticus 1)
The distinctive feature was the burning of the whole animal. The Hebrew name for the sacrifice conveys the idea of 'going up', and the phrase a 'pleasing odour to the Lord' is common. These points taken together suggest that the burnt-offering symbolized the worshipper's homage and total dedication to God. In laying his hand on the animal he identified himself completely with the sacrifice. The offering had to cost him something – one of his herd of cattle or flock of sheep and goats (a bird was permitted for the poor), and it had to be of the best – a male without blemish.

Peace-offering (Leviticus 3)
The outstanding feature is the sharing of the sacrifice. Part was burnt in acknowledgement of God, part belonged to the priests and part was eaten by the offerer and his family. The Hebrew name indicates 'peace' or 'well-being', and these sacrifices are sometimes seen as communion or fellowship rites. On the whole they are best regarded as expressing a desire to maintain and demonstrate right relations

between God, man and his neighbour. This harmony might be expressed as an offering which accompanied a vow of some kind (Leviticus 22:21), or as a thank-offering (Leviticus 22:29) or free-will offering (Leviticus 22:21). The offerings expressed the individual's gratitude to God for his goodness, or were simply spontaneous expressions of devotion.

Cereal-offering (Leviticus 2)

The Hebrew word has the sense of 'gift' or 'tribute'. No distinct meaning is evident; the offering probably expressed homage and thankfulness.

Sin and guilt-offerings (Leviticus 4 - 6:7)

The procedure is similar for both these sacrifices, and it is difficult to pin-point a difference of meaning. It may be that the sin-offering deals with infringements of God's laws, whereas the guilt-offering, since it raises the question of compensation, deals with situations where human injury is involved. Both offerings demonstrate the need for sin to be dealt with objectively, and give prominence to the use of the blood. Both sacrifices deal with unwitting or unavoidable breaches of law. Hence 'sin' in these contexts often has a purely ritual meaning – as with the sin-offering after childbirth (Leviticus 12:6). In this case the sacrifice brings the offerer back to full membership of the holy community.

In various parts of the Bible all these offerings are said to 'atone' – to cover sin – indicating that any act of worship was set squarely in the context of God's forgiving grace.

The sacrificial system was clearly open to abuse, and on more than one occasion was criticized by the prophets (e.g. Amos 5:25; Isaiah 1:11-12; Jeremiah 7:22) probably in the light of contemporary attitudes.

And a number of other texts stress the fact that obedience counts for more than sacrifice (e.g. 1 Samuel 15:22-23; Psalm 40:6-8). It was only too easy to assume God's acceptance of the offering and neglect the moral obligation to obey him. By making sin a purely external thing its seriousness was minimized.

On the other hand the sacrificial system did demand a right inward attitude. The sin-offering had to be accompanied by confession, and, where possible, a genuine attempt to put things right (Leviticus 5:5; Numbers 5:7). On the Day of Atonement the high priest confessed the sins of the whole community before the scapegoat was released (Leviticus 16:21). Furthermore the law provides no sacrifice for sin 'with a high hand', i.e. wilful and deliberate sin (Numbers 15:27-31).

Each sacrifice, upheld by God's promise and power, had real effect and potency, but this was not a power that could be manipulated by man. On the contrary, it was recognized that the system was divinely appointed from beginning to end. It was a God-given area of contact between God and man, bringing man into fellowship with God. Viewed in this light, a meticulous observance of these laws could inspire confidence in God. In any case, human activity was not the only factor in the observances. The priests, as God's representatives, were required to declare God's acceptance or rejection of the worshipper and his offering.

The letter to the Hebrews makes it clear that the Old Testament sacrifice was at best an incomplete answer to the problem of sin. The sacrifices themselves have disappeared, but they go far to help us understand the meaning of the cross, the sacrifice of Jesus Christ.

See too 'The Meaning of Blood Sacrifice' and 'Feasts and Festivals'.

A pleasing odour to the Lord (1:9): a human way of expressing God's satisfaction with the offering. The people knew God did not need to be fed by them – *he* was feeding *them* with manna.

No leaven nor any honey ... you shall offer salt (2:11ff.): leaven (yeast) or honey caused fermentation. Perhaps the part played by wine in the excesses of Canaanite religion lay behind this ruling. Salt, on the other hand, is a preservative and a reminder of the solemn covenant meal.

You shall eat no blood whatever (7:26): the reason is given in 17:10-14; and see article 'The Meaning of Blood Sacrifice'.

8 - 10 THE CONSECRATION OF AARON AND HIS SONS

8 The investiture

Now that the priest's sacrificial duties have been listed, Moses implements the instructions given in Exodus 29. In an elaborate and impressive ritual Aaron and his sons are instituted to the priesthood. Moses performs the priestly duties on their behalf. The blood on Aaron's ear, hand and toe indicate the dedication of the whole man to God's service.

9 Aaron and his sons take office

The order of their first sacrifices is significant:

1. A sin-offering: obtaining cleansing and forgiveness.

2. A burnt-offering of dedication to God.

3. A peace-offering: fellowship and communion with God is restored and enjoyed.

10 Sacrilege

The rejoicing is short-lived. In no time Aaron's sons are deciding to do things *their* way: and God reduces the priesthood to three. Perhaps they were under the influence of drink (10:9). Whatever the reason, God's terrifying holiness cannot allow disobedience in those dedicated to his highest service. His commands are absolute; no man may tailor them to suit his fancy.

Verse 6: mourning is forbidden.

Verse 9: God's priests are to avoid the excesses of Canaan, where wine featured prominently.

Verse 16: the people's sin-offering should have been eaten by the priests in the holy place as a sign that God accepted the offering – Aaron's excuse is not clear, but Moses accepts it.

11 - 15 LAWS FOR DAILY LIFE: PURITY AND IMPURITY

Today we are more able to understand and appreciate the sound principles of diet, hygiene and medicine which these laws express. God works in and through the processes he has built into the natural world.

11 Food-laws: clean and unclean creatures

Israel may eat:
— Animals which chew the cud *and* have cloven hoofs.
— Sea creatures with both fins and scales.
— Birds not listed as forbidden.
— Insects belonging to four classes of the locust family.

Amongst those banned are:
— Carnivorous animals – which readily transmitted infection in a warm climate where flesh decayed rapidly.
— Pork – specially dangerous in this respect, as the old British saying about eating it only when there is an 'r' in the month (i.e. the cold months) bears out. Pigs are also hosts to various parasites.
— Vermin and predatory birds – likely disease-carriers.
— Shellfish – even today these often cause food-poisoning and enteritis.

Verses 32-40 set out measures to prevent contamination of food and water supplies. The same principles govern present-day public health regulations.

12 Purification after childbirth

In Canaan, prostitution and fertility rites were all mixed up with worship. In Israel, by sharp contrast, anything suggesting the sexual or sensual is strictly banned from the worship of God – as this chapter and chapter 15 make plain. The intention is not to write off this side of life as 'dirty', as is plain elsewhere in Scripture. The purpose is to ensure its separation from the worship of God. The rule of strict cleanliness in all sexual matters was also a positive safeguard to health.

13 - 14 Uncleanness due to skin diseases

Although the word 'leprosy' is used throughout, true leprosy as we would define it is only one of the diseases mentioned here. Chapter 13 is written in technical jargon – a professional textbook on diagnosis for the priest-physician, enabling him to distinguish between 'acute' and 'chronic' forms of the various diseases. This is the earliest formulation of quarantine

THE MEANING · OF BLOOD SACRIFICE

J.A. Motyer

The practice of sacrifice, the shedding of the blood of animals, goes back to the very beginning of God's dealings with sinful man (see Genesis 4:4). It pervades the whole of the Bible. In the New Testament it provides the terms in which the death of Jesus Christ is explained (see for instance Hebrews 9:11ff.).

The key verse, Leviticus 17:11, says that sacrifice is something that God has given to man: it is his provision for human need. It is a contradiction of this to say (as many Old Testament specialists do) that the basic meaning of sacrifice is an offering or gift to God. The word translated 'offering' certainly means gift. So, it is said, the person bringing the offering gains possession of the life, the blood, of the sacrificed animal, and can give it to God. By this means he injects new life into his relationship with God. Or else he is able to interpose a living screen between himself as a sinner and God the holy One. But how can that which God gives to man be interpreted as something man gives to God?

Leviticus 17:11 gives us two great clues to the meaning of blood and sacrifice. First: the purpose of the blood is to make atonement. Whenever the word translated 'atonement' was used it meant paying a price – a ransom price. So it is not sufficient to say that the blood 'screens' the offender. One must say that it does so by providing a price sufficient to pay off a debt of sin before God.

So here, as always in the Bible, 'the wages of sin is death'. No sin, no sinner, can come into the presence of an utterly holy God. To be cut off from God is death. Only if this price can be paid, the penalty taken, the sentence borne, can sinful man hope to be forgiven and come again into God's presence. This, says Leviticus 17:11, is precisely what the blood does.

We are told, second, that the blood can do this 'by reason of the life'. 'By reason of' translates a Hebrew preposition regularly used to express price or expenditure (e.g. 1 Kings 2:23; Proverbs 7:23; Lamentations 5:9). It is found in a basic legal passage on the necessity for exact justice, in the phrase 'life for life' (Deuteronomy 19:21), i.e. 'life in payment for life'. So in Leviticus 17:11, just as 'to make atonement' means 'to pay the atonement/ransom price', so 'by reason of the life' means 'by reason of the payment of life'.

In other words 'blood' means death – the termination of life – just as it does in ordinary metaphorical usage (see, for instance, Genesis 9:5, 37:26; etc.). In the sacrifice, life was terminated. The flowing blood was the symbol and proof that life had been taken in payment for the sins of the guilty and as a substitute for his own guilt-stained life.

Animal sacrifice expressed the principle. The full reality took place in the death of the Lord Jesus Christ. In the Old Testament the people had a God-given preview of the shed blood of Jesus, his substitutionary death on our behalf, for our sins, the just for the unjust, once and for all.

regulations and preventive medicine relating to these diseases so far recovered from the ancient Near East.

As far as clothing and buildings are concerned, the 'leprosy' is a mould, or fungus.

14:34ff.: we have a similar system of house inspection and treatment for dry rot today.

Cedarwood (14:49): contains a substance used in medicine for skin diseases.

Hyssop (14:49): a herb, possibly marjoram, containing a mild antiseptic.

15 Uncleanness due to bodily discharge

See under chapter 12. Regulations are given for both normal (seminal and menstrual) and abnormal, possibly malignant, discharges. Washing is prescribed both to prevent and sterilize infection.

16 THE DAY OF ATONEMENT

The 10th day of the 7th month (Tishri – September/October) was to be the annual Day of Atonement ('at-one-ment') for the nation. Only on this occasion was Aaron allowed into the innermost part of the tabernacle, where the ark of the covenant was housed. He must first obtain forgiveness and cleansing for his own sin. Only then might he cleanse the tabernacle and offer on behalf of the people's sins. For a New Testament look at the Day of Atonement, see Hebrews 9 and 10.

Azazel (8,10): a place in the wilderness to which the scapegoat was sent, symbolically carrying away the sins of Israel. The meaning is uncertain, but it cannot refer to an offering to a demon, as some suggest, for this was strictly forbidden (see, e.g., 17:7).

Outside the camp (27): neither offering might be eaten, since no one was to eat any of his own sin-offering, and Aaron identifies himself with the people in their sin-offering.

17 FURTHER REGULATIONS ABOUT SACRIFICE

As a safeguard against apostasy (17:7), sacrifice might be offered only in the proper place, and to the proper Person. On 17:10ff. see 'The Meaning of Blood Sacrifice'.

18 - 20 ETHICAL AND MORAL LAWS

18:3 provides a key to these chapters. From what we know of Canaanite and Egyptian religions it is clear that many of these laws are directed against the specific practices of Israel's neighbours.

18 Sexual offences

6-18: marriage between those closely related by blood or by marriage is forbidden in Israel. In Egypt, which had no marriage-laws, such marriages were common.

19-30: adultery, child-sacrifice, homosexuality, bestiality (perhaps a hangover from animal cults) were all part of the indescribably debased religions of Canaan. Israel is to shun behaviour which is bringing God's judgement on the land (compare Genesis 15:16).

19 Various laws

19:2 stands at the heart of the moral law for Jew and Christian alike (see 1 Peter 1:15-16). God's holiness, the holiness we are to reflect, shows itself in concern for the under-privileged (9-10, 14, 20), in honesty, fair dealing and impartial justice (11, 13, 15) and in respect for life and reputation (16-18).

Verses 23-25: the likelihood of heavy cropping is greatly increased by this practice.

Verses 26b-31: these are all heathen practices.

20 Serious offences and crimes punishable by death

Verses 6-21 list the penalties for disobedience to laws in chapters 18 and 19 (compare, e.g., 6 with 19:31; 9 with 19:3; 10 with 18:20). That such a wide range of offences should be punishable by death seems incredibly harsh to the modern reader. It is worth noting, however, that the offences listed are either in deliberate defiance of God's holy law, or offences against people – not property.

Molech (2-5): an Ammonite god. Amongst the Phoenicians live infants were placed in the arms of an idol, and died in the flames burning inside it. Some equally horrible practice is in mind here.

21 - 22 RULES FOR THE PRIESTS

Because of their position and duties the priests are subject to particularly stringent regulations on ritual purity. Any defilement disqualified them from contact with the holy things. The rules for the high priest (21:10-15) are even stricter (compare 11 with 1-2; 13-14 with 7). No one with any physical defect may serve as priest, though he may share in eating the

FEASTS AND FESTIVALS

Philip Budd

From very early times the Jewish year was punctuated by the great festivals – the 'feasts of the Lord'. Some were timed to coincide with the changing seasons, reminding the people of God's constant provision for them, and providing an opportunity to return to God some token of all that he had given. Others commemorated the great events of Israel's history, the occasions when in an unmistakable way God had stepped in to deliver his people. All were occasions of whole-hearted delight and enjoyment of God's good gifts, and at the same time sober gatherings to seek his forgiveness and cleansing.

They were never intended to be observed out of mere formality and empty ritual. The prophets had sharp words for those who reduced them to this level. The purpose of the festivals was spiritual: a great and glorious meeting of God and his people.

There were probably many local festivals (Judges 21:21), but on three occasions in the year all the men were required to attend great national celebrations:

1. Passover and the Feast of Unleavened Bread (Exodus 12:1-20; 23:15). These two feasts, combining pastoral and agricultural elements, were observed together to commemorate Israel's departure from Egypt (see on Exodus 11-12). The observance began on the fourteenth day of the first month and lasted for a week.

2. The Feast of Weeks (Harvest) (Exodus 23:16; Leviticus 23:15-21). Later known as Pentecost, it was celebrated 50 days after the beginning of Passover. It was essentially an agricultural celebration at which the first-fruits of the harvest were offered to God.

3. The Feast of Ingathering (Tabernacles) (Exodus 23:16; Leviticus 23:33-43). An autumn festival at the end of the fruit-harvest. The people lived for seven days in

Israel's religious festivals marked the high points in the farmer's year. The diagram shows the months of the Jewish calendar and how they relate to the calendar we use today.

shelters made of branches – essentially as an agricultural thanksgiving, but also as a reminder of their tent-dwelling days in the wilderness (Leviticus 23:43).

All of these festivals were regarded as 'holy', occasions when all ordinary work stopped. There were also other celebrations (all in some way connected with the number seven).

4. Sabbath. On the seventh day all work was forbidden and the daily sacrifices were doubled. This observance was connected with the completion of God's work of creation (Exodus 20:11), the deliverance from Egypt (Deuteronomy 5:15), and man's simple need for rest and refreshment (Exodus 23:12). After the exile the sabbath rules were strictly enforced (Nehemiah 13:15-22), and their observance became one of the outstanding features of Judaism.

5. New moon. This is often mentioned along with the sabbath (e.g. Isaiah 1:13). Special sacrifices (Numbers 28:11-15), and the blowing of trumpets (Numbers 10:10) were distinctive features of the new moon festival. There were also special meals and family sacrifices in early times (1 Samuel 20:5, 24), and sometimes prophets were consulted (2 Kings 4:23). On the new moon of the seventh month there was a special **Feast of Trumpets.** (Numbers 29:1).

6. Sabbatical year. By law, every seventh year the land lay fallow (Leviticus 25:1-7), and every fiftieth year was a **Jubilee Year** (Leviticus 25:8-34) when mortgaged property was returned to its owners and Hebrew slaves were freed.

7. Day of Atonement (Leviticus 16). On the tenth day of the seventh month there was a special annual ceremony of confession and atonement for sin.

There were other feasts not mentioned in the biblical laws. One was the **Feast of Purim** (Esther 9) to commemorate the Jewish deliverance from Haman, and later the **Feast of Dedication** (John 10:22) celebrating the purification of the temple after its desecration by Antiochus Epiphanes in 168 BC.

offerings. Only the best man can give – whether in the priesthood or sacrificial offerings – is in any measure worthy of God.

23 THE SET FEASTS

Israel's special festivals, like the weekly sabbath, reflect a pattern of sevens – pointing back to God's hallowing of the seventh day at the creation.

1. The sabbath: one day of rest in seven.

2. Passover, followed by the seven-day Feast of Unleavened Bread (March/April).

3. Firstfruits (April), followed seven weeks later by

4. The Feast of Weeks (Pentecost): the harvest festival (June).

5. The Feast of Trumpets: first of three festivals in the seventh month (September/ October); the others being

6. The Day of Atonement; and

7. The Feast of Tabernacles (Booths): a perpetual reminder of the nation's tent-dwelling days following the deliverance from Egypt.

24 THE LAMP, SHEWBREAD, AND THE SIN OF BLASPHEMY

Chapter 24 turns from special festivals to two regular duties: the lamp which must be kept burning, and the weekly offering of 12 loaves. The loaves remind the tribes of their complete dependence on God's provision. They are not put there for God to eat (as in pagan religions). Aaron and the priests are openly instructed to eat the bread themselves.

Verses 10-23 record the ruling about a breach of the third commandment. The emphasis is on one law for Israelite and resident foreigner alike. **The law of retaliation (lex talionis, verses 15ff.):** the principle this law expresses is of exact public justice, as opposed to individual revenge. In the event, compensation for injury often took the form of a fine (as the exception made in the case of murder implies – Numbers 35:31ff.). The fact that literal retaliation by bodily mutilation was legally allowed does not necessarily mean it was practised. It was a strict, legal statement against such practices as family feuds (the evils of which are shown, for instance, in Greek drama).

25 THE SEVENTH AND FIFTIETH YEARS: SABBATH AND JUBILEE

The pattern of sevens reflected in the festivals (chapter 23) is now extended to the land. One year in seven it is to lie fallow: a year in which the people, freed from much of their ordinary work, are to be taught and trained in God's law (Deuteronomy 31:10ff.). The fifieth year, following the seventh seven, is an extra fallow year for the land, which reverts to its original owner. It is a time when those who have fallen on bad times have their freedom and property restored. Jubilee serves a dual purpose: It reminds the people that the land belongs to God; and it prevents the wealthy from amassing land.

26 PROMISE AND WARNING: BLESSING AND CURSING

The reward of obedience is pictured as an idyll of peace and plenty. Best of all, God will walk amongst his people, as he walked in the garden with the first man. This is Eden restored. Disobedience, on the other hand, will bring calamity on the nation: fatal disease, famine, wild beasts ravaging the land, and war leading to exile. The cursings are more detailed than the blessings: human nature being what it is, fear brings a readier response than love. Yet even after all the disobedience, God still promises to respond to the call of genuine repentance.

27 VOWS AND TITHES

Firstborn sons, the firstlings of flocks and herds, and firstfruits of the field are God's by right (he accepts part for the whole). One-tenth of all cattle and produce are also his due. Over and above this, men might vow individuals or possessions to God as a dedication or thank-offering. Normally these would be redeemed for their set valuation, plus one-fifth.
Devoted to the Lord (28): deliberately set apart for God and therefore no longer available to man. Verse 29 presumably refers to someone 'set apart' under a death sentence.
Verse 34 brings us back to the source of authority for these and all the laws in Leviticus. The commands are God's, given through Moses, at Sinai.

LITERARY CRITICISM AND THE OLD TESTAMENT

Gordon Wenham

'Criticism' is an indispensable aid to interpreting the Old Testament. In everyday speech it is a decidedly negative word. But in the specialized sense it covers a range of disciplines which apply to most types of literature, and it has made a very positive contribution to the understanding of the Bible.

The six main branches of biblical criticism are textual, source, tradition, redaction, form and historical criticism. The first five are basically concerned with the structures of literature and the various ways in which an author expresses himself. The last, historical criticism, is more concerned with the meaning and truth of the author's statements.

Textual criticism
Textual criticism is concerned with recovering the original text of a document. Mistakes are liable to creep into every document copied by hand, and it is the task of the textual critic to spot these errors and – wherever possible – correct them. By studying numerous manuscripts, textual critics have been able to work out a set of principles which can be applied to many different sorts of document.

For the most part the scribes who copied the Pentateuch were very careful, and it would seem that very few errors crept into the Hebrew text. In the case of other Old Testament books – notably Samuel and Jeremiah – there are passages where it is more difficult to re-establish the original text.

The discovery of the Dead Sea Scrolls was therefore very important, since they give us a Hebrew text of much of the Old Testament about a thousand years older than anything we had before.

Source criticism

Source criticism is the attempt to discover and define the written material on which the different biblical writers drew. It has important bearings on the reliability of the Bible books. Some Old Testament books describe events that occurred many years before they were written. The book of Kings for instance must have been written after the last event it mentions – the release of King Jehoiachin from prison in 562 BC – yet it also relates the accession of Solomon, some 400 years earlier, as well as numerous events in between. Stories simply handed down by word of mouth over that length of time are likely to be less accurate than those written down from the beginning. But source critics, prompted by the recurring refrain 'And the rest of the deeds of King X, are they not written in the Book of the Chronicles of the Kings of Judah/Israel?', have concluded that much of the early material in the book has in fact been taken from royal annals and other trustworthy contemporary records.

It is extremely difficult to distinguish different literary sources within a document unless some of those sources have actually survived. In that case the source material may be subtracted from the document in question to leave the author's own contribution or material taken from another source. In the Bible we rarely possess two or more parallel documents where we can see how one writer used another as his source. The Synoptic Gospels (Matthew, Mark, Luke) in the New Testament and the Old Testament book of Kings with its parallel in Chronicles are the exceptions.

Elsewhere, though it is a reasonable assumption that the biblical writers used sources, there is little or no objective evidence that this is so. More subjective, less dependable criteria, such as variation in style or vocabulary, have to be used to distinguish the sources. Using such criteria it has become customary to distinguish at least four sources in the Pentateuch (commonly designated J,E,D and P). More recently, however, it has been argued that the differences in Hebrew style which are used to define the pentateuchal sources have no significance in the light of ancient literary conventions, and that a fresh approach to this aspect of the criticism of the Pentateuch is required.

Tradition criticism

Tradition criticism attempts to trace the development of a biblical story or tradition from the time it was first told to the time it was written down. For instance, the stories of Abraham were probably passed on by word of mouth for several generations before being incorporated in a written source later used by the author of Genesis. A historian concerned to reconstruct the life of Abraham as exactly as possible wants to know what changes the story of Abraham went through in the process of retelling. Tradition criticism tries to pin-point and explain such changes. However, except where the precise means and circumstances in which a story was transmitted are known, the results of tradition criticism are open to question and must be treated with caution.

Redaction criticism

The task of redaction criticism is to determine how the editor (redactor) of a biblical book utilized his sources, what he omitted and what he added and what his particular bias was. Only when the critic has access to all the sources which were at the disposal of the editor can his findings be absolutely certain. And in the Old Testament the critic has, at best, only some of the sources (e.g. the book of Kings used by the author of Chronicles). Elsewhere the sources are precariously reconstructed out of the edited work itself. Then redaction criticism is of limited value, but its methods can help to bring out the special interests of the editor and so lead to a fuller appreciation of the theology expressed in his work.

Form criticism

Form criticism is concerned with the study of literary form in the

Bible. Different writings have different forms. An essay differs in form from a poem. The form of a law differs from that of a psalm. Often the form of a piece of literature may throw light on the nature of the piece and its background, or 'life-setting'. The basic method of form criticism is to compare like with like, to determine the characteristic features of a particular type of literature, and then to suggest reasons for these features.

Form criticism has been most profitably used in the psalms and has revolutionized our understanding of them. The psalms fall into different categories, such as hymns, thanksgivings, laments, royal psalms, pilgrimage songs, etc. It used to be held that most of the psalms were personal poems of pious Jews after the exile. Now, thanks to form criticism, it is recognized that most of the psalms were sung in the public worship of the temple prior to its destruction in 587 BC.

Historical criticism

Historical criticism is a very broad discipline covering all aspects of history writing. There are two aspects of it which are of particular concern to biblical studies.

First, historical criticism has determined the techniques used for dating a document. How do we know when it was written, and the date of the copy we possess? Unless we have the original, the date of composition will of course always be earlier than a copy. The latter is relatively easy to determine with modern methods in palaeography and archaeology. However, our earliest manuscript of Exodus dates from about 250 BC, and all agree that it is not an original and that Exodus must have been composed much earlier. To discover that date is a much more involved process. If its author were named in the text, this would help. But a forgery could always claim to be written by Moses in the same terms as an authentic Mosaic document. A second clue to the date of a book lies in the events it records. Obviously its date of composition must be later than the last event mentioned – in the case of Exodus, the erection of the tabernacle. But this only tells us the earliest date at which the book could have been written, not the latest date, which is of more interest.

If there are no explicit statements in the text itself about its date of composition, we have to rely on indirect evidence, such as the assumptions of the writer. The author of the book of Judges shows when he was writing by remarking several times, 'In those days there was no king in Israel; every man did what was right in his own eyes.' The obvious implication is that the writer had experienced the order a just king could create, and was writing after the establishment of the monarchy.

The second important task of historical criticism is to verify information found in the biblical sources. When a document says something, how do we know it is telling the truth? This basic question may be broken down into a number of smaller ones. How close is the document to the events it describes? Are its statements backed up by other sources, biblical or non-biblical, or by archaeology? Could the events have occurred just as they are described? In trying to answer these questions the historian will be able to build up a fuller and richer picture of what happened. Discovering the author of a source may greatly illuminate the meaning of a narrative; and non-biblical sources can often fill in the background to the biblical account.

In these various ways biblical criticism has been of use in interpreting the Old Testament and defending its integrity against those who question its truth. Only too often Old Testament criticism, especially historical criticism, has been marred by the introduction of unjustified rationalistic assumptions (e.g. that miracles do not happen). But on the whole, the value of criticism has been proved by its generally positive conclusions. Certainly all who believe in the value of the Old Testament must take criticism seriously, as they will be the first to want to establish an accurate text and be sure of its meaning.

NUMBERS

Numbers covers 38 years in the history of Israel: the period of desert wandering in the Sinai peninsula. It begins two years after the escape from Egypt. It ends on the eve of entry into Canaan. The title comes from the 'numbering' (census) of Israel in the early chapters and chapter 26. The book might have been called 'The grumblings of a nation'. It is one long sad story of complaining and discontent. As a result, of the entire generation that had seen the marvels of God's deliverance from Egypt, only three men – Moses, Joshua and Caleb – survive to the end of the book. And only two – Joshua and Caleb – were to enjoy the promised land.

1 - 10:10 ISRAEL IN THE WILDERNESS OF SINAI

1 The general census

The purpose of the census is to list all men over 20 fit for military service. The Levites, by virtue of their other duties, were exempt. Moses and Aaron, the civic and religious heads, are in charge of the count, assisted by one representative from each tribe. In the second census (chapter 26), taken 38 years later, after Aaron's death, his son Eleazar takes his place. The later total, 601,730, is slightly less than the figure here, 603,550. In Egypt Israel's population rose rapidly, but now the tough desert conditions and the judgements their disobedience brings upon them keep the figures static.

The problem of high numbers: a military force of over 600,000 would mean a total population of some 2-3 million. The Bible account makes it plain that the numbers involved were considerable. Israel could not have survived in the desert without God's miraculous provision. Even so, 2-3 million would equal the entire population of Canaan. And other passages imply that the Canaanites were more numerous than the Israelites (Deuteronomy 7:7, 17, 22). For this reason, various attempts have been made to reduce the numbers. Some

believe, for example, that the word translated 'thousands' should be 'captains'; others that it should be 'families'. It is also possible that the numbers are used as symbols of power and importance, rather than a literal count of heads. See further 'Large Numbers of the Old Testament'.

2 The encampment

When the nation moved, the three eastern tribes, headed by Judah, led the way. 10:17 gives a slightly different order for the middle section – Gershonites and Merarites carrying the tabernacle, then Reuben, Simeon and Gad, followed by the Kohathites with the sanctuary. The northern tribes, Dan, Asher and Naphtali bring up the rear. The tribal leaders are the same as those who helped in the census. Ramesses II of Egypt (Moses' contemporary) used this same hollow rectangular formation in his Syrian campaign, so it looks as if Moses was making good use of his earlier Egyptian military training.

The standards (2:2): according to Jewish tradition, a lion for Judah, a human head for Reuben, an ox for Ephraim and an eagle for Dan.

3 God chooses the Levites for special service

God's claim to the firstborn goes back to the night of the Passover (Exodus 12). Now God accepts the Levites instead of the firstborn of all Israel. The first census pairs them off man for man, leaving a surplus of 273 who are redeemed by money.

Shekel of the sanctuary (3:47): a weight of about 10gms, not a coin.

4 The Levitical families are assigned their jobs

The second census of Levites lists those between 30 and 50, eligible for the service of the tabernacle. (The age-limits varied at different times: see 8:24; 1 Chronicles 23:24.)

Verses 1-20: the **Kohathites** are responsible for carrying the sacred objects of the sanctuary after the priests have dismantled and covered them.

Verses 21-28: the **Gershonites** are in charge of transporting the curtains and coverings of the tabernacle and forecourt under Ithamar's supervision.

Verses 29-33: the **Merarites** are to look after and transport the framework – pillars, pegs, cords – also under Ithamar's supervision. Wagons drawn by a yoke of oxen are provided for the Gershonites and Merarites (7:7-8).

5 Various laws; the jealousy ordeal

Verses 11-31 describe the trial by ordeal for suspected infidelity. Trials of this kind were not uncommon in ancient times, and they are also well known from Africa and India. This one is mild by some standards – and also less heavily weighted than many towards a verdict of guilty. It is not clear whether the water contained some herb which would induce miscarriage if the woman were guilty and pregnant, or whether it worked simply by psychological suggestion.

6:1-21 The Nazirite

A special vow gives the Nazirite his (or her) spiritual status. The outward marks of consecration to God are:
— abstinence from wine and strong drink;
— uncut hair;
— special care to avoid defilement through contact with a dead body (see on chapter 19).

The vow was usually for a limited time, but Samson (a somewhat unorthodox Nazirite) had a lifelong vow (Judges 13-16). Samuel may also have been a Nazirite. It is not known how or when these practices originated.

6:22-27 Aaron's benediction

7 The tribes bring their offerings

The dedication of the altar preceded the events of Numbers 1 by a month. On successive days the leader of each tribe brings a silver plate and silver basin filled with a cereal offering, a golden dish of incense, and animals for burnt-offering, sin-offering and peace-offering (see on Leviticus 1-7).

8 Consecration of the Levites

Those who serve God must be clean through and through. Washing and shaving ensure outward cleanliness. The blood of sacrifice cleans man of the inward stain of sin.

9:1-14 Rulings about the Passover

No one may opt out of celebrating the Passover (see Exodus 12). But the absentee and anyone ritually unclean at the time may observe the feast one month later.

9:15-23 The cloud and the fire

God's guidance in the wilderness was a clear and visible reality. Cloud by day and fire by night marked his presence at the tabernacle, which was quite literally in their midst. When the cloud lifted they moved on. Where it settled again, they encamped: no movement of the cloud, no movement of the people.

10:1-10 The silver trumpets

These sounded the alarm, summoned the assembly, and announced the feasts and new months. Long trumpets like these were common in Egypt about 1400-1300 BC. Some were buried with the Pharaoh Tutankhamun (about 1350 BC).

10:11 - 12:16 FROM SINAI TO KADESH

10:11-36 The journey begins

About three weeks after the census they strike camp and leave Mt Sinai. (See on chapter 2 for the marching order.) Moses' brother-in-law goes with them as guide. The direction and company of the Lord is a very real thing (33-36).

11 Complaints about the monotonous diet

The first delicious taste of manna (see Exodus 16) was like wafers made with honey. Now sheer monotony makes it stick in the gullet like sawdust. Mouth-watering thoughts of all the fish and vegetables that abounded in the Egyptian delta soon produce an irresistible craving. God gives them what they want – till they are sick of it! And with it comes judgement for the attitude which lay behind the outcry.

Verse 29: a remarkable attitude in a leader – power without a streak of corruption (see 12:3).

A flock of quails, on their migration flight, satisfied the Israelites' craving for meat.

Quails (31): as in the previous year (Exodus 16), this was a migratory

flight returning in spring to Europe.
Homer (32): 'a donkey load'; 10
homers is the measure of their
gluttony.

12 Miriam and Aaron challenge Moses' leadership

The real bone of contention is not
Moses' marriage, but his position. As
Miriam is the one to be punished,
presumably she was the instigator.
Moses is silent, but God's answer is
a remarkable tribute to the man (6-8).
Cushite (1): this is usually taken to
mean 'Ethiopian'.

13 - 20:21 IN THE KADESH AREA

Details are few, but it seems that the
best part of 38 years – a whole generation – was spent around here.

13 - 14 The twelve spies and their reports; mutiny

From Deuteronomy 1:19-25 it seems
plain that Moses intended to go
straight on into the promised land at
this point; it was the people's suggestion that they should send spies
ahead. No doubt Moses afterwards
wished he had not listened. The two
men of faith put the true interpretation on the facts (Numbers 13:30),
but the people listened to the ten
prophets of doom, with their tales of
giants and grasshoppers. God, and
the good land, was forgotten. Within
sight of the goal, a whole generation
cut itself off from all that was
promised. Moses' prayer at this point
is staggering. Only God's intervention
has saved him from death by stoning.
Yet here he is, pleading for the life
of the stubborn nation that caused
him nothing but trouble! Time and
time again he stands between Israel
and utter destruction (Exodus 32:7-
14; Numbers 11:1-2; 16:41-48; 21:5-9).
Now his plea involves him in sharing
their sentence with them.
The Anakim ... the Nephilim: see
Genesis 6:4. Nothing is known of
them outside the Bible, but they were
evidently a race of Goliaths.
Caleb never lost his whole-hearted
trust in God. Forty-five years later,
at the age of 85, he chooses Anakim
territory to conquer as his possession
(Joshua 14:6-15).

15 Various laws

Verses 1-31: offerings to be made
after the conquest of Canaan.
  Verses 32-36: the seriousness of
sabbath-breaking.
  Verses 37-41: the border of tassels
to remind forgetful Israel of God and
his commands.

16 The rebellion of Korah, Dathan and Abiram

This unholy alliance has a two-
pronged attack. Korah the Levite's
grievance is Aaron's monopoly of the
priesthood (10b). Dathan and Abiram
challenge Moses on the grounds of
high-handedness and his failure to
bring them into the promised land
(13-14). But at root the attack is on
God (11), and it is God who puts the
rebellion down.
Put out the eyes (14): New English
Bible 'hoodwink' gives the sense.
Our equivalent of the Hebrew idiom
is 'to pull wool over the eyes'.
The earth opened its mouth (32): God
makes use of natural forces to
execute judgement (as in the nine
plagues of Egypt). The phenomenon
here may be the breaking up (perhaps
by storm) of the hard crusty surface
which forms over deep lakes of liquid
mud in the Arabah rift valley where
this incident occurred.

17 Aaron's rod produces the fruit

Like all biblical miracles, this one has
a very practical point. Everyone can
see where God's choice falls, and
there is no more room for dispute.

18 - 19 Duties and dues of the priests and Levites; the purification ritual

Neither priests nor Levites share in
the inheritance of the land. Instead,
God gives the priests the remainder
of all the sacrificial offerings, firstfruits and firstlings. The Levites are
given the nation's tithes (one tenth of
all the flocks and herds and produce),
of which they in turn give one tenth
to the priests.
  The ritual with the red heifer (19:1-
10) is the remedy for defilement by
contact with a dead body, described
in verses 11-22. To minimize the risk
of accidental defilement, tombs were
later painted white (see Matthew
23:27).

20:1-13 Miriam's death; water from the rock

Miriam, Aaron (20:25ff.; 33:38f.) and
Moses (Deuteronomy 34:5-8) all died
in the same year – on the brink of
entry into Canaan. The best part of
38 years has passed since 13:1.
  Verses 2-13: Moses' sin seems to
be his failure to give God credit for
the water-supply. It cost him the land
he had so longed to enter. Even the
greatest of God's servants, after a
long lifetime of trust and obedience,
can fall. Nothing seems to cure the
people's grumbles. They were moaning when they first left Egypt. They

are moaning still, after all the years of God's providing.

Water out of the rock: Sinai limestone is known to retain water (see on Exodus 17:6).

20:14-21 Edom refuses a safe-conduct

Your brother Israel (14): not just a manner of speaking, the Edomites were descendants of Esau, Jacob's brother.

King's Highway (17): Edom's refusal to let Israel pass along this main road involves them in a long detour south and round.

20:22 - 21:35 DETOUR TO AVOID EDOM

20:22-29 The death of Aaron

Mt Hor may be Jebel Madeira, north-east of Kadesh, on the north-west border of Edom.

21 Victories over Arad and Sihon; the incident of the poisonous snakes

Complaints begin again on the trek south to the Gulf of Aqaba (the 'Red Sea' here) to clear Edom's territory. Jesus used the incident of the bronze serpent to explain his own death in his discussion with Nicodemus (John 3:14). In the wilderness the people had only to look, and they lived.

The well (16): water lies close to the surface in some parts of the Sinai peninsula and southern Transjordan. The Israelites often had only to dig shallow pits to find it.

22 - 36 ISRAEL IN THE PLAINS OF MOAB

22 - 24 Balak and Balaam: the blessing of Israel

With the Israelites encamped on his doorstep, the king of Moab sends to Pethor (probably Pitru, near Carchemish) on the Euphrates for Balaam the diviner to come and curse his enemies. It was a routine business arrangement for the prophet, in a day when everyone believed in the power of words (especially formal 'blessings' and 'cursings') to influence events. What is surprising is the disclosure that the source of Balaam's knowledge is God himself. And neither bribe nor threat will budge him from the truth as God reveals it to him.

Three times they go through the same ritual (22:41 - 23:10; 23:13-24; 23:27 - 24:9). Three times Balaam blesses Israel, to the increasing anger of Balak. The fourth oracle tops all (24:15-24) – a remarkable prediction

of Israel's future.

The incident of the ass: God's purpose seems to be so to impress Balaam, that no matter how hard Balak works on him, the prophet will stick to the truth.

The origin of these oracles: it is not known how these oracles came to be included in Numbers. But linguistic and other factors indicate that the oracles were written down by the 12th century BC.

25 Idolatry at Peor

It was on Balaam's advice (31:16, Revised Standard Version) that the Midianite women brought Israel low at Peor. And he paid for it with his life (31:8).

Play the harlot (1): they did so literally and also as far as religion was concerned. By joining in pagan worship, Israel broke faith with God.

Baal of Peor (3): the local deity of the place. 'Baal' (meaning 'master') gradually became a proper name for the great fertility god of the Canaanites. The events described here already show a blend of sexual and religious practices.

Moabite ... Midianite: the interchange of terms sounds confused, but from late patriarchal times on, there was in fact a good deal of overlap in the use of the terms 'Midianite', 'Ishmaelite', 'Medanite', 'Moabite'.

26 The second census

See on chapter 1.

27:1-11 The right of daughters to inherit

Women could not normally inherit in other ancient Near Eastern countries, but in Israel the ruling is given that brotherless daughters may inherit. However, to safeguard the tribal inheritance, they must marry within their own tribe (see chapter 36).

27:12-23 Joshua appointed as Moses' successor

Moses' life is almost over. Joshua, his right-hand man (Exodus 17:9ff.; 24:13; 33:11; Numbers 11:28) and one of the two faithful spies (14:6ff.), is now invested with authority to lead the nation in his place.

Mt Abarim (12): the name of the mountain range. Mt Nebo, overlooking Jericho, was the actual summit from which Moses viewed the land.

You rebelled against my word (14): see on 20:2-13.

28 - 30 Rules for public worship and vows

28: 1-8, daily offerings; 9, 10, sabbath offerings; 11-15, offerings for each new month; 16-25, offerings for Passover and Unleavened Bread; 26-31, the Feast of Weeks (Firstfruits).

Chapter 29: the feasts of the seventh month. Verses 1-6, offerings for the Feast of Trumpets; 7-11, for the Day of Atonement; 12-38, for the Feast of Booths.

For feasts, see Leviticus 23, and article. For offerings see on Leviticus 1-7, and article.

Chapter 30: vows. Men in Israel are unconditionally bound by vows of any kind (1, 2). Verses 3-15: the terms under which vows made by women are binding.

31 Vengeance on the Midianites; dealing with the spoil
The Midianites are punished for their sin in inducing Israel to worship false gods (see chapter 25 and notes). Army and nation divide the spoil fifty-fifty. One five-hundredth of the army's share goes to the priests; one fiftieth of the nation's share to the Levites. Verses 48-54 record the army's special offering given in gratitude for their safe return.

32 Reuben, Gad and half Manasseh settle east of the Jordan
See map. This is permitted only on condition that they help in the conquest of Canaan before returning to a settled life.

33 A list of the stages of the journey from Egypt to the plains of Moab

Figured stones ... high places (52): i.e. stone carvings, and hilltops or artificial 'high places' where shrines were built. The intention is to wipe out everything associated with idolatrous religions.

34 The ideal boundaries of Israel
See also Joshua 13-19.

35 Cities and pasture for the Levites: the six cities of refuge for those who cause death by accident
See also Joshua 20-21.

36 Safeguards in the case of daughters' inheritance
See on 27:1-11

THE LARGE NUMBERS OF THE OLD TESTAMENT

John Wenham

The Old Testament at various places records numbers which seem impossibly large. It has often been assumed that these figures were simply invented, and are evidence that the Bible is historically unreliable. But who would make up figures which are patently absurd? Would any man in his senses invent a story of a bus crash in which 16,000 passengers were killed? It is much more likely that these Old Testament numbers were faithfully copied out, despite the fact that they did not seem to make sense. Invention does not satisfactorily account for them. The explanation must lie elsewhere. And in fact patient research has gone a long way towards resolving this knotty problem.

The corruption of numbers
There is evidence that the Old Testament text is on the whole marvellously well preserved. There is also evidence from the parallel passages in Samuel, Kings and Chronicles and (especially) in Ezra 2 and Nehemiah 7 that numbers were peculiarly difficult to transmit accurately. We have instances of extra noughts being added to a number: 2 Samuel 10:18 reads '700 chariots', 1 Chronicles 19:18 reads '7,000'. A digit can drop out: 2 Kings 24:8 gives the age of Jehoiachin on accession as 18, whereas 2 Chronicles 36:9 gives it as 8. An entire numeral can drop out: 1 Samuel 13:1 says 'Saul was years old'. In Ezra 2 and Nehemiah 7 the digits often vary by one unit.

And there are other errors of copying, many of which are easily explained.

The confusion of words

In the modern Hebrew Bible all numbers are written out in full, but for a long time the text was written without vowels. The absence of vowels made it possible to confuse two words which are crucial to this problem: 'eleph and 'alluph. Without vowel points these words look identical: 'lp. 'eleph is the ordinary word for 'thousand', but it can also be used in a variety of other senses: e.g. 'family' (Judges 6:15, Revised Version) or 'clan' (Zechariah 9:7; 12:5, 6, Revised Standard Version) or perhaps a military unit. 'alluph is used for the 'chieftains' of Edom (Genesis 36:15-43); probably for a commander of a military 'thousand'; and almost certainly for the professional, fully-armed soldier.

Military statistics

At certain periods warfare was conducted by two sharply distinguished types of fighting men – the Goliaths and the Davids – the professional soldiers who were fully armed, and the folk army, whose only weapons were those of the peasant shepherd. It seems clear that in a number of places the word for professional soldier has been misunderstood as meaning 'thousand'. Take, for example, the attack on the little town of Gibeah in Judges 20. Verse 2 says that 400,000 footmen 'that drew the sword' assembled. If these were in fact 400 fully armed foot-soldiers, the subsequent narrative makes excellent sense. The Benjamite forces (verse 15) consist of 26 soldiers armed with swords, together with 700 men armed only with slings. At the first attack (verse 21) the Israelites lose 22 of their crack soldiers, the next day (verse 25) they lose a further 18; on the third day (verses 29,34) an ambush is set, consisting of, or led by, 10 of them. (Could 10,000 men take up their positions undetected?) The losses begin again (verse 31) 'as at other times' – and in this case the scale of loss has been clearly preserved, for about 30 Israelites (not apparently sword-armed soldiers).

25 Benjamite soldiers and 100 others are killed. Eighteen of them were killed in the first stage of the pursuit, 5 were later 'cut down in the highways' and 2 more at Gidom. The remaining 600 slingers took refuge in the rock of Rimmon. Similarly, in the assault on Ai (Joshua 7-8) the true proportions of the narrative become clear when we realize that the disastrous loss of 36 men is matched by the setting of an ambush, not of 30,000 men of valour, but of 30.

David's feast in Hebron in 1 Chronicles 12 appears to be attended by enormous numbers, not of ordinary men, but of distinguished leaders – some 340,800 of them. In this case it looks as though in fact there were 'captains of thousands' and 'captains of hundreds', and that by metonymy or by abbreviation 'thousand' has been used for 'captains of thousands' and 'hundreds' for 'captains of hundreds'. 'Thousand' and 'hundred' have been treated as numerals and added together. When these figures are unscrambled, we get a total of roughly 2,000 'famous men', which seems eminently reasonable.

Along these lines most of the numerical problems of the later history fall into place. In 1 Kings 20:27-30, the little Israelite army killed 100 (not 100,000) foot-soldiers, and the wall of Aphek killed 27 (not 27,000) more. The Ethiopian invasion had a thousand, not a million, warriors (2 Chronicles 14:9). 10 (not 10,000) were cast down from the top of the rock (2 Chronicles 25:12).

The size of the Israelite nation

The most interesting, most difficult and (from the historian's point of view) the most important question is the size of the Israelite population at the different stages of its history. The present texts indicate that the 70 souls of Joseph's day had risen to two or three million at the time of the Exodus (Numbers 1) and to at least five million in the time of David (2 Samuel 24:9; 1 Chronicles 21:5). With regard to the latter, R. de Vaux rightly says: '(2 Samuel) lists 800,000 men liable for military service in Israel, and 500,000 in Judah ... The lower total, in 2 Samuel, is still far too high: 1,300,000 men of military age would imply at least five million inhabitants, which, for Palestine, would mean nearly twice as many people to the square mile as in the most thickly populated countries of modern Europe.'

The solution of the problem of the Exodus numbers is a long story. Suffice it to say that there is good reason to believe that the original censuses in Numbers 1 and 26 set out the numbers of each tribe, somewhat in this form:

Simeon:
57 armed men; 23 'hundreds' (military units).
This came to be written:
57 '*lp*; 2 '*lp* 3 'hundreds'.

Not realising that '*lp* in one case meant 'armed man' and in the other 'thousand', this was tidied up to read 59,300. When these figures are carefully decoded, a remarkably clear picture of the whole military organization emerges. The total fighting force is some 18,000, which would probably mean a figure of about 72,000 for the whole migration.

The figures of the Levites seem consistently to have collected an extra nought. The mystery of Plato's Atlantis has been solved by recognition of this same numerical confusion. Plato obtained *from Egyptian priests* what now turns out to be a detailed account of the Minoan civilization and its sudden end. But as all the figures were multiplied by a factor of ten, the area was too great to be enclosed in the Mediterranean, so he placed it in the Atlantic; and the date was put back into remote antiquity, thousands of years too early. This same tenfold multiplication factor is found in the figures of the Levites in the book of Numbers. When it is eliminated Levi fits into the pattern as a standard-size tribe of about 2,200 males. These figures agree remarkably well with the other indications of population in the period of the conquest and the judges.

David's census
The discrepancy between the two sets of figures for David's census can be accounted for by recognizing at different stages in transmission, first, the addition of noughts, and then, a misunderstanding of '*lp*. If we postulate original figures: Israel: 80,000 plus 30 '*lp*; Judah: 40,000 plus 70 '*lp*, the present text of both Samuel and Chronicles can be accounted for thus:

Chronicles
Stage 1
Israel: 80,000 plus 30 '*lp*
Judah: 40,000 plus 70 '*lp*

Stage 2
Israel: 800,000 plus 300 '*lp*
Judah: 400,000 plus 70 '*lp*

Stage 3
Israel: 1,100,000
Judah: 470,000

Samuel
Stage 1
Israel: 80,000 plus 30 '*lp*
Judah: 40,000 plus 70 '*lp*

Stage 2
Israel: 800,000 plus 30 '*lp*
Judah: 470,000

At this stage it would seem that the copyist was perplexed by the floating '30 '*lp*', which he took to be 30,000. He wrongly combined it with the Judah figure, so producing:

Stage 3
Israel: 800,000
Judah: 500,000

If the original figures totalled 120,000 men of military age, together with 100 professional soldiers, the entire population would have been nearly half a million, which again tallies well with other indications in the text.

By the use of these methods a very large proportion of the numerical difficulties can be resolved.

DEUTERONOMY

Deuteronomy is the record of Moses' farewell addresses to Israel, given about 1260 BC on the plains of Moab, on the eve of entry to the promised land. The title, which comes from the Greek translation, implies a second law-giving, but in fact the book contains a restatement and reaffirmation of the Sinai covenant. It follows a specific treaty-pattern (see article 'Covenants and Near Eastern Treaties'):

1 *Introduction* 1:1-5
2 *Historical prologue* 1:6 - 4:49
3 *Stipulations* 5:1 - 26:19
4 *Curses and blessings* 27:1 - 30:20
5 *Succession arrangements and public reading* 31:1 - 34:5

The laws recorded in Exodus, Leviticus and Numbers are brought together and applied specifically to the settled life of Canaan which is about to begin.

1:1-5 INTRODUCTION

Time and place are carefully specified. Forty years after the exodus, at the end of the wilderness wanderings, in the plains beyond Jordan, Moses gives God's message to Israel.

Eleven days' journey from Horeb ... **(2):** the journey from Jebel Musa (traditional site of Mt Sinai/Horeb) to Dahab on the east coast of Sinai, up the coast and across to Kadesh (the Ain Qudeirat area) has recently been shown to take just this time.

1:6 - 4:49 HISTORICAL PROLOGUE: MOSES LOOKS BACK

1:6-46 Sinai to Kadesh; the spies and the revolt

Verses 9-18: Moses recalls how he found relief from the solitary burden of leadership in delegating responsibility. The wise advice to do so came from his father-in-law, Jethro (see Exodus 18:13-26).

Verses 19-46: see on Numbers 13-14.

That great and terrible wilderness (19): 'wilderness' simply means uninhabited land. North of Sinai the land is barren and desolate, with rugged

peaks and the earth covered with stones and flints. But there are oases, with a surprising amount of vegetation after the winter rains.

Amorites (44): Numbers 14:43 uses the wider term 'Canaanites'.

2 Edom, Moab, Ammon; war against the Amorites

Verses 1-8: see Numbers 20:14-21. Although the Edomites refused Israel passage along the King's Highway, it seems that some were willing to sell them food. The friendliness shown to Edom (Esau's descendants), Moab and Ammon (Lot's descendants, see Genesis 19:36-38) on grounds of kinship is characteristic of patriarchal and Mosaic times. God keeps his word down the ages, and he expects his people to keep theirs.

Verses 26-37: see Numbers 21:21-35.

Seir (8): the mountains of 'Seir', i.e. Edom, rise to the south and east of the Dead Sea.

Made his heart obstinate (30): the Old Testament sees no conflict between God's sovereignty and man's freedom. God is never described as 'hardening the heart' of a good man. See also on Exodus 6-10.

3 War against King Og; settlement of the two and a half tribes

See Numbers 21:33-35, and chapter 32. Og's land was part of the Amorite kingdom. Bashan, famed for its cattle, with the area around was an attractive proposition to the stockmen of Reuben, Gad, and Manasseh.

His bedstead (11): probably a coffin. The 'common cubit' was about 18 inches or 450 mm.

The Arabah (17): the rift valley which runs from the Sea of Galilee south to the Gulf of Aqaba. 'Chinnereth' is Galilee: the word comes from the harp shape of the lake. The 'Salt Sea' is the Dead Sea.

Verses 23-26: the price of disobedience was a heavy one. What Moses longed for above all was to lead his people into the promised land. 'On your account' is not merely an attempt to shift the blame. It was the people's provocation which stung him to anger.

4:1-40 Moses' warning and call to obedience

Moses has recounted the history of God's dealings with Israel over the past 40 years. Now he reminds them of God's character as shown in his acts, and warns of the inevitable consequences of disobedience to him.
'The Lord is God in heaven above and on earth below; there is no other ... Keep his statutes ... then all will be well with you.'
Baal-peor (3): see Numbers 25.
Statutes (8): permanent rules of conduct;
ordinances/judgements: case-laws, judicial decisions.
4:41-43 Three cities of refuge for Transjordan
4:44-49 Historical and geographical setting of the covenant restated

5 - 11 BASIC COMMANDMENTS

5 The Ten commandments and the law-giving at Sinai
See also Exodus 19:16 - 20:21 (and the notes on Exodus 20 above).
Moses does not hesitate to modify the application, so that it relates more closely to a settled life (14-16,21).

6 The great commandment; instruction to teach future generations
Jesus said that the whole law could be summed up in the words of verse 5 and Leviticus 19:18 (see Matthew 22:37-40).

An orthodox Jew wears his phylactery (passages from the law, in a small box) bound to his forehead in literal obedience to Deuteronomy 6:8.

You shall write them (9): ordinary people possessed no copy of the law, so it was to be taught by word of mouth, and important parts written down where they could not fail to see

COVENANTS AND NEAR EASTERN TREATIES
Gordon Wenham

Hebrew uses the same word for an international treaty and a covenant between God and his people. Recent study has shown that similarities between ancient Near Eastern treaties and Old Testament covenants extend much further than this, and considerable light has been shed on the characteristics of Old Testament covenants, and our understanding of the Old Testament generally, by comparing them with treaties.

Most of the ancient treaties discovered this century date from about 1500 to 600 BC, a period in which much of the Old Testament was composed. It therefore seems likely that the writers would have been familiar with the way in which treaties were drafted. Furthermore their use of treaty terms and ideas shows that they found the relation-

ship between treaty-partners an apt picture of that between God and his people.

The earliest covenant recorded in Scripture was made with Noah (Genesis 9). Covenants were also made with Abraham (Genesis 15, 17). But by far the most important covenant in the Old Testament is the covenant of Sinai (Exodus 19ff.). Though Sinai is commonly thought of as the occasion when God's law was made known to Israel, in fact the law-giving was only one part of a much larger event, the call of Israel to be a holy nation owing exclusive allegiance to the Lord. The new relationship was termed a covenant. The covenant made at Sinai was the decisive step in the creation of Israel as a nation; all subsequent covenants looked back to Sinai as their model, and in a sense were regarded as renewals of it.

Covenants resemble treaties in three principal respects: in language, form and ideology.

Language
The purpose of a treaty is to secure the entire allegiance of a vassal-king or state to the other partner in the treaty, whether it be a king or an empire. To this end florid and rhetorical language is used in the treaties to stir the emotions of the vassal and impress on him the importance of obedience. Rhetorical style has long been regarded as characteristic of Deuteronomy, a work that in other respects bears a close resemblance to a vassal treaty. Certain terms are used in treaties to describe an obedient vassal's behaviour. A good vassal should 'go after', 'fear', 'love', 'hearken to the voice of his lord'. A rebellious vassal 'sins'. This phraseology is often echoed in the Old Testament.

Form
The most striking similarity between treaties and Old Testament covenants is in their form, in their basic outline structure. The classical Near Eastern treaty used by the Hittites had six parts:
1. **A preamble** naming the author of the treaty.
2. **A historical prologue** setting out the relations between the parties prior to signing the treaty.
3. **Stipulations** explaining the mutual responsibilities of the partners.
4. **A document clause** describing the treaty document and arranging for the vassal to read it at regular intervals.
5. **A list of gods** witnessing the treaty.
6. **Curses and blessings** threatening the vassal with illness, death, deportation, etc. if he breaks the treaty, but promising him prosperity and blessing if he remains faithful.

Old Testament covenants have a similar though not identical structure. For instance, believing in one God, they omitted the list of gods as witnesses. Deuteronomy contains most elements of the treaty form:

1-3 Historical prologue
4-26 Stipulations
27 Document clause
28 Blessings and curses.
Exodus 19-24, Joshua 24, and 1 Samuel 12 are other shorter examples of the treaty form in the Old Testament.

Ideology
Treaties and covenants both begin with history and both insist on the grace and mercy of the author of the covenant. The Hittite king can remind his vassal of his kindness in allowing him to continue as king of the vassal state in spite of his recent rebellion. God in similar tones reminds Israel of his mercy, 'I am the Lord your God, who brought you out of the land of Egypt' (Exodus 20:2).

In both treaties and covenants, the basis of the stipulations is the undeserved favour of the overlord. Stipulations or laws come after the vassal has been reminded of what the treaty-lord has done for him. He is expected to obey the stipulations out of gratitude. Similarly in the Old Testament, law follows grace. Because of the way God has saved them, Israel is encouraged to obey.

Blessing and prosperity are promised if the vassal remains obedient, but curses are invoked on him if he rebels. Drafters of treaties and the authors of the Old Testament, well knowing the human heart, tend to dwell much more on the curses than the blessings. Appalling pictures are drawn of the sufferings the people will endure if they disregard the demands of the covenant (see Deuteronomy 28:15-68). Prophetic threats of coming judgement often echo these covenant curses. The prophets remind the people that the covenant relationship involves responsibility as well as privilege (e.g. Amos 3:2).

The Dead Sea Scrolls show that covenant ideas continued to be important in Jewish theology up to the New Testament era. Jesus himself clearly assumed that his disciples were familiar with covenant thinking, when he referred to his death as inaugurating the new covenant (Mark 14:24).

it. The whole law was also engraved on plastered stones and set up in public places (see 27:1-10; Joshua 8:32).

Cisterns (11): pits for storing water collected from rainfall or from a spring. The inside was coated with waterproof mortar. The pits narrowed at the top to reduce evaporation.

Massah (16): see Exodus 17:6-7.

7 - 11 Moses calls the nation to faith and obedience

Moses turns from the past to the present and future. Israel will soon be right in amongst the pagan nations. They will taste the heady glory of victory (chapter 7). Prosperity will bring an unprecedented rise in the standard of living. There will be much to enjoy (chapter 8). And all these things bring dangers: the danger of losing their identity as God's people; the danger of false pride (chapter 9), of patting themselves on the back for all they have achieved; the danger of leaving God out of account.

But if they will let it, the past can keep them on the right lines for the future. So Moses urges them: 'Remember'; 'Do not forget.' Remember Egypt (7:18). Remember the wilderness (8:2). Remember what you were really like (9:7). Remember God's love, his power, his provision, his law, his judgements. And let that memory keep you humble, faithful, obedient (chapters 10-11).

Not like the land of Egypt (11:10): there the vegetable crops depended on irrigation, using water from the Nile.

Blessing and curse: Gerizim ... Ebal (11:26ff.): see on chapter 27.

12 - 26 DETAILED LAWS

12 - 13 Idols to be destroyed; the place for offerings; dealing with offenders

12:1-14: all the places where the Canaanites practised their depraved rites are to be wiped out. Israel is not to use them. When the nation is settled God will select a specific place for the sacrifices.

12:15-32: meat was not a staple food for the ordinary Israelite, but all enjoyed it at feasts and sacrifices. On the matter of the blood, see Leviticus 17:10ff. and article 'The Meaning of Blood Sacrifice'.

13:1-18: the danger of being enticed away to false religions was very real. Anyone encouraging this must be summarily dealt with. It was a case of drastic action to prevent contagion.

14 Clean and unclean animals; tithes

Verses 3-21: see on Leviticus 11.

Verses 22-29: see also Leviticus 27 and Numbers 18. All man's wealth is God's gift. To remind him of this, a proportion is regularly set aside. Jewish writers generally see the tithe (one tenth) here as a 'second tithe', the first being given to the Levites. It provides an occasion for enjoyment, for entering into the result of one's labour, and for generous sharing with others.

15 The seventh year

Every seventh year is a year of release for Hebrew slaves, and cancellation of debts contracted by fellow-Israelites. See on Leviticus 25.

Verses 19-23: see on Leviticus 27.

16 The three main feasts

See the full list, Leviticus 23, and article 'Feasts and Festivals'. Three times each year – Passover, Weeks (Pentecost), Booths (Tabernacles) – all Jewish men were required to present themselves at the chosen place of assembly.

Asherah ... pillar (21-22): wooden images, and symbols of pagan deities.

17 The death-penalty for idolatry (1-7); legal problem-cases (8-13); the future king (14-20)

Verses 14-20: God permits the monarchy, but does not set it up. The dangers foreseen here – military aggression, and sensuality leading to idolatry – became an uncomfortable reality in Solomon's reign, 300 years later.

18 Revenue for priests and Levites (1-8); witchcraft (9-14); the future prophet (15-22)

Verses 1-8: see also Numbers 18.

Verses 9-14: compare Leviticus 18:3, 24-30; 20:1-6.

A prophet like me (15): God raised up many prophets in succeeding centuries. But the New Testament seems to see in this a reference to the prophet *par excellence*, Jesus himself (John 5:46; Acts 3:22-26).

19 Cities of refuge (1-3); provisions covering accidental death and murder (4-13); prohibition of acquiring property by fraud (14); witnesses (15-21)

Three cities of refuge in Canaan are added to the three in Transjordan (4:41-43). Joshua 20 lists them as: Kedesh, Shechem, Kiriath-arba (Hebron), Bezer, Ramoth and Golan.

Avenger of blood (6): the dead man's next of kin, whose duty it was to avenge his death. The regulations here are designed to prevent the development of a blood-feud.

Landmark (14): a stone inscribed with the boundaries of the property.

The law of retaliation (21): see on Leviticus 24.

20 Rules for war

Those who have built a new house or planted a new vineyard, the newly married, and the fainthearted are excused military service. Verses 10-18 make a distinction between the treatment of Canaanite nations and those further afield.

You shall utterly destroy ... (17): in contrast to the compassion and humanitarianism of verses 1-11 and the concern for conservation in verses 19-20 this ruling seems incredibly harsh. But there is nothing arbitrary about it. The evil and corrupt religious practices of the Canaanite nations – child sacrifice, prostitution and much else – were highly contagious and therefore highly dangerous to the new nation of Israel. And God, in his patience, had given these nations long centuries in which to change their ways (Genesis 15:16).

21 Murder by an unknown hand (1-9); women captives (10-14); the right of the firstborn (15-17); sons beyond parental control (18-21); execution by hanging (22-23)

God sets a basic value and dignity on every human life – even of the individual society sets least store by.

Shave her head (12): either a sign of purification from heathenism, or a mourning.

Right of the firstborn (17): already ancient custom. The trouble in Jacob's family stemmed from this kind of favouritism.

The stubborn and rebellious son (18) was casting off the authority not only of his parents but of God himself.

Accursed by God (23): see Galatians 3:13-14.

The Law-Code of King Hammurabi of Babylon (about 1750 BC) is inscribed on this dark stone obelisk.

22 Lost animals and lost property (1-4); keeping the sexes distinct (5); birds-nesting (6-7); building, farming, clothing (8-12); sexual relations (13-30)

These are rules which encourage attitudes of mutual help and care, and a concern for purity.

Verse 5: a rule intended as a protection against perversion and immorality.

Verses 9-11: man should not obliterate the clear distinctions God has made in nature.

Tassels (12): see on Numbers 15:37-41.

Tokens of virginity (14): a blood-stained cloth from the wedding-night is still displayed as proof of the bride's chastity in some places in the Near East.

23 Membership of the congregation (1-8); social rules (9-25)

The Lord's community is both inclusive (7-8) and exclusive (1-6). It is marked by purity and holiness (10-14, 17-18) and practical humanity (15-16, 19-20).

Verses 1 and 17-18: a protest and safeguard against Canaanite cultic practices. 'Dog' (18) refers to a male prostitute.

Verse 2: a condemnation, not of the individual concerned, but of the illicit sexual relationship in which he was conceived.

Balaam (4): see Numbers 22-24.

Verse 15: Paul's letter to Philemon provides an interesting New Testament comment.

24 Divorce (1-4); humanitarian laws (5-22)

Verses 1-4: Moses is not instituting divorce, but regulating ancient practice, first by insisting on a definite grievance, and second by issuing a formal document.

Verses 5-22: even in exercising their rights, God's people are to be thoughtful of others. To take away one millstone, for example, left the other useless for grinding flour to make the day's bread.

Leprosy (8): the term includes various skin diseases. See on Leviticus 13 - 14.

Miriam (9): see Numbers 12.

25 Corporal punishment (1-3); compassion for working animals (4); the Levirate marriage law (5-10); fights (11-12); fair weights (13-16); punishment of the Amalekites (17-19)

Verses 1-3: the lash is to punish guilt, not extract confession. It must never take away human dignity or self-respect. The 'forty stripes' later became 39, for fear of inadvertently overstepping the limit (see 2 Corinthians 11:24).

Verses 5-10: the Levirate ('husband's brother') law was intended to prevent the calamity of the family name dying out. See Ruth (and for the sandal custom, Ruth 4:7).

Muzzling the ox (4): the New Testament extends this principle – see 1 Corinthians 9:3-14.

26 Firstfruits and tithes (1-15); concluding plea (16-19)

See on 14:22-29. The firstfruits ceremony includes the recital of a lovely prayer of remembrance and praise summarizing Israel's career.

Verses 16-19: blessing comes through obedience.

A wandering Aramaean (5): after leaving Ur, Abraham stayed in Aram-naharaim, where part of his family settled (becoming Aramaeans) while he journeyed on to Canaan.

27 - 30 CURSES AND BLESSINGS

The curses and blessings are an integral part of the ancient Near Eastern covenant. See 'Covenants and Near Eastern Treaties'.

27:1-10 The law is recorded

See on 6:9.

27:11-26 The curses

Gerizim and Ebal are the two most prominent hills in the natural centre of Palestine. With six tribes on either side, the Levites are to pronounce a curse on twelve infringements of the law, and the people to add their assent. See Joshua 8:30-35.

28:1-14 Blessings

Obedience will bring the benefits of victory, peace, fruitfulness, prosperity.

28:15-68 Solemn curses

Disobedience will result in disease, famine, defeat, subservience, and ultimately exile, loss of homeland and all the joys of life. This is no idle threat, as events later proved, even to the horrors of siege (see 2 Kings 6:24-30; Lamentations 2).

Powder and dust (24): sandstorms and duststorms in place of rain.

27 - 30 Moses calls the nation to a new commitment

Moses' life is fast drawing to a close. He puts his whole heart into this final appeal. He pleads (29:2-15). He warns (16-28). He encourages (30:1-14). He confronts them with the choice: life or death, blessing or curse (15-20).

Moist and dry alike (29:19): New English Bible, 'this will bring everything to ruin' catches the spirit of the proverb.

Sodom and Gomorrah, Admah and Zeboiim (29:23): cities at the southern end of the Dead Sea engulfed in the catastrophe of Genesis 19:24ff.

Secret things (29:29): certain matters of eternal significance are known only to God (see also Acts 1:7).

30:11-14: Moses speaks of the accessibility of God's word. Paul (Romans 10:5-8) takes the thought and applies it to Christ, the Word made flesh.

31 THE COVENANT PLACED IN SAFE-KEEPING: THE SUCCESSION ASSURED

The law is safely deposited with the Levites, and provision made for regular public reading. Throughout their subsequent history, Israel prospered in so far as they listened to God's word and obeyed it. Joshua is formally appointed as Moses' successor (see Numbers 27:12-23).

Go out and come in (2): New English Bible 'move freely' gives the sense. The phrase is used of citizens who 'go in and out' of a city, etc.

32:1-47 MOSES' SONG

God is the best of teachers. He instructs Moses to warn his people of their future treacherous disloyalty in song, to make it unforgettable (31:19).

Apple of his eye (10): the pupil, on which sight depends.

Jeshurun (15): a poetic name for Israel.

32:48 - 34:12 MOSES' BLESSING AND DEATH

32:48-52 Moses receives his last orders

33 Moses blesses the tribes

After all the warnings, this last blessing looks forward to a great and glorious future for Israel. Simeon is omitted from the tribes: his people were later absorbed by Judah. (Compare Jacob's blessing in Genesis 49.)

Verses 2-5: the law-giving at Sinai is pictured as an eastern sunrise.

Let Reuben live (6): the tribe's numbers were reduced through the rebellion of Dathan and Abiram (Numbers 16).

Thummim and Urim (8): two objects kept in the high priest's breastplate by which he ascertained God's will (see Exodus 28:30).

Massah, Meribah: see Exodus 17 and Numbers 20.

Makes his dwelling between his shoulders (12): either a picture of God as Shepherd, carrying his lamb, or a reference to God's house at Jerusalem, which would be built on Benjamite territory.

Choicest fruits (14): the valleys of Ephraim and Manasseh were laden with fruit, year by year.

Your going out … in your tents (18): Zebulun's success was in commerce, Issachar's in agriculture and domestic life.

The lake and the south (23): the fertile land south and west of the Sea of Galilee.

Oil (24): Asher's territory was famous for its olives.

34:1-8 The death of Moses

At last Moses sees the land he has for 40 years longed to enter. Israel sees him no more. But we meet him once again in Scripture – on a mountain, talking to the Lord (Mark 9:2-4)

34:9-12 Conclusion

The action now passes to Joshua – but the book closes with a simple and moving tribute to the greatest of all Israel's leaders. There would be no prophet to match him until Elijah; no one to surpass him but Christ himself.

THE HISTORICAL BOOKS

Introduction/John Taylor

In the Hebrew Bible the account of Israel's history was in two separate sections:

The Prophets included Joshua, Judges, 1 and 2 Samuel, 1 and 2 Kings;

The Writings included 1 and 2 Chronicles, Ezra and Nehemiah.

PROPHETIC HISTORY

The historical narrative from Joshua to 2 Kings was in fact given the title 'The Former Prophets' in Hebrew. This was to distinguish the books from the Latter Prophets – Isaiah, Jeremiah, Ezekiel and the twelve minor prophets. What is interesting is that it was called prophecy at all.

There are two possible reasons for this. Either it was because the main aim of the books was to teach; or else because they are the history not so much of the nation as of the way God's message was fulfilled in the nation's life.

This group of six books (not counting Ruth, which belongs to 'The Writings' in the Hebrew Bible) has been regarded by many scholars as one complete historical work. Some call it the 'Deuteronomic history', because the theological viewpoint expressed is similar to that of Deuteronomy.

If the books are treated as a basic unity in this way, the earliest date that could be given to the entire work would be shortly after the last event in 2 Kings – the release of King Jehoiachin from prison in 561 BC. However, this would apply only to the latest editorial work. Most of the material is much earlier and contemporary sources were often used.

Sources quoted in the text include the Book of Jashar (perhaps an ancient national song-book of Israel), the Book of the Acts of Solomon and the Chronicles of the Kings of Judah and Israel (unconnected with the Books of Chronicles in our Bibles). These were court archives, or popular histories based on them. They illustrate two things: the amount of historical writing that had gone on in Israel during the monarchy; and the number of written sources which were available to the biblical authors. It is fair to assume that the sources quoted were not the only ones used, and that other writings – such as a Court-history of David and a collection of Elijah-Elisha stories – were also freely drawn upon.

The period covered by these books extends from Joshua's entry into the land of Canaan until the middle of the exile. Most scholars prefer the late 13th century date for the conquest to an earlier one (1400 BC has been suggested on the basis of 1 Kings 6:1) and would see the events of Joshua and Judges as taking place between 1240 and 1050 BC.

Joshua covers the life-span of Moses' successor and describes the conquest of Canaan from the crossing of the River Jordan to the covenant-renewal ceremony at Shechem which established the tribes in a united allegiance to the Lord. Space is also given to a detailed description of the apportionment of Canaan among the twelve tribes (Joshua 13-21).

Judges begins with a reminder that the conquest under Joshua was by no means complete and that almost every tribal allotment still contained pockets of enemy resistance. In fact, this was the setting for the whole book, for throughout the period of the Judges individual tribes suffered from the incursions of hostile neighbours (or former residents!) and the judges, or 'liberators', were raised up to lead the tribes against them in open battle or guerilla warfare.

Chief among these were *Deborah and Barak*, who led the combined forces of Zebulun and Naphtali against the Canaanites under Sisera; *Gideon* of Manasseh who defeated the Midianites and Amalekites; *Jephthah* the Gileadite who subdued the Ammonites; and *Samson* the Danite who successfully baited the Philistines. The book ends with two bizarre episodes. The first describes the establishment of a new sanctuary for the tribe of Dan (Judges 17-18). The second deals with the punishment of Benjamin for an outrage committed by the people of Gibeah (Judges 19-21).

So far the historical element in the writings has been relatively small: the style has been episodic, occasionally moralistic, and owing a good deal to the art of story-telling. With **1 and 2 Samuel** (the division between them is artificial and probably due only to the length of a scroll) we begin to have a more chronological record of events, and this is particularly true of the story of David. *Samuel* is an important figure at the start, being judge and prophet combined, but the interest is really focussed on the question of kingship, and Samuel fades into the background as first *Saul* and then *David* dominate the scene. Saul probably reigned from shortly after the defeat at Aphek in 1050 BC, when the ark was captured by the Philistines, until about 1011 BC. David reigned from then until 971 (from Hebron for the first seven years and then from Jerusalem).

1 and 2 Kings continue the record, from the accession of *Solomon* to his father's throne, through the break-up of the kingdom 40 years later, and the continuing rivalry between the northern and southern kingdoms of Israel and Judah. This lasted until Israel became absorbed into the Assyrian Empire after the fall of Samaria in 722 BC. After that, Judah survived precariously for over a century, experiencing a miraculous deliverance from an Assyrian siege in the reign of *Hezekiah* and enjoying the extensive reforms of *Josiah's* reign (640-609). Then came collapse before the combined weight of God's displeasure and Nebuchadnezzar's armies, and exile in Babylon. The gloom of defeat is alleviated only by the concluding words of 2 Kings which tell of the release of King *Jehoiachin* from his Babylonian prison-cell. The hope of a survivor from David's line had not been totally extinguished.

As we have seen, one of the main points of interest in this prophetic and 'deuteronomic' history is **kingship**, and in particular King David's dynasty. In Judges 9 there was the abortive attempt of Gideon's son, Abimelech, to establish himself as hereditary monarch in Shechem. In Judges 17-21, the evils of the day were attributed to the fact that 'there was no king in Israel; every man did what was right in his own eyes'. In 1 Samuel, five chapters (8-12) are devoted to the setting up of a monarchy. It appears to have been rather grudgingly accepted by the historian, since Israel was a theocracy, and the Lord her only rightful King. But with the rise of David all such hesitations disappear, even though his personal morality often left much to be desired. The high point of his reign was God's promise of a lasting succession (2 Samuel 7). The fulfilment of this word can be traced in the lives of the subsequent kings of Judah.

A second main interest was prophets and **the word of the Lord**. The writer's treatment of Deborah and Samuel, Nathan and Gad, Ahijah and Micaiah, Elijah and Elisha, bears witness to the importance he accorded to the office of prophet. These men could make and break kings. They acted as court advisers and political watchdogs. They were the men of power because they in turn were controlled by the word of God. And, in the view of the writer, it was the word of God which controlled history. A word once spoken – the curse on the house of Ahab, for instance – inexorably worked its way to fulfilment.

A third interest of the writer was the **temple** at Jerusalem. From the beginning of 1 Samuel we can trace a special concern about the welfare of the ark of the Lord as it moved from Shiloh to Philistia, back to Kiriath-jearim and eventually was brought to Jerusalem. It was David's desire to build it a more permanent home that provided the occasion for Nathan's prophecy of the hereditary kingship. And in Solomon's time the temple was finally erected.

Finally, there was the fixed standard against which all kings were assessed. This was primarily a matter of **worship**. Was the Lord worshipped at Jerusalem in purity, or were foreign, idolatrous influences allowed in? Were high places (the old, pagan shrines) stamped out or allowed to continue? By the nature of the evaluation, all the kings of Israel came short because they perpetuated worship at the Bethel and Dan sanctuaries which Jeroboam had set up. Kings of Judah also were found wanting when for political reasons they incorporated the religious practices of a foreign overlord as a mark of submission to him. Only Hezekiah and Josiah receive unqualified commendation. So it is reasonable to conclude that the historian's own theological standpoint was influenced by their reforms.

THE CHRONICLER

The second part of the account of the history of Israel, included in 'The Writings' in the Hebrew Bible, was originally one book. The author or compiler is often called the Chronicler. The period before the exile was covered by 1 and 2 Chronicles, and the first hundred years after the exile by Ezra and Nehemiah. At first only the second section was incorporated into the Hebrew Bible, probably because of the overlap between Chronicles and Samuel-Kings, but subsequently 1 and 2 Chronicles were admitted. That is why in the Hebrew Bible Ezra-Nehemiah precedes Chronicles. In order to make their original unity apparent, the opening verses of Ezra were tacked on to the end of 2 Chronicles.

A summary of contents clearly shows the Chronicler's particular interests and the ground covered.

1 Chronicles 1-9: genealogies from Adam to Saul.
1 Chronicles 10-29: reign of David.
2 Chronicles 1-9: reign of Solomon.
2 Chronicles 10-36: the history of Judah from Rehoboam to the exile.
Ezra 1-6: the rebuilding of the temple after the exile.
Ezra 7-10: Ezra's arrival in Jerusalem and reforms.
Nehemiah 1-7: Nehemiah's rebuilding of the walls of Jerusalem.
Nehemiah 8-13: Ezra's reading of the law and Nehemiah's reforms.

From this it can be seen that the northern kingdom, Israel, is ignored, and that most space is given to David and Solomon and matters to do with the Jerusalem temple. To this extent the author was following in the same steps as the deuteronomic historian. He was a strong advocate of David's dynasty and did not regard the northern kingdom after its secession from Judah as belonging any more to the true people of God. Similarly, when the rebuilding operations were in progress on both the temple and the city walls, he was careful to note that the Samaritans – descendants of the mixed Israelite population – were debarred from participating in the work, or were actively hostile to it.

The Chronicler was also a devotee of David as the chief architect of the temple, its worship and its organization. Even though Solomon was the builder, the ideas were all from David's mind. This resulted in what some have called an idealized picture of David, very different from the fallible guerilla-leader-turned-monarch of the Samuel-Kings version. But it is not fair to accuse the Chronicler of deliberately whitewashing David. He was not writing a political history of Israel. He ignored events and records which had no bearing on the temple. His prime concern was to trace the temple and its worship back to its earliest origins and to tell as much of David's and Solomon's contributions as would enhance its glory.

Unlike the author of Samuel-Kings, however, the Chronicler was fascinated by the part played by priests and Levites, and their importance was frequently emphasized. So too was the uniqueness of their position as cultic officials.

The evaluation of the individual kings of Judah tallies with that of 1 and 2 Kings. But the Chronicler was keen to give reasons for unusual features where a strict law of retribution did not appear to work out – for instance in the tragic death of a good king such as Josiah, or the long reign of a bad king such as Manasseh. Again, there is no evidence to show that he twisted or invented the facts to make his point, but he clearly used his material selectively because he was writing as an ecclesiastical, not a political, historian.

His interest in things priestly did not cut him off from the world of prophecy. For in addition to his extensive use of the annals – e.g. 'the book of the kings of Israel and Judah' and many similar records – he also made use of many collections of the sayings of prophets, such as Samuel, Nathan, Gad and Iddo. This encourages us to respect the painstaking care with which he assembled and selected his material.

In the Ezra-Nehemiah period he was able to use memoirs of both these men (notice the use of the first person singular in Ezra 7:27-9:15 and Nehemiah 1:1-7:5; 13:6-31). Indeed Jewish tradition has held that Ezra was himself the Chronicler, and this is by no means impossible. Otherwise we can say at least that the Chronicler was almost certainly on the temple staff, that he was a man of deep piety and that he wrote in the late 5th or early 4th century BC.

JOSHUA

The book of Joshua takes the story of Israel's history on from the death of Moses, through the conquest of Canaan, to the death of Joshua. Chapters 1 - 12 cover the first five or six years after Moses' death. The events recounted in the last two chapters probably took place about 20 years later. The conquest probably began somewhere about 1240 BC, according to recent archaeological and other evidence. It seems likely that this account was written down in the early days of the monarchy (1045 BC), during Samuel's lifetime, and before David captured Jerusalem (see Joshua 15:63).

Joshua himself was born in Egypt. He became Moses' right-hand man during the exodus and desert wanderings. He was a fine military commander (Exodus 17:8ff.). In the law-giving at Sinai he was Moses' companion (Exodus 24:13). Joshua was one of the 12 spies sent by Moses to reconnoitre the land. He and Caleb alone had the faith and courage to recommend advance (Numbers 14:6ff.) – and in consequence were the only ones to survive the 40 years of wandering. When Moses died, Joshua was an obvious choice to succeed him in leading the nation (Deuteronomy 34:9).

1 - 4 ISRAEL ENTERS THE PROMISED LAND

1 Joshua takes over as leader

This account of Joshua's accession is one of the great chapters of the Bible. Moses is dead: but God's purpose for the nation continues. The keynote of this prelude to the conquest is the repeated call to be strong and take courage (6, 7, 9, 18).

This book of the law (8): see Deuteronomy 31:24-26. Joshua was with Moses when the law was given at Sinai.

Within three days (11): either the events of chapter 2 have already taken place, or the meaning is simply 'soon'.

Remember the word ... (13): see Numbers 32.

2 Rahab and the spies

Jericho, the 'city of palm trees', lies just west of the River Jordan. Joshua's intention was to make his first thrust into the centre of Palestine, driving a wedge between north and south. Jericho stood directly in his path, an obvious first target. See article 'The Cities of the Conquest'.

Rahab's action in harbouring the spies stemmed not from fear, but from belief that Israel's God is the *true* God (see Hebrews 11:31, which commends her faith, not her immorality). Rahab's house was built on or into the city walls, with a flat roof on which produce could be spread out to dry – in this case flax, from which she would spin linen thread. Her house was somewhere the spies might go with no questions asked; and no doubt a good place to pick up information. The Israelites kept their promise to her (6:22ff.). Rahab was naturalized, married Salmon, and through her son Boaz (see Ruth 2-4) became an ancestress of David, and of Jesus himself (Matthew 1:5).

3 The Israelites cross the Jordan

It was spring, and the river swollen with melted snows, when God took his people across Jordan. As the priests stepped into the flood-water, a blockage at Adam, 16 miles up river, dammed the stream, leaving 20 or 30 miles of river-bed dry. (In 1927 earth tremors caused a collapse of the high clay river-banks at the same spot, and the Jordan was dammed up for over 21 hours.)

The ark of the covenant (3): containing the tablets inscribed with the law. It was a visible symbol of God's presence with his people – and of his leading and guidance.

Sanctify yourselves (5): i.e. 'prepare yourselves before God', by ritual purification and moral self-scrutiny.

4 The memorial stones

Two piles were made. One where the priests had stood in the eastern edge of the river, the other at Gilgal, their base-camp on the west. Both were to serve as a perpetual reminder of the greatness of God. (This is the same stretch of Jordan where John the Baptist's ministry and Jesus' baptism took place.)

For you ... for us (23): not many of those who had crossed the Red Sea now remained. Of the over-20s at the time the spies were sent out, only Joshua and Caleb still lived.

5:1-12 GILGAL: ISRAEL CIRCUMCISED

The rite of circumcision had not been practised because the convenant itself was, so to speak, in suspension for 40 years as a result of the people's disbelief and disobedience (Numbers 14). Now the circumcision of the new generation marks the renewal of the old relationship between God and his people.

Flint knives (2): bronze tools had superseded stone by this time, but the traditional tools are used for the religious rite.

The manna ceased (12): see Exodus 16:13ff. This special provision of God had never failed through all the years in the wilderness. Now it was no longer needed.

5:13 - 6:27 THE FALL OF JERICHO

The conquest of Canaan was a holy war. God was at the head of the army. No one knew this better than Joshua, after his experience of 5:13ff. Israel knew it, as the ark of God's presence led the forces. And Israel's enemies knew it, and quaked (2:10-11; 5:1). It was a war of nerves for the men of Jericho; day after day the encircling troops, the trumpet-blasts, the silent army, building up to the great climax of the seventh day.

Things devoted to destruction (18): the city and all its contents are dedicated utterly to God. It becomes sacrilege then, for anyone to take anything for himself.

Outside the camp (23): until such time as they were 'cleansed' by a period of purification.

Cursed ... be the man (26): the mound lay in ruins for 400 years, until Ahab's reign. Then Hiel rebuilt Jericho – and fell heir to the curse (see 1 Kings 16:34).

7 ACHAN'S DEFIANCE

Because of Achan's sin (see on 6:18) 36 men died at Ai, and the whole nation was shamed before their Canaanite enemies. God requires absolute obedience; and the disobedience of one individual affects the whole people of God.

THE CITIES OF THE CONQUEST
Alan Millard

The Bible's accounts of Israel's entry into Canaan record the actual destruction of only a few cities. Throughout, they emphasize that Israel drove out the former inhabitants and took over (inherited) their property. A desolate land with its towns in ruins would be of little benefit to the Israelites, just emerging from 40 years of semi-nomadic life. What *had* to be destroyed were the pagan shrines of the Canaanites with their cultic paraphernalia.

Jericho was a special case. The city was an offering to God, a 'first-fruit' of the conquest. Ai and Hazor were also sacked. But again they were exceptional cases, perhaps as focal points of opposition. If the biblical record is to be believed, then, we shall not expect to find much physical evidence of the Israelite conquest. The change of ownership probably left few recognizable marks except in the religious sphere. More cities may have been sacked at that time than Joshua and Judges indicate, but the Hebrew accounts do not demand it.

So it is misleading to try to link all signs of destruction in Canaanite cities of the Late Bronze Age with the Israelite invasion. Excavations at the sites of Bethel, Beth-shemesh, Debir? (Tell Beit Mirsim), Hazor and Lachish have all revealed signs of violent destruction during the 13th century BC, but the dates are only approximate and the cities may not all have been destroyed at the same time. After their destruction the cities were deserted, or else reoccupied on a less elaborate scale.

Smaller towns and villages, with mud-brick houses, would have offered little resistance to Joshua's army. The village pictured here is in Syria.

It is important to realize that Israel was only one of the Canaanites' enemies, although ultimately the worst. The history of the 13th century BC includes major military actions, invasions, and a general decline in cultural standards. Egypt's pharaoh was lord of Canaan, and of Lebanon and Damascus. His governors and officials resided in major cities (e.g Gaza, Megiddo), and other places served as garrison towns. There were periodic rebellions which were quelled by loyal neighbours or by Egyptian forces. Following a period of Egyptian weakness, Pharaoh Seti I campaigned in Canaan and east of the Jordan about 1300 BC. Archaeologists often identify his invasion with destruction levels in ruined cities, as at Hazor. Shortly afterwards, his son, Ramesses II, had to curb a revolt following an unsuccessful battle with the Hittites in Syria. He penetrated as far as Moab at this time (about 1285 BC).

Perhaps as a result of these firm measures, once Ramesses had made peace with the Hittite king (in about 1270 BC), there was no further invasion from Egypt for over half a century. Trouble came again in the reign of Merneptah, Ramesses' son. Little is known beyond the fact of Egyptian intervention in Canaan, and indirect evidence of continuing Egyptian control there. One record supplies the oldest non-biblical reference to Israel, as one of a number of defeated foes. Merneptah had halted a wave of invaders from the north-west, the 'Peoples of the Sea'. Egypt was safe until another wave repeated the threat, marching through Syria and Canaan as well as coming against Egypt by sea.

This wave was stemmed by Ramesses III who destroyed the fleet and stopped the advance before it reached the frontier, re-establishing his control of Canaan for a while. But many of the invaders remained, some seizing certain cities. The Philistines, for example, took over Ashdod, Ashkelon, Ekron, Gath, and Gaza; and another group took control of Dor. All these events, and others unknown to us, brought pillage and destruction to the towns of Canaan around the time of the conquest. Neighbouring princes could create as much devastation as an invading force.

Nevertheless, we are told that three cities – Jericho, Ai and Hazor – were set on fire by Israel. At Hazor in Galilee, there is evidence that the last city of the Late Bronze Age was violently destroyed at some time in the 13th century BC. The ruins of the last Canaanite city were not well preserved, partly because of exposure to the elements and damage by ploughing. But enough remained to show a city of importance, even if past its zenith. Other towns of the same date are closely similar. All were well fortified, although the city walls often incorporated (or were renovations of) earlier defences. Cities on the main roads – Megiddo, for example – tended to be far wealthier. On the other hand the relative poverty of such sites as Tell Beit Mirsim (Debir?) concentrated the excavators' attention on details of pottery styles, on which Palestinian archaeology depends for its comparative chronology.

At Jericho, the site where the clearest evidence of Israel's attack might have been expected, nothing has been found to show the existence of a city there in the middle of the 13th century BC. Severe erosion of the mudbrick ruins has left little trace of some earlier periods in the city's life. For this reason, the possibility of a fortified city standing there later in the century cannot be discounted. Its ruins would have disappeared during the long desertion of the site from Joshua's time to Ahab's (about 400 years; see 1 Kings 16:34). The city walls, thought at one time to be evidence of Joshua's attack, in fact date from a much earlier period; the excavations show a city which had already been frequently destroyed and rebuilt before the time of Joshua.

Ai also presents a problem. Excavations have revealed that the city was derelict from about 2500 BC until after 1200 BC, although it was important in the earlier period. The name Ai means 'ruin', and many see the Joshua story simply as an attempt to explain the very impressive ruins. But even accepting the archaeological evidence, it is still possible that a group of Canaanites made use of the old fortifications of this strategic stronghold in their fight against the Israelites. Such a brief occupation would have left little or no trace.

In short, we need not expect to find widespread and unmistakable signs of a specifically Israelite conquest in the ruins of Canaan. Israel's mission was in any case not totally destructive. And there were other causes of destruction. Towns may have lain deserted as a result of general turmoil, or have been only partially inhabited, until the Israelites were established in the land and able to exploit it. This they could not do fully while they were menaced by the Philistines and enemies from across the Jordan. The poor remains in several post-Canaanite (early Iron Age) sites attest this situation.

Many scholars have explained Israel's possession of the promised land in terms of a gradual infiltration by nomadic herdsmen. Or they see it as a combination of infiltration and a movement of a few tribal groups from Egypt, perhaps on more than one occasion and over several generations. Or they even envisage a general revolt of the people of the land. These widely varying opinions are all connected with theories involving the documentary analysis of the Pentateuch. These assign stories to a number of different sources, so proposing separate origins for them, and fostering views of unrelated tribal histories. Closely linked with this is a theory that the concept of Israel as a nation was formed long after the 'conquest', and read back into early times by later Israelite historians.

The idea of a gradual process is supported by analogy with other invasions and movements with peoples. It is emphasized that the occupation was limited. (Judges 1 for example lists the main Canaanite cities on the major roads as unconquered, or only occupied jointly with the native citizens.) The stories in Joshua are attributed to tribal or cultic sources. They are thought to describe what were really small, local events, or to relate folk-tales woven around the origin of ruined cities whose real history was forgotten.

It always pays to be cautious in arguing from analogies and this is certainly so in the case of the 'conquest'. The analogies of nomadic infiltration are used in order to fit Israel into a known pattern. But all her records claim that Israel was different. At best such approaches should be regarded as experimental, not factual. To rule out the account actually given in the Bible on the grounds that it is unusual is prejudiced and unscientific.

Ai (2): 'The Ruin'. See article 'The Cities of the Conquest'.

Sanctify yourselves (13): see on 3:5.

Which the Lord takes (14): the guilty man was discovered by means of the sacred lot, the two stones kept in the high priest's breastplate. It is not now known exactly how this was done.

Stoned him ... burned them (25): i.e. the stolen goods, unless his family were also in the know and therefore to blame (see Deuteronomy 24:16).

8 AI CONQUERED

The evidence of the mound at Et-Tell is difficult to accord with the biblical record here – which suggests that this may not in fact be the correct site of Ai. But see 'The Cities of the Conquest'. Joshua's flight and ambush strategy makes capital out of Israel's previous defeat.

From Ai, Joshua moves north to establish himself at Shechem, in the valley between Mts Ebal and Gerizim. In God's name he takes possession of the land. And the covenant is sworn as Moses had commanded (Deuteronomy 27).

30,000 (3): This may refer to the total force, unless there were two ambushes (12). But high numbers in the Old Testament present a real problem. See on Numbers 1, and 'The Large Numbers of the Old Testament'.

Bethel (9): the place where Jacob had his vision. A well-fortified and prosperous city during Israel's early days in Egypt; somewhat declined by Joshua's day. Either on this campaign (Bethel and Ai were only 1½ miles apart) or later, the king of Bethel was defeated (12:16).

9 - 10 THE CAMPAIGN IN THE SOUTH

9 Gibeon tricks Israel into a treaty
Gibeon was an important city about six miles north of Jerusalem. The treaty obtained by such cunning (even to the pretence that news of the recent victories at Jericho and Ai had not reached them, 9-10) also included three other cities (17). Israel could not draw back from a treaty sealed in friendship (the meal eaten together, 14). It still held good in David's day. The worst they could do was reduce the Gibeonites to slave status (21).

10 Alliance of the five Amorite kings; the 'long day'
The treaty with the Gibeonites promptly involves Israel in war. All five Amorite kings are killed at Makkedah and their city-states (all except Jerusalem) destroyed in the campaign following the rout at Beth-horon. All the strategic cities of the south fall before Joshua's army. Israel now controls the land from Kadesh-barnea in the south to Gaza on the west, and as far north as Gibeon.

The long day (12-14): usually taken as an extension of daylight (not necessarily by a literal standing still of the sun). But it may be a prolongation of *darkness*. Recently it has been suggested that there may have been an eclipse of the sun. Joshua's surprise attack was at dawn (as the positions of sun and moon in verse 12 also indicate) and the hailstorm increased the gloom and consequent confusion. 'Go down' (13) may simply mean 'come' or 'go'.

Book of Jashar (13): a book of songs praising national heroes.

Put your feet upon the necks (24): customary gesture of total subjection.

Goshen (41): a town south of Hebron, not Goshen in Egypt.

THE CONQUEST OF CANAAN

Mt Hermon △
Kedesh
Merom Brook
Hazor
Achshaph
Madon
Shimron
Mt Ebal △
Mt Gerizim △
Gilgal
Beth-horon
Bethel Ai
Gezer
Gibeon
Jericho
Acacia
Jerusalem
Libnah
Makkedah
Eglon
Lachish
Hebron
Debir

11 THE NORTHERN CAMPAIGN

The powerful king of Hazor, commanding his vassals, assembles an even more formidable alliance than that of the south. But with no more success. Although the strategic cities were in Israel's hands within a short time of their entry into Canaan, mopping-up operations took a great deal longer (18).

Hazor (1): a vast metropolis of 40,000 people, many times the size of Jerusalem in David's day. The lower city which Joshua destroyed was never rebuilt. See 'The Cities of the Conquest'.

As far as Great Sidon (8): Tyre had evidently not yet risen to prominence.

The Anakim (21): the colossal race who struck fear into the hearts of the spies (Numbers 13:33).

Gaza, Gath, Ashdod (22): all Philistine strongholds. Gigantic Goliath came from Gath (1 Samuel 17:4).

12 LIST OF THE DEFEATED CANAANITE KINGS

Thirty-one kings are listed, including those defeated under Moses. The list rounds off the section on the conquest.

13 - 21 DIVISION OF THE LAND

Not all the land allocated had been completely subdued – and not every

THE LAND DIVIDED AMONG THE TWELVE TRIBES

tribe realized its ideal by conquering all its allotted territory. In several places the writer comments on the situation in his own day (e.g. 15:63).

13:1-7 Land still unconquered
13:8-14 The land east of Jordan
13:15-23 The tribe of Reuben
13:24-28 The tribe of Gad 13:29-33 The half-tribe of Manasseh 14:1-5 The land west of Jordan

The inheritance of each tribe is decided by lot, by the high priest.

14:6-15 Caleb claims Hebron

Forty-five years after the spy episode (Numbers 13-14) Caleb remains a man of unwavering faith. Despite 10:21ff. there are still Anakim survivors to deal with (15:14; Judges 1:10-15, 20). Hebron became Levite property (21:11-13), but Caleb retained the surrounding land and villages.

15 The tribe of Judah

Judah's inheritance included Caleb's lands – and also Jerusalem, or part of it (18:28). But the city remained unconquered when Joshua was written (63).

16 - 17 Joseph's sons: the tribes of Ephraim and Manasseh

They were to have extended their territory by clearance and conquest. But the horses and chariots of the Canaanites holding the plains deterred them.

18:1-10 The move to Shiloh; the land survey; the inheritance of the seven remaining tribes
18:11-28 The tribe of Benjamin

Jerusalem seems to have been partly on Judah's land, partly on Benjamin's (15:63; Judges 1:8,21).

19:1-9 The tribe of Simeon

Simeon's people, whose land was part of Judah's territory, became absorbed into the larger tribe.

19:10-16 The tribe of Zebulun
19:17-23 The tribe of Issachar
19:24-31 The tribe of Asher
19:32-39 The tribe of Naphtali
19:40-48 The tribe of Dan
19:49-51 Joshua's city
20 The cities of refuge

See Numbers 35:6-34; Deuteronomy 19:1-13. The cities were a safeguard against vengeance and blood-feud, protecting those who caused accidental death.

21 The cities of the Levites

The Levites receive no tribal inheritance: God is their inheritance. But they are given 48 cities, with pasturage, by the other tribes. This ensures that the leaders of the nation's faith and worship are dispersed amongst the tribes.

22 THE TRIBES SETTLED ON THE EAST OF THE JORDAN RETURN HOME; THE ALTAR OF WITNESS

Reuben, Gad and Manasseh have fulfilled their obligations to help in the conquest. Now they return home, with Joshua's blessing, and a share of the spoil. Fear that, once across Jordan, Israel may at some future time disown them prompts the building of the altar which caused such misunderstanding. This was neither a sign of idolatry, nor a second sanctuary. It was a token of solidarity with the rest of Israel to whom they were bound by faith and worship of the one God.

The sin at Peor (17): when Israel worshipped Baal (Numbers 25).

Achan (20): for his sin 36 men died (chapter 7).

The Mighty One, God, the Lord (22): a solemn oath, twice repeated, and using all three names of God: El, Elohim, Yahweh. (See article 'The Names of God'.)

23 - 24 JOSHUA'S LAST DAYS

23 Joshua counsels the leaders

Some years have elapsed since the division of the land. Joshua has reached the end of a long life, and is appointing no single successor. It is therefore vital to ensure that the leaders keep the law and remain faithful to God – the God who keeps his promises (23:14; see 21:45).

24 Joshua and the nation renew the covenant

Here, as in Deuteronomy, the covenant pattern follows that of contemporary treaties (see article, 'Covenants and Near Eastern Treaties'). The King's title (2a) is followed by a rehearsal of his past favours (2b-13). The stipulations are made in 14-15, with warnings on the consequences of disobedience (19-20). Joshua's own readiness to commit himself wholly to God remains unwavering at the end of a long life. The eagerness of the people to follow him in renewing the covenant is in itself sufficient tribute to his leadership. Verse 31 is an indication of the strength of this man's influence for good.

Balak ... Balaam (9): see Numbers 22-24.

I sent the hornet (12): a vivid image of the panic and confusion into which God threw Israel's enemies.

JUDGES

Judges covers the period in Israel's history between Joshua's death and the rise of Samuel – roughly 1220 to 1050 BC. It was a time of transition, when the scattered tribes were held together only by their common faith. Loyalty to God meant a strong united nation. Turning to the gods around brought weakness and division.

The writer looks back, probably from the days of Israel's first kings – Saul or David – to the time when the nation had no king. He wrote after the destruction of the sanctuary at Shiloh (18:31), but before David captured Jerusalem (1:21). He weaves together the stories of the nation's heroes; and Deborah's song, written just after the battle, he quotes verbatim. Six of the 12 judges mentioned are described in some detail: Othniel, Ehud, Deborah/Barak, Gideon, Jephthah, Samson. These 'judges' of Israel were not simply legal advisers. They were men of action who delivered tribe or nation from subjection to the nations around and became local or national rulers.

The human scene in Judges is a depressing one. The nation's fortunes follow a monotonous, repetitive cycle. Israel deserts God for the heathen gods. In consequence God allows them to suffer at the hands of the Canaanites. Israel cries to God for help. God sends a deliverer. All is well until his death: then the old pattern of infidelity reasserts itself. Nowhere in Scripture is man's essential bias to sin more graphically portrayed – a bias which shows itself even in those who know God.

The wonder is God's constant love and concern in the face of all this. Despite their past unfaithfulness, and what he knows will happen again, as soon as Israel turns to him he answers. And he uses the most unpromising people: Jael, who breaks all the sacred laws of hospitality; Ehud, who stoops to assassination; Samson, who leads a life of sexual promiscuity; a nation that gloats over acts of cruel revenge against the enemy. *And the Bible nowhere commends these things* or whitewashes the individuals who committed them. God took and used them because of their faith (Hebrews 11:32ff.), and despite their morals. So, because God is a God like this, there is hope for sinful man.

Chronology. Eastern writers do not show the same preoccupation with precise time-order as modern western historians. Added together, the figures in Judges total 390 years. Yet, with the most probable date for the conquest at about 1240, the period covered must be under 200 years. One of the reasons for this seeming discrepancy is the overlap between the periods of the different judges. We know, for example, from 10:7 that the Ammonite oppression in the east and the Philistine oppression in the west occurred at the same time. It is likely there is considerable overlap elsewhere. A further factor is the frequent use of 'forty years' as a round figure for 'a generation' rather than a precise length of time.

A. E. Cundall suggests the following approximate chronology:

1200	Othniel
1170	Ehud
1150	Shamgar
1125	Deborah and Barak
1100	Gideon
1070	Jephthah
1070	Samson

1 - 2:5 EXTENT AND LIMITS OF THE CONQUEST FOLLOWING JOSHUA'S DEATH

1:1-21 Campaigns in southern Canaan

Verses 10-15: see Joshua 15:13-19.

City of palms (16): Jericho.

Chariots of iron (19): this was the beginning of the Iron Age. The Philistines introduced and controlled the iron industry in Palestine and guarded it jealously (see 1 Samuel 13:19-22). Until the days of David, Israel were at a disadvantage against the superior iron weapons and chariots of their enemies.

1:22-26 Capture of Bethel
1:27-36 Unconquered cities
2:1-5 God's judgement on disobedience

The angel of the Lord (1): mentioned a number of times in Judges (here and in the stories of Gideon and Samson) as well as in other Bible passages. He always comes as God's representative, with a special message from God. He speaks in God's name, and is virtually identified with God by those to whom he appears (see e.g. 13:22). Sometimes he shows himself as an ordinary man, sometimes as an awesome heavenly being (see chapter 13). But none who see him are left in any doubt of his authority.

2:6 - 16:31 ISRAEL UNDER THE JUDGES

2:6 - 3:6 Introduction
Verses 11-23 set out the repeated pattern of events which began once the conquest generation had died out (10). As a result of disobedience the surrounding nations are not driven out. They remain to test Israel and keep her a fighting nation (2:20 - 3:6).
Baals and the Ashtaroth (2:13): local male and female fertility/vegetation gods.

Five lords of the Philistines (3:3): rulers of the city-states of Ashdod, Ashkelon, Ekron, Gaza, Gath (see the Samson story, chapters 13 -16, and 1 Samuel 17:1-54). Judah did not hold her three cities for long (1:18).

3:7-11 Othniel
If Cushan-rishathaim was indeed king of 'Mesopotamia' (8: i.e. modern east Syria, north Iraq) the attack must have come from the north – which makes his defeat at the hands of a southern champion surprising. But some would emend the name to 'Cushan chief of Teman' (in Edom).
The Spirit of the Lord came upon him (10): the same phrase is used of Gideon, Jephthah and Samson. The might of these champions was a special gift from God.

3:12-30 Ehud
Eglon of Moab headed an eastern alliance which included Ammonites and Amalekites. They not only overran the land east of Jordan, but crossed the river to set up an outpost at Jericho.

Like Ehud, many of the Benjaminites were left-handed or ambidextrous – the tribe's left-handed slingers had a high reputation (see 20:16; 1 Chronicles 12:2). On this occasion

BARAK DEFEATS SISERA AND THE CANAANITES
•Kedesh
•Hazor
△Mt Carmel
•Harosheth-of-the-Gentiles
△Mt Tabor

it meant that the movement aroused no suspicion.

3:31 Shamgar
This isolated action did not restrain the Philistines long. See chapters 13-16.

4 - 5 Deborah and Barak
Deborah is the judge in the judicial sense, Barak the military leader. Deborah's song – one of the most ancient pieces of writing in the Old Testament – provides the clue to the victory. A cloudburst changed the Kishon to a raging torrent (5:21). Many of the chariots were swept away, the rest completely bogged down in the mud.
Hazor (4:2): Joshua defeated an earlier Jabin, and destroyed the city. The lower part was never rebuilt, but the mound (tell) was re-fortified by the Canaanites, and later by Solomon.

6 - 8:28 Gideon
Bedouin from the east, the Midianites, swept through southern Israel as far as the Philistine city of Gaza. The terror spread by these fierce camel-riders is vividly pictured in 6:11. Gideon is forced to thresh his meagre grain harvest secretly, in the confines of the wine press. The faith of this man, for all his initial caution, is seen in his preparedness to face the Midianite hordes with a force of only 300 men. Gideon used his wits in the surprise attack, and the victory in the ensuing rout is God's.
The Asherah (6:25): a wooden image of the Canaanite mother-goddess.
An ephod (8:27): probably an image of God, which the law forbade. The place then became a rival to Israel's official sanctuary.

8:29-35 Gideon's later years
9 The rise and fall of the usurper Abimelech
Gideon, with some claim to kingship, firmly rejected it. Abimelech, his brutal and ambitious son, shows no such scruples.

The scene of Gideon's surprise attack on the Midianites.

Gideon's camp
at the spring of Harod

Hill of Moreh

Midianite
camp

Shechem (1): in the heart of Palestine; see map. Shechem was the central sanctuary of Israel in Joshua's day. But now it had a temple to Baal (for 'house', verses 4 and 46, read 'temple' with New English Bible). The city's history goes back to Jacob's day and earlier.

Sowed it with salt (45): symbolically consigning the city to permanent desolation. It was in fact rebuilt 150 years later in the time of Jeroboam 1.

Upper millstone (53): grain was ground between two heavy circular stone slabs about 18 inches across.

10:1-2 Tola

10:3-5 Jair

10:6 - 11:40 Jephthah

Southern Israel is now caught in a vice between the Philistines on the west and the Ammonites on the east. Against Ammon, the new champion is the brigand-chief, Jephthah. Numbers 20-21 describes the events referred to in the parley of 11:12-28. Moab in fact had the better claim to the land, as part of it had been theirs until Sihon dispossessed them.

Three hundred years (11:26): i.e. it was now the third century since the events described (in fact about 160 years).

Jephthah's vow, and other moral problems in Judges: the vow is an indication of how little the Israelites understood God at this time. Human sacrifice might please the heathen gods, but never the God of Israel. Yet, though ignorant and mistaken, the vow was made in good faith, and kept, though it cost Jephthah his only child. And the New Testament writer of Hebrews commends this man's faith – as he commends the faith of Samson, Gideon and Barak (Hebrews 11:32). This instance of child-sacrifice, Jael's hideous murder of Sisera, Ehud's assassination of Eglon, Samson's selfish, sensual and irresponsible behaviour (see Introduction) are a real source of embarrassment to many Christians. How can people like these be commended for their faith? How could God use them? There can be no completely satisfactory answer to questions like these. The 'heroes' of Judges are people of their age – an age which the Bible plainly shows was one of religious decline, falling far short of the standards of the Old Testament law, let alone those which Christ sets. The fact is – the wonder is – that God did and still does use men whose lives are far from blameless, who may even be acting from completely wrong motives. We are not meant to imitate their shortcomings. Their immorality is neither condoned nor glossed over in Scripture. Only their

SAMSON'S RAIDS

Sorek •
Timnah • • Eshtaol
• Lehi
Zorah
Ashkelon •
• Hebron
Gaza

faith and courage are commended. God does not permit his ultimate purposes to be thwarted even in an age of seemingly hopeless decadence.

The dark ages of a period like that of Judges may be followed by a time of real spiritual advance.

12:1-7 Ephraimite jealousy
Where Gideon used soft words to placate these touchy tribesmen (8:1-3), Jephthah takes up the sword. At the fords the men's dialect pronunciation of 'Shibboleth' gives them away.

12:8-10 Ibzan
12:11-12 Elon
12:13-15 Abdon
13:1 - 16:31 Samson
The champion against the enemy in the west (see 10:7) is set apart for the task from the moment of his conception. For Samson the Nazirite vow (see Numbers 6) was lifelong. Yet he treats it with a casualness amounting to contempt, eventually allowing Delilah to shave off the long hair which was the sign of his dedication to God. Moral weakness robs the strong man of both spiritual stature and physical prowess – since his strength is God-given for an explicit purpose.

Samson's marriage: not the usual Jewish type, although formally arranged by the parents. Instead of the bride returning to Samson's home she stayed with her family and her husband visited her, bringing gifts. Because of the deceit over the riddle there was no consummation at the end of the seven-day feast. A hasty second marriage to the best man was an attempt to lessen the bride's disgrace.

Three hundred foxes (15:4) more

probably jackals, who hunt in packs and would therefore be easier to catch in large numbers than the solitary fox.

17 - 21 APPENDICES
This closing section differs from the rest of Judges. The writer turns from Israel's heroes to two incidents which illustrate the low state of religion and morality in the days when Israel had no central government and everyone 'did what was right in his own eyes'.

17 - 18 Micah, the Levite and the Danite migration
This story relates to the time when Philistine pressure on their southern territory led to the mass migration of the Danites to the far north of Israel. The image set up by Micah was strictly forbidden by the law the Levites were supposed to administer. 'Ephod and teraphim' were used as means of divination – equally strictly prohibited.

19 - 21 Rape of the concubine at Gibeah; punishment of the Benjaminites
When the Benjaminites refuse to hand over the men of Gibeah – their fellow tribesmen who committed the outrage – civil war results. The outcome is the near-extinction of Benjamin, and great national grief. Chapter 21 relates the lengths to which the tribes go to circumvent the rash oath made at Mizpah (21:1).

The writer has no need to point a moral. The simple statement of verse 25 is sufficient. The whole book makes plain the disastrous consequences of breakdown of authority, when men become a law unto themselves, setting their own standards of permissiveness.

RUTH

This quiet tale of ordinary life stands in strong contrast to the war and strife of Judges, which relates to the same general period. No doubt many people lived just such a normal peaceful life during this age. And although religion generally was at a low ebb, the book of Ruth makes it clear that the personal faith of many in Israel remained strong. The most striking feature of this simple and beautiful story is the sense of God's intimate concern in humble affairs. He is the One who orders all the circumstances of daily life, even for the most unimportant people. And so the new-found faith of a Moabite girl, and her sacrificial love for her mother-in-law are woven into the great tapestry of God's plan of salvation. For descended from Ruth is King David, and from the line of David comes the Messiah himself.

1:1-5 Elimelech takes his family to Moab
The journey was about 50 miles, to the far side of the Dead Sea.

1:6-22 The widowed Naomi returns to Bethlehem with Ruth, her daughter-in-law
The famine is over: God has again shown his care for his people. Orpah, sorrowfully, returns home to the hope of a second marriage. But Ruth will not leave Naomi to a lonely old age. Her choice is Naomi's people, and, significantly, Naomi's God. The two reach Bethlehem in April.

2 Ruth goes gleaning and wins Boaz' protection
There were not many ways for widows to earn a living, and Ruth and Naomi were poor. But the law (Leviticus 19:9-10) laid down that the gleanings of the harvest must be left for the poor. By 'chance' in the common open field, Ruth gleans in the part belonging to Boaz, Elimelech's kinsman. His kindness goes far beyond the law's demands (9, 14-16).
Parched grain (14): fresh ears of barley roasted in a pan.
An ephah of barley (17): the ephah was a large container holding about 22 litres. Ruth had gleaned about $\frac{1}{2}$ cwt of barley by her own hard work and Boaz' generosity.

3 The threshing-floor; appeal to Boaz as next of kin
Under the Levirate law (referred to by Naomi in 1:11-13), when a man died childless his brother was bound to raise an heir to him by the widow. This law extended to the next of kin, hence Naomi's plan. Ruth, by her action in verse 7, was claiming this right. The issue is complicated by the fact that Boaz is not in fact Elimelech's closest kinsman, but he promises to take up her case.

4:1-12 The transaction between the kinsmen
The city gate was the place for important assembly. It was also the place where legal business could be publicly transacted, as here. The elders acted as witnesses. In addition to his obligation to raise an heir to carry on the dead man's name, the next of kin also had to buy his land, to keep it in the family. Boaz discusses the land first, then the widow. The kinsman would have bought the land to add to his own inheritance. But when he hears it will in fact go to Ruth and her son, and that he will have Ruth to provide for, he declares himself unable to purchase.
Perez (12): ancestor of Boaz; son of Tamar by her father-in-law, Judah, because of his refusal to honour the custom later formalized as the Levirate law.

4:13-22 Ruth marries and becomes the great-grandmother of King David
So Boaz fulfils his own prayer of 2:12. God rewards Ruth with the gift of a husband and a son. And Naomi finds solace for her grief in this grandson. When God steps in, the ordinary events of life take on extraordinary significance. The child Obed became grandfather to the founder of the royal line of Israel from which Christ himself took human flesh, in another birth at Bethlehem.

THE OLD TESTAMENT AND THE ANCIENT NEAR EAST

Alan Millard

The Bible is an ancient text, a historical record. As such it is very helpful to study it in the light of our knowledge of the world in which it was written.

There is nothing un-Christian in doing this. The Christian faith depends on historical events, things which actually happened. The events recorded and explained in the Bible can be set alongside other events known from other historical sources. The Bible itself consists of documents as ancient and as historically verifiable as any others.

Checking the accuracy of the Bible

Its accuracy can also be tested and checked against other known historical sources. However, this is not always as simple as it may seem. Documents are often damaged or incomplete. Archaeological evidence is in many cases open to more than one interpretation. We possess very few ancient writings which describe the same events the Bible describes, and in any case two observers will rarely describe the same event from an identical standpoint.

The Hebrews were a relatively insignificant people. Their career made little impact on the major powers whose records we possess. Hardly any of the biblical characters appear in other writings, apart from some of the later kings of Israel and Judah. None the less, where we are able to make comparisons, the accuracy of the biblical writers is impressive. Although we seldom find parallel accounts of the same events, we often find examples of customs and occurrences very like those described in the Old Testament, even though they are in no way connected. A superficial similarity can of course be misleading, so we have to be cautious. And a knowledge of the ancient Near East can help, even when it provides neither direct nor circumstantial evidence of the Bible's historical accuracy: the study of Israel's neighbours – customs, culture, literature, history – gives us an idea of what to expect in the case of the Hebrew nation.

These three types of evidence – direct evidence, circumstantial evidence and the evidence of analogy – must be taken in turn to show how they shed light on the Bible.

Direct evidence

As we have seen, direct references to Israel are rare, and almost solely limited to royal names. Amongst those we do have is the record of an invasion by Shishak who was king of Egypt – he ruled about 945-924 BC (1 Kings 14:25f.). His inscription at Thebes, badly preserved, lists many towns conquered in Palestine – evidence of his campaign there. Tiglath-pileser III (about 745-727 BC) re-established Assyrian rule over Syria and Palestine following some decades of weakness, when Jeroboam had made Israel prosperous and Uzziah had built up Judah. The Assyrian records the tribute paid by Menahem of Samaria and claims to have been responsible for replacing Pekah by Hosea (2 Kings 15:19-20, 30). In 2 Kings 15:19 (see also 1 Chronicles 5:26) Tiglath-pileser is called Pul and he was known by that name to Babylonian chroniclers of the 6th century BC, when it is believed 1 and 2 Kings were finally compiled. Subsequently Assyrian rule in Samaria involved Judah as a vassal, but her kings preferred to struggle for independence, seeking Egypt's aid. So Hezekiah rebelled, and Sennacherib brought his forces to overwhelm Judah and lay siege to Jerusalem. The Assyrian tells of this in many inscriptions. He relates how Hezekiah sent tribute to him in Nineveh (the amounts seem to differ slightly from 2 Kings 18:14ff.), yet lays no claim to the capture of Jerusalem, nor, naturally enough, does he mention his army's fate.

In the account of Solomon's

building projects, 1 Kings 9:15 names three major cities besides Jerusalem – Hazor, Megiddo and Gezer. Excavations at each one have uncovered city walls of the 10th century BC, all of the same pattern. Each city wall is pierced by a massive gateway, and all are identical in plan and in measurement, to within a few inches. Here is a material record demonstrating the truth of the biblical text. Here, also are physical signs of an overall planning authority, a central power. Indeed, Solomon's glory, fabulous though it may appear, becomes more and more credible when set in its ancient context.

Circumstantial evidence

Most of the discoveries which feature in books on archaeology and the Bible fall into the class of circumstantial evidence – matters which make no direct reference to biblical events, but supply examples of practices or incidents apparently comparable with passages in the Bible. In this way we learn that Abraham's marriage to the slave-girl Hagar because of Sarah's childlessness, and his later refusal – until reassured by God – to send her from his household, agree with requirements in the contemporary Laws of Hammurabi of Babylon. The names of the patriarchs of Israel also accord with names generally used in the 2nd millennium BC, now known from thousands of contemporary documents.

Another of Solomon's glories gains evidence from Egyptian sources. According to 1 Kings 9:16, he married the pharaoh's daughter. Yet two or three centuries earlier, in Egypt's heyday, the princesses of Egypt did not leave the court, and when an important foreign king requested one as his bride he was refused. In the 10th century BC however, under the less glorious 21st dynasty and its successor, this rule was broken. So it was that Solomon received his bride.

A little before Solomon's time, the hero Gideon called on a boy to write down the names of trading men in Succoth – apparently just a boy who happened to be available (Judges 8:14). That names could be easily written and recognized then

is shown by copper arrowheads, found near Bethlehem, and in other places, inscribed with their owners' names and dated to the 12th and 11th centuries BC.

The evidence of analogy

The fact that we have virtually no written record of ancient Hebrew life, thought and history apart from the Old Testament means that many aspects of life can hardly be known at all. Normal processes of decay have destroyed any documents on leather or papyrus buried in the cities of Palestine along with furniture and clothing. Where such items are preserved in neighbouring cultures, it is possible sometimes to attribute similar usages to ancient Israel. Each case needs thorough testing to ensure that the circumstances really are parallel, but some are sufficiently clear to help us evaluate the Old Testament.

No literature has survived from Israelite towns, but there is no doubt it existed. The Old Testament itself is witness to that, although scholars debate just how old its written form is. In Egypt and Babylonia the complicated writing-systems gave the scribes a monopoly. In Israel (and adjacent states) the simple 22-letter alphabet was learnt easily by any who wanted, so writing was more widespread amongst the population, although professional scribes still had an important role. Evidence from various minor written documents demonstrates this fact for ancient Israel. If writing was used for daily affairs, this implies it could be used for works of literature, too. The written word was treated with respect. Valuable old books were copied with great care. They could be revised or edited, but the way this has been done is seldom detectable unless the older copies survive for comparison.

Egypt, Assyria and Babylonia, the Hittites and Canaanites all had elaborately-arranged religious rites, sacrifices, and priestly orders. Their temples were finely built and lavishly furnished, especially by successful kings. If Israel had been different in this they would have been the odd ones out, but in fact they were not. These analogies show that the tabernacle, Solomon's temple, and the Levitical regulations were Israel's counterparts. As in neighbouring nations, moreover, the mass of the people toiled and suffered to provide for the magnificence demanded by the king.

We would expect Israel, as a nation among nations of related stock, to share similar modes of thought and expression. When Babylonian or Egyptian literature shows features strange to modern thought, we take great pains to understand them – to account for inconsistencies, paradoxes, and apparent contradictions without impugning the accuracy of the texts which are our only sources of information (unless there are firmly-founded objective reasons for doing so). Israel's literature may be expected to contain similar quirks, and they too should be treated with respect. Some are clear, for instance the narration of events out of chronological order, or the collecting of items without evident relation to the context.

Similarities and differences

These examples are sufficient to show the value of gathering, studying and applying whatever the ancient Near East affords by way of background to the Bible. The direct and indirect evidence agrees so strikingly with the Old Testament that it makes attempts to discredit its picture of Israel's culture and career very dubious indeed. No discovery has been proved to contradict the Hebrew records. There may be discrepancies, uncertainties, unanswered questions. The incomplete nature of all our evidence makes this inevitable. New discoveries solve old problems, frequently revealing false premises in modern theories. At the same time they may raise fresh questions and stimulate deeper study, new approaches, and better understanding.

If the similarities between Israel and her neighbours form the bulk of the contribution made by biblical archaeology, the differences merit attention as well. The Old Testament proclaims an unbridgeable gap between Israel and her neighbours. Whereas her language and culture shared so much, her faith stood apart. To find material traces of Israel's monotheistic faith, imageless worship, centralized cult, is difficult. Her neighbours reckoned her God as no more than a national god like their own (Chemosh of Moab, or Milcom of Ammon), unaware of his unique place. To make things more complicated, Israel never remained entirely faithful, so pagan religious objects can be found in the ruins of her cities.

It is in comparing biblical teaching with contemporary texts that the distinctions are best seen. The absolute demands of the Ten Commandments, the exclusive devotion to Israel's electing God, the equality of individuals balancing their corporate responsibility, the altruism of the prophets – all these, and many others, find no true echo in the world of the Old Testament.

Some may find them incredible, yet we possess actually preserved manuscripts which guarantee them an antiquity of over 2,000 years.

Some may find them unacceptable, but although so old they still speak sense to modern man.

If the historical and cultural aspects harmonize with our knowledge of ancient times, as in fact is the case, the ethical and religious distinctions need explanation. The Old Testament gives one: God spoke.

1 AND 2 SAMUEL

These two books were originally one volume in the Hebrew Bible. They provide a history of Israel from the end of the Judges period to the last years of David, the nation's second and greatest king – roughly 100 years (about 1075-975 BC). This is essentially religious history: the story of God and the nation – particularly, God and the nation's leaders. Samuel gives his name to the books, not as author, but as the dominating figure of the early chapters, and Israel's 'kingmaker' under God's direction. It was he who anointed first Saul and then David as king.

The historian may well have drawn his material from Samuel's own writings (1 Samuel 10:25) and those of the prophets who followed him (1 Chronicles 29:29). He certainly knew some of David's poems (which he quotes in 2 Samuel 1:19-27; 22:2-51; 23:1-7). And he was himself a born storyteller and master of suspense. He must have written some time after the division of the kingdom. (He several times refers to the separate kingdom of Judah, but the nation was not yet in exile: see, e.g. 1 Samuel 27:6.) 900 BC is therefore the earliest likely date for the books as we know them. Critics have argued for several authors, largely because of the 'duplicate' accounts of various events (e.g. the two sparings of Saul's life; the two occasions when Samuel announced God's rejection of Saul). On closer inspection, however, most of the so-called duplicates emerge quite clearly as two separate if similar events, recounted by the author in order to emphasize certain points. Repetition is a feature of his literary technique.

1 - 3 SAMUEL'S BIRTH AND EARLY YEARS

1 God answers Hannah's prayer for a child

In the Old Testament, when God has a special purpose for a man there is often something special about his birth. Like Hannah, Sarah and Rebekah in the Old Testament and Elizabeth in the New experienced the bitterness of being childless. Like Samuel, Isaac and Jacob and John the Baptist were the God-given answers to many years of prayer. Each had a special role to play in the great plan of God. When God gave Hannah the son she longed for he also gave Israel the last and greatest of the judges, and the first (after Moses) of the great prophets – the man who was to usher in the kings.

To sacrifice ... at Shiloh (3): the centre of worship in the Judges period; the place where Joshua had set up the tabernacle (Joshua 18:1). (The 'temple' proper – verse 9 – was not built till Solomon's day.)

I will give him to the Lord ... (11): the child is dedicated to God for life under a Nazirite vow (see Numbers 6, and compare the vow made by Samson's parents in Judges 13).

Only her lips moved (13): it was usual to pray aloud. Eli is quick to jump to the wrong conclusion. Religious life must have been at a low ebb if worshippers came drunk to the tabernacle. Compare the conduct of Eli's own sons, 2:12ff.

When she had weaned him (24): Samuel would have been two or three years old.

2:1-10 Hannah's song of thanksgiving

Hannah's song is echoed by Mary in the New Testament (Luke 1:46-55). In the small mirror of her own experience Hannah sees reflected all the wonder of God's character. God has reversed her fortunes (1). Penninah's taunts have been silenced (3, 5). Emptiness, misery, shame are gone – in their place, life, joy, honour. And what God can do for one, he can and will do for all his people.

Sheol (6): the shadowy land of the dead.

His King (10): this is either inspired prophecy on Hannah's part, or verses 2-10 are part of a psalm added by the narrator, as being singularly appropriate to her experience.

2:11-36 Eli the priest and his no-good sons

The priests were entitled to a share in the sacrificial offerings (see Numbers 18:8-20; Deuteronomy 18:1-5). But what is going on here is a travesty of the law. Eli's sons seize the best bits before the offering has even been given to God (15). What is more, they are bringing prostitution into the worship of God, in the worst traditions of Canaanite religion (22). On his death these two will be the nation's 'archbishops' – and all Eli can do is reason with them!

Verses 27-36: the man of God's prediction is fulfilled in the death of Eli's sons in battle at Aphek (4:11). The priesthood passed from Eli's family to the line of Zadok in David's day (2 Samuel 8:17).

A linen ephod (18): a tunic worn by the priests (see verse 28).

It was the will of the Lord to slay them (25): the writer puts it this way because God is sovereign in every circumstance. It is equally true that their death is a direct outcome of their own free choice to disobey God. The Bible sees no conflict between God's sovereignty and man's free will. See on Exodus 6:28 – 10:29.

3 Samuel hears God's call

In the early hours (before the oil for the lamp ran out, as it would at dawn), when he is on duty near the ark, inside the tabernacle, Samuel hears God speak to him for the first time – a message of judgement for Eli. From this time on, Samuel is God's messenger, and the whole nation knows it, from Dan in the far north to Beersheba on the edge of the southern desert.

4:1 - 7:1 THE PHILISTINES AND THE ARK OF GOD

4:1-11 The Philistines defeat Israel and capture the ark

The ark (see Exodus 25 - 27) was Israel's most precious possession, the focal point of the tabernacle. A copy of the law was kept inside it. Its lid was the mercy seat, symbol of the presence of God.

But now the nation wants to use it as a talisman, the ultimate protection against the Philistines. The result is total disaster: the army defeated, the ark in enemy hands.

Philistines (1): one of a group known as the Sea Peoples, who migrated into the Near East from the Aegean area in the 14th-13th centuries BC.

This plaster-cast of the head of a Philistine soldier is from Thebes in Egypt, 12th century BC.

They were defeated by the Egyptians and settled the southern coastal area of Palestine.

4:12-22 Death of Eli

The ark never returned to Shiloh. Although there is no mention of it here, the Philistines probably followed up their victory by destroying this city (see Jeremiah 26:6). These verses record the fulfilment of God's judgement on Eli's family (2:27-36; 3:11-14).

He had judged Israel forty years (18): most of Israel's judges were warrior-leaders (see Judges). But the last two, Eli and Samuel, were religious leaders and administrators of justice.

5 The ark in Philistine hands

To the Philistines' way of thinking, Dagon, their god, has given them victory. So they place the ark as a war-trophy at his feet. But Dagon is not in the same class as the God of Israel. God is no man-made idol. He treats the figure of Dagon as they might have treated a captive king (see Judges 1:6-7). As a further demonstration of his power there is an outbreak of plague (bubonic plague, carried by the rat-flea; see verse 6 and 6:4, New English Bible). Moving the ark simply spreads the disease.

6 - 7:1 Return of the ark

After seven months of this, the Philistines have had enough. The religious leaders advise the ark's return – but in a way which will show, once for all, whether or not Israel's God is responsible for the disasters. The cows, not trained for the yoke, are unlikely to pull together. In the nature of things they would also be expected to stay near their calves. Yet they respond to the yoke like a team of oxen, and head straight for the border.

Verse 19 (Revised Standard Version) sounds a sombre note in all the rejoicing. Even Israel must learn not to overstep the mark. It is not safe to treat God as an object of idle curiosity.

7:2-17 NATIONAL REVIVAL: SAMUEL AS JUDGE

Twenty years pass, and there is a genuine turning to God (verse 2, New English Bible). The old idols – Baal and Ashtoreth, the Canaanite fertility gods – are destroyed. And Samuel, judge and religious leader in Eli's place (see 15-17), leads the nation in an act of repentance and cleansing. Immediately the test comes. The Philistines are advancing, and God uses the occasion to show Israel just what he will do for a people who keep faith with him. Israel is needed only for the mopping-up operation. The name of the place of a former defeat (4:1) is chosen to mark the present victory (12). It is God's help which makes such a dramatic reversal possible.

All the days of Samuel (13): this includes most of Saul's reign. War continued, but Saul and David kept the Philistines at bay until the great battle of Gilboa when Saul and Jonathan lost their lives.

From Ekron to Gath (14): the two inland Philistine city-states. Israel won back their border towns.

Bethel, Gilgal, Mizpah, Ramah (16-17): Samuel did an annual circuit of the four sanctuary towns.

8 - 12 SAUL BECOMES ISRAEL'S FIRST KING

8 The people ask for a king; Samuel's warning

History repeats itself in the case of Samuel's sons. They turn out little better than Eli's (2:12). This provides the people with a ready-made excuse to ask for a king, like the nations around. Samuel warns of the cost. They have only to look at their neighbour states to see that having a king means conscription, forced labour, taxation, and loss of personal liberty. But even this does not deter them.

9 - 10:16 Saul becomes king: the private anointing

A search for lost donkeys, of all things, brings Israel's future king from Gibeah to Ramah, and the meeting with Samuel. All Israel knows the prophet, but not, apparently, this young provincial.

The oil (10:1) sets Saul apart for his high office. The detailed fulfilment of Samuel's predictions assures Saul of the prophet's authority. Saul goes home a new man (10:9).

The high place (9:12): the shrine; the phrase has not yet acquired the idolatrous associations of later times.

A bed ... upon the roof (9:25): a pleasantly cool place in the summer heat.

Down ... to Gilgal (10:8): the instruction seems to relate to mustering for battle. When this took place (chapter 13) Saul disobeyed.

When they came to Gibeah ...(10:10): Saul's ecstatic experience took place in his own home town.

10:17-27 The public proclamation

God chooses Israel's king; it is not left to the people.

11 Saul's first victory melts the opposition

God moves Saul to make his appeal (6) and the people to respond (7). For perhaps the first time since Joshua the nation is united: a good beginning to the new king's reign.

12 Samuel cautions the people at Gilgal

Samuel has always been alert to the dangers of monarchy (8; 10:17ff.). Politically the move to choose a king was no doubt wise. Religiously, it was a step in the wrong direction, a step away from the ideal of God alone as Israel's King. And if God ceases to be King for his people, both nation and monarchy will be swept away (25).

Verse 9: *Sisera* defeated by Deborah and Barak (Judges 4 - 5); *the king of Moab* – Eglon, assassinated by Ehud (Judges 3:12-30).

Verse 11: *Jerubbaal* – i.e. Gideon (Judges 6 - 8); *Jephthah* – Judges 11 - 12; *Samuel* – this seems odd coming from his own lips. Perhaps we should read 'Samson' (New English Bible; Judges 13 - 16).

13 - 15 SAUL DISOBEYS AND IS REJECTED

13 - 14 War with the Philistines: Saul's disobedience and stupidity

Saul musters his troops and waits seven days, during which time the army steadily dwindles. But he fails to see the seventh day out. And his disobedience and arrogance in taking over the function of the prophet costs him his dynasty.

Chapter 14: Jonathan and his armour-bearer seem to have been taken for deserters, so they were able to catch the Philistines on the hop.

Earth tremors add to the panic and confusion. And Israelite deserters change sides to help Saul to victory. Jonathan is seen as a man of outstanding faith and courage. By contrast, the narrative begins to bring out those flaws in Saul's make-up which later developed into serious mental disorder.

13:1: the text is incomplete. Acts 13:21 puts Saul's reign in round figures at 40 years. Possibly a tens-unit has dropped out here and the text should read 32 years (but see article 'Unravelling the Chronology of the Kings'). We know from 9:2 that Saul was a young man when he came to the throne. By this time he must be in his thirties since he has a son old enough to fight. When he died, a younger son, Ishbosheth, was himself 40 (2 Samuel 2:10).

Thirty thousand (13:5): more probably 3,000 – see article 'The Large Numbers of the Old Testament'.

The people hid themselves (13:6): the atmosphere is much the same as it was in Gideon's day, when the people went in fear of the Midianites (Judges 6:2).

Bring hither the ark (14:18): perhaps in view of Saul's command to the priest in verse 19, New English Bible translates 'ephod' rather than 'ark'. This was the tunic with the breastpiece containing the Urim and Thummim (41), the lots which were cast to discover God's will.

Sinning ... by eating with the blood (14:33): forbidden in Leviticus 17:10ff.

Ishvi (14:49): short form of Ishbosheth.

Abner (14:50): he later set up Ishbosheth as king in opposition to David (2 Samuel 2:8 - 3:39).

15 God orders the destruction of the Amalekites; Saul again disobeys

This time the disobedience is deliberate (9). Saul is personally rejected by God as king, and Samuel pays him no more official visits. The prophet had foreseen trouble. He might well have relished Saul's downfall. Instead he went home grieving.

Amalek (2): the Amalekites were old enemies whose punishment had long been forecast (Exodus 17:8-16; Deuteronomy 25:17-19). Even so, we find it hard to swallow the order to destroy them completely – notwithstanding the unparalleled atrocities of our own century. In the more realistic, less individualistic world of

Saul's day the whole community was held responsible for the misdeeds of its members, and suffered the consequences. Saul's disobedience (for the lowest of motives) left his people open to continued harassment from the Amalekites.

Kenites (6): a nomadic Midianite tribe into which Moses had married. The Kenites acted as Israel's guides in the desert (Numbers 10:29-33).

To obey is better than sacrifice (22-23): Samuel's declaration became a major theme of later prophets.

16 - 31 SAUL AND DAVID

16:1-13 Samuel anoints David king

With the anointing, as in Saul's case, comes spiritual power (13). Again God chooses his man and prepares him long before he becomes a national figure.

16:14-23 David finds a place at court

When the Spirit of God leaves Saul, evil forces take charge. Saul is at the mercy of his own ungovernable temperament. His disordered mind plunges him into black depression and violence. But music can push back the shadows, and so Saul's need becomes David's opportunity.

David's harp was a 'kinnor', the first musical instrument mentioned in the Bible. This reconstruction is from the Haifa Music Museum.

An evil spirit from God (15): to the observer, Saul is 'possessed' by a spirit sent by God in punishment.

17 David and Goliath

The Philistine champion is ten feet tall, fully armed and mailed. But David's time in the hills alone with the sheep has taught him faith – and deadly accuracy with the sling. The giant doesn't stand a chance.

Verses 55-58: this is difficult to tie in

with 16:18ff. The events of chapter 17 may have taken place while David was still attending court only occasionally, when Saul's black moods came on him. 16:21-22 then refer to a later time. Or possibly the enquiry is a purely formal one concerning David's family background. The victor had, after all, been promised the king's daughter in marriage (17:25).

18 The friendship with Jonathan; Saul grows jealous

David was to look back on his friendship with Jonathan as one of the best things in his life (2 Samuel 1:26). Nothing could shake the amazing bond between the king's son and the man who, humanly speaking, was to rob him of the throne.

As David's prestige grows, Saul's jealous suspicion increases, and he plots David's death. David's poverty gives Saul the chance to suggest a bride-price which is likely to cost him his life. Such a toll could be exacted only from the Philistines, Israel's number one enemy; the other nations practised circumcision. David doubles Saul's demand and returns unharmed, to claim his royal bride.

19 - 20 Attempts on his life force David to leave Saul's court

Jonathan's first attempt at reconciliation succeeds (1-7). But one of Saul's black moods follows and only Michal's deception saves David's life (8-17). For a time he joins Samuel and his school of prophets at Ramah (18-24). Jonathan tries to secure David's safe return, but his father only turns on him (20:30-33). And the two friends are forced to part (35-42). **Is Saul also among the prophets? (19-24):** compare 10:10-13. So irresistible is the power of the Spirit of God that not only is Saul's evil plan frustrated, but the king himself becomes 'infected'. Like his messengers, he too – for the time at least – turns prophet.

Tomorrow is the new moon (20:5): the first day of each new month was a feast day.

21 Ahimelech helps David to escape

The priest pays dearly for David's deception (22:11-19). But David is fed and armed, and makes good his escape to the Philistine city of Gath. In danger of recognition he feigns madness and plays the part so effectively that Achish is completely convinced (see also 27:5-12).

Nob (1): Israel's central shrine at that time.

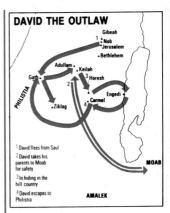

DAVID THE OUTLAW

Gibeah
Nob
Jerusalem
Bethlehem
Adullam
Keilah
Horesh
Gath
PHILISTIA
Engedi
Carmel
Ziklag
MOAB
AMALEK

1 David flees from Saul
2 David takes his parents to Moab for safety
3 In hiding in the hill country
4 David escapes to Philistia

Holy bread (4): each sabbath twelve fresh loaves were placed on the altar and the twelve stale ones removed. Only the priests were entitled to eat them.

Vessels (5): i.e. 'bodies' (New English Bible). Israelite soldiers abstained from sexual intercourse during campaigns. If Uriah had not steadfastly stuck to the rules, David would have had no occasion to resort to murder (2 Samuel 11:11).

22 David the outlaw; Saul's revenge on Ahimelech

He left them with the king of Moab (4): for safety. David had Moabite blood in his veins (see Ruth).

Doeg (9ff.): the title of Psalm 52 relates it to this episode.

23 The hunt is on: Keilah, Ziph, Maon

David welds his band of outlaws into an effective military force. But Saul's relentless pursuit keeps them continually on the move.

The ephod (6): see on 14:18.

24 David spares Saul's life in the cave at Engedi

Saul is completely at David's mercy. His refusal to take a short-cut to the throne brings the king to his senses. But Saul's word cannot be relied on.

25 The death of Samuel; David and Abigail

Not until Elijah will there be another religious leader to equal Samuel. The old prophet had anointed Israel's greatest king, but did not live to see him reign.

David's request to Nabal is not unreasonable. He is not demanding protection money, but asking some return on past services (15-16). After all, the man was rich and it was sheep-shearing, a feast time. Abigail's quick action saves the lives of her husband and household (22). She evidently made a good impression on David (see verse 39). God attends to Nabal's punishment. He dies of a double stroke.

26 David again spares Saul's life

The pro-Saul Ziphites again lay information against David. And once again it is Saul who finds himself at David's mercy and is shamed into repentance. No doubt Macbeth would have seen this as a heaven-sent opportunity for advancement. David knew God could and would put him on the throne without any assistance from him.

Abishai the son of Zeruiah (6): Abishai, Joab, and Asahel, David's military leaders, were all sons of his step-sister. Though brave, they caused him a great deal of trouble when he was king (2 Samuel 3:39; 18:14; 20:10).

27 Back in Philistine country

Achish is once again completely taken in (see 21:10-15). While pretending to raid Israel and her allies (10), David in fact wipes out enemy cities (8), leaving no one alive to tell the tale (11).

28 Saul consults a medium

Saul can get no reply from God (6). Witchcraft had always been forbidden in Israel (Leviticus 19:31). But in desperation he sets out at night and in disguise on a dangerous journey, close to the enemy camp at Shunem, to consult the medium at Endor. However, he finds Samuel no more reassuring in death than he had been in life.

29 David is not trusted

The other Philistine overlords are less gullible than Achish, so David is spared the awkward predicament of facing his fellow countrymen in battle. This chapter refers to earlier events than chapter 28. The Philistines muster at Aphek. They have not yet moved north to Shunem.

30 The Amalekite raid on Ziklag; David's successful reprisal

David's return is well-timed, and the slave's information more than a stroke of luck. All is recovered. And Judah and the Calebites, also victims of the raid (14), share in the spoil.

31 The battle of Gilboa; death of Saul and Jonathan

The writer of Chronicles (1 Chronicles 10) found this account of Saul's death more credible than the Amalekite's story (2 Samuel 1:4-10). The latter may well have adjusted the facts to suit his own ends. Fittingly, it is the men of

Jabesh who rescue the bodies. They have not forgotten what they owe to Saul's first great victory (chapter 11).

2 SAMUEL 1 - 4 THE EARLY YEARS OF DAVID'S REIGN

(The reign of David is also recorded in 1 Chronicles 11 – 29.9)

1 News of Saul's death; David's lament

The Amalekite's story differs from the account of Saul's death in 1 Samuel 31. If he twisted the facts in hope of a reward, he did not know David. After the Amalekite raid on Ziklag (1 Samuel 30) David had no cause to love this race. But it was his strong conviction that the king's life was sacred (14; and see 1 Samuel 24 and 26), not racial discrimination, that led to the death sentence.

The lament for Saul and Jonathan is one of the most moving and beautiful of all David's poems. His regret for the king seems wholly sincere; his distress at the loss of Jonathan, deep and genuine.

On the third day (2): it was 100 miles from Gilboa to Ziklag.

The book of Jashar (18): a lost anthology (see Joshua 10:13).

The shield ... anointed with oil (21): the shield was leather; oil prevented it drying and cracking.

2 Civil war; Abner kills Asahel

Only Judah (by this time probably including Simeon) acclaims David as king. The other ten tribes follow the lead of Abner, Saul's army commander, and give allegiance to Ishbosheth, Saul's son. For two years the nation is divided.

An attempt to settle the issue by representative single combat (14, see New English Bible) at Gibeon is inconclusive, and full-scale civil war follows.

Sons of Zeruiah (18): see on 1 Samuel 26:6.

The butt of his spear (23): Abner did not intend to kill Asahel. But the butt was sharp so that it would stick in the ground, and the blow proved fatal.

The Arabah (29): the long rift valley from Galilee to the Dead Sea and beyond; here, the Jordan Valley.

3 Abner makes terms; Joab avenges his brother

Ishbosheth is not the man his father was. Abner is the real power. If he transfers his support to David, he carries the nation with him. But he reckons without the implacable hatred of Joab. David leads the nation's mourning for Abner. Despite a public declaration of innocence, the taint of the murder remains with him all his life (1 Kings 2:5).

Saul had a concubine (7): a king's harem normally passed to his heir, which makes Abner's action tantamount to a claim to the throne. Compare Absalom's action, 16:20ff. Rizpah appears again in chapter 21.

A dog's head of Judah (8): i.e. 'one of David's contemptible supporters'.

Dan to Beersheba (10): the whole country, north to south (in Britain one would say, from John o' Groat's to Land's End).

My wife Michal ... (14): see I Samuel 18:20-27. Saul had given David's wife to another man.

One who has a discharge ... (29): who is defiled and therefore disqualified from religious service; *holds a spindle*: fit only for women's work.

4 The assassination of Ishbosheth
A second incident (compare 1:1-16) which shows the complete failure of David's supporters to understand his attitude to Saul and the royal family. Ishbosheth is given honourable burial, the two murderers are publicly disgraced.

5 - 12 DAVID'S KINGDOM ESTABLISHED
5 David, king of all Israel; the new capital at Jerusalem
The writer makes it clear that David is no usurper. God has given him his title to the throne: a fact recognized by Saul (1 Samuel 24:18-20), by Abner (3:9-10) and finally by the whole nation (5:2).

Although part of Jerusalem fell to Judah at the conquest (Judges 1:8), the fortress itself had never been taken (Joshua 15:63; Judges 1:21). The Jebusites had some ground for their boast that a garrison of blind men and cripples could hold it (6). But they underestimated David. Jerusalem was held by Judah until Nebuchadnezzar destroyed it 400 years later. It was a first-rate choice of capital.

The Millo (9): part of the fortifications.

Hiram, king of Tyre (11): contemporary with David and Solomon (1 Kings 5). Hiram reigned about 979-945 BC. The sea-port of Tyre was capital of the Phoenician kingdom. Hiram's reign was a golden age of political expansion and commercial prosperity, when arts and crafts flourished. His craftsmen helped to build the temple.

6 The ark is brought to Jerusalem
See also 1 Chronicles 13, 15-16. After the Philistines returned the ark (1 Samuel 4 - 6), it remained at Kiriath-jearim (Baalah in Judah; see 1 Chronicles 13:6). Now David brings it to his new capital. The occasion is marked with all the exuberance of Jewish worship. Even the king dances for joy. Only Michal stands aloof and outside it all, cold and

Part of the modern city of Jerusalem.

The temple area

The Valley of Hinnom

The Kidron Valley

Site of David's city

unmoved by the presence of God.
Uzzah put out his hand to the ark (6):
which not even the Levites might
touch. David blames himself for not
following the instructions Moses laid
down (1 Chronicles 15:2-15). At the
next attempt the Levites carried the
ark on poles.

7 The house of God and the throne of David

David is not the man to build God's
temple – that is for his son, a man of
peace, not a warrior (1 Chronicles
22:7ff.). But God compensates for
the disappointment by promising a
'house' for David, a dynasty which
will be 'for ever' (16). On this
promise rests a hope which runs right
through the Old Testament, the hope
of a Messiah. And when he came,
the promise was fulfilled. Christ was
born in David's birthplace, Bethlehem, and 'of the house and lineage
of David' (Luke 2:4). The angel tells
Mary: 'The Lord God will give to
him the throne of his father David,
and he will reign over the house of
Jacob for ever; and of his kingdom
there will be no end' (Luke 1:32-33).
Your son ... shall build (12-13): Solomon did build (1 Kings 5-7). But
David contributed a great deal: he
drew up the plans and provided
materials (1 Chronicles 28:11ff.;
22:2ff.).

DAVID'S WARS

REHOB
MAACAH
GESHUR
Helam
TOB
Mahanaim
AMMON
Rabbah
Jerusalem
Hebron
MOAB
PHILISTIA
AMALEK
EDOM

8 David's victories

This chapter predates the events of
chapter 7 (see 7:1).
Moab (2): previously David was on

good terms with them (1 Samuel
22:3-4).
Valley of Salt (13): probably in the
barren section of the great rift valley
south of the Dead Sea.
Cherethites ... Pelethites (18): Philistine mercenaries.
David's sons were priests (18):
although not from a priestly family,
David was himself something of a
priest-king (see chapter 6), like
Melchizedek, a much earlier king
of Jerusalem (Genesis 14:18).

9 David and Mephibosheth, Jonathan's son

The events of chapter 21 may pre-
date this chapter. If so, no doubt the
king's summons terrified
Mephibosheth. But David's motives
are wholly good, 'for Jonathan's
sake' (see 1 Samuel 20:42). He re-
stores the family estates (7) and treats
the young man as his own son (11).
Lo-debar (4): in north Gilead, not far
from Jabesh.
Verse 10: this sounds contradictory,
but being at court would mean an
increase in general expenses, even if
meals were provided.

10 Defeat of the Ammonite/Syrian alliance

See also 1 Chronicles 19. Hanun provoked the war by his outrageous
treatment of the ambassadors. But no
doubt neighbouring nations were
suspicious and afraid of Israel's
powerful king.
    The campaign in verses 16-18 may
be the one mentioned in 8:3ff.

11 David's adultery with Bathsheba

His army is fighting the Ammonites,
but this spring the king is not with
them. He is taking an after-siesta
stroll in the cool, on the palace roof.
And from his vantage-point he can
see down into the open inner courtyard of a nearby house, where Bathsheba is going through the purification ritual. The events that follow –
adultery and murder – are the water-
shed in David's life. From this point
on he reaps the bitter harvest of his
sin.
Rabbah (1): present-day Amman,
capital of Jordan.
Uriah the Hittite (3): to make matters
worse, Uriah was one of David's special guard (23:39), away on the king's
war.
Verse 11: the army is on campaign,
under canvas, and the rule is that the
men abstain from sexual intercourse.
Had Uriah been a man of less principle he would have gone home to his
wife. The child could then have

passed as his and he would not have been killed. But maybe he already suspected the truth.

Jerubbesheth (21): i.e. Jerubbaal/ Gideon (Judges 9). 'Baal' being a pagan name, the scribes later substituted the word 'bosheth'/'besheth', 'shame'. So Jerubbaal became Jerubbesheth; Eshbaal became Ishbosheth; Meribbaal, Mephibosheth, and so on.

12 Nathan's visit; death of the child

Uriah is dead; the wedding over; the child born. It all seems to have blown over very nicely – until Nathan arrives. And then the whole sordid episode is exposed. David is made to see himself as God sees him: a humbling experience for a king (see Psalm 51). God forgives him, but he is punished, and the child dies.

Restore ... fourfold (6): see Exodus 22:1.

Verses 10-11: the prophecy was fulfilled. Three of David's sons were murdered, two by their own brothers. And in the rebellion Absalom took over his father's harem (16:22).

Sent a message ... (25): presumably to reassure David that this child would not die.

A talent of gold (30): about 66 1lb/ 30kg.

13 - 20 DAVID AND HIS ELDEST SONS: ABSALOM'S REBELLION

13 Amnon and Tamar; Absalom's revenge

Faced with the appalling rape of his daughter by her half-brother, David does nothing at all. The strong king is a fatally weak father (see 1 Kings 1:6). Had David taken action he might have prevented both the murder and the later rebellion.

Speak to the king (13): Tamar does not think marriage out of the question (though in view of Leviticus 18:11 they would have needed a special dispensation). The 'impossibility' of verse 2 lies in her careful seclusion – Amnon only wanted to satisfy his lust, he had no thought of marriage.

14 The woman from Tekoa; Absalom forgiven

Joab pierces the king's defences much as Nathan had done (chapter 12), but with a fake law-suit. This time the appeal is to waive the next-of-kin's obligation to avenge her murdered relative. The application to David is obvious. He is willing to overrule in the case of one of his subjects: why not for his heir?

ABSALOM'S REBELLION

Mahanaim

Jerusalem.

.Hebron

■■ Absalom
■ David

Joab wins his point, and Absalom returns from exile. But two long years pass before he is admitted to his father's presence.

Verse 26: it was Absalom's hair which eventually brought about his death (18:9). The weight is 3½-4lb.

15 Absalom's rebellion; David leaves Jerusalem

With Amnon out of the way, and Abigail's son dead, Absalom is next in line to the throne. But Solomon is David's chosen heir. For four years Absalom lays his plans (1-6), gradually winning the people over. When he does come into the open (7-12) the challenge to David is extremely serious.

The king is caught unprepared. To save the city, and gain time, he leaves Jerusalem. But he organizes a spy-ring. And Hushai is sent back to outwit Ahithophel, whose far-sighted council is otherwise likely to win the day for Absalom.

The gate (2): where the city's business and legal transactions took place (see Ruth 4:1ff.).

Hebron (7): David's former capital, in Judah.

The Mount of Olives (30): the place where Jesus spent the night of his betrayal.

Ahithophel (31): Bathsheba's grandfather; wisest of all David's advisers.

16 Ziba and Shimei; Hushai and Ahithophel

Ziba (1-4) clearly has an eye to the main chance. Mephibosheth later denies the charges made against him (19:24-30). Shimei (5-14) takes a vindictive pleasure in the downfall of the man who robbed his family of the throne (5-8).

In Jerusalem (15-19) Hushai succeeds in convincing Absalom of his loyalty. Verses 20-23 provide an example of Ahithophel's political strategy. By taking over David's harem, Absalom will convince his followers that reconciliation with his father is impossible. No king could forgive such a public insult.

17 Absalom rejects Ahithophel's plan

Ahithophel's advice is to strike quickly, and only against the person of the king – so avoiding civil war. But Hushai gains time for David by a scheme which appeals to Absalom's vanity (11ff.). Ahithophel has the foresight to realize the probable consequences – hence his suicide (24). Meantime Jonathan and Ahimaaz, on their way to David with the information, narrowly escape discovery by hiding in a dry cistern – one of many hollowed out for storing rain-water (17-20).

18 - 19:8 Defeat and death of Absalom; David's grief

Joab is shrewd enough to see that only the death of the pretender – or the king – can settle the issue. But David still loved his son, and he did not forgive Joab for ignoring orders (see 19:13). It was ironic that Absalom's beautiful hair (14:26) should tangle in the oak and leave him a helpless prey to Joab.

18:33 - 19:8: grief and remorse (see 12:10) blind the king to the effect of his conduct on the people. Joab's harsh words bring him to his senses and save him from political disaster. **Great heap of stones (18:17):** a cairn marked the grave of a criminal. **I have no son (18:18):** presumably those mentioned in 14:27 died young. **Ahimaaz and the Cushite (18:19-32):** Joab chooses the dark-skinned Sudanese to take the bad news. The king would naturally have assumed (as he does in 27) that the priest's son brought good news. Joab may also have been thinking of the fate of earlier messengers (1:11-16; 4:9-12). But the direct hill-route proved slower than the route Ahimaaz took along the Jordan Valley (23).

19:9-43 The aftermath of rebellion

Judah had backed Absalom. David's attempt to win them back, and his appointment of Amasa (Absalom's army commander, and his own nephew) in Joab's place lead to further trouble (41-43 and chapter 20). David is in effect punishing loyalty and rewarding rebellion. Now that the king is back in power, there are some who are anxious to get back into favour (Shimei, 16-22, see 16:5-14; Mephibosheth, 24-30, see 16:1-4; on Shimei and Barzillai, see also 1 Kings 2).

20 Sheba's revolt; Joab kills Amasa

Despite the statement in verse 2, those who actively supported Sheba, when it came to it, were few (14ff.). Joab is as quick to kill Amasa (a member of his own family) as he was to kill Abner, when his own position was threatened before. In both cases his treachery is despicable. The kiss and the sword thrust bring to mind Judas' betrayal of Jesus. David did not forget, or forgive (see 1 Kings 2:5-6).

Your lord's servants (6): the men of David's special guard (7 and 23:18ff.), led by Abishai.
It fell out (8): into Joab's hand.
Adoram (24): in a post not likely to win friends! He was stoned to death in the reign of Solomon's son.

21 - 24 RECORDS OF EVENTS IN DAVID'S REIGN

With Sheba's death, the nation is once more united and at peace. The writer now brings together events and information belonging to various periods of David's reign.

The old titles to the Psalms link many of David's psalms to events in his life.

Escape from the palace: 1 Samuel 19:11ff.: Psalm 59
David feigns madness: 1 Samuel 21: Psalm 34 (though the difference in names may indicate a further occasion not recorded in Samuel)
David in hiding in the cave: 1 Samuel 22:1ff.: 24:3ff.: Psalms 57, 142
Doeg's betrayal of the priests at Nob: 1 Samuel 22: Psalm 52
The Ziphite informers: 1 Samuel 23:19ff.: Psalm 54
David in the Judean desert: 1 Samuel 24:1-2,22; and again in 2 Samuel 15ff.: Psalm 63
Defeat of the Edomites: 2 Samuel 8:13: Psalm 60
David's sin over Bathsheba: 2 Samuel 11-12: Psalm 51 (and probably 32)
Absalom's rebellion: 2 Samuel 15:13ff.: Psalm 3
David's song of deliverance: 2 Samuel 22: the same poem as Psalm 18

21 The appeasement of Gibeon; defeat of the Philistine giants

Verses 1-14 probably precede Mephibosheth's welcome at court (chapter 9). The story of Israel's pact with Gibeon is told in Joshua 9:3-27. Saul had broken the treaty, despite close family connections with the city (1 Chronicles 8:29ff.).

That you may bless ... (3): and so remove the curse that brought the famine.

Hang (6): the hebrew does not specify the manner of death.

Merab (8): the daughter who had been promised to David as wife.

Took sackcloth and spread it ... (10): to form a tent. Rizpah may have been there as long as six months. The coming of rain brought an end to the famine, and to the curse, leaving David free to act.

Elhanan ... slew Goliath (19): this seems to conflict with 1 Samuel 17. The text here may be confused. R. K. Harrison suggests it should read, 'Elhanan, the son of Jairi the Bethlehemite, slew the brother of Goliath', which ties in with 1 Chronicles 20:5. Another possibility is that a new champion took the name of the one killed by David.

22 David's victory song

This is virtually identical with Psalm 18, and can be compared with Moses' song in Deuteronomy 32. It belongs to the period of David's great early victories. Verses 21-25 contrast with the deeper self-knowledge which followed the Bathsheba/Uriah episode, expressed in Psalm 51.

23:1-7 David's 'last words'

These may be the last words he set down in poetry (see 1 Kings 2 for his final charge to Solomon). His thoughts centre on what makes a good ruler, on his own standing before God, and on the promised dynasty – a fitting close to the life of the king who was 'a man after God's own heart'.

23:8-39 Annals of the men of David's special guard

The exploits of 'The Three' against the Philistines (8-12) are followed by an incident from the campaign described in 5:17-25 (13-17; Bethlehem was David's home town). Then come the exploits of two leaders (Abishai, leader of 'The Thirty', and Benaiah, leader of the Philistine mercenaries), followed by a list of the special guard. The group was probably formed at Ziklag, and helped to put David on the throne (1 Chronicles 12:1; 11:10). More than thirty are listed – those killed (e.g. Asahel, Uriah) were replaced by others.

Ariel (20): 'lion of God'; either lions of exceptional size, or a metaphor for great warriors.

24 The census and the plague

It is not clear why it was wrong to take the census. Perhaps it indicated reliance on numbers, instead of on God. Satan does the inciting in 1 Chronicles 21:1. Here it is God, since all is ultimately under his control.

Verses 8-25: the first readers did not need to be told the tremendous significance of David's purchase, explicitly mentioned in 1 Chronicles 21:18 - 22:1. On this threshing-floor the temple was built, close to the place where Abraham offered up Isaac (2 Chronicles 3:1; Genesis 22:2).

1 AND 2 KINGS

Four centuries of Israel's history are covered by the books of Kings. We move from the close of David's reign, through the golden age of Solomon and the rift between Israel and Judah, to the fall of Samaria in 722 BC and the destruction of Jerusalem in 587 BC. The account begins with a stable, united kingdom under a strong king and ends with total collapse and mass deportation to Babylon. It is a sombre story, and one in which the writer sees a clear moral. God is the Lord of history, actively involved in the affairs of men. When the nation and its leaders look to him and obey his laws, peace and prosperity follow. Political and economic disaster overtake Israel and Judah as a direct consequence of the weakening of the nation's moral and religious fibre.

The writer is unknown; probably a prophet in Babylon during the exile, about 550 BC. He mentions a number of his sources (e.g. 1 Kings 11:41; 15:31): court and official records and cycles of stories about the prophets. He wrote his account as one volume, to be read through from beginning to end. Much of the material is paralleled in Chronicles.

1 - 2 DAVID'S LAST DAYS: SOLOMON'S ACCESSION

1 Adonijah and Solomon; rivals for the throne

King David is now an old man. Thoughts turn to his successor. With his three elder brothers dead, Adonijah is heir apparent. He has the backing of Joab, the army commander, and Abiathar, one of the two chief priests. But the throne has been promised to Solomon (1:13, and see 1 Chronicles 22:9). And thanks to some quick thinking by the prophet Nathan, and even quicker action by the old king, Adonijah is out-manoeuvred. Solomon is made king, co-regent with David.

Abishag the Shunammite (3): from Shunem near Nazareth. Although Abishag is sometimes identified with the heroine of the Song of Solomon, there are no real grounds for this.

Knew her not (4): did not have sexual intercourse with her. The verb 'know' often has this sense in the Old Testament (Genesis 4:1).

Verses 7-8: Zadok and Abiathar, see 2 Samuel 15:24ff.; Benaiah, 2 Samuel 23:20-23; Nathan, 2 Samuel 12. The mighty men: David's special guard, 2 Samuel 23:8-39.

Gihon (33): a spring just outside the eastern wall of Jerusalem, in the Kidron Valley.

Cherethites and Pelethites (38): foreign (Philistine) mercenaries.

The tent (39): in which the ark was kept.

Horns of the altar (50): curved pieces at the four corners.

2:1-12 Last instructions to Solomon; David's death

High-toned advice (1-4) is abruptly followed by worldly wisdom of doubtful morality (5-9).

Joab (5): see 2 Samuel 3:26-30; 20:8-10.

Barzillai (7): see 2 Samuel 17:27-29; 19:31-40.

Shimei (8): David did not regard his pledge to Shimei as binding on Solomon. See 2 Samuel 16:5-14 and 19:16-23.

The basins on wheeled stands used in the temple courtyard may have resembled this bronze stand, from 1200 – 1100 BC.

2:13-46 Solomon secures his position

This time Adonijah pays dearly for what may have been an unthinking request. Solomon interprets it as a claim to the throne, since possession of his predecessor's harem was part of the eastern king's title to the throne (compare Absalom's action, 2 Samuel 16). Abiathar and Joab are dealt with at the same time. And Shimei, another potential trouble-maker, is put on parole in Jerusalem to keep him away from fellow-Benjaminites. When he breaks parole, even though for an innocent reason, Solomon has him killed.

The word ... concerning the house of Eli (27): see 1 Samuel 2:27-36.

3 - 11 THE REIGN OF SOLOMON

3:1-15 Solomon's dream; the gift of wisdom

Solomon is at Gibeon, the town six miles from Jerusalem where the tabernacle and altar are kept, when God appears to him. His reign is outstanding for wise judgement, economic prosperity and fame – the very things God promised.

Verse 1: 'the city', i.e. the citadel on Mt Zion.

High places (2): the old Canaanite shrines (often, but not always, on hill-tops) which the Israelites took over. It was not long before the worship of God in these places became mixed with crude pagan practices. The later prophets condemned them.

Burnt offerings (4): for sacrifice generally, see on Leviticus 1 - 7.

3:16-28 Solomon the wise judge

We are given one example to illustrate Solomon's God-given gift. Where it is a case of one woman's word against another, special insight into human nature is needed to uncover the true facts. The incident shows the king's accessibility to ordinary folk, even two prostitutes.

4 State officials: arrangements for provisioning the court

Solomon's harem alone was enormous (11:3). His court – which included not only the royal family, but ministers, civil servants and domestics – must have numbered several thousand. No wonder elaborate arrangements are necessary for their maintenance (7-28).

The king outshone his greatest contemporaries in wisdom, which he expressed, as did, in proverbs and songs and sayings based on

natural and animal life (see, for example, Psalms 72 and 127, both of whose titles ascribe them to Solomon, and Proverbs 10:1 - 22:16).

Verses 1-6: Azariah was head of inland revenue, in charge of those who collected taxes (in kind). 'King's friend', i.e. king's councillor.

Every man under his vine ... (25): a proverbial phrase indicating idyllic conditions of peace and plenty.

5 The trade-pact with Hiram; work on the temple begun

Friendship with Tyre (see on 2 Samuel 5:11) is further cemented by the agreement that Hiram should supply raw materials for the temple in return for foodstuffs.

Cedars of Lebanon (6): the finest timber available. Few of these great trees remain today, but Lebanon was once densely forested.

Cor (11): a measurement of capacity. A cor of wheat: a donkey-load. A cor of oil: 48 gallons.

6 The building of the temple

In size the temple was a chapel rather than a cathedral. It was intended as a house for God, not a building to hold vast gatherings of people. It measured about 90ft long x 30ft wide x 45ft high, divided into two sections, with part of the inner section curtained off to form the sanctuary. In front was a 15ft entrance porch, and along the sides were store-rooms.

480th year (1): the exodus probably took place something over 300 years before Solomon built the temple. The figure here (12 x 40) may indicate twelve generations rather than a precise number of years.

Neither hammer nor axe was heard (7): even at this stage the place was regarded as holy. The stone was quarried close to the site, but so deep underground that no sound would carry.

7 Other building projects; cast bronze furnishings for the temple

Verses 1-12: Solomon builds the House of the Forest of Lebanon (possibly an armoury, see 10:17; Isaiah 22:8), the Hall of Pillars, Hall of Judgement, and palaces for himself and for pharaoh's daughter (his queen; it may also have housed the rest of the harem).

Verses 13-51: Hiram, the craftsman from Tyre, supervises the casting in bronze of two decorative pillars for the entrance to the temple (15-22); a huge bowl able to hold nearly 10,000 gallons of water (23-26); ten wheeled

THE TEMPLES
Alan Millard

In the journey through the wilderness, when the nation was living in tents, Israel had a 'tent' shrine, the tabernacle. The basic idea of a portable pavilion is attested in Egypt from before 2,000 BC. Surviving examples have a framework of wooden beams and rods, plated with precious metal and made with joints and sockets for easy erection. Ancient pictures show how they were once hung with curtains.

Israelite craftsmen trained in Egypt would have known how to make such a structure, and all the materials used were obtainable in Sinai, or already in their possession (the gold and silver, for example).

The tabernacle was built to a simple plan. A courtyard contained the two-roomed holy place, the altar for burnt offerings and the basin for ritual washings. The two rooms were about 15 feet wide. The inner one, the 'holiest place', was square; the outer about 30 feet long. After the conquest of Canaan, the tabernacle was moved from one place to another until Solomon laid it up in the temple.

It was David's great ambition to build a temple, though this was only realized by his son. It was natural for a powerful king to honour his God in this way, and the existing tabernacle provided the pattern for a simple central sanctuary. The hill-top David bought is the site now covered by the 'Maram es-Sherif', the Mosque of Omar, in Jerusalem. The central rocky crust was perhaps the site of the altar of burnt-offering.

The detailed descriptions in 1 Kings 6 - 7, and 2 Chronicles 3 - 4, give a fairly complete picture of the temple. This is supplemented by evidence from archaeological discovery. The tabernacle plan was extended by an entry porch, the resulting three rooms forming a scheme similar to some Canaanite temples (e.g. at Hazor and Ras Shamra). This may have been the work of the Phoenician builders whose skill Solomon utilized. A series of storage chambers three storeys high ran round the outside of the holiest place and the middle room (the 'holy place'). The doorway was flanked by two giant free-standing pillars whose function is uncertain.

Comparison with Ezekiel's temple suggests that the whole building stood on a platform above the level of the courtyard. An officiating priest would have crossed the courtyard, passing the great bronze altar for the sacrifices (about 33 feet square, 10 feet high) and the enormous bronze basin for water supported by twelve bronze bulls, before climbing the steps to the shrine. Apparently the porch had no doors; gates may have closed the passage, but he would have faced a pair of folding doors at the entrance to the 'holy place'. These were made of cypress wood, carved with flowers, palm-trees, and cherubim, and plated all over with gold, as was all the woodwork. In this room he would see the golden incense altar, the table for showbread, and five pairs of lampstands. Additional light came from a row of windows high in the wall. Beneath his feet was a golden floor. And if he could see into the 'holiest place' the whole room would have shone a dim gold in the light admitted through the doorway. But these doors were opened rarely, perhaps only for the annual Atonement ceremony. The decorative motifs are well known from Phoenician ivory-carvings and bronze-work of the centuries around Solomon's time. And Egyptian and Babylonian kings boast of ornamenting their temples with golden pavements, doors and furnishings.

Solomon's temple was destroyed by Nebuchadnezzar in 587 BC. Much of its glory had already been torn away and paid as tribute when foreign conquerors menaced Judah. The disconsolate exiles in Babylonia were heartened by Ezekiel's vision of a new temple (Ezekiel 40 - 43), described with minute attention, and including facts about the courtyard which hardly occur in the account of Solomon's work. This sanctuary was never built, but the exiles who returned about 537 BC, after some delay, completed the rebuilding of the old one in 515 BC. The little we know about it shows it followed the old design closely, however inferior its appearance. Nothing has survived from the first temple. But a length of stone walling above the Kidron Valley, on the east of the site, may be a part of the platform on which this second temple was erected, and which Herod incorporated into his walls.

The cosmopolitan nature of Jerusalem after the exile caused trouble to Nehemiah by bringing non-Jews into the sacred precinct (Nehemiah 13:4-9). It probably resulted in dividing off an outer courtyard from an inner one which only Jews could enter. This was certainly true of Herod's temple. Two stone blocks have been found inscribed with a warning to non-Jews that they passed in at their own risk (see also Acts 21:17ff.).

Herod's temple was the Idumaean king's attempt to curry favour with his Jewish subjects.

Most of it was built between 19 and 9 BC, although work continued until AD 64. The Romans destroyed it in AD 70. Parts of its massive substructure are still visible on the west (the 'Wailing Wall') and east sides, and some blocks from the parapets have been recovered in excavations.

Descriptions by the Jewish historian Josephus, and notes in rabbinic writings, supply us with information about this splendid building. The great courtyard was surrounded by a portico where schools were held, and business transacted (John 10:23; Luke 19:47; John 2:14-16). Beyond the barrier mentioned was the Women's Court where the money-boxes stood (Mark 12:41-44), then the Court of Israel, and finally the Priests' Court in which the altar and the temple proper stood. This last was a larger version of Solomon's design.

The 'holiest place', however, was empty, as in the second temple. The ark holding the terms of the covenant, upon whose covering lid (the 'mercy-seat') God had appeared, was no longer in existence. Significantly, the temple, too, disappeared with the establishment of the new covenant and the new Israel.

Stevens' reconstruction of King Solomon's temple.

stands to support more bowls (27-39), and numerous smaller items of equipment (40).

8 Dedication of the temple; Solomon's prayer

Work complete, the ark is brought from the citadel and installed in the inner sanctuary. And the whole building is filled with the glory of God's presence – the cloud that once rested on the tabernacle in the desert (Exodus 40:34-38).

Solomon's prayer, for the royal house (23-26) and for the nation (27-53), echoes the language of Moses. He asks that God will hear the prayers and forgive the sin of his people when they focus on the temple – even though no building on earth could ever contain the God of heaven.

Prayer is followed by blessing (54-61); blessing by sacrifice (62-64); sacrifice by feasting throughout the land (65; see on 2 Chronicles 7).

That my name might be there (16): God himself is present in a special sense in the temple, as he was in the tabernacle. But in contrast to the heathen temple, Israel's contained no statue to represent their God.

An oath (31): in which he solemnly swears his innocence.

9:1-9 God once again speaks to Solomon

He speaks in promise (3-5) and in warning (6-9).

As ... at Gibeon (2): when Solomon was given the gift of wisdom:3:3-14.

9:10-28 Trade and commerce; building and public works

For all his wealth, Solomon has his balance of trade problems. On this occasion (10-14) he makes 20 cities over to Hiram of Tyre as security against a loan.

Verses 15-22: the vast labour force needed for new building and defence works is raised from two sources. Native Canaanites provide permanent slave-labour. And the Israelites are pressed into short-term forced labour.

Verses 26-28: Solomon is the first of Israel's kings to create a merchant navy. His ships traded with Arabia and beyond.

Ophir (28): suggestions include South Arabia, East Africa, and even India.

10:1-13 The visit of the Queen of Sheba

Intriguing reports of Solomon's wisdom and splendour bring the queen from the Yemen to Jerusalem. Unlike the people of Christ's day (Matthew 12:42) this woman was prepared to undertake a long journey to find out for herself the truth of what she had heard.

Almug wood (11): possibly the red sandal-wood of Ceylon and India.

10:14-29 Solomon's wealth and power

Solomon's revenue through trade and taxed (including a lucrative tourist trade, 24-25) is enormous. But consumer spending more than keeps pace. The country's position made him a convenient middle-man for chariots from Egypt and horses from Turkey (Kue=Cilicia).

Talent (14): about 66lb/30kg. The purchasing-power of the bullion is not known.

Shekel (16): $\frac{1}{2}$oz/11.4gm.

Mina (17): $1\frac{1}{4}$lb/500gm.

Ships of Tarshish (21-22): large deep-sea cargo vessels.

11 Solomon's folly, and his enemies

Verses 1-13: Solomon's political marriage-alliances no doubt contribute to the country's peace and security. But foreign wives bring with them foreign gods. And Solomon in his old age turns from God to worship idols – a sin which costs his son the greater part of his kingdom and divides the nation.

Solomon's reign is not wholly trouble-free. In the south there is trouble from Hadad of Edom (14-22; a story reminiscent of Joseph's); in the north from Rezon of Damascus (23-25); and within his own nation there is Jeroboam (26-40), the man destined by God to rule over the ten break-away tribes after the king's death.

Ashtoreth, Milcom, Chemosh, Molech (5, 7): worship of these gods involved perverted and gruesome practices – child sacrifice, fertility rites, prostitution, sexual deviations.

One tribe (13): the southern state of Judah also included the much smaller tribe of Benjamin (12:21). The other ten tribes broke away to form the northern kingdom of Israel.

House of Joseph (28): the tribes of Ephraim and Manasseh.

Shilonite (29): from Shiloh, sanctuary-city of Israel in Eli's day.

Book of the acts of Solomon (41): otherwise unknown.

Verses 41-43: this formula, with slight variations, is repeated throughout Kings at the end of each reign.

12 - 14 THE KINGDOM SPLITS IN TWO

It was never easy to hold the twelve tribes together. Ephraim, in particular, envied Judah's power. A split had threatened in David's day (2 Samuel 20). The secret of national unity and strength always lay in the bond of common worship of the one God. The monarchy in itself was no substitute. Without the religious tie, king and people would go down together, as Samuel so clearly foresaw at Saul's coronation. 'If both you and the king ... will follow the Lord your God, it will be well; but if you ... rebel against the command-ment of the Lord, then the hand of the Lord will be against you and your king' (1 Samuel 12:14-15). The nation's history as recounted in Kings fully bears this out. The divi-sion is a direct consequence of Sol-omon's idolatry. And as Israel strays further and further from the law and worship of God, things go from bad to worse. Internal strife weakens both kingdoms. The nation becomes prey to stronger neighbours, and is eventually devoured by the great powers.

THE DIVISION OF THE KINGDOM

12:1-24 Rehoboam succeeds Solomon; the revolt

The northern tribes find a leader and spokesman in Jeroboam. But negotiations break down in face of Rehoboam's strong-arm tactics. The rebel tribes declare independence and set up the rival kingdom of Israel, but this kingdom never enjoyed the stability of a single dynasty as did Judah.

The division is permanent, with a constant state of hot or cold war between the kingdoms. Only in the reigns of Ahab-Ahaziah-Joram in Israel and Jehoshaphat-Joram-Ahaziah in Judah was the breach temporarily healed through a mar-riage alliance. And that resulted in the near-extinction of the royal house of Judah at the hands of Queen Athaliah.

Scorpions (11): barbed whips used on slaves.

Adoram (18): the Adoniram of 4:6; 5:14.

A hundred and eighty thousand (21): the figure seems too high. See article 'The Large Numbers of the Old Testament'.

12:25-33 Jeroboam king in Israel; a new capital and new religious centres

Jerusalem had been the religious centre of the united kingdom. Jer-oboam now creates two new sanc-tuaries for the northern kingdom to counter its draw and prevent the people from going to Jerusalem and coming under the influence of the king of Judah. But his action encour-aged idolatry, and as time went by Israelite worship became more and more degenerate.

13 The man of God and the prophet

The man of God is wrong to accept the prophet's word when it contra-dicts God's own word to him. His death is a sign to Jeroboam and Israel of the severity with which God deals with disobedience. But there are none so blind as those who will not see (33).

Josiah (2): the king who initiated the most thoroughgoing reform in Judah. See 2 Kings 23.

Dried up (4): paralysed.

A lion (24): lions roamed Palestine, particularly the Jordan Valley, until the Middle Ages. Here the strange sight of the lion standing by its prey but leaving both the body and the ass untouched marks the event as having special significance. It is a 'sign' to Israel.

14:1-20 Ahijah's prophecy against Jeroboam

Ahijah had predicted Jeroboam's rise (11:29ff.). Now he announces his downfall.

He only ... shall come to the grave (13): meaning that all the rest will die violently.

Scatter them beyond the Euphrates (15): Israel was taken into exile by Assyria after the fall of Samaria (2 Kings 17).

Tirzah (17): capital of Israel in Baasha's day (15:33).

Book of the Chronicles ... (19): not the same as Chronicles in the Bible.

14:21-31 Rehoboam's reign in Judah

The southern kingdom also turns back to pagan gods. The weakened state loses the temple treasures to the invading Egyptian pharaoh. See 2 Chronicles 12:1-12.

Shishak (25): Sheshonq, Libyan founder of the Egyptian 22nd dynasty. He left a record of his campaign carved on a temple in Karnak, Egypt.

This bracelet could well have been made from gold plundered from the temple. It belonged to Nemoreth, son of the Pharaoh Shishak who defeated Rehoboam and stripped the temple of gold.

15 - 16:28 KINGS OF ISRAEL AND JUDAH

The dates for the kings of Judah in this section include a number of periods of co-regency between one king and his predecessor. Almost all the dates given can only be approximate. See articel 'Unravelling the Chronology of the Kings'.

15:1-24 Abijam and Asa of Judah

The writer of Kings defines a good king as one who promotes the worship of God; a bad king as one who strays into idolatrous practices. On this definition, Abijam's three-year reign (about 913-911) was a bad one (see 2 Chronicles 13). Asa, by contrast, was a good king. He ruled for

41 years, about 911-870. The war with Israel continued but he made an alliance with Syria. See 2 Chronicles 15-16.

The matter of Uriah the Hittite (5): see 2 Samuel 11.

Maacah (10, 13): Asa's grandmother.

Ramah (17): Only a few miles north of Jerusalem.

15:25 - 16:28 Kings of Israel

All Israel's kings were automatically bad by the writer's definition, though some were worse than others. After ruling for two years (910-909) Nadab (15:25-32) was murdered by Baasha.

15:33 – 16:7 Baasha introduces a new dynasty and rules Israel for 24 years, about 909-886.

16:8-14: his successor, Elah, rules for two years (886-885) before his assassination by Zimri.

16:15-20: Zimri introduces a short-lived new dynasty (885) and commits suicide when under siege by Omri.

16:21-28: although only briefly mentioned here, Omri was one of Israel's most powerful kings politically. He introduces a new dynasty and rules for 12 years, about 885-874, fortifying Samaria as his new capital. For 150 years from this time, Assyria refers to Israel as 'the land of Omri'.

According to the word of the Lord (15:29): see 14:6-16.

Jehu (16:1): a prophet, not the later king.

16:29 - 2 KINGS 1, KING AHAB AND THE PROPHET ELIJAH

Religious life in Israel reached an all-time low in Ahab's 22-year reign. He and his thoroughly evil wife, Jezebel of Tyre, introduced the corrupt worship of the Phoenician god Melqart

One of the famous ivory carvings from Samaria. This winged creature is typical of decoration from the period of King Ahab.

(the 'Baal' of these chapters). Into this crisis situation God sent Elijah, the greatest of all the prophets (see Matthew 17:3 and 10-13).

16:29-34 Ahab of Israel 874-853
Verse 34: see Joshua 6:26.

17 Elijah predicts drought; the widow of Zarephath
Baal was worshipped as a weather-god. God therefore stages a demonstration to show that he alone has power over sun and rain. And he provides for Elijah in Baal's own country, at Zarephath near Sidon!
Verse 21: Elijah may have used the 'kiss of life'; but the cure was the result of his prayer, not just a particular method of resuscitation.

ELIJAH'S JOURNEYS

Zarephath

Mt Carmel

Jezreel

Cherith Brook

Tishbe

Samaria

Beersheba

To Sinai

The contest with the prophets of Baal on Carmel challenged them on their own ground: Baal as a weather-god is shown here holding axe and thunderbolt; 8th century BC, from Syria.

18 The contest with the prophets of Baal on Mt Carmel
After three years, in which Jezebel has done her best to eliminate the worship of God in Israel (4), Elijah returns with a challenge. Baal should have been able to produce fire as

readily as rain. But the result of the contest provides tangible evidence that God is God, and Baal is impotent. Even so, there was no deep and lasting religious reform.
He ... ran before Ahab (46): 17 miles to the summer palace at Jezreel.

19 The escape to Sinai; Elisha's call
Elation passes. Spiritual and physical strain leave Elijah in the grip of depression, fear, disappointment. Jezebel still holds the whip hand. Elijah escapes south to the desert and Sinai (Mt Horeb). In the place where God made himself known to Moses, he speaks to Elijah, out of the stillness. Self-pity is dealt with, a sense of proportion restored, and the path ahead mapped out. Elijah had felt himself intolerably alone, his work finished. He is given a companion and successor, Elisha. God's work goes on.
Anoint Hazael ... and Jehu ... and Elisha (15-16): Elisha is 'anointed', called to become a prophet, by Elijah's symbolic action in throwing his

cloak around him. But Elijah leaves the anointing of Hazael and Jehu to Elisha (2 Kings 8-9).

20 War between Israel and Syria Benhadad of Syria and the allied kings of 32 city-states attack Samaria. The diplomatic exchange (2-9) is difficult to follow. But Benhadad has to eat his words in face of Israel's double victory. Ahab spares his life, but in doing so stores up trouble for Israel. (Israel and Syria fought as allies against Shalmaneser III of Assyria at Qarqar in 853, but later fell out – see 22:1-2.)

All ... Israel, seven thousand (15): presumably representatives of all Israel.

WARS WITH SYRIA

SYRIA

1st Syrian attack on Israel

2nd Syrian attack

• Israel defeats Syrians at Aphek

• Jezreel

Ramoth-gilead

Samaria •

ISRAEL

Ahab and Jehoshaphat set out to take Ramoth-gilead but are defeated by the Syrians. (1 Kings 22)

• Jerusalem

JUDAH

100,000 ... 27,000 (29-30): the figures seem exaggeratedly high. See article 'The Large Numbers of the Old Testament'.

My father ... your father (34): meaning ancestor, not actual father.

21 Ahab takes Naboth's vineyard; Elijah pronounces judgement Seizure or compulsory purchase of land was illegal in Israel. A man's heritage had to be handed on to the next generation. But other people's rights do not bother Jezebel. While

her husband sulks like a spoilt child, she quietly arranges for Naboth's liquidation. She has only to contrive a blasphemy charge – backed of course by the statutory number of witnesses – and the 'criminal's' lands are forfeit. Elijah, the old prophet of doom, is the only fly in the ointment. But Elijah speaks true (see 22:37; 2 Kings 9:30-37).

22:1-40 The alliance with Judah; Micaiah's prophecy; Ahab's death See also 2 Chronicles 18. Jehoshaphat's son Jehoram has married Ahab's daughter Athaliah. Israel and Judah are, temporarily, allies against Syria. It is Jehoshaphat's request which brings Micaiah to the king with his fateful prophecy. The warning is ignored, and Ahab meets his death in battle at Ramoth-gilead, east of the Jordan. (For true and false prophets, see on 2 Chronicles 18.)

22:41-50 Jehoshaphat of Judah 873-848 See 2 Chronicles 17-20. Jehoshaphat was a 'good' king. He reigned 25 years.

Verse 48: see on chapters 9 and 10. The strong north winds may have blown the fleet on to the rocks.

22:51 - 2 Kings 1, Ahaziah of Israel 853-852 Ahaziah reigned two years during which time Moab seized independence. Ahaziah consults the Philistine god after a fall and Elijah pronounces God's judgement on his idolatry. It takes three military posses to bring Elijah to the king. But nothing can alter the sentence.

Baalzebub (3): 'Lord of the flies', a derogatory pun on the god's real name, Baalzebul.

2 - 8:15 STORIES OF ELISHA
2 Elijah's dramatic exit Elijah seems to want to face this last experience alone. But Elisha stays with him right through the journey. The final scene – the whirlwind which catches up the prophet, and Elisha's vision of a fiery chariot and horses – is played out east of the Jordan, close to the place where Moses died. It is a remarkable end to a remarkable life. Elijah's reappearance at the transfiguration of Jesus (Matthew 17) underlines the unique position of this man amongst all the prophets of God. Elisha, left alone, takes up his task straight away.

Sons of the prophets (3): groups possessing ecstatic gifts; not always men of high spiritual calibre.

UNRAVELLING THE CHRONOLOGY OF THE KINGS

Arthur Cundall

At first glance there seems to be quite enough data on the kings of Israel and Judah to construct an accurate time-chart.

The reign of each king is clearly given (except for Saul: 1 Samuel 13:1 is uncertain); and during the period after the split between Israel and Judah, the accession of each king is related to the reign of the king in the other kingdom.

There are also 'check-points', where one event simultaneously affected both kingdoms, such as Jehu's slaying of Joram of Israel and Ahaziah of Judah on the same day (2 Kings 9:21-28). The historian has carefully integrated the chronologies of the two kingdoms. He keeps both histories parallel by dealing with the whole reign of one king from his accession until his death, and then returning to deal with the kings of the other kingdom whose reigns *began* during this period. The only exception is in 2 Kings 8-9 where Jehu's murder of Joram and Ahaziah made it necessary for the historian to mention Jehoram and Ahaziah of Judah (2 Kings 8:16-29), who would not normally have been dealt with until after the death of Joram of Israel.

Problems

However, serious problems arise on closer inspection. For instance, in Judah, the total from Rehoboam to Ahaziah's death is 95 years, whereas the identical period of Israel, from Jeroboam to Joram's death, totals 98 years.

A greater discrepancy appears in the period from Jehu's coup to the fall of Samaria. There the combined total for Judah's kings is 165 years and that for Israel is only 144 years. A further minor problem is that although we are told Queen Athaliah the usurper reigned for six years (2 Kings 11:3), she was not included in the normal chronological scheme.

We have another headache in the apparently conflicting dates for the accession of Jehoram of Israel (2 Kings 1:17 and 3:1). It is reasonably certain that Solomon's death cannot have been earlier than 930 BC, which makes the period between this event and the fall of Jerusalem in 587 BC about 343 years. But the lowest total we can set to the biblical figures supplied for this period is about 372 years.

Clues

Three factors, however, greatly increase our understanding of the apparent problems of the chronology of the period and go a long way towards resolving them completely.

Two different methods of reckoning the reigns of the kings were used in the ancient Near East. One was the 'non-accession-year' method, the other the 'accession-year' method.

In the non-accession-year (or ante-dating) system the death of a king meant that a year was counted twice, since the portion of the year falling to the king who died was counted as a full year to him, whilst the remainder of the year was counted as a full year to his successor. To reduce this system to an accurate chronological reckoning, one year must be deducted for each king who reigned.

The accession-year (or post-dating) system did not count any *portion* of a year in the total years of a king's reign. The portion of the year falling to a king *before* his first, full calendar-year, was regarded as his accession year. This system allowed for an accurate chronological reckoning.

It is clear that, in the early period of the divided monarchy Israel used the first method and Judah the second. The discrepancy in totals between the two kingdoms corresponds to the greater number of Israelite kings in this period. A possible further complication is evidence suggesting that the year in Judah (in the earlier part of the period at any rate) began in the month of Tishri (September/ October), whilst the year in Israel began in the month Nisan (March/ April).

Some reigns overlap because of the practice of co-regencies. The precedent for this is found in the case of David and Solomon, which effectively prevented Adonijah seizing power (1 Kings 1). Another clear instance is the case of Jotham, who acted as co-regent when his father Uzziah was smitten with leprosy (2 Chronicles 26:21). No doubt this practice, which appears to have been confined to Judah, lent stability to David's dynasty.

Most scholars accept co-regencies between Asa and Jehoshaphat, Jehoshaphat and Jehoram, Amaziah and Uzziah, Jotham and Ahaz, Ahaz and Hezekiah, and Hezekiah and Manasseh. In certain cases the younger man (for example, Hezekiah) outshone his father (Ahaz) and this led to events being dated by reference to the co-regent rather than to the actual reign (e.g. 2 Kings 18:9-10).

An awareness of this custom means a reduction of the over-all total of the reigns of Judean kings, and also helps us to understand the significance of the biblical figures. For example, Manasseh of Judah reigned from 687 to 642 BC. 2 Kings 21:1 says he reigned for 55 years, which leads us to assume a co-regency from 697 to 687, made the more plausible by Hezekiah's severe illness (2 Kings 20:1).

Some reigns may have taken place at the same time as each other. This is probably what happened in the northern kingdom of Israel during the last turbulent decades after the death of Jeroboam II. The combined reigns of the six kings of this period is 41 years 7 months, whereas historically the period cannot have been more than 31 years; indeed, most scholars hold that it was only about 24 years. The probability is that, in a period of near-anarchy, there were occasions when rival kings were 'ruling' over different parts of the kingdom at the same time.

External checks

By a careful application of these factors, the chronologies of Judah and Israel can be integrated. But the process of relating the resultant chronology to the events of the surrounding world, to obtain an absolute rather than a relative chronology, has been made possible largely by archaeological discovery. The most significant finds are as follows:

The Assyrian Limmu or Eponym lists. In Assyria an official holding annual office gave his name to that particular year. Remarkably complete lists of these officials have survived covering the period 892-648 BC, and significant events during their period of office were noted down. An eclipse of the sun is mentioned in the month Simanu when Bur-Sagale was *Limmu*, which astronomers have fixed as occurring on 15 June 763 BC. This provides a reliable basis for determining all other dates in the *Limmu* lists. Since biblical and Assyrian histories converge at various points, biblical events can also be dated accurately.

The Khorsabad king list. This, and duplicate copies, gives a complete list of Assyrian kings until 745 BC, often including the length of their reigns. This list agrees with the *Limmu* list.

The Canon of Ptolemy. Although this work dates from the 2nd century AD, its accuracy has been demonstrated beyond any reasonable doubt. It preserves the names and lengths of reign of the Babylonian kings from the accession of Nabonassar in 747 BC.

The Babylonian Chronicle. These tablets, some only recently published, deal with Babylonian history during the period from Hezekiah to the fall of Jerusalem. They are of special interest to biblical scholars for the period when Judah was subject to Babylon, i.e. after 605 BC. Many facts which before were not clear have now been resolved. For instance, it was not known what encouraged the Judean king, Jehoiakim, to rebel against the Babylonians in 601/600 BC, or why the revolt was not put down until 598/597 BC. The Babylonian Chronicle tells us that in November/December 601 BC there was a fierce encounter between Babylonia and Egypt on the borders of Egypt. Although the battle was indecisive, Babylonian losses were great and meant a withdrawal from the area and a regrouping of the army. It was this apparent weakness which led Jehoiakim to rebel. The Chronicle gives the only exact date for an event in Old Testament history, the capture of Jerusalem on 15-16 March 597 BC.

One minor problem remains. It is not certain whether the Hebrew civil year uniformly followed the Babylonian pattern. This makes for an uncertainty of one year in dates during the reign of Zedekiah, the last king of Judah. The fall of Jerusalem, for example, is given as either 587 or 586 BC. The two modes of reckoning appear in Jeremiah 52:12 and 29, where, on first sight, the prisoners were taken from Jerusalem a year before it was captured!

A bronze cast of the original Seal of Shema, which is inscribed: '(belonging) to Shema, Servant of Jeroboam'.

Numerous contemporary inscriptions also relate to particular events: such as the battle of Qarqar in 853 BC, fought between Assyria and a coalition of small states including Israel under King Ahab; or Jehu's payment of tribute to the Assyrian king, Shalmaneser III in 841 BC; or the fall of Samaria to the Assyrians in 722/721 BC. These records supply reliable pegs on which to hang the biblical information.

By carefully applying the principles underlying the biblical chronologies, and correlating them with the fixed chronology made possible by contacts between Judah and Israel and contemporary world-powers, we can establish an absolute chronology, including all the biblical data, which is accurate to within a year for the greater part of the period of the kings. The reign of Saul remains an exception. The 40 years given in Acts 13:21 is probably a round figure, and seems to be too high. Since '2' is the only figure remaining in the Hebrew text, most scholars accept that a tens-unit has dropped out and suggest a reign of 12, 22 or 32 years. Twenty-two is probably the most acceptable since it fits in best with the other chronological data, such as the period of the Judges.

ELISHA'S JOURNEYS

SYRIA

△ Mt Carmel

Shunem •
Jezreel • 3

4

Samaria • 2

Gilgal

Bethel • Jericho 1

Jerusalem

MOAB

EDOM

1 Elisha goes to
Mt Carmel and
on to Samaria

2 Elisha and the
march against
Mesha of Moab

3 Elisha and the
woman from
Shunem

4 Elisha meets
Hazael of
Damascus

A double share (9): i.e. the portion which fell to the heir, the eldest son, who inherited twice as much as anyone else. So Elisha asks, not for twice Elijah's spiritual power, but for the share which would mark him out as the prophet's spiritual heir.

Chariots of Israel ... (12): meaning that Elijah was of more value to the nation than its armed forces.

Some small boys (23): young men – local louts, yelling abuse at the prophet and his God, telling him to 'Go up' like Elijah.

3 Jehoram of Israel, 852-841, and the Moabites

Jehoram reigned 12 years. A punitive expedition against Moab by the allied forces of Israel, Judah and Edom is made hazardous by drought. Elisha, his faculties stimulated by music (a common prophetic custom), promises an end to the drought, and victory.

Who poured water (11): i.e. who served Elijah.

There came great wrath (27): the sacrifice of the king's son so heartened the Moabites, or so terrified the Israelites, that the advance was halted.

4 Four of Elisha's miracles

Elisha's miracles, like the Lord's, show God's care for ordinary people and their needs. Verses 1-7: the

widow whose children were to become slaves to discharge her debts; 8-37 the childless woman of Shunem who gave Elisha generous hospitality; 38-41 and 42-44 the feeding of the hungry. These are not necessarily recounted in chronological order.

Oh, my head ... (19): the child had sun-stroke.

Neither new moon nor sabbath (23): special times of religious observance when it would be natural to visit a holy man. The woman did not tell her husband the child was dead.

Wild gourds (39): in the famine one man gathered colocynths, a powerful laxative, bitter and poisonous in large quantities.

Bread of the firstfruits (42): the offering normally made to the priests at the beginning of the harvest.

5 The healing of Naaman the leper

God's concern is not limited to Israel (see Luke 4:27; Syria was often at war with Israel, and Naaman was the army commander). A young Israelite slave-girl, captured in a border raid, tells her Syrian master of Elisha's power. A visit is arranged through diplomatic channels. The prophet's instructions are not what Naaman expected. But his staff persuade him to try, and he is healed. Deeply impressed by the cure and Elisha's refusal of payment, the army chief of Syria becomes a follower of the God of Israel. Gehazi's greed might have undone it all, and could not go unpunished.

Talents, shekels (5): there were no coins as yet; these were weights: see on 1 Kings 10.

Two mules' burden of earth (17): he took soil from the land of Israel's God so that he could worship him in his own land, not realizing his character as God of the whole world.

6:1-23 Elisha and the Syrian army

Verses 1-7: the floating axe-head. The thick woods of the Jordan Valley provide a ready source of timber for the new community building needed by the prophets. Elisha's miracle was simply an act of disinterested kindness.

Verses 8-23: God's people are under his protection, and this is a very real thing. Elisha seemed at the mercy of the Syrian army. In fact he has them in the palm of his hand – and shows *them* mercy.

Dothan (13): ten miles north of Samaria.

6:24 - 7:20 The siege of Samaria

The peace secured by Elisha (23) did

not last for ever. Samaria is besieged by the Syrians and reduced to starvation and cannibalism. The king blames Elisha for telling him to hold out and promising deliverance (33). The lepers, who depended on gifts of food, are worse off than most. Their desperate hunger makes them the first to discover the truth of Elisha's prediction. The Syrian army fled at the approach, so they thought, of a relief force.

6:25: the ass was an 'unclean' animal, forbidden food; dove's dung, some kind of weed. In the famine, both fetched astronomical prices.

8:1-15 Elisha and Hazael of Damascus

Verses 1-6 belong in time after 4:8-37 and before Gehazi's leprosy, 5:25-27.

Verses 7-15: Elisha fulfils God's commission to Elijah (1 Kings 19:15). Hazael, like Macbeth, resorts to murder to turn prediction into fact and seize the throne.

8:16 - 17:41 KINGS OF ISRAEL AND JUDAH TO THE FALL OF SAMARIA

The writer returns to the history of the kings which has been interrupted by the stories of Elisha.

8:16-24 Jehoram of Judah 853-841

Jehoram was a 'bad' king, influenced by his wife Athaliah, daughter of Ahab and Jezebel. He reigned eight years plus a co-regency, during which time successful revolts by Edom (to the south-east) and Libnah (on the Philistine border, south-west) crippled Judah. See 2 Chronicles 21.

8:25-29 Ahaziah of Judah 841

Ahaziah was another king who turned from God and went his own way. He reigned only one year. See 2 Chronicles 22.

9 Jehu anointed king of Israel (841-814); death of King Joram and Jezebel, the queen mother

Elisha carries out the last of Elijah's commissions (1 Kings 19:16) while the armies of Israel and Judah are defending Ramoth-gilead against Syria. With the king conveniently recovering from his wounds at Jezreel, 35 miles away, the time is ripe for Jehu's coup.

This mad fellow (11): the man's ecstatic state enables the army officers to recognize him as a prophet.

The property of Naboth (21): the vineyard seized by Ahab, 1 Kings 21.

Verse 26: see 1 Kings 21:19.

She painted her eyes (30): women's make-up, even in those days, was

THE BLACK OBELISK

Shalmaneser III erected an obelisk in honour of his own victories. It includes a panel which reads:

The tribute of Jehu, son of Omri. Silver, gold, a golden bowl, a golden vase, golden cups, golden buckets, tin, a staff for the royal hand (?), puruhati-fruits.

The scene from the Black Obelisk which specifically mentioned Jehu. The king is shown bowing before Shalmaneser.

sophisticated: black kohl to outline the eyes; blue eye-shadow from lapis lazuli; crushed cochineal to serve as lipstick; and scarlet henna to paint finger- and toe-nails. There were also powders, and an array of perfumes and ointments.

You Zimri ... (31): King Elah's assassin, 1 Kings 16:8-10.

The word of the Lord ... by ... Elijah (36): 1 Kings 21:23.

10 Jehu's purge

Jehu's reign opens with a blood-bath in which all Ahab's family (1-11), many of the royal house of Judah (12-14), and the prophets, priests and worshippers of Baal (18-27) lose their lives. Objects connected with Baal-worship are destroyed. But Jeroboam's shrines at Bethel and Dan are left and God's law neglected. Jehu reigned 28 years, starting a new dynasty. During his reign, territory east of Jordan was lost to Syria.

11:1-20 Queen Athaliah of Judah 841-835

Athaliah reigned six years. See 2 Chronicles 22:10 - 23:21. These are some of the darkest days in the nation's history. The royal line of David is all but wiped out; only the baby Joash survives. The priest Jehoiada (husband of princess Jehosheba, who rescued Joash) leads the well-planned and virtually bloodless coup which puts Joash on the throne. The constitutional monarchy is restored, and loyalty to God reaffirmed in the swearing of a new covenant-pact.

11:21 - 12:21 Joash of Judah 835-796; the temple repaired
Joash was one of Judah's best kings, ruling for 40 years. See 2 Chronicles 24. Under Jehoiada's guidance Joash rules well. But for some years money intended for temple repairs gets no further than the priests. A new method of collection is devised and the work put in hand. Funds come from tax (2 Chronicles 24:6; Exodus 30:11-16) and freewill offerings. Joash's later years see a decline in political (17ff.), moral and religious spheres (2 Chronicles 24:17ff.). Syria makes inroads into Judah and threatens Jerusalem. The king dies at the hands of his servants.

13:1-9 Jehoahaz of Israel 814-798
Jehoahaz reigned 17 years during which time Israel fell under Syrian domination.
A saviour (5): various suggestions have been made: Adad-nirari of Assyria, who took tribute from Damascus and from Jehoash of Israel; Jeroboam II; Elisha.
Verse 7: contrast Ahab's 2,000 chariots.

13:10-25 Jehoash of Israel 798-782
Jehoash reigned 16 years. There was war with Judah. Elisha's last prediction of victory over Syria is realized. The prophet dies.
Chariots of Israel (14): see on 2:12.

14:1-22 Amaziah of Judah 796-767
Amaziah was a 'good' king who reigned 29 years. See 2 Chronicles 25. Victory over Edom goes to his head. The disastrous challenge to Jehoash brings the forces of Israel right into Jerusalem, looting the temple and other treasures. The people make Azariah co-regent. A further conspiracy against Amaziah ends in his death at Lachish.
In the book of the law (6): Deuteronomy 24:16.
Valley of Salt (7): the area south of the Dead Sea.
A thistle on Lebanon (9): Joash replies in sneering parable to Amaziah's fool-hardy challenge to battle.
Elath (22): Ezion-geber on the Gulf of Aqabah, naval base of Solomon's

Red Sea fleet. The port fell into the hands of the Edomites but was recovered by Amaziah's victory.

14:23-29 Jeroboam II of Israel 793-753
Jeroboam II ruled for 41 years, including a time as co-regent. He was politically strong, dominating the land from north of Lebanon (Hamath) to the Dead Sea (Sea of Arabah). He defeated a weakened Syria.
Jeroboam's reign is Israel's Indian summer. After his death the nation falls apart. Amos (2:6ff.) and Hosea reveal the corruption within Israel: extremes of wealth and poverty: the grinding down of the poor and the weak.
How he ... are they not written (28): the meaning of the text is not clear.

15:1-7 Azariah (Uzziah) of Judah 791-740
Azariah, a 'good' king, reigned 52 years, including a time as co-regent. See 2 Chronicles 26. Azariah was a strong king who defeated the Philistines and Arabs and reduced Ammon to a vassal state. But pride brought him to an unpleasant end (5; 2 Chronicles 26:16ff.).

15:8-31 The succession in Israel 753-732
Verses 8-12: Zechariah son of Jeroboam rules six months and is assassinated by Shallum, 753-752.
    Verses 13-16: Shallum rules only one month before his assassination by Menahem.
    Verses 17-22: Menahem introduces another new dynasty, rules 10 years (752-742) and becomes vassal to the powerful Tiglath-pileser III (Pul) of Assyria.
    Verses 23-26: Pekahiah son of Menahem rules two years and is overthrown by an army coup led by Pekah, 740.
    Verses 27-31: Pekah introduces a new dynasty and rules 20 years, dating his reign from Menahem's accession, 752-732. His anti-Assyrian policy leads to mass deportation of the people by Tiglath-pileser. He is assassinated by Hoshea.

15:32-38 Jotham of Judah 750-732
Jotham was a godly king. During his 16-year reign (and co-regency) he encountered opposition from Syria and Israel.

16 Ahaz of Judah 735-716
Ahaz was one of Judah's worst kings. See 2 Chronicles 28; Isaiah 7. During his 16-year reign and co-regency Judah was under attack from all quarters: Syria and Israel to the

King Tiglath-pileser III, depicted on the palace walls at Nimrud.

north; Edom and Philistia to the south. The temple was stripped of silver and gold to pay the heavy tribute demanded by Assyria in return for help. Some of Isaiah's prophecies date from this time.

17 Hoshea, last king of Israel, 732-723; Samaria falls to Assyria
Hoshea reigned nine years as Assyria's vassal. An attempt to win Egyptian support proved fatal. Samaria fell after a three-year siege, and the whole remaining population was deported. Israel's fate is seen as the direct consequence of long-standing idolatry, of pursuing heathen practices, disobeying the law, and ignoring the prophets (7-18).

Assyria repopulated the land with other conquered peoples, each with its own religion. But troubles are attributed to their failure to placate the local god, and an Israelite priest is sent back as a missionary. From this strange hotch-potch of religions a purer form of worship emerged amongst their descendants, the Samaritans.

Verse 6: the people were deported to north and east Mesopotamia (Halah, Gozan, Media): i.e. north-east Syria/Turkey and Iran.

18 - 25 KINGS OF JUDAH TO THE FALL OF JERUSALEM

18:1-12 Hezekiah's reign begins
Hezekiah was one of Judah's finest kings, and ruled for 29 years plus a co-regency, 729-687. See 2 Chronicles 29-32.

The bronze serpent (4): see Numbers 21:4-9. This goes to show how easily an object which is innocent in itself can be misused once it has served its purpose.

18:13-37 Sennacherib attacks Jerusalem
Eight years after the fall of Samaria,

the Assyrians turn their attention to rebel Judah. Lachish, in the lowlands 30 miles south-west of Jerusalem, is besieged, and messengers sent to Hezekiah. The three Assyrians (the 'Tartan', commander-in-chief of the army; 'Rabsaris', high military official; 'Rabshakeh', probably high civil dignitary) are masters of psychological warfare. They refuse private talks with Hezekiah's cabinet, and insist on a public harangue. And they play on the people's fears by speak-

An Assyrian soldier, from the palace of Sargon II. He wears a curled beard, and carries a quiver and bow, sword and heavy club.

ing Hebrew – not the diplomatic language, Aramaic – so that everyone understands. But their boast that God cannot save Judah from Assyria seals their fate.

19 Hezekiah consults Isaiah; death in the Assyrian camp
See Isaiah 36-39; 2 Chronicles 32:9-23. Crisis brings out the best in the king. God answers his prayer and vindicates his trust. Isaiah's prophecy is fulfilled. Jerusalem is saved.

Isaiah (2): one of the great prophets

SENNACHERIB'S PRISM

Sennacherib's own views about the siege of Jerusalem may be read on this hexagonal clay prism, inscribed with the details of his eight campaigns. It is also known as the 'Taylor Prism', and stands 15in/375mm high.

But as for Hezekiah, the Jew, who did not bow in submission to my yoke, forty-six of his strong walled towns and innumerable smaller villages in their neighbourhood I

besieged and conquered by stamping down earth-ramps and then by bringing up battering rams, by the assault of foot-soldiers, by breaches, tunnelling and sapper operations. I made to come out from them 200,150 people, young and old, male and female, innumerable horses, mules, donkeys, camels, large and small cattle, and counted them as the spoils of war. He himself I shut up like a caged bird within Jerusalem, his royal city. I put watch-posts strictly around it and turned back to his disaster any who went out of its city gate. His towns which I had despoiled I cut off from his land, giving them to Mitinti, king of Ashdod, Padi, king of Ekron, and Sillibel, king of Gaza, and so reduced his land. Moreover, I fixed upon him an increase in the amount to be given as katre-presents for my lordship, in addition to the former tribute, to be given annually. As for Hezekiah, the awful splendour of my lordship overwhelmed him, and the irregular and regular troops which he had brought in to strengthen Jerusalem, his royal city, and had obtained for his protection, together with 30 talents of gold, 300 talents of silver, precious stones, antimony, large blocks of red stone, ivory (inlaid) couches, ivory arm-chairs, elephant hide, elephant tusks, ebony-wood, box-wood, all kinds of valuable treasures, as well as his daughters, concubines, male and female musicians he sent me later to Nineveh, my lordly city. He sent a personal messenger to deliver the tribute and make a slavish obeisance.

of Judah. According to Isaiah 1:1 he prophesied during the reigns of Uzziah, Jotham, Ahaz and Hezekiah. His home was in Jerusalem. See further under the book of Isaiah.

Libnah (8): ten miles north of Lachish.

Tirhakah (9): Pharaoh Taharqa, of Ethiopian descent; in charge of the army, but not yet on the throne.

Gozan (12): in north-east Syria; *Eden:* the Aramaean city-state of Bit-Adini on the Euphrates.

My hook (28): God will lead them meekly captive as a man leads a bull or a horse. The Assyrians drove rings

through the noses of captive kings.

The angel of the Lord went forth (35): it is not clear what happened, possibly an outbreak of bubonic plague. See 2 Chronicles 32:21; Isaiah 37:36.

20 Hezekiah's illness; the embassy from Babylon

Verses 1-11: to men of the Old Testament hope of life after death was vague. The prospect of death fills Hezekiah with distress (see also his poem, recorded in Isaiah 38:9-20).

Verses 12-21: Babylon at this time was a small state south of Assyria, looking for allies. Isaiah predicts its future power, and the fate of Judah.

A cake of figs (7): a fig poultice was routine treatment for ulcers and boils.

Verse 11: 'made the shadow go back ten steps on the steps of Ahaz' (Jerusalem Bible; similarly New English Bible) – a staircase used as a form of sundial.

21:1-18 Manasseh 696-642

Manasseh was Judah's Ahab. He reigned 55 years, part of the time as co-regent, and brought Judah to the point of no return; a degradation worse than that of the Canaanite nations the Israelites had destroyed. The prophets declare God's inevitable judgement. Jerusalem will share the fate of Samaria. See also 2 Chronicles 33, which records a complete change of heart before the end of Manasseh's life (33:10-13).

21:19-26 Amon 642-640

Amon was another evil king. After ruling two years he was assassinated by his own house servants. See 2 Chronicles 33:21-25.

22 Josiah 640-609; Hilkiah discovers the book of the law

Josiah reigned 31 years. He was the best of Judah's kings, carrying out thorough-going religious reform. See 2 Chronicles 34-35. A book of the law (probably a copy of Deuteronomy) is found in the course of repairing the temple. Reading it shows just how far short of the standards Judah has fallen – and the penalty.

23:1-30 Josiah's reformation

Public reading of God's law is followed by renewal of the covenant-pact with God (1-3). Then comes a purge of public places, ridding the land of objects associated with pagan worship (4-14). The clean-up extends beyond Judah to former Israelite territory (15-20). The neglected Feast of Passover is celebrated once more (21-23; see 2 Chronicles 35), and private malpractices dealt with (24-25). God's judgement is delayed but not reversed: the nation's heart is not changed by an official reformation. Josiah dies in futile conflict with Pharaoh Necho, who was marching to join forces with Assyria, after the Assyrian capital (Nineveh) had fallen to the Babylonians.

23:31-35 Jehoahaz 609

Jehoahaz was on the throne for an evil reign of three months. Then he was deported to Egypt by Necho. See 2 Chronicles 36:1-4.

23:36 - 24:7 Jehoiakim 609-597

Josiah's son Eliakim, renamed Jehoiakim as a sign of his subjection, was put on the throne by Pharaoh Necho. He ruled for 11 years. At first subject to Egypt, Jehoiakim became Babylon's subject after Egypt was defeated at Carchemish in 605. Judah remained a vassal of Nebuchadnezzar for three years, then defected to Egypt again. This brought more attacks from the Babylonians, and repeated warnings from the prophet Jeremiah. See also 2 Chronicles 36:5-8.

24:8-17 Jehoiachin 597

Jehoiakim's son, Jehoiachin, was removed from the throne after three months by Nebuchadnezzar. He was taken to Babylon with the treasures of Jerusalem and all the leading men of Judah.

24:18 - 25:30 Zedekiah 597-587; the destruction of Jerusalem

See also 2 Chronicles 36:11-21; Jeremiah 37-39. The new puppet king also rebels. Jerusalem suffers a terrible 18-month siege. Zedekiah attempts to escape south but is caught and taken to Babylon. The city falls to the Babylonian army, is looted and utterly destroyed. All but the poorest people, left under the governor, Gedaliah, are taken into exile. But Gedaliah is murdered and the people escape to Egypt to avoid the inevitable wrath of Babylon. 25:27-30 conveys a glimmer of hope. Under a new king in Babylon 35 years later, Jehoiachin, the deposed king of Judah, is released from prison and kindly treated.

BABYLONIAN ACCOUNT OF THE FALL OF JERUSALEM

The capture of Jerusalem is described on a Babylonian tablet as follows:

In the seventh year, in the month of Kislev, the Babylonian king mustered his troops, and, having marched to the land of Hatti, besieged the city of Judah, and on the second day of the month of Adar took the city and captured the king. He appointed therein a king of his own choice, received its heavy tribute and sent (them) to Babylon.

KINGS OF ISRAEL AND JUDAH

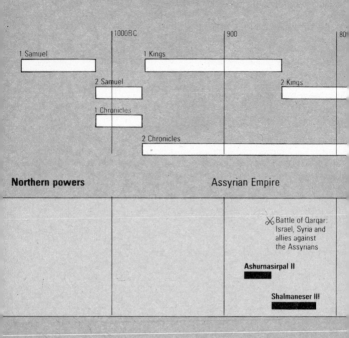

| | 1000BC | | 900 | | 80° |

1 Samuel

1 Kings

2 Samuel

2 Kings

1 Chronicles

2 Chronicles

Northern powers   Assyrian Empire

✂ Battle of Qarqar:
Israel, Syria and
allies against
the Assyrians

Ashurnasirpal II

Shalmaneser III

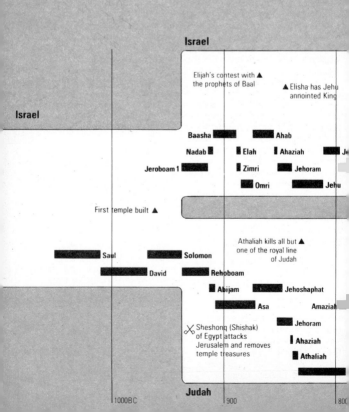

Israel

Elijah's contest with ▲
the prophets of Baal

▲ Elisha has Jehu
annointed King

Israel

Baasha **Ahab**

Nadab **Elah** **Ahaziah** **J**

Jeroboam 1 **Zimri** **Jehoram** **Jehu**

Omri **Jehu**

First temple built ▲

Athaliah kills all but ▲
one of the royal line
of Judah

Saul **Solomon**

David **Rehoboam**

Abijam **Jehoshaphat**

Asa **Amaziah**

✂ Sheshonq (Shishak) **Jehoram**
of Egypt attacks
Jerusalem and removes **Ahaziah**
temple treasures
Athaliah

Judah

| 1000BC | | 900 | | 800 |

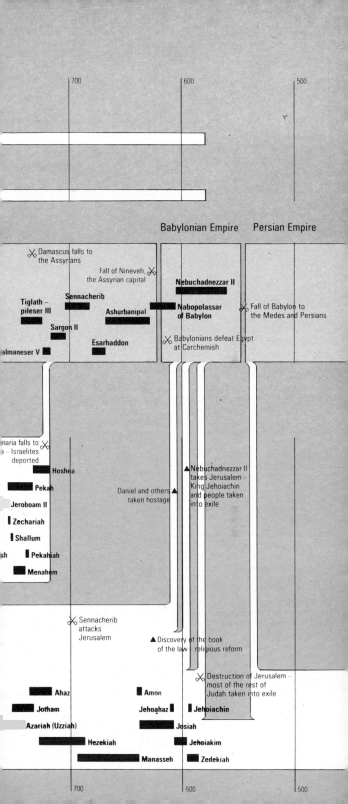

| | 700 | 600 | 500 |

Babylonian Empire   **Persian Empire**

✂ Damascus falls to
the Assyrians

Fall of Nineveh, ✂
the Assyrian capital

Nebuchadnezzar II

**Tiglath –
pileser III**

Sennacherib

**Nabopolassar
of Babylon**

✂ Fall of Babylon to
the Medes and Persians

Ashurbanipal

Sargon II

Esarhaddon

✂ Babylonians defeat Egypt
at Carchemish

almaneser V

..aria falls to
..a – Israelites
deported

Hoshea

Pekah

▲Nebuchadnezzar II
takes Jerusalem –
King Jehoiachin
and people taken
into exile

Jeroboam II

Daniel and others ▲
taken hostage

Zechariah

Shallum

...h

Pekahiah

Menahem

✂ Sennacherib
attacks
Jerusalem

▲ Discovery of the book
of the law – religious reform

✂ Destruction of Jerusalem –
most of the rest of
Judah taken into exile

Ahaz

Amon

Jotham

Jehoahaz

Jehoiachin

Azariah (Uzziah)

Josiah

Hezekiah

Jehoiakim

Manasseh

Zedekiah

| 700 | 600 | 500 |

1 AND 2 CHRONICLES

On the face of it, Chronicles seems to repeat in duller and more moralistic fashion what we already have in 2 Samuel and Kings. In fact, the Chronicler was writing for those who knew the earlier books. He had no need to repeat, except in so far as it suited him. He was free to follow particular themes within a roughly chronological historical framework. And he was specially interested in two themes – true worship and true kingship in Israel – so he selected his historical material accordingly. (After the division of the kingdom, for example, he follows the fortunes of the kings of David's line only, ignoring the northern kingdom. And even in the introduction – the family-trees of chapters 1-9 – he concentrates on the southern tribes, Judah and Benjamin, and the tribe of Levi, which gave Israel her priests and ministers.) This is not to say, as some have done, that the Chronicler twists the facts of history to suit himself. A book does not have to be a history text-book to be historically reliable.

The Chronicler chose these particular themes with his original readers in mind – the men who had returned from exile to rebuild Jerusalem under Ezra and Nehemiah. (He may have written about 400 BC; and his books form part of the longer series, Chronicles-Ezra-Nehemiah.) The new community needed to be linked with the past. They needed to know the right lines on which to re-establish patterns of worship. And, if history was not to repeat itself, they needed most of all to be reminded of the greatest lesson their history had to teach: that prosperity and well-being depend absolutely on faithfulness to God. Idolatry and neglect of God's law always has and always will result in judgement and disaster.

To assert the essential historical reliability of Chronicles is not to deny that there are problems. The Chronicler does not mind 'modernizing' – describing events in terms of the people of his own day would understand. His high statistics are also a difficulty to modern (though not ancient) man. See article 'The Large Numbers of the Old Testament'. And names are often spelt differently in Chronicles from the earlier books, though changes made by those who copied the text must account for some at least of these. (It does no harm to remind ourselves of the wide variety in English spelling before Johnson compiled his dictionary – witness the various ways of spelling 'Shakespeare'.)

1 - 9 SKELETON FAMILY-TREE OF ISRAEL: ADAM TO THE EXILE AND AFTER

The lists are not intended to be complete. In line with his purpose the Chronicler gives most attention to the family of David, and the tribes of Judah, Benjamin and Levi (see introduction above). The family-trees provide a lead-in to the history which begins at chapter 10 and a link with those for whom the book was first written.

1:1 - 2:2 Adam to Israel and his family

1:1-27: Adam to Abram; Noah's descendants through Japheth, Ham and Shem. The list is drawn from Genesis, though the spelling of many names is slightly different here.

1:28-54: Abraham, Isaac, Israel (Jacob); descendants of Ishmael and Esau. Attention narrows down to the father of the nation.

2:1-2: the twelve sons of Israel.

2:3 - 3:24 The royal line

2:3-55: the descendants of Judah: David's ancestors.

3:1-16: David's dynasty to the exile.

3:17-24: the royal line from the exile on.

Achar (2:7): Achan. See Joshua 7.
Chelubai (2:9): Caleb. Not necessarily Joshua's contemporary, who was not an Israelite, although he was adopted into the tribe of Judah.
Father of Kiriath-jearim (2:50): i.e. founder of the town.
Bathshua (3:5): Bathsheba.
Elishama (3:6): Elishua.

Johanan (3:15): not a king of Judah.
Zerubbabel (3:19): a leader in the return from exile. See Ezra.

4 - 7 The tribes of Israel
4:1-23 Judah; 4:24-43 Simeon; 5:1-10 Reuben; 5:11-22 Gad; 5:23-26 the half-tribe of Manasseh.

6 Levi. Verses 2-15: the line of the high priests; 16-30 the families of Gershom, Kohath and Merari; 31-48 families of the singers; 49-53 descendants of Aaron; 54-81 list of Levitical cities.

7:1-5 Issachar; 7:6-12 Benjamin (this does not tie in with chapter 8; it has been suggested that 6-11 is Zebulun and 12 is the end of an otherwise lost list of Dan); 7:13 Naphtali; 7:14-19 Manasseh; 7:20-29 Ephraim; 7:30-40 Asher.

Reuben (5:1): the reference is to Genesis 35:22.
Tilgath-pilneser (5:5): Tiglath-pileser.
5:26: Pul and Tiglath-pileser are one and the same.
6:27: 'Samuel his son' should be inserted after Elkanah. The reference is to the prophet Samuel.

8 The line of Benjamin; Saul's family 9:1-34 Those who returned from exile to live in Jerusalem 9:35-44 Saul's family-tree

10 - 29 THE REIGN OF DAVID
10 The death of Saul

See on 1 Samuel 31 and 2 Samuel 1. The story of Saul's rise and fall is told in 1 Samuel 9ff. For the Chronicler the history of the monarchy begins with David – 10:13-14 is sufficient comment on Israel's first king.
11 - 12 David made king

11:4-9: the capture of Jerusalem. Verses 10-47: David's special guard – see on 2 Samuel 23. 12:1-22: David's supporters at Ziklag. Saul's own kinsmen went over to David, and the warriors from Gad were so eager to join him that they crossed the River Jordan when it was in spate. Verses 23-40: the troops who made David king at Hebron.

Ariel (11:22): probably means great warrior, or hero.
12:21: see 1 Samuel 30.
13 The first attempt to bring the ark to Jerusalem

See on 2 Samuel 6. In line with his purpose of outlining the *religious* history of the nation, the Chronicler assigns this event first place in the record of David's reign. In actual point of time it came somewhat later.
14 Foreign affairs

See 2 Samuel 5. David was well able

to handle the nations around. His family life was his weak point, as the other records make plain (2 Samuel 13ff; 1 Kings 1:6).
15 - 16:16 The Levites bring in the ark

See also 2 Samuel 6. After three months, David brings the ark to Jerusalem and installs it in the tent he has had made. The original tent (the tabernacle) and altar remain at Gibeon. The Chronicler details the role of the levites in the ceremony. Proper worship is characterized by both orderliness and joy. From earliest times music has held a special place in worship.
16:7-43 A call to praise; regular offerings reinstituted

Extracts from various psalms are brought together in verses 8-36. These may be typical of what Asaph's choir sang before the ark, rather than the actual words. At Jerusalem and at Gibeon provision is made for daily sacrifices and praise to God in words and music.
17 David's request to build the temple

See on 2 Samuel 7. It seems wrong to David that he should have a palace to live in while the ark of God is still housed in a tent. And his attitude is right (contrast Haggai 1:4). God refuses the request, none the less. But he expresses his love and approval of David in the promise of a dynasty which will never die out, and in allowing Solomon to build the temple. David does not let disappointment shadow his glad acceptance of God's answer.
18 David's victories; expansion of the kingdom

Verse 4: the numbers are large. This problem is not unique to the Old Testament. Other contemporary documents give similarly large numbers of soldiers and chariots. Statistics given by the opposing sides in a war rarely tally – even today! See further 'The Large Numbers of the Old Testament'.

Chief officials (17): the writer of Samuel calls them 'priests', but by the Chronicler's time the word priest had acquired a technical meaning, hence the change.
19 - 20 Wars with the Ammonites, Syrians and Philistines

Chapter 19: see on 2 Samuel 10. The Bathsheba and Uriah episode took place between 20:1 and 20:2. This is not an attempt to whitewash David; the Chronicler regularly omits details of private life, in line with his purpose. In any case, these incidents were already known from the earlier records.

19:18: 2 Samuel 10:18 says 700 chariots, a more likely figure. But the word chariot here can mean simply 'mounted men'. The foot-soldiers here are the 'horsemen' of Samuel, since at this time in the ancient Near East horsemen dismounted to fight.

21 - 22:1 Census and plague: the purchase of the temple site
See on 2 Samuel 24. For the Chronicler the census and plague are significant simply as the lead-in to David's decision (22:1) to build the temple on the site of Ornan's threshing-floor, a fact not even mentioned in Samuel.

Satan (21:1): 'God' in 2 Samuel. Satan has power only within the limits set by God (see Job 1-2). His existence in God's world, and God's use of him, remain a mystery.

Guilt upon Israel (3): national solidarity is a fact. When the king as leader sins the people suffer.

Verse 5: these numbers differ from 2 Samuel 24:9. The Chronicler may have taken his figures from a different source.

Verse 18: the threshing-floor was a flat open space where the sheaves could be spread out. Oxen pulling studded sleds loosened the grain, which was then winnowed by tossing it into the wind. 'Ornan' is the 'Araunah' of Samuel. Difficulty may have arisen because it was a foreign name.

Hid (20): perhaps in the cave beneath the rocky floor, which now lies under the Dome of the Rock mosque, erected on the temple site.

Verse 25: 2 Samuel records the price paid for the threshing-floor, this verse apparently the price paid for the whole site.

22:2-19 Preparations for the temple
This section has no parallel in Samuel. It follows naturally from the mention of the temple in verse 1. In point of time it probably belongs to the period of Solomon's co-regency with his father (23:1; 1 Kings 1), which may have lasted some years. David never stopped longing to build God a house fit for him. He accepted the set-back of God's refusal and turned all his energy and enthusiasm to the things he *could* do: selecting the site; amassing materials; deciding the plan.

Aliens (2): the Canaanites who remained in the land were pressed into a permanent slave-force of navvies.

You have shed much blood (8): this does not imply that Solomon was morally better than David, or that David's wars were not justified (God is often stated to have been with him in his campaigns). These very wars bought Solomon's reign of peace in a strong kingdom, and with it the freedom for king and nation to concentrate at last on the great task of building God's temple.

Verse 14: taken literally, this would make David far richer than Solomon. The meaning is clear: David had laid up colossal supplies: a fortune in gold; fantastic wealth of silver; a vast mass of bronze and iron.

23 The duties of the Levites
Chapters 23-27 record David's organization of the nation's religious and civil administration.

From the earliest days of desert-wandering, the job of the Levites had been the care and transport of the tabernacle. They had also served the priests – in later times at the many shrines scattered throughout the land. Now the ark was to have a permanent home, and worship was to be centralized in the temple at Jerusalem. So David allocates new duties to the Levites: the care-taking and maintenance of the temple; appointments as magistrates, janitors, musicians and choristers; and general assistance of the priests.

Verses 3, 27: the age at which a Levite qualified to serve had been 30. David ordered that once the temple was completed it should be 20.

Verse 13: the sons of Amram were descendants of Aaron and Moses.

24 Divisions of priests
Twenty-four groups of priests were to be in charge of the temple sacrifices, each serving for two weeks a year. The order was decided by lot.

Nadab, Abihu (1): see Leviticus 10.

Verse 4: the fact that Eli's family was descended from Ithamar partly accounts for the reduced numbers. Because of the sins of Eli's sons, many of their descendants met a violent death (see 1 Samuel 2:30ff.).

25 The musicians
Music, both instrumental and vocal, was important in Jewish worship, as it was in social life generally. The temple musicians were 'leaders in inspired prophecy' (25:1, 3, New English Bible). Asaph, Heman and Jeduthun were amongst the famous: they are named in the Psalms. But

Musicians from Carchemish, 8th century BC.

status does not come into the temple service. Teacher and pupil alike share an equal place (8). David, himself a skilled musician (1 Samuel 16:15ff.; 2 Samuel 23:1), must have taken special delight in this part of the arrangements, over which he exercised personal supervision (2,6).

26:1-19 The janitors
These were to take turns on guard outside the temple and store-house.
Verse 18: the meaning of 'parbar' is not known; New English Bible gives 'colonnade'.

26:20-32 Temple treasurers, clerks and magistrates
The temple treasuries – gifts and taxes from the people, and the spoils of war – were vast.

27 Army commanders, tribal leaders, civil service and government officials
All twelve army chiefs seem to have come from David's special guard of 'mighty men' (see chapter 11). Verses 26-31 list those in charge of the royal estates, each specializing in a particular branch of agriculture.
Below twenty (23): under-twenties were not eligible for military service and were never counted in the census.
Verse 32: Jonathan and Jehiel were tutors to the king's sons.
Verse 33: Ahithophel and Hushai both appear in the story of Absalom's rebellion, 2 Samuel 15:31ff. 'King's friend' is an official title.

28 - 29 The government passes to Solomon; plans and instructions for the temple
A formal public assembly marks Solomon's official coronation, after the hasty affair of 1 Kings 1 (see 29:22). David presents his son to the people (1-8) and gives him a solemn charge (9, 10) before committing the plans for the temple building fund to his care (11-19). The design is God-given, closely following the pattern given to Moses for the construction of the tabernacle. At the same time, David hands over the lists of temple duties (21; see chapters 23-36).

Chapter 29: in addition to all he has put by over the years, David makes a last lavish personal gift for the temple building fund (1-5). His example and appeal (5) calls forth a willing, joyful response from the people, and the gifts pour in (6-9). Deeply moved, David thanks God from his heart that such giving is possible from men who apart from God's goodness have nothing. His prayer is one of the greatest in the whole of the Old Testament. It shows, as perhaps no other passage does, just why this man could be described as 'a man after God's own heart'.
Verse 4: see on 22:14.
Darics (7): a Persian gold coin; anachronistic for David's day, but a clue to the date at which the Chronicler wrote.
All the sons of King David (24): ear-

lier, Adonijah had attempted to wrest the throne from Solomon (1 Kings 1); later, Solomon put him to death. But for the present there was concord.

2 CHRONICLES 1 - 9 THE REIGN OF SOLOMON

1 Solomon established on the throne

See on 1 Kings 3 and 10.

Shephelah (15): the low hills between Judea and the Philistine coastal plain.

2 Trade arrangements with Huram over building materials for the temple

See on 1 Kings 5.

Huram (3): the 'Hiram' of Kings. See also on 2 Samuel 5.

Huramabi (13): elsewhere shortened to Huram or Hiram.

3 The construction of the temple

See on 1 Kings 6 - 7, and illustrations.

Mt Moriah (1): it was on a mountain in the land of Moriah that Abraham was told to offer up Isaac (Genesis 22:2).

Parvaim (6): not known; possibly in Arabia.

The veil (14): the sanctuary in which the ark was kept was divided off from the main part of the building by this curtain.

4 - 5:1 The temple furnishings

See on 1 Kings 7.

3,000 baths (5): i.e. about 14,500 gallons, on the usual reckoning of 4 gallons 6¾ pints/22 litres to one bath.

1 Kings 7:26 gives 2,000 baths (10,000 gallons).

5:2 - 6:11 The dedication of the temple

See on 1 Kings 8. The ark is installed with joyful music and singing and great thanksgiving. The glory of God's presence fills the temple (2-14). Solomon speaks to the people (6:3-11).

The Levitical singers ... (12): see on 1 Chronicles 25.

Verse 2: in the desert days, when they themselves lived in tents, the people made a tent for God (the tabernacle). Now that they are settled in houses, the temple is built as a house for God. It was not a cathedral in which they met for worship. Assemblies took place in the open, in front of the temple, where the altar and great basin stood.

6:12-42 Solomon's prayer

See on 1 Kings 8. The ground for this prayer, and all prayer, is the fact that God and his promises are utterly dependable. The requests are based on other vital facts about God: his love for his people; his absolute moral standards; his readiness to hear and forgive those who genuinely turn away from sin.

Verses 41-42: a free quotation of Psalm 132:8-10.

7 The dedication feast; God's answer to Solomon

See on 1 Kings 8 - 9. Flame burns up the sacrifices in token of God's pre-

Model of a merchant ship from King Solomon's fleet, from the Maritime Museum, Haifa, Israel.

Horses from Cilicia

Horses and chariots exported to Hittites and Syrians

King Ḥiram of Tyre supplied cedar and pine for Solomon's building projects

Jerusalem

The strategic position of Solomon's kingdom enabled him to control the major north-south caravan routes

Egypt supplied chariots

Copper mining near Ezion-geber

Ocean-going fleet (joint operation with Hiram) brought back gold, silver, hardwood, ivory and jewels

Queen of Sheba brought spices, gold, jewels

KING SOLOMON'S TRADE

sence and approval. The seven days of festivity run on into the week-long Feast of Tabernacles, with a final day of solemn meeting before they all disperse (this clarifies 1 Kings 8:65-66).

Verses 11-22: God agrees to all Solomon's requests. But in return he expects loyal obedience.

8 Solomon's building and trading operations

See on 1 Kings 9:10ff.

Verse 2: the cities of 1 Kings 9:10-14, redeemed from Hiram by Solomon.

Verse 10: the 250 officers plus 3,600 overseers (2:18) add up to the same total as the 550 plus 3,300 of 1 Kings 9:23; 5:16.

Law of Moses (13): for the set feasts see Leviticus 23; the sacrifices, Leviticus 1-7.

Verse 14: David's instructions are given in 1 Chronicles 23-26.

9:1-12 The visit of the Queen of Sheba

See on 1 Kings 10. The Chronicler includes the visit as an illustration of Solomon's widespread fame and reputation.

Algum (10): a foreign word, the 'almug' of 1 Kings.

9:13-31 Solomon's wealth and glory

See on 1 Kings 10:14-29.

Verse 21: a voyage from Elath, round Africa, to Tarshish (Tartessus) in Spain is highly unlikely. In Kings the phrase 'ships of Tarshish' describes the type of vessel – deep-sea cargo ships.

Prophecy of Ahijah (29): this source is now lost, but two of Ahijah's prophecies are recorded in 1 Kings 11 and 14.

10 - 36 THE KINGS OF JUDAH

The dates and length of reign of each king are given in the parallel sections of 1 and 2 Kings. Many of them include a period of co-regency with a predecessor, so there is often some overlap. See article 'Unravelling the Chronology of the Kings'.

The Chronicler does not recognize the kings of Israel. Only David's descendants are the nation's true kings. From the time of the split he therefore largely ignores the northern kingdom, and frequently refers to Judah as 'Israel'. Even so, the ten tribes are still considered part of the Israelite nation, and contain elements which continue loyal to God and to the rightful king.

10 King Rehoboam and the split between Israel and Judah

See also 1 Kings 12. Rehoboam

inherited from Solomon a wealthy kingdom beginning to show signs of weakness. By the time of his death only a fraction of that land and income remained to be handed down to his successor.

In Egypt (2): see 1 Kings 11:26ff.

The word spoken by Ahijah (15): 1 Kings 11:30-39.

Hadoram (18): the Adoram (Adoniram) of Kings.

11 Rehoboam strengthens Judah's defences

A timely word from Shemaiah averts civil war (1-4). Instead, Rehoboam concentrates on fortifying his tiny kingdom against attack from her larger and stronger neighbours, particularly Israel and Egypt. Refugee priests flock to Judah from Israel following Jeroboam's measures to break the religious ties with Jerusalem (see 1 Kings 12:26-33).

Satyrs (15): the goat-like desert-demons of the old nature worship.

Abijah (20): the Abijam of Kings.

Daughter of Absalom (20): the Old Testament often uses 'son of', 'daughter of', in the wider sense of 'descendant'. Maacah was Absalom's granddaughter (see 13:2).

12 Rehoboam turns unfaithful; Shishak's invasion

Invasion, here and later, is seen as a direct consequence of disloyalty to God. National repentance limits its effects, but Judah remains under Egyptian domination for some years. See also 1 Kings 14.

All Israel (1): the Chronicler means the true Israel, i.e. Judah.

Shishak (2): Sheshonq 1, Libyan founder of the 22nd dynasty of Egypt.

13 King Abijah; full-scale war with Israel

See also 1 Kings 15:1-8. The fuller account here enlarges on what constitutes 'proper' worship, and on the reason for Judah's victory.

Micaiah (2): Maacah (11:20; 1 Kings 15:2).

Covenant of salt (5): salt had a ceremonial use in the ratification of treaties. It stood for faith, loyalty and long-lastingness (particularly in 'pacts' made with God).

500,000 (17): best taken as meaning simply 'a large number'.

14 Peace under King Asa; Zerah's invasion

See also 1 Kings 15:9-24.

Zerah (9): Ethiopia/Cush is modern Sudan. Zerah was probably an Egyptian or Arabian chieftain (the earlier identification with Pharaoh Osorkon has now been abandoned).

A million (9): best taken to mean simply 'an enormous number'.

15 Azariah's message from God encourages religious reform

Ephraim, Manasseh and Simeon (9): loyal men from the two northern tribes migrated to Judah. But Simeon's territory had always been in the south, and the tribe had been assimilated long ago by Judah.

Maacah (16): Asa's grandmother. See on 11:20.

Verse 17: on the face of it, a contradiction of 14:3. But Asa probably destroyed the shrines where foreign gods were worshipped and left the others.

16 The alliance with Syria against Israel

Asa's faith weakens under test in his later years. He calls in foreign aid. And he turns to medicine-men whose cures were effected by magic. Nonetheless, in death, his people honour him.

Fire (14): not a cremation, but the burning of spices (see Jeremiah 34:5).

17 Jehoshaphat: a king to be reckoned with

See also 1 Kings 15:24; 22:1-50.

Jehoshaphat builds up a strong army and defences. He arranges for the people to be taught the law. And he is much respected by the surrounding nations.

The Arabs (11): former nomads settling in Edom and Moab.

Verse 14: as they stand, the figures for the muster are over-high. It is possible that the term 'thousand' is a group term rather than a numeral. See article 'The Large Numbers of the Old Testament'.

18 Military and marriage alliance with Ahab; battle at Ramoth-gilead

A repetition of the story in 1 Kings 22.

The marriage alliance (1): Jehoshaphat's son Jehoram married Athaliah, Ahab's daughter. Far from reuniting the kingdom, this link brought near-disaster to Judah in later years (22:10).

True and false prophets (4ff.): it was never easy to distinguish between the two. Here Jehoshaphat senses from the shallow optimism of their message that these prophets are merely telling Ahab what he wants to hear. The false and the true can only be distinguished by their life and message, not by methods or manner (see Deuteronomy 18:17-22). No true prophet made a prediction which failed to happen; practised or encouraged immorality; or led people away from God and his law.

19 Reform of the legal system

After Ramoth-gilead, Jehoshaphat concentrates on home affairs. He appoints civil judges, sets up local law-courts and a mixed court of appeal in Jerusalem.

Jehu (2): probably grandson of the Jehu in 1 Kings 16:1. It was not unknown for names to alternate like this within families.

Law of the Lord (8): cases covered by the law of Moses; the other law-suits ('disputed cases', Revised Standard Version) are civil matters.

Brethren (10): fellow judges, not kinsmen as in New English Bible.

20 War with the allied forces of Ammon, Moab and Edom

Judah's trust in God is amply vindicated. The invaders quarrel among themselves and leave the spoil to Judah. Only the alliance with Israel spoils the good record of Jehoshaphat's reign.

Meunites (1): from a district of Edom near Mt Seir.

The Sea (2): the Dead Sea.

Verse 33: this agrees with 1 Kings 22:43; but contradicts 17:6. (See on 15:17.) The high places (often but not always on hills) were simply platforms on which cult objects stood. As the places themselves were regarded as holy, nothing short of the desecration carried out by Josiah could stop people using them.

Tarshish (36): see on 9:21.

21 King Jehoram

See also 2 Kings 8:16-24. The evil influence of Jehoram's wife (Athaliah was the daughter of Ahab and Jezebel) proved stronger than his father's good example. Jehoram lost control over Edom and Libnah (on the Philistine border), and led the nation into idolatry. No one regretted his death (20): a terrible epitaph.

Elijah's letter (12): it would appear from 2 Kings 3:11 (in Jehoshaphat's reign) that Elijah was no longer alive, though we cannot be certain. Possibly, foreseeing how things would go, the prophet left a written message which was delivered by a successor.

Jehoahaz (17): an alternative way of writing Ahaziah (22:1). Both are a compound of 'Ahaz', meaning 'he has hold', or 'possession' and the name of God (written Jeho- or Jo- as a prefix; -iahu or -iah as a suffix). The whole name thus means 'God

has possession'. Most of Judah's kings have names compounded in this way.

22:1-9 King Ahaziah

See also 2 Kings 8:25-29. Ahaziah learnt nothing from his father's horrible end. Friendship with Israel led directly to his death in Jehu's purge.

Verse 2: 42 should be 22, as 2 Kings 8:26.

Verse 9: this seems to be at variance with 2 Kings 9 and 10, where Ahaziah dies at Megiddo, and before his nephews' deaths. It is possible that 'Samaria' is used here of the kingdom rather than the city itself.

22:10 - 23:21 Athaliah seizes the throne; the rising in favour of Joash

See also 2 Kings 11. Ahaziah's infant son Joash is the rightful heir. But so many of the royal family have been wiped out (21:17; 22:8) that the queen mother is able to make her bid unchallenged. After six years the usurper is overthrown. The Chronicler lays his stress on the role of the priests and Levites in restoring the rightful monarch to the throne.

24 King Joash; the repair of the temple

See also 2 Kings 11:21 - 12:21. Under Jehoiada's influence, Joash began well. After the priest's death the king came under less healthy influences, till he sank to the murder of Jehoiada's son for his outspoken criticism. In consequence his own life ends in ignominious defeat and assassination.

The tax (6): see Exodus 30:12ff.

25 King Amaziah

See also 2 Kings 14. Amaziah's cruel victory over Edom leads to his downfall. He brings home the foreign gods. And in his bumptious pride he throws down the gauntlet to powerful Israel. Defeat turns the people against him. It seems that Uzziah, the 'Azariah' of 2 Kings, was made co-regent. And an eventual conspiracy succeeded in ending Amaziah's life.

Verse 4: Deuteronomy 24:16.

100,000 (6): a round figure indicating a large number.

Israel ... Ephraimites (7): the Chronicler makes it clear that in this instance he means the northern kingdom.

26 King Uzziah

See also 2 Kings 15:1-7. A strong king, Uzziah begins well, seeking God and extending his sovereignty as far south as the Red Sea. He loves the land and protects the cattle from desert raiders (10). He sees that his army is well-equipped and armed with the latest in guided missiles (14-15). But as with many a good man before and since, power and success are his undoing. In his pride he takes on the role of priest. God strikes him with leprosy, a visible token of that unseen defilement of sin which made him unfit for God's presence.

27 King Jotham

See also 2 Kings 15:32-38. Jotham proves a good king. He maintains and increases his father's power, adding Ammon to his tributary-states. But the religion of the people remains mixed.

28 King Ahaz

See also 2 Kings 16; Isaiah 7. The terrible apostasy of Ahaz brings Judah near to destruction. God even uses the idolatrous northern kingdom to punish his people – and to show them up by almost unheard-of clemency to the prisoners-of-war. There were still some 'Good Samaritans' in Israel. Crisis brings some people to deeper faith, but not Ahaz.

Valley of the son of Hinnom (3): the Valley of Gehenna, south of Jerusalem.

King of Syria (5): Rezin, see 2 Kings 16.

Tilgath-pilneser (20): Tiglath-pileser. This is not an invasion, but the imposition of crushing tribute.

Altars (24): to pagan gods.

29 King Hezekiah

See also 2 Kings 18-20. Hezekiah's first concern is to restore the temple

HEZEKIAH'S CONDUIT

To secure his water-supply from the invaders, Hezekiah channelled the water from the Spring of Gihon to the Pool of Siloam. The tunnel is over 1,700ft/620m long, and winds to follow the lie of the rock.

In 1880 a boy who had been bathing in the Pool of Siloam found an inscription which tells its own story:

... And this is the story of the piercing through. While (the stone-cutters were swinging their) axes, each towards his fellow, and while there were yet three cubits to be pierced through, (there was heard) the voice of a man calling to his fellow, for there was a crevice (?) on the right ... And on the day of the piercing through, the stone-cutters struck through each to meet his fellow, axe against axe. Then ran the water from the Spring to the Pool for twelve hundred cubits, and a hundred cubits was the height of the rock above the head of the stone-cutters.

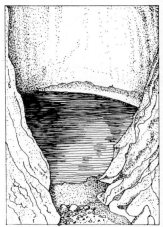

The Spring of Gihon, from which Hezekiah's conduit was channelled.

The inscription carved by workmen on the tunnel wall.

to its proper use. The detailed account of the cleansing and rededication of the desecrated temple is characteristic of the Chronicler. When the building has been made ready, king, priests and people are themselves made clean from sin by the offering of sacrifices.

Verse 25: see 1 Chronicles 25. Gad and Nathan were both prophets of David's day.

The song to the Lord (27): many of the psalms were written for use in the temple on various occasions.

30 The great Passover celebration (For the origin and meaning of Passover see on Exodus 11-13.) Samaria had fallen to Assyria in the reign of Ahaz (when Hezekiah was co-regent) – see 2 Kings 17. Most of the northern Israelites had been taken captive and their land re-settled. Hezekiah's appeal is to the few remaining Israelites to join with Judah for the feast (9). Despite the poor response, there had been no Passover to equal this since Solomon's day. And such was the general rejoicing that they extended the feast an extra week.

Verse 3: the normal date was the 14th of the first month, but Numbers 9 also allows the later date.

Verse 15: many priests and Levites were slow to return to the reformed worship (29:34).

Verse 19: the Chronicler, who set great store by proper forms of worship, makes it clear that it is the attitude of heart that matters most.

31 The priests resume their functions; tithes and offerings brought in
The old laws governing worship and the support of the priests are reintroduced. The sheer volume of produce

raised by the tithe takes everyone by surprise. Special care is taken to see that it is properly distributed.

Verse 7: people began to give in May/June at the grain harvest and continued to the end of the fruit and vine harvests in September/October.

32 Sennacherib's invasion
See also 2 Kings 18-19. Having wiped out the northern kingdom, the Assyrians make inroads into Judah, who have shown signs of independence. But Sennacherib fails to take Jerusalem. The reason, says the Chronicler, is that in the crisis Judah's king put his trust wholly in God.

Verse 12: the Assyrian emissary misunderstood Hezekiah's reforms.

Verse 18: they used Hebrew. The people would not have understood Aramaic, the diplomatic language.

Verse 31: see 2 Kings 20:12ff. 'Left to himself' Hezekiah exhibits his treasures with foolish pride.

33:1-20 Manasseh's evil reign
See also 2 Kings 21:1-18. For almost all of his long reign Manasseh was one of Judah's worst kings, responsible for desecrating the temple and practising human sacrifice. But the Chronicler relates a change of heart not mentioned in Kings. Possibly Manasseh was caught up in the revolt of Ashurbanipal's brother, vassalking of Babylon, and was called to account there after Ashurbanipal was victorious. God answered the king's desperate prayer, and his release and return changed him, but not the people.

Verse 6: the Valley of Gehenna.

Hooks (11): kings conquered by the Assyrians had hooks or rings driven through their noses.

THE ASSYRIAN EMPIRE

Black Sea

Caspian Sea

Carchemish • Nineveh

ASSYRIA

Mediterranean Sea

Euphrates Tigris

Damascus • Babylon • Susa PERSIA

Jerusalem ISRAEL BABYLONIA

EGYPT JUDAH

Persian Gulf

Assyrians invade the Eastern Mediterranean. Samaria conquered 722-721 BC

Red Sea

33:21-25 Amon

See also 2 Kings 21:19-26. Amon reigned two years, 642-640. He followed Manasseh's evil example and was murdered by his servants.

34 Josiah: Judah's last and greatest reformer

See also 2 Kings 22-23. Josiah desecrates and demolishes places and objects of pagan worship, and repairs the temple. During his reign the book of the law is discovered, and a measure of true repentance follows. But, despite the king's lead, the people's response is too little and too late to avert judgement. There are some differences between the accounts in Kings and Chronicles, mainly in the order of events, but neither writer is primarily concerned with chronology. The real significance of the events lies in what they teach.

Verse 3: Assyrian power was declining, and Scythian hordes attacking her in the north, so Josiah became gradually freer to take the politically dangerous step of ridding his land of the Assyrian gods.

35 Josiah's Passover; the tragic end to his reign

See 2 Kings 23:21-30. Passover had been neglected during the monarchy. Now the celebration forms the climax to the reforms. The nation remember their deliverance from slavery in Egypt – within a few short years of a second slavery, to Babylon.

Verse 20: Necho was marching north in 609 to help Assyria fight off Babylon. On his way home he deposed and deported Josiah's successor, Jehoahaz. But in 605 he was defeated by Nebuchadnezzar of Babylon at Carchemish.

Jeremiah (25): the prophet's lament has not been preserved.

36:1-4 Jehoahaz

See also 2 Kings 23:31-35 See on 35:20.

36:5-8 Jehoiakim

See also 2 Kings 23:36 - 24:7. Jehoiakim began as a puppet of Egypt, and ended as a captive in Babylon.

36:9-10 Jehoiachin

See also 2 Kings 24:8-16. After only three months Jehoiachin was deposed and taken captive to Babylon. (He was 18 when he became king, not 8; and Zedekiah was his uncle.)

36:11-21 Zedekiah; the destruction of Jerusalem

See also 2 Kings 24:18 - 25:30. God gave Zedekiah and the nation many warnings through Jeremiah and the other prophets, but they were all ignored. The judgement that came spelt death or exile for the whole nation. The exile lasted until the Persians took over the Babylonian Empire.

Sabbath (21): the Chronicler implies that these sabbaths were not kept under the kings. See Leviticus 25:1-7; 26:34-35.

36:22-23 New hope

When the book of Ezra was detached from Chronicles, these verses were retained at the end of Chronicles and repeated at the beginning of Ezra. Chronicles could not end at verse 21. God had not utterly abandoned his people. Jeremiah had spoken scalding words of God's judgement and condemnation. But he had also spoken of God's continuing love for his exiled people, and of their eventual return (Jeremiah 24:4-7).

THE BABYLONIAN EMPIRE

EZRA

Ezra, Nehemiah and Esther cover the last century of Old Testament Jewish history, roughly 538-433 BC. Ezra follows on from Chronicles (2 Chronicles 36: 22-23 and Ezra 1:1-3 are identical), which ended with the destruction of Jerusalem and the people being taken into exile in Babylon by Nebuchadnezzar (587). Ezra and Nehemiah describe the three-stage return: the main party, who returned with Zerubbabel in 538/7; the party that returned with Ezra 80 years later, in 458 (on the traditional dating – but this does raise some major problems, and debate on the subject continues); and Nehemiah's party in 445. Esther's story belongs to the time between the rebuilding of the temple at Jerusalem and Ezra's return (Ezra 7:1).

On the wider plane, the Jewish events belong to the time following the overthrow of the Babylonian Empire by Cyrus, king of Persia, in 539. Ezra and Nehemiah span the reigns of five Persian kings.

The writer. It is not clear who wrote what, or when. The compiler may have been the Chronicler. But it seems plain that the personal memoirs of Ezra and Nehemiah make up the bulk of the books named after them.

1 - 2 THE EXILED JEWS RETURN TO JERUSALEM
1 Cyrus' proclamation
The policy of the Babylonian kings had been to deport the peoples they conquered. But Babylon has now fallen to Persia (as the prophets predicted). And one of Cyrus' first actions is to repatriate the exiled peoples, and allow them to reinstate their national gods. Among those who benefit from the change of policy are the Jews. (See Isaiah's remarkable prophecy, Isaiah 44:26-28; 45:1-13.)
Verse 1: see on 2 Chronicles 36:22-23.
Verse 6: God saw to it that the exiles did not return empty-handed, as he had done at the exodus (Exodus 12:35-36).
2 The list of those who returned
See also Nehemiah 7.
Jeshua (2): the Joshua of Haggai 1:1.
Nehemiah (2): not the same individual as the later governor.
Verse 59: family-trees were reckoned of great importance. Those unable to prove their ancestry were barred from the priesthood.
Barzillai (61): 2 Samuel 17:27; 19:31ff.
Verse 64: the figures given do not add up to this total. There may have been mistakes in copying or interpreting the numbers.

3 - 6 REBUILDING THE TEMPLE
3 The foundation is laid
The first thing to be rebuilt is the altar, so that worship and sacrifice may begin again, on the pattern laid down by Moses (Leviticus 1 - 7). Lebanon again provides choice cedarwood for the building (see 2 Chronicles 2). But the work makes little progress beyond the foundations.
Verses 10-11: see 1 Chronicles 25. There are two choirs (or choir and soloist) singing alternately.

Cyrus 559-530
The return from exile. Ezra 1
End of Daniel's life (1:21; 10:1)

Cambyses 530-522
Not mentioned

Darius I 522-486
The temple rebuilt. Ezra 4:5, 24;5
Haggai and Zechariah

Xerxes I 486-465 (Ahasuerus)
Ezra 4:6. The king who made Esther his queen and Mordecai his grand vizier

---

Artaxerxes I 464-423
Ezra 4:7-23; 7:1ff.; Nehemiah 2:1. The king who sponsored the return of Ezra and of Nehemiah. Jerusalem rewalled. Reforms. Malachi

Verse 12: the older men wept for the glories of the temple that had been destroyed.

4 Work is halted

Verses 1-5,24: the opposition succeeds in bringing the work to a standstill for 15 years, until Darius is king. Verses 6-23 interrupt the chronological sequence to carry the account of the opposition through to the time of Ezra and Nehemiah. Here the bone of contention is the rebuilding of the city walls (12).

Judah and Benjamin (1): it was mainly exiles from the southern kingdom who returned. Their 'adversaries' are the mixed people Esarhaddon settled in the land, later known as Samaritans. They worshipped God, but alongside other 'deities' (2 Kings 17:24-41).

Verse 7: Aramaic was the international diplomatic language of the Persian Empire.

Osnappar (10): An Aramaic version of Ashurbanipal. 'Beyond the River'/ 'Beyond Euphrates': title of the fifth 'satrapy' or province, which included all Palestine and Syria.

Eat the salt (14): i.e. they were maintained by the king; his paid officials.

Verse 23: this is the situation recounted in Nehemiah 1:3.

5 - 6 The temple completed

Urged on by the prophets Haggai and Zechariah, the people again start building. This time an attempt to get the new king, Darius, to stop it has the opposite effect. In four years the temple is finished and the people are able to celebrate Passover. For a nation recently delivered from a second 'bondage', this must have had special meaning.

6:11: a common form of execution in Persia; in effect crucifixion.

King of Assyria (22): i.e. king of what was once Assyrian territory.

7 - 10 EZRA'S RETURN TO JERUSALEM

Nearly 60 years separate 7:1 from 6:22, during which time Esther is able to avert a complete massacre of the Jewish people and, indirectly, to save the lives of Ezra and Nehemiah.

Artaxerxes is favourably disposed towards the Jews, and Ezra the scholar and teacher (direct descendant of the high priests) is given official sanction to teach the law and appoint magistrates in his homeland, to offer sacrifices and beautify the temple. (Ezra's own memoirs, written in Hebrew, begin at verse 27.)

Verse 9: the 900-mile journey took four months.

8 The men who accompanied Ezra

Ezra's party of over 1700 includes priests, people and, somewhat reluctantly, Levites. With them they take gifts valuing more than £1,000,000. Ezra is faced with a long and dangerous journey at a time of great unrest. And having boasted his confidence in God, he can hardly now apply to the king for an escort! His prayer is heartfelt, and his faith rewarded by God's own safe-conduct.

Satraps (36): very powerful governors; usually only one to each 'satrapy' or province, with several subordinates.

9 - 10 The problem of mixed marriages

Since their return, priests and Levites, rulers and people alike have intermarried with the heathen peoples around, a thing forbidden by God (Deuteronomy 7:1-5), not out of racial prejudice but because it led to idolatry. This very practice had been a major factor in the nation's downfall under the kings. Yet even the horrors of defeat and exile have not taught the people their lesson. Small wonder Ezra's bitter distress at the disclosure. His close identification with the offenders and the deep grief of his prayer move the nation to prompt action, despite the time of year (heavy December rains, 10:9). His lead saves the whole nation from extinction. The blame for all the unhappiness of broken marriages rests not on Ezra, but on those listed in 10:18-44 – the men who contracted those marriages in defiance of God's law. And some of them (as Malachi 2:10-16 makes clear) had even broken former marriages to Jewish wives in order to marry pagans. See also under Nehemiah 13.

NEHEMIAH

See introduction to Ezra.

1 - 2 NEHEMIAH RETURNS TO JERUSALEM
1 Bad news; Nehemiah's prayer
In December 446, Nehemiah's brother Hanani (see 7:2) brings sad news of the colony in Jerusalem (see Ezra 4:23). Nehemiah holds the trusted position of king's cup-bearer at the Persian court, at that time resident in the winter capital of Susa. It is his job to taste the king's wine, in case it is poisoned. Although far from his homeland, he is so concerned for his people that for four months he continues to grieve and pray over the situation. And, characteristically, when the opportunity comes he has a practical plan to put to the king.

Remember the word (8): e.g. Deuteronomy 30:1-5.
This man (11): the Persian king.
2 The king consents; Nehemiah's tour of inspection
The sorry state of Jerusalem is a direct consequence of Artaxerxes' decree that building should cease (Ezra 4:7-23). Nehemiah therefore takes his life in his hands in cham-

pioning a city which has been represented to the king as a hot-bed of rebellion. Even by letting his grief show in the king's presence he places himself in grave danger. But Nehemiah's concern for his people outweighs self-interest. God answers his prayer, and Artaxerxes grants his request.

On arrival in Jerusalem he mentions his plans to no one until he has made a secret personal inspection of the city.
Verse 6: Nehemiah returned after 12 years as governor (5:14), but the term agreed on here was probably shorter.
Sanballat, Tobiah (19): see also 4:1-9; 6:1-18; 13:4-9. *Geshem* (Gashmu, 6:6): tribal chief of Kedar in north Arabia.

3 - 6 THE BUILDING OF THE WALLS
3 A list of the builders
People of all sorts join together in the work of rebuilding. The list mentions priests and perfumers, goldsmiths and merchants, rulers, even women. Some undertook a double section. Nehemiah, astute as always, sets the people to work on sections near their own homes, for which they naturally have a special concern. The leaders named are citizens of long standing; neither Ezra nor the men of his party are mentioned.
4 Enemy opposition
The people have a will to work, and a dynamic leader. Nonetheless they have to face first ridicule, then terrorism from powerful opponents. Nehemiah's reply is prayer and faith, plus practical action: 'we prayed ... and set a guard' (9); 'Remember the Lord ... and fight' (14).
Verse 2: the walls had been burned, and fire made the local limestone disintegrate.
Verses 4-5: Old Testament prayers like this one fall short of Christ's standards. But the motive behind them is not personal vengeance, but concern for God's honour which is at

JERUSALEM IN NEHEMIAH'S TIME

Tower of Hananel
Fish Gate
Sheep Gate
Tower of the Furnaces
Temple area
Horse Gate
Valley
Water Gate
Gihon Spring
Kidron
Pool of Siloam
Fountain Gate
Valley Gate
Dung Gate
Valley of Hinnom

200 m

stake when his people are under attack.

5 Internal troubles

While Nehemiah has been buying back Hebrew slaves and loaning money and food to the poor (even providing his own support as governor), rich Jews have been exacting interest from their fellow countrymen, contrary to the law (Exodus 22:25) and selling them as slaves to foreigners. Nehemiah takes firm action to set this right.

6 The wall is finished

The opposition realize that their only chance of stopping the work is to get rid of Nehemiah. Their first move is to try and persuade him to leave Jerusalem for talks (2). When that fails they try blackmail (5-7) and intimidation (10). Nehemiah's replies (3, 8, 11) are superb. He will allow nothing to deflect him from his God-given task. And in under two months the walls are finished – such a fantastic achievement that even Israel's enemies are forced to acknowledge God's hand in it.

7:1-73a LIST OF THOSE WHO RETURNED WITH ZERUBBABEL

Verses 6-73: see also the practically identical list in Ezra 2. It refers to the first, and main, party of Jews to return home in 538 following Cyrus' decree.

7:73b - 8:18 EZRA READS THE LAW TO THE PEOPLE

The request comes from the people (8:1). Ezra reads and the Levites explain, possibly also translating for some who knew no Hebrew. When they learn the full measure of God's standards the people are overwhelmed with grief at the extent of their failures (just as King Josiah had been, long before; 2 Kings 22).

In the course of study, they rediscover the original instructions for the Feast of Tabernacles. And for the first time since Joshua's day they make leafy shelters to live in, as a reminder of the time of desert-wandering.

9:1-37 THE PEOPLE'S CONFESSION AND EZRA'S PRAYER

The nation's repentance is genuine. Wrongs are righted and the people turn to God in confession and worship. Ezra's prayer – the prelude to renewal of the covenant – recalls

God's loving and faithful dealings with his rebellious people from the time of Abraham to his own day.

9:38 - 10:39 THE COVENANT IS RENEWED

Nehemiah the governor, priests, Levites and leaders sign the renewed covenant-agreement on behalf of the nation. It is ratified with a curse (on those who break it) and an oath (of loyalty to God). The people pledge specifically to keep the law's requirements on marriage, the sabbath, and taxes, tithes and offerings for the upkeep of the temple services, priests and Levites.

11 - 12:26 LISTS OF RESIDENTS

11:3-19: probably a list of those already living in Jerusalem (it is substantially the same as 1 Chronicles 9:2-17). The number was increased by a 10 per cent levy on the villages around.

Verses 25-36: a list of occupied villages.

12:1-9: the priests and Levites who returned with Zerubbabel.

11:23: see 1 Chronicles 25.

12:9: there were two choirs who sang or chanted in reply to one another.

12:27-47 THE DEDICATION OF THE WALLS

Two processions, each led by a choir, make their way in opposite directions along the broad top of the wall, meeting in the temple area for the concluding thanksgiving and sacrifices. It is an occasion of tumultuous joy.

13 ABUSES AND REFORMS

Verses 1-3 seem more closely linked with 4-9 than with 12:44. In 433 Nehemiah went back to the court of King Artaxerxes. On his return he finds that various abuses have arisen in his absence. The high priest, of all people, has given Nehemiah's old enemy, Tobiah (who is not even an Israelite) quarters in rooms attached to the temple. The income for the Levites has not been forthcoming. Sabbath laws are being flagrantly broken. And yet again (see Ezra 9-10) the Israelites have contracted marriages with foreign women. Nehemiah adopts strong measures to deal with the abuses, and the offenders.

The achievements of Ezra and

Nehemiah in the crucial years following the return of their decimated nation from exile are notable. Without the teaching of the law, without the invincible faith and fearless action of these two leaders, it is doubtful if a distinctive Jewish religion and community – with all that means for the world through the birth and death of Christ – could have survived. To this end their strong line on mixed marriage was essential. The objection to foreign women was not on the grounds of race, but because of their debased religions. (The Old Testament does not condemn interracial marriage if both partners worship the God of Israel.) History had taught them that the admixture of paganism, with its easy standards and its appeal to the lowest in human nature, could quickly bring the Jewish faith to the brink of extinction.

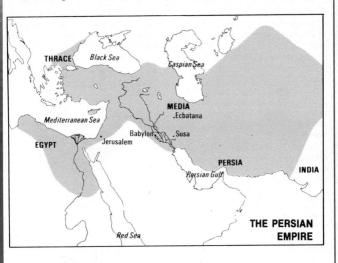

THE PERSIAN EMPIRE

ESTHER

Esther tells the story of a plot to exterminate the entire Jewish nation in the days of the Persian king, Ahasuerus (Xerxes), and how it was thwarted. It also explains the origin of the Jewish Feast of Purim. Estimates of the book vary – largely on account of the seeming improbability of the events. Some regard it as pure fiction. Others see it as a historical novel. Others again think that the knowledge we have of Persian affairs in the 5th century BC gives good grounds for treating Esther as history.

The writer is unknown, but his nationalism and accurate knowledge of Persian ways make it likely that he was a Jew who lived in Persia before the empire fell to Greece.

Although the book does not mention God by name, it speaks plainly of his over-ruling in the affairs of men, and his unfailing care for his people. Had Haman's plot succeeded there would have been no Nehemiah and, far more important, no Christ.

1 Ahasuerus dethrones his queen
Ahasuerus reigned over an empire stretching from the Indus to northern Sudan (see map). His winter capital (unbearably hot in summer) was Susa, a city in Elam, 150 miles east of Babylon. The Greek historian Herodotus describes him as a cruel, capricious, sensual man – which fits well with his character in this book. In 483 he gives a huge feast, the climax to a six-month display of his wealth and power. But his queen (we are not told why) refuses to play along with his wish to make her part of the exhibition. And on the advice of his astrologers the king deposes her.

Queen Vashti (9): Herodotus says Amestris was Ahasuerus' queen. It may be she succeeded both Vashti and Esther. The king may have had more than one wife, but there would have been only one queen.

He sent letters (22): Darius had set up an excellent fast-courier postal service which operated throughout the empire.

2 Esther becomes queen; Mordecai saves the king's life
The years of the disastrous Greek war – the battles of Thermopylae and Salamis – intervene between chapters 1 and 2. Four years pass before the king is able to get round to choosing a new queen. Among the beautiful

A Persian guard, in multi-coloured glazed brick, from the palace walls at Susa.

girls rounded up to be taken to the capital for twelve months' beauty treatment, sampled by the king, and then for the most part forgotten, is a young Jewish girl, Esther, Mordecai's cousin. When her turn comes, she delights the king and he makes her his queen.

Verses 5-6: Mordecai would have been nearly 120 if he personally had been taken captive in 597. It probably means that his family was among the captives.

Hadassah/Esther (7): some make much of the fact that the names 'Esther' and 'Mordecai' are similar to those of the Babylonian gods 'Ishtar' and 'Marduk'. But this is not surprising if both were names given to them in captivity, as this verse says Esther's was.

Tebeth (16): December/January 479.

Verse 23: this record in the court diary later proves important (6:1-2).

3 Haman's promotion and plot against the Jews

We are not told why Mordecai refused to make obeisance. He must have considered that Haman's demand went beyond court courtesy. To have complied would have involved idolatry. In his unreasoning fury Haman plans the destruction of an entire race. Superstition insists he must choose a 'lucky day'. And fortunately for the Jews it was eleven months off. The king's assent is easily won by accusing the Jews of rebellion and promising a £3,000,000 rake-off. (Haman plans to raise the money by plundering Jewish goods and confiscating their lands.)

A Persian gold armlet, decorated with griffins, from the Treasure of the Oxus, Persia.

4 Esther hears the news

Esther is the only one of her people with access to the king, and she has not been summoned to him for a month. The only way open is the dangerous step of going to him unbidden. Anxiously she agrees to take the risk.

Verses 14-16: although God is not mentioned, Mordecai's faith is plain. The fast would involve prayer.

5 Esther gives a dinner-party

The king permits an audience. But Esther proceeds cannily. She invites the king and his favourite to dinner. In the mellow after-dinner atmosphere she gives a second invitation. Haman – suspecting nothing, knowing nothing of Esther's relationship to Mordecai – is greatly flattered. He goes home and builds a gallows topping the city wall, on which he intends to hang his enemy.

6 The king honours Mordecai

A sleepless night and the reading of the court diary give events a new twist. To his mortification Haman finds himself heaping on his enemy honours he had thought were intended for himself. His superstitious advisers see in this the beginning of his downfall.

7 Haman's villainy unmasked

After dinner on the second evening Esther makes her request. Haman is dumbfounded. And his action in throwing himself at Esther's feet as she reclines on her couch only succeeds in adding attempted rape to the charges against him. In the supreme irony of things, he ends his life on the gallows he himself had made.

They covered Haman's face (8): i.e. in token of the death sentence.

8 Mordecai becomes grand vizier; a new edict

There still remains the problem of Haman's edict. Since it was issued in the king's name and under his seal it cannot be revoked (8). But in answer to Esther's further plea the king authorizes a second decree permitting the Jews to defend themselves against attack.

Verse 11: the Jews were allowed to treat their enemies exactly as they were to have been treated themselves (see 3:13).

9 Jewish vengeance; the Feast of Purim

When the appointed day arrives, the Jews rid themselves of their enemies, including Haman's ten sons; but they take no plunder. There can be no excuse for Esther's vindictive request. She shows herself to be a child of her age. The bodies of Haman's sons are hanged to make their fate public knowledge.

In commemoration of the nation's deliverance, the 14th and 15th Adar become annual feast days, preceded by a fast on the 13th. To this day the Jews celebrate Purim, reading the book of Esther aloud, and remembering many more recent miracles of deliverance.

10 Conclusion

The author closes with a final historical note, attesting the good use Mordecai made of his power.

POETRY AND WISDOM LITERATURE

Introduction/Derek Kidner

POETRY

The word 'poetry' may suggest to us a highly specialized branch of literary art, produced by the few for the few. But this would be a misleading term for any part of the Old Testament. A closer modern equivalent would be the measured oratory of, for instance, a Winston Churchill –

We shall fight on the beaches,
We shall fight on the landing-grounds,
We shall fight in the fields and in the streets

– in which reiteration (or other devices) and rhythm join to make a passage doubly memorable and impressive.

Reiteration was a favourite Canaanite technique, and is also a mark of some of the earliest biblical poetry:

Proverbs is paralleled in contemporary cultures by other collections of wisdom. *The Wisdom of Amenemope*, on this papyrus from Thebes, Egypt, dates from about 1000 BC.

Spoil of dyed stuffs for Sisera,
Spoil of dyed stuffs embroidered,
Two pieces of dyed work
    embroidered for my neck as spoil
    (Judges 5:30).

The rhythm, though tighter than this in the original, is a flexible matter of stresses, or beats, not of fixed numbers of syllables. Most often there will be three stresses to a line, matched by another three in the following line which pairs with it to form a couplet. But this pattern may be varied by an occasional longer or shorter couplet, or by a triplet, in the same passage; or again the predominating rhythm may be of couplets in which a three-beat line is answered by another of two beats:

How are the mighty fallen
in the midst of the battle!

This last rhythm, with its touch of fading or drooping, is often used for taunts or laments (as in the book of Lamentations), and this has suggested the name *Qinah* (lament) for it, although its use is not confined to such themes.

What is almost the hallmark of biblical poetry, in contrast to our own, is parallelism: the echoing of the thought of one line of verse in a second line which is its partner:

Has he said, and will he not do it?
Or has he spoken, and will he not fulfil it? (Numbers 23:19)

There are many varieties of this, from virtual repetition to amplification or antithesis. It has a dignity and spaciousness which allows time for the thought to make its effect on the hearer, and often also the opportunity to present more than one facet of a matter:

For my thoughts are not your thoughts,
neither are your ways my ways, says the Lord (Isaiah 55:8).

Bishop Lowth, whose lectures on Hebrew poetry in 1741 first introduced the name 'parallelism' for this poetic style, pointed out that this structure, based as it is on meaning, survives translation into the prose of any language with remarkably little loss, unlike the poetry that relies on complex metre or a special vocabulary. There are, of course, such points of style in Old Testament verse, and occasionally such devices as assonance, rhyme, refrains, word-plays and acrostics; but they are secondary. The essence of this poetry is that it has great matters to convey forcibly to people of all kinds. It is therefore unselfconscious, and remarkably free from artificialities of language.

For this reason, poetry is not segregated into a few poetical books, but breaks out in various contexts at moments of special importance. The examples quoted above are drawn from books we might call histories (but the Jews called them the 'Former Prophets') and from prophecy. In fact nearly all prophetic utterances are in this form, and are rightly set out as lines of poetry in recent translations of the Bible.

Three books of the Old Testament, however, were given a more elaborate system of accents than the rest by the Jewish grammarians, to mark them out as distinctively poetic. These were Job, Psalms and Proverbs. To our ears, a better candidate than Proverbs would have been the Song of Solomon; its pure lyric poetry a third example of Hebrew poetry to stand beside the rich eloquence of Job and the singable verse of the Psalms. On Job, more will be said under the heading of Wisdom, below; but purely as poetry it has been hailed as one of the masterpieces of world literature, for the wealth and energy of its language and the power of its thought. In the Psalms, poetry is put to work, to be 'the way to heaven's door' in worship or in teaching, furnishing inspired words for public festivals and royal occasions, and for the individual who might come to confess his sins, or plead for healing, or rejoice over some deliverance or revelation. The Song of Solomon, by contrast, scarcely gives the name of God a mention, but responds rapturously to his creation and to its crowning glory, the gift of love between man and woman. Its

presence in the Bible is the most graceful of tokens that God's world is not properly divisible into secular and sacred, and that holiness cannot be indifferent to beauty.

WISDOM LITERATURE
Wisdom, in the Old Testament, is the voice of reflection and experience, rather than of bare command or preaching. We are persuaded, even teased, into seeing the connection between God's order in the world and his orders to men, and the absurdity of going against the grain of his creation.

It takes many forms. A vivid comparison, perhaps expanded into a parable or an allegory, is a favourite device; the Hebrew word for it, *mashal*, does duty for any of these, and equally for a proverb or a taunt. A riddle or an enigmatic saying is another means of pricking a person into thought. At a deeper level there will be searching reflection on the way God governs the world, and on the ends for which men live.

Like poetry, Wisdom is not confined to the books which we group under this name (in the Old Testament, Proverbs, Job, Ecclesiastes), for proverbs and pointed sayings are part of every culture, and Israel's was no exception. In the narratives we have, for instance, Jotham's fable of the trees, Samson's riddle, and various proverbs; while in the Psalms and prophetic oracles the teaching style of the Wise makes itself clearly heard from time to time (e.g. Psalm 1; Isaiah 28:23ff.; Jeremiah 17:5ff.; Hosea 14:9). We are confirmed in identifying this as a distinct ingredient in Scripture by the fact that Israel itself heard it as a third voice alongside Law and Prophecy. There was even a proverb to this effect: 'The law shall not perish from the priest, nor counsel from the wise, nor the word from the prophet' (Jeremiah 18:18).

Of all reputations for wisdom, Solomon's is pre-eminent; and it rests not only on his own brilliance but on his patronage of learning and the arts. The Queen of Sheba was but one of a stream of visitors who poured into Israel to hear him and put him to the test. The names and places of 1 Kings 4:30-33 give a glimpse of an intellectual world that briefly found its capital in Jerusalem; and this openness to foreign enquirers finds some reflection in the authorship of Proverbs 30 and 31:1-9, which are apparently the work of non-Israelite converts.

Israel's Wisdom literature, then, never professed to have developed in an intellectual vacuum. Just how rich was the surrounding culture is becoming clear as the wisdom of Egypt and Mesopotamia comes increasingly to light. Some of their fables, popular sayings and precepts have been preserved, and they are largely concerned with the common stuff of life that occupies the biblical proverbs: teachability, sobriety, wise speech, kindness, trust in divine help, magnanimity, friendship. There is a certain amount of mere worldly wisdom here, but much, too, that is sound and high-principled, although the biblical material moves at a consistently higher level of informed faith. Another class of literature from these countries wrestles with the problems of suffering and the meaning of existence, arguing the points at considerable length in skilfully constructed poetic monologues and dialogues.

The fact that questions of this depth were being debated in writing, not only in the time of Solomon but for a thousand years before him, and that the Israel of his day was anything but a cultural back-water, should dispose of the idea (still current in some circles) that Israel's stock of wisdom consisted at this time of short popular sayings, which supposedly developed by degrees into longer and more religious units, and only in the latest period into the connected discourses of Proverbs 1-9 or the probings of Job and Ecclesiastes. The dating of these calls for better criteria than a scheme of religious evolution.

But while it is illuminating to see how high a level of discussion existed from these early times, the Old Testament treatment of these themes remains distinctive. In the book of Job, God is recognizably the faithful, righteous Lord whose ways, while they are past finding out, are to be trusted to the end. Job does not have to conclude, like one of the Babylonian sufferers, that what is evil on earth may be counted good in heaven; nor is there any question of placating God with gifts; still less of throwing in one's hand and renouncing him. And in Ecclesiastes the apparent pessimism of the book has only a surface resemblance to the deep-dyed cynicism of the Babylonian Dialogue between Master and Servant, where nothing has meaning or value, and only caprice remains. Ecclesiastes does indeed reduce everything the world offers to a mere breath, but this is done precisely because man was made for something bigger than time and space: the fear of God, whose assessment of every deed and 'every secret thing' as good or evil invests the whole of life with meaning (Ecclesiastes 12:13-14).

That expression, the fear of God, to which Ecclesiastes moves as its conclusion, is the starting-point of Proverbs (1:7) and the pivot of all the Wisdom literature (see Job 28:28; Psalm 111:10; Proverbs 9:10). Secular philosophy tends to measure everything by man, and comes to doubt whether wisdom is to be found at all. But the Old Testament with this motto turns the world the right way up, with God at its head, his wisdom the creative and ordering principle that runs through every part; and man, disciplined and taught by that wisdom, finding life and fulfilment in his perfect will.

JOB

The book of Job stands alone amongst the books of the Old Testament. It forms a part of the 'Wisdom' material (Proverbs, Ecclesiastes; see 'Poetry and Wisdom Literature', Introduction), but in form and theme it is unique. No one knows who wrote it, or just when it was written, but the story is set in the days of the patriarchs. Job is a wealthy and influential sheikh – wealthy in terms of flocks and herds rather than cash. Part of the year he is a man of the city; for the rest, on the move with his cattle. He belongs to the days before the priesthood and organized religion or to a region where these things were not needed. He reminds us very much of Abraham: a man of the east.

A prose prologue introduces the great debate between Job and his friends which the author records in magnificent poetry. The subject is as old as the hills and as modern as the space-age. If God is just and good, why does he let innocent people suffer? (Why the casual victims of war and terrorism? Why the child dying of cancer?) As a man Job is *really* good: about the best any man could ever hope to be. Yet calamity overwhelms him. Loss of possessions and family is followed by grim, prolonged physical suffering that shakes his faith to the depths.

As they tussle with the problem, both Job and his friends are hampered by ignorance of the larger issue, the challenge of Satan related in the prologue. They have no assurance of a future life. For them death is the end. So justice must be seen to be done in this life. According to orthodox theology – the position championed by the three friends – prosperity was God's reward for good living, calamity his judgement on the sin of the individual. Generally speaking this held good. But the friends reduced a general truth to a rigid, invariable rule. If Job suffers, then he must be a wicked man. But Job knows this is untrue. So the argument goes back and forth, neither side shifting position, until they reach complete impasse, at which point God himself intervenes. He does not answer Job's questions. But, seeing God, Job is satisfied. If his friends' theology had been too narrow, his own concept of God had been too small.

The book leaves much unsettled. It is only in the New Testament that we approach an answer to the problem. As we look at Christ on the cross we see the suffering of the only really innocent Man. And we see a God who cares so much for us he is prepared to shoulder the whole burden of human sin and suffering. Yet the book of Job is not out-dated. Even today, suffering men and women find that this book speaks to their need as no other book in the Bible.

1 - 2 PROLOGUE

1:1-5: Job is introduced (see introduction).

1:6-12: in the court of heaven Satan accuses Job of serving God for what he can get out of it. God allows him to test this out – a measure of his confidence in Job – but Job himself is to be spared.

1:13-22: in the space of a single day Job loses everything –

Transition from wealth to poverty can be swift for any nomadic people. But Job's misfortunes were out of the ordinary.

possessions, servants, family – but his confidence in God remains unshaken (compare verse 21 with Paul's words in Philippians 4:11-12).

2:1-6: Satan has lost the first round. Now he says Job is only really concerned for his own skin. So God allows a further test, stopping short only at Job's life.

2:7-13: Job's body breaks out in running sores. The great man becomes an outcast. His wife fails him. The three friends who remain loyal sit in silence, appalled at what has happened. But still Job holds fast to God.

Uz (1:1): a town to the east of Palestine – in Edomite territory, or possibly in the Hauran, south of Damascus.

Sons of God (1:6): angels of God's court in heaven. Satan is among them, under God's authority.

Sabeans (1:15): nomads of south-west Arabia; *Chaldeans* (17): nomads from south Mesopotamia, Abraham's homeland.

Job's friends (2:11): wise men from towns in Arab and Edomite territory, a region renowned for its sages.

3 - 14 THE FIRST ROUND IN THE DEBATE

3 Job's first speech: the bitterness of life
Job's suffering makes him wish he had never been born. He longs to find peace and release in death.

Verse 8: Job refers to magicians who can make a day 'unlucky'. Leviathan may be the monster supposed to have been imprisoned by God at creation. In chapter 41 Leviathan is the crocodile.

Verse 24: sighs and groans are his daily diet.

4 - 5 Eliphaz' first speech
Job has often helped others in trouble; now he should be prepared to swallow his own medicine. God destroys the guilty, not the innocent (4:7). No one is blameless before him (17). Trouble is an inevitable part of life (5:7). The best course is to turn to God (8), accept his reproof (17), and wait to be restored to favour.

There is much in what Eliphaz says, but his diagnosis happens to be wrong in Job's case.

5:4: cases were tried and contracts made at the town gate; it was the hub of public life.

6 - 7 Job's reply
It is nauseating advice (6:6-7) to tell a man at the end of his tether to be patient (11-12). Job wants only to cease to be. His friends have failed to show sympathy when he needed it most (14ff.). He has done nothing to deserve suffering (30). Life is a succession of pain-filled days and sleepless nights (7:3-6).

7:11-21: Job turns to God and pours out his heart to him – his fear, his longing for death. Why won't God leave him alone? If sin is the trouble, why won't he forgive?

6:18-19: the caravans of traders crossing the desert come looking for water, and not finding it move on to die of thirst.

7:5: Job's sores breed maggots. 8

Bildad's first speech
Eliphaz had begun gently. Bildad takes a firmer line as Job's words grow wilder. God is just. He rewards the good and punishes the wicked. Bildad's words are salt to an open wound (4).

Papyrus (11): the reed which grew in the Egyptian marshes and from which paper was made.

9 - 10 Job's reply
Job believes as Bildad does in the justice of God. But his own case will not square with his belief. God has condemned an innocent man. How can anyone call him to account?

Good, bad – it is all one (9:22). Disaster strikes both. Why (10:2)? The Creator has turned Destroyer (8). Will he allow no respite before life is over (20-22)?

Rahab (9:13): the legendary monster of chaos.

God as an unjust judge. Like many a man before and since, Job's basic problem was to get a hearing at all (19), and even if he got as far as the court he could not be sure of a fair hearing and impartial administration of the law.

11 Zophar's first speech
Zophar's words are harshest of all. Does Job think himself innocent? God is letting him down lightly (6). Job must put away his sin (13-14); then God will restore him.

12 - 14 Job's reply
Job is stung to sarcasm. His friends are not the only ones who can work things out. God is all-wise, all-powerful. If he turns the norms of wisdom and justice upside-down, what can anyone do about it (12:7-22)? Job's experience gives the lie to the arguments of his friends (13:1-4). He will put his case to God direct, and God will acquit him (18). What are the

charges against him (23)? Life is short and there is no waking a man from the sleep of death (14:1-12). Job cries to God to hide him away in the land of the dead until his anger is past, and then to restore him (13-17). But despair floods back – what hope is there (19)?

15 - 21 THE SECOND ROUND

15 Eliphaz' second speech

The debate grows more heated. Job has needled his friends, and they make no allowances for the stress he is under. It never crosses their minds he may really be innocent. They go on doggedly defending their position and trying to bludgeon Job into submission.

Job is a self-opinionated old wind-bag (2)! All he has said – his wild accusations against God; his attempts to justify himself – merely serve to prove his guilt (6). Job is wrong in saying that the wicked get off scot-free. Their fate is a terrible one (17-35).

16 - 17 Job's reply

It is cold comfort his friends have to give. How easy for them to talk, when it is Job who bears the pain. (Like many since, their silent sympathy, 2:13, helped more than their well-meaning words.) God has worn him out with suffering and the cruelty of his fellow men. The pictures Job paints (16:9, 12-14) convey his intense, unbearable agony – a tortured body and a mind tormented at the thought that God could do all this to him. Even now he cannot believe God is unjust: there must be one who will plead his cause in heaven (19; see 1 John 2:1). If his case rests till he is dead, what hope is there (17:13-16)?

17:3: Job speaks to God.

18 Bildad's second speech

Bildad bitterly resents Job's angry rejection of their advice. He replies by painting a terrible picture of the fate of the wicked, meant to put Job in his place. But Job is innocent, and Bildad's tirade irrelevant.

19 Job's reply

Job's friends have become his tormentors, levelling false accusations and offering no answer to his desperate questions. He is shut in on himself (8), despairing (10), utterly alone (13-16). He has become an object of loathing to those he loves most (17). Even pity is denied him (21-22).

Yet even in his darkest moments, faith and hope still well up inside

him. He is certain of vindication. One day God himself will take up his case and clear him – and he will be there to see it (25-27). Then those who have maligned him will find themselves answerable to God.

20 Zophar's second (and last) speech

Zophar takes up Bildad's theme: the fate of the wicked. Their prosperity is short-lived, their punishment certain. We hear no more from him after this: either he has nothing further to add, or a section of the third round of speeches has been lost. It is possible that 27:7-23, which sounds so strange coming from Job, belongs in fact to Zophar.

21 Job's reply

Zophar's theology is all very well, but it flies in the face of experience. The condition of Job, the good man, is pitiful (5). Yet more often than not, evil men flourish, live happily and die peacefully (7-18). The friends will argue that God's vengeance falls on their children (19). But what kind of justice is that? Their so-called comfort is nothing but a pack of empty lies.

22 - 31 THE THIRD ROUND

22 Eliphaz speaks for the third and last time

It is still the same stubborn line of argument. Job is in the wrong – Eliphaz even lists out his sins (5-9)! Job had thought he could hide the fact from God (14). Let him return to God, put away his sin, and all will be well again.

Ophir (24): so famous for the export of gold (see 2 Chronicles 8:18) that 'Ophir' and 'fine gold' became synonymous. The location is unknown.

23 - 24 Job's reply

If only he could find God and put his case to him. But God is not to be found, and his ways are inexplicable.

'Mines where copper is smelted': in the mountains near the port of Eilat the ancient mines are being worked again today.

Chapter 24: look what goes on in the world. Life is neither fair nor just. God delays judgement, and those who trample the helpless underfoot seem to get away with it. **Remove landmarks (24:2):** i.e. seize lands. The landmark was a stone sometimes inscribed with the landowner's title-deeds and boundaries. **Take in pledge (24:3, 9):** take as security for credit, or seize in payment of debt.

25 Bildad speaks for the third and last time

If the speech is complete as it stands, Job's friends have exhausted their argument. They have nothing more to say. Bildad merely reiterates the obvious truth that no man is 100 per cent perfect in God's sight. This does not help Job. What point is there in godly living if God's punishment falls equally on good and bad?

26 - 31 Job's last reply

Chapter 26: in the created universe we catch a glimpse of God's dynamic power. But who can think to comprehend that power in all its fullness?

Chapter 27: his friends want him to deny his integrity, but Job will not perjure himself. Verses 7-23 sound strange coming from Job. This has previously been the argument his friends have put forward. Either Job's thinking has changed, or this passage really belongs to one of the others (perhaps Zophar's missing third speech).

Chapter 28: Job's mind turns again (see 26:14) to the question of wisdom. This is the heart of his problem: how to understand the inscrutable ways of God. But no miner can uncover a vein of wisdom; all the wealth in the world will not buy it. Only God knows where to find it. And man becomes wise through reverence for God and by rejecting evil.

Chapter 29: Job looks back on the golden days of God's favour – past enjoyment of home, of success in business, of universal respect.

Chapter 30: 'But now': he returns to the bitter present, which has made him the butt of all, an outcast, incessantly gnawed by pain.

Chapter 31: all this has befallen a man who has avoided immorality, even in his thinking (1); who has played fair with his employees (13); been generous in relieving need (16); never become obsessed with money (24) or turned idolater (26-27); turned no one from his door (32); harboured

no secret sins (33); never kept quiet for fear of what others might think or how they might react (34). Job is prepared to swear to all this before God. How many of us could honestly do the same?

Abaddon (26:6; 28:22): another word for 'Sheol', the shadowy land of the dead.

Rahab (26:12): see on 9:13.

Ophir (28:16): see on 22:24.

32-37 ELIHU'S TIRADE

Chapter 32: Elihu is the original angry young man. His elders are lost for words, but he is simply bursting with indignation at Job's attitude, dying to have his say.

Chapter 33: Job has declared himself the innocent victim of God (9-11); but God will not answer his charge (13). Elihu says God speaks to man through warning dreams (15) and through suffering (19) – in order to save, not destroy him (30).

Chapter 34: Job has said God is in the wrong (5-6), and there is nothing to be gained by making him our delight (9). But God is the judge of all men: supreme, just, impartial (10-30). Job has added to his other sins resentment and rebellion against God (36-37).

Chapter 35: Elihu (wrongly; see 2 Samuel 11:27; 12:13) sees good and bad conduct as a matter between men (8): God remains high above, untouched by either. People cry out to him in their need (9). But they are concerned for their own skins, not for him (10-12). This is why he does not answer (13).

Chapter 36: God is almighty, all-wise (5). He is a Teacher who uses suffering to open men's ears to listen and learn where they have gone wrong (8-10). Job should not be longing for death (20), but learning his lesson (22).

Chapter 37: God is great. He commands the thunder and lightning, rain and snow. He spreads out the clouds and the shining skies. Man is as nothing beside God's awesome splendour, his unassailable holiness. Men are right to fear him (24). He pays no attention to people (like Job!) who grow too big for their boots.

38 - 42:6 JOB FINDS SATISFACTION IN GOD'S ANSWER

God breaks in just when Elihu has finished his list of excellent reasons why Job cannot expect an answer! God *is* almighty, far and away above humanity. But he is also near. He hears, and he cares. Job had imagined himself putting his case to God, asking his questions. But imagination is not reality. It is God, not Job, who asks the questions now. And through the succession of searching questions Job finds his opinion of himself shrinking, his concept of God expanding. His mental image of God had been altogether too small. The God who confronts him is God on a different scale altogether.

Chapters 38 and 39: where was Job when God made the world, light and darkness, wind and rain, the constellations in their courses? What does Job know about the creatures of the wild – the lion, the goat, the wild ass and ox, the ostrich, the horse, the eagle? Did he make them? Can he feed them, tame them – *as God can?*

Chapters 40 and 41: is Job God's equal, that he calls him to book, and questions his justice? (Job's wild words had brought him dangerously near the sin of the first man.) Look at just two of my creatures, says God – Behemoth (the hippopotamus) and Leviathan (the crocodile). Look at their strength (40:16; 41:27); their sheer untameability (40:24; 41:1-2). Man is utterly powerless to control them. What folly then to claim equality with God who made them!

42:1-6 contains Job's reaction, the climax of the book. Job now realizes he had been dabbling in things beyond his understanding, totally out of his depth. Before, he had gone by hearsay; now he has seen God for himself, as he longed to do. There is now no question of putting his case; seeing God is enough. His questions remain unanswered, but he is satisfied. It is unthinkable that this God could ever let him down or act inconsistently. He can trust, where he does not understand. Now he can accept what comes. Self-righteousness melts away. Job regrets the bitter things he has said. As he looks at God and worships, he sees himself and his problem in perspective.

42:7-17 EPILOGUE

Verses 1-6 are the high point in the story. This final passage in prose merely rounds things off. Job has been vindicated, and this must be visibly demonstrated. (There is no promise of a fairy-tale ending to every case of suffering.)

God has taken Job to task for his reaction to suffering, but his integrity is beyond question. Job's good name is as clear as his conscience. It is the three friends who have been wrong. Job's was an honest search for truth. They would not allow for truth being bigger than their understanding of it – and so they were guilty of misrepresenting God. They must obtain Job's forgiveness before God will forgive them.

Significantly, it is at the point when Job has accepted his suffering and forgiven his friends, that God reverses his fortunes. Friends, prosperity, family are all restored to him, with a long life in which to enjoy them.

PSALMS

The psalms express the whole range of human feeling and experience, from dark depression to exuberant joy. They are rooted in particular circumstances, yet they are timeless, and so among the best-loved, most-read, parts of the Bible. In our modern age we are stirred by the same emotions, puzzled over the same fundamental problems of life, cry out in need, or worship, to the same God, as the psalmists of old. We find it easy to identify with them. And we find their sheer, dogged faith, the depth of their love for God, both a tonic and a rebuke.

Psalms, the Old Testament hymnal, is a collection of five books: 1 - 41, 42 - 72, 73 - 89, 90 - 106, 107 - 150. At the end of each section (e.g. 41:13) the break is marked by a 'doxology' (a formal ascription of praise to God), Psalm 150 forming a doxology to the whole collection. Within the five books the psalms are often grouped, according to common themes, a common purpose, or a common author/collector. Most of the psalms are prefaced by a title or heading (these are omitted in the New English Bible and the Jerusalem Bible) which is later than the psalm itself but preserves very ancient Jewish tradition. Some name the author or collector, and relate to specific events in history (those linked with David's life-story have already been listed). Seventy-three psalms bear David's name – some, no doubt, dedicated to him as king; some collected by him; and a good many, surely, the work of his own pen. (1 Samuel 16:17-23 and 1 Chronicles 25:1-8 are not the only indications that the king was a gifted poet and musician.) Many other titles concern the musicians, instruments, musical settings, or indicate the type of psalm ('Maskil', 'Miktam'), although the meaning of many of the terms used can now only be guessed at.

There have been many attempts to classify the psalms, and they can be grouped in a number of ways, for example by theme. There are psalms which plead with God and psalms which praise him; appeals for forgiveness, or the destruction of enemies; prayers for the king, or for the nation; 'wisdom' psalms and psalms which probe life's problem-areas; and psalms (such as 119) which celebrate the greatness of God's law. Many psalms are a blend of several of these common themes. All are part of the religious life of Israel.

Perhaps one of the most helpful ways of grouping the psalms is by the main literary types:

— Hymns, in praise of God's character and deeds (e.g. Psalms 8; 19; 29).
— Community laments, arising out of some national disaster (44; 74).
— Royal psalms, originating in some special occasion in the life of the reigning king (2; 18; 20; 45).
— Individual laments (3; 7; 13; 25; 51).
— Individual thanksgivings (30; 32; 34).

It is very difficult to date individual psalms, or to discover just how and when they were collected and compiled, though the process began with David, if not before, and continued into the days after the exile. Manuscripts found at Qumran have shown that the whole collection as we have it must have been finalized some time before the Maccabean period (2nd century BC).

The words of C.S. Lewis underline one further important point:
'*The psalms are poems, and poems intended to be sung: not doctrinal treatises, nor even sermons ... They must be read as poems if they are to be understood ... Otherwise we shall miss what is in them and think we see what is not.*'

Before turning to the psalms themselves, read the introduction to the Poetry and Wisdom section, which explains the conventions of Hebrew poetry.

BOOK 1

Psalm 1 The blessing which results from the study and practice of God's law

Verses 1-3 depict the happy man, who resolutely turns his back on evil and sets his heart and mind on God's law. 4-6, in terrible contrast, picture the present life and future fate of the wicked.

Verse 3: compare the picture here with Jeremiah 17:7-8.

Psalm 2 Rebel man – sovereign God

Verses 1-3: the world-rulers enter into a futile conspiracy. 4-6 depict the power of God and his chosen man (primarily the king, ultimately the Christ, see note on Christ in the Psalms). 7-9: God delegates authority. 10-12: the psalm ends on a note of solemn warning.

Zion (6): the citadel of Jerusalem.

Psalm 3 A cry to God in time of danger

The title refers the psalm to the specific time of Absalom's rebellion against his father, King David, 2 Samuel 15.)

Verses 1-2 outline the situation. 3-6: in God, the God who answers, is security and freedom from fear. 7-8: the psalmist calls on God to save him.

Psalm 4 A prayer for the night

Trust in God sets mind and body at rest.

Verse 1: past answers to prayer give grounds for present confidence. 2-5: a reprimand is followed by command. 6-8 describe the joy and peace which nothing can shake.

Psalm 5 A prayer in the morning

Beset by men who lie and flatter

CHRIST IN THE PSALMS

The primary meaning of the psalms is always to be sought first of all in their immediate, historical context. But this does not exhaust their significance. No one can read the psalms without becoming aware that certain psalms and individual verses have a deeper, future significance beyond the simple meaning of the words. The Messiah is not mentioned by name, but his figure is foreshadowed, as later generations of Jews came to realize. And the New Testament writers are quick to apply these verses to Jesus as the prophesied Messiah.

Some psalms, particularly the 'royal psalms' (of which 2, 72, 110 are the most striking) picture an ideal divine king/priest/judge never fully realized in any actual king of Israel. Only the Messiah combines these roles in the endless, universal reign of peace and justice envisaged by the psalmists.

Other psalms depict human suffering in terms which seem far-fetched in relation to ordinary experience, but which proved an extraordinarily accurate description of the actual sufferings of Christ. Under God's inspiration, the psalmists chose words and pictures which were to take on a significance they can hardly have dreamed of. Psalm 22, the psalm Jesus

quoted as he hung on the cross (verse 1, Matthew 27:46), is the most amazing example. Compare verse 16 with John 20:25; verse 18 with Mark 15:24. (See also Psalm 69:21 and Matthew 27:34, 48).

There are also many other verses in the psalms which New Testament writers apply to Jesus as the Christ:

Psalm 2:7, 'You are my son': Acts 13:33

Psalm 8:6, 'all things under his feet': Hebrews 2:6-10

Psalm 16:10, 'not give me up to Sheol ...': Acts 2:27; 13:35

Psalm 22:8, 'let him deliver him': Matthew 27:43

Psalm 40:7-8, 'I delight to do thy will': Hebrews 10:7

Psalm 41:9, 'my bosom friend ... has lifted his heel against me': John 13:18

Psalm 45:6, 'your divine throne endures for ever': Hebrews 1:8

Psalm 69:9, 'zeal for thy house has consumed me': John 2:17

Psalm 110:4, 'a priest for ever after the order of Melchizedek': Hebrews 7:17

Psalm 118:22, 'the stone which the builders rejected ...': Matthew 21:42

Psalm 118:26, 'blessed be he who enters in the name of the Lord': Matthew 21:9

while they plot his downfall (6, 8-10), the psalmist appeals to the God who loathes every semblance of evil (1-5), the Defence and Rewarder of the good (11-12). This is the God he will worship and serve (7).

Psalm 6 A cry of anguish

Sick at heart (disturbed in mind, ill in body), the psalmist pleads with God for his life (1-7), and is assured of God's answer (8-10).

Sheol (5): the shadowy world of the dead. Although the psalmists thought in terms of some kind of continued existence beyond the grave it was largely negative. Death cut a man off from all he could experience of God during his life. His tongue was still; he could no longer sing God's praises.

Psalm 7 A prayer for protection and the just judgement of God

The psalmist casts himself on God, knowing his cause is just (1-5). He calls on God to clear his name, to support the right and break the wicked (6-11). He describes the terrible fate awaiting those who refuse to repent (12-16) and closes on a note of thanksgiving.

Psalm 8 God – and man

Verses 2-4: as he contemplates the great expanse of the universe the psalmist is overwhelmed by a sense of man's littleness. He marvels that God not only bothers about man, but has set him over all other creatures (5-8). The psalm ends, as it began, with a refrain of praise to God (1,9)
Verses 4-6: see also Hebrews 2:6-9 and Genesis 1:28.

Psalm 9 A song of praise

One of a number of 'acrostic' psalms, in which the first letter of each verse follows the order of the 22-letter Hebrew alphabet. Only the first 11 letters (with one omission) are used here, and the acrostic seems to continue (imperfectly) in Psalm 10.

Verses 3-8 give the reason for the outburst of praise. God has executed justice and upheld the right. He is an unassailable fortress (9-10). Praise him (11)! Trouble is by no means over (13), but past experience gives ground for fresh hope (15-20). 'Thy kingdom come'!

Psalm 10 A prayer to God to defend the helpless

Verses 1-11: times are bad. Evil men defy God and disregard his laws and get away with it. The poor are their helpless victims. 12-18: the psalmist calls on God to act, confident that he will break oppression and defend those who have no one but himself to turn to.

Psalm 11 A declaration of faith

No matter what the danger, the man who trusts in God has no need to panic (1-3). He knows God is still sovereign: the champion of justice, the Judge of evil (4-7).

Psalm 12 A prayer for God's help

Surrounded by men whose word cannot be trusted (1-4), the psalmist puts his faith in the utterly dependable promises of God.

Psalm 13 From despair to hope

In his misery it seems to the psalmist that God has forgotten him. How much longer must he bear it? Will only death bring an end to it (1-4)? No! All his past experience assures him he will again have cause to thank God for his goodness (5-6).

Psalm 14 The folly of godless man

Society is corrupt: the bias to sin universal (1-3). In wilful blindness men pit themselves against a God who not only exists but punishes and avenges every aggressive act against his people (4-7).

Verses 1-3: Paul uses these verses to support his case that no human being is sinless when measured by God's standards (Romans 3).

Jacob ... Israel (7): the psalmist calls the nation by the two names of its founder. The wily Jacob was given the new name 'Israel' after his momentous encounter with God at Peniel (Genesis 32:28).

Psalm 15 Testimonial of the man of God

What does God require of the individual who seeks his company? He expects right conduct, right speaking (2-3a), right relationships with others (3b-4), and a right use of wealth (5). See also Psalm 24.

Who swears ... (4): i.e. who keeps his word whatever the cost.
Verse 5: one of the Jewish laws, see Leviticus 25:36-37. It was not a total ban on lending at interest, but applied to fellow Israelites.

Psalm 16 The way of faith

The man who sets his heart on God and puts his life in God's hands (1-6) finds joy and security for the present and need not worry about what lies ahead (7-11).

The lines (6): used to measure out the plot of land a man inherited.
Verse 10: the psalmist is probably thinking of premature or sudden death. Paul, applying the words to Christ, sees their deeper significance (Acts 13:35-37).

Psalm 17 Appeal to God from a clear conscience

This psalm raises two problems which occur in a number of other psalms: self-justification and vengeance. See note below.

Apple (8): the pupil; the part of the eye a man instinctively protects.

Psalm 18 Praise to God for deliverance

This is a revised version of David's victory song (2 Samuel 22). The outburst of love and praise (1-3), and the cataclysmic terms in which he describes God's rescue (7-19), give some idea of his previous desperation. He owes his life, his triumphs, his throne, everything to God (28-50).

Sheol (5): see on Psalm 6.

Verses 20-24: for the problem of self-justification see special article.

Psalm 19 God's wonderful creation; his perfect law

God's universe describes his glory in speech without words (1-4). The psalmist's thought leaps straight from the sun, with its all-pervading, searching rays, to the law of God – pure and clean, bringing joy and wisdom, instruction and enlightenment to man's heart (4b-11); and to his own need of protection and cleansing from sin (12-14).

Psalm 20 Prayer for victory for the king

A national prayer; the king himself speaks in verse 6.

Psalm 21 Thanksgiving for the king

Verses 1-7 rejoice in all God's goodness. Verses 8-12 look to the future. With God's help the king will put down all his enemies. King and people join to praise him (13).

Psalm 22 Suffering and salvation

It was the opening words of this psalm that Jesus used to express his anguish on the cross (Matthew 27:46). And the terms the psalmist chose to describe his own agony of mind and body became an extraordinarily precise description of the last hours of the Messiah. The psalmist only *felt* himself deserted by God (confidence returns, verse 22), but the separation Jesus experienced was real – the crushing, suffocating weight of human sin which shut him out from the Father's sight.

Despair at God's silence (1-2) and his own situation (6-8, 12-18) alternates with hope – hope that springs out of every recollection of God's past dealings with him (3-5, 9-11). The final prayer (19-21) brings new inward assurance, expressed in open praise (22-31). If, at the deepest level, the early verses of Psalm 22 speak of Christ's suffering, surely the closing verses speak of the worldwide deliverance he made possible.

Bulls of Bashan (12): Bashan, north of Gilead on the east of the Jordan, was famous cattle country.

Psalm 23 Sheep and Shepherd

This best-known, best-loved of all psalms pictures God, the Good Shepherd (see also John 10). He provides all that his people need. He leads them through life. He secures them from all harm (1-4). Verse 5 introduces a second picture: God, the perfect host, feasting his people with good things.

His name's sake (3): i.e. because this is his nature. God's love and care are wholly in keeping with his character.

Psalm 24 Worship

This psalm is a processional hymn, possibly written for that great occasion in David's life when the ark was first carried into Jerusalem (2 Samuel 6:12-15).

The whole world and everything in it is God's. Who then is worthy to stand in his presence (1-3)? The answer (4, and see Psalm 15) would lead to despair if God were not 'the God of Jacob' (6) – the twisted character God took up and made the founder of Israel. Verses 7-10: the ark is at the gates of the city: open the doors for God himself to enter!

Psalm 25 Prayer of a troubled man

An acrostic psalm (see on Psalm 9). The psalmist is harassed by the incessant attack of his enemies, and disquieted in his own conscience (1-3, 16-21). Deeply aware of his need, he turns to God for his help and leading, asking to experience again his love and forgiveness (4-15). What more reassuring verse for any of God's children than verse 10?

Psalm 26 Prayer of a good man

The psalmist is not claiming perfection but a consistent life of trust and

The shepherd leads his sheep to fresh pasture.

obedience to God. Compare this self-portrait with the first part of Psalm 1.

Psalm 27 Trust and commitment to God

The man whose priorities are right (4,8) has nothing to fear (1-3, 5-6). He knows where to turn in trouble (7-12) and his hope is well founded (13-14).

Psalm 28 Prayer – and its answer

Danger leads to a cry for help, and a plea for the punishment of those evil men who are the source of the trouble (1-5). Prayer turns to praise at the assurance that God has heard and answered (6-9).

Psalm 29 The thunder of God

In the torrent of rain, the ear-splitting thunderclaps, the blaze of lightning, the roaring wind that sets the great forests in motion, the psalmist hears God's voice. For God made and orders them all (3-10). Let the hosts of heaven sing his glory (1-2) – and may he bless his people on earth (11).

The style of this psalm is very similar to ancient Canaanite poetry.

Sirion (6): 9,000 ft Mt Hermon, on the Israel/Lebanon border.

Kadesh (8): a place in the desert south of Beersheba.

Psalm 30 Thanksgiving for a new lease of life

(The events in 1 Chronicles 21 may possibly provide the background to this psalm.) The dark days when life was in danger are past (2-3, 6-10). Easy times bred self-reliance (6). But this experience has put life into perspective (5) and shown the psalmist his own helplessness (7-10). Now that the danger is behind him, he gladly

A blind harpist, from Egypt. The psalms were part of the temple music. Many of their titles refer to musicians and instruments.

and openly acknowledges his debt of gratitude to God (11-12).

Psalm 31 Trial and trust

Verses 1-8: the psalmist turns to God for refuge (1-5); trust deepens as he recalls God's past dealings with him (6-8). 9-13: his mind returns to the painful present. 14-24: from his own trouble he turns to God again, with such renewed trust in his goodness and love that he is able to give encouragement to others (23-24).

Verse 5: with his dying breath Jesus echoed these words (Luke 23:46).

Psalm 32 Confession and the joy of God's forgiveness

Guilt suppressed becomes an intolerable burden (3-4). Confession and forgiveness bring a joyous lightness of heart (1-2, 5). Out of his own experience the psalmist encourages others to pray to God with confidence. (In verses 8-9 God himself speaks.)

Psalm 33 Everybody sing!

Tune up the instruments. Sing aloud in praise of God's character (4-5) and his great power (6-7). Stand in awe of him (8-9). Praise his sovereign rule in the affairs of men – his unfailing care for all who honour him (10-19). Sing a song of trust in him (21-22).

A new song (3): to surpass the best of the old. Every fresh experience of God calls forth new praise. John, in his vision, heard a new song in heaven (Revelation 5:9-10; 14:3).

Psalm 34 God's care for his people

An acrostic poem (see on Psalm 9). The title seems to refer to the incident in 1 Samuel 21:10 - 22:1, although the king's name there is Achish.

A man with such a story to tell of God's faithfulness cannot help sharing it. He owes it to God and his fellow believers (1-10). In the psalmist's experience, the man who honours God finds life (11-14). His misfortunes may be many, but God brings him through them all (19-22).

Psalm 35 A prayer to God to uphold the right

(For the ethical problems raised by the psalm see note on Self-justification, below.) Confident that right is on his side (he states his case in 7, 11-16, 19-25), the psalmist calls on God to pay back his enemies in their own coin (1-6, 17, 26) and clear his good name. Then he will praise God and tell others of his righteousness (9-10, 18, 28).

Psalm 36 The unfailing love of God

Verses 1-4 portray a man dedicated

to his own evil ways. 5-10 contrast the character of God – loving, faithful, good; the source of life and light and all the good that man enjoys. 11-12: a personal prayer.

Psalm 37 Good and evil

An acrostic poem (see on Psalm 9) full of the proverbial sayings that the wisdom writers loved (see 'Poetry and Wisdom Literature', Introduction).

Wherever one looks, people are flagrantly disobeying God's law, and getting away with it. Don't be tempted to envy them, says the psalmist. Things are not what they seem (1-2, 7b-9). The wicked are in a far from enviable position. Their time will soon be up, but blessing and security await God's people (the message drummed home by the proverbial sayings of 10-40, which paint the contrast between the wicked and the good). Go on doing good; be patient; and trust God to act (3-7a).

Psalm 38 In great distress: a prayer for forgiveness

Sin has resulted in physical sickness (3, 5, 7), as well as mental anguish (2, 4, 6, 8). Friends and family stand aloof (11), and the opposition have the chance they have been waiting for (12, 16). The psalmist admits his sin, with bitter regret, and cries to God for help (21-22).

Psalm 39 Man's 'little life'

The psalmist struggles to contain his thoughts, for fear of dishonouring God, but they burst out (1-3). He feels death at his shoulder; life as insubstantial as a puff of wind (5-6). And he cries out to God to reassure (4) and forgive him (8), and to remove his troubles (10-13).

Psalm 40 Praise and prayer from a full heart

The psalmist has openly declared God's marvellous dealings with him (9-10). He looks back with deep thankfulness (1-3), and spells out for others the things he has learnt about God (4-8). But his troubles are not yet over (11-17). He is still conscious of his need. And he appeals afresh to God for his help. (Verses 13-17 are repeated in Psalm 70.)

Psalm 41 'Prayer of a sick and lonely man'

Verses 1-3 state a general truth. Happy the man who helps those in need; when trouble hits *him* he finds that God is at hand to help. 4-12 outline the psalmist's own case: his illness, his isolation, his reliance on God. Verse 13 is a formal stanza of praise

to God, added to mark the end of the first book of psalms.

BOOK 2

Psalms 42 and 43 Longing for God

These two psalms share the same theme and the same refrain (42:5, 11; 43:5), and probably began as a single poem.

The psalmist is in exile in the north (42:6), surrounded by godless men who mock his faith (42:3, 10; 43:1-2). Deeply dispirited, he contrasts past joys (when he led the pilgrim throng to the sanctuary, 42:4) with the unhappy present. He is filled with longing for God's presence (42:2; 43:3-4). And, black as things are, faith and hope still break through (42:5, 11; 43:5).

Verse 6: the River Jordan rises near the foot of Mt Hermon on Israel's northern border. 'Mount Mizar' remains unidentified.

Psalm 44 National lament

This psalm is prompted by a disastrous defeat. Israel is bewildered. After all the stories of God's amazing actions in their early history (1-3), and their complete reliance on him (4-8, 17-18), now this defeat! God has deserted them (9-12). They are disgraced (13-16), and cannot understand why (17-22). Verses 23-26 are a real cry from the heart for God's help.

The switch to 'me' and 'my' in 4, 6, 15 may indicate a single voice (that of the king or high priest) leading the public prayer.

Verse 19: 'the place where jackals live', i.e. the desert.

Verse 22: Paul quotes these words, describing the experience of Christians (Romans 8:36).

Psalm 45 A royal wedding song

The actual occasion may have been the wedding of King Ahab of Israel to Jezebel, princess of Tyre (12, and see on 8 below). If so, the king's reign soon changed for the worse (1 Kings 16:29-33).

Verses 1-9: the poet's eloquent praise of the king's majesty and godly rule. 10-15: a word to the bride in all her finery. Verses 16 and 17 are addressed to the king.

Ivory palaces (8): a further possible link with Ahab. Archaeologists have discovered beautiful carved ivories in his palace at Samaria.

Ophir (9): see on 1 Kings 9:28.

Tyre (12): important sea-port and city-state; modern Sour in Lebanon.

Psalm 46 'A mighty fortress is our God'

This psalm – the one on which Luther based his famous hymn – may have been written following Sennacherib's attack on Jerusalem (2 Chronicles 32), some natural disaster, or in anticipation of the events heralding Messiah's coming. Verses 4-5 have a parallel in Revelation 22:1-5, where the ideal is perfectly realized. The psalmist glories in God's presence with his people (1, 4-5, 7, 11), and his real and unassailable protection.

Psalm 47 Shout and sing!

A psalm acclaiming God as Israel's King and Lord of the world. Let everyone rejoice and sing his praises.

Psalm 48 Zion, glorious city of God

An outburst of relief and joy at the city's reprieve from invasion (perhaps Sennacherib's, see 2 Chronicles 32).

The far north (2): Mt Zion in Jerusalem is in the south of Israel. The psalmist may have used this phrase because the north was the traditional seat of the gods.

Verse 7: New English Bible, 'like the ships of Tarshish when an east wind wrecks them'. For 'ships of Tarshish', see on 1 Kings 10:22.

Psalm 49 Meditation on life and death

A typical piece of 'wisdom' on life's inequalities. At the end of the line death waits for the materialist – not even he can buy himself off. The 'moral' is similar to that of Jesus' parable of the rich man (Luke 12:16-21).

Generally speaking the psalmists have no clear concept of life after death, and verse 15 is therefore often taken as a reference to premature death. But this undermines the reasoning, which requires an ironing out of this life's inequalities beyond the grave.

Psalm 50 God calls man to account

In verses 1-4 the summons comes. 7-15: God speaks in warning to his loyal people. It is not enough to go through the ritual motions. It is the thankful heart, not just the token thank-offering, that counts. 16-21: there are serious charges against those who mouth God's commands, yet disobey them; who take up with crooks but are prepared to ruin a member of their own family, leaving God out of account.

Psalm 51 Plea for forgiveness

The title links this psalm with Nathan's confrontation with David following his adultery with Bathsheba and the death of Uriah (2 Samuel 12). But verses 18-19 seem to be later, belonging to the time after Jerusalem fell to the Babylonians.

The psalm itself is profoundly moving. It lets us see right into the soul of a man who has loved God yet fallen into grievous sin. He has been made to see himself through God's

The people of Israel looked to God as all-powerful against the forces of evil. This relief illustrates the fears of the nations around. The Assyrian god Ninurta, armed with a thunderbolt, drives a demon from his temple.

eyes, and he is heart-broken. He makes no excuse, simply accepts God's judgement and admits his guilt. All he can do now – knowing God's love and mercy – is ask forgiveness and the chance of a fresh start.

Verse 5: the meaning is not that conception or childbirth are sinful in themselves, but that sin is ingrained from the very first moment of existence.

Hyssop (7): the herb used in the purification ritual described in Numbers 19.

Bloodguiltiness (14): this certainly fits David's case. He arranged for Uriah's death in order to cover up his own sin (2 Samuel 11).

Psalm 52 The doom of the wicked
Verses 1-4 describe man's guilt; verse 5 God's certain reprisal. 8 and 9 are a personal expression of trust and thanksgiving. The occasion of the psalm, according to the title, is Doeg's betrayal of David (1 Samuel 22).

Psalm 53
A revised version of Psalm 14, see above.

Psalm 54 Cry for help
According to the title, this is David's appeal to God after the Ziphites betrayed his position to Saul (1 Samuel 23:19ff.).

Psalm 55 Prayer of a man in trouble
The title attributes the psalm to David. The content fits in well with the time of Absalom's rebellion (2 Samuel 15-17), when Ahithophel, David's most trusted adviser, defaulted.

On top of all his other trouble (1-4, 9-11), a friend and fellow believer's treachery is the last straw (12-14, 20-21). The psalmist is full of conflicting emotions: fear and longing to opt out of the whole situation (4-8); and the desire to see his enemies worsted (9, 15). But trust eventually wins (16-18, 22) – for friends may be faithless, but not God.

Psalm 56 'In God I put my trust'
The psalmist has plenty to worry him and shake his nerve (1-2, 5-6). But he knows the answer to fear (3-4, 10-11). And he can safely and thankfully (12-13) leave God to deal with his enemies (7-9).

The title refers to the incident described in 1 Samuel 21:10-15.

Psalm 57 Prayer from among ferocious enemies
Circumstances may be black (4, 6), but the man who fills his mind with

God can sing his praise, come what may (1-3, 5, 7-11). Traditionally the prayer belongs to the time when David was in hiding from Saul (1 Samuel 22:1; 24), but Paul and Silas also knew the truth of it (Acts 16:19-25).

Psalm 58 'There is a God who judges'
The psalmist calls down God's terrible judgement on corrupt and evil men in power. See note on cursing and vengeance in the Psalms.

Gods (1): a sarcastic reference to the rulers and judges.

Adder (4): 'deaf' because it does not respond to the snake-charmer.

Verse 8a: in popular belief, slugs and snails left slimy trails because they melted as they moved.

Psalm 59 Prayer for protection and punishment
The title links the psalm to the incident in 1 Samuel 19:11-17, echoed in the refrain 'Each evening they come back ...' (6, 14). The psalmist addresses his very personal prayer (1-4, 9-10, 16-17) to the Lord of all the nations (5,8,13).

Jacob (13): i.e. the nation of Israel.

Psalm 60 The nation in defeat
The title associates the psalm with the campaign recorded in 2 Samuel 8, when the faith of verse 12 and God's word in verse 8 were realized in eventual victory.

Verses 6-8: God's power over Israel – Shechem, in the heart of the country, between Mts Ebal and Gerizim; Succoth, a city east of the Jordan; Gilead, Israelite land east of the Jordan; Manasseh, Ephraim, Judah, the 'big three' of the twelve tribes – and over Israel's traditional enemies – the Moabites, east of the Dead Sea; Edomites, to the south-east; and Philistines, on the Mediterranean coast.

Psalm 61 Prayer of a burdened king
Precarious on his throne (2, 6-7), the king craves the safety and security only God can give (1-4).

Psalm 62 A psalm of longing and trust
Humbly, trustingly, the psalmist commits his cause to God. Man is bent on destruction (3-4), but what *is* he (9-10)? Power belongs to God, who wields it with love and justice (11-12).

Psalm 63 The thirsting heart
Having tasted the full joy and satisfaction of God's presence (2-8), who can bear to lose it (1)?

Verses 9-10: in sharp contrast to the

SELF-JUSTIFICATION, CURSING AND VENGEANCE IN THE PSALMS

Christians reading the psalms are bound to come across two special problem areas. One is the self-justification of the psalmists. The other is their tendency to call down and spell out the most terrible vengeance. We cannot simply discard the offending passages. They are part of God's word, alongside passages no one would question. Nor will it do to excuse the psalmists on the grounds that they did not possess the teaching of Christ. Because they did possess the law. They knew as well as we do that no man is perfect by God's standards; and they were taught to behave in a loving way to others (Leviticus 19:17-18), even their enemies (Exodus 23:4-5). The law did not license retaliation, it set limits to it (an eye for an eye, *and no more*).

Self-justification . Two comments may help. First, the psalmist is claiming comparative, not absolute righteousness (i.e. in comparison with other people, not measured by God's standards). 'A good man may sin and yet be a good man.' There is all the difference in the world between those who endeavour to do right and those who deliberately set aside the common laws of God and society. David, in particular, was well aware of his shortcomings before God (see Psalms 51 and 19:11-13). Deep repentance features alongside self-justification in the psalms.

Second, the psalmist is very often picturing himself as 'the indignant plaintiff' putting his case before God the Judge. And, however much we dislike his self-righteous tone, from this point of view he is unquestionably 'in the right'.

Cursing and vengeance. Before we rush to condemn these passages as utterly 'unchristian', there are a few points worth bearing in mind.

The first concerns God's holiness. In emphasizing God's love we tend today to be over-sentimental about rank evil. But the psalmists knew God as One 'whose eyes are too pure to look upon evil', who cannot countenance wrongdoing. And this is what motivates their call for vengeance on the wicked. God's own character – his good name – demands it.

Second, the psalmists are realistic in recognizing that right *cannot* triumph without the actual overthrow of evil and punishment of wrong. We pray 'Thy kingdom come'. But we are often horrified when the psalmists spell out what this means – perhaps because we are less in love with good, less opposed to evil than they were; or because many of us have never known real persecution for our faith; or because we value life more than right.

However, if the psalmists are guilty of actually gloating over the fate of the wicked, if personal vindictiveness creeps in under the cloak of concern for God's good name, we are right to condemn it – and beware. We can ourselves so easily be guilty of the same thing. But in the psalmist's case the wrong thinking (if wrong thinking there is) never carries over into wrong action. There is no question of him taking the law into his own hands; no Inquisition. Vengeance is always seen as God's province, and his alone.

---

rest of the psalm. See note on vengeance.

Psalm 64 Prayer for protection
In verses 1-6 the psalmist pictures his trouble. In 7-9 he expresses his certainty that God will punish all who plot and scheme and slander. The punishment will fit the offence exactly (compare verse 7 with verses 3-4).

Psalm 65 Hymn of thanksgiving
All praise to God who hears and forgives (1-3), who blesses, satisfies and saves (4-5). Praise to God the Creator and Controller of the natural world (6-8). Praise to God who gives the harvest and makes the whole earth ring with joy (9-13).

Psalm 66 Praise and worship: national and individual
Praise God for national deliverance, from the earliest days (5-7) until now (8-12). And thank him for his love

and care for every individual (13-20).

Psalm 67 Harvest
At the sight of God's blessing poured out on Israel every nation will sing his praise.

Psalm 68 Israel's song of triumph
A battle-march cum processional hymn, sung as the ark was carried into Jerusalem (2 Samuel 6), or at the ceremony commemorating that event (see the allusions in verses 1, 7, 17-18, 24-25). The psalm paints a series of vivid pictures of God's victorious power.

Verses 1-6, a tribute to God; 7-10 God leads the nation through the desert; 11-14, the conquest of the land; 15-18, God chooses Mt Zion in Jerusalem to be his home; 19-23, salvation to Israel – death to the enemy; 24-27, the procession; 28-31, may God make a show of his strength to subdue the nations; 32-35, let everyone sing the power and majesty of Israel's God!

Verses 14-15, 22: 'Bashan' is the Golan Heights area, north-east of the Sea of Galilee. In the wide sense the region stretched as far as Mt Hermon, which may be the mountain referred to here. 'Zalmon' is probably another of the mountains in this region.

Psalm 69 Prayer of a man overwhelmed by suffering
A psalm often quoted in the New Testament (John 2:17; 15:25; Romans 15:3). The psalmist's picture in verses 2, 14-15 could be taken for an actual description of Jeremiah's case (Jeremiah 38:6). Verse 35 seems to pinpoint a time following the wholesale destruction of Judean cities, but before the fall of Jerusalem itself.

The psalmist is in desperate trouble, through no fault of his own. His suffering is borne for God's sake (1-12). He prays that God, in his love, will rescue him (13-18). The guilt of his tormentors is clear (19-21): may they be punished for all they have done (22-28). May God set him free to praise him; let the whole earth ring with praise at the restoration of God's people (29-36).

Psalm 70 An urgent call for help
These verses also appear at the end of Psalm 40.

Psalm 71 A prayer in old age
At the end of a long and troubled life (9, 20) there is still no let-up (4, 10-11). But trouble has schooled the psalmist in trust (6-7). Nothing can make him despair. As long as God is with him (9, 12, 18), the future is full of hope (14-16, 19-24).

Psalm 72 Prayer for the king
This last psalm in Book 2 is a fitting one for Solomon's reign (see title) – Israel's golden age of peace, prosperity and power. But it also looks beyond it to the perfect ideal: an endless reign (5) over the entire world (8, 11); a rule of God-like justice and righteousness (7, 12-14); a time of unequalled fruitfulness (16).

The River (8): Euphrates.

Tarshish, Sheba (10): meaning 'the remotest outposts of empire'. Sheba may be a region in Arabia. Tarshish is probably Tartessus in Spain.

Like Lebanon (16): for a small country Lebanon produces an amazing abundance and variety of fruit and vegetables.

BOOK 3

Psalm 73 This unjust world
How is it that those who flout God's laws prosper, and trouble falls on those who least deserve it (3b-14)? It is enough to make a good man envious and bitter (3, 21), and tempt him to say things better left unsaid (15). Only as he turns to God does he learn to see beyond appearances (16, 17). In reality, God's people have

The psalmists cry out for judgement. God's people suffered cruel atrocities at the hands of enemies like this Assyrian soldier who holds a decapitated head.

everything that matters (1, 23-26, 28). The wicked – for all their wealth – are destined for destruction (17-20, 27).

Psalm 74 Lament for the destruction of the temple

God has turned against his people (1-2). The temple has been desecrated and destroyed (3-8). How long will the anti-God enemy remain master (9-11)? The psalmist thinks of the power of his God (12-17) and pleads with him to keep his promise to Israel (19-20) and sweep the blasphemous enemy away (18, 22-23).

Verses 13-15: a description of the deliverance from Egypt, pictured first as a dragon, then as Leviathan, the crocodile of the Nile.

Psalm 75 God is Judge

Israel rejoices in God's sovereign justice. He alone has power to judge all men.

Verses 2-5: God is speaking.

Verse 5: a picture of arrogant power.

Psalm 76 A song of deliverance

Israel marvels at the terrible glory of the God who overthrows all the might of the enemy.

Salem, Zion (2): Jerusalem.

Psalm 77 Past and present

The psalmist calls to mind all God's great deeds on behalf of his people (11-20). But now he seems no longer to care for them (5-10), and there is no comfort in the present troubles (1-4).

Verses 2-6: the trouble which sets the psalmist thinking may be a personal, or a national, crisis.

Psalm 78 Lessons from Israel's history

For a long time Ephraim was the most powerful of the twelve tribes. Joshua was an Ephraimite, and the tribe had great prestige under the judges (Judges 8:2; 12). But with David's accession Judah took the lead. The psalmist thinks over the reasons for Ephraim's rejection, and finds them in Israel's history.

God gave Israel the law to remind them of him (5-8). But Ephraim disobeyed (9-11). They forgot what had happened in Egypt and the desert – the miracles (13-16, 23-29, 44-53), the rebellions and the punishments (17-22, 30-43). They forgot the pattern that repeated itself after the conquest of the land (54-66). And God chose Judah instead – a city of Judah (Jerusalem) as capital and a man of Judah (David) to be king (67-72).

Verse 9: this seems to be a reference to the defeat of Saul and Israel on Mt Gilboa (1 Samuel 31:1).

Zoan (12): an ancient capital of Egypt.

Verses 13-16: see Exodus 14 and 17.

Verses 24-31: see Exodus 16; Numbers 11.

Verses 44-51: see Exodus 7-12.

Ham (51): one of Noah's three sons, ancestor of the Egyptian people.

Shiloh (60): for a long time the principal sanctuary in Israel – presumably destroyed when the ark was captured by the Philistines (1 Samuel 4).

Psalm 79 Jerusalem in ruins

A lament for the destruction and bloodshed of the fall of Jerusalem (1-4; the city fell to Babylon in 587 BC, see 2 Kings 25:8ff.). The people call on God to forgive and help them (5, 8-10a, 11), and to destroy the pagan enemy (6-7, 10b, 12).

Psalm 80 A prayer for the restoration of Israel

The time may be after the exile of the northern kingdom of Israel (2 Kings 17) but before the fall of Jerusalem (2 Kings 25). (The psalmist mentions two northern tribes, and Benjamin, but not Judah in the south.)

Israel is pictured as a great vine planted by God (8-16), stretching out to the mountains and cedars of Lebanon in the north (10), west to the Mediterranean and east to the River Euphrates (11).

Walls (12): i.e. the walls enclosing and protecting the vineyard.

Verse 17: the name 'Benjamin' means 'son of the right hand'.

Psalm 81 God's message at harvest

Verses 1-5: the people are summoned to celebrate the Feast of Tabernacles. God reminds his people of all he has done for them (6-7) and all he longs to give (10, 14-16). Yet in obstinate disobedience they refuse him and choose trouble (8-9, 11-13).

A voice I had not known (5): a puzzling statement, unless it refers back to the time before Moses' day (see Exodus 6:3).

Verse 6: a description of Israel's slave-labour in Egypt.

Meribah (7): see Exodus 17:1-7.

Psalm 82 The justice of God

There is corruption and injustice in the law-courts: God calls the judges to account.

The gods (1): probably meaning those men who exercise God's right of judgement over others.

Psalm 83 Prayer for help

The nation is in grave danger from an alliance of all the old enemies, plus powerful Assyria (2-8). The people call on God's aid, remembering past victories (9-18).

Children of Lot (8): Lot fathered Moab and Ammon (see Genesis 19:36-38).

Verses 9-12: see Judges 4 and 5. Oreb and Zeeb, Zebah and Zalmunna, were Midianite princes put to death by Gideon (Judges 7 and 8).

Psalm 84 A pilgrim's song

He comes with a heart singing for joy at the prospect of worshipping God in his temple. The happiest people in the world – it seems to him – are those who can be there always (4, 10).

Baca (6): possibly an actual valley the pilgrim passes on his way to Jerusalem. But New English Bible 'the thirsty valley' gives the sense.

Psalm 85 Thanksgiving and a prayer

Praise for God's forgiveness in the past (1-3) and prayer for restoration in the present (4-7). All he knows and has experienced of God's love and faithfulness fills the psalmist with optimism (8-13). What God has yet to give will far exceed his past goodness.

Psalm 86 Prayer of a man in trouble

Because he knows God – and all his love and goodness (5, 7, 13, 15) and power (8-10) – he can be confident in putting his case (1-4, 6-7, 14), and trust God for the answer.

Poor and needy (1): a 'bankrupt', not financially, but before God.

Psalm 87 Zion; city of God, mother of nations

A prophecy of the holy city's glorious future: a capital whose citizenship includes even former enemies (4). The Old Testament sees this largely in material and geographical terms, the New in spiritual (Revelation 21:1 - 22:5).

Rahab (4): a poetic synonym for Egypt.

Psalm 88 Cry of a desperate man

This is the darkest of all the psalms. Here is a man who feels life ebbing away (3-9a), and he has no hope beyond death (10-12). There is no one to turn to but God, who is crushing him with trouble (7-8, 13-18). He is in the grip of the blackest depression. Yet faith lives on – how else can one account for his persistent cry to God?

Sheol, the Pit, Abaddon (3, 4, 11): all meaning the shadow-land of the dead.

Psalm 89 A hymn and prayer

The psalmist sings the story of God's faithful love to Israel; his covenant and promise to the line of David (1-37). But now, in a very different present, God is angry with his people; the covenant is broken. Where is his 'steadfast love of old' (38-51)?

Rahab (10): see on Psalm 87.

Tabor and Hermon (12): Tabor, the rounded hump of mountain near Nazareth from which Deborah and Barak swept down to victory (Judges 4 - 5); Hermon, the 9,000 ft peak on the border with Lebanon.

Verse 52: the 'doxology' (see Introduction) added to mark the end of Book 3.

BOOK 4

Psalm 90 A short life and a hard one

The title links this psalm with Moses, who must often have felt like this in the long years of desert wandering. Ecclesiastes also shares the psalmist's mood.

The everlasting God (1-4) – and man, as transient as a blade of grass (5-6). His span of life is short, yet even this must be worked out under God's judgement (7-10). The psalmist appeals to God's pity as he begs for the return of joy and gladness (13-17).

Psalm 91 Trust God and rest secure

In this psalm the voice of encouragement (1-13) and the voice of God (14-16) speak to the man of faith. Under God's protection nothing can touch him – neither man nor beast, by day or by night; not war, nor disease. (This is not to say his life will be all roses, or verse 15 would have no meaning.)

Verses 11-12: the devil quoted these verses to tempt Jesus (Luke 4:9-12). But Christ had no need to test the truth of God's word, neither had he come into the world to take the soft option.

Psalm 92 'A song for the sabbath'

A joyous thanksgiving in music and song for all that God has done (5-9); his goodness to each individual, and to all his people (10-15).

Psalm 93 'The Lord reigns'

– eternal, almighty; his laws and his holiness unchanging.

Psalm 94 God's justice

The starting-point is the wicked – how fully they deserve God's judgement; their stupid lack of understanding (1-11). But as he thinks of God, though the thought of vengeance is never far away, the psalmist moves on to all the help and love and blessing God pours out upon his afflicted people (12-22).

Psalms 95-100 are a group of psalms written in exultant praise of the God who reigns over all his creation.

Psalm 95
Let us praise and worship God our Maker (1-7a), remembering that he expects obedience (7b-11).
Verse 8: see Exodus 17:1-7.
Psalm 96
A song of God's salvation, of his greatness and his glory. A song of universal joy at his coming in judgement.
Psalm 97
In praise of God – supreme, triumphant; the Saviour and delight of all who hate evil.
Psalm 98
A song to God the Victor. He comes to rule his kingdom. Let the whole world go wild with joy.
Psalm 99
God the King, the Holy One, is on his throne; God who forgives and disciplines his people, from the least to the greatest.
Psalm 100
'The Lord is God; 'the Lord is good'. Let the whole earth sing and be glad.
His gates, his courts (4): i.e. the temple.
Psalm 101 The king's manifesto
The king pledges himself to root out evil from private and public life and to reward integrity.
House (2): household and court.
Verse 8: most probably a reference to his daily administration of justice in Jerusalem.
Psalm 102 The cry of man on the rack
Verses 1-11 describe his suffering: ill in body, sick at heart, taunted by enemies, cast off by God. His life is slipping away (11), but God is not subject to time (24, 27). He is Sovereign for ever (12). Surely he will pity his city and free his people (13-22). Surely he will answer the psalmist's prayer (23-28).
Psalm 103 The love and mercy of God
A psalm of humble, heartfelt gratitude to God for all his goodness, but above all for his mercy and his unchanging, unchangeable love. What he has done for one (1-5), he does for

all (6-18): so let everyone, everywhere praise him.
Psalm 104 To God the great Creator
The psalmist marvels at the grandeur and the detail, the perfection and completeness of God's work in creation (1-24 – verse 24 sums it all up). Earth and sea (25-26), with everything in them, are his work, and depend entirely upon him (27-30). The train of thought leads into a song of praise (31-35).
Badgers (18): probably the Syrian rock hyrax, a shy little animal about the size of a rabbit, which lives among the rocks.
Leviathan (26): usually the crocodile (see Job 41), but here used more generally of large sea-creatures.
Psalm 105 Praise to God for his covenant with Israel
The call to praise (1-11) is followed by a history of how God chose Israel and gave them the land (12-45): the patriarchs (12-15); Joseph's story (16-23; Genesis 37-46); the deliverance from Egypt (23-38; Exodus 1-12); God's provision in the desert (39-42; Exodus 16-17) and the possession of Canaan (43-45).
Psalm 106 Israel's disobedience
The psalm begins with praise (1-5), but from verse 6 on becomes a confession of the nation's sin, from the very beginning to the psalmist's own day.
Verse 7: the first instance of rebellion, see Exodus 14:10ff.
Wanton craving (14): for the good food of Egypt. God gave them meat but punished them with a plague (Numbers 11).
Verses 16-18: see Numbers 16.
A calf in Horeb (19): Horeb=Mt Sinai. While Moses was in the mountain receiving God's instructions, the people made a golden calf to worship after Egyptian custom (Exodus 32).
Land of Ham (22): see on Psalm 78.
Baal of Peor (28): the people turned to idol worship and laid themselves open to God's judgement (Numbers 25).
Meribah (32): see Numbers 20:2-13.
Did not destroy ... but mingled (34-35): Judges 1 and 2 summarize this part of Israel's history. From that time on (40-46) the story became a repetitive pattern of rebellion against God, followed by enemy occupation, followed by repentance, followed by freedom, followed by further rejection of God.
Verse 48: the 'doxology' which

closes the fourth book of psalms.

BOOK 5
Psalm 107 In praise of God the Redeemer
A single theme (man is beset by troubles of his own choosing or making, but God rescues him from them all) is spelt out in four word-pictures (the traveller, 4-9; the captive, 10-16; the sick man, 17-22; the sailor, 23-32). Circumstances differ for each individual, but all share the same experience: as they cry out to God in their need, he hears and answers. All have equal cause to praise him. Verses 33-43 describe God's unchanging love in dealing with his people.

Psalm 108 A hymn to God
The psalm combines extracts from Psalm 57:7-11, and Psalm 60:5-12.
Verses 7-13: see on Psalm 60.

Psalm 109 A cry for vengeance; a call for help
People the psalmist has loved and treated well have returned evil for good. They have no excuse for the attack which has reduced him to a shadow (1-4; 22-25). His bitterness is understandable, but the tirade of 6-20 seems to overstep the mark. See note on cursing and vengeance in the Psalms.

An ancient harp, the 'nevel', reconstructed here in the Music Museum at Haifa, Israel.

Psalm 110 'King and priest for ever'
This psalm speaks of the ideal, fully realized only in Christ, as the New Testament writers make plain (Matthew 22:41-46; Luke 22:69; Hebrews 5:8-10; 10:12-13). See 'Christ in the Psalms'.
Melchizedek (4): the mysterious priest-king to whom Abraham gave a

tenth of his possessions (see Genesis 14:17-20).

Psalm 111 In praise of God
This psalm is identical in form with Psalm 112. Both consist of 22 phrases each beginning with a successive letter of the Hebrew alphabet.

The psalmist rejoices in God's greatness; his faithfulness and justice; his integrity and trustworthiness; his provision and his redemption. Respect for God is the true starting-point of all human wisdom.

Psalm 112 Happy the man who respects and obeys God
For the form, see on Psalm 111 above.

The man who obeys God and cares for his fellow men is sure of reward. He can withstand life's knocks, secure and unafraid.
Verses 2-3: the psalmist describes the reward in material terms because in his day there was no clear concept of the afterlife. What he says is *generally* (but not invariably) true. God's people have their full share of trouble, but are given resources to meet it (7-8).

Psalms 113-118 are a group of psalms linked traditionally with the Jewish feasts of Tabernacles (Harvest) and Passover. In Jewish homes Psalms 113 and 114 are sung before the Passover meal; Psalms 115-118 after it (see Matthew 26:30).

Psalm 113 Our incomparable God
He is above and beyond his creation, yet closely concerned for the humblest of his people.
Ash heap/dunghill (7): the rubbish dump, the place for outcasts (see Job 2:8).

Psalm 114 Passover hymn: God present with his people
The nation recalls God's marvels on their behalf at the time of the exodus.
Verses 3,5: the reference is to the crossing of the Red Sea (see on Exodus 14) and the later crossing of Jordan (Joshua 3).
Verse 8: see Exodus 17:1-6.

Psalm 115 The living God: lifeless idols
A psalm which gives an indication of the way many psalms must have been sung – with a single voice leading and the congregation joining in the response (9-11, etc.).
House of Aaron (12): i.e. the priests.
Verse 17: meaning that praise is for

the living: death stills all tongues.

Psalm 116 Hymn of thanks

A psalm for the individual as he comes to make his thank-offering in the temple. God has heard his prayer and brought him through dark days. Now he pours out his heart in gratitude.

Cup of salvation (13): this is vivid picture-language. God gave him back his life; now he offers it up to God in thanks.

Psalm 117 Call to praise

Psalm 118 A hymn for the Feast of Tabernacles

The hymn was sung in procession by king, priests and people. As they approach the temple, the king recalls God's victory for his people (1-18).

Verses 19-27: the procession, carrying branches, moves from the gateway to the altar.

Verse 22: the despised nation of Israel has become the great power. By Jesus' day Israel, in turn, had forfeited her privileged position (Matthew 21:42-43).

Psalm 119 In praise of the word of God

This is the longest psalm of all – and the most formal and elaborate in concept. There are 22 eight-verse sections. Each section begins with a successive letter of the Hebrew alphabet, and each verse within the section begins with the same letter. Within this stylized pattern the psalmist makes a series of individual, though not isolated or disconnected, statements about the 'law' (God's teaching) and the individual – interspersed with frequent prayers. He uses ten different words to describe it: God's law, his testimonies (instruction), precepts, statutes, commandments, ordinances (decrees), word, ways (paths), promises and judgements (rulings). And one or other of these descriptions occurs in all but a very few verses. He seems to have taken the same delight in the discipline set by this complex poetic form, as he did in the study of the law itself. In the psalm we see how eagerly and persistently he applies himself to the task of understanding the law. He learns it by heart. He longs for more. Nothing is allowed to deflect him from it. God's word rules his life and conduct, gives him hope and peace, leads him into life. His confidence in it is unbounded, and to see it broken genuinely distresses him. We possess far more of God's word than the

psalmist did. But his love and regard for it often puts us to shame.

Psalms 120-134 (the 'Songs of Ascents') are a collection of songs thought to have been sung by pilgrims on their way to Jerusalem to celebrate the three great annual feasts. In many of them the thought and imagery focusses on the holy city.

Psalm 120 The whiplash of wagging tongues

The psalms are full of references to the sins of the tongue – lies, scandal, slander, hypocrisy. The man of God may suffer as much from what people say as from what they do.

Verse 5: a poetic way of saying he is living among barbarians!

Psalm 121 God, the Guardian

The man who trusts God knows where to turn in trouble. With God to guard him he can come to no harm.

The hills (1): perhaps those on which Jerusalem stands.

Psalm 122 Jerusalem, city of God

The pilgrim prays for the peace of the city, the centre of worship and seat of government for the whole nation.

Psalm 123 Plea for mercy Psalm 124 God, the Rescuer

Without God's help the nation could not have survived the onslaught of their enemies. The credit is his alone. (How many times this has been true in Israel's history!)

Psalm 125 Secure in God

Those who trust in God enjoy complete security. But let the wicked be warned.

Psalm 126 Laughter and tears

A psalm often associated with the return from exile and the hardships that followed. Verses 1-3 express the people's exuberant joy at God's blessing; verses 4-6 the need to experience this yet again (or a prayer for the restoration of the nation as a whole).

Verse 4: for most of the year the riverbeds in the southern desert (Negev) are dry, but when the rain comes the water rushes down them in torrents.

Psalm 127 The futility of human effort without God

Verse 5: disputes and business deals were settled at the city gate. Here the grown-up sons support their father in maintaining the family's interests.

Psalm 128 Blessings of the man who respects and obeys God

The psalmist's picture describes

everything the man of his own day asked of life. But see also on Psalm 112:2-3.

Verse 3: the vine and the olive are symbols of peace and plenty – the fullness of God's blessing.

Psalm 129 A prayer for the downfall of all who have crushed God's people

Verses 5-8: see note on cursing and vengeance in the Psalms.

Psalm 130 Praying, waiting, hoping for God's redemption

Psalm 131 A psalm of simple trust

Psalm 132 In commemoration of the day the ark was brought to Jerusalem

Verses 1-10: see 2 Samuel 6:12-15; 11-12: God's promise of a royal dynasty (see 2 Samuel 7:11-16); 13-18: Jerusalem is chosen as the religious centre of Israel.

Ephrathah (6): Bethlehem, David's birth-place.

Jaar (6): an abbreviation for Kiriath-jearim, where the ark was kept for 20 years following its return by the Philistines.

Psalm 133 The family-unity of God's people

Verse 2: at the high point in his consecration ceremony the high priest was anointed with oil (Exodus 29:7).

Verse 3: the dew is seen as a symbol of blessing. Mt Hermon has an exceptionally heavy dewfall, which meant greater fertility there than elsewhere in the days before piped water and mechanical sprinklers.

Psalm 134 A psalm for those on night-watch in the temple

Psalm 135 Hymn of praise for public worship

This psalm echoes many earlier ones. God is to be praised for choosing Israel (1-4), for his greatness (5-7, 15-18) and his mighty works (8-14). Let priests and people sing his praise (19-21).

Sihon ... Og (11): see Numbers 21.

Psalm 136 The 'Great Praise' (Hallel)

The description of God's great works in creation (4-9) and history (10-24) alternate with the people's refrain to God's unchanging, timeless love.

Verse 13: see Exodus 14.

Verses 19-20: see Numbers 21.

Psalm 137 Lament of the exiles in Babylon

The old joyful songs stick in the exiles' throats at the memory of the terrible destruction of their city and temple. Instead they cry out for the punishment of the barbarian invaders.

Edomites (7): descendants of Esau and therefore closely related to Israel, but centuries-old hostility divided the two. The Edomites gloated at the news of Jerusalem's ruin (Obadiah 8-14).

Verse 9: see the note on cursing and vengeance in the Psalms. The Israelites had no doubt witnessed just such atrocities committed in Jerusalem by the Babylonian army (8).

Psalm 138 A song of thanks

God has answered prayer. Once again he has shown his faithful love. He is great and high, yet he cares for insignificant men and women. The psalmist has a continuing story to tell of God's protective care for individuals.

Psalm 139 The God who is there

The psalm is concerned with God's all-knowingness and 'everywhere-presentness', not in an abstract, but

These Egyptian musicians wear disks of perfume which melt and 'drip' down their cheeks; from the Tomb of Nebamun, Thebes, about 1400 BC.

in a highly personal way. God is all-knowing: he knows *me* through and through, even my thoughts. He has known me from the day I was born (1-6, 13-16). God is present everywhere: wherever *I* go, he is there. He is always with me (7-12, 18b). I will align myself with him in the fight against evil. Let him search out and deal with all that is wrong in me (19-24)

Psalm 140 Prayer for help
The psalmist is in real trouble from the plotting of violent men, and from their venomous tongues. He prays that God will guard him (1-8) and punish them (9-11), in the confident knowledge that God is for the right and implacably opposed to evil (12-13).

Verses 9-11: see the note on cursing and vengeance in the Psalms.

Psalm 141 A prayer for right reactions
The pull of evil is a force to be reckoned with. The psalmist asks that God will keep him from the very things he condemns in others, in thought and word and action.

Psalm 142 Prayer of a man alone and in trouble
The title links this psalm with the time when David was on the run and in hiding from Saul (1 Samuel 23:19ff.). He cries to the One who knows all about him: the Lord, his refuge.

Psalm 143 Prayer for God's help
The psalmist has reached the end of the line: no more reserve or resources (3-4). But in a desperate situation one refuge remains: God himself (5-12). 'O Lord ... teach me ... deliver me ... lead me ... bring me out of trouble.'

Psalm 144 A song for the God of victory
What is man that the great God should spare him so much as a passing thought (1-4)? Yet time and again God comes to the rescue (5-11). The song closes with a prayer for peace and prosperity for the future generation (12-15).

Psalms 145-150 are a group of psalms in praise of God, probably intended for public worship. They are used by Jews today in daily prayer. Psalms 146-150 each begin and end with an Alleluia – 'O praise the Lord'!

Psalm 145 'Great is the Lord'
An acrostic (see on Psalm 9). One letter, missing from the Hebrew text, has been taken into the English versions from the Greek Septuagint as 13b.

Praise is poured out to God for his greatness and power (1-7, 10-13a), and for his character: loving, forgiving, good and faithful, just and kind, satisfying the needs of his creation (8-9, 13b-21).

Psalm 146 Praise from the individual
The focus is on God, the hope and help of his people, utterly dependable, caring for all in need.

Psalm 147 Praise from the nation
God commands the universe (4), the seasons (8), the nations (14), the elements (16-18), with a power that puts him utterly above and beyond mankind. Yet his heart goes out to individuals; all who are hurt and unhappy (2-3). He takes pleasure in those who love and respect him (11). And he gives his people his word to live by (19). Praise the Lord!

Psalm 148 Universal praise
Everything that is owes praise to the Creator: the angels in heaven; sun, moon and stars; nature; the deep; every creature on earth and all mankind.

Waters above the heavens (4): i.e. the rain.

Horn (14): symbol of power. New English Bible 'he has exalted his people in the pride of power' gives the sense.

Psalm 149 The song of God's faithful people
His people rejoice in the victory God has given, and exult at the judgement of the opposing nations.

A new song (1): see on Psalm 33.

Two-edged swords (6): in the New Testament the two-edged sword is a metaphor for the word of God (Hebrews 4:12; Revelation 1:16).

Vengeance (6b-9): see note above. Victory for the downtrodden *must* entail defeat for the forces of oppression.

Psalm 150 Choral symphony of praise
This is the grand climax and finale to the whole collection of Psalms. Every instrument in the orchestra, everything with life and breath in the whole creation, joins in a mighty crashing paean of praise to God.

PROVERBS

Proverbs is a book of wise sayings: not simply an anthology, but an oriental textbook, schooling young men in wise and right living by the repetition of wise thoughts. It is wisdom distilled into short, sharp phrases, dramatic contrasts, and unforgettable scenes from life. It sets out what is right and what is wrong (not just a slick formula for success), because 'wisdom' in Proverbs is based on reverence for God and obedience to his laws. The 'fear of the Lord' is the essence of all true human wisdom. This is the starting-point. Proverbs applies the principles of God's teaching to the whole of life, to relationships, home, work, justice, decisions, attitudes, reactions, everything man does and says, and even thinks. God has taught what is best for man. Experience proves it.

The book divides into eight main sections: a general introduction on wisdom (chapters 1 - 9); six collections of sayings (10:1 - 31:9); and an acrostic poem on the perfect wife (31:10-31). For details see below.

It is now fairly generally agreed that in content the proverbs belong to the days of Israel's first kings, although editing continued for some centuries. King Hezekiah, who organized some of the editorial work (25:1), reigned 250 years after Solomon. The book as we have it was finalized, at the latest, by Ben Sira's time (180 BC).

The precise part Solomon played in all this is not known. His name appears in the title, and he is the author/compiler of the two longest collections (10:1 - 22:16 and chapters 25 - 29). Solomon was a man of outstanding wisdom (see 1 Kings 3; 4:29-34) and his court became an international centre for the exchange of learning. 1 Kings 4:32-34 tells us that Solomon 'uttered three thousand proverbs; and his songs were a thousand and five. He spoke of trees ... he spoke also of beasts, and of birds, and of reptiles, and of fish.

And men came from all peoples to hear the wisdom of Solomon, and from all the kings of the earth, who had heard of his wisdom'. Through marriage with pharaoh's daughter, Solomon had close links with Egypt, and perhaps knew the *Teaching of Amenemope* which is so closely paralleled in Proverbs 22:17 - 23:14, as well as other collections of wise sayings. He and his wise men culled the wisdom of the east, but they incorporated nothing that was not in line with God's standards. See 'Poetry and Wisdom Literature', introduction.

From chapter 10 on, Proverbs is best digested a few sayings at a time. It may also be a help to study them under themes. This way we can weigh one saying against another, and get an idea of the general teaching on a particular topic. It is important to bear in mind that proverbs are by nature *generalizations*. They state what is *generally*, not *invariably*, true. The writers do not deny that there are exceptions. But exceptions are not within the scope of proverbial sayings. For instance, Proverbs states that those who live by God's standards will prosper in the world. This is generally the truth. But it is not an unqualified 'promise'. Job, and above all the life of Jesus, show the other side of the coin.

1:1-7 INTRODUCTION

Proverbs opens with a statement of its purpose (2-6) and basis (7). It is aimed especially at the young and uninstructed – but no one is too old or too wise to learn.

Verse 1: best taken as the title to the whole book, not just the first section. Solomon's own proverbs begin at 10:1.

Fear of the Lord (7): an important recurring phrase in Proverbs (see themes, below). It describes a wholesome awe and respect for God which expresses itself in obedience, reliance on God and deliberate avoidance of evil (3:7).

1:8 - 9:18 LESSONS ON WISDOM

The teacher addresses his pupils as a wise father would his son. The young man has a vital choice to make: between the right course and the wrong one; between wisdom and folly; between going God's way through life and going his own. The teacher describes the two alternatives, and shows where each leads. The theme of every lesson is the same: 'Get wisdom'. Repetition is still a good teaching method!

Chapter 1
Resist the blandishments of violent men (10-19). Listen instead to the voice of wisdom (20-33). All who disregard her call will live to regret it.
Verse 12: the Pit of death, 'Sheol' – the place of the dead.
Wisdom (20): the teacher pictures wisdom as a great lady. She competes for Everyman's attention with another woman – Folly – who is no lady at all (see chapter 9). See note on Wisdom under themes.

Chapter 2
Wisdom is to be found through knowing God. It is hard-won, but worth every effort (1-10). It is a safeguard against wrong company, both male (12-15) and female (16-19). It sets men's feet on the right path (20).

Chapter 3
Take wise teaching to heart; stay humble; trust God (1-12). Wisdom offers the things that money can't buy: peace, happiness, security (13-26). Wisdom was at work in creation. It continues to be worked out in the do's and don'ts of everyday life and relationships (27-35).

The 'woman at the window' seen in this ivory carving was a popular subject with Near Eastern craftsmen. Proverbs warns young men against the shameless seduction practised by some married women.

Chapter 4
The teacher passes on his own father's instruction. Wisdom is the thing to go for: it leads to life. Steer clear of wrong-doing and the company of wrongdoers.

Chapter 5
Be wise when it comes to women. Don't fall for a cheap line, especially from a married woman. She is a *femme fatale* in more than name. Find your pleasure in your own wife: see that you stay in love with her.

Chapter 6
This chapter gives some timely warnings. Beware of accepting unlimited liability for anyone (1-5). Beware of idleness (6-11). Beware the fate of a 'bad lot' (12-19). Keep God's commands. They will save you from the schemes of seductive women.
Six things ... seven (16): see on 30:15.
Eyelashes (25): this seems a surprisingly modern touch! But long before Solomon's time women wore the equivalent of mascara, if not of false lashes.
Verse 27: the Jerusalem Bible translates 'can a man hug fire to his breast ...?'

Chapter 7
The teacher describes a young man falling for a married woman's shameless seduction. To judge by the number of warnings in Proverbs this was common enough. Even Solomon, with all his wisdom, was as weak as any at this point – and in the end his foreign wives led him into idolatry (1 Kings 11:1-13).

Chapter 8
In marked contrast to the sly woman of chapter 7, slipping out at dusk to catch her man, Wisdom makes an open appeal to all men as they go about their daily business. She is straight and true, the value of her instruction beyond any earthly fortune (6-21). She stands at the head of God's creation, the very first of all created things (22-31).

Chapter 9
All the teacher's previous lessons are crystallized in this vivid picture of Wisdom (1-6) and Folly (13-18). Each invites man – empty-headed, wayward man – to a feast. Wisdom sets life before him. On Folly's menu there is only death.

10 - 22:16 PROVERBS OF SOLOMON

The young man has been faced with the choice and urged to choose wisdom. Now the instruction begins; practical instruction that ranges over every aspect of life. In this first collection, the sayings get their punch from contrast. The second line, or half, of each saying is the antithesis of the first. Each proverb is complete in itself, though some are linked by words or themes into series. They reveal sound psychology and accurate observation of life. They demonstrate the out-working of wisdom and folly in the practical business of living. For the teaching in 10:1 - 31:9, see under themes.

15:11: even the realms of the dead (Sheol and Abaddon) are open to God.

17:8: the man is confident his bribe will work, but the practice is wrong (see verse 23).

18:18: in Old Testament times it was common practice to discover God's will by casting lots.

20:10: Leviticus 19:35 condemns the giving of short weight, and the prophets also denounce all such cheating in business.

22:17 - 24:34 TWO COLLECTIONS OF SAYINGS OF WISE MEN

It seems likely that in this section Proverbs makes creative use of material from abroad (see introduction, and 'Poetry and Wisdom Literature'), in addition to material from Israel's own 'wise men'. The sayings in this section are more connected than in the previous one. They begin with 'things to avoid' (22:22-29). Then come the hazards of social climbing (23:1-8); father and son – discipline and advice (23:12-28); a portrait of a drunkard (23:29-35); teaching on wisdom and folly (24:1-14), and right living (24:15-22). The group of additional sayings (24:23-34) focusses on justice and hard work, with a sketch of the lazy man in verses 30-34. See also under themes.

Thirty sayings (22:20): the Hebrew has several possible meanings, but it seems to imply a book of sayings which consists of (roughly) 30 paragraphs or chapters.

Ancient landmark (22:28): stones set up to mark out boundaries.

Narrow well (23:27): i.e. one it would be difficult to get out of.

25 - 29 MORE OF SOLOMON'S PROVERBS (HEZEKIAH'S COLLECTION)

Under King Hezekiah Israel returned to the old neglected patterns of worship. He repaired the temple and resumed the sacrifices, restoring the temple music along the lines laid down by David (2 Chronicles 29). What is more likely than that he should then have turned his attention to the classic wisdom of Solomon? At any rate, it was his men who published this collection of Solomon's proverbs. There is more grouping here than in 10:1 - 22:16, and the proverbs rely more on comparison than contrast for effect. For the teaching, see under themes.

25:6-7: Jesus uses the same theme in Luke 14:7-10, but he broadens it to cover a whole attitude to life.

26:4-5: these two verses are probably meant to be complementary, not contradictory. It is usually pointless to argue with a fool, but there are times when his false reason must be shown up for what it is.

26:8: what could be more nonsensical than fixing a stone to a sling so that it can't come out?

The ideal wife, amongst many other virtues, spins her own thread and weaves her own cloth.

30 SAYINGS OF AGUR

Both Agur and Lemuel (31:1) are non-Israelites. 'Massa' was an Arab tribe descended from Abraham's son Ishmael. The east was famous for its wisdom, right down to Christ's own day (see Matthew 2:1). Agur is a man whose close observation of life and nature have taught him humility.

Three ... four (15): a device indicating that the list is not exhaustive. See also 18, 21, 29 and 6:16.

Verse 19: he finds four sources of wonder: how the eagle can soar; how the serpent can move without legs;

how the ship can ride the waves; and the mysterious attraction which draws a man to a woman.

31:1-9 SAYINGS OF KING LEMUEL

See under chapter 30 above. Lemuel outlines his mother's teaching. We seem to catch a tone of mild reproach in verse 2.

Son of my vows (2): the vows made when she prayed for a son.

31:10-31 THE PERFECT WIFE

Proverbs paints a remarkable picture of the power of woman, for good and for ill. It closes with this lovely acrostic poem (see on Psalm 9) about the ideal wife: responsible, capable, hardworking and completely trusted. Not only do her husband, family and household depend on her provision and foresight for their physical needs; they owe her their well-being at a much deeper level (11, 12, 26). Her influence extends beyond this immediate circle to society at large (20). And she finds ample scope for all her gifts in the wider spheres of buying and selling and business trans-actions (16, 18, 24). Where does her secret lie? In that same 'fear of the Lord' in which all true wisdom has its roots.

IMPORTANT THEMES IN PROVERBS 10-31

Wisdom and folly – the wise man and the fool

This is the main strand of the whole book, the subject of the first nine chapters. The sayings point the contrast between wisdom – living by God's standards, keeping to what is right, and folly – man wilfully going his own way. Wisdom leads to life and all that is good; folly is a mere half-life that ends in death. The verses listed below detail the wise course of action in many different circumstances. They outline the wise man's character, in contrast to the life and character of the 'fool', who shuts his mind to God and reason.

10:8, 13-14, 23; 12:1, 15-16, 23; 13:14-16, 20; 14:1, 3, 7-8, 15-18, 24, 33; 15:5, 7, 14, 20-21; 16:16, 21-23; 17:10, 12, 16, 24, 28; 18:2, 6-7, 15; 19:25, 29; 21:22; 22:3; 23:9; 24:3-7, 13-14; 26:1, 3-12; 27:12, 22; 28:26; 29:8-9, 11.

The righteous and the wicked

The individual's response to life's alternatives determines which of these two groups he joins. The wise man, on Proverbs' definition of wisdom, will be righteous. The gullible fool is always teetering on the edge of wrongdoing. It is more than likely he will end up among the wicked. The proverbs below describe the righteous life – the life of integrity – and the blessing it brings to the individual and the community. God loves and protects the righteous. The wicked are subject to his wrath. If they flourish, it is only for a short time. They are heading straight for death and destruction.

10:3, 6-7, 11, 20-21, 24-25, 27-32; 11:3-11, 17-21, 23, 28, 30-31; 12:2-3, 5-7, 10, 12-13, 21, 26, 28; 13:5-6, 9, 21-22, 25; 14:9, 11, 14, 19, 32; 15:6, 8-9, 26, 28-29; 16:8, 12-13; 17:13, 15; 18:5; 20:7; 21:3, 7-8, 10, 12, 18, 26-27; 24:15-16; 25:26; 28:1, 12, 28; 29:2, 6-7, 16, 27.

Words and the tongue

Proverbs places tremendous stress on the power of words and speech, for good and for ill. What we say, and how we react to what others say – advice, or rebuke, or gossip, or tempting suggestions – betrays what we are (see Matthew 12:34-37). The tongue is an incalculable force: it takes a wise man to master it (see also James 3). The proverbs below are full of sound advice and timely warning.

10:18-21, 31-32; 11:9, 11-14; 12:6, 14, 17-19, 22; 13:2-3; 14:5, 25; 15:1-2, 4, 23; 16:1, 23-24, 27-28; 17:4, 7, 27; 18:4, 6, 13, 20-21; 19:5, 9; 20:19; 21:6, 23; 22:10; 25:11, 15, 23, 27; 26:20-28; 27:2; 28:23; 29:20.

The family

Fads and fashions change, but the basic structure of family life, its joys and sorrows, remain constant.

There are still unfaithful husbands, and wives who bicker and nag their husbands out of existence. There are still children from good homes who go off the rails. Proverbs' wise advice on the things that make for a happy and stable home-life, and the things that undermine it, is as sound today as ever.

Parents and children: 10:1; 13:1, 24; 17:21, 25; 19:13, 18, 27; 20:11; 22:6, 15; 23:13-16, 19-28; 28:7, 24; 29:15, 17; 30:11, 17.

Wives: 12:4; 18:22; 19:13-14; 21:9, 19; 25:24; 31:10-31. (The main advice to husbands comes in the earlier section, e.g. chapter 5.)

Laziness and hard work

Proverbs contains a good many sketches of the lazy man, too idle to begin a job, too slack to see it through, yawning his way through life until it is too late, and poverty and hunger are on him. There is nothing to commend slackness, but 'in all toil there is profit'.
10:4-5, 26; 12:11, 24, 27; 13:4; 14:23; 15:19; 18:9; 19:15, 24; 20:4, 13; 21:25; 22:13; 24:30-34; 26:13-16; 28:19.

SOME SECONDARY THEMES
Rich and poor; poverty and wealth:
10:15; 11:4, 24-25; 13:7-8, 11; 14:20-21, 31; 18:11, 23; 19:4, 7, 17; 21:13, 17; 22:1-2, 7, 16, 22-23; 23:4-5; 28:3, 6, 11, 20, 22; 30:8-9.

The world of business and affairs; plans and decisions:
11:1, 15, 26; 15:22; 16:3, 9-11, 33; 17:8, 18, 23; 18:16; 19:21; 20:10, 14, 16, 18, 23; 21:14; 22:26-27; 27:23-27; 28:8.

The proud and the humble:
11:2; 12:9; 15:25; 16:18-19; 18:12; 21:4, 24; 22:4; 29:23.

Friends:
17:9, 17; 18:24; 19:4, 6; 27:6, 10; **and neighbours:** 25:8-10, 17-18; 26:18-19; 27:10, 14; 29:5.

Masters and servants:
11:29; 14:35; 17:2; 29:19-21; 30:10, 22-23.

Kings and rulers:
16:13-15; 19:12; 20:2; 23:1-3; 24:21; 25:1-7; 28:15-16; 29:12, 14; 31:4-5.

Hopes and fears; joys and sorrows:
12:25; 13:12-19; 14:10, 13; 15:13, 30; 17:22; 18:14; 25:20; 27:9.

Anger:
14:17, 29-30; 15:18; 16:14, 32; 19:11-12, 19; 20:2; 22:24-25; 29:22.

The 'fear of the Lord'
(although the phrase does not occur all that often, this is no secondary theme; as the basis of all wisdom, it is absolutely fundamental to the whole book): 10:27; 14:26-27; 15:16-33; 16:6; 19:23; 22:4; 23:17; 24:21. See also in the earlier section, e.g. 1:7; 3:7.

ECCLESIASTES

Ecclesiastes is a piece of 'wisdom literature' (see 'Poetry and Wisdom Literature', Introduction), a popular form of writing in Near Eastern countries in Old Testament times. It is not a familiar form today, and can seem disjointed to us, with its apparently disconnected thoughts and sayings and observations on life. But the theme of Ecclesiastes is singularly 'modern': it is shared by any number of 20th-century novels and plays.

The book simply observes life around and draws the logical conclusions. This is life 'under the sun', life as man sees it. The author imposes no preconceptions. Life as man lives it, without God, is futile, meaningless, purposeless, empty. It is a bleak picture. Nature and history go round in circles: there is nothing new. Add up the profit and loss of human life and you are better off dead. Life is unfair; work is pointless; pleasure fails to satisfy; good living and wise thinking are rendered futile by death. 'Be realistic', says the book. 'If life without God is the whole story, see it for what it is. Don't pretend. Don't bury your head in the sand. This is the truth about life.'

But this is not – like so many modern writings – just cynicism and despair. God never intended man to leave him out of the picture. God can inject joy into every aspect of living: from food and work to home and marriage (2:24-26; 3:10-15; 5:18-20; 9:7-10). He intended man to find ultimate satisfaction not in life but in him. The wise man dies like the fool, it is true, but wisdom is still good and right (2:13). And God will judge the just and the wicked (3:17). Enjoy life, not as an Epicurean ('eat, drink, for tomorrow we die'), but as a man of God, because you depend on him for life and for enjoyment (3:13; 5:19). An empty, futile existence is not inevitable: remember God while you are still young (12:1); fear him and keep his commandments (12:13).

'Ecclesiastes' is the Greek translation of 'Qoheleth' (Revised Standard Version 'the Preacher'; New English Bible 'the Speaker'), a word which seems to indicate the author's official title rather than his name. It could be a pseudonym for Solomon, who was 'son of David, king in Jerusalem' (1:1, 12) and the embodiment of wisdom. What man was better qualified to pronounce on life, having tasted it

'What do we gain from our work?' asks the Philosopher. This Assyrian workman, carrying a rope, is depicted on the walls of King Sennacherib's palace.

to the full – power, fame, riches, women, all that any man could wish for – and tested out what life was like both under God and without him?

Chapter 1

The author states his theme: the emptiness and futility of life. Men come and go. The cycles of nature and history are constantly repeating themselves. There is nothing new. Even the search for wisdom – man's highest goal – is futile, for 'the more a man knows, the more he has to suffer'.

Verses 1, 12: see introduction.
Under the sun (3, 9, 14): a recurring phrase in Ecclesiastes. It indicates 'the world, seen simply from a human stand-point'.

Chapter 2

What is man to do with his days (3)? If he lives for pleasure – all that wealth and status can afford – life is still empty (10-11). Wisdom is far better than folly, but in the end death makes fools of us all. The things we work for must be left behind for others to enjoy. This is the futility of life 'under the sun'. For there is no joy or satisfaction in life apart from God (24-26).

Chapter 3

There is a time for everything in life (1-9). God has made it so. Man understands time, but he cannot comprehend the whole of God's work (11). So he learns to stand in awe of God. There is injustice and corruption in life (16ff.), but God has set a time for just judgement, although all men must die.

Chapter 4

Such are the oppressions in life that man is better dead; better still never to have been born (1-3). Men wear themselves out with work, trying to outdo one another, never stopping to ask what it's all for (4-8).

From this point in the book the thoughts and observations are more frequently interspersed with advice and teaching, in the proverbial manner adopted by the 'wise'. Wisdom may look foolish in the world's eyes (1:17, 18; 2:14-17) but 'Qoheleth' clearly still believes in it and intends men to live by it (see 12:9-11).

A threefold cord (12): three are even better than two. A rope made of three strands is hard to break.

Chapter 5

Sound advice on promises made to God (1-7) and attitudes to money (10-

12). Another of life's evils (13-17) is the business crash. The way to live is to enjoy work, and to enjoy prosperity if it comes, for these are God's gifts. Enjoyment is the antidote to gloom about the passing of the years (20).

Verses 8-9: the meaning is not clear. New English Bible translates verse 9, 'The best thing for a country is a king whose own lands are well tilled.'

Chapter 6

What value is long life to a man, without the chance to enjoy all he has worked for (1-6)? Better be stillborn or miscarried (3). The man who is ruled by his appetite and desires will never be satisfied (7-9).

Chapter 7

The wise man takes account of death as well as life (2). His outlook on life is serious (1-6). He knows how to enjoy good times and learn from bad ones (14). 'Qoheleth' observes another of life's anomalies (15). There are good men who die young, and wicked men who grow old in their wickedness. Everything is brought to the test of wisdom (23), but life will not add up. Man as God made him was all right; his troubles are all of his own making (29).

Verse 18: the advice is to avoid extremes. Verses 16-17 sound like the cynical tones of worldly wisdom. God would never say we were overdoing real goodness, or advise a little wickedness!

Verse 28: he has found only one man in a thousand worth the name, and not one woman!

Chapter 8

Faith cannot resolve the problem of evil: good men getting what the bad deserve; wicked men admired and having a cushy time. The man of God can only assert what he knows is true, though all the evidence is against it (12). Enjoyment is the best thing in life, says 'Qoheleth' (15). Yet he applies his own energy to wisdom, even though God has concealed from man the answer to life's mysteries (16-17).

Chapter 9

One fate – death – comes to all men, good and bad alike (with this one difference, that the good are in God's hands, 1). There is no knowing how long any man has (11-12). So work hard and enjoy life while it lasts, for death cuts men off from all the world has to offer (7-10). Wisdom may not pay, yet it is still worth more than power (13-18).

Chapter 10
A collection of proverbs on wisdom and folly, wise sayings and practical advice, continued in chapter 11.

Chapters 11 and 12
Practical advice leads straight in to the author's conclusions. If life is long, rejoice in it. Rejoice in the light before the dark night of death begins. Let the young rejoice in their youth, always mindful of God who calls all men to account. Don't wait till old age. Don't wait till life has become futile and empty and there is nothing ahead but death. Fear God – hold him in awe – and obey him.

12:2-6: verse 2 depicts life drawing to an end, the darkness of death closing in. Verses 3-5 are a series of pictures of old age, when strength fails, teeth are few, sight grows dim. Moffatt translates verse 5: 'When old age fears a height, and even a walk has its terrors, when his hair is almond white, and he drags his limbs along, as the spirit flags and fades.' The 'silver cord ...' (6): metaphors of death.

Verses 9-14: the author's (or editor's) postscript. He has spoken the truth about life, shown it up for what it is without God. His constructive advice is scattered through the book. Now he pinpoints the one thing on which man's life turns: his attitude to God. There is a judgement, when good and evil will be sorted out. Man must live in the light of it. The 'fear of the Lord' (as Proverbs makes so plain) is where true wisdom – and real life – begins.

THE SONG OF SOLOMON

This 'song of songs' is a series of lyric poems on the theme of love between man and woman. The setting is pastoral: the poems are full of images from the countryside. The time, appropriately, is spring. They are full of the passion and delight of human love.

The poems defy complete analysis and, partly for this reason, have been subject to all kinds of interpretation. Jews and Christians alike have seen them as allegories – of God's love for Israel; of Christ's love for his bride the Church. But the poems themselves give no direct warrant for this. Some see the poems as a drama with two characters: bride and royal bridegroom; some say three: Solomon, the girl, and her shepherd lover. There is, however, no evidence apart from the Song that this kind of literature existed in Israel. Others regard the poems as a series of songs sung during the week-long wedding-feast, as in Syria today, with the bride and groom crowned king and queen.

Whatever the form, the poems as they stand celebrate the beauty and wonder of human love. There is a frank and open delight in physical attraction, which underlines the fact that God intends man to enjoy physical love within the laws he has given.

The notes below provide only a general outline of the Song. Both the New English Bible and the Jerusalem Bible give a detailed analysis.

Chapter 1
The Song begins (2-8) with a dialogue between the bride, a country girl, and the women of Jerusalem (probably the court or harem). The bride and bridegroom then converse (9-17).
Song of Songs, which is Solomon's (1): the title may imply that Solomon wrote it, or that it was written for, or about, him. He was as renowned in the field of love (1 Kings 11:1-3) as he was in the field of wisdom. But he can hardly be taken as the ideal of single-minded devotion! Nor does the country-shepherd image suit him, unless the language is pure literary-

pastoral convention. Hence the appeal of the three-character interpretation of the Song, in which Solomon attempts to win the heart of the girl, who remains true to her shepherd lover.

The king and his bride: The Egyptian King Tutankhamun and his queen are pictured on the backrest to the throne found in his tomb.

Kedar (5): a nomadic Arab tribe. Bedouin tents are made of black goatskin.
My own ... (6): she is talking about her complexion, burnt brown by the sun.
Pharaoh's chariots (9): Solomon ran a thriving import-export trade in the horses and chariots for which Egypt was famous (1 Kings 10:26-29).
Verses 12-13: 'nard': spikenard, a perfumed ointment. Those women who could afford such luxuries wore sachets of fragrant myrrh, suspended from the neck, beneath their dresses; or on their cheeks.
Verse 14: a red cosmetic dye was made from henna. 'Engedi': a beautiful freshwater 'oasis' close to the barren shores of the Dead Sea.

Chapter 2
The bride's thoughts are filled with the sweetness and longing of love. The bridegroom calls to her in the idyllic beauty of springtime (10ff.). It

is all in a country setting. Only verse 7 contains any hint of the court.

Verse 7: see also 3:5; 8:4. The significance of this refrain seems to be that love must be allowed to grow naturally, in its own time. It is not to be forced or given an artificial stimulus.

The foxes (15): jackals. If they damage the blossom there will be no fruit.

Chapter 3

In a dream sequence the bride describes the desolate feelings separation brings, and the joy of reunion. Verses 6-11 describe the grand procession of King Solomon.

Wood of Lebanon (9): the famous cedar, imported for building the temple and palaces.

Chapter 4

The bridegroom glories in the beauty of his bride. The imagery is oriental, but love the world over shares the same delighted appreciation of the human form.

A flock of goats (1): their silky black coats gleam in the sun as they ripple over the hillside.

Verses 2-4: her teeth are white and even; her cheeks full and rosy; her neck like a tower hung with trophies.

Senir, Hermon (8): the 9,000 ft mountain on the Israel-Lebanon border.

Verse 16: the voice of the bride inviting the bridegroom to enjoy his 'garden' – herself.

Chapter 5

The bride dreams again (2-8). This time the bridegroom comes and she is too slow in letting him in. And again joy turns to desolation. In reply to the women (9) she describes what he looks like. He is as 'altogether desirable' to her as she is to him.

Myrrh ... (5): she is perfumed as a bride on her wedding night.

Chapter 6

The women question; the bride replies – and the bridegroom again describes the beauty of his one and only love. Not all the queens and concubines can rival her.

Tirzah (4): a beautiful city, the early capital of the northern kingdom of Israel.

Verse 12: New English Bible translates, 'I did not know myself; she made me feel more than a prince reigning over the myriads of his people.'

Shulammite (13): if 'Shulam' is a place, its location is not known. There are no grounds for linking the girl here with Abishag the Shunammite (1 Kings 1:3-4), as some have done.

Chapter 7

Again the bridegroom marvels at the physical beauty of his bride. He cannot tear his eyes away. Every detail is perfection. The bride loves him utterly, without reserve (10-13), in all the glory of the springtime.

Carmel (5): the mountain of Elijah's contest with the prophets of Baal, which today makes an impressive backcloth to the port of Haifa.

Mandrakes (13): a plant considered from very early days to have aphrodisiac powers.

Chapter 8

The bride longs to display her affection openly. At verse 5 the scene changes, and the two are together at last. There is *nothing* that can destroy true love.

Verses 8-9: the girl's brothers debate how to preserve her honour. This she declares she has kept (10).

Verses 11-12: the 'vineyard' is probably a poetic allusion to Solomon's harem and all its attendants. Let him keep it! The bride's love and person is her own to give: it is not for sale.

THE PROPHETS
Introduction/Alec Motyer

The people of Israel had become a nation. They had been redeemed from slavery in Egypt. They had been given the law. They were committed to a life of obedience to God, and a religion which constantly reminded them of their dependence on God's forgiveness and mercy.

But they were constantly falling down on their calling and their promises. With idol-worship, civil war, immorality, complacency, the nation needed to be recalled again and again to the whole point of their existence.

The call to obedience

The prophets were men raised up by God to do just this – to call the people back to God and his way. Slackness had grown into forgetfulness. God's holy law for life had ceased to be an effective force moulding men and society.

Sometimes the fault was more a reversal of right priorities. The sacrifices were intended to make provision for lapses into disobedience. But there were periods in Old Testament history when they were seen as substitutes for the life of obedience – ritual techniques for keeping God happy.

When the nation's religion was corrupted into this sort of non-moral ritualism, the prophets raised their protest. This explains a whole series of verses in which the prophets at first sight seem to deny the divine authority behind the sacrifices (Isaiah 1:11ff.; Jeremiah 7:21ff.; Hosea 6:6; Amos 5:25; Micah 6:6-8). Their intention is rather to recall the people from false priorities; to insist on God's primary requirement that his people should obey his commands and live out his standards.

Distinguishing false from true

Our world today is full of conflicting voices, all claiming to be authoritative pronouncements. Religious opinion varies so widely that quite often there is headlong collision between different views, all of which are put forward in the name of God. How can we tell where the truth lies?

What the prophets said in a similar situation was that what accords with Scripture can be taken as God's truth. In Deuteronomy 13 the false prophet is one who calls people away after 'other gods' and speaks 'rebellion against the Lord your God, who brought you out of the land of Egypt ... to make you leave the way in which the Lord your God commanded you to walk'.

In other words, the truth about God spoken by Moses stands as a test of the truth of people's opinions. This passage specifically mentions the commandments of the Lord: does a prophet subscribe to the old morality of Mt Sinai, or is he preaching a new morality?

We can see this test at work in Jeremiah 23:9-22. Both in his personal life (verses 9-15) and in his public ministry (verses 16-22). the false prophet subscribes to another morality and encourages his hearers to do likewise. Consequently, Jeremiah infers, this man cannot have 'stood in the council of the Lord' (verses 18, 22).

The prophet's call

The true prophet claimed the privilege of being in the Lord's 'council', a word which conveys the idea both of consultation (see 1 Kings 22:19-22) and of close companionship with God.

It is this experience of being brought into close fellowship with God and learning his mind 'in council' that lies behind the three words describing the prophet. All three appear in 1 Chronicles 29:29.

The word translated 'prophet' signifies 'called (by God)', with the consequent task of proclaiming the message of God to men. God's call is not an invitation but an appointment. For instance, the Lord 'took' Amos (7:15) in order to make him a prophet 'to my people'.

The two other Hebrew words are both translated 'seer', meaning 'one who sees'. These words point to the fact that by God's inspiration the prophets have an altogether unique ability to 'see': both into the affairs of men and into the mind of God.

The three words are used synonymously throughout the Old Testament (though 1 Samuel 9:9 points back to a time when some distinction was observed in usage). Taken together, they show the two sides of the prophetic experience. 'Seer' refers to the change God makes in the man he 'takes' for this task (see 2 Peter 1:21). 'Prophet' indicates God's revelation of his mind and will to and through that man (see 2 Timothy 3:16).

'Thus says the Lord'

The prophets, then, were essentially men whom God chose to bring close to himself. The prophet's calling was not hereditary, like the priest's. And God chose his men from many different walks of life. Some, like Jeremiah and Jonah, were very reluctant recruits, especially when they learnt what God wanted them to do.

But out of their fellowship with God (see 1 Kings 17:1) the prophets came with his message for their contemporaries, and for us too (see Acts 7:38). Sometimes they emphasized their message by means of dramatic action (e.g. Jeremiah 19; Ezekiel 4; see 2 Kings 13:14-19). But mostly their messages were presented in carefully constructed spoken discourses which bear all the marks of premeditation and preparation.

The prophets are very reticent about how they received these messages. We are often told no more than that 'the word of the Lord came' (e.g. Jeremiah 47:1; Ezekiel 17:1; Zechariah 8:1). 'Came' translates the Hebrew verb 'to be', meaning that 'the word of the Lord became a living, present reality', which tells us the content but not the nature of the experience.

However, there is no doubt that the prophets intended their claim to be taken seriously. 'Thus says the Lord' meant precisely what it said. They received from the Lord the very 'words' (note the plural, Jeremiah 1:9; Ezekiel 2:7; 3:4) which they spoke.

We can offer no logical description of their experience. We must simply observe the facts. On the one hand they themselves claimed to speak words which God gave to them; on the other hand they were clearly not impersonal 'tape recorders' of an external 'message'. On the contrary, they were great and colourful personalities.

From the far more remarkable personality of the Lord Jesus – Son of God, Son of man – we can only conclude that when man is wholly at one with God then true humanity, full individual personality comes to perfection. So, in the case of the prophets, God brought them into such close intimacy of fellowship with himself, such harmony of mind and will, such consecration of life (and all by means of the characteristic experiences of salvation) that they both grew to full maturity themselves and by his unique inspiration became the mouthpieces of God (see Exodus 4:15-16; 6:28 - 7:1).

The present and the future

A glance at the accompanying chart will show that these remarkable men were rooted in history. They were deliberately placed by God at crisis-points.

Amos spoke at a time when financial affluence and religious formalism combined to produce a high-tide of social decadence and permissiveness (see Amos 3:15 - 4:1; 4:4-5; 2:6-8).

Hosea addressed an era in which established social forms were dissolving before men's eyes.

Isaiah, according to God's estimate of the situation, preached to a people who by rejecting his message would have passed the point of no-return and condemned themselves out of hand (Isaiah 6:9ff.).

Jeremiah belongs in the thick of the final agonies of Jerusalem, and Ezekiel in the first traumatic experiences of exile.

They spoke in the name of the God who is neither an observer nor an occasional visitor but always the active Ruler of human history. Inevitably, therefore, the prophets not only explained the past (Amos 4:6ff.) and exposed the tendency of the present (Isaiah 5:11-13) but declared above all what God was about to do.

To predict what was about to happen was to them an essential consequence of their fellowship with the Lord of history (e.g. Amos 3:7). When in his presence they felt obliged to ask the vital question 'How long?' (Isaiah 6:11) and to wait to hear the answer. But when they proclaimed that answer it was not in order to satisfy men's curiosity about the future; it was to use their certainty about what was to come as a lever to bring people to repentance here and now.

The characteristic prophetic use of

prediction is seen in the words of John the Baptist, the last and most privileged of the prophets. He did not say, 'Repent, in order that the kingdom of God may come,' but, 'Repent, for the kingdom of heaven is at hand' (Matthew 3:2). The sure facts of the future call for a present moral re-alignment, a getting right with God (see Isaiah 2:5, 10, 22; 3:1ff.; 31:6-7; etc.).

The message of the prophets

God rules in history, he calls men and women to repentance. These are two of the prophets' themes. With three others they constitute the core of their teaching.

The Lord as Ruler of all history. The prophets took this so seriously that they were prepared to risk depicting the mighty empires of their day as 'tools' in the hand of God (Isaiah 10:5-15). This constitutes a problem for Habakkuk (1:5-11, 12-17): how could the holy God use unholy, corrupt instruments? The only answer the Bible offers is to re-affirm God's sovereign control of the world, a control so intricately exercised that sinners act responsibly according to the dictates and pressures of their own natures, but over all the just and holy Ruler presides, governs and guides (see 2 Kings 19:25, 28; Ezekiel 38:3-4, 10-11, 16; 39:2-3).

The primary need to be right with God. Since it is God who determines the outcome of every situation, the important thing is not to have the best and strongest human allies (see Isaiah 30:1-2; Hosea 5:13) but to side with God, to get right with him (see Isaiah 30:15). God is always at work to bring his people back to himself (Amos 4:6-11); and the prophet summons men and women to personal readiness to meet with God (Amos 4:12).

The moral foundation of religion and society. We have already mentioned Jeremiah's rejection of a religion without morality (Jeremiah 7:1-15). The prophets as a whole insist that to be right with God men and women must live in obedience to his standards and commands, and that this produces a sound society. Once people are alienated from God they cannot maintain right relationships with each other (compare Amos 2:7-8 with 9-12).

A blend of judgement and hope. Time and again, as we hear the prophets analyse the situation in which they live, we see that God's judgement is inevitable. The whole landscape is filled with threatening clouds of gathering wrath, and yet, suddenly, surprisingly, a bright shaft of hope pierces through (Isaiah 6:13; 28:5; 29:5; 31:5; Amos 9:11ff.; etc.). This blending of darkness and light, judgement and hope is more than a fact of the prophetic message: it is a necessity, for they spoke in the name of Yahweh, the Lord, the God who-saves-his-people-and-judges-his-enemies, the God of the exodus (see the article 'Names of God').

The messianic kingdom. We use this heading as a general description of the bright future state God has in store for his people. It is seen as the setting up of the perfect covenant relationship (Isaiah 54:10; Jeremiah 31:31-34; Ezekiel 37:26-27), and in many other ways also. But it is chiefly described as centring upon some great coming Person. He is:

The new 'David': Ezekiel 37:24
The 'branch' of David's line (or, to stress his divine ancestry) the 'branch of the Lord': Isaiah 11:1; Jeremiah 23:5-6; 33:14-16; Zechariah 3:8; 6:12; Isaiah 4:2
Immanuel, 'God with us': Isaiah 7:14
The 'mighty God' occupying David's throne: Isaiah 9:6-7
The servant, dying for his people's sins: Isaiah 53
The anointed Conqueror of his people's foes: Isaiah 63:1-6
The Lord himself coming in the wake of the appointed forerunner: Malachi 3:1
Born in Bethlehem, born of a virgin: Micah 5:2; Isaiah 7:14

It is the crowning glory of the Old Testament prophets that God permitted and enabled them to see this radiance afar off. It sets the seal on their prophecies as God's word to men, that all was so perfectly fulfilled in the Lord Jesus. And what greater incentive could we have to get to know the writings of these men than Jesus' own statement that without them we cannot understand him, but that with them we can both know him (Luke 24:27, 32) and preach him to the world (Luke 24:44-48)?

THE PROPHETS IN THEIR SETTING

800BC			700	
2 Kings				
14	15	16	21	
2 Chronicles				
26		27 28	29	33

Northern powers   Assyrian Empire

Tiglath-pileser III ♔   ♔ Sennacherib   Nabopolass
of Babylon
♔ Shalmaneser V
Sargon II ♔   ♔ Esarhaddon
Ashurbanipal ♔   Nebuch

Edom becomes ▲   ✂ Tyre falls   Nebuch
Assyria's vassal   to the   dream
Assyrians
✂ Tyre falls

?Jonah ▬▬▬
takes God's message   ✂ Damascus falls to
to Nineveh   the Assyrians

Israel

Jeroboam II ♔

Zechariah ♔   ♔ Pekahiah

Shallum ♔   ♔ Hoshea

Menahem ♔   ♔ Pekah

Fall of ✂
Samaria,
Israelites
taken to
Assyria

Amos ▬▬▬
the farmer from Judah
denounces Israel

Hosea ▬▬▬▬▬▬
expresses God's love
for his faithless people

Judah

♔ Ahaz   ♔ Hezekiah   ♔
♔ Jotham   ♔ Manasseh   ♔
♔ Azariah (Uzziah)

✂ Sennacherib   **Nahum** ▬▬
▲ Uzziah dies: besieges   prophesies a
Isaiah's vision   Jerusalem
Zephaniah ▬
pronounces
judgement

Isaiah ▬▬▬▬▬▬   **Haba**
speaks to the nation   debat
under the threat of Assyria

Micah ▬▬▬▬   **Jere**
denounces Samaria and Jerusalem   spea
facin

800BC		700	

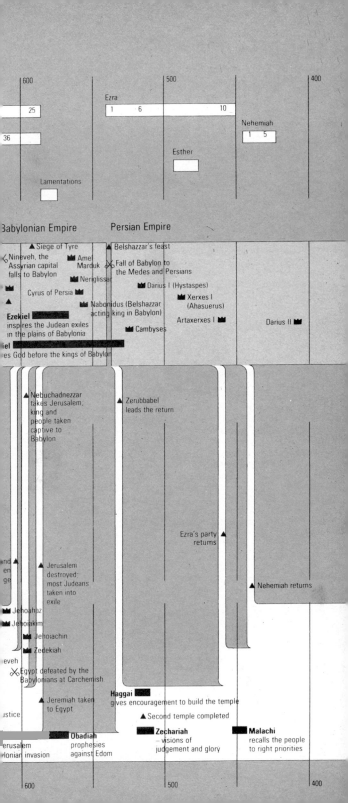

600 500 400

Ezra
1 · 6 · · 10

Nehemiah
1 · 5

25

36

Esther

Lamentations

Babylonian Empire　　　Persian Empire

▲ Siege of Tyre　▲ Belshazzar's feast
Nineveh, the　▟ Amel
Assyrian capital　Marduk　✗ Fall of Babylon to
falls to Babylon　　　the Medes and Persians
▟ Neriglissar　▟ Darius I (Hystaspes)
Cyrus of Persia 👑　　Xerxes I
▟ Nabonidus (Belshazzar　(Ahasuerus)
acting king in Babylon)　Artaxerxes I ▟　　Darius II ▟
Ezekiel inspires the Judean exiles
in the plains of Babylonia　▟ Cambyses

iel
es God before the kings of Babylon

▲ Nebuchadnezzar　　▲ Zerubbabel
takes Jerusalem,　　leads the return
king and
people taken
captive to
Babylon

Ezra's party ▲
returns

▲ Jerusalem
destroyed;　　　　　▲ Nehemiah returns
most Judeans
taken into
exile

nd ▲
en
ge

▟ Jehoahaz
▟ Jehoiakim
▟ Jehoiachin
▟ Zedekiah

eveh
✗ Egypt defeated by the
Babylonians at Carchemish

▲ Jeremiah taken　**Haggai**
to Egypt　gives encouragement to build the temple

ustice　▲ Second temple completed

Obadiah　**Zechariah**　**Malachi**
erusalem　prophesies　– visions of　recalls the people
lonian invasion　against Edom　judgement and glory　to right priorities

600 500 400

ISAIAH

The prophets. Isaiah stands at the head of 'The Prophets', the third great section of the Old Testament. Sixteen prophets are named, and we have 17 books of their visions and prophecies (the odd one out being Lamentations: known in the Greek versions as the 'Lamentations of Jeremiah'). The four 'major' prophets are Isaiah, Jeremiah, Ezekiel and Daniel; the twelve 'minor' prophets, Hosea, Joel, Amos, Obadiah, Jonah, Micah, Nahum, Habakkuk, Zephaniah, Haggai, Zechariah, Malachi.

The books of the prophets belong to the time of the nation's decline, the exile and the return to their homeland. They span, altogether, a period of 250-300 years. Most of them address their messages primarily to the southern kingdom of Judah – Isaiah, Joel and Micah before Jerusalem fell to Babylon in 587 BC; Jeremiah, Habakkuk and Zephaniah at the time of the fall and during the exile; Haggai, Zechariah and Malachi at the time of the return, 538 BC and after. Of the others, Hosea and Amos had a special mission to Israel (the northern kingdom which fell to Assyria in 722 BC); Jonah and Nahum to the Assyrian capital, Nineveh; Daniel in Babylon; Ezekiel to the Jewish exiles in Babylon; and Obadiah to Edom, Israel's long-standing enemy.

God sent these prophets on a daunting and sometimes dangerous mission. They were for the most part despatched at the eleventh hour, to try to halt the people's headlong rush to destruction; to warn them of judgement; to call them back to God in repentance – and after the great crash came, to comfort the survivors with the assurance of God's continuing love and purpose for them. To a man, the prophets went out in the burning conviction that they had a message from God. Some braved death to make it known.

The book of Isaiah. Isaiah's place at the head of the prophetic books is well deserved. There is nothing to

equal his tremendous vision of God and the glory in store for God's people until we reach John's book of Revelation, at the end of the New Testament. Other prophets came before him historically, but there was none greater.

Isaiah lived in Jerusalem in the 8th century BC. (For the historical background see article 'The Threat of Assyria'). In chapter 6 he describes his call from God in the year of King Uzziah's death (about 740 BC). He prophesied for over 40 years, through the reigns of Jotham (a godly man like his father), Ahaz (one of Judah's worst kings) and Hezekiah. He may have lived on into the dark days of the evil King Manasseh. He knew from the outset that his words would fall on deaf ears, but he did have one great triumph. When Sennacherib's Assyrian army was hammering at the gates of Jerusalem in Hezekiah's reign (701 BC) the king took Isaiah's advice and the city was saved (chapters 36 - 37).

The initial vision of God in all his glory in the temple (chapter 6) coloured Isaiah's whole mission. He had seen God as the 'Holy One of Israel' and he never forgot it. He had seen human sin for the appalling thing it is, and he never forgot that either. And he had been forgiven and taken into God's service. Throughout his life, he preached God's righteousness, warned of the judgement on sin, and comforted his people with the knowledge of God's love, his longing to forgive, and all the glories in store for those who remained faithful to him.

In the book of Isaiah we have a collection of visions and prophecies belonging to various periods of the prophet's life. It is not always easy to follow – partly because we are unfamiliar with the language and ways of prophets and visionaries; partly because we do not know the principles which determined the present arrangement of material. In places there is clearly a time-sequence. Other parts seem to be

THE PROPHETS

NAHUM prophesies to Nineveh

EZEKIEL and DANIEL prophesy as exiles in Babylonia

HOSEA prophesies in Israel

ISRAEL

JONAH sails from Joppa – and then goes to preach to Nineveh

Samaria

Anathoth

Jerusalem

From Tekoa AMOS is sent to prophesy to Israel

From his home in southern Judah MICAH speaks to Jerusalem and Samaria

JUDAH

Prophets in Judah: ISAIAH and JEREMIAH in Jerusalem; JOEL, ZEPHANIAH, ?HABAKKUK; after the exile, HAGGAI, ZECHARIAH, MALACHI

EDOM, subject of the prophecy of OBADIAH

arranged according to subject. Also, because Isaiah was a visionary, his thoughts range freely over the whole scale of time. One minute he is describing God's judgement on the Jerusalem he knows (the Assyrians about to pounce); the next it is God's universal judgement on evil – the end of the world as we know it; the beginning of a reign of perfect peace and justice. What he sees happening in his own time is the outworking of principles which are eternal and universal. And he moves in a flash from the particular to the universal and back again.

We do not know how the book was eventually put together. No doubt Isaiah himself wrote down at least some of his prophecies (see 30:8, and the use of the first person in chapters 6 and 8). Over the past century there has been a great deal of discussion over the differences between chapters 1 - 39 and 40 - 66. These have led many scholars to argue for more than one author – even allowing for the fact that the book was always written on a single scroll, and that

the New Testament (which quotes Isaiah more than any other Old Testament book) assumes a single author. Some of the theories on authorship, in the past at least, have been open to criticism on the grounds that they have grown out of a basic presupposition that prediction in the prophets can simply be discounted. On this view, the 8th-century Isaiah could not have predicted with such accuracy events which took place long after his death (notably the fall of Babylon to Cyrus the Persian, 44:28ff.). But this runs counter to one of the main themes of Isaiah 40 - 48: that God demonstrates that he and he alone is God by announcing in advance the events which he as Lord of history will bring about. However, this by no means accounts for all the arguments about authorship. The debate continues.

1 - 5 GOD'S MESSAGE FOR JUDAH AND JERUSALEM

1 The sordid corruption of Judah
Although Jerusalem was not finally destroyed until 587 BC, by Isaiah's

time the nation has already virtually reached the point of no return. They have rejected God. And God is sickened by their moral degradation, social injustice and religious hypocrisy. Yet he still offers forgiveness (18). Swift and terrible judgement will fall on all who persist in refusing.

The vision (1): Isaiah describes what God enables him to see in his mind's eye. 'Amoz' is not the same as the prophet Amos.

Holy One of Israel (4): Isaiah's special title for God. It is used only twice in other parts of the Bible.

Verses 7-9: the Assyrians have overrun Judah. The northern kingdom of Israel has already fallen. Only Jerusalem (the 'daughter of Zion') remains. Genesis 19 describes the destruction of Sodom and Gomorrah, two utterly corrupt cities at the southern end of the Dead Sea.

New moon and sabbath (13): the first day of each new month and the weekly sabbath were holy days.

Scarlet ... crimson (18): both fast colours; only God could 'wash' these out.

Oaks (29): the sacred groves where Canaanite rites took place; symbols of the nations' idolatry.

2 - 4 God's coming day: peace and judgement

In these chapters Isaiah looks far ahead to the time when Jerusalem will become the city of God for people of all nations (2:1-5). But before that God will execute fierce judgement on all the wickedness and pride which pollute his people (2:6 - 4:1). For evil has no place in the renewed city; only the few who are faithful to God will survive to enjoy it (4:2-6). The theme is developed in chapters 11 - 12.

Mountain (2:2): Mt Zion, i.e. Jerusalem.

2:6: the practice of magic (forbidden in Leviticus 19:31) and foreign alliances both led to idolatry.

2:13-16: symbols of pride. Solomon used the famous Lebanese cedarwood for his temple. The ships of Tarshish were great ocean-going vessels, the pride of the fleet.

The vineyard (3:14): symbol of the nation, see chapter 5.

Baldness (3:24): heads were shaved as a sign of mourning or degradation.

4:1: so many men have been killed in battle that the women offer to provide their own keep (unheard of in those days), if only the man will marry them.

The branch (4:2): new growth shooting from the old roots (see 11:1); the community is to be reborn.

4:5: cloud and fire – the symbols of God's presence when they journeyed through the desert (Exodus 13:21).

5 The song of the vineyard

The Jewish nation is the vineyard of God. He has done everything necessary to ensure a heavy yield. But the vintage is bitter; so God will abandon the vineyard (but not for ever, see chapter 27). Jesus uses the same picture in Matthew 21:33-41.

In the land of Judah the vast estates built up at the expense of the poor (8) will become waste land. Ten acres of vines will yield only 22 litres; the harvest will be only a tenth of the seed sown (10). Again the prophet denounces pride, luxury, drunkenness, injustice. God will give the signal for the enemy invasion (26ff.) – Assyria first and then Babylon – to destroy them.

Sheol (14): the shadowy world of the dead.

6 ISAIAH'S VISION OF GOD AND CALL TO SERVICE

For the effect this had on his mission, see introduction to the book. Isaiah had many visions, some so terrible, some so wonderful, he could hardly put them into words: but none to equal this. The knowledge that he had seen God with his own eyes, experienced his forgiveness and been sent out in his service would sustain him all his life. And he would need it: for God sent him to a nation deaf and blind to his entreaties (9-10); a nation that would be destroyed and taken captive (11-12). Yet there was hope: the germ of a new nation would survive (13).

Verses 9-10: we trip up here, as elsewhere, over the Hebrew idiom which expresses result as if it were purpose. God did not intend to stop people repenting. He sent Isaiah out with the express purpose of saving people from judgement. But when they heard him they shut their ears and refused to act.

7 - 12 PRESENT AND FUTURE

7 The threat from the north: God warns King Ahaz

The date is about 735 BC. The new king, Ahaz, defied God (2 Kings 16), and in consequence his kingdom came under attack from all quarters. When he refused to join the Israel/

Syria alliance against Assyria, they attacked Judah. It is at this point that Isaiah goes to him with God's message (3-9). In the crisis, Ahaz turned to Assyria, not God, for help. But Assyria would soon become a razor (20) in God's hand, to shave his rebel people of their pride and strength.

House of David (2): the royal household.

Syria and Ephraim (2 and 5ff.): Syria (strictly speaking at this date, Aram) was ruled from Damascus. As predicted, the kingdom was crushed by Assyria in 732. 'Ephraim' is the northern kingdom of Israel, which also fell to Assyria. 734-722 BC.

Shearjashub (3): the name means 'a remnant shall return'. The names of both Isaiah's sons stood as a constant reminder of his teaching – see chapter 8 and on 10:20.

Fuller's Field (3): the fuller needed to be near water for his job of cleaning and whitening cloth.

Verses 14-16: the sign seems to have both present and future significance. 1. In the few years it takes for a child conceived now to reach an age when he can choose for himself, Israel and Damascus will cease to be a threat. 2. There will one day be born a child who will truly be 'Immanuel', 'God with us' (see Matthew 1:23).

Curds and honey (15, 22): these symbols of natural plenty, here stand for a waste land where cattle and bees afford the only remaining food supply.

8 Isaiah's own family becomes a sign

God has any number of ways of getting his message across. This time, the fact that Damascus and Samaria are riding for a fall is embodied in the name of Isaiah's baby son. (Maher-shalal-hashbaz means 'Speed spoil, hasten plunder'.) When Assyria has dealt with the rebels she will sweep on into Judah, till Jerusalem itself is surrounded (see chapters 36 - 37).

The prophetess (3): Isaiah's wife.
Shiloah (6): probably an aqueduct outside Jerusalem. Hezekiah's Siloam tunnel had not yet been constructed.
The River (7): Euphrates.

9:1-7 The prince of peace

Isaiah sweeps his listeners far into the future with this glorious vision. Zebulun and Naphtali in Galilee were the first of the tribes to be crushed by Assyria. They will be first to see the light, to taste the joy, to be set free by the prince of peace. Nazareth, in Galilee, was the home of Jesus; Cana in Galilee the place where his public ministry began with the very first miracle.

The way of the sea (1): the main highway between Egypt and Syria passed through Galilee.

Day of Midian (4): the day of Gideon's great victory against the Midianites, Judges 7.

9:8 - 10:4 God warns Israel of what is coming

Isaiah switches abruptly to the present. Israel (the breakaway northern kingdom) stands condemned for her arrogance and rebellion, injustice and oppression. She has already had a taste of judgement, but learnt nothing from it. Therefore God will not spare her.

(The Assyrians took many Israelites captive in 734, but Samaria held out till 722. Israel had turned a deaf ear to the warnings of Amos and the appeals of Hosea (Isaiah's contemporary), the two prophets God had specially sent them.)

The prophecy is written in four stanzas, each ending with the same refrain (12, 17, 21, 10:4).

10:5-34 God sends Assyria against his people

God makes use of a proud and cruel nation to punish his people. But Assyria's excessive ferocity is not excused: it will be punished. Even at the height of judgement God never loses sight of his purpose to save. A remnant – pathetically few – of his people will survive to trust and serve him.

Verse 9: a list of cities and city-states conquered by Assyria – all Syrian except for Samaria.

There is none ... (14): a vivid way of expressing the total absence of any resistance.

The remnant (20): this is one of the key themes in Isaiah. It goes back to the day God called him into service (6:13), and runs as a thread of hope through the darkest messages of judgement. This same faithful remnant is to realize all the glorious promises for the future.

Verse 26: see Judges 7 and Exodus 14.

Verses 28ff.: Gibeah, just north of Jerusalem was Saul's capital; Anathoth, a few miles east, the home of Jeremiah. Isaiah pictures an attack on Jerusalem from the north, the usual route of invading armies from countries to the north or east.

Sennacherib actually approached from Lachish, to the south-west.

11 - 12 The perfect king: the perfect kingdom

The theme of earlier passages (2:2-4; 4:2-6; 9:1-7) is developed more fully here. The coming king will be from David's family ('Jesse', 1, was David's father). He will possess the Spirit of God himself: just, righteous, faithful, like God. His will be an international kingdom, free of enmity and evil, utterly transformed. There will be a great gathering in of all God's people, and the song of God's salvation will be on everyone's lips. Isaiah pictures it all in physical terms. But what he sees is a radical change. This is a new, God-centred earth (see 65:17ff. and Revelation 21).

13 - 23 GOD WARNS THE NATIONS OF JUDGEMENT

A collection of prophecies against foreign nations given at various times. God's concern is not limited to Israel. The world was his then; it is his now, and his people should realize that.

13 - 14:23 Babylon

See also chapters 46 - 47. In Isaiah's day Babylon was struggling for independence from Assyria. Here he steps forward 100 years to see Babylon at the height of her power – and to look beyond, to the day when Babylon in turn would be brought down. In 539 Babylon fell to the Medes and Persians led by Cyrus. Xerxes destroyed the city in 478, and it was finally abandoned in the 4th century BC. In the New Testament, Babylon is universalized, as the city of rebel man, implacably opposed to God (Revelation 17; it also serves as a cover-word for Rome).

Ophir (13:12): see on 1 Kings 9:28.

13:21-22: a list of repulsive creatures. The 'satyrs' are demons of desert places.

King of Babylon (14:4): the taunt-song is addressed, not to a particular king, but to the dynasty, representing the whole kingdom.

14:13: the very same thoughts which brought God's judgement on Babylon's predecessor, Babel (Genesis 11:1-9).

14:24-27 Assyria

Assyria's fate is also sealed (see on 10:5-34). Ultimately Babylon will break the power of Assyria. But before that there will be a signal defeat in God's own land (25; see chapters 36 - 37).

14:28-32 Philistia

The date is probably 716 BC. Assyria is in trouble, and the Philistines (old enemies of Israel, occupying the coastal plain) try to persuade Judah to join them in rebellion. But the Assyrians are far from finished (29, 31); and the Philistines are doomed. God's people must learn to trust in him.

15 - 16 Moab

The Moabites were descendants of Abraham's nephew, Lot. They occupied the plateau land east of the Dead Sea. It was from Moab that Ruth came. At times the Moabites were on good terms with the Israelites, but they had no share in Israel's faith. Isaiah is stirred to sympathy at the spectacle of Moab's suffering (15:5), now only three short years away (16:14). Moab sends to Jerusalem for help, and God urges his people to take the fugitives in (16:1-5).

The cities of Moab fell to Assyria in successive campaigns. They were to fall again to Nebuchadnezzar of Babylon.

15:1-9: these are all towns in Moab. 'Nebo' is the mountain from which Moses viewed the promised land; 'Zoar' a town at the southern end of the Dead Sea, spared in the overthrow of Sodom. The 'Brook of the willows' is probably the boundary between Moab and Edom to the south.

Baldness (15:2): see on 3:24.

Sela (16:1): 'the rock', the fortress in Jordan where Petra now stands.

16:3-5: these verses may be Moab's plea to Judah or God's word to his people.

Vine of Sibmah (16:8ff.): a region famous for its wine – here a symbol of national prosperity.

Years of a hireling (14): the hired man works no more than the time contracted for; so, 'three years, and barely that'.

17 Damascus

A prophecy from Isaiah's early days – see on chapter 7. In response to King Ahaz' appeal for help against the Syria/Israel alliance, the Assyrians launched a series of raids in which Damascus was plundered and King Rezin met his death. This prophecy also attacks Israel for siding with Syria against their own brother-nation of Judah.

Asherim ... (8): Canaanite cult-images and altars.

Hivites, Amorites (9): tribes

destroyed by the Israelites in the conquest of Canaan.

18 Ethiopia/Cush

This is modern Sudan. In Isaiah's day Egypt was ruled by an 'Ethiopian' dynasty. The Assyrian threat brings envoys from afar. But God will deal with the invader on the very eve of victory (5 - 6 – see 37:36ff.). And the far-off nation will send gifts in grateful homage to God (7; see 2 Chronicles 32:23).

19 Egypt

Isaiah foretells the disintegration of Egypt: internal strife, followed by conquest, a ruined economy and breakdown of leadership (1-15). Egypt was defeated by Assyria when Sennacherib's army besieged Jerusalem (701 BC). Further defeats culminated in the sack of Thebes in 663 BC when the Assyrians pillaged centuries of temple treasures. But God uses the sword for surgery, not anarchy. Verses 16-24 reveal his ultimate purpose, the conversion of Egypt. 'That day' (i.e. the day of God's judgement – both temporal and final – a frequent phrase throughout Isaiah) is the day of God's final intervention in judgement and salvation on a worldwide scale. That day, the New Testament tells us, is the day of Christ's return.

After Jerusalem fell in 587 there were numerous influential colonies of Jews in Egypt and in Assyria. A copy of the Jewish temple was even constructed at Leontopolis in Egypt about 170 BC. But all that was only a pale shadow of what Isaiah envisages here.

Zoan (11) ... Memphis (13): respectively the current and ancient capitals of Egypt. Zoan (Tanis) was in the delta region; Memphis just south of it on the Nile.

City of the sun (18): Heliopolis = On; centre of Egyptian sun-worship

20 Egypt and Ethiopia

'The year' (1) is 711 BC, when the Assyrians crushed the Philistine rebellion at Ashdod. The support expected from Egypt had not materialized. God instructs Isaiah to play the role of a slave (2) to illustrate the coming captivity of Egypt and warn his people to place no reliance on help from that quarter. In 701 BC (see on chapter 19 above) Egypt was defeated by Assyria.

Naked (2): i.e. wearing only a loin-cloth.

21 Babylon; Dumah (Edom); Arabia

The 'wilderness of the sea' (1) is Babylon (9). See on chapters 13 - 14. The downfall of Babylon will be good news to the captives from Israel (10). Even so, Isaiah is appalled by what he foresees. There is temporary respite for Edom (Dumah, 11-12) – but judgement was to follow (see 34:5). Not even the remote tribes of Arabia (13-16) will escape the long arm of Assyria. This prophecy became reality when Sargon attacked Arabia in 715 BC.

Verse 16: 'Kedar', a powerful Bedouin tribe; 'years of a hireling', see on 16:14.

22 Jerusalem, the 'valley of vision'

Jerusalem was Isaiah's base, the place where he had his visions. The city is surrounded by valleys and mountains, and he may have had a particular spot in mind. Despite the reprieve in Hezekiah's day (chapters 36 - 37), Isaiah foresees the future destruction of Jerusalem. (Nebuchadnezzar II of Babylon eventually took the city after a terrible siege in 587 BC. The walls were broken down and the temple destroyed.) The people's reaction in the face of disaster is a mixture of frenzied activity and sheer escapism (8-13). Verses 15ff. relate to Isaiah's own day. Shebna, a high official in Hezekiah's court (36:3) is to be demoted, and Eliakim promoted. But he will find himself unable to cope with his hangers-on, and his authority will be short-lived.

Elam ... Kir (6): outposts of the Assyrian Empire which no doubt supplied conscripts to the army.

House of the forest (8): an arsenal, see 1 Kings 7:2; 10:17.

Verses 9, 11: it was vital to any city to ensure its water supply in the event of siege. See 2 Chronicles 32 for the Siloam tunnel, Hezekiah's solution to the problem.

The lintel of a tomb, found at Siloam in Jerusalem, with the name of a royal steward, possibly Shebna. The inscription is one of the longest in ancient Hebrew so far discovered.

23 Tyre

For centuries Tyre (modern Sour in Lebanon) dominated the sea-trade in the eastern Mediterranean. Her colonies, of which Cyprus was the nearest, were widespread. And her merchantmen ventured as far afield as the Indian Ocean and the English Channel. A major tradeline was Egyptian grain (3). Tyre was a city corrupted by her own wealth and success, and Isaiah warns of the approaching end. He spoke truly. In 722 the city fell to Sargon of Assyria. In 701 the ruler of Tyre fled to Cyprus as Sennacherib approached. As Assyria declined, Tyre regained her power, only to lose it again to the Babylonians.

Tarshish (6): probably 'Tartessus' in Spain.

Chaldeans (13): Chaldea was part of south Babylonia, but when Chaldean kings came to power in Babylon the term was used of the Babylonian kingdom as a whole.

Seventy years (15): probably a round figure, meaning a lifetime.

24 - 27 GOD'S FINAL JUDGEMENT AND VICTORY

From the particular – God's judgement on specific nations – we move to the universal – his judgement on the whole world and everyone in it. Life will not go on for ever just as it is. There will come a point when God will step in and end the world as we know it; when the earth will rock on its foundations. Isaiah was in no doubt about it. Neither was Jesus (see Matthew 24). But God's purpose is not just to condemn. One chapter (24) on judgement is followed by three (25-27) on his glorious salvation.

A song of joy in God, who makes the weak and helpless his concern (25:1-5), leads into a description of the joys awaiting God's people on the far side of judgement (25:6-12). Chapter 26 breaks into song again. Its theme is trust. In life there is waiting (8ff.), suffering and failure (16-18). But God holds fast his own, even through death (19). The song of the vineyard in 27:2-13 contrasts with chapter 5. The day will come when God's purpose for his people will be fulfilled. The present punishment is intended as a corrective. The exile will end. In the final harvest all God's people will be brought home.

That day (24:21, etc.): see on chapter 19 above.

Moab (25:10): the current enemy of God's people stands for all such enemies.

Thy dew (26:19): a picture of God's power to revive the dead.

Leviathan … (27:1): the dragon/serpent figure from pagan mythology. God's judgement extends to the superhuman realm (see 24:21). The same figure is used in Revelation 12:9 to depict Satan.

Asherim (27:9): see on 17:8 above.

27:10-11: refers to the oppressors, whose suffering will be far greater than that of God's people.

28 - 31 MORE WARNINGS TO GOD'S REBELLIOUS PEOPLE

28 Woe to Samaria and Judah's leaders

Attention is turned once again to the sins of Isaiah's own day. Verses 1-6, addressed to Israel, belong to the time before Samaria fell. The pleasure-loving, luxury-loving city is ripe for the plucking – and Assyria's hand is outstretched to take it. Yet a remnant (see on 10:20 above) will remain.

The leaders come under special attack (7ff.). Religious leaders and rulers alike have not led but misled the people. They are so cocksure, they think they can dictate terms to death itself. They will discover how wrong they are (18). Real security rests with God.

Verses 9-13: J. B. Phillips translates 10, 13: 'The-law-is-the-law-is-the-law, The-rule-is-the-rule-is-the-rule.' Isaiah's hearers are deliberately making nonsense of God's message; 9-10 may be their sneering reply to the prophet. To those who treat God's words as gibberish, Isaiah says that God will deliver his next message in Assyrian!

Verse 21: refers to David's victories; see 1 Chronicles 14:8-17.

Verses 23-29: a parable, meaning there is method in the 'madness' of God's present actions, just as the farmer has good reason for the way he works.

29 Woe to Jerusalem

'Ariel' stands for Mt Zion/Jerusalem (8). The city will be besieged (3) and then reprieved (5ff. and see 37:36). God's word to his people has become a closed book, because they pay him only lip-service (11-16). But the day is coming (17ff.) when those who are deaf and blind to his message will hear and see, when God's people will once again fear and obey him.

Verse 17: a picture of things suddenly reversed: the forests become fields and fields forests. The same thought continues in the verses that follow.

The meek … the poor (19): people

loyal to God, not simply the victims of social injustice (see Matthew 5:3, 5).

30 - 31 Woe to the rebels who rely on Egypt

Judah is in league with Egypt and thinks herself secure against Assyria (28:15), despite all Isaiah's earlier warnings. But when it comes to the crunch Egypt will sit tight (7) while the Assyrians invade Judah (chapters 36 - 37). It is God – the One they would not trust (9-12) – who will save them in the end (27-33; 31:5-9; 37:36). He calls on them yet again to turn to him (31:6).

Zoan (30:4): see on 19:11.

30:6: the gifts are carried through the Negev desert to Egypt.

Rahab (30:7): a poetic synonym for Egypt.

30:33: the oppressor will be utterly destroyed. 'Topheth' ('a burning place') is in the valley of Hinnom, just outside Jerusalem, where in Israel's darkest days children were sacrificed to the pagan god Molech. The valley later supplied the name for hell, 'Gehenna'.

32 - 35 THE GLORIOUS FUTURE – AND THE DARK DAYS PRECEDING IT

32 The future king; peace by a hard road

Isaiah sees far into the future (1-8), returns to his own day at verse 9, and at verse 15 looks forward again to a time of lasting peace, justice and righteousness brought about by the working of God's Holy Spirit in his people. But before the king comes, present evil must be swept away, and people shaken out of their complacency. They will lose all that they now enjoy – until God steps in once again (15).

Verse 9: the cossetted women of Jerusalem typify the society of Isaiah's day.

Verse 19: the meaning is not clear; 'forest' and 'city' may refer to enemies.

33 When God intervenes

This is a chapter with many changes of speaker and mood. Isaiah does not name the destroyer (1). His description (7-9) can apply to many times beside his own. Only those who live by their faith in God remain unshaken in circumstances like these (2-6; 15-16). God never deserts his own; the city defended by him is unassailable (17-24). His presence guarantees stability, prosperity, security (20-21).

34 Judgement on the nations

God will one day avenge the wrong done to his people (8; see also chapter 24). Edom – the enemy par excellence – is singled out as an example. The destruction is total: the whole land rendered uninhabitable for man.

Bozrah (6): at various times Edom's capital city.

35 Salvation for God's people

This chapter stands in striking contrast to the horror of 34. Destruction gives way to re-creation. God is coming to bring his people home by a safe highway. At the sight of him everything is changed. The dry and lifeless desert, bursting for joy, becomes a paradise of flowing streams, great trees and the glowing colours of flowers.

36 - 39 CONTEMPORARY EVENTS: CRISES IN HEZEKIAH'S REIGN

See on 2 Kings 18 - 20, an almost identical account apart from Hezekiah's poem (38:9-20). See also 2 Chronicles 32. Hezekiah's illness and the embassy from Babylon probably preceded the siege (about 705-702 BC). The events may have been reversed here to provide a lead-in to the following chapters, which are

Assyrian soldiers return from a victory.

focussed on Babylon as the world power she later became. 'Peace in my time' was Hezekiah's reaction to the terrible prediction of conquest and captivity (39:5-8). Isaiah could draw no comfort from the thought.

40 - 48 ON THE BRINK OF FREEDOM

Up to this point Isaiah has been largely taken up with the threat from Assyria. Now that particular crisis is behind him. He is given a new vision for a new situation. Jerusalem has been saved from Assyria, but the city *will* fall to Babylon and the captive people will be taken into exile. This will not be the end of the nation, though it will seem like it. In due course Babylon itself will be overthrown by Cyrus the Persian, and he will return the exiles to their homeland. All this God reveals to the prophet, so that he may comfort and encourage the people, reassuring them for the bitter times ahead. So clear is all this in Isaiah's mind that from now on he leaves current events behind. In 40 - 48 he stands with the captives in Babylon at the end of their long exile.

40 A message of comfort: God's forgiveness and his infinite power
There is comfort for God's people: he is coming as he promised (1-11; see chapter 35). Israel's God is God the Creator: incomparable, eternal. He never stops caring for his people (12-31).
Double (2): not twice as much, but an equal measure.
Verses 3-5: these verses sum up the mission of John the Baptist, see Luke 3:1-6.
Verse 11: Jesus took up this picture, describing himself as the good shepherd, see John 10:11.

41 'Fear not ... I will help you'
God's tone is stern as he brings the nations to book (1). But with his own people he is infinitely loving and tender (8ff.). He is at hand to help. They have nothing to fear.
One from the east (2) ... one from the north (25): 44:28 names the new conqueror, Cyrus the Persian (from Israel the route was north, then east).
Verses 21-24: the pagan gods – who are no gods – cannot predict things to come. Only God, the one true God, can do that.

42 A light for the nations
A new theme begins to unfold, alongside the forecast of Babylon's downfall: God's plan to open the eyes of the whole world and bring salvation to all mankind. This was, from the very beginning, the intended role of Israel (Genesis 22:18). So, to begin with the servant of God in Isaiah's series of 'songs' is the nation (or faithful remnant) of Israel. But Israel failed to be God's true servant in the way he intended (19-25). And so, in the series of portraits which follow (49:1-13; 50:4-9; 52:13-53:12; 61:1-4), the realization gradually dawns that God's purpose will ultimately be fulfilled not through the nation but through one who will be his true servant. The New Testament writers are in no doubt that the servant Isaiah foresaw – who would save men by suffering on their behalf – was Jesus Christ (Matthew 12:15-21). They have Christ's own authority for saying so (Luke 4:16-21).

43 God's unfailing love and care
By their constant disobedience, God's people have forfeited all right to his care (22-24) – yet he forgives (25). In all their sufferings he is beside them (2). He will set them free again, simply because he loves them (4ff.).
Verses 16-17: this refers to the exodus from Egypt.

44 - 45 No God but God; the forecast of Israel's return
These chapters continue the themes that run through the whole section: Israel as God's servant, the object of his love (44:1-5); God as Lord of history, the only Person able to draw back the veil on the future (44:6ff.); the lifeless no-gods that men worship; God's promise that he will set

The superstition and fear involved in idol-worship is expressed by this colossal statue, which stands about 15ft/5m high.

his people free. 44:26 - 45:13 take us a stage further. The general promise becomes specific. In the reign of Cyrus, Jerusalem and its temple will be rebuilt (see on Ezra 1:1-4ff.).

Cyrus (44:28): many find it hard to believe Isaiah could actually have named the king so far in advance. God can reveal what no man could possibly predict (41:21-24, 26-27; 42:9; 43:12-13; 44:6-8; 45:18-21).

45:22-25: God's love reaches beyond Israel to the world. The New Testament applies verse 23 directly to Christ; see Philippians 2:10-11.

46 - 47 The downfall of Babylon

See also chapters 13 - 14 above. The indictment of pagan gods reaches its climax in the passive submission of the Babylonian gods Bel and Nebo. These dumb idols burden the backs of their worshippers. The real God is One who carries his people's burdens, who has power not only to speak but to act. Chapter 47 (like 14:4-21) is a taunt-song. Babylon will be shown as little mercy as she has shown others.

47:1: 'Virgin daughter', the city of Babylon; 'Chaldeans', see on 23:13.

48 God's patient love for faithless Israel

The history of Israel is one long tale of hypocrisy, rebellion, scepticism, idolatry. She has fully deserved all she has suffered. God always purposed peace for his people (18), but there could be 'no peace for the wicked'. Now the moment of liberation has come: he says 'Go forth'. **Verse 16:** there is a change of speaker here; the voice may be the prophet's or that of the servant/Messiah, as in 49:1, etc.

49 - 55 THE SERVANT OF GOD AND THE REDEMPTION OF HIS PEOPLE

These chapters give us a series of portraits of God's servant and his mission (see on chapter 42 above) in the course of God's message to his people. The context generally indicates when the term 'servant' refers to Israel, and when it refers to that individual representative of the true Israel who was yet to come

49 - 50 A word to put new heart into Israel

God's servant has a mission to Israel – and beyond Israel to the world (49:6). Comfort, compassion and restoration are the keynotes of 49:14 - 50:3. 50:4ff. returns to God's servant, and for the first time we glimpse his

suffering and rejection (see chapter 53). But nothing can deflect him from his purpose.

50:1: God did not divorce his unfaithful 'wife', Israel; he brought her lovingly home (see Hosea 3:1; Hosea was declaring his message to Israel at the same time as Isaiah proclaimed God's word in Judah.)

51 - 52:12 Israel released and restored

God urges his people to draw comfort from past history, and to look forward to a greater exodus yet. It is time to shake off grief and lethargy. There is good news. God is about to escort his people home.

Rahab (51:9): see on 30:7.

52:13 - 53:12 God's servant suffers for his people

The scene shifts from the joyous home-coming to the lonely figure who paid the price of it. He bore the whole burden of sin which estranged humanity from God, and it cost him his life. Isaiah, eight centuries before Christ, clearly foresaw him. He knew why he must come and what he would do. He saw the Saviour giving his life for mankind. He saw God raise him high in exaltation. (Compare 53:5-9 with Matthew 27:11-13, 26-31, 41-43, 57-60. Compare 53:4-6, 10-12 with Romans 5:6-9, 18-19; 1 Peter 2:21-24; Philippians 2:5-11.)

54 - 55 The expanding kingdom; salvation for all nations

God pledges himself in tender, unswerving, enduring love to his people. In peace and security the foundations of a new and dazzling city are laid (54:11ff.; and compare Revelation 21:18ff.). The gates stand wide in welcome to men of every nation who respond to God's invitation (55:1-7).

The vision in the later chapters of Isaiah (as earlier, at 2:2-4; 4:2-6; 9:2-7; 11 - 12; 25; 35) goes far beyond the events of the actual return from exile. The restoration of Israel which took place then, merges into a vision of the final glorious day when sin and sorrow will be no more, and the whole Israel of God (see Romans 9 - 11; Galatians 3) will be for ever at home with the Lord (Revelation 21).

56 - 66 ISRAEL'S SHAME AND ISRAEL'S GLORY

Isaiah turns back from Babylon and the exile to the land of Israel. In these final chapters scenes of sin and failure mingle with scenes of future glory.

56:1-8 Welcome for the outcasts
There is nothing exclusive about the love of God. There is a place among his people for all who will follow and obey him (1-8), even the most despised.

56:9 - 59:21 God's accusations against Israel
59:1-2 gets right to the heart of the matter: sin cuts men off from God. Israel has been guilty of many sins – the charges are quite specific. Spiritual and secular leaders alike have gone soft and failed in their jobs (56:9-12). The nation has gone running after pagan gods, joining in sexual rites and child-sacrifice (57:4-13; see 2 Chronicles 33:1-9). Their religious observance is a hollow mockery: the people love neither God nor their fellow men (58). Society is rotten to the core, riddled with lies, dishonesty, injustice, malice and violence (59:1-13). It has no time for truth and justice, or for the individual who upholds them (59:14-15). All these things stand in stark contrast to all that God, in his amazing love, wants for his people (57:14-19; 58:6-14; 59:20-21).

Beds (57:2): i.e. their graves.
57:5-8: the pagan rites involved prostitution. Idolatrous Israel unfaithful to God, is pictured as a prostitute.
Molech (57:9): see on 30:33.
Public squares (59:14): the 'lawcourt' of the day, where cases were heard and justice was dispensed.
59:21: compare this with the new covenant described in Jeremiah 31:31-34.

60 - 62 The nation's glory
In the unbridgeable gap between the shame of Israel and her glory stands the figure of God the Avenger and Redeemer (59:16-21). Chapter 60 pictures the incredible transformation. Isaiah sees the return to God's favour in very 'earthly' terms: fabulous wealth, power, influence. But it is very different from the earth we know (17-22); and the New Testament translates Isaiah's concept into spiritual and universal terms (see on chapters 54 - 55 above).

Although unnamed, the voice in 61:1-4 is that of the servant (see Luke 4:16-21). In 61:5-9 God's people become the nation of priests he always intended them to be (Exodus 19:6; and see 1 Peter 2:9), breaking into a song of praise (10-11). The day is coming (62) when God will be able to rejoice and delight in his people: a day to long for, pray for, prepare for.
60:6-7: 'Ephah', a Midianite tribe; 'Kedar' and 'Nebaioth', Arabian tribes. Their wealth lay in their camels, sheep and goats.
Double portion (61:7): here Isaiah has in mind the share of the firstborn son.

63:1-6 A vision of the Avenger
See also 59:16ff. Edom (which means red) and its capital, Bozrah, represents all the enemies of God's people. This is an appalling picture; but until the enemy is defeated, God's people cannot be set free (see Revelation 19:11-16).

63:7 - 64:12 Prayer for God's people
The recollection of all God's past goodness and faithfulness (63:7-14) leads into an impassioned appeal for his response to the crying need of his people.

65 - 66 God's answer: new heavens and a new earth
God will answer the prayer for his people in a way which exceeds their wildest dreams. But the answer will be two-edged: for those who align themselves against him, total destruction, the sweeping away of every vestige of evil; for his faithful ones, life, joy, peace beyond imagining, in a heaven and earth made new. So the final prophecies of Isaiah highlight the contrasting destinies of men, in a sharp play of light and darkness. God cannot overlook evil. Those who go their own sinful way (65:1-7, 11-14), who refuse to listen to God (66:3-4), will be punished. But God has a place reserved in his new world for men of humble faith: not only for faithful Israel, but for people of all nations (66:18-23).
65:8: the bunch is poor, but it contains some good grapes which are not to be wasted.
Fortune, Destiny (65:11): pagan gods of fate, Gad and Meni, to whom sacrificial offerings were made.
65:25: see 11:6-9.
66:19: Isaiah pictures men streaming in from distant lands – from Spain (Tarshish) in the far west, from Africa (Put, Lud) to the south, from the far north, Anatolia (Tubal) and across from Greece (Javan).

THE THREAT OF ASSYRIA

Alan Millard

Sculpture in bas-relief representing Ashurbanipal, King of Assyria, from Nineveh.

For 200 years, from about 850 to 650 BC, the kingdoms of Syria and Palestine were over-shadowed by Assyria. Her kings had reached the Mediterranean in the days of Israel's Judges, but pressure from Aramaean tribes then establishing themselves in Syria stopped them keeping control so far afield.

In 853 BC Shalmaneser III led Assyria against a coalition including Ben-hadad of Syria and Ahab of Israel, although he gained no clear victory until 841 BC. Ahab brought Israel into direct conflict with Assyria, who now looked upon her as a tributary state. Jehu's embassy is shown on Shalmaneser's Black Obelisk, bringing valuable gifts.

Assyrian activity gave Israel some relief from oppression by Damascus. Although the usurper Hasael briefly reimposed this yoke (see 2 Kings 8:12; 12:17ff.), it was broken by an Assyrian campaign about 800 BC when Jehoash paid tribute; and Israel rapidly expanded. Jeroboam II and then Uzziah of Judah seem to have become the principal monarchs of southern Syria and Palestine while Assyria's fortunes varied.

However, in 745 BC Tiglath-pileser III began to restore Assyria's imperial state. Menahem of Israel paid tribute, but anti-Assyrian elements replaced his son by their nominee Pekah, only to see him displaced in due course by the Assyrian-approved Hoshea. It was Hoshea's defection that resulted in the Assyrian capture of Samaria in 722 BC and the deportation of its people.

The policy of exile had always been employed by powerful kings, and was an ever-present threat to smaller nations. Assyrian kings did not apply it indiscriminately; it was a final weapon against obstinately rebellious states. Where a vassal and people were loyal they lived undisturbed, even helped by Assyria when enemies attacked. It is in this light that Assyria's relations with Israel and Judah should be seen.

Pekah's anti-Assyrian stance pushed Ahaz of Judah into Assyria's arms for protection, and so Hezekiah's independent policies brought harsh retribution from Sennacherib (701 BC). Thereafter, Manasseh remained loyal to Assyria, following an enforced visit to Babylon (2 Chronicles 33:11), and enjoyed a long reign (about 687-642 BC). Josiah profited from Assyrian complacency to strengthen Judah, but he lost his life trying to hinder Egyptian troops going to help the last Assyrian king (609 BC; 2 Kings 23:29). It was to these situations that the prophets Amos, Hosea, Micah and Isaiah spoke. They showed that God's people could not escape the consequences of faithlessness in human affairs, any more than the other nations they quoted as examples. They showed, too, that God's people could not escape the consequences of disloyalty to their alliance with God. He could use other nations to chasten them in furthering his purpose.

JEREMIAH

Jeremiah appears on the scene about 100 years after Isaiah. He was born into a priestly family at Anathoth (Anata), a few miles north of Jerusalem, about 640 BC, and was called to be God's prophet in 627. 2 Kings 22 - 25 and 2 Chronicles 34 - 36 provide the historical background to Jeremiah's prophecies.

The power of Assyria was already crumbling when he began to declare God's message to Judah. For 40 years – through the reigns of Judah's last five kings – Jeremiah warned of coming disaster and appealed in vain to the nation to turn back to God. With the death of godly King Josiah in 609 religious and political affairs worsened. Judah was caught in the crossfire between the contending world powers: Babylon to the north, and a resurgent Egypt to the south. Babylon emerged supreme, to become the instrument of God's

JUDAH'S LAST KINGS

```
                1
             Josiah
             640-609
    ┌───────────┼───────────┐
    2           3           5
Jehoahaz    Jehoiakim    Zedekiah
  609        609-597      597-587
                │
                4
            Jehoiachin
               597
```

judgement on his godless people. In 587 the army of Nebuchadnezzar of Babylon broke into Jerusalem, destroyed the city and took the people captive into exile. Jeremiah was offered a comfortable life at court, but chose instead to remain in Judah. When Gedaliah (the governor appointed by Nebuchadnezzar) was murdered, the people fled to Egypt, taking Jeremiah with them. As far as we know he ended his days there, still declaring God's words to men who refused to listen.

Jeremiah was not the only prophet of his day. Among his contempor-

MAJOR EVENTS OF JEREMIAH'S LIFETIME

627 Jeremiah called to be God's prophet. Death of Ashurbanipal, last great king of Assyria.

621 Discovery of the book of the law. King Josiah's great reformation begins.

612 Nineveh, capital of Assyria, falls to Babylon.

609 The Egyptian army marches north to bolster collapsing Assyria. Josiah intercepts it at Megiddo and is killed. On his return from Assyria, Pharaoh Necho deposes the new king, Jehoahaz, placing Jehoiakim on the throne.

605 Egyptian forces routed at Carchemish by Nebuchadnezzar of Babylon.

604 Nebuchadnezzar subdues Syria, Judah and Philistine cities.

598 Alliance with Egypt brings the Babylonian forces down on Judah again.

597 King Jehoiakim dies. Jerusalem falls to Babylon after a two-month siege. The new king, Jehoiachin, is deported with others to Babylon. His uncle, Zedekiah, is put on the throne.

588 Under pressure from the pro-Egypt party, Zedekiah breaks faith with Babylon. Jerusalem under siege for 18 months.

587 The Babylonian army breaks into Jerusalem. The people are deported; the city plundered and burned. Three months later, governor Gedaliah is murdered. Jeremiah is taken to Egypt.

aries were Habakkuk and Zephaniah; Daniel, at the Babylonian court; and Ezekiel, among the exiles in Babylon. But he stands out, a lonely figure: isolated by a message from God which made him increasingly unpopular; branded a traitor for advocating submission to Babylon. He was imprisoned and often in danger of his life. Yet this sensitive, unselfconfident man never once compromised his message from God. He could not help but declare the terrible fate he saw in store for his nation. And he grieved over their stubborn refusal to take notice. The times were dark; his message sombre; yet to write him off as a born pessimist does him injustice. There is a strong streak of hope running through his prophecies. After the judgement, after the exile, God will restore the joy and prosperity of his people in their homeland.

Jeremiah's book (which grew from the scroll dictated to Baruch, chapter 36) is a glorious mixture of literary forms: prose and poetry, taunt and lament, acted parable, biography and history. He added bits to it at various times, and not all of them are dated. The material is not arranged in historical order, which makes some of it difficult to set against the right background. The key events of Jeremiah's lifetime are listed, and dates are indicated in the text wherever possible.

1 - 25 GOD SPEAKS TO JUDAH AND JERUSALEM

1 Jeremiah's call to be God's prophet

The date is 627 BC. Jeremiah is a young man, probably in his early twenties, and as reluctant to become

God's spokesman as Moses before him (Exodus 3:10 - 4:17). But about one thing he had no doubt. His message was a word from God himself. 'The word of the Lord came to me' runs as a refrain right through the book, from first to last. In this lay his certainty, and his compulsion.

Verses 1-3: see introduction.

Almond ... watching (11-12): there is a play on words in the Hebrew. The almond is the first tree to blossom in spring. God's actions follow his words equally swiftly.

Verse 13: the forces of Babylon are like a cauldron about to pour its scalding contents on Judah. In this period of Jewish history trouble always came from the north: the powerful armies of Assyria first; then, in Jeremiah's day, the Babylonians.

2 - 3:10 God charges his people with unfaithfulness

The heathen nations are at least loyal to idols (10-11). Not so the people of the living God. Their offence is set before them in a series of vivid pictures. They prefer their own polluted water to God's fresh spring (13). They would sooner turn to Egypt and Assyria for help than to God (18). The vine of Israel has gone wild (21). Like a wife turned common prostitute, the nation has run after foreign gods (20, 23-25, 33; 3:1-10).

Baal (2:8): the Canaanite god

Cyprus ... Kedar (2:10): from west to east (Kedar is in Arabia): the whole pagan world.

2:13: compare Jesus' words: John 4:13-15; 7:37.

Memphis ... Tahpanhes (2:16): cities of Egypt – Memphis near Cairo; Tah-

A pagan altar at Byblos, Lebanon.

panhes a frontier town in the eastern Nile delta, on the route to Palestine.

Strangers (2:25): pagan gods.

3:1 such a thing was unlawful; see Deuteronomy 24:1-4.

3:6-10: 'Israel' here refers to the northern kingdom whose people had been carried into exile a century before, in 722 BC (verse 8). King Josiah's religious reforms (beginning in 621 BC), far-reaching though they were, did not change the heart of the nation.

3:11 - 4:4 'Return, O Israel, says the Lord'

Even now God will save his people if they repent. He will bring them back from exile a united nation (18) whose worship is a living reality, not a mere ritual (16; 4:4; and compare 31:31-34).

The ark (16): in which the law was kept in the inner sanctuary of the temple. It is no longer needed when God's law is written on every heart.

The shameful thing (24): a euphemism for 'Baal'.

4:4: all Jewish boy babies were circumcised when they were eight days old, as a sign that they had entered into covenant relationship with God (Genesis 17:1-14). But no external mark can make a man God's child without an accompanying 'circumcision' of heart, mind and will.

4:5-31 Approaching disaster

Destruction and devastation are about to fall on Judah. Jeremiah is given a preview of the nation's collapse before the Babylonian army which fills him with unspeakable horror (19-31).

Verse 11: the scorching desert wind is a symbol of destruction.

Dan (15): the northernmost town in the land; first in the path of the invader.

Verse 23: God is unmaking the earth; see Genesis 1:2.

Verse 30: a picture of Jerusalem (the 'daughter of Zion'), unrepentant still; still seeking foreign aid.

5 National corruption

God searches in vain for a vestige of truth and justice among his people. The nation is steeped in idolatry; happy with a rotten society; untroubled by conscience. God and his prophets alike are disregarded. It is false prophecy the people want to hear. God has no option but to punish.

6 Declaration of war

All God's warnings have fallen on deaf ears. His call to men to walk 'the good way' (16) has met with flat refusal. So God has rejected his

people (30) and turned them over to the invading armies. Even Jerusalem will be besieged.

Tekoa, Beth-hac-cherem (1): two hills south of Jerusalem.

Shepherds (3): a picture of the enemy encampments.

Noon (4): it was not usual to attack in the heat of the day.

Sheba (20): in Arabia; famous for the incense it exported.

Assayer (27): testing the nation, as precious metals are tested.

7 - 8:3 In the temple

The people had a superstitious faith in the temple. They thought Jerusalem could not fall because of the temple; but they were wrong. God knows the difference between religious ritual and real religion (10). He sees all that goes on (9). Jerusalem is no more sacrosanct than Shiloh, the sanctuary the Philistines destroyed (see on 1 Samuel 4). Security and well-being rest on obedience to God (23).

Verse 11: Jesus quoted these words of the temple in his day (Matthew 21:13).

Ephraim (15): the leading tribe of the breakaway northern kingdom.

Queen of heaven (18): the fertility goddess Ashtoreth/Astarte/Ishtar, whose worship involved sexual immorality.

Verse 22: Jeremiah is not denying that the system of sacrifices was instituted at God's command (see Leviticus 1 - 7). But the people were substituting sacrifice for obedience. Jeremiah is urging them to get their priorities right. As Samuel said long before, 'to obey is better than sacrifice' (1 Samuel 15:22).

Topheth (31): see on Isaiah 30:33.

8:4-17 A false sense of security

The people refuse to repent, and the men of religion aid and abet them with their smooth words. The scribes (professional interpreters of God's law), the wise men who applied God's laws to the practical matters of life, prophets and priests, are all alike motivated by self-interest.

8:18 - 9:26 Lament for the coming destruction

Jeremiah shares God's own deep grief at his people's sin and its tragic consequences. Society is sick (9:3-6, 8): sick as a direct result of the nation abandoning God and his laws and going their own way (12-14). So inevitable has judgement become (15-16) that the professional mourners can already be called in (17).

Balm (8:22): Gilead was famous for its healing ointment from very early times (Genesis 37:25).

Wormwood (9:15): a bitter-tasting plant, and so a symbol for sorrow.

9:25-26: despite the outward mark of his covenant (see on 4:4), God's people have made themselves like the pagan nations around. And like them they will be punished. See chapters 46 - 51.

10 The living God – and idols made by men

The idols man creates – no matter how elaborate – are lifeless, powerless, motionless, speechless. Not so the God of Israel. This was one of Isaiah's great themes: Isaiah 40:18-20; 44:9-20.

Tarshish ... Uphaz (9): Tarshish, Tartessus in far-away Spain; Uphaz may be Ophir (as New English Bible), famous for its gold.

Gather up your bundle (17): get ready to flee.

Shepherds (21): leaders.

Verses 23-25: Jeremiah's prayer on his people's behalf.

11:1-17 The broken covenant

The terms of God's covenant-agreement with his people, made at Sinai after the exodus (see Deuteronomy 5ff.), are still in force. By persistent disobedience to God's law, and by idol-worship, Judah has broken that agreement and come under the curse (see Deuteronomy 11:26-28; 27).

This chapter seems to belong to the period of reaction following Josiah's reforms (2 Kings 23).

11:18 - 12:17 The plot against Jeremiah's life

Jeremiah's message aroused such intense anger that the men of Anathoth, his hometown, were prepared to kill him (18-23). The discovery leads Jeremiah to question God about the way evil men get on in the world (12:1-4). He is neither the first, nor the last, to puzzle over this (see Psalm 73; Habakkuk 1:12-13). In answer, God tells him there is worse to come (5-6)! Nonetheless, he *will* punish (7-13), and afterwards restore (14-17).

Jungle of Jordan (12:5): the Jordan runs below sea-level from the Sea of Galilee to the Dead Sea; and in Old Testament times the river was bordered by dense, steamy thickets which were the haunt of wild animals.

House, heritage (7), vineyard (10): metaphors for the nation.

13 The loin-cloth: a dramatic parable

God makes use of every teaching method in the book to get his message across. The prophets often act out their message (see chapters 18, 19, 32). Actions often speak louder than words, and stick in the mind. Jeremiah got no joy from announcing God's vengeance (17), though he had earlier cried out for it (11:20).

Verse 4: the Euphrates represents the captivity and exile of the nation. It is some 350 miles from Jerusalem.

King and queen mother (18): almost certainly Jehoiachin and Nehushta (see 2 Kings 24:8-16).

14 - 15 The drought; Jeremiah's prayer

There is severe and prolonged drought (14:1-6). The people once again appeal to God (7-9). but God

Looking south from the walls of the present city of old Jerusalem, with the Kidron Valley.

will not listen (10-12). Neither will he listen to Jeremiah's pleas that they have been duped by the lies of false prophets (13ff.). Yet Jeremiah goes on praying for them (13-22) though God is deaf and the people reward him with hatred (15:10). His self-pity (15:15-18) is understandable. Its cure lies in turning away from himself to God, in renewed confidence.

Sword, famine, pestilence (14:12): all regarded, from earliest times, as punishments from God. The three together imply full-scale judgement (see also 16:4; 24:10; Ezekiel 14:21; Revelation 6:8; 18:8).

Thy glorious throne (21): the temple.

Moses and Samuel (15:1): both interceded successfully for the nation (Exodus 32; 1 Samuel 12:19-25).

15:4: under Manasseh the nation reached an all-time low; see 2 Kings 21; 2 Chronicles 33.

16 Jeremiah forbidden to marry
By remaining single, in a society where this was almost unheard of, Jeremiah becomes a living symbol of God's message. Very soon there will be the most terrible famine and slaughter in Jerusalem. This is no time, no place, to raise a family. As God removes his peace and his love from them (5) the people will at last know him as the Almighty (21). Yet he still has a future for them (14-15).

Verses 6-7: customs connected with mourning, some of them pagan (see Leviticus 19:27-28).

17 God and the human heart;
the sabbath
Judah's sin is indelible (1). Yet God still sets the alternatives before them (5-8; see Psalm 1). If only the people will listen (24) judgement can be averted.

Disregard for the day of rest which God instituted (19-27; see Exodus 20:8-11) is symptomatic of the nation's general disobedience.

Verse 1: an iron stylus was used to incise inscriptions on rock or stone. The nation's sin is just as permanently engraved on her hard heart.

Asherim (2): see on Isaiah 17:8.

Verses 14-18: this is Jeremiah's prayer.

18 The potter and the clay;
more plots against the prophet
Another dramatic parable (see on chapter 13). Like the human potter, God has the unquestionable right to remould the spoilt nation. We can never simply assume that things will always be the way they are (7-10).

In verses 18-23 Jeremiah is so

A potter works his wheel.

touched on the raw by those who spurn his God-given message that he comes out with a really vengeful prayer (very different from his reaction in 13:17).

Sirion (14): Mt Hermon, usually capped with snow all year round.

East wind (17): see on 4:11.

19:1-13 The shattered jug
Again, an acted parable: God will break the city and people as surely and as irreparably as the jug the prophet shatters before their eyes.

Ben-hinnom (2), Topheth (11): see on Isaiah 30:33.

19:14 - 20:18 Jeremiah in the stocks
Jeremiah goes straight from the Hinnom Valley to the temple; and there his message lands him in trouble. With hands and feet made fast in the wooden stocks he pours out his heart to God. Jeremiah was not a thick-skinned man; it hurt to be hated and ridiculed (20:7-8). Yet he was continually driven by an inner compulsion to make God's word known (9). His role as prophet put him under tremendous pressure. And his mood fluctuates between confident faith (11, 13) and utter misery (14-18).

21 King Zedekiah's enquiry
The date is about 589, when Judah was involved in her final struggle with Babylon. Zedekiah turns to the prophet, hoping for a word of comfort. But none is forthcoming. The only hope lies in surrender.

22 A warning for King Jehoiakim
This prophecy is earlier than chapter 21. Jehoiakim reigned from 609 to 597 – the year Jerusalem first surrendered to Babylon, and 18-year-old Jehoiachin (Coniah, 24) was taken into exile with the first batch of captives. Verses 13ff. contrast Jehoiakim – who sees his kingship in terms of cedarwood palaces – with his godly father, Josiah.

Him who is dead (10): probably King Josiah, killed at Megiddo.

Him who goes away (10), Shallum (11): King Jehoahaz, taken to Egypt by Pharaoh Necho on his return from Assyria in 609.

Lebanon, Bashan, Abarim (20): mountain ranges to the north, northeast and east of Judah.

23 Against the leaders and false prophets

The government (1-8) and religious leaders (9ff.) alike receive a stinging rebuke. Misrule, and the lies pronounced in God's name, will not go unpunished. God will set on the throne a king of his own choice (5-8). With such a message against the men of religion (9-40), it is not surprising that Jeremiah encountered bitter hatred from the priests and prophets – as Jesus himself did (26:11; compare Matthew 21:45-46; 26:66).

Branch (5): see on Isaiah 4:2; 11:1.

Adulterers (10): those who played God false by turning to pagan gods whose worship involved sexual rites and prostitution.

Burden of the Lord (33): i.e. a message from God.

24 The two baskets of figs

The date is some time after 597 (verse 1; 'Jeconiah' is Jehoiachin). The exiles are the pick of the bunch of God's people. (Ezekiel was among these first captives, and Daniel had been taken to Babylon earlier still.) And God is shaping a future for them. For those who remain in Judah there is no future but destruction. Yet through Jeremiah God still perseveres with his 'bad figs'.

25 Prediction of Nebuchadnezzar's invasion and the exile

The year is 605 (1), when Nebuchadnezzar routed the Egyptians at Carchemish. For 23 years Jeremiah has been repeating God's message, and still the people remain unmoved. Now he tells them that the city will fall and they will serve the Babylonians for 70 years in exile. The judgement of God will also fall on the pagan nations who so richly deserve it, and on Babylon itself (12-38).

Verse 13: for Jeremiah's prophecies against the pagan nations, see chapters 46 - 51.

26 - 45 JEREMIAH'S LIFE AND TIMES

26 Jehoiakim's reign: Jeremiah's life in danger

The date is 609 or after; the situation has links with chapter 7. It was one of those times when it is dangerous to declare the plain truth of God (15), and Jeremiah's straight speaking almost cost him his life. The priests and prophets wanted him dead (11), but the name of God still counted for something among the rulers and people (16). Uriah (20ff.; known only from this passage) was less fortunate.

Shiloh (6): see on chapter 7.

Verse 18: see Micah 3:12. The prophet's words are remembered a century later (Micah was Isaiah's contemporary).

27 - 28 Zedekiah's reign: the yoke of Babylon; Hananiah's false prophecy

It is 597: the Babylonians have taken the first captives from Jerusalem and placed Zedekiah on the throne. But already there is subversion. Jeremiah walks the streets of the city wearing a wooden yoke in token of submission to Babylon. Only by servitude can Judah (27:12-15) and the nations (27:3-11) escape destruction. It was not a popular message, and provoked a head-on clash with the false prophets. Hananiah flatly contradicted Jeremiah; broke the yoke (28:1-5, 10), and told the people what they wanted to hear. But time proved the truth of Jeremiah's words (28:15-17; and compare 27:19-22 with 52:17-23).

29 Jeremiah's letter to the exiles

The exiles to whom Jeremiah wrote were the captives deported with King Jehoiachin, among them Ezekiel. The false prophets predicted a swift return. Jeremiah advises the exiles to settle down and live a normal life: the exile will last 70 years. Then they will return. But even from Babylon his enemies stir up trouble for him (24ff.).

30 - 31 The promise of a new covenant

The message of hope comes at the nation's darkest hour. When it looked like total extinction, God promised his people a future. They would be saved (30:10ff.) and restored (18ff.). The exiles would return rejoicing to their homeland (31:7ff.). And a new covenant would replace the old one made at Sinai, which they had broken. This time God will remake them from within, giving them the power to do his will (31:31-34; and compare Romans 8:1-4; 2 Corinthians 5:17). Like Isaiah before him, Jeremiah here telescopes future events. He is talking, in the short-term, of the actual return from exile; in the long-term he looks forward to the new covenant brought in by Christ himself (see Hebrews 8ff.).

Ramah, Rachel (31:15): Rachel, mother of Joseph and Benjamin, died at Ramah near Bethlehem. Jeremiah pictures her weeping for her exiled sons. Matthew 2:18 sees this as a prophecy of the grief caused by Herod's slaughter of the young children.

32 Jeremiah buys land

It was 588/7, when Jerusalem was under siege, and Jeremiah's home town, Anathoth, under enemy occupation. Hanamel must have been an opportunist to try to sell land then! But Jeremiah's purchase spoke louder than words: 'God has a future for Judah.' And everyone in the city must have heard about it. Jeremiah acted under orders from God; only afterwards does he admit his puzzlement (25). In answer God outlines his immediate, and his ultimate purpose for the nation.

Verse 8: land was a family heritage; it never came up for sale on the open market. See Leviticus 25:25.

Baruch (12): Jeremiah's secretary; see 36:4ff.

Verse 35: see on Isaiah 30:33.

33 God's unbreakable promise

The theme is still future restoration. Where God has destroyed, he will rebuild (6ff.). Joy and prosperity will return (10-11), and an ideal king will rule (14-16). It will happen as surely as night follows day (20).

Verse 21: see 2 Samuel 7 and Numbers 25.

Two families (24): judging by verse 26, this means the family of Jacob (the nation) and the family of David (the kings).

34 The Jewish slaves

The date is still 588/7. After receiving God's message (1-7), King Zedekiah issues an order to free all slaves, hoping that this will win God's favour (see Deuteronomy 15:12ff.). But their owners quickly go back on it. And God condemns them as law-breakers.

Verses 4-5: see 39:7. There is no record of Zedekiah's death.

Verses 18-19: the ceremony invoked a similar fate on whoever broke the covenant. See Genesis 15.

Withdrawn (21): there was a temporary let-up while Nebuchadnezzar dealt with pharaoh's army (37:5).

35 The Rechabites

Chapters 35 - 36 take us back ten years to the earlier siege of Jerusalem. The Rechabites were bedouin descendants of Jehonadab, who took God's part against the Baal-worshippers in 2 Kings 10:15-23. Fear of the invading army brings them to the city (11), where their obedience to a pledge made 200 years before puts the people of God to shame.

36 King Jehoiakim burns Jeremiah's scroll

This is one of the most vivid and dramatic chapters in the whole Bible. The year is 605/4. Jeremiah is banned from the temple (5; no doubt to prevent him repeating what he said earlier, chapter 26). But the word of God cannot be stifled. The message is written; the prophet bides his time; and then within a single day it is read aloud in the hearing of the people, the rulers, and the king himself. Jehoiakim may burn the scroll, but not even he has power to destroy the message, or prevent its fulfilment. Patiently, Jeremiah and Baruch write the words again.

Beneath Jerusalem, even today, are ancient cisterns designed to conserve every drop of water. In Jeremiah's time they were mostly round, carved out of rock. This one is below the Ecce Homo Convent in Jerusalem.

Verse 30: within three months of Jehoiakim's death his son was deported to Babylon.

37 - 38 Jeremiah's imprisonment

Zedekiah is king; the year, 588 (5). Jeremiah's counsel to surrender (38:2) lands him in his deepest trouble yet. He is flung into prison as a subversive influence and a traitor. Only through the prompt action of a

Assyrians besiege a city; relief from the palace of Ashurbanipal at Nineveh.

good friend, and the intervention of the king, is his life saved (37:20-21; 38:7-13). Zedekiah is anxious to know God's word (37:3, 17; 38:14), but lacks faith and courage to act on it. So Jeremiah's terrible vision (38:22-23) becomes reality (39:6-8). But even in the midst of judgement, God does not lose sight of individuals. Ebedmelech's life is saved (39:15-18).

39 - 40:6 Jerusalem falls; Jeremiah's choice
See also chapter 52; 2 Kings 25; 2 Chronicles 36. God's warnings finally give way to judgement (39:1-10) and Jeremiah is the only man to have any say in his own future (39:12; 40:1-5). Offered a place of honour at the Babylonian court, he chooses instead to throw in his lot with the have-nots, left behind in the land of Judah.

Riblah (39:5): Nebuchadnezzar's base was a town to the south of Hama in Syria.

Gedaliah (39:14): son of the man who earlier saved Jeremiah's life (26:24).

Because you sinned (40:3): the nation, not Jeremiah.

Mizpah (40:6): a town a few miles north of Jerusalem; a place of national assembly from Samuel's time.

40:7 - 41:18 Assassination of the governor, Gedaliah
Gedaliah made a good start as governor. Those who had fled before the army returned and they gathered in a good harvest, after the hungry days of occupation. But after three months he was murdered, and the people, fearing reprisals, made ready to escape to Egypt.

41:9: see 1 Kings 15:16ff.

42 - 43:7 Escape to Egypt
For all their declared willingness to obey God's word, when the message came telling them to stay put, they disobeyed. Egypt seemed safer. They took Jeremiah and Baruch with them. And as God had predicted (15-18) in due course the long arm of Nebuchadnezzar, king of Babylon, reached down into Egypt (568 BC). According to Josephus, there were Jews among the captives he took back with him.

43:3: Baruch had obviously already warned them against going to Egypt.

Tahpanhes (43:7): see on 2:16.

43:8 - 44:30 In Egypt: Jeremiah's last appeal
Jeremiah enacts his last recorded parable (43:8ff.). But despite all that has happened, the people still refuse to listen. They will go back to worship-

JEREMIAH IS TAKEN TO EGYPT

Mizpah
Gibeon
Anathoth
Jerusalem
Bethlehem

JUDAH

Tahpanhes

EGYPT

ping the 'queen of heaven' (see on 7:18), and all will be well again! We hear no more of Jeremiah after this. Tradition has it he was stoned to death in Egypt.

The pavement (43:9): archaeologists have uncovered a large area of brick paving on the site.

Heliopolis (43:13): see on Isaiah 19:18.

45 Baruch

This short chapter relates to the writing of the scroll in 605 (chapter 36). Baruch shared something of the prophet's distress. God promises him life in the coming slaughter (as he promised Ebed-melech, 39:15-18). That is enough.

46 - 51 PROPHECIES AGAINST THE NATIONS

See 25:13. Jeremiah, like Isaiah before him, sees God controlling the history of the world, not just one corner of it. God deals with evil wherever it occurs. These chapters contain some of the most magnificent poetry in the book.

46:1-26 Egypt

Verses 1-12 describe the defeat at Carchemish in 605. Verses 13-26 forecast Nebuchadnezzar's invasion of Egypt (which took place in 568). Isaiah and Ezekiel also prophesied against Egypt: Isaiah 19-20; Ezekiel 29-32.

Verse 9: these are the mercenaries: from Sudan (Ethiopia) and Libya (Put).

Balm (11): see on 8:22.

Apis (15): the Egyptian sacred bull. God has overthrown the gods of Egypt.

Amon (25): god of Thebes.

46:27-28 Comfort for Israel

47 Philistia

See also Isaiah 14:28-32. Pharaoh Necho controlled Gaza at the time of

his march north in 609, but the city often changed hands. Calamity is predicted from the Babylonians in the north. Nebuchadnezzar must have overrun the Philistine cities when he quelled Judah in 587. Other prophecies: Ezekiel 25:15ff.; Amos 1:6-8; Zephaniah 2:4-7; Zechariah 9:5-7.

Gaza, Ashkelon (1, 5): Philistine cities.

Caphtor (4): Crete, the island from which the Philistines originally came.

Anakim (5): people of giant height who had some connection with the Philistines (Joshua 11:22). But this may not be the right word here.

48 Moab

See on Isaiah 15-16. Moab, Ammon and Edom seem to have joined forces with Judah in rebelling against Nebuchadnezzar (27:1-3). Presumably he dealt with them when he dealt with Judah. Other prophecies: Ezekiel 25:8-11; Amos 2:1-3; Zephaniah 2:8-11.

Nebo (1): the city, not the mountain.

Chemosh (7, 13): chief Moabite god. Bethel was the sanctuary set up in the northern kingdom of Israel to rival Jerusalem.

Arnon (20): the river which was once Moab's northern boundary.

Dibon (22): the capital.

Horn (25): an image of power, strength, might.

Kir-heres (31): original capital of Moab; present-day Kerak in Jordan.

Verse 37: a picture of mourning.

49:1-6 Ammon

See on Moab above; also Ezekiel 25:1-7. Ammon is condemned for seizing Israelite land, but will later be restored.

Milcom (1): the Ammonite god.

Rabbah (2): the capital; modern Amman, capital of Jordan.

49:7-22 Edom

Other prophecies: Isaiah 21:11-12;

EXILE TO BABYLON
Alan Millard

At about the time Jeremiah began to prophesy, the Assyrian Empire crumbled. Nabopolassar, Chaldean governor of southern Babylonia, took control of Babylon (626 BC) and gradually ousted the Assyrian garrisons from other towns. Then, allied to an army of Medes and Scythians from the Persian hills, he attacked Assyria, finally sacking Nineveh in 612 BC (see Nahum). The last vestige of Assyrian power was destroyed two years later, and the forces of the Egyptian Pharaoh Necho routed at Carchemish in 605 BC (see Jeremiah 25).

Thus the Chaldeans became masters of the 'Fertile Crescent', although the northern provinces of the Assyrian Empire fell under Median rule. The famous Nebuchadnezzar became king in 605 BC. His first 20 years saw much fighting as he subdued rebellious provinces, Judah among them.

After Carchemish, he retained Jehoiakim (the Egyptian nominee) as king in Jerusalem, exacting an oath of loyalty, and taking hostages (Daniel 1:1). The Judean disregarded his oath and linked his country to Egypt again. In righteous fury, Nebuchadnezzar brought his forces to besiege Jerusalem, whose king refused to surrender, despite Jeremiah's pleas.

The king died. His son, Jehoiachin, reigned a month or two until the city fell and he was taken into exile in Babylon (597 BC). There, according to ration-lists found in the ruins, he and his family were supplied from the royal stores. The throne of Judah was given to Zedekiah, yet he failed to learn the lesson, falling prey to Egypt's lures as his predecessors had done.

Judah's fate was inevitable. Babylonian forces attacked again, took Jerusalem and sacked it (587/6 BC). Large numbers of surviving citizens were settled in Babylonia, and the territory of Judah was placed under a governor.

The exiles seem to have been moved to Babylonia itself, living in various towns and villages as well as in the capital city. They were free to establish themselves as part of the community, so far as can be discovered, to maintain their own traditions and to practise their own religion as they wanted. No doubt the new surroundings and the refurbished splendour of ancient Babylon (justifying Nebuchadnezzar's boast, 'Is not this great Babylon, which I have built'; Daniel 4:30) awed the men of Judah. Some may have felt that Marduk of Babylon and his host of attendant gods was superior to the God of Israel. Others certainly found a profitable way of life in their new surroundings. Others longed to return to the promised land

The impress of Babylonian culture can be seen in the figures of Ezekiel's visions and in the stories of Daniel. It was an amalgam of native concepts and foreign. In the streets and workshops of the city, exiles and visitors from Egypt, Syria and Palestine rubbed shoulders with others from Cilicia and Caria and Ionia, all speaking a common language, Aramaic.

Yet the empire of the Chaldean kings was not to last. As Isaiah, Jeremiah and Daniel foresaw, the hill-men of the east and north would overcome it. The picture, vague in Isaiah and Jeremiah, is clear in Daniel. Media grew ever more powerful after ridding herself of Scythian rule. By 585 BC the Median yoke extended half-way across Anatolia. And Media was clearly a rival to Babylon when, in 550 BC, her vassal, Cyrus the Persian, seized the throne.

In Babylon, Belshazzar governed while his father Nabonidus lived in northern Arabia. The king returned only to see his realm fall to Cyrus in 539 BC. The new king's policies were generally peaceable, and he liberally allowed Jews to return and restore Jerusalem's temple as he restored many other shrines.

A line of prisoners. The Babylonians (like the Assyrians pictured here) removed whole nations from their homelands, taking them into exile.

Obadiah (who seems to have borrowed some passages from Jeremiah). Edom's judgement will be total: see on Isaiah 34.

Verse 18: see Genesis 19.

Jungle of the Jordan (19): see on 12:5.

49:23-27 Damascus

See also Isaiah 17.

Hamath, Arpad (23): Hama, in Syria; and a town just north of Aleppo.

Ben-hadad (27): the name or title of a number of Syrian kings.

49:28-33 Kedar

As predicted, Nebuchadnezzar routed these nomadic tribes in 599.

Hazor/Hazer (30): probably nomad settlements; not the city in northern Galilee.

49:34-39 Elam

Jeremiah spoke in 597. Within a year Elam, east of Babylon, was attacked by Nebuchadnezzar.

50 - 51 Babylon

See on Isaiah 13 - 14 and 46 - 47. Jeremiah's impressive prophecy was sent with the delegation that went to Babylon in the fourth year of Zedekiah's reign, six years before the fall of Jerusalem. It was given a public reading, then sunk in the Euphrates, as Babylon itself would sink before its conqueror (51:59-64). The Medes (51:11) would pour in on Babylon from the north like the sea. God's people are warned in advance to be out of harm's way when it happens. Cyrus, at the head of an army of Medes and Persians, took Babylon in 539. Babylon was God's instrument

to punish his people (as the Assyrians had been earlier), but God could not overlook her sinful pride. He cannot ignore evil; judgement must always come.

Bel, Merodach (Marduk) (50:2): the Babylonian gods.

50:21: there is a play on the names Merathaim and Pekod, two Babylonian tribes.

Vengeance for his temple (50:28; 51:11): Jeremiah wrote this prophecy before the temple was destroyed: this note was probably added after the destruction in 587.

51:27: Ararat in eastern Turkey; Minni in north-west Iran; Ashkenaz, the Scythians, in the same area. All were subject to the Medes.

Her sea (51:36): Babylon's prosperity and security depended on her elaborate system of canals and lakes.

Seraiah (51:59): Baruch's brother (32:12).

Thus far ... (64): taking the reading of the Revised Standard Version margin, this note seems to belong to the end of verse 58, making 59-64 and chapter 52 additions.

52 HISTORICAL APPENDIX

See on 2 Kings 24 - 25, which are almost identical with this chapter; and Jeremiah 39.

Verses 28-30: the captives were deported in 597, 587 and 581.

Verse 31: with the accession of Nebuchadnezzar's son (562-560), things improved for Jehoiachin, a token of new hope for the nation.

LAMENTATIONS

We do not know who wrote these laments – although the Greek versions name Jeremiah. They are anonymous in the Hebrew text. And they differ in style and content from Jeremiah's prophecies. But the author must at least have been a contemporary of the prophet. The first four poems were obviously written by an eye-witness to the destruction of Jerusalem by Nebuchadnezzar's Babylonian army in 587 BC.

To the people of Judah, the fall of the city meant more than the loss of their beautiful and almost unassailable capital. It was more than just the destruction of a nation's capital city: because Jerusalem was in a very special sense God's city. His temple was there. This was where he chose to live with his people. And when Jerusalem was burned, the temple destroyed, the people deported, they knew that God had given them up to the enemy. It could not have happened otherwise. So these laments express the poet's grief, not simply over the suffering and humiliation of his people, but over something deeper and far worse, that God had rejected his people because of their sin.

The first four poems have the rhythm of the dirge, and they are written as acrostics. In 1, 2 and 4, each of the 22 verses begins with a new letter of the Hebrew alphabet. In 3, there are three verses to each letter. The fifth poem (chapter 5) also has 22 verses, but is neither a dirge nor an acrostic.

The poems are still read aloud in Jewish synagogues in mid-July to mark the anniversary of the destruction of the temple in 587, and remembering the later destruction in AD 70.

Chapter 1 The first lament
Jerusalem is alone, deserted, mourning; the people gone; the temple defiled and destroyed. God has judged and punished her for the enormity of her sin. Now, at last, she cries out to him.

Chapter 2 The second lament
The poet sees again the outpouring of God's anger: the starving children; the slaughter; the ruin of city and sanctuary. He hears again the taunts of old enemies, gloating over the fate of Jerusalem. Let her call out to God to look, and pity.

Chapter 3 The third lament
We see the agony of the nation focussed in the experience of a single individual. In the darkness, crushed and battered to the point where all hope dies (18), faith still rekindles at the thought of God in all his love and mercy (19-33). When he is all but lost, there comes the knowledge that God is near (54ff.) But he cannot forgive the bitter provocation of his enemies (59-66).

Chapter 4 The fourth lament
The city's former glory – and the horrors of siege. The cries of starving children; wizened faces; shrivelled bodies; never to be forgotten. The sins of the people, the prophets and the priests, have brought the city low. And Edom – the old arch-enemy – gloats, not knowing that her punishment is yet to come (21-22).

Chapter 5 The fifth lament – a prayer
The poet vividly depicts defeat: the loss of freedom, loss of land, loss of respect; rape and cruelty; forced labour; near-starvation. And all because of sin. He prays to God for restoration.

EZEKIEL

In 597 BC King Jehoiachin surrendered Jerusalem to the Babylonian army, and was taken into exile. With him went 10,000 men – statesmen, soldiers, craftsmen (2 Kings 24:14). And among them was Jeremiah's younger contemporary, Ezekiel, then in his mid-twenties. Ezekiel was in training as a priest, looking forward to service in the temple like his father before him. Exile in the plains of Babylonia, far from Jerusalem, meant the end of all his hopes.

But five years later, when he was 30 (the age at which he would probably have taken up his duties as a priest – Numbers 4:3; and see on 1:1), God called him into service as a prophet. The call was accompanied by a vision of God which coloured his entire ministry (just as Isaiah's had done nearly 150 years earlier). He saw God in all his awesome majesty, above and beyond the world of men, all-seeing, all-knowing. It was a vision of fire and glory. And against this dazzling brilliance Ezekiel saw his people's sin in all its blackness. He saw the inevitability of judgement. And for six years this was his message. Only after the city and temple of Jerusalem were destroyed in 587 did he really begin to stress God's intention to 'resurrect' (chapter 37) and restore Israel, and to look forward to the time when the ideal would be realized: to the new temple in which God's people would offer him perfect worship (chapters 40ff.).

As he declared God's message to the exiles, a great weight of responsibility rested on Ezekiel. He saw himself as a 'look-out', who must give warning of danger or be held accountable. One of his most characteristic themes is that of individual responsibility before God. Ezekiel was an extraordinary man, a visionary, imaginative, by training a man who appreciated and understood ritual and symbol. He was passionate, dedicated, utterly obedient to God. The most hardened onlooker could not fail to be impressed as Ezekiel acted out his sobering messages.

The book – written entirely in the first person, apart from the note in 1:2-3 – is in keeping with the man. The prophecies are meticulously ordered and dated, even to the day of the month. Message and language are consistent (often repetitive) throughout the book. Characteristic themes and phrases run right through. And although some scholars have questioned the authorship and background of Ezekiel, the various arguments tend to cancel one another out. Ezekiel's message is very close to that of Jeremiah (another prophet given to acted parables), whom he may have heard as a young man in Jerusalem. But although he writes for the most part in 'cold' prose, Ezekiel is more flamboyantly visual than the other prophets. With him, prophecy merges into 'apocalyptic' (see Revelation). The Bible book closest in spirit to Ezekiel is Revelation, which borrows many of his images.

For many Christians Ezekiel is a closed book, apart from a few familiar passages (the watchman; the valley of dry bones; the vision of the temple). It is easy to give up at the first chapter – the vision of flashing lights and peculiar creatures and wheels with eyes. But this is our loss. Because in our materialistic, man-centred world, we need Ezekiel's vision of the almighty God. We need to see sin as God sees it. We need to be reminded of our own accountability. We need to know that God is God – before we learn it the hard way, as Israel did, through judgement. Reading the Old Testament also helps us to understand the New. We need to be acquainted with Ezekiel in order to understand Revelation.

1 - 3 EZEKIEL'S CALL AND VISION OF GOD

Ezekiel is a book of visions and symbolic actions – beginning with this great vision of God. As Ezekiel gazed out over the plain, he saw what looked like an approaching storm: thunder, lightning, black clouds. Then he made out the figures of four cherubim (see 10:15), angelic creatures, standing wing-tip to wing-tip, forming a hollow square. At the centre, fire glowed; and above, under the blue vault of the heavens, was the Lord of glory in human form, seated on a throne, encircled by a dazzling rainbow. Beside each four-faced cherub was a terrifying, whirling wheel, moving like a castor and full of eyes. Who could look on this and live?

The Almighty, the God of Israel was present in all his power in the far-flung lands of Babylon. He came to make Ezekiel his messenger to the exiles, the watchman sent to warn the remnant of God's rebel people (2:1-7; 3:16-21). And the words of God, though they were hard, were satisfying (2:8 - 3:3). It became Ezekiel's life-mission to let God's people know that he is the Lord. They would learn it first through the terrors of judgement (7:4). Afterwards they would see his power to restore and renew (36:8-11).

Thirtieth year (1:1): most probably Ezekiel's own age. If, as seems likely, this was the age at which a priest took up his duties, it would have been a year of special significance for the prophet. But to become eligible at last for his life's work as a priest, when in exile, hundreds of miles away from Jerusalem and its temple, must have been a bitter experience.

Chebar (1:1): usually identified as the great canal which ran from the Euphrates north of Babylon, close to the city of Nippur.

Verses 2-3: a note added to explain Ezekiel's opening sentence. The date was 593 BC (see introduction).

Living creatures (5): cherubim (10:15), the figures which spread their wings over the mercy-seat above the ark of the covenant (Exodus 25:18ff.). As the son of a priest, Ezekiel may have been familiar with the figures of cherubim which decorated Solomon's temple. Similar winged, sphinx-like creatures frequently appear in Babylonian art.

Verse 26: although it was normally reckoned that no one could see God and live, there were some who shared Ezekiel's privilege and described what they saw – see Exodus 24:9-11; Isaiah 6; Daniel 7; Revelation 4.

Son of man/man (2:1): Ezekiel is addressed in this way throughout the book. It simply means 'human being'. This is the term Jesus most often used to describe himself.

Briers and thorns … scorpions (2:6): a vivid picture of the hostile reception.

2:10: normally a scroll had writing on only one side; perhaps the implication is that there was no room left for Ezekiel to add anything of his own.

3:7: the call of Isaiah, and of Jeremiah, was equally daunting: see Isaiah 6:9-12; Jeremiah 1:17-19.

3:25-27: the meaning seems to be that Ezekiel would be dumb except on the occasions when God had a message for him to give. But some take this as a self-imposed, ritual dumbness, rather than an actual loss of speech. Either way, it gave added force to the utterances he did make. The dumbness lasted until news reached him of the fall of Jerusalem (24:27).

4 - 24 ISRAEL'S SIN: GOD'S JUDGEMENT

4 - 5 Ezekiel enacts the siege and destruction of Jerusalem

The 'props' for the drama were ready to hand: a large sun-dried brick on

Winged creatures carved in ivory to decorate a piece of furniture.

which Ezekiel drew an outline of the city; and the metal plate on which they baked their flat loaves of bread. The people watched, and got the message. They watched with growing horror as Ezekiel weighed out his meagre measure of mixed grain and eked out his water ration. They saw the prophet wasting away, as the population of Jerusalem would do under siege. They watched him shave his head, sharing Jerusalem's disgrace. They saw him burn the hair and toss it away, till only a tiny handful – representing the exiles themselves – remained. It was a telling lesson.

4:5-6: the Greek version has 190 days; from the fall of Samaria in 722 BC to the return of the exiles in 538 is 184 years. From the fall of Jerusalem in 587 to 538 is 49 years. 40 may represent a generation, rather than being an exact figure.

4:9: under siege no one is fussy about the ingredients they use to make bread.

Twenty shekels (10): about 8 ozs/220 gms.

Sixth part of a hin (11): about a pint/ 0.6 litre.

Unclean (13ff.): using dung for fuel defiled the food, according to Jewish regulations. It was hard for Ezekiel, a man trained to maintain ritual cleanness, to do as God instructed. Compare Peter's reaction in Acts 10:9-16.

6 - 7 Against the land of Israel: the end has come

The acted message is reinforced by the spoken word. The people's flagrant idolatry is about to bring destruction upon them – judgement from which there is no escape. Then they will know that the Lord is God indeed. Terrible, total calamity is befalling the land.

From the wilderness to Riblah (6:14): from south to north. Riblah, on the River Orontes, is near Israel's northern boundary.

The seller mourn (7:12): because he has been forced to sell the land which was his heritage.

7:18: shaven heads were a sign of disgrace as well as of mourning.

Cast their silver (7:19): their money is useless.

8 - 11 Ezekiel's vision of Jerusalem – its guilt and its punishment

September 592. Ezekiel is transported in vision (or, as John would have said, 'In the Spirit') to Jerusalem,

and set down beside the temple (8:1-4). What he sees may be actual practices, or the description may be symbolic. Either way the meaning is plain. There has been a total departure from the true religion of Israel. In the temple of God an image of the Canaanite goddess Asherah/Astarte (the 'image of jealousy', 3) has been set up, as in the days of King Manasseh. The nation's leaders are secretly practising animal worship (8:7-13). The women are mourning the Sumerian god Tammuz, who was supposed to die with the old year and rise again with the spring. Men turn their backs on God to worship the sun (8:16-18).

Contrary to popular belief (8:12), God both sees and judges (9:9-10). Only those who grieve for the loss of the true faith will be spared (9:4-6).

Chapter 10: following the terrible slaughter which made Ezekiel cry aloud for his people (9:8), he sees again the vision of the cherubim, the glory, the whirling wheels, that he first saw on the plains of Babylon (chapter 1). What greater contrast imaginable than this sight of God in all his glory – and the loathsome scenes of idolatry in his temple (chapter 8). Because of all this the glory of God will finally depart from Jerusalem.

But first Ezekiel sees two men he recognizes, rulers who are advocating resistance to Babylon, despite the insistence of God's prophets that this would prove fatal (11:1-4). Ezekiel pronounces God's judgement, and as he speaks, to his alarm, Pelatiah falls dead (11:5-13) in confirmation of God's word. But God is not making a 'full end' (13). The future lies with the exiles. And on this note, and with this message (25), the vision ends.

Jaazaniah (8:11): his father was King Josiah's secretary of state; his brother Ahikam, Jeremiah's friend. Not the same man as in 11:1.

The branch ... (8:17): possibly a reference to some pagan practice.

A mark (9:4): Jeremiah, Baruch and the foreigner, Ebed-melech, were among those 'marked' to be spared (Jeremiah 40:4; 45; 39:15ff.). In Revelation God's men are marked (14:1), and so are those who sell out to the forces of evil (13:16). The 'mark' here is the last letter of the Hebrew alphabet, *taw* written as a cross in the oldest script.

11:3: a difficult verse, most likely meaning that this was not the moment for peace-time building. The cauldron protects the meat from the flames.

A new spirit (11:19): compare Jeremiah 31:33-34; Ezekiel 36:26.

12 Ezekiel plays the part of an exile
Although most people refuse to listen, the prophet continues to make God's word known (1-3). As he put together the bare necessities, ready for flight, and as he broke through the mud-brick wall at night, Ezekiel was playing the part, not just of any exile, but of King Zedekiah ('the prince', 10). Compare 12-13 with Jeremiah 52:7-11. Ezekiel's prophecy proved accurate to the last detail. It was as God said it would be, and within a very short space of time (21-28).

The exiles provided useful slave labour. Here timber is hauled for building King Sargon's new capital at Khorsabad, Assyria.

13 False prophets
The work of Jeremiah and Ezekiel was constantly undermined by false prophets, who told people what they wanted to hear, and claimed God's authority for their message of false hope. They were like plaster, concealing the crumbling structure of the nation, but unable to stop it falling (10-16); for what God says will happen, always happens. Among them were prophetesses, practising magic and holding helpless individuals in thrall (17ff.).

Souls (18): the whole person; the idea of disembodied spirits was completely alien to Jewish thinking.

14 Idolatry and its consequences
God claims a unique place in the hearts of his people. Those who deny him his rightful place, worshipping other 'gods' alongside, are destined for destruction. The majority regard the few godly men among them as an insurance against disaster. But at this point in time not even a Noah or a Job could save anyone but himself.

Daniel/Danel (14): probably an otherwise unknown Jewish patriarch, and not Ezekiel's contemporary in exile.

The name of the biblical Daniel is spelt differently. There is also a hero of this name in an ancient Canaanite epic.

Verse 21: these judgements represent the worst fears of ancient peoples (see on Jeremiah 14:12).

15 The parable of the vine
The vine was a popular symbol for Israel. There is by this time no question of it bearing fruit, and as wood the vine is useless. Israel is already partially destroyed (4): there is nothing for it now but total destruction (6-8).

16 The unfaithful wife: an allegory
God took Israel up when she was nothing – an abandoned waif – and lavished his love on her, making her into a great and glorious nation. She owed him everything. But prosperity turned her head and, like a wife turned prostitute, she played fast and loose with foreign nations. She 'courted' them and worshipped their gods, with all the hideous practices that involved (20-29). God was forgotten; the covenant (like the marriage-vow) broken. He must punish Israel (35-43): but he will also restore (53,60).

Amorite … Hittite (3): the reference is to moral, not literal, parentage. Israel had become as decadent as the nations she destroyed at the conquest of Canaan.

Verse 4: these were the midwife's duties.

Spread my skirt (8): with this symbolic gesture he claimed her in marriage. See Ruth 3:9. God sealed the contract with the Sinai covenant.

Verse 38: adultery was punishable by death.

Verse 46: 'Samaria': capital of the northern kingdom; destroyed in 722. 'Sodom': the city at the southern end of the Dead Sea, wiped out for its gross immorality (Genesis 19).

17 The eagles and the vine
The first eagle is Nebuchadnezzar of Babylon, who took King Jehoiachin captive (3,4; see introduction). The seed he plants (5, 13) is Zedekiah. But Zedekiah soon turned to Egypt (the second eagle) for help (7,15), bringing the Babylonians back to destroy Jerusalem. In 587, within three or four years, the prediction of 17-21 came true (see Jeremiah 52). But God will take a 'cutting' from the line of Israel's kings (the cedar) which will take root (22-24).

Verse 8: it seems best to take this as stressing the fact that Zedekiah was well off under Nebuchadnezzar (as in 5).

18 Each individual accountable to God

Contrary to popular belief (2), God is not so unjust as to punish one generation for the sins of another (20). He holds every man answerable for his own sins. It gives God no pleasure to sign the death warrant for any man (23). His concern, always, is that men should turn away from evil and live (30-32). And he makes his standards plain (5-9; 14-17).

Soul (4): see on 13:18 above.

Verse 20: Ezekiel is redressing the balance, not denying the basic principle that in life children do suffer the consequences of their parents' wrongdoing (Exodus 20:5).

19 A lament for Israel's rulers

The poem is written in the familiar dirge-rhythm. The lioness is Judah; the kings her cubs. The first (3) is Jehoahaz, carried off to Egypt by Pharaoh Necho in 609. The second (5) is Jehoiachin (see introduction). Now, thanks to Zedekiah's rebellion, both the nation and its line of kings will be destroyed (10-14).

20:1-44 A history of the nation's rebellion

July/August 591. Ezekiel turns from allegory to historical fact. From the time in Egypt and the wilderness right down to his own day, Israel's history has been a weary repetition of idolatry and rebellion against God. All along, God held back from making an end of the nation. But now he will cut off the rebels (38). His own, he will restore (40-44).

I gave them ... (25-26): these difficult verses seem best understood in the light of Romans 1:24, etc. God 'gave them up' to the evil things they wanted.

Bamah (29): high place. There is a play on words in this verse.

Verse 37: Jerusalem Bible translates: 'I mean to make you pass under my crook and I will bring a few of you back.'

20:45 - 21:32 Fire and sword

God's judgement will sweep across the land from south to north like a forest fire (20:45-48). The sword of God is drawn against Israel. It is in the hands of the king of Babylon (21:19), who will destroy the capital cities of both Ammon and Judah (21:20). (Five years after Jerusalem fell, Nebuchadnezzar attacked Ammon.)

Negeb (20:46): today this region is arid desert, but Palestine as a whole was more wooded in Old Testament times.

Rabbah (21:20): Amman, present capital of Jordan.

Until he comes ... (21:27): see Genesis 49:10. There is one coming to whom the kingship rightly belongs.

22 The charges against Jerusalem

God's people are guilty – guilty of bloodshed, oppression, extortion, bribery, and sexual sin; they have made a mockery of their religion (6-12). When God tests them by fire, no trace of genuine metal will be found (17-22). Every section of society shares the guilt: rulers, priests, prophets and common people alike (23-31).

Unclean and clean (26): see on Leviticus 11.

Verse 28: see 13:8-16.

23 Parable of the two sisters, Oholah and Oholibah

Oholah is Samaria, capital of the northern kingdom of Israel. Oholibah is Jerusalem. Both sisters have behaved like common whores. Their appetite for their lovers (the pagan gods) is insatiable; their behaviour utterly disgusting. They have run, in turn, after Egypt and Assyria. Now Judah, outdoing her sister, is running after Babylon. Jerusalem will share Samaria's fate – shame and destruction at the hands of her latest lover. Her punishment is fully deserved (45).

Verse 10: the Assyrians destroyed Samaria in 722 BC.

Verse 23: Pekod, Shoa and Koa were probably tribes on the eastern borders of the Babylonian Empire. The Babylonians and Chaldeans were not separate peoples.

24 Jerusalem besieged; Ezekiel's wife dies

The date is the same as in 2 Kings 25:1; Jeremiah 52:4 – usually thought to be 15 January 588 BC. Jerusalem is like a rusty cooking-pot, set on the fire to burn. The behaviour of the people has polluted the city. The very same day that the siege is laid, Ezekiel's much-loved wife is suddenly taken from him. But God forbids him the customary forms of mourning. Ezekiel's personal loss is part of a grief beyond expression. Men will eat their hearts out for the fate of Jerusalem, though they go about dry-eyed, like the prophet. And when news of the city's fall reaches them, Ezekiel will at last be able to speak freely (27; see 3:26-27); the judgement will be over.

Verse 17: the mourning customs of the day: noisy lamentation; bared head sprinkled with dust and ashes; bared feet; veiled face; and the funeral meal provided for the mourners.

25 - 32 PROPHECIES AGAINST FOREIGN NATIONS

Although the prophets concentrated mainly on Israel/Judah, all of them were very conscious that God was Lord of the whole world. There is no nation beyond the reach of his judgement; and what he condemns and punishes in his own people, he condemns and punishes in other nations too. This collection of prophecies effectively marks the break in Ezekiel's ministry before, and his ministry after, the fall of Jerusalem in 587 BC.

25 Ammon, Moab, Edom, Philistia
For other prophecies, see on Jeremiah 47 - 49. These four nations were Israel's closest neighbours, and her oldest enemies. All took a vengeful delight in Israel's downfall, for which God will punish them. Shortly after this, Ammon, Moab and Edom were overrun by Nabataean tribesmen. The Philistines disappeared from history after Maccabean times.

26 - 28:19 Tyre
See on Isaiah 23. The date of Ezekiel's prophecy is probably the end of the 11th year – February 586 – assuming that Ezekiel learnt of the fall of Jerusalem that year, rather than the following one (see on 33:21). The forecast of chapter 26 proved all too true. Tyre did not laugh long over Jerusalem's fate. Within a few months Nebuchadnezzar's army was at her own gates, and for 13 years she was under seige.

Tyre was a tempting prey. The city lay at the foot of the Lebanese mountains and possessed the finest natural harbour in the eastern Mediterranean. It was in fact a double harbour, as the main city was built on an offshore island (26:5). As a centre of trade and commerce Tyre was fabulously wealthy, and her own glassware and purple dye were world famous. Ezekiel fittingly pictures the city as a great trading vessel (chapter 27) laden with the choicest of cargoes, and commanding human skills and resources from far and wide. News of her wreck will put the world into mourning. Chapter 28 is a lament for the king of Tyre, whose pride has proved his downfall.

Senir (27:5): Mt Hermon.

Gebal (27:9): Byblos, now Jubail, in Lebanon.
Daniel (28:3): see on 14:14.
28:12ff.: much of the imagery is drawn from Genesis 2-3.
28:20-26 Sidon
Another famous Old Testament seaport, Sidon is in Lebanon, 20 miles north of Tyre. Today both Tyre (Sour) and Sidon are small fishingports. The charge against Sidon is, again, contempt for God's people (24). Sidon, like Tyre, fell to Nebuchadnezzar. Verses 25-26 are a message of hope for Israel.
29 - 32 Egypt
A collection of seven prophecies, all (except the one beginning at 30:1) carefully dated.
29:1-16, January 587. By his insufferable pride in placing himself among the gods, Pharaoh has exposed his whole land to God's anger. But he will learn who is God!
29:17-21, New Year's day, 571 (the latest prophecy in the book). The long and costly siege of Tyre ended about 574. Ezekiel declares that Egypt will be Babylon's next prey.
30:1-19, undated. Ezekiel depicts the judgement Nebuchadnezzar will execute on Egypt and her allies. God will put an end to Egypt's wealth (10-12) and her 'gods' (13ff.).
30:20-26, April 587. Pharaoh Hophra's army had made a half-hearted attempt to relieve besieged Jerusalem, but had been defeated. His power will be yet further broken.
31:1-18, June 587. Egypt is likened to a great cedar tree (2-9). Because of its over-bearing pride the tree will be felled (10-14). Egypt will be removed to the place of the dead (15ff.).
32:1-16, March 585 (after the news of Jerusalem's fall had reached the exiles). A lament for Pharaoh.
32:17-32 (? March) 585. Egypt will join the other fallen nations: Assyria, Elam, Meshech, Tubal, Edom, Sidon. They are consigned to a great burialchamber full of graves.
Pharaoh (29:2): the particular pharaoh is Hophra. All the pharaohs were worshipped as gods. So also was the Nile crocodile ('dragon', 3).
Migdol to Syene (29:10): i.e. from north to south – the whole land. Migdol was a city on the Nile delta; Syene is modern Aswan.
Pathros (29:14): upper Egypt.
30:5: Egypt's allies.
31:3: although the Authorized Version, Revised Version and New English Bible name Assyria

here, the Revised Standard Version and Jerusalem Bible translations make better sense.

32:22-30: 'Assyria', the great power in Isaiah's day, overthrown by Babylon. 'Elam', a nation east of Babylon. 'Meshech and Tubal', little-known nations on Assyria's northern frontier. 'Princes of the north', presumably city-states north of Palestine.

33 - 48 ISRAEL RESTORED

33:1-20 The watchman
These verses reiterate the teaching of two earlier passages, 3:17-21; 18:5-29.

33:21-33 The exiles hear that Jerusalem has fallen
The news did not take Ezekiel by surprise. God had already given him back his speech, as promised (24:27), by the time the messenger arrived. Some texts have 'eleventh year' for 'twelfth' in verse 21, in which case the news takes the more likely time of six months to reach them. Those left behind in Judah, far from repenting, were busy annexing other people's property. And in Babylonia the exiles who seemed to lap up Ezekiel's words came simply for entertainment. They neither believed them nor acted on them: a depressing state of affairs after all that had happened!

34 God denounces the leaders and people of Israel
Both 'shepherds' (1-10) and 'sheep' (17-22) come in for condemnation.

Phoenician figure of a shepherd.

They have greedily, cruelly, selfishly exploited those committed to their care. But God will be a true shepherd, bringing his scattered flock back to good pasture in their homeland (11-16; and see Luke 15:4-7). He will appoint a good shepherd – a new David – to care for them (23-24; and see John 10:11), and the flock will dwell secure.

35 Prophecy against Edom
Edom is marked out for destruction, because of her callous reaction to Israel's downfall. She not only gloated, but planned to make capital out of it by seizing the land (10; the two nations are Israel and Judah). See 25:12-14 above. Other prophecies against Edom: Isaiah 21:34; Jeremiah 49:7-22; Obadiah.

36 The return to the homeland
God tells the desolate land it will soon be inhabited. His people are coming home. Israel's defeat has made men despise the God of Israel as powerless. Their return will vindicate his honour. The nations will know, and God's people will know, that he is the Lord. Those who returned from exile were truly and permanently cured of idolatry (25). But the total transformation of a 'new heart' is realized only 'in Christ' (2 Corinthians 5:17). Ezekiel was thinking of something far more complex than a heart transplant: the heart, in Jewish thought, stood for the whole personality, the essential man.

37 The vision in the valley of dry bones
After ten years in exile, and with Jerusalem destroyed, the people have given up hope. Not all Ezekiel's promises of restoration can raise a spark in his hearers. The nation is dead. But God can take even skeletons and make them into a living army. Ezekiel plays his part by making God's word known, but it is the Spirit of God who gives life. Israel will be re-made and live again. The two warring kingdoms will become one nation under one king – a new David. And here (21-28) the promise to the exiles merges into the full blessing of the future golden age. The return is only a foretaste of all God has in store for his people.

Into one (17): Ezekiel holds the two ends together in his clenched fist, making the two sticks look like one.

David (24): the ideal, messianic king, who will rule for ever in peace and righteousness.

38 - 39 The prophecy against Gog
Magog, Meshech, Tubal (2) and
Gomer (6) were all sons of Japheth
(Noah's son). They gave their names
to Indo-European peoples living in
the Black Sea/Caucasus region, on
the northern fringe of the then-known
world. Ezekiel pictures an invasion
of these barbaric hordes from the
north, led by the unidentified Gog,
who may personify the cosmic forces
of evil. Allied with armies from far
and near (Persia, Sudan and north
Africa) he will wage war on the
Lord's people. And God will demonstrate his power in the sight of all by
taking on all the forces of evil single-
handed, and destroying them once
and for all. 'Gog' is responsible for
the plan, but the Lord's hand is
always in control.

Chapter 39 repeats and enlarges on
38. So vast is Gog's army that the
weapons provide Israel with seven
years' fuel supply. And the carnage
is so great it takes seven months to
clean up the land. (For the Jews, the
number seven symbolized perfection
and completeness.) The judgement of
God is a terrible thing, and Ezekiel
conjures it up in horrifying pictures.
The fact that these chapters immediately precede Ezekiel's vision of the
new temple in which God dwells
among his people, gives added point
to John's choice of Gog and Magog
to represent all who oppose God in
the last great battle instigated by
Satan at the end of time (Revelation
20:8).

*Ezekiel's vision of the temple was a
detailed reconstruction of the temple
area in Jerusalem. But through it
flowed the 'river of life'.*

40 - 48 The vision of the temple
These chapters were written some
years after the rest (except for 29:17-
21), in 573 BC. Although, for the
most part, they make rather dull
reading, they are in a very real sense,
the climax to the whole book. Ezekiel began with a vision of God in the
plains of Babylon. It ends with a
vision of God returning in glory to a
new temple – God in the midst of his
people once again, never to depart.

For all the detail, Ezekiel's
description is no mere blueprint for
the second temple. It was not the old
Jerusalem, but a structure *like* a city
that he saw (40:2). It is true that the
new temple follows much the same
layout as Solomon's temple, and is
all set out for the sacrifices
(40:38ff.). But when God returns in
all his glory it is to live for ever in a
temple and among a priesthood and
people cleansed from evil (chapter
43). Everything is perfect. This is the
ideal. Yet it is not as far-reaching as
the vision in Revelation. It is still
envisaged in earthly terms: there is
still a temple and sacrifices; the
people of God are synonymous with
Israel (44:6ff.); the laws continue, so
does death, so does the need for a
sin-offering (44:15-27). Again there is
the subtle blending and telescoping of
near and distant future which is characteristic of the prophets. The laws,
the offerings, the feasts of Exodus
and Leviticus are reinstated (chapters
45 and 46). Yet suddenly, in chapter
47, we are given something gloriously
new. Out of God's temple flows a
great life-giving river bordered by
trees whose fruit is for food and
whose leaves are for healing (see
Revelation 22:1-2). The new tribal
boundaries with which the book concludes (47:13ff.) are stylized, rather
than geographically feasible. And at
the very end the city is named. It is
not now Jerusalem, but 'The Lord is
there' (compare Revelation 21:22ff.).
Long cubit (40:5): about 20.4in/
520mm.
Sons of Zadok (40:46): Zadok, who
replaced Abiathar (1 Kings 2:26-27,
35), was the first high priest to
officiate in the temple.
43:3: see chapter 10 and chapter 1.
47:9-10: the salt water of the Dead
Sea is made fresh. The 'Great Sea' is
the Mediterranean.

DANIEL

Daniel was a Judean exile at the court of Babylon. He was taken there as a boy a few years earlier than Ezekiel and the first main batch of exiles. He belonged to a noble (possibly royal) family and was exceptionally able and intelligent. Strictly speaking, Daniel was a statesman rather than a prophet, but his book rightly belongs among the prophetic writings. The first six chapters relate to historical events in Babylon over a period of 70 years. The remaining chapters, written in the first person, record a series of visions of future events. Two languages are used: 2:4 - 7:28 is in Aramaic, the international language; the rest in Hebrew. Right at the beginning of Israel's history God had his man – Joseph – at the Egyptian court. Now again, at this great crisis-point, God placed Daniel in a position of influence at the political centre of the Babylonian Empire, for the whole period of the exile.

To help explain a number of historical difficulties in Daniel (see in the text below), many think that the book as we have it was written in the 2nd century BC by an unknown author who used Daniel's name to give his work added authority. But the book of Daniel was widely accepted as Scripture in that same century, and the Jewish authorities were scrupulously careful about examining writings before they were given official approval. So either they

had no objection to the real author adopting the name of the 6th-century prophet; or they were themselves taken in by one of their own contemporaries. There is the added problem that although these men lived only 400 years after the events recorded in Daniel, they failed to spot (or at least failed to challenge) the book's historical inaccuracies. At the heart of the issue is the question of prediction, since Daniel alludes to events long after his own day. If the possibility of genuine prediction in prophecy is allowed, the book can be taken as it stands, as the record of the life and visions of Daniel himself. Only if it is denied is one bound to conclude that the book cannot be earlier that the 2nd century BC.

1 - 6 DANIEL AT THE BABYLONIAN COURT

1 Daniel and his friends win a place at Nebuchadnezzar's court

Daniel arrived in Babylon in 605 (see below). Good looks and natural ability ensured a place for him and his friends among those selected for special training. But the Babylonians did not observe Jewish rules on clean and unclean food (Leviticus 11), nor did they drain away the blood when they slaughtered animals (Leviticus 17:10ff.). Young as they were, Daniel and his friends were determined not to compromise their religion. So their only course was to restrict them-

An artist's impression of 'great Babylon', based on archaeological excavation.

selves to a vegetarian diet – and they thrived on it. What is more, they graduated from the king's school with honours!

The third year ... (1): the date is 605. After defeating Egypt at Carchemish, Nebuchadnezzar attacked Jerusalem. Daniel and others were taken hostage for the good behaviour of King Jehoiakim, who had been placed on the throne by the Egyptian pharaoh. Daniel uses the Babylonian reckoning for Jehoiakim's reign, beginning the year following the accession year. So 'the third year' here is the same as the fourth year (Jeremiah 25:1; 46:2) in Palestinian reckoning.

Shinar (2): the old name for Babylonia.

Verse 7: the endings of the Hebrew names (-el, -iah) link them with the name of Israel's God. At least one of the new names (Belteshazzar) is linked to that of a Babylonian god (see 4:8).

First year of King Cyrus (21): mentioned not because it was the year of Daniel's death (see 10:1), but because it was the year of the decree repatriating the exiles (Ezra 1:1-4).

2 Nebuchadnezzar's dream

Daniel had only just graduated when he was faced with this test. Nebuchadnezzar had either genuinely forgotten his dream, or he was deliberately making things difficult. It is clear from this chapter that Daniel's faith went much deeper than mere observance of the law. With his own life and the lives of many others at stake, he turns in complete trust to God. Astrology and divination, at which the Babylonians excelled, are not for him.

The image stands for four world empires: Babylonian (with Nebuchadnezzar as head), Medo-Persian, Greek and Roman. In the days of the Roman Empire, God would begin to carve out a new, everlasting, kingdom which would become universal. See further in chapters 7ff. (Those who think in terms of a 2nd-century writer looking back on events cannot include the Roman Empire, and are forced to make separate Median and Persian Empires. In point of historical fact, although there were Median kings, there was never a dominant Median Empire.)

Chaldeans (2): in its general sense the term simply means 'Babylonian'; later it was used in a restricted sense of a class of wise men. Daniel uses the word in both ways.

Verse 4: the Aramaic section starts here, and ends at 7:28. We do not know if the original used both languages.

3 The golden image and the fiery furnace

The years pass and Nebuchadnezzar, forgetting he once acknowledged Daniel's God as supreme, sets up his 90 ft idol, demanding that all his people worship it. But Daniel's companions will not compromise. They know God is *able* to deliver them from a terrible death; they do not know if he *will* (17). But come what may, they will not deny him (18). In the event, the flames killed those who flung them in, and burned through their own bonds; but they came out with not so much as a smell of burning about them. And a god-like figure walked through the fire with them. Again the king is compelled to worship.

Satrap (2): one of a number of Old Persian words which occur in Daniel. There is no reason why Daniel should not have used them; they were known before his day, and he lived on into the period of Persian supremacy. Or it may be that this Aramaic section (see on 2:4) is a later, or updated, translation.

Lyre, trigon, harp (5, Revised Standard Version): these are all Greek words. The instruments themselves

Assyrian musicians.

are Mesopotamian, but Greek cultural influences had spread across this part of the world before Nebuchadnezzar's time. Greek colonies were widespread, and Greek mercenaries served in many armies.

Furnace (6): a kiln (probably for baking bricks) with an open top and an open door at the side through which the king could see the men.

4 The king's madness

Nebuchadnezzar himself authenticates this extraordinary story (1-18, 34-37). Perhaps sensing that this dream is against himself, he does not turn to Daniel straight away (6-8). It is clear from Daniel's dismay that he does not wish the king ill. But the king's pride in his achievements (and archaeology shows they really *were* something to be proud of) overrides Daniel's wise advice. He is stricken with a rare mania, believing himself to be an animal. (Other cases are known, where patients have exhibited precisely the same symptoms: roaming out of doors, and living on a diet of grass and water.) Yet God is at work in the depths of his now humble mind, and as he worships the one true God his reason returns.

One would hardly expect to find open reference to such a seemingly shameful illness in contemporary official records. But events of the later years of Nebuchadnezzar are not known from ancient texts.

Verses 3 and 34-35: the echoes from Psalms and Isaiah may reflect Daniel's influence on the king.

Seven times (16): the length of time here as elsewhere in Daniel is unspecified. It was a definite, limited period of time fixed by God.

5 Belshazzar's feast

Strictly speaking, Nabonidus (556-539 BC) was the last king of Babylon. But he retired to Arabia early in his reign, leaving his son Belshazzar acting king in Babylon (hence the fact that Daniel could be made only 'third ruler', 16).

The date is 539, 23 years after Nebuchadnezzar's death. The great feast at the palace is going with a swing, when a mysterious hand begins to write on the wall. Three words are written. They are weights, or units of money: 'a mina, a mina, a shekel and a half-shekel'. Daniel, now an old man, is summoned to interpret; and he goes to the root meanings of the words: 'number', 'weigh', 'divide'. The king's days were indeed numbered. That very night Cyrus the Persian took the impregnable city of Babylon, so the ancient historians tell us, by diverting the course of the River Euphrates and entering along the dry river-bed, while the Babylonians were at a feast of their gods.

Gold drinking vessel of the time; Persian, from the Oxus Treasure.

Father (2): i.e. ancestor, predecessor. The word often has this sense in the Old Testament.

The queen (10): as Belshazzar's wives were there already, this may have been Nebuchadnezzar's widow.

Darius the Mede (31): no other historical record so far found mentions anyone of this name, or places any ruler between Nabonidus/Belshazzar and Cyrus. Darius has been variously identified, but none of the suggestions is completely satisfactory. This does not mean we can write Darius off as a fictional character. Since Cyrus was so well known the author could hardly have hoped to get away with such an invention.

6 Daniel in the lion's den

All his life Daniel has been a man of God. He is now in his eighties, and his enemies still cannot fault him. They can only attack him through his religion (4-5). Daniel could have stopped praying for a month, or he could have prayed in secret. But he is no more ready to compromise now than he was as a boy. So his enemies have him. The king's hands are tied by his own decree, but God's hand is not. Daniel was as safe from harm in the lion-pit as his friends had been in the furnace.

Verses 8, 15: see Esther 1:19; 8:8.

The den (16): most probably an enclosure with an open top around which was a spectator's gallery. There was also a small entrance at the side, which Darius sealed up (17).

7 - 12 THE RECORD OF DANIEL'S VISIONS

7 The four beasts

Like chapter 2 this is a pictorial representation of history. Again there are four successive empires, and then the kingdom of God is established. The winged lion is Babylon; and verse 4 has Nebuchadnezzar particularly in mind. Verse 6 depicts the Greek Empire of Alexander the Great, on his death divided among his four generals. Seleucus founded a dynasty in Syria. Ptolemy founded a dynasty in Egypt. The other two kingdoms were Greece and Asia Minor. The 'ten horns' (7, 24) equate with the toes of the image in chapter 2, though the precise identification has been much debated. Verses 9-12 picture God's judgement of the world empires. In 13-14 God gives total dominion to 'one like a son of man', Jesus' favourite title for himself. The kingdom inaugurated at Christ's first coming will be finally realized when he returns (see Matthew 26:64). Opposing God's people in different guises throughout history is the 'little horn' (8, 20-21), until God finally removes its power. It is from this chapter that Revelation 13 draws its imagery.

A time, two times, and half a time (25): often taken to mean $3\frac{1}{2}$ years; but see on 4:16. Evil is given its head, but for a strictly limited time.

8 The ram and the he-goat
The vision focusses on the second and third empires. The two-horned ram which symbolizes Medo-Persia will be superseded by the swift-footed goat – Alexander's Greek Empire. Alexander himself is the 'great horn'. The 'four horns' are the kingdoms into which his empire was divided (see on chapter 7). The little horn, in this chapter, refers to Antiochus IV, who ruled Syria 175-164 BC. Verses 9-14 vividly depict the atrocities of his reign (see on chapter 11), which resulted in the Maccabean revolt. 1 Maccabees 1 - 6 (in the Apocrypha) recounts this period of Jewish history.

Susa (2): east of Babylon; one of the four capitals of Persia.

Prince (11, 25): God himself. In attempting to wipe out the Jewish religion Antiochus was directly challenging the God of Israel.

Verse 14: i.e. 2,300 days (see Genesis 1). Antiochus first meddled in Jewish affairs in 171; he died in 164.

Gabriel (16): this is the first time God's messenger-angel is named. It was Gabriel who appeared to Zacharias, father of John the Baptist, and again to Mary before the birth of Jesus.

The end (17): this usually refers to the winding-up of history, and God's final judgement. But verse 26 relates the vision to the distant future, and 19 to the period when the suffering will be over. The Bible writers often seem to step clear of time, and view contemporary and future events as one aspect of the total, final events of 'the end'.

9 The seventy weeks; Daniel's prayer
The date is 538. Babylon has virtually ruled Judah since the Battle of Carchemish in 605. The 70 years' captivity spoken of by Jeremiah is almost up. Daniel pleads with God for the return of his people to their homeland. He is completely one with his people, sharing the blame for sin (5ff.), and his request rests solely on God's mercy (18). He saw the answer to his prayer that same year, but Israel's troubles were not over. God now shows Daniel something of what lies ahead.

Verses 24-27 are very difficult, and numerous interpretations have been suggested. God has ordained a period of 70 x 7 ('seventy weeks of years') in which the salvation of his people will be completed (24). For the Jews, the number seven itself symbolized completeness, perfection. And it may be best to take the numbers symbolically. But the period of time between the decree to rebuild and restore Jerusalem and the beginning of Jesus' ministry (25) comes very close to the 7+62 weeks=483 days, standing for the same number of years – the total reached if we take the figures literally (though there is more than one possible starting-point, and even the end-date is not absolutely fixed). Verse 26 seems to point to the death and rejection of Christ and the destruction of the temple which followed in AD 70 - with a wider reference at the end. But the subject of verse 27 is not at all clear. 'He' is taken by some to be the Messiah, by others to be the destroying prince of the previous verse.

10 - 11:1 Vision and conflict
After a long fast, Daniel receives an awe-inspiring vision of a glorious figure: very like John's vision of Christ in Revelation 1:12-16. He is given insight into the continual battle raging in the spiritual realm between those protecting God's people and those bent on their destruction (see Ephesians 6:12). Michael is the special guardian angel of the Jewish people (12:1). The 'princes'

in this chapter are patron angels of the various nations.

11:2-45 The struggle for power
This chapter claims to set out the course of future history in detail. And from our vantage-point in time we can look back on its amazingly accurate fulfilment in the history of the Greek Empire. There are to be three more Persian kings (2; Cambyses, Gaumata and Darius I), followed by a fourth (Xerxes). Xerxes invaded Greece but was defeated at Salamis in 480 BC. The power then passed to Greece (3-4; see on chapter 7). Verse 5 refers to Egypt (the 'king of the south') and to Ptolemy's one-time general, Seleucus, who became 'king of the north' – the powerful kingdom of Syria and the east. Fifty years later (6) the daughter of Ptolemy II married Antiochus II of Syria. But she was divorced and murdered, and her brother avenged her by attacking Syria (7). Verses 9-13 reflect the struggles between the two powers at the end of the 3rd century BC. The Jews then joined forces with Antiochus III of Syria to defeat Egypt (14-15). They gained their freedom from Egypt (16), and Antiochus made a marriage alliance with Ptolemy V (17). Antiochus invaded Asia Minor and Greece but was defeated by the Romans at Magnesia in 190 BC (18-19).

The 'exactor of tribute' (20) was his son Seleucus IV, who was shortly succeeded by his brother Antiochus IV, the persecutor of the Jews. Verses 21-24 aptly portray his character and policies. Through the treachery of Ptolemy's own men, Antiochus briefly gained control of Egypt in 173. On his return he attacked Jerusalem and slaughtered 80,000 Jews (25-28). The next time he attacked Egypt he was thwarted by the Roman fleet (29-30). He turned on Jerusalem again and desecrated the temple (31). He was aided and abetted by some Jews, but others refused to compromise their faith, though they died for it (32-33). Judas Maccabaeus instigated a successful revolt, so helping the faithful (34).

Verses 36-45 do not describe actual events at the end of Antiochus' life. They may refer to the end of Syrian domination, at the hands of Rome, the new king from the north. Or they may anticipate events at the end of time (see on 8:17), which the sufferings of God's people under Antiochus foreshadow. This then leads in to chapter 12.

12 Deliverance
Daniel is the first Old Testament book to speak explicitly of resurrection, though he is thinking only of the Jewish nation ('your people'). When that day comes, and all the terrible troubles are past, those who have shown themselves wise by their faithful obedience to God will rise to shine like stars for ever. All evil will be done away. But as for times, those are in God's hand. Not even Daniel understands this (6-8) – so a cautious approach to these matters may still be the wisest course!

HOSEA

Hosea was one of Isaiah's contemporaries, a prophet of God in the 8th century BC. But Hosea, unlike Isaiah, was a northerner. His message was for Israel, the northern kingdom, although he occasionally refers to Judah. And Israel in his day was in a mess. Hosea became a prophet at the end of the reign of the nation's last powerful king, Jeroboam II. He prophesied for the next 40 years, until just before Samaria fell to Assyria in 722 BC. And during that time the country went rapidly down hill. Rejection of God and the wholesale adoption of pagan religious practices brought about a moral and political landslide. 2 Kings 14:23 - 17:41 gives the history of the period. But the fact that after Jeroboam's death Israel had six kings in just over 20 years, and four of them assassinated their predecessors, gives some idea of the state of the country.

What Israel's idolatry meant to God – how he continued to love and long for his people's return to him – Hosea learnt through bitter personal experience, as his own wife betrayed and deserted him. His message comes straight from the heart. And this is what makes the book unique.

1 - 2:1 Hosea's wife and children
God instructs Hosea to marry Gomer, a woman God knows will prove unfaithful. (This seems to be the only tenable interpretation of verse 2.) Three children are born, and each is given a name which speaks God's message to Israel (compare Isaiah 8). Through the prophet, God is giving his people a last opportunity to repent before judgement breaks on the land (2 Kings 17:13-14). Yet even though they refuse, his loving purpose is not thwarted (1:10 - 2:1).

Jezreel (4): the site of many bloody battles; here the reference is to the slaughter recounted in 2 Kings 10.

2:2-23 Unfaithful Israel; God's steadfast love
Hosea's voice, pleading with his unfaithful wife through his children, becomes one with the voice of God addressing Israel. The people are worshipping Baal, the Canaanite fertility god, thinking he is the one who gives good crops and plentiful harvests; when all the time it is God. Israel will be taught by punishment, and afterwards become God's dearly loved bride again (19-20).

Achor (15): near Jericho; the place where Achan sinned and was punished (Joshua 7).

My Baal (16): a substitute word must be used because 'baal', which was the everyday word for 'lord/master/husband' was also the name of the Canaanite god.

Jezreel (22): the word means 'God sows'.

3 Probation
Gomer, now seemingly the slave of another man, is bought back and put on probation. Again Hosea's action, and his continuing love, provide an object-lesson. For a while, Israel too will be deprived of the things she

The background to Hosea is one of idolatry. This tile from Assyria shows a worshipper standing before a statue of his god.

counted on – her king and her religious emblems – but in time she will turn back to God.

Cakes of raisins (1): offered to pagan gods.

Verse 4: sacrifice and ephod (part of the priest's regalia) belonged to the legitimate religion; pillar and teraphim (household gods) were part of the pagan admixture.

4 Idolatry in Israel

From now on there is no further mention of Hosea's family. But the experience is there – and it colours the rest of the book. Real faith in God issues in obedience to his standards. The prostitution of Israel's religion led to literal prostitution (11-14). Paganism brought in its wake sexual degradation (13-14) and the breakdown of law and order in society (1-2). It still does. The priests – who failed to make God's laws known, and feathered their own nests into the bargain (4-10) – and the men of Israel (14) are responsible for what has happened. And God holds them accountable.

Beth-aven (15): a derisory name for Bethel, one of the religious centres in the northern kingdom.

Ephraim (17): Israel. Ephraim was the leading tribe.

5:1-14 Judgement

A generation has grown up to whom God is a stranger (7). The alarm is sounded on Judah's borders, for Judah shares the sin to which Israel has become addicted (8-12). Not even the great king of Assyria (13; Tiglath-pileser III – see 2 Kings 16:5ff.) can save them from God's judgement.

Mizpah, Tabor, Shittim (1-2): places where there were shrines for Baal worship.

5:15 – 6:6 A change of heart

Suffering turns the people to God again. But there is no deep change. Their 'love' evaporates as quickly as dew in the hot sun. It is lasting love and real knowledge of him that God looks for.

6:7 – 7:16 Catalogue of evil

Priests have turned butcher. At the heart of the nation's religion, at Shechem, there is intrigue and murder (6:7-10). At court it is the same. Kings fall at the hands of hot-heads and conspirators (7:6-7; see introduction). Israel turns to foreign peoples (8-9), foreign powers (11), foreign gods (16): but never to the Lord.

Oven (4-7): they baked their flat loaves on saucer-shaped 'hot-plates' placed upside down over the embers.

The 'cake' (8) must be turned over to cook both sides.

8 God is forgotten

Israel will be caught up in the whirlwind of God's judgement. They have made gods, made up laws, set up kings to suit themselves: as if God and his laws did not exist. But neither idols nor allies will avail when the God they have forgotten strikes.

Calf (5): Israel's first king set up two images at shrines in his own land to rival Jerusalem as religious centres (1 Kings 12:28). The calf had a long association with pagan cults in Egypt and in Canaan.

9 A terrible destiny for Israel

It was probably at the height of the festival to mark the grape-harvest that Hosea spoke out (1-5). The people may call him a fool, but he knows he is God's watchman, and he will not hold his tongue (7-8). Israel will become a slave-nation to Assyria, as she once was to Egypt (3, 6). Sin has become habitual, ingrained, to the point where God finally withdraws his love (12, 15).

Gibeah (9): see Judges 19.

Baal-peor (10): see Numbers 25.

Gilgal (15): the place where Saul was acclaimed king (1 Samuel 11:14-15). The people's eagerness to have a king had in it the seeds of danger. Some of the later kings would usurp God's place as the true Leader of his people.

10 Under the yoke

Outwardly, affluent Israel made a great show of religion (1), but inwardly the people moved further and further away from God. The calf-image at Bethel had become the nation's only 'king' (3-5), a king marked for destruction (6-8). Now they are reaping what they have long sown (13). Yet they could still sow an altogether different crop (12).

Shalman (14): probably a reference to the recent invasion of Gilead by Salamanu of Moab.

11 The Father's love

This chapter lets us see right into the infinitely loving heart of God. All down the long years of history, from Egypt on, and despite all he has done for them, Israel has rejected God's love (1-4). The nation deserves no mercy (5-7). Yet God still shrinks from destroying them (8-9). He is torn between love and justice, neither of which can be denied. This is the pain he took to himself in the cross of Christ.

Admah and Zeboiim (8): two cities to

the south of the Dead Sea, presumably destroyed with Sodom and Gomorrah (Genesis 19).

12 Lessons from history

This is not an easy chapter to follow. Israel needs to be reminded of scheming Jacob (3-6, 12), and how he learnt to lean on God – and forget her proud independence and reliance on foreign powers. The people deride the prophets of their own day. They need the reminder that it was through a prophet (Moses, 13) that God brought the nation into being.

Verses 3-4, 12: incidents recounted in Genesis 25:21-26; 32:22-32; and 29.

13 The east wind of God's judgement

Israel may turn to Baal and other idols, but there is in fact no God but God (what was true then is still true now). Men may forget him, or discount him, but he exists: and he has power to carry out all that he has warned of.

East wind (15): the scorching wind from the desert which dries and shrivels everything in its path.

14 'Return, O Israel'

After the fierce tones of chapter 13, this last chapter is full of love and pleading. The way is open. There is no need to pass through the fire of judgement. Men have only to give God their loyalty (2-3) to find his love and forgiveness, and embark on a new, transformed life (4-7). This is the truly wise course (9).

Hosea makes the way so plain. It is more than sad to realize that his contemporaries ignored it all – until the Assyrians swept down and destroyed their splendid capital, Samaria; took the remaining Israelites into exile; and repeopled their land with foreigners. When God gives warning of judgement, he is not playing with words. How many of the practices he condemned in Israel do we see all around us in our own society? How long do we expect his patience to last?

JOEL

We know nothing at all about this prophet, apart from his father's name (1:1). And the prophecy contains few clues to the date when it was written. Joel is obviously familiar with themes which also occur in Isaiah, Amos and Ezekiel – particularly the 'day of the Lord', when God will finally judge the world and his own people. We may guess at dates – and guesses range from the 8th century BC to the 4th century BC and later – but the book itself is timeless.

1 The disastrous plague of locusts

Even in our own century Jerusalem has been stripped of all vegetation by a plague of locusts like the one Joel describes so vividly. The swarm of several million insects is carried into Palestine by the desert wind from Arabia. The locust grows rapidly from larva to winged adult (4), and at every stage its appetite is insatiable. It is worse than an invading army: when it moves on there is no green or growing thing left (6-12). There is nothing to offer to God (9,13), or so little that the people are using all they have to ward off starvation. For Joel, the locust swarm is an object-lesson, a warning of the terror of God's approaching judgement day (15). He calls for a national day of prayer (14).

2:1-27 The coming day of the Lord; repentance and restoration

The locust-army becomes a picture of the invading army of God on the day of his judgement: the sky black with insects (2); the 'scorched earth' in their wake (3); their inexorable, totally irresistible, onward march (4-9). This is what God's judgement will be like. Who can bear it (11)? But no one need endure God's judgement. He is still calling all men to repent (12). Joel calls the whole nation to

turn to God and plead for mercy (13-17). And in response God promises to restore in profusion all that the locusts have robbed them of. He will rid the land of his great army (25), which is now identified with all his enemies ('the northerner', 20: see on Ezekiel 38 - 39; it is very unlikely that the locusts actually came from the north).

2:28 - 3:21 The outpouring of God's Spirit: judgement on the nations

Joel foresaw a day when God's Spirit would be poured out, not just on priests and prophets, but on ordinary people, regardless of sex, age, or class. He little dreamt that God spoke not just of Israel, but of all nations (Acts 2). Equally, God's judgement awaits men of all nations who refuse his call, including Israel (32). But all who call out to him, and whom he calls, will escape.

The nations will be punished for all they have inflicted on God's people (3:2-8). Multitudes will be gathered to God's judgement. There He will decide their destiny (14). All evil will be done away on that momentous, earth-shaking day. God will make his home in a city and among a people at last made holy; and the whole land will share in this abundant blessing (16-18).

Tyre, Sidon, Philistia (3:4): see on Ezekiel 25 - 28. Artaxerxes III sold the Sidonians as slaves in 345 BC, and in 332 Alexander the Great sold the people of Tyre and the Philistine city of Gaza into slavery.

Sabaeans (8): famous Arabian traders.

3:10: Joel reverses Isaiah's famous words (Isaiah 2:4).

Valley of Jehoshaphat (12): probably a symbolic name; it means 'the Lord judges'.

AMOS

Amos was a layman, a shepherd and dresser of fig-trees. His home was in Tekoa, about 12 miles south of Jerusalem, on the edge of the Judean desert. But God sent him as his prophet to the northern kingdom of Israel. His base was the religious centre of Bethel, where Jeroboam I had set up a calf-image when the nation had first split into two rival kingdoms. Amos lived in the reign of Jeroboam II (793-753), Israel's Indian summer of prosperity and influence. But beneath the affluence the nation was rotten. Amos was sent to denounce the social and religious corruption, and warn of God's impending judgement. But the people turned a deaf ear, as they did to his contemporary, Hosea. And the king's chaplain told him to get back to Judah (7:10ff.)! Thirty years after Jeroboam's death the Assyrians destroyed Samaria and took the people into exile. Israel ceased to exist. But the prophet has a word for any nation in Israel's condition. Put his descriptions in 20th-century dress and they still strike home.

1 - 2:5 The indictment of Israel's neighbours

Syria, Philistia, Tyre, Edom, Ammon, Moab and Judah are each condemned in turn. Their offences are many (the formula 'For three ... for four' indicates an indefinite number). They stand condemned for their crimes against humanity. Only Judah is judged against the full standard of God's law. The Syrians are guilty of wanton cruelty (running studded threshing-sledges over the bodies of their captives, 3); the Philistines of selling their fellow men. Tyre and Edom have transgressed the laws of kinship. Ammon's atrocities have been committed simply to gain more land. By desecrating a corpse Moab has violated one of the most universal of all ancient unwritten laws. God will punish each and every one.

Hazael, Ben-hadad (1:4): kings of Syria. Hazael seized the throne in Elisha's time and founded a dynasty.

Kir (5): the place the Syrians originally came from.

Gaza, Ashdod, Ashkelon, Ekron (6-8): four of the five Philistine cities.

His brother (11): Edom and Israel were descendants of two brothers, Esau and Jacob.

Rabbah (14): the Ammonite capital; modern Amman, capital of Jordan.

2:6-16 Israel's crimes

The other prophets make it plain that Israel's basic sin was in turning away from God to worship idols. But Amos emphasizes the moral and social decline which resulted. They have grown hard and callous in their dealings with others; young and old make use of temple prostitutes; and they have gagged God's spokesmen. None will escape God's punishment.

Verse 8: the law humanely ordered that garments taken in pledge be returned by nightfall (Exodus 22:26-27).

Amorite (9): here an umbrella term for the original inhabitants of Canaan.

Nazirites (11): men consecrated to God by a special vow which involved renouncing wine.

Cart/wagon (13): more likely the threshing-sledge (as in the Jerusalem Bible).

3 Punishment

Israel has broken the covenant-agreement with God and must suffer punishment. It is simple cause and effect (like the other instances given in verses 3-6). God has spoken; he will act. Of beautiful Samaria, with its great stone houses and exquisite ivory panels, only a trace will be left; just enough to show that the city once existed. And God will demolish the trappings of debased religion at Bethel (verse 14).

4 God's warnings

The luxury-loving women of Samaria ('cows of Bashan'), living it up at the expense of the poor, will be led away with hooks. (The Assyrians actually did this to their captives.) While they crushed their fellow men, the people still kept up the religious facade (4-5). But 'insurance policy' religion is a mockery of the real thing (see James 1:26-27). By famine and drought, blight and disease God warned them where they were heading – all to no avail.

Amos protested against the 'houses of ivory' being built by the rich while the poor were oppressed. Many ivories of the period have been found. This one is from a palace in Assyria.

5 'Seek me and live'

The lament (1-3) is quickly followed by an appeal. God calls on his people to save their lives by seeking him. And this means, not yet more sacrifices at the nation's corrupt sanctuaries (5, 21-23, 25-26), but reformed living – a return to God's standards of justice and right conduct in public as well as private life. Otherwise the 'day of the Lord' (18ff.), the day on which they expect to enter into God's blessing and see their enemies destroyed, will be a terrible day of condemnation for God's people.

The gate (10): the city gate was the place for business transactions and the administration of justice.

Joseph (15): Ephraim and Manasseh (descended from Joseph's two sons) were leading tribes in the northern kingdom.

Verse 25: the meaning seems to be 'Was it *only* sacrifice and offerings you brought to me...? Was it not also right living and obedience?'

Sakkuth, Kaiwan (26): Assyrian gods associated with the planet Saturn.

6 Exile

Affluence and comfortable living (then as now) insulate men from the real issues, and breed false security. Self-sufficiency and pride have been man's downfall from first to last (e.g. Genesis 11:1-9; Ezekiel 28).

Calneh, Hamath (2): two towns in Syria; Hamath is modern Hama.

Lo-debar, Karnaim (13): towns east of the Jordan, which Israel took from the Syrians.

Arabah (14): the dry valley running south from the Dead Sea to the Gulf of Aqaba.

7 The plumb-line

Twice Amos prevails on God to stay his hand; but judgement cannot be delayed for ever. Israel does not begin to measure up against the straight line of God's standards.

God's man and 'official religion' meet head-on in the confrontation between Amos and Amaziah. (10-17). The prophet has God's authority for his message and will not be silenced. Amaziah will die in exile. The invading army will abuse his wife, kill his children and seize his land.

The Lord repented (3, 6): i.e. he mercifully changed his mind (this does not imply that his original intention was wrong).

Sycamore (14): a kind of fig-tree; not the tree we call sycamore.

8 Israel ripe for ruin

Men like to think their 'little' sins too small for God to notice. But he sees everything: greed and sharp practice; short weight and sub-standard goods. And the poor, who always come off worst, are his special concern.

Ephah ... shekel (5): this was a double cheat; the trader reduced the size of the measure for the grain (ephah) *and* increased the weight of the silver paid for it (shekel).

Ashimah (14): a Syrian goddess worshipped in Israel. Dan, in the far north, was the town where Jeroboam I erected his second calf-image.

9 Evil destroyed; the faithful remnant restored

For the nation as a whole judgement will be inescapable. God will deal with them like any foreign nation (7a). But for the faithful few the future holds unimagined blessing (11-15).

Caphtor (7): Crete, where the Philistines originally came from.

OBADIAH

A prophecy of Edom's downfall (for other prophecies against Edom, see Isaiah 34:5-15; Jeremiah 49:7-22; Ezekiel 25:12-14; 35:1-15; Amos 1:11-12). Edom occupied the mountainous region south-east of the Dead Sea. The capital, Sela (now Petra), was perched high on a plateau above a sheer rock cliff approached by a narrow gorge. It was virtually impregnable. From mountain strongholds like this the Edomites launched their raids on Palestine. As Esau's descendants they were in fact kin to Israel, but there was never any love lost between the two. The final outrage – and the occasion of Obadiah's prophecy – was their invasion of Judah while Jerusalem was being sacked by the Babylonians in 587 BC.

Obadiah denounces Edom's pride. The Edomites thought their strongholds invincible, but they would be utterly destroyed. In the 5th century BC Arabs took Edom, and in the 3rd century the region was overrun by the Nabataeans (who built the rock-city of Petra in present-day Jordan). Some Edomites settled in southern Judah. Herod the Great, ruler of the Jews at the time of Jesus' birth, was one of their descendants. After AD 70 the Edomites entirely disappeared from history. In contrast to dispossessed Edom, Obadiah foretells the return of Israel to possess a greatly extended land including former Edomite territory.

Teman (9): an important town in Edom, home of Job's friend Eliphaz; Mt Esau is Mt Seir.

Verse 19: 'Negeb', the southern desert; 'Shephelah', the hill-country behind the western coastal plain; 'Ephraim and Samaria', the northern kingdom of Israel; 'Gilead', east of the Jordan.

Verse 20: 'Halah', in Mesopotamia; 'Zarephath', modern Sarafand in Lebanon.

JONAH

2 Kings 14:25 is the only other mention of this prophet, and that would place him in the mid-8th century BC. Nineveh, capital of powerful Assyria (Israel's enemy) and subject of this book, was destroyed by the Babylonians in 612 BC. If Jonah did not write the story himself, it was probably written after this date (see 3:3). Whether we take the book as 'history with a moral' or as parable (and the Bible contains many parables, though none as long as this), there is no doubt about the main message. God's concern extends beyond Israel to the whole world. Jesus focussed attention on two further points: the parallel with the three days between his own death and resurrection; and the ready repentance of the Ninevites in contrast to his hearers (Matthew 12:40; Luke 11:32).

1 Jonah runs away

4:2 tells us why. Jonah was not afraid to go to Nineveh (verse 12 shows plenty of courage!). But he knew God: he knew that if the Ninevites changed their ways God would forgive them. And Jonah wanted this cruel threatening enemy nation destroyed. So in deliberate disobedience he sets out in the opposite direction. By trying to save his life, the heathen sailors display more humanity than the man of God (13).

A great fish (17): although sperm whales and large sharks capable of swallowing a man are not unknown in the eastern Mediterranean, this incident is clearly intended to be seen as a miracle. It is one of the many things God 'appoints' in the story (see 1:4;

4:6-8). Argument over this must not be allowed to blind us to the whole point of the story.

2 Jonah's prayer

This psalm records Jonah's cry to God when he was at death's door ('the belly of Sheol', 2). At last he comes to his senses, remembering his 'true loyalty' (8). And God, who has already saved him from death, gives him a 'second life'.

3 Nineveh's response

Given a second chance, Jonah leaps to obey. And his message produces a remarkable effect. The whole city, from the greatest to the least, repents. And God spares them.

Three days' journey (3): this applies to the district of Nineveh as distinct from the city: 'Greater London', so to speak.

God repented (10): see on Amos 7:3.

4 A hard lesson for Jonah

Jonah wanted God to confine his love and mercy to Israel. Let the heathen get their deserts. Far from being delighted that his message provoked such a fantastic response, he was furious. And it wasn't simply that he didn't want to look a fool. There was no spark of compassion for the people of Nineveh in Jonah's heart. And so God used a plant (the shady castor-oil plant) to make him feel something of his own pity for men and women: 'Should I not pity Nineveh?'

Verse 11: the city could well have housed this number of people. The inner wall formed a circuit of 7¾ miles. Not knowing their 'right hand from their left' expresses their utter ignorance of God and his laws.

MICAH

Micah was one of the 8th-century BC prophets, contemporary with Amos and Hosea (in the northern kingdom of Israel) and Isaiah (in Jerusalem). He was a countryman, from a town in south-west Judah, on the Philistine border. His message is for Samaria and Jerusalem, capital cities of the two kingdoms. And from a comparison with Amos it is clear that Judah had become infected with the same sins that beset Israel. So Micah, too, denounces rulers, priests and prophets; deplores the money-grubbing exploitation of the helpless; dishonesty in business; sham religion. God's judgement will fall on Samaria and Jerusalem; only after that will there be restoration. But Micah also sees a glorious future, when Jerusalem will become the religious centre of the world, and Bethlehem give birth to a greater David who will rule over all God's people.

1 The two cities

God is pictured coming down from heaven, treading upon the mountains, to destroy Samaria for her persistent idolatry. The gangrene has spread into Judah, and God's judgement is at the gates of Jerusalem. Micah pictures the approach of the invading army, coming from the coastal plain through the hills of Judah to Jerusalem (10ff., where the place-names frequently conceal a play on words). The parents in Judah will mourn for their exiled children. In 722 BC the Assyrians destroyed Samaria. In 701 they besieged Jerusalem, and the city escaped by a miracle (see 2 Kings 18:9 - 19:37). Micah most probably lived through both.

Verse 1: Jotham (750-732) and Hezekiah (729) were good kings; Ahaz (735-716) was one of the worst, introducing terrible heathen practices, including child-sacrifice. (Overlapping dates indicate periods of co-regency.)

2 - 3 Exploitation; misrule; a perverted priesthood

The men with power and influence are all of them on the make, and they are not fussy about the means. So property is seized and families made destitute; and the preacher is told this is none of his business. (2:12-13 moves abruptly to the future, picturing God at the head of the remnant of his people.) The ordinary people are just so many animals to the rulers (3:1-3). Every man has his price: judge and priest and prophet alike (3:11).

4 Future greatness

Micah is full of contrasts. Verses 1-8 sweep us on to a new Jerusalem, from which God's word goes out to all men, and to which the nations flock, in an era of peace and plenty. Verses 9-10 return us to the condemned city, to a nation in exile, to God's judgement: not on his people alone, but on all nations around (11-13).

Verses 1-3: almost identical with Isaiah 2:2-4.

Babylon (10): the enemy in Micah's day was Assyria, but like Isaiah he looks 100 years ahead to the power which would destroy Jerusalem.

5 The king from Bethlehem

In the midst of the Assyrian siege, Micah speaks of a deliverer – *the* ultimate deliverer – who would come, like David of old, from Bethlehem (see Matthew 2:1-6). Historical perspectives blur, as so often in the prophets, and current events melt into those of the near and far distant future. In the messianic peace, even the Assyrian will be overcome. But Judah too will be purified 'in that day' (10ff.). All that she has relied on in place of God will be destroyed: armies, defences, witch-craft and false gods.

Ephrathah (2): the district around Bethlehem.

Seven ... eight (5): idiomatic, for 'an indefinite number': no matter how many leaders are needed they will be forth-coming.

Nimrod (6): Assyria (see Genesis 10:8-12).

6 What God requires of his people

Verse 8 gives us the essence of true

worship. God accepts no substitute. Though men may try to buy him off with all kinds of impressive gifts, he sees and will punish their sharp practice, their violence and deceit.

Verse 5: see Numbers 22 - 24.

Shittim to Gilgal (5): i.e at the crossing of the Jordan (Joshua 3 - 4).

My first-born ... (7): the sacrifice of the firstborn crept into Israel with other pagan practices in the dark days of the nation's last kings.

Verse 11: see on Amos 8:5.

Omri ... Ahab (16): two kings of Israel notorious for introducing Baal-worship.

King Sennacherib recorded his victory over the fortress city of Lachish in Judah in a series of scenes carved in stone which lined his palace walls at Nineveh.

7 Darkness and light

Micah watches the breakdown of society in his country. The rot which began at government level has permeated the whole nation. And now all human relationships are crumbling. Friendship and family count for nothing. The human scene is black. But with God there is still light. He may still be relied on. His promise will not fail. He will build again. He will deliver again. In his compassionate love he will forgive again.

Watchmen (4): the prophets were posted as watchmen to warn of coming judgement (see Ezekiel 3:17-21).

NAHUM

The subject of Nahum, like that of the earlier book of Jonah, is Nineveh, the great capital city of Assyria. But whereas Jonah records the city's reprieve, Nahum predicts its destruction. The date is somewhere between the fall of Thebes to the Assyrians in 663 BC (3:8-10), and the fall of Nineveh to the Babylonians and Medes in 612 BC. Nahum seems to have been a Judean, but apart from this we know nothing about him, except that he was capable of writing the most graphic poetry in the whole of the Old Testament.

1 Vengeance on God's enemies; comfort for his people

Nahum starts, not with Nineveh, but with God: his power, his anger, his goodness. The days of Assyria, whose armies had destroyed Israel and threatened Jerusalem itself less than a century before, are now numbered.

An overflowing flood (8): impregnable Nineveh eventually fell when floodwaters breached her walls, making way for the attacking army.

One (11): perhaps Sennacherib, the Assyrian king who took Lachish and then laid siege to Jerusalem in 701 BC (see Isaiah 36 - 37).

2 The assault on Nineveh

Once, God had used the armies of Assyria to punish his people. Now the forces attacking Nineveh are his instruments. Blood and thunder; plunder and desolation; the den of the Assyrian lion is no more. Nahum pictures the final assault in all its horror.

Mantelet (5): a siege-engine armed with battering-ram.

Verse 6: see on 1:8.

Its mistress (7): this may be Ishtar, the Assyrian goddess of love and war.

A siege-engine with battering-ram is shown being used by the Assyrians in this relief at Nimrud.

3 Destruction

Nahum pictures the city as a prostitute, enticing the nations into submission. Now she will receive a prostitute's punishment (5-6). She will share the terrible fate she inflicted on the Egyptian city of Thebes (No-Amon). (At Thebes, city of Amun, state-god of Egypt, the treasures of centuries had been accumulated. The Assyrians took the city with fire and slaughter and plundered all its wealth.) Though the nation is as great as a swarm of locusts they will vanish like a swarm that has flown. For all its might, Nineveh fell quickly into ruin, leaving no trace but a mound which is known today as Tell Kuyunjik, 'the mound of many sheep'.

Ethiopia (9): present-day Sudan, which supplied a dynasty of Egyptian kings. 'Put' may be Libya or possibly Somalia.

HABAKKUK

The prophet Habakkuk is battling with much the same problem as Job and the writer of Psalm 73: the fact that while God's people suffer, the wicked go free. Current events faced him with this problem in a particularly acute form. God had announced that he would use the Babylonians – a far more wicked nation – to punish his own people. So Habakkuk, the man of faith, questions God.

The book belongs to the latter part of the 7th century BC, when Jeremiah was prophesying in Jerusalem. Some would place it before, some just after, the fall of the Assyrian Empire (Nineveh was taken by the Babylonians in 612 BC) and the defeat of Egypt at Carchemish in 605. Babylon is on the march, but so far Judah has escaped. In 597 BC, not long after this, Jerusalem fell into enemy hands, and the city was destroyed in 587.

1 The prophet's dilemma

In response to Habakkuk's first question (2-4), God presents him with an

'I will climb my watch-tower,' says Habakkuk. From towers like this a constant watch was kept over the vineyards as the fruit ripened.

even greater stumbling-block (5-11). How can God, who is just and good, who hates evil, send against his people a nation that he openly admits makes a god of its own might? Will he let Babylon ('the Chaldeans', 6) fish the sea of humanity forever (17)?

2 God's answer

The answer is no. When the final scores are added up, only the man who trusts God and remains loyal to him will live. God will punish all man's arrogant pride. Woe betide those who greedily grab what belongs to others; who for selfish ends justify the cruellest means; who climb to power on the backs of others; who destroy and dehumanize; who give their worship to man-made idols. The lives of all such men are forfeit whatever their nationality.

3 The triumph of faith – Habakkuk's prayer

The musical form of this prayer has led some to believe that Habakkuk was a Levite, attached to the temple. Its focus is on God himself; God approaching from the mountains of the southern desert (Teman is in Edom; Paran part of Sinai); God wrapped about with thunder and lightning in the storm of his wrath; God setting the world trembling with a glance. Habakkuk sees the inevitability, the fury of judgement. Yet though it means the loss of every good thing in life, God is still to be trusted. The prophet will wait for the day when God deals with the invader (16). He will rejoice in God, though life is stripped of all that gives natural joy and satisfaction.

ZEPHANIAH

Zephaniah prophesied in King Josiah's reign (640-609 BC), about the time Jeremiah's ministry began. From his stern words, it seems he spoke before Josiah launched his great programme of reform in 621, following the discovery of the law-book in the temple. The two previous kings, Manasseh and Amon had brought the religion and morality of the nation to an all-time low. Zephaniah himself seems to have been of royal blood, tracing his ancestry back to Hezekiah, who was king in Isaiah's day, 70 years or so before.

1 The great and terrible day of judgement
In popular thinking the 'day of the Lord' would bring untold blessing to all God's people, and destruction to their enemies. Amos, years before this, had warned that on that day all evil would be punished, making it a black day for many in Israel. Zephaniah spells out the same message, in detail, to Judah. The day is close at hand when all who are guilty of idolatry (4-6), violence, fraud (9), all who sit by in idle indifference (12), will be set apart for destruction (this is the meaning of verse 7). And their cry will be heard in every quarter of the city of Jerusalem (10-11).

Baal (4): the Canaanite god of fertility whose worship involved sexual licence and prostitution.
Milcom (5): the national god of the Ammonites.
The hills ... the Mortar (10-11): districts of Jerusalem.
Thickening upon their lees (12): a picture drawn from wine-making; one of the secrets in making wine is not to let it settle.

2 Judgement on the nations
The only hope for God's people is to seek him, and begin living by his standards. If they do not, they will share the fate of the nations around: Philistia (4-7) to the west; Moab and Ammon (8-11) to the east; Ethiopia (12) to the south; Assyria (13-15) to the north.

Gaza, Ashkelon, Ashdod, Ekron (4): the four remaining Philistine city-states.
Cherethites (5): the Philistines, who originally came from Crete.
Sodom, Gomorrah (9): cities at the southern end of the Dead Sea, destroyed by God for their wickedness (Genesis 19).
Ethiopians (12): from modern Sudan; at this time the ruling dynasty in Egypt.
Nineveh (13): capital of Assyria; see on Nahum, particularly chapter 3.

3 Jerusalem condemned; a remnant saved
The city (1-7) is not named, but it is clearly Jerusalem. Beginning with rebellion against God, and the corruption of religion, the rot spreads into every sector of society. In the end, God has no alternative but to wipe the city out – but not completely. Zephaniah has already spoken of 'a remnant' (2:7, 9). Now he enlarges on God's purpose for the humble, faithful few who will survive when all human pride and self-sufficiency is done away. There is cause for great rejoicing. God is in the midst of his people: he will pour out his love on them. He will change and make them into those who are 'pure of heart' (9, 13). With exultant song they will be brought home and restored to favour. All the nations of the world have their share in this (9).

HAGGAI

The last three books of the Old Testament take us on past the exile to the time when the Jews were repatriated, the time of Ezra and Nehemiah. Haggai delivered his 'word from the Lord' in 520 BC, Zechariah in 520-518. When the first party of exiles returned to their homeland under the leadership of Zerubbabel (grandson of King Jehoiachin) in 538, they made an enthusiastic start on rebuilding the temple which had been destroyed by the Babylonians in 587. But opposition and apathy very soon brought the work to a standstill (Ezra 4:4-5). For years nothing was done, until Haggai and Zechariah began to stir things up (Ezra 5:12). Thanks to them, by 516 the temple was completed. Haggai's little book is one of the gems of the Old Testament. It has permanent relevance, because its basic concern is not with the rebuilding of the temple but with priorities.

Four times Haggai comes to the people with a message from God (1:2-15; 2:1-9; 2:10-19; 2:20-23). 1:2-15: life is hard, with food and clothing in short supply, and prices soaring. Why? Because the people have their priorities wrong. Every man is wrapped up in his own selfish concerns. God is neglected. And so the very things man works for evade him. For all the good things of life are God's to give or withhold. Haggai's words strike home to the nation's conscience. Within three weeks, work on the temple is resumed.

2:1-9: Solomon's fabulous temple had been demolished 70 years before. Few of those now building would have seen it – but all had heard of it. And the glory had lost nothing in the telling. The new temple seems a feeble thing in comparison. But let the builders take heart. The present building is just a foretaste of the splendour and glory of the end-time, the era of peace and prosperity to which the prophets all looked forward.

2:10-19: work on the temple has been resumed, but this in itself will not make the workmen 'holy' (right with God). It is rottenness, not soundness that is contagious (Haggai makes his point from the ritual law). Their previous neglect of God brought all kinds of unpleasant consequences. But from the day they begin to put first things first, God will bless every aspect of life.

2:20-23: a word for Zerubbabel. It is to Zerubbabel the heir to David's throne, rather than to Zerubbabel the individual, that these messianic promises are made. He stands in the line from David to Christ.

ZECHARIAH

Zechariah came from a family of priests, and with Haggai was closely involved in the rebuilding of the temple following the return from exile (see on Haggai, and Ezra 5 - 6 for the historical background). Like Daniel and Ezekiel he was a visionary. And his book at one and the same time distils the wisdom of many of the earlier prophets, and brings the events of the far future into sharp focus. It contains detailed references to the Messiah which are clearly fulfilled in the life of Christ. There is a marked break (some would say a change of author – someone writing much later) between the visions of the first eight chapters and the spoken messages of chapters 9 - 14.

1:1-17; The four riders

In point of time, verses 1-6 slot in between Haggai 2:9 and 10; the vision of verses 7-17, two months after Haggai's last recorded message. Zechariah is probably a young man (his grandfather, Iddo, returned with the exiles less than 20 years before: Nehemiah 12:4). Verses 2-6 retell past history, warning the present generation not to behave as their fathers had done. Zechariah's first vision (7-17) is of four horsemen patrolling the world on God's behalf, like the mounted patrols which 'policed' the Persian Empire. (The significance of the colours, if any, is now lost.) The message is one of comfort and encouragement for God's people. Jerusalem will be rebuilt; prosperity will return.

1:18-21 The four horns

The second vision is a vivid picture of the destruction of the hostile powers which had ground the nation down. ('Four' indicates completeness – the four quarters of the earth.)

2 The measuring-line

The man may be Zechariah's projection of his own image, measuring up the city for rebuilding. The walls had been destroyed in 587. They were not rebuilt until Nehemiah's day (445, 75 years after this prophecy). But God pledges himself to protect Jerusalem.

He calls to the remaining exiles to return.

The land of the north (6): Babylon; in point of fact, east, but the invading armies of Assyria and Babylon all entered Palestine from the north.

3 The investiture of the high priest

The taints of exile, when strict observance of dietary and other laws was impossible, are removed. And Joshua – high priest and partner with the ruler Zerubbabel in the exiles' return – is fittingly robed for office. God promises to send the long foretold Messiah, the Branch (8, and see Isaiah 11) from the family of David; the all-seeing, all-knowing 'stone' (the seven facets are literally seven eyes). He will usher in a day of universal peace and prosperity (this is the meaning of the vine and fig-tree idiom, 10).

4 The lamp and the olive-trees

Both these images are taken up in Revelation (1:12, 20; 11). The seven-branched lampstand stood in the tabernacle and temple. Here it may represent God's people or their worship, supported and 'fed' by the royal and priestly leaders, Zerubbabel and Joshua (the two olive-trees). From small beginnings (the start already made on the temple) great things will be accomplished, through the power of God's Spirit. Zerubbabel will lay the last stone in the temple building, as he had laid the first.

5 Sin removed

In ancient thinking a curse possessed destructive power. This is the concept behind the picture of the scroll. The woman in the great measure, or barrel, is sin personified; perhaps particularly the sin of idolatry, since she is removed to Babylon (Shinar is the old name) where a temple is built for her.

6 The four chariots

This last vision is like the first (1:7-17). God is keeping watch over the whole world. He is actively in control. His 'patrol' has power to execute judgement (this time there are chariots, not just reporting horsemen). In verses 9-14 the crowning of

Joshua prefigures the dual role of the Messiah, as priest and king.

7 The question of fasts

The fast in the fifth month (July/August) commemorated the fall of Jerusalem in 587. The fast in the seventh month was in memory of the murdered governor, Gedaliah (2 Kings 25:25). Now that the temple was being rebuilt, need the fasts continue? In reply, God questions *them* about the spirit in which the fasts were kept, and reminds them of the standards they refused to keep before the exile (8-14). They still apply.

8 Hope burns bright

God promises a glorious future for his people and for Jerusalem. His purpose is wholly good. Judgement is past. God will return to make his home in the city. His people will enjoy peace and plenty. Right will prevail. And men and women of every nation will flock to Jerusalem seeking God. At the time of the prophecy only a few had returned from exile; the building was scarcely begun. But it was a foretaste of the wonderful days to come.

Verse 19: the two additional fasts were probably to mark the beginning of Nebuchadnezzar's siege of Jerusalem (the tenth month) and the breaching of the walls 18 months later (the fourth month). In answer to the question in 7:3, Zechariah replies that God wants all these fasts to be turned into feasts. The future for God's people is one of rejoicing.

9 - 11 Israel and the nations

For the break at this point, see introduction. Chapter 9 pictures the joyous arrival of the Messiah, riding an ass (not a war-horse), inaugurating a rule of peace (9-10; see Matthew 21:5). Before him Israel's old enemies will fall (1-8). There will be no more oppression. The Philistines (5-7) will be absorbed into Israel, as the Jebusites (from whom David captured the city of Jerusalem) had been long before. The Jewish captives will be released, and Israel's military power will equal even that of rising Greece. God is his people's protection and salvation.

Chapter 10 condemns the careless leaders of God's people. He is full of pity for the straying flock. Every one

will be brought home.

In chapter 11 the prophet becomes shepherd to God's flock – but the people prefer exploitation to genuine care. They get what they want (15-16). The covenant with God is broken and the nation divided.

9:1-7: many relate this to Alexander's advance after defeating the Persians in 333 BC.

10:2: in the absence of any real spiritual lead, the people are dabbling in magic. The old household gods (teraphim) were used in divination.

11:1-3: the 'clearance' in preparation for the returning Israelites. In Old Testament times the thickets fringing the Jordan were the haunt of lions.

Thirty shekels (11:12): the prophet sarcastically calls it a 'lordly price' – this was the price of a slave (Exodus 21:32; and see Matthew 26:15; 27:3-5).

12 - 14 Israel's future

Chapter 12 pictures God strengthening his people for a great battle against the nations (1-9). But in the midst of triumph there is national mourning – the people weep as the pagans wept for their dying vegetation-god (11). The phrase 'him whom they have pierced' inevitably makes us think of Christ. But if Zephaniah is speaking of the Messiah, this national Jewish remorse for the One they crucified is yet to come.

13:1 takes our thoughts to Christ again. Verses 2-9 describe the 'refining' of God's people; the removal of everything that offends God. 'The prophets' are false prophets; the 'wounds' are self-inflicted – part of the religious frenzy of the old prophets of Baal (1 Kings 18:28).

Chapter 14 pictures the last battle and the age to come. God himself will appear, ushering in perpetual day. The idea of life-giving water flowing from Jerusalem echoes Ezekiel 47. The whole earth will become God's kingdom. Those who set themselves against God will be destroyed. All who survive will worship him. Everything will be sacred. But the world is still not perfect. The possibility of disobedience and punishment remains. It is not yet the new Jerusalem of Revelation.

MALACHI

The name means 'My messenger', which may have been the prophet's actual name or a pseudonym. From the conditions reflected in the book it is usually dated around 460-430 BC – either just before Nehemiah became governor of Jerusalem, or during his absence later on. This is about 80 years after Haggai and Zechariah spurred the people on to rebuild the temple. And since then disillusionment had set in. Times were hard, and the promised prosperity had not been realized. The people tended to feel that the prophets had been shooting them a line; that God was a bit of a let-down. This showed in an increasingly casual attitude to worship and the standards God had set. Malachi's message about God's claims on his people was needed. It still is.

1 The very best for God

Malachi's starting-point is God's love. His people, struggling with economic hardship and persistent sniping from the opposition (see e.g. Nehemiah 1:3; 4), cannot see much evidence of it. In answer they are told to look at their brother-nation, Edom – overrun like themselves by Babylon, but not restored (see on Obadiah). Israel enjoys a unique Father-son relationship with God. He is in a special sense their Lord. But their attitude over the sacrificial offerings shows their contempt for him. The left-overs are good enough for God, although they know the rules (Leviticus 22; Deuteronomy 15, 17). They dishonour and belittle his greatness. It would be better to close the temple and stop the sacrifices altogether (10).

Love ... hate (2-3): the Hebrew idiom is over-strong in English. It means, not literal love/hate, but the special choice of one and not the other.
Verse 11: God is receiving more acceptable worship from the Gentiles – a statement intended to shock Malachi's Jewish hearers.

2:1-9 God's charges against the priests

The task God committed to his ministers, the Levites, was to teach the truth, and by their own lives to set an example (6). But instead of turning people away from wrong, they have actively misled them.

2:10-16 Marriage and divorce

See on Ezra 9-10 and Nehemiah 13. When God and his laws are respected, so are our fellow men. Indifference towards God is soon reflected in callousness towards one another. The Jews were marrying pagan women (11), which was forbidden (on religious, not racial, grounds). What is more, the older men were cruelly discarding their ageing wives for these attractive young foreigners – a situation not without parallel! And family life, as always, suffered. God cares about these things. He requires faithfulness from his people: faithfulness to himself and faithfulness in human relationships.

2:17 - 3:18 Justice; and giving

God's people can always look around and see godless men and women flourishing. It seems unfair (2:17; 3:13-15). But in the final winding-up of things there will be absolute justice (3:1-5). The Lord is coming, first to purify, and then to judge. And a messenger will be sent on ahead to prepare the way (see on 4:5).

God does not change; nor do his people (6, New English Bible). They have been fickle from first to last. God gives them all they have, yet they rob him even of his legal dues. (The tithe was a sort of income tax to provide for the upkeep of the temple and the 'salaries' of the ministers.) Anything we give to God is only a small return on all we owe him. When we hold back from giving, through self-interest, we deprive ourselves of all the good things God would otherwise give us.

Verses 16-18 warm the heart. There are still some who encourage one another in the love of the Lord; and he knows and honours them.

4 The Day of the Lord

The day is coming when God will even things out once and for all. For some (the wicked) the fierce brilliance of that day will burn like fire. But those who honour God will rejoice in its healing rays.

Verses 4-5 serve as postscript, not just to Malachi but to the Old Testament as a whole. They look back to the laws given at Sinai (Horeb), and these must always be kept in mind. They look forward to a new age, to the reconciling work of Christ and the end of all things. With Malachi the voice of Old Testament prophecy falls silent. Four hundred years later, God sent one last prophet, John the Baptist (the promised 'Elijah'), to herald the coming Messiah (Matthew 17:10-13).

Sun (2): Malachi draws his picture (but not his theology) from the winged disk which represented the sun-god in Persian and Egyptian art.

THE APOCRYPHA

David Clines

To most people the word 'apocrypha' means, quite simply, a work of fiction. An apocryphal story about a historic personage is a fabricated, and often a far-fetched, tale. However, that is not the meaning of the term when applied to the ancient writings which we know as the 'Apocrypha' of the Old Testament.

The word means in Greek 'the hidden', that is, 'the hidden books', and its use for these writings goes back to the great biblical scholar Jerome (died AD 420). He held that these books, which were to be found in Greek and Latin Bibles but not in the contemporary Hebrew Bible, should not be regarded as equally authoritative with the canonical books, though they might be read in church for edification. In using the term 'apocryphal', he was probably alluding to a distinction made in 2 Esdras 4:14ff., one of the apocryphal books, between the 24 canonical books of the Old Testament (39 by our reckoning), and others containing esoteric knowledge and mysteries suitable only for the wise and therefore to be 'hidden' from the general public.

The church's attitude

Jerome's view was a minority one, though a number of scholars both before his time and since have made the same distinction between the books of the Hebrew canon and the apocryphal books. However, from the 1st century AD the churches used some at least of the apocryphal books as if they were Scripture, and continued to do so until the Reformation.

Luther, in his Bible of 1534, extracted the apocryphal books from their accustomed places among the biblical books, and grouped them together at the end of the Old Testament under the heading:
'Apocrypha: these are books which are not held equal to the Sacred Scriptures and yet are useful and good for reading.'

The Anglican statement was very similar: Article VI of the Thirty-Nine Articles, after listing the canonical books of the Old Testament, says:
'And the other Books (as Hierome [Jerome] saith) the Church doth read for example of life and instruction of manners; but yet doth it not apply them to establish any doctrine.'

This statement in the Westminster Confession of Faith (AD 1647) is typical of the lower status given to the Apocrypha in the Reformed churches:
'The Books commonly called Apocrypha, not being of divine inspiration, are not part of the canon of Scripture; and are therefore of no authority in the Church of God, nor to be any otherwise approved, or made use of, than other human writings.'

The Roman Catholic Church, on the other hand, partly as a reaction against the Reformers' affirmations, and partly to perpetuate what had long been customary in the church, declared at the Council of Trent (AD 1546) that the Old Testament contained 45 books, i.e., in addition to the 39 books universally recognized, most of those known as the Apocrypha. Catholics refer to the disputed books as the 'deutero-canonical' books, and reserve the term 'Apocrypha' for the books Protestants call the 'Pseudepigrapha' – works of similar character and date to the Apocrypha which were never considered canonical.

The books of the Apocrypha

The Apocrypha, which is about a quarter the length of the Old Testament, contains 15 books:
First Esdras (otherwise **Third Esdras)**
Second Esdras (otherwise **Fourth Esdras)**
Tobit (Tobias)
Judith
The rest of the **Book of Esther**
The Wisdom of Solomon (The Book of Wisdom)
Ecclesiasticus (The Wisdom of Jesus the Son of Sirach)
Baruch the Prophet
The Letter of Jeremiah

The Song of the Three (Holy) Children
The Story of Susanna (Daniel and Susanna)
Of Bel and the Dragon (New English Bible, Daniel, Bel, and the Snake)
The Prayer of Manasseh (Manasses)
The First Book of Maccabees
The Second Book of Maccabees

The Letter of Jeremiah is missing from the list in the Thirty-Nine Articles since it is there counted as the sixth chapter of Baruch. Catholic Bibles do not contain First or Second Esdras or the Prayer of Manasseh; the additions to Esther are included in Esther and the Letter of Jeremiah in Baruch; and the Song of the Three Children, Susanna, and Bel and the Dragon form part of Daniel.

The books of the Apocrypha form a very varied collection of Jewish literature from the period between about 300 BC and AD 100. The majority of the books were written in Hebrew, but in many cases the original Hebrew has disappeared since the Jews themselves eventually refused to recognize these writings as inspired. Most of the books have survived only through their use in Greek and other versions by the early Christian church.

Historical books

1 Esdras (the Greek form of the name Ezra) is largely identical with our canonical Ezra, though it begins its story with the events of 2 Chronicles 35 (Josiah's Passover celebrations) and ends with the story of Ezra's reading of the law (Nehemiah 8). Its major addition to the biblical account is the 'debate of the three young men' (1 Esdras 3-4) which purports to explain how Zerubbabel gained permission from the Persian king to rebuild the temple.

1 Maccabees is a much more valuable book, since it is our chief source for the history of the Maccabean revolt against foreign and Jewish purveyors of Greek culture. Apart from his obvious desire to eulogize the family of the Maccabees, the author has no axe to grind, and provides us with an essentially reliable as well as graphic history of the years between 175 and 134 BC.

2 Maccabees covers much the same ground as 1 Maccabees, but is less reliable. It is written from a distinctly Pharisaic point of view, and tends to lay greater weight upon moralizing and doctrinal observations than upon historical accuracy.

'Religious fiction'

Tobit is a charming tale of domestic piety. It was so popular among early Christians that it was translated from Hebrew into Greek, Latin, Armenian, Syriac and Ethiopic. The story tells how Tobias, a righteous but afflicted Jew, is healed of his blindness and his son Tobit is saved from an unpleasant death. It has many folk-tale motifs, and is plainly not a historical work.

Judith contains the tale of an altogether more daunting heroine, who used her charm to lure the invading Assyrian general Holofernes to his death by decapitation. This rather horrific story not without its lighter moments contains some gross historical blunders, but these would not have detracted from its purpose of stiffening the resolve of Jewish freedom fighters in Maccabean times.

The additions to **Esther** are popular

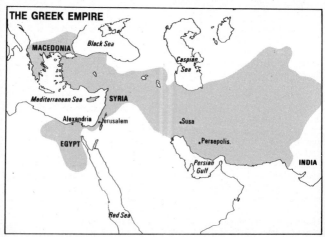

THE GREEK EMPIRE

MACEDONIA
Black Sea
Caspian Sea
Mediterranean Sea
SYRIA
Alexandria
Jerusalem
Susa
EGYPT
Persepolis
Persian Gulf
INDIA
Red Sea

expansions of the biblical story, partly designed to introduce some religion into that apparently secular book, which does not even mention the name of God.

The additions to **Daniel** are partly legends about Daniel the sage and Godfearer (**Susanna, Bel and the Dragon**), and partly liturgical texts: **The Song of the Three Children** contains a historical prayer attributed to Daniel's companion Azariah, and a doxology (the *Benedicite* of Christian worship) attributed to the three in the fiery furnace.

'Wisdom'

'Wisdom' literature is represented in the Apocrypha principally by Ecclesiasticus and the Wisdom of Solomon. **Ecclesiasticus,** composed by Joshua (or Jesus) ben Sira (Sirach) about 180 BC, offers advice on practical and godly living in the spirit of the Proverbs. Chapter 44 contains the memorable lines beginning, 'Let us now praise famous men.' A great favourite in the early Christian centuries (James 1:19, for example, probably alludes to Ecclesiasticus

5:11), the book, earlier known as the Wisdom of Jesus ben Sira, became entitled the 'church-book' (Ecclesiasticus).

The Wisdom of Solomon, a 1st-century BC composition, more indebted to Greek ethics and rhetoric than any other Jewish wisdom book, pays homage in its title to the traditional founder of wisdom literature without seriously claiming to be written by Solomon.

Baruch, likewise ascribed in honorific manner to an Old Testament notable, contains a prayer of confession, a poem in praise of wisdom, and songs of comfort. Its appendage, the **Letter of Jeremiah,** is an attack on idolatry cast in the form of a letter to the exiles (compare Jeremiah 29); and the **Prayer of Manasseh** is a free composition based on 2 Chronicles 33:13, 19.

Apocalyptic

Only one example of this fourth category is included in the Apocrypha: **2 Esdras.** Written probably in the 1st century AD, 2 Esdras comprises some Christian chapters 'predicting'

Alexander the Great riding to the rescue of a subject king. A detail from his tomb at Sidon.

the rejection of the Jews in favour of the church, and a Jewish book of visions of the future ascribed to Ezra.

The Apocrypha today

What is the Christian today to make of the Apocrypha? The theological problem of its authority remains. Here we must acknowledge the fact that Christians have never been in complete agreement over the precise limits of the Old Testament, though they are at one in affirming its authority and inspiration. There is some evidence that the Bible which Jesus and the apostles held as authoritative was the Hebrew Bible of 39 books, which did not include the apocryphal books. Even those who regard the Apocrypha as Scripture would admit that its authority is secondary to, and derived from (or dependent on), that of the 39 books.

But even though the Christian may not give the Apocrypha the same standing as the books of the Hebrew Old Testament, he will find within it passages of deep piety and thoughtful spirituality.

In *Grace Abounding*, John Bunyan recounts how, searching for the verse, 'Look at the generations of old, and see, did ever any trust in God and were confounded', he was at first daunted to find it came from the Apocrypha (Ecclesiasticus 2:10). But he came to realize that 'as this sentence was the sum and substance of many of the promises, it was my duty to take the comfort of it, and I bless God for that word, for it was of God to me'. The person who reads the Apocrypha devotionally will know how to handle it, for he will discriminate, as he does when he reads any religious literature, between what conforms and what does not conform to the essentials of his faith.

Part Three
NEW TESTAMENT

Tyre

△ Mt Hermon

PHOENICIA

• Caesarea Philippi

GALILEE   ITURAEA

Ptolemais   TRACHONITIS
3

Chorazin •
Capernaum
Gennesaret • • Bethsaida
Magdala   Lake Galilee
Sepphoris • 2 • Tiberias
Nazareth • • Cana
△ Mt Tabor   • Gadara
Nain •

DECAPOLIS

Caesarea

Scythopolis •

Aenon
(near Salim)
• Gerasa

Sebaste
(Samaria) •
• Sychar
△ Mt Gerizim

Joppa •
• Antipatris

• Arimathea
SAMARIA   PEREA
2
• Lydda   1

Jericho •
• Bethany
beyond
Bethphage • Jerusalem   Jordan
• Azotus   Bethlehem • • Bethany

Judean
wilderness

JUDEA   Dead
Sea   • Machaerus

• Gaza

Masada •

NABATAEA

IDUMAEA

1 Judea: Roman province
2 Galilee and Perea:
kingdom of Herod Antipas
3 Tetrarchy of Philip

0   10   20   30   40 Km
0   5   10   15   20   25 M

NEW TESTAMENT HISTORY AT A GLANCE

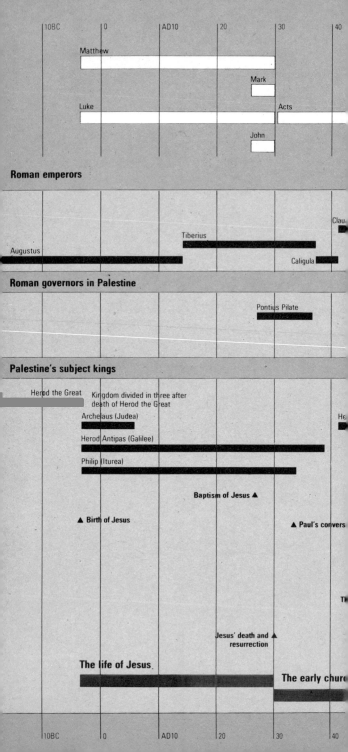

10BC	0	AD10	20	30	40

Matthew

Mark

Luke

Acts

John

Roman emperors

Augustus

Tiberius

Caligula

Clau

Roman governors in Palestine

Pontius Pilate

Palestine's subject kings

Herod the Great — Kingdom divided in three after death of Herod the Great

Archelaus (Judea)

Herod Antipas (Galilee)

Philip (Iturea)

He

▲ Baptism of Jesus

▲ Birth of Jesus

▲ Paul's convers

The life of Jesus

Jesus' death and ▲ resurrection

The early churc

Th

| 50 | 60 | 70 | 80 | 90 | 100 |

'General' letters James, 1, 2 Peter, 1, 2, 3 John, Jude

Hebrews

Revelation

Paul's letters

Nero

Vespasian

Galba

Otho

Titus

Vitellius

Domitian

Festus

Felix

ippa I

Herod Agrippa II

First missionary journey

Paul at Rome

▲ **Council at Jerusalem**

Persecution of the church under Domitian

Second missionary journey

▲ **?Death of Paul**

Paul in prison at Caesarea

ssionary journey

▲ **Fall of Jerusalem**

?Death ▲ of John

| 50 | 60 | 70 | 80 | 90 | 100 |

THE GOSPELS AND ACTS

The Gospels and Jesus Christ/Howard Marshall

Virtually all we know about the earthly life of Jesus is to be found in the four Gospels contained in the New Testament. The life of a travelling preacher in an obscure corner of the Roman Empire was not likely to find its way into the writings of Roman historians, who had (as they thought) more important things to occupy their attention. Tacitus refers very briefly to Jesus, and then only by way of explanation of the name of the 'Christians' who were put to death by Nero.

Even Jewish historians offer us little more. The standard history of the Jews was written by Josephus towards the end of the 1st century, and he does refer to Jesus at one point in his narrative as a miracle-worker who was the Messiah; he was put to death by Pilate but later reappeared to his disciples. The passage may have been tampered with by later Christian scribes (for would Josephus have called Jesus the Messiah?), but is probably genuine in essentials.

Other Jewish traditions about Jesus have been preserved in the writings of the rabbis. They tell us that he practised magic, beguiled the people, and said that he had not come to destroy the law or add to it. He was hanged on the eve of Passover for heresy and misleading the people, and had five disciples who healed the sick. This gives some idea of how Jesus would have been regarded by people who shared the outlook of the Sanhedrin, the Jewish council that condemned him to death.

More recent discoveries do not alter the picture. The Dead Sea Scrolls, the library of a Jewish sect living just before and during the time of Jesus, shed light on the thought-world of ancient Palestine, but they make not the slightest reference to Jesus. What is recorded of the members of the sect and their enemies in no way affects the historicity of Jesus.

A more promising source of information lies in various 'gospels' which were not included in the New Testament. Such works have long been known, but in recent years interest has been rekindled by the discovery of the 'Gospel of Thomas' at Nag-Hammadi in Egypt. This work contains a set of sayings ascribed to Jesus. They have obviously been worked over by radical Christians, but it is possible that here and there in this and other similar documents fragments of genuine tradition about Jesus may be preserved. However, the fact that the early church excluded them all from the canon of Scripture is some indication that the hunt is not likely to be very successful.

This means that for all practical purposes our knowledge of Jesus must come from the New Testament alone. Within the New Testament itself the field narrows down to the Gospels. The letters of Paul and the other apostolic writers make very little reference to the life of Jesus as such – though this is not because they did not attach great importance to his ministry as a historical fact, or were not strongly influenced by what he had taught.

The Gospel records

It is, then, to the Gospels that we must turn for the written record of the life and teaching of Jesus. The Gospels were not composed until at least 30 years after the death of Jesus. During this period the material for them was preserved and handed down both by word of mouth and by written records that no longer survive.

The tradition would have been handed down carefully. The Jewish rabbis were extremely careful to hand down oral material accurately, and we may presume that the Christians did the same. The Gospel material was originally taught in Aramaic, the language spoken by Jesus, and in a poetic form which was easy to memorize.

People remember what they want to remember. This does not mean that Jesus' hearers conveniently forgot what they found disturbing and unpalatable. On the contrary, there is much in the Gospels that must have been challenging and difficult, and yet it has been faithfully preserved. The story of Jesus was remembered and retold because it was relevant to the life of the church. For example, the first Christians had to argue with the Jews, so it was essential to remember how Jesus had debated with them. Faced with decisions on ethical issues such as marriage and divorce, they needed his teaching as their authority on such matters. So it is good, when we read a passage in the Gospels, to ask what significance it had for the early church. The story of Jesus was not preserved out of an academic interest in history for its own sake, but because of its practical relevance for the first Christians. It was not 'pure' but 'applied' history.

People also tend to remember and pass on stories and teaching in a certain pattern. Stories of healing miracles, for example, describe in turn the condition of the sufferer, the way in which the cure was effected, and the results it produced. Many stories about Jesus describe a situation in which he was placed, or a question which was put to him, and culminate in the essential point; an authoritative saying of Jesus on the topic at issue.

The article on 'The Gospels and Modern Criticism', shows how these factors have been used to try to explain the actual composition of the Gospels. The clearest example is John's Gospel. For the author has to some extent interpreted the story of Jesus to show its significance for his readers. He has offered a kind of commentary on the ministry of Jesus in which it is hard to distinguish between the original 'text' and its 'interpretation'.

The important point, however, is that there really is a 'text' which he is explaining for us; he is not commenting on something that never existed. Behind the Gospel stands the figure of John the apostle, just as apostolic testimony is the basis of the other Gospels. It is also being increasingly recognized by scholars that it is one and the same Jesus who is described in all four Gospels. Whereas the critics of a former era argued that the Gospel of John had little or no basis in history, it is now seen that all four Gospels build on historical tradition, each preserving different aspects of it.

The purpose of the Gospel writers John's Gospel raises the question of the relation of the Gospels to history. Did what is described in the Gospels really happen? We have already indicated that the Gospels rest on reliable tradition, handed down with care in the church. At the same time we must bear in mind that the Gospels are concerned to present the Christian significance of Jesus. Their basic purpose is to preach the gospel in order to convert the unbeliever and to build up the believer in his faith.

This means that they are not simply historical reports, as for example the biography of some famous soldier might be. The writers were not biographers, giving a detailed historical account of Jesus' life with everything in proper chronological order. We have only to compare the order of events in Mark 4 - 5 with Matthew 13; 8; 9 to see this fact plainly. Or again, the Gospels record very little of some aspects of Jesus' life: scarcely anything is mentioned before he reached the age of 30; and even the account of his ministry is incomplete. There is by no means enough incident to fill the whole time it lasted. We have no right to blame the Gospel writers for not doing something they never intended.

But this does not mean they were unconcerned about history. The Gospels are not invention. In the preface to his Gospel (Luke 1:1-4), Luke lays particular stress on the fact that he was making use of authentic eyewitness testimony. History certainly mattered for him, and there is no reason to think that the other writers thought differently.

What, then, were they trying to do? They were preaching the gospel, the good news. They were presenting Jesus as the Christ, the Son of God (Mark 1:1). They wrote in order that their readers might believe in him and so have eternal life (John 20:31). They therefore portrayed Jesus as his followers saw him. To them he was no ordinary man, not even a unique prophet. He was the Lord whom God had raised from the dead and who was now alive and active in heaven. They knew no other Jesus than this. They might have thought differently about him before the resurrection (see Luke 24:19-24), and even the resurrection did not compel everybody who heard about it to believe. But they had come to believe in Jesus as a result of the total impact which he had made upon them, and so they could not present him in any other way.

So the history in the Gospels is history as seen by Christians. A non-Christian would see it differently; he would claim, for instance, that the resurrection could not have happened. It might be interesting to have an account of Jesus written from that point of view, but none has come down to us. What we have are the Gospels, written by Christian believers, written to persuade men to believe, but none the less historical for that.

Four portraits of Jesus

Each of the Gospel writers presents Jesus to us in his own characteristic way. The greatness of this person could not have been captured in one picture. So we have four portraits, each bringing out its own distinctive facets of the character of Jesus.

Matthew concentrates on the relationship of Jesus to the Jewish faith. He shows how Jesus came to fulfil the Old Testament, but at the same time to judge the Jews for their unfaithfulness to their religion. No other Gospel denounces so forcibly the hypocritical outlook of the Pharisees. The Jews are called to see Jesus as the promised Messiah, the Son of David; and judgement is pronounced upon them for their failure to respond to him. Matthew portrays Jesus very much as a teacher. He has given us systematic accounts of Jesus' teaching for the church's inner life and evangelistic mission.

Mark emphasizes action rather than teaching. He stresses how Jesus taught his disciples that the Son of man must suffer and be rejected, and that they must be prepared to tread the same path. Those who tried to understand Jesus other than as a crucified Saviour would misunderstand him. The Jews expected a Messiah who would be a political leader and a figure of glory. They found it hard to recognize Jesus as the Messiah because he chose the path of humble service and suffering. Only at his second coming would he appear as the King in his glory.

The Gospel of Luke stresses the blessings of salvation brought by Jesus. It emphasizes the signs of the coming of the Messiah, prophesied in the Old Testament, and seen in Jesus' healing of the sick and preaching of the gospel to the poor and needy. Luke especially brings out the grace of God revealed in Jesus and

bestowed upon those who seemed least worthy of it, sinful women and rapacious tax-collectors; for this is precisely what grace means, that men and women can do nothing to deserve it.

Finally, the Gospel of John reveals Jesus as the One sent by God the Father into the world to be its Saviour. As the Son, he has his Father's authority, living in close communion with him. John goes deepest into the things God has revealed and brings out the eternal significance of the 'God-become-man'.

An outline of the life of Jesus

Behind these four accounts stands a figure who is recognizably the same in all of them. Jesus was the son of the virgin Mary, born at Bethlehem shortly before the death of Herod the Great (4 BC). He spent his early life in Nazareth where he worked as the village carpenter. When John the Baptist began to preach beside the River Jordan (about AD 27), Jesus came and was baptized by him. He immediately received the gift of the Spirit, commissioning him for his work. In the strength of the Spirit he withstood Satan's inducements to divert him from his calling. He then commenced a ministry of preaching and healing, mainly in Galilee. This was preceded by a period in Judea (John 1 - 3) and included visits to Jerusalem. It concluded with a journey to Jerusalem which culminated in his arrest and death at Passover time (about AD 30).

Jesus' message was concerned with the good news of the rule (or kingdom) of God. In the Old Testament the prophets looked forward to a future era when God would act in power and set up his rule over Israel. This hope was associated with the coming of a king (or Messiah; Greek, 'Christ') who would belong to the kingly line of David. In the time of Jesus, the people had come to expect a warrior-king to deliver them from their Roman over-lords.

Jesus taught that this hoped-for era was already dawning. He looked forward to the future consummation of God's rule, with himself as King. But the coming of God's rule was to be seen not in military victories but in Jesus' mighty works of healing and his preaching of salvation. God was already acting in the ministry of Jesus.

This good news demanded a

response from men. Jesus called them to repent of their sin; he offered forgiveness to the penitent; and he summoned men to become his disciples. To accept the good news of the rule of God meant accepting Jesus as Master. Out of the many who responded, Jesus appointed twelve men to be the leaders of the new people of God who were to replace the old Israel which rejected the message of God, and to be associated with his missionary work.

Jesus taught his disciples a new way of life. It is summed up in the Sermon on the Mount (Matthew 5 - 7). Jesus took over the Old Testament commandments to love God and one's neighbour and filled them with new life and vigour.

Jesus taught with such self-confident authority that men asked who he thought he was. Some people dismissed him as mad. Others were prepared to see him as Messiah, but when he showed no inclination to lead them to war against Rome they turned away from him. This was probably why Jesus did not claim the title of Messiah openly. He preferred to speak of himself cryptically as the 'Son of man', a phrase which he took from Daniel 7:13 and filled with new content. For him it meant a figure who would one day be invested with power and glory by God (Mark 14:62), but who was for the time being humble and unknown (Matthew 8:20) and destined for suffering and death (Mark 8:31).

After his disciples had realized who he was, he began to teach them that he must die, although they were slow to take it in. Jesus saw himself fulfilling the role of the Servant of the Lord who suffers humiliation and death (Isaiah 52:13 - 53:12). He laid down his life as a ransom for men to save them from death (Mark 10:45; John 10:11). Only to his closest disciples did he reveal that he was the Son of God in a unique, intimate manner. And he shared with them his privilege of addressing God in prayer by the name of 'Abba', 'Father' (Matthew 6:9; 11:25-27; Mark 14:36).

Throughout his ministry Jesus was involved in conflict with the religious authorities, mainly because of his scorching criticisms of their man-made traditions which diverted men from the real purposes of God's law. He attacked the hypocrisy which substituted tradition for the law of Moses. His messianic claims spurred the Jewish leaders on to arrest him. They feared he might be the centre of a popular uprising against Rome which would lead to grim reprisals and the loss of their own positions (John 11:47-53). So when Jesus came to Jerusalem and flung down the gauntlet by his attitude to the temple, they took steps to arrest him with the connivance of one of his followers.

Meanwhile Jesus held a last meal with his disciples. He filled a familiar table ritual with new content by using the bread and wine as symbols: his body was about to be broken in death on their behalf, and his blood about to be shed sacrificially, to ratify God's new covenant with men and to bring in his kingdom. After the meal, he went out to pray – and to meet his enemies. He was put through a trial which appears to have broken the appropriate legal rules. When the witnesses failed to produce sufficient evidence to condemn him, he was forced to make what his judges regarded as the blasphemous statement (to Christians it was the simple truth) that he was the Messiah. He was condemned to death. The Jews handed him over to the Roman governor as a political rebel against Rome, and although the governor was privately convinced of his innocence he allowed him to be put to death by the Roman punishment of crucifixion.

From the third day after his death, however, many of his disciples claimed that his tomb was empty and that he had himself appeared to them. God had raised him from the dead. The appearances took place over a period of 40 days, at the end of which time Jesus gave his final command to his disciples to be his witnesses throughout the world, and ascended from their presence as a symbol of his return to be with God and as a promise of his second coming to them at the end of the world.

That is the gospel story in brief. There is no other Jesus. The attempts of sceptical scholars to peel off the Christian interpretation and leave behind an ordinary, human person as the real 'historical' Jesus have proved fruitless.

It leaves with us the picture of a person about whom men must make up their minds. Throughout the Gospels Jesus appears as more than a man. His message, his deeds, and his person force the reader to decision.

MATTHEW

Each of the four Gospels has its own special emphasis. Matthew, writing for his fellow Jews, concentrates on Jesus as the long-awaited Messiah – the Christ predicted in the Old Testament (see article 'The Religious Background of the New Testament'). Many Jews were expecting a political leader who would free them from Roman domination. So Matthew is careful to record what Jesus said about his kingdom – the kingdom of heaven. He gives us a great deal of Jesus' teaching, which he collects together into five main sections. These alternate with sections of narrative in the Gospel, and include the famous 'Sermon on the Mount'. Matthew's Gospel, more than any other, is the link between the Old Testament and the New, the old Israel and the new world-wide church of God's people.

The writer. The Gospel does not name its author, but from earliest times it has been attributed to Matthew, the apostle and one-time tax collector. Little is known of him. And beyond the fact that it belongs to the period between AD 50 and AD 100 no one knows for certain when or where the Gospel was written. Much of Matthew's material is almost identical with Mark's – and Mark's source of information was Peter. Scholars today mostly believe that Matthew drew on Mark – not vice-versa; see article 'The Gospels and Modern Criticism'.

STORIES AND EVENTS FOUND ONLY IN MATTHEW

Parables
The tares
Hidden treasure
The pearl
The drag-net
The hard-hearted servant
The workers in the vineyard
The two sons
The marriage of the king's son
The ten 'bridesmaids'
The talents

Miracles
The two blind men
The dumb man who was possessed
The coin in the fish's mouth

Incidents
Joseph's dream
The visit of the wise men
The escape to Egypt
Herod's massacre
Pilate's wife's dream
The death of Judas (also in Acts)
The 'saints' resurrected in Jerusalem
The bribing of the guard
The great commission

Some of Jesus' **teaching** is found only in Matthew, including his wonderful invitation to 'Come unto me'.

1 - 2 JESUS, THE MESSIAH, IS BORN

1:1-17 Christ's family line
See also Luke 3:23-38. The two lists are in reverse order and give a different set of names from David onwards (only Zerubbabel and Shealtiel appear in both). Matthew is showing Jesus as Messiah, descended from the royal line of David. He may be listing the heirs to the throne, while Luke lists Joseph's particular line. Matthew's list is stylized and abbreviated to fit his pattern: 14 names from Abraham to David; 14 from David to

Jechoniah; 14 from Jechoniah to Jesus. This pattern of '14s' may have been suggested by the fact that the Hebrew letters in the name 'David' add up to that number. (The letters of the alphabet also served as numbers.)

Son of David (1): King David was promised an unfailing succession. But Israel ceased to be a monarchy at the time of the exile. And the promise came to be understood as referring to the Messiah.

Verses 3-6: it was unusual to list women. And if God's love and pur-

Modern Bethlehem, the small hill-town where Jesus was born.

poses had been limited to decent people of a particular race none of these would have been included. *Tamar* had children by her father-in-law, Judah (Genesis 38); *Rahab* was a Jericho prostitute (Joshua 2); *Ruth* a foreign Moabite woman (Ruth 1 - 4); and *Uriah's wife* was Bathsheba, with whom David committed adultery (2 Samuel 11).

Verse 11: 'father', like 'son' (verse 1), can be used in a wider sense. Josiah was Jechoniah's grandfather.

1:18-25 Mary and Joseph
Luke's fuller account of the birth focusses on Mary; Matthew's on Joseph. It takes little imagination to appreciate the very human dilemma. But Mary's pregnancy had a supernatural beginning. Matthew recalls Isaiah's words, giving them a significance the prophet could not have dreamt of. 'Jesus' means 'the saviour'; 'Emmanuel', God with us, in the world of men. (See also article 'The Virgin Birth'.)

Betrothed (18): betrothal, unlike modern engagement, was legally binding and could be broken only by divorce.

Verse 25: the implication is that after the birth Mary and Joseph lived a normal married life (see also 13:55-56).

2 The arrival of the wise men; the massacre; escape to Egypt
The wisdom of these men lay in the stars and their meanings. They were astrologers. And they had no doubt what the new star meant – the birth of the promised king in Judah. Tradition, not the Gospels, says there were three kings and that the presents they gave the baby had special significance – gold for a king; incense for God; myrrh for mortal man.

The news was not so welcome at the palace. Herod was king of the Jews (this is Herod the Great, who reigned 40-4 BC). He wanted no rivals. The massacre is in keeping with other cruelties mentioned in the historical records. The little family escape to Egypt, as Jacob's family had done long before when famine struck.

Verse 6: Matthew part-quotes, part-interprets Micah's words.

The house (11): some time has passed; the cave where the animals were stabled was only temporary shelter.

Rachel (18): mother-figure of Israel; Jacob's much-loved wife who died in child-birth at Ramah on the way to Bethlehem.

Archelaus (22): inherited one third of Herod's kingdom, but his repressive measures soon led the Romans to depose him and take control of Judea.

3 - 4 JESUS' BAPTISM AND TEMPTATION
3 The preaching of John the Baptist; Jesus' baptism
See also Mark 1:2-11; Luke 3:2-22. Luke 1 tells the story of John's birth. John's compelling preaching – calling men to make ready for the Messiah – draws the crowds out to the desert to hear him. Peter's brother, Andrew, was one of those baptized by John, following genuine repentance for past

wrong-doing. The 'washing' of baptism symbolized a radical cleaning up of a man's life – wiping the slate clean of all previous wrong – in preparation for the coming rule of God. This was not necessary in Jesus' case. He was baptized, not in order to be forgiven, but to identify himself completely with men. When he stepped into the Jordan, it was as if he was asking to take on the responsibility for human sin. He was accepting his destiny with all that that involved. God's words (17), combining Psalm 2:7 and Isaiah 42:1, proclaim Jesus as his Son, the Messiah, and the Servant who would suffer for his people.

Verse 4: see note under Mark 1:1-8.
Pharisees and Sadducees (7): see article 'The Religious Background of the New Testament'.

4 The temptation; the call of the first disciples; Jesus begins to teach

See also Mark 1:12-13; Luke 4:1-13. In the temptations that follow his 40-day fast, Jesus faces up to all he will have to go through in his ministry. He now has power – power to feed the hungry, heal the sick, raise the dead. How will he use it? To satisfy his own needs? To try God out? To compel a following? When it comes to it, will he use his power to save himself, or will he trust himself entirely to God and tread the path to the cross? Jesus replies to Satan's test questions in words from Deuteronomy (8:3; 6:16; 6:13) – key passages from Israel's 40 years in the desert, when God tested their obedience to him (Deuteronomy 8:2).

After John's arrest, Jesus travels north, making the lakeside town of Capernaum his base. Here he calls his first disciples and begins his public ministry.

Decapolis (25): ten free Greek cities south-east of Galilee.

5 - 7 THE SERMON ON THE MOUNT: STANDARDS OF DISCIPLESHIP

See also Luke 6:20-49. The 'sermon' is the first and longest of the five sections in which Matthew gathers together the Lord's teaching. Jesus shows his followers how man ought to live – not simply according to a set of rules but by an inner revolution of attitude and outlook. The glorious thing is that having set a seemingly impossible standard, he went on to give men the power to live up to it.

5:1-16 Where true happiness lies
Jesus turns ordinary human ideas about happiness upside down. Contrary to general opinion, it is not the go-getters, the tough ones, those who bend the rules, who are the real successes. The truly happy ones are those who recognize the spiritual poverty (verse 3) of self-reliance and learn to depend wholly on God.

Many of Jesus' healings and much of his teaching took place in the area around Lake Galilee. The view here is the north-eastern corner of the lake, from Tiberias.

Everything else follows from this. The people who can be certain of a future are the humble, the forgiving, the pure, those who set their hearts on what is right, who try to heal the rifts. And here and now, these are the ones who put the seasoning into life, who stop the rot, who light up the way. By what they do and say and how they react, they show men something of what God himself is like.

5:17-48 The old law and the new

Nothing can ever supersede or do away with the law God gave through Moses. But the law is a minimum standard. It can only deal with actions, not with the thoughts that give rise to them. Jesus takes five examples to show what the principles expressed in the law involve at the personal level. Sin begins in the mind and will. That is where it must be rooted out. The standards of the new society – God's kingdom – are way above the standards of the law-courts.

The five case-studies: murder (21-26; Exodus 20:13); adultery (27-32; Exodus 20:14); oaths (33-37; Numbers 30:2 – and see Matthew 23:16-22); retaliation (38-42; Exodus 21:24); loving others (43-48; Leviticus 19:18; see also Luke 10:29-37).

The law and the prophets (17): i.e. all the Old Testament precepts. There were three divisions in the Jewish Bible – the Law (Genesis to Deuteronomy); the Prophets (Former: Joshua, Judges, Samuel, Kings; and Latter: all the prophets except Daniel); and the Writings (the rest of our Old Testament).

Verse 22: the progression is difficult to understand, unless 'fool' should be 'apostate' – meaning that any man who calls another an outcast of God is in danger of being cast out himself.

Verse 23: a sacrifice offered by an individual was of no value if he had not put right an offence committed against a fellow man.

Verses 31-32: in Moses' day a wife could be dismissed at whim. His law gave her some security. Jesus goes back to the fundamental meaning and purpose of marriage. The bond made when the two become 'one flesh' is indissoluble. Divorce is unthinkable, except where one of the partners has broken the bond already. See 19:3-9.

6:1-18 Warnings against a mere parade of religion

Motives, thoughts, intentions, what goes on deep inside, are what matter in religion, too. God gives no prizes for an outward show of piety. So Jesus tells us to give and pray and fast without drawing attention to ourselves – and God will reward us. Our prayer is to be simple, trusting. We are to come as children to our Father, eager to please, conscious of our failings. (Luke 11:2-4 also records the Lord's Prayer.)

6:19-34 Singlemindedness

Men can choose what to set their hearts on. They can go all out for money and material things, or for God and spiritual things. But not for both. Everyone must decide his own priorities. Those who put God first can rest assured he knows all their needs and will not fail to supply them. They can be free from worry. **Verses 22-23:** the eyes were thought of as windows, letting light into the body.

7 Instructions and warnings

Do not be harshly critical (1-5); do be discriminating (6). Never give up praying (7-11). Always treat others as you would like them to treat you (12). Make sure you are on the right road to eternal life (13-14), there are plenty of people out to mislead (15-20). And many more are self-deceived (21-23). Words are not enough, the only safe course is to act on what we hear Christ say (24-27).

At the end of the teaching, it is the note of authority that most impresses the listeners. They have heard no one before like this man.

8 - 9:34 HEALING AND TEACHING

8:1-17 Miracles of healing

Verses 1-4: the leper. To the Jew lepers were unclean, untouchable. Jesus could have healed the man with a look, or a word – instead he reached out and touched him. (For the leprosy regulations, see Leviticus 13-14: the term 'leprosy' in the Bible covers a number of skin diseases.)

Verses 5-13: the centurion's boy. Jesus' mission is to Israel, but nowhere among his own people has he found faith to equal that of the Roman officer who recognized authority when he saw it.

Verses 14-17: Jesus cures physical, spiritual and psychological ills at Capernaum.

8:18-27 Storm and calm

Son of man (20): a phrase Jesus often uses to describe himself. It emphasizes his humanity (Psalm 8:4), yet points beyond it (Daniel 7:13-14).

Verses 21-22: the disciple wants to wait till after his father's funeral before joining Jesus. This need not mean that his father is dead. 'I must first bury my father' is a colloquial way of saying, 'I will follow you sometime – when my father is dead and I am free to go'. Jesus' reply stresses the urgency of his work. It calls for a response now, not sometime in the future.

Verses 23-27: see also Mark 4:36-41, with some differences of detail.

8:28 - 9:8 Further healings

Verses 28-34: two men possessed by demons. In their accounts, Mark and Luke focus on just one of the men, 'Legion' (Mark 5:1-17; Luke 8:26-37). Here Matthew tells how Jesus restored both men to sanity. But the residents of Gadara – a town six miles from the lake – would rather turn Jesus away than run the risk of losing more pigs.

9:1-8: the man with paralysis. Jesus uses the physical healing as proof that the spiritual cure, the man's forgiveness, is equally real.

His own city (9:1): Capernaum – see 4:13.

9:9-17 Matthew's call; questions about fasting

In Mark (2:13-17) and Luke (5:27-32) the tax collector is called Levi, and they make it clear that the feast is held at his house. 'Matthew' may have been Levi's 'Christian' name, as 'Peter' was Simon's. Jesus' presence in such company scandalizes the religious Pharisees. John's followers are also puzzled. Why does Jesus feast whereas John fasted? Luke (5:36-37) gives Jesus' answer most clearly. His radically new teaching cannot be squeezed into the mould of the old legalism. It must find new forms of expression – or else the old will be destroyed and the new spoilt. Luke 5:39 is a perceptive comment on human nature – the conservatism which mistrusts anything new.

9:18-34 More healings

Verses 18-26: Jairus' daughter; the woman with a haemorrhage (see on Mark 5: 21-43; Luke 8:40-56).

Verses 27-31: two blind men. The reason for secrecy (30) is not explained. Presumably Jesus is anxious to avoid his miracles giving people the wrong ideas about his mission.

Verses 32-34: the dumb man who was possessed.

Flute players (23): musicians were often hired to play dirges at a house where someone had died.

9:35 - 10:42 JESUS' CHARGE TO THE TWELVE

The second teaching section. See also Mark 6:7-13; Luke 9:1-6, and other parallel passages. The choice and training of the Twelve was a vital part of Jesus' mission. The task of spreading the good news about eternal life would rest with them after his death. Now he sends them out for the first time, with power to heal. He gives them their instructions (some only temporary – see Luke 22:35-36) and warns them of the kind of reception they are likely to get, both now and in the future. They are to expect hardship; trust in God's care; and fear no one.

The tax collector (10:3): it seems Matthew could never forget he was once a social outcast.

Verse 23: Jesus said that even he did not know when his second coming would be. The reference here may be to his triumphant return from death at the resurrection.

Beelzebul (25): see 12:22-24.

The housetop (27): a favourite place for gossip and discussion.

Verse 28: only God, not Satan, has this power.

Verses 34-35: the division is a *result* of Jesus' teaching. The Bible often expresses consequences as if they were deliberate intention.

Verse 39: 'he who finds' – i.e. the man who denies his faith to save his skin.

11 - 12 THE CLAIMS OF JESUS

This is one of Matthew's narrative sections – but it contains a good deal of teaching.

11:1-19 Messengers from John the Baptist

John – imprisoned by Antipas, younger son of Herod the Great, and ruler of Galilee and Perea – is puzzled by reports of Jesus. He expected the Messiah to come in judgement. Jesus' reply reminds him of the other aspect of Messiah's work (predicted in Isaiah 35:5-6; 61:1), which he is fulfilling. John is the last and greatest of the Old Testament prophets – the latter-day Elijah predicted by Malachi (4:5). Jesus thinks no less of him for his doubts. But the humblest Christian enjoys far greater privileges (11).

Verse 12: it is difficult in retrospect to see exactly what Jesus meant. He

may be referring to Zealot militants, from whom he disassociated himself; or to the fact that the kingdom opens its gates to those who are desperate, not just drifters (see Luke 16:16).
Verses 16-17: like sulky children, Jesus' contemporaries refuse to 'play weddings' with him, or to 'play funerals' with John. They will listen neither to good news – nor to warnings.

11:20-30 'Come to me'
Most of Jesus' miracles took place in the small area at the north of the sea of Galilee – around Capernaum, Chorazin and Bethsaida. They evoked so little response from the people that God's judgement on their stubborn disbelief was inevitable. Tyre and Sidon – the prosperous, godless sea-ports denounced by the prophets (see Isaiah 23) – even Sodom, that byword for evil (Genesis 19), could not have seen what they had seen and remained unmoved.

It was the ordinary folk who received Jesus – and he was glad. To all who are worn down by burdens he offers relief. Those who enter his service will find him no crushing task-master.

12:1-14 The Lord of the sabbath
See on Mark 2:23 - 3:6.
12:15-37 Hope of the nations? Or devil's emissary?
The Pharisees see Jesus as the devil's agent (24), despite the transparent goodness of his work (22-23). If they were right, Satan would be set on a suicide course (25-29) – as are all who, like the Pharisees, call good evil. They are stubbornly denying the Holy Spirit's work, and making their own forgiveness impossible (31-32).
12:38-50 'Give us a sign'
After all Jesus' miracles of healing, the lawyers and Pharisees have the effrontery to demand a spectacular sign. Only one such sign will be given – Jesus' resurrection from the dead – the incontrovertible proof that he is who he claims to be.

Verses 43-45: the story is a warning to those who have repented as a result of what they have seen and heard. Unless they take the further step of whole-hearted commitment, they are in grave danger.
Verse 40: by Jewish reckoning any part of the 24 hours which make up day and night could count as the whole. So Friday afternoon to Sun-

THE KINGDOM OF GOD AND THE KINGDOM OF HEAVEN
David Field

The two expressions 'kingdom of God' and 'kingdom of heaven' represent exactly the same idea. To a devout Jew the word 'God' was far too sacred to be used lightly or frequently. Matthew, writing primarily for Jewish readers, therefore normally speaks about the 'kingdom of heaven', whereas Mark and Luke prefer the alternative 'kingdom of God', as an easier expression for non-Jews to understand.

It is surprising to find that neither expression is used at all in the Old Testament. And even in the New Testament the phrases seldom occur after the first three Gospels. This highlights the important part the theme of the kingdom played in the teaching of Jesus himself. We are told that it was right at the heart of his gospel message (Mark

1:15), and when the disciples were sent out on their first missions it was the message of 'the kingdom' that they were to proclaim (Luke 9:2; 10:9-11).

The meaning of 'kingdom'
Jesus never defined exactly what he meant by the kingdom of God. But in answering the charge of rebellion before Pontius Pilate he was careful to disown all claims to temporal, territorial dominion. 'My kingdom', he said, 'is not of this world' (John 18:36). Some modern versions translate 'kingdom' in this verse as 'kingship' or 'kingly authority'. The kingdom of God, in the Bible, normally means God's active reign in the world. Sometimes Jesus could talk about 'entering' the kingdom (e.g. Mark 10:23), much as we might speak of enter-

ing a country, but the idea behind the word he used is far more often that of 'rule' than of 'realm'. Perhaps the Lord's Prayer comes closest to an exact definition when it equates the coming of God's kingdom with the doing of his will. Where God's will is done with perfect submission, there, according to the New Testament, is his kingdom revealed.

Although the Old Testament authors did not write about the 'kingdom of God' as such, they eagerly anticipated the great Day when he would display his glory (Isaiah 24:23) in such a dramatic way that all men would acknowledge his rule (Zechariah 14:9). This keen sense of anticipation, both a cosmic hope and a longing for the liberation of the land, persisted well into Jesus' time. (Joseph of Arimathaea, Mark tells us, was one man who was 'looking for the kingdom of God'.) So when John the Baptist announced 'the kingdom of heaven is at hand' (Matthew 3:2), he was immediately surrounded by crowds of excited people who had come to witness the long-expected display of God's ruling power in history.

God's kingdom – present and future

Jesus' first preaching was apparently couched in very similar terms to John's, but according to Mark he prefaced his announcement of the kingdom's imminence with the words 'The time is fulfilled' (Mark 1:15). This declaration of fulfilment strikes a note which sounds right through the Gospels, that in Jesus the kingdom of God has become a living reality. His miracles, and especially his exorcisms, testify to the fact that God's sovereign rule is breaking in upon man (Matthew 12:28). His preaching, with its unique note of authority, is evidence of the kingdom's arrival (Mark 1:27; Matthew 11:5). Because 'the kingdom of God is in the midst of you', he tells his disciples (Luke 17:21), the kingdom's blessings – forgiveness, salvation and eternal life – are theirs to enjoy, not only for the future but in the present. For centuries the prophets had forecast a time when God's kingly power would be displayed on earth; now, in the person and ministry of Jesus, that time had come.

If Jesus taught that the kingdom had actually arrived in his own person, it is equally clear that he looked to the future for a final demonstration of God's ruling power. His disciples must *pray* 'Thy kingdom come' and watch alertly to see 'the kingdom of God come with power' (Mark 9:1; Matthew 25:1). The miracles they saw him perform – and performed themselves, in his strength – were a mighty token of the kingdom's presence, but the battle with Satan still raged and the result, though not in doubt, awaited the final show-down (Matthew 25:41). Forecasts of a great future consummation intertwine, therefore, with clear evidence of the kingdom's present arrival, and it is obvious from the 'parables of the kingdom' in Matthew 13 that Jesus intended his disciples to grasp both truths. The seed is sown and grows before the climax of harvest is reached.

The demands of the kingdom

Whether present or future, God's kingly rule demands man's obedient submission. Men are not called upon to build or establish the kingdom for themselves, but only to seek for it and enter it (Matthew 6:33; Mark 9:47). Its ethical standards are exacting – far above those of the scribes and Pharisees (Matthew 5:20) – and they call not only for theoretical knowledge but for practical expression (Mark 12:34). In short, entry into the kingdom requires the unquestioning obedience of a child (Mark 10:15) and makes absolute demands on the disciple's loyalty and devotion. Yet submission to God's rule is in man's very best interests, because his kingdom, like hidden treasure or a pearl of great price, is the one thing of supreme value in life, for which any sacrifice is worth while (Matthew 13:44-46).

day morning is spoken of as three days and nights.

Verse 42: the Queen of Sheba (1 Kings 10:1-10).

Verse 49: presumably younger children of Mary and Joseph (see on 1:25). It is usually thought that Joseph was dead by this time.

13:1-52 PARABLES ABOUT GOD'S KINGDOM

The third teaching section. Jesus made many of his points by means of parables – stories that could be taken at two levels, the superficial or the more perceptive. They were a means of sorting out his followers; discovering who had come just because of the miracles, and who really wanted to understand his teaching. The former were happy to listen to stories; the latter were prepared to look for the deeper meaning and ask him to explain. There was so much misunderstanding – even among the disciples – about the nature of his kingdom that he needed to straighten them out one point at a time.

Verses 1-9: the seed and the soils (explained in 18-23) pictures the varied response his message will bring.

Verses 24-30: the wheat and the weeds (explained in 36-43) is concerned with the mixture of good and bad in this life, to be sorted out at the judgement.

Verses 31-33: the mustard-seed, and the yeast. From small beginnings, quietly and unnoticed, the kingdom will make great growth.

Verses 44-45: the treasure, and the pearl. So valuable is the kingdom, it is worth giving all we have to make sure of it.

Verses 47-50: the fisherman's net. This describes the sorting out of good and bad at the end of time.

Verse 52: New English Bible, 'When, therefore, a teacher of the law has become a learner in the kingdom of Heaven ...'

13:53 - 14:12 NAZARETH REJECTS JESUS; THE DEATH OF JOHN THE BAPTIST

See on Mark 6:1-6 and 14-29.

14:13 - 17:27 TEACHING AND MIRACLES IN GALILEE AND THE NORTH

14:13-36 5,000 people fed; Jesus walks on the water

See on Mark 6:30-56. See also Luke 9:10b-17; John 6:1-21.

15:1-20 The Pharisees and the question of tradition

See also Mark 7:1-23. From the first, Jesus' teaching on religion (6:1-18) brought him into conflict with the Pharisees. For them 'tradition' (the oral teaching of the rabbis which supplemented and interpreted Scripture) was binding. But Jesus never hesitated to denounce tradition wherever it watered down or undermined scriptural principles. Their ruling on vows is a case in point. Exemption from his duty to maintain his parents was allowed a man if he dedicated the money to God. That way he could still enjoy the proceeds himself. It is not clean hands (2) but a clean heart (18) that matters.

15:21-39 The Canaanite woman; further healings; 4,000 fed

Tyre and Sidon (21) lay outside Jewish territory. Jesus could not refuse a request made with such tenacious faith.

Verses 29-39: the differences of detail between this passage and 14:13-21, and the fact that Mark also records both miracles, make it unlikely that this is a second account of the same event, despite the basic similarity.

The dogs (26): an abusive term for Gentiles. Jesus is testing the woman out, leading her to faith.

Magadan (39): the location is not known.

16:1-12 Jesus warns against the teaching of the Pharisees and Sadducees

See also Mark 8:11-21. The Pharisees had demanded a sign once before (12:38ff.). Now the Sadducees, the rationalists, join them. Jesus' answer is still the same.

16:13-28 Peter's great declaration: Jesus predicts his death

Simon speaks for all the apostles in asserting his belief that Jesus is the Messiah. And Jesus sees in him the man of rock (Peter) he will become after the shattering experience of denial and forgiveness (26:69-75). It is Peter the natural spokesman who will be responsible, more than any other, for the formation of the church at Pentecost (Acts 2 - 5).

Verses 21-28: Jesus begins to prepare his disciples for the suffering that lies ahead. But the recent promise has gone to Peter's head. The rock becomes an obstacle. God's spokesman turns devil's advocate.

Verse 19: the authority given to Peter is given equally to the others (see 18:18). The idea of the keys echoes Isaiah 22: 22. God is not bound by whatever Peter may say. But anything done by the disciple in accordance with Christ's will is to have permanent validity.

Verse 28: see on 10:23.

17 The transfiguration and what follows

See on Mark 9:2-32; Luke 9:28-45.

Verses 24-27: as Son of God, the one on whose behalf the tax is levied, Jesus is exempt. But as Man, identified with men, he pays it.

18 LIFE IN GOD'S COMMUNITY

This is Matthew's fourth teaching section. God's kingdom operates by totally different standards from the world's. Status-seeking is out (1-4). So is the policy of 'the weakest to the wall'. On the contrary, the spiritually weak are the special responsibility of the strong (5-14). In the new community wrongdoing matters; every effort must be made to set the defaulter right (15-20). Unlimited forgiveness is expected from those whom God has forgiven (21-35).

Verses 8-9: see on Mark 9:44-45.

Verses 24, 28: 'millions' and 'a few pounds' (New English Bible): the point being the immeasurable extent of our 'debt' to God, compared to anything we may have to forgive our fellow men.

Those who led 'little ones' astray, Jesus said, were fit only to have a millstone tied round their necks and be cast into the sea. These millstones are in the Agricultural Museum, Jerusalem.

19 - 20 THE JOURNEY TO JERUSALEM

19:1-15 Marriage and divorce

See also 5:31-32; Mark 10:2-12; Luke 16:18. The rabbis disagreed about divorce. Some allowed it for anything that displeased the husband; others only for unfaithfulness. Jesus goes back to God's purpose for man and woman at the very beginning. That is the ideal. Moses, dealing with a situation that fell short of the ideal, placed a restriction on divorce. Jesus says that unfaithfulness is the only legitimate reason for it.

Verses 10-12: see New English Bible or Good News Bible.

19:16 - 20:16 Eternal life; the disadvantage of wealth; rewards

9:16-30: see also Mark 10:17-31; Luke 18:18-30. Jesus' first answer is the one any Jewish teacher would have given. And the man – a ruler in the synagogue – could claim he had kept the commandments. But Jesus pinpoints the root of this man's trouble. His commandment-keeping is not wholehearted. His possessions mean too much to him. Because of them he is failing to love God and his neighbour without reserve. So Jesus tells him to sell up. It is better to possess nothing than to love things more than God.

20:1-16: this story, illustrating Jesus' words in 19:30, comes only in Matthew. He is not talking about pay structures, or saying that all will be equal in heaven. The point is that many who expect to be made much of will be in for a rude shock in God's kingdom. God will honour some very unexpected people. Eternal life is for all who will receive it: 'good' and 'bad', young and old. The remarkable thing is the landowner's (God's) generosity – not his unfairness.

19:24: there have been various 'explanations' of the 'Needle's Eye'. But it seems that Jesus is being deliberately humorous in suggesting the impossible – a camel going through the eye of a literal needle.

19:25: they were surprised because they thought riches were a reward for goodness – an index of a person's spiritual state.

19:28: the apostles have a special place in the new kingdom. Only Matthew records these words.

19:29: those who follow Christ will be repaid many times over, here and now – but 'with persecutions' (see Mark).

20:2: New English Bible gives the meaning, 'the usual day's wage'. The denarius was a Roman silver coin.

20:3-6: the times are 9 a.m. (the third hour), 12 noon, 3 p.m. and 5 p.m. – an hour before sunset, which was when the men were paid for the day's work.

20:17-34 Jesus again predicts his death; status in God's kingdom; two blind men healed

See also Mark 10:32-52; Luke 18:31-43. Jesus' patience is amazing. Over and over again he explains that the kingdom is for the humble. There is to be no lording it. Yet even when he speaks of his death the disciples are taken up with their own status. The place at the top is reserved for the disciple who – like his master – is prepared to live for others and if need be to die for them.

Sons of Zebedee (20): i.e. James and John.

The cup (22): i.e. the cup of suffering. James was the first of the loyal apostles to meet a violent death (Acts 12:2).

Verses 29-34: Mark and Luke mention only one blind man – perhaps because Peter knew one of them personally (Bartimaeus – see Mark).

21 - 25 JESUS IN JERUSALEM

It was spring, and people from far and near were crowding into Jerusalem for Passover, the great feast commemorating the nation's liberation from Egypt. Not all could find lodgings in the city itself. Jesus and his friends stayed at nearby Bethany, where Martha, Mary and Lazarus had their home. Each day they walked the two miles into Jerusalem, over the shoulder of the Mount of Olives and down through the thick groves of trees.

21:1-11 His triumphant arrival
See on Luke 19:28-44. See also Mark 11:1-10. Characteristically, Matthew quotes the prophecy from Zechariah 9:9.

21:12-17 The purging of the temple
See also on John 2:13-25. The dealers operated in the outer court of the temple, the Court of the Gentiles. Jews from abroad were not allowed to use their own currency to pay the annual temple dues. And the money-changers fixed a high rate of exchange. (The annual revenue from the temple tax is estimated at £75,000: the moneychangers' annual profit at £9,000.) Poor people, who could only afford the cheapest sacrifice (two pigeons), were charged extortionate prices. The priests turned a blind eye to all this. Yet their indignation knows no bounds at the 'irreverence' of Jesus. He actually healed people in the temple courts and let the children chant the earlier tributes of the crowds!

21:18-22 The fig-tree
See also Mark 11:12-14, 20-24. A healthy fig-tree bears fruit for ten months of the year. Since the tree was in leaf, there should have been green figs. Mark makes it clear that it was the following day when the disciples found the tree withered. Jesus uses the incident as an object lesson: faith can move insurmountable obstacles. It also indicates the fate of the spiritually barren nation of Israel.

21:23-46 The priests question Jesus' authority
The question is natural, in the light of

Jerusalem in New Testament times

Hinnom Valley

Pool of Siloam

Herod's palace

Kidron Valley

Herod's temple

Fort of Antonia

Pool of Bethesda

Gethsemane

what has happened (12-17). Jesus makes no direct answer, but it is clear that he and John derive their authority from the same source. In the three parables that follow his critics find themselves under fire.

Verses 28-32: the two sons. The first represents the religious leaders, with their mock obedience; the second the social outcasts, who have made a genuine response to John and to Jesus.

Verses 33-41: the vineyard (the nation of Israel whose owner is God – Isaiah 5:1-7). The men to whom God has entrusted spiritual leadership have abused the prophets and are about to kill his Son.

Verses 42-43: see Psalm 118:22-23. Jesus transfers the picture from Israel to himself – cast aside, crucified, by the nation, but reinstated by God.

22:1-14 The parable of the wedding-guests

Jesus illustrates what he has just said (21:43). The day will come when God no longer invites those who repeatedly refuse him. The invitation will go to others. Verses 11-13 are a warning to the new-comers. Those who come must come on God's terms.

22:15-46 Test questions; the Pharisees plot against Jesus' life

See on Mark 12:13-44.

23 Jesus denounces the lawyers and Pharisees

Chapters 23 - 25 contain the fifth and last teaching section. The subject is judgement. Jesus launches into a scathing attack on Israel's legalistic, but much-respected religious leaders. The man who cared so deeply and had such patience with ordinary people – even the wicked, the weak-willed and the stupid – could not stomach the religious sham, the self-righteous pride, the hair-splitting pedantry of the Pharisees and scribes. Proud and selfish hearts still lurk beneath such 'proper' exteriors. How he must hate to see Pharisaic hypocrisy in his own followers.

Verse 2: in the synagogue they stood to read the law, but sat to expound it.

Verse 10: New English Bible 'teacher' gives the sense. The same Greek word is used today of a 'professor'.

Verse 15: New English Bible 'twice as fit for hell' gives the sense. New converts are often more fervent than those brought up in the faith.

Mint, dill, cummin (23): common garden herbs.

Verse 27: tombs were specially white-washed for Passover to prevent people inadvertently touching them and becoming ceremonially defiled.

Verse 35: this may be Zechariah son of Jehoiada, as there is no record of the prophet Zechariah being murdered. Genesis 4:8; 2 Chronicles 24:20-21.

Verses 38-39: Jesus may be predicting the destruction of the city. Verse 39 refers to his return in glory and judgement.

24 - 25 The fall of Jerusalem and Jesus' return in judgement

24:1-44: questions and answers. See also Mark 13; Luke 21 and 17:23ff. Jesus is answering questions about when the temple will be destroyed and what indications there will be that the age is coming to an end. Jerusalem and the temple were actually to be destroyed by the Romans in AD 70. The disciples seem to think of the end closely following. And Jesus does not clearly separate them – both are part of the total judgement of God (although more than 1900 years already separate the two events). The disciples are not to be misled – there will be many wars and natural disasters, persecutions and false Messiahs (4-13, 23-27). These are not signs of the end. There will be time for world-wide preaching of the gospel (14). And when the end does come, it will be totally unexpected (36-44). But there will be clear warning signs of the destruction of Jerusalem (15-22, 32-35)

24:45 - 25:46: parables of judgement. Jesus uses stories to drive home the points of the previous chapter.

24:45-51: the good and bad servants. Because his return will be unexpected, Jesus' followers must always be ready.

25:1-12: the wise and foolish girls. The same lesson, but stressing that one day time will run out, and preparedness is an individual thing. It cannot be borrowed from someone else.

25:14-30: the 'talents'. The talent was a large amount of money – not a coin. Each man is entrusted with a capital sum in line with his business ability, and he is expected to trade with it. Our future depends on how we use what we have been given in this life.

25:31-46: the sheep and the goats. At the judgement God takes account of how we have treated others in this life. In the parable, the 'goats' are punished for failing to do what they should have done.

Verse 15: Daniel 11:31. An alternative rendering, in line with Luke's paraphrase is 'so when you see the abominable sign spoken of by the prophet Daniel (let the reader understand)'. This could be a reference to the emperor's image on the ensign carried by the Roman soldiers.

Verse 21: over 1,000,000 people lost their lives in the fall of Jerusalem, and Herod's magnificent cream stone and gold temple was razed to the ground.

Verse 28: the picture seems to be of the 'eagles' of the Roman army converging on the 'corpse' of the city.

Verses 29-31: symbolic language used of Christ's return. In the light of verse 36, 'immediately' cannot be taken literally. Jesus is again telescoping the two 'comings in judgement'.

Verse 34: a reference to the destruction of the temple within the lifetime of his hearers. It took place about 40 years after Jesus' prediction.

Jesus' words about the destruction of Jerusalem were dramatically fulfilled in AD 70. The Romans destroyed the city and plundered the temple. The scene is pictured on the triumphal arch of Titus in Rome. The seven-branched candlestick was taken from the temple.

THE PASSOVER AND THE LAST SUPPER

The Passover meal followed a fairly standard pattern in every Jewish household. First comes the opening prayer – the blessing of the cup (the first of four cups of wine passed round during the ceremony). Then each person takes herbs and dips them in salt water (see Matthew 26:23). The head of the family takes one of the three flat cakes of unleavened bread, breaks it and puts some aside. Then, in response to a question from the youngest member of the family, the story of the first Passover is recounted and Psalms 113, 114 sung. The second cup (see Luke 22:17) is filled and passed round.

Before the meal itself, all wash their hands (probably the point at which Jesus washed the disciples' feet, John 13:4-12), grace is said and bread broken. Bitter herb dipped in sauce is distributed (this was when Jesus gave the sop to Judas, John 13:26). The climax of the ritual is the festive meal of roast lamb.

It was after this that Jesus instituted the Lord's Supper, breaking the bread laid aside earlier and passing round the third cup of wine, the 'cup of blessing'. (The words 'this is ...' (Matthew 26: 26, 28) must mean 'this represents ...' since he was himself there, giving the disciples the bread and wine.) The ritual concludes with the singing of the remaining 'Hallel' (or Hallelujah) psalms (115 - 118) and the 'Great Hallel', Psalm 136. These psalms are probably the 'hymn' Matthew mentions (26:30). Then the final cup of wine is drunk.

The setting of the Lord's Supper at the heart of the Passover meal explains its meaning. Jesus is thinking of himself as the Passover lamb, offered up for the deliverance of his people. The wine speaks of his death, and of the new covenant it ratifies, reconciling God and man. Until he comes again, we are to remember the significance of what he has done for us.

26 - 27 THE FINAL CLASH: JESUS' TRIAL AND CRUCIFIXION

26:1-5 Jesus forewarns his disciples; the Jewish leaders plot his death

26:6-13 A woman anoints Jesus
See on Mark 14:3-9.

26:14-29 Judas turns traitor; the Last Supper
See also Mark 14:12-25; Luke 22:7-38; John 13 - 14.

On the first evening of the festival, Jesus and his close friends meet as a family to eat the Passover meal together. At the exodus each Jewish household sacrificed a lamb or kid and daubed the blood over the door to ensure their safety as death struck the firstborn of every Egyptian family. Now the Lamb of God (John 1:29) is about to offer himself, to secure life for the whole world. The old Passover is transformed into the Lord's Supper. At the exodus, the nation of Israel was born. By Christ's sacrifice, the church is born, a people drawn from all the nations. The Passover looked back. The Lord's Supper is also a reminder for us today of a past event. It looks forward, too, to the joyous day when Christ will come and make his home with his people, in a new world which has no place for sin or death or pain.

26:30-56 The garden of Gethsemane; Jesus is arrested
See also Mark 14:26-52; Luke 22:39-53. It is Luke who depicts most vividly the agony of Christ's prayer in the garden. So intense was Jesus' last plea that – God willing – he might be spared the terrible suffering about to begin, that his sweat fell like great drops of blood. What was it he shrank from? Surely not simply physical suffering. We can never know just what he faced during that lonely hour. But the prospect which filled him with such horror was God's judgement on *our* sin – the penalty which would have been ours had Christ not paid it for us (1 Peter 2:24).

The moment passes, and as the mob comes out to arrest him he is once more utterly in command. He expresses only love for the traitor. When Peter draws his sword (John 18:10), Jesus heals the injured man (see Luke). No man can ever have been so completely in control of such a situation. He had come to fulfil the scriptures. He knew it must be so – even when everyone deserted him.

26:57-68 Trial before the high priest
See on Mark 14:53-65.

26:69-75 Peter denies all knowledge of Jesus
See on Luke 22:54-65.

27:1-26 Judas commits suicide; Jesus before Pilate
Only Matthew records Judas' remorse. He flings back the money – but a clear conscience is not so easily bought. (Acts 1:16-20 has a slightly different version of the story.) For the trial before Pilate, see on Luke 23:1-25.

27:27-56 Mockery and crucifixion
See on Mark 15:16-41.

27:57-66 Jesus' burial; a guard is set
See on Mark 15:42-47. Matthew is the only one to mention the guard; see also 28:11ff.

28 THE RESURRECTION

See on Luke 24 and 'The Accounts of the Resurrection'.

Verses 1-10: the women hear the news and see the Lord. Verses 11-15: the guards are bribed to lie. The penalty for falling asleep on duty was death. But perhaps Pilate could also be squared with a bribe. Verses 16-20: Jesus' last command. This most Jewish of all the Gospels closes with a word from the Lord that throws the kingdom open to men of every nation.

THE RELIGIOUS BACKGROUND OF THE NEW TESTAMENT

Richard France

Jesus was a Jew. The Christian church began its life in Palestine, and its first members were Jews. So the most important element in the religious background to the New Testament is the Jewish religion itself.

JEWISH RELIGION

The last of the Old Testament prophets lived 400 years or more before John the Baptist appeared. Since that time the Jewish religion had not stood still. The classical religion of the Old Testament had evolved (some might say, degenerated) into Judaism.

Some important institutions in Judaism

The temple. The simple temple built by the Jews who returned to Jerusalem after the exile had been replaced by a magnificent structure commissioned by Herod the Great (40-4 BC). It was begun in 19 BC; it was still not complete in the time of Jesus (John 2:20), and was not finished until AD 64 – six years before it was destroyed by the Romans! It was this imposing complex of buildings in huge cream-coloured stones, marble and gold, which evoked the admiration of Jesus' disciples (Mark 13:1). Here the age-old ritual of sacrifice and worship continued, with its elaborate establishment of priests and temple servants, though all under the watchful eye of the Roman garrison in the fortress of Antonia, which overlooked its courts (Acts 21:31ff.). Here too, in the Court of the Gentiles (beyond which no Gentile dare venture, on pain of death – Acts 21:28-29; Ephesians 2:14), was the thriving market in sacrificial animals and sacred money for the temple offerings which was the object of Jesus' anger. And here in the shaded porticos men would gather to listen to any teacher who cared to set up his stand.

The synagogue. There was only one temple, but each community had its synagogue. Here there was no sacrificial ritual. It was the local centre for worship and study of the law. On the sabbath day the community would meet, men and women seated apart, to listen to the reading and exposition of the set passages from the Law and the Prophets (Luke 4:16ff.), and to join in the set liturgical prayers. But the synagogue was more than a place of worship. It was the local school, the community centre, and the centre of local government. Its elders were the civil authorities of the community, the magistrates and guardians of public morals.

The law and the traditions. Israel had always had a law, since the days of Moses. But from the time of Ezra (5th century BC; following the exile in Babylon which the prophets saw as a direct result of the nation's disobedience to the law) greater emphasis had been placed on the study of the law, until the Jews had become 'the people of the book'. This intensive study had resulted in an increasing body of 'traditions', which came to be regarded as no less binding than the law itself. *Scribes*, professional students and exponents of the law and traditions, were needed to prescribe exact regulations for every occasion. There were, for example, 39 types of action prohibited on the sabbath: reaping and threshing were forbidden – this included plucking ears of corn and rubbing the grain out in the hands (Luke 6:1-2); a 'sabbath day's journey' (Acts 1:12; about two-thirds of a mile) was the maximum travel permitted. Sadly, in their meticulous care over details of tradition the scribes sometimes forgot the more fundamental concerns of the law itself (Mark 7:1-13; 3:4-5; Matthew 23:23).

Parties, sects, and movements in Judaism

The Pharisees. These were the religious purists – a party which grew from the 2nd century 'Hasidim' (God's loyal ones) and concentrated on control of religious, rather than political, affairs. Their supreme concern and delight was to keep the law (including, of course, the traditions) in every exact detail. (Most scribes belonged to the Pharisee party.) Judged by this standard, they were model Jews (Philippians 3:5-6). To this end, they kept themselves as far as possible apart from other men: they could not eat with a non-Pharisee in case the food had not been tithed (i.e. one tenth given to God).

Inevitably, perhaps, this policy of separation led to disdain for all lesser mortals, a 'holier-than-thou' attitude which has made their name a term of reproach today. This arrogance, combined with a dry legalism which put exact ritual observance before love and mercy, led them into conflict with Jesus. He did not dispute their orthodoxy, but the proud and unloving way in which they upheld it. The influence of the Pharisees was out of all proportion to their numbers, which were seldom large. It was the Pharisees who laid down the lines along which Judaism developed after the destruction of Jerusalem in AD 70. They ensured a continued emphasis on individual piety and strict ethical standards, as well as their better-known rigid legalism. They were respected, if not loved, by other Jews.

The Sadducees. The Sadducees were the other main party at the time of Jesus, though they were already declining in influence. They were drawn largely from the rich landowning class who in earlier days, by shrewd manipulation of political advantage, had secured a dominant position. They still controlled a roughly equal proportion of the seats in the Sanhedrin (the Jewish supreme council) with the Pharisees (Acts 23:6-10). Many of the chief priests were Sadducees, or worked closely with them. Their religious position was conservative, to the extent of refusing to accept any revelation beyond the Five Books of Moses (Genesis to Deuteronomy). They thus rejected more recent religious ideas, such as the belief in immortality, resurrection, angels and demons, which were fostered by the Pharisees (Mark 12:18; Acts 23:8). As an aristocratic minority, they enjoyed little popular support.

The Essenes. This rather shadowy 'party' has come dramatically to light with the discovery of the Dead Sea Scrolls since 1947. These scrolls are from the library of the *Qumran Community*, a monastic sect living in isolation in the barren desert near the shores of the Dead Sea. Although this sect cannot firmly be identified as Essenes, it was certainly very similar. The sect was founded by the otherwise unknown 'Teacher of Righteousness', probably about 165 BC, and survived until AD 68, when it was destroyed in the Jewish revolt. They regarded themselves as the true people of God, and all others, including the Jewish leaders at Jerusalem, as his enemies. They were the 'Sons of light', and they lived for the day when in the final battle against the 'Sons of Darkness' they would be given the victory and dominion which was their due.

Meanwhile they kept themselves to themselves, occupied in the diligent study of the scriptures, bound by a strict monastic discipline, loving one another and hating all those outside. They produced elaborate biblical commentaries, applying every phrase of the Old Testament passages to their own situation and expectations. They looked forward to the coming of two Messiahs, of Aaron (priestly) and of Israel (royal) – or possibly one Messiah combining both roles. The importance of the Qumran documents is not so much for the sect in itself, but that they give evidence of an ascetic, apocalyptic strain in Judaism, far removed from the Jerusalem establishment, which may well have been much more widespread than this single isolated group. If before 1947 we were tempted to think of Pharisees and Sadducees as constituting 'the Jews', we must now recognize that the situation was not so simple.

The Zealots. While Pharisees and Sadducees tried to make the best of Roman rule, and the men of Qumran dreamed of the mighty intervention of God to deliver them, many Jews sought salvation more actively. The Zealots, as they later came to be called, were the freedom fighters, the revolutionaries of the Jewish people. It was they who eventually sparked off the great rebellion which led to the Roman destruction of Jerusalem in AD 70. By the time of Jesus abortive revolts had already occurred (Acts 5:36-37; and possibly Barabbas), and the people were ripe for revolutionary propaganda. Intensely patriotic, the Zealots founded their appeal on the belief that subjection to Rome was treason to God, the true King of Israel. At least one of the apostles was a former Zealot.

The apocalyptic movement. In this atmosphere the type of literature known as the 'apocalypse' (revelation) flourished. Many apocalypses were written in Palestine from the 2nd century BC onwards. They are marked by a strong dualism: good and evil, God and Satan, light and darkness, are irreconcilably opposed and on a collision course. The present world-order is under the control of the forces of evil, but the final battle is about to be fought, and then the tables will be turned. God will crush all opposition, destroy all evil for ever, and create a new blessed order, in which his faithful people will be released from their oppression and reign in glory.

This message is conveyed in often extraordinary visions, with symbolic numbers, and a careful calculation of dates and times, usually in cryptic form. It is a message of hope for a people near despair, a triumphant appeal to the sovereignty of the one true God, the God of Israel. The New Testament book of Revelation is in many ways a typical apocalypse (though written from a Christian standpoint), except that its author uses his own name, whereas Jewish apocalyptists attributed their visions to such famous Old Testament figures as Enoch, Moses, Elijah, or Ezra. Another important difference is that Jewish apocalyptists wrote past history as if it were prophecy, whereas Revelation concentrates on the future.

Messianic hopes. The extravagant visions of the apocalypses were only one among the many hopes currently cherished by the Jews. Many messianic figures from the Old Testament had taken firm root in popular expectation: the prophet like Moses (Deuteronomy 18:15-19); the returning Elijah (Malachi 4:5-6); but above all the Son of David, a great king and warrior, whose mission it would be to bring victory, peace, and glory to Israel. Some saw a place for the Gentiles in this hope, others were exclusively nationalistic. Some thought of spiritual restoration, most of victory over the Romans. To utter the word 'Messiah' (Greek, 'Christ') would inevitably stir up hopes of political independence, so it is no wonder that Jesus was cautious in letting others call him 'Christ'. He came to a people who, if they were not agreed quite *what* they were hoping for, were united in eagerly 'looking for the consolation of Israel' (Luke 2:25). But none expected it to come by way of a cross.

'The Dispersion'. So far we have thought only of the Jews in Palestine. But the Christian church soon spread outside Palestine, and there, too, its first contacts were with Jews. At least since the exile in the 6th century BC Jews had begun to scatter around the world of the Middle East and the eastern Mediterranean, so that by the 1st century AD there were a million Jews in Egypt alone. In Alexandria Jews made up a considerable part of the population, and in most of the main cities a Jewish colony, with its own synagogue (or at least a place for prayer, Acts 16:13), was to be found. These are the Jews of the Dispersion (Greek, *Diaspora*), sometimes referred to, a little inaccurately, as the Hellenistic Jews.

'Hellenism', the wave of Greek culture and ideas which had rolled over the Mediterranean world and far beyond with the conquests of Alexander the Great, was still the dominant strand in the culture of the Roman Empire, and these dispersed Jews, away from the more conservative atmosphere of Palestine, adapted more readily to the Greek way of life. Not that they abandoned their distinctive religion and culture, and ceased to be Jews; but they were more willing to learn from and enter into dialogue with Greek ideas. Many of the later Jewish writings, particularly those from Alexandria (e.g. the Wisdom of Solomon, or the writings of Philo) are deeply influenced by Greek philosophy. Apollos, the learned Jew from Alexandria (Acts 18:24), no doubt belonged to this school, before his gradual conversion to Christ.

Proselytes. The Jews are often unjustly charged with a rigid exclusivism. In fact, particularly among the Dispersion, they recognized their mission to the Gentiles, and there was a sincere attempt to win converts. To accept the Jewish religion was no light matter for a Gentile. He must accept circumcision and baptism, and agree to keep the whole law of Moses, including such ritual prescriptions as the sabbath and the laws about unclean food. He must in fact renounce his own nationality. There were a considerable number who took this drastic step, and it is to them that the term 'proselyte' applies.

Many more were attracted by the monotheistic faith and the strict morality of Judaism in contrast with the decadent polytheism of Rome. They were prepared to identify themselves with the faith and ideals of the Jews, but stopped short of the proselyte's full commitment. These fellow-travellers, many of them rich and influential officials, are known in the New Testament as 'those who fear God' or 'the devout' (Acts 13:26, 43, 50; 17:4).

The Samaritans. The Samaritans were descendants of the surviving Israelites of the northern kingdom who intermarried with the newly imported alien population after the fall of Samaria in 722 BC. They never effectively made common cause with Judah, and in the time of Nehemiah the rift was clearly irreparable. The building of the Samaritan temple on Mt Gerizim, overlooking Shechem (John 4:20), set the seal on the Jewish rejection of this heretical sect. It was the Jewish king Hyrcanus who destroyed the Samaritan temple in 128 BC. Yet the Samaritans worshipped God, as the Jews did. Their authority was the Five Books of Moses (Genesis to Deuteronomy;

but not the rest of the Old Testament), hardly altered from the Jewish version. Like many of the Jews, they awaited the coming of a prophet like Moses. Jewish hatred and disdain for the Samaritans sprang more from historical and racial considerations than from any fundamental difference of religion.

GREEK AND ROMAN RELIGION

The old classical religion of the Greeks, with its pantheon of gods and goddesses who loved, quarrelled and fought like men and women, had become effectively fused with the similar polytheism of Rome. It was preserved and officially fostered as part of Greek and Roman culture. Most Greeks and Romans would still give a formal assent to the old beliefs, and take part in the rituals, but the heart had gone out of them.

Further east in the Empire these gods were associated with local deities, sometimes producing absurd results, such as the identification of the earthy fertility-goddess of Ephesus with the severely chaste Artemis of the Greeks (Roman Diana; Acts 19:24ff.). The Lycaonian worship of Zeus and Hermes (Roman Jupiter and Mercury; Acts 14:11ff.) was probably a similar dignifying of a local cult with the classical Greek names.

It was from the East that new religious ideas came. One such was the worship of the emperor. This was not officially encouraged by the Roman emperors until Domitian (AD 81-96) insisted on being addressed as 'Lord and God'. But it was freely practised in the East by their grateful (or flattering) subjects throughout the New Testament period. Even before the birth of Christ, Herod the Great had renamed the city of Samaria 'Sebaste', in honour of Augustus (Greek, *Sebastos*, 'The one to be worshipped'), and built in it a temple of Augustus.

Those who wanted a more personal and emotional faith gravitated to the mystery religions. The Greek mysteries – those of Eleusis, or the Orphic cult – had long been known in the West, but the spread of the Empire brought to light similar cults from Egypt (Isis and

Osiris/Serapis), Persia (Mithras), and elsewhere in the East. Although these religions differed in detail, they shared the element of personal commitment by initiation into what amounted to a secret society, whose rites were never divulged to an outsider. The rites often centred on a mythology of the death and resurrection of the god (Persephone, Orpheus, Osiris, and the rest), which was re-enacted in a drama in which all participated. They inspired a spirit of warm, personal devotion, far removed from the cold intellectualism of the official state religion.

Also from the East came the fascination of astrology (still very much with us today), divination, magic, demon-worship, and other occult practices, all trying to bring a reality and a practical efficacy into religion.

About the time the New Testament letters were being written there began to develop a number of sects which later (in the 2nd century) came under the general heading of 'Gnosticism'. They varied considerably in detail, but shared the basic belief that 'matter' was evil and spirit was good. It followed that God could not have created the world out of matter, nor could his Son have become incarnate in it. So they envisaged a whole range of subordinate beings between God and the world. Men share in the evil of the material world, but they also (or some of them) contain a divine spark which can be set free and thus redeemed. In order to be redeemed men need to have knowledge (Greek *gnosis*) of their heavenly origin. These views were expressed in fantastic myths and made known to initiates in sects like those of the mystery religions.

The world was, as Paul put it, '*very* religious' (Acts 17:22). Men wanted a faith worth following, not an empty mythology. It was a world searching for God, eagerly trying every avenue which might lead to a real, practical, satisfying religion.

HEROD'S TEMPLE

An artist's drawing, from a reconstruction at the Bible Museum, Amsterdam; style and decoration are guessed.

1 Porticos
2 Court of the Gentiles
3 'Wall of Partition' (no non-Jew might go beyond this point)
4 Beautiful Gate
5 Court of the women
6 Court of Israel
7 Court of the priests
8 Altar
9 Bronze laver
10 The Holy Place (and Holy of Holies)

MARK

Matthew is formal and stately. Mark is bustling with life; full of action. Matthew collects Jesus' sayings. Mark concentrates on the marvellous things Jesus did, and the places he went to.

This is the shortest of the Gospels, and probably the first to be written (AD 65-70 or even earlier). There is a strong early tradition that John Mark wrote it in Rome, setting down Jesus' story as he had heard it direct from the apostle Peter. This would certainly account for the Gospel's extraordinary vividness. And Mark often explains Jewish customs, so he obviously had non-Jewish readers in mind.

He tells the story roughly in the order things happened – moving swiftly through from Jesus' baptism to the critical events of the cross and resurrection. Within this framework the material tends to be grouped by subject. Only four paragraphs in these 16 chapters are unique to Mark. All the rest appears again in either Matthew or Luke, or both. Yet to lose Mark would be to lose something beyond price. In Mark we see Jesus in action. And as we watch, the things he does convince us that he is the Son of God himself.

The writer. The name 'John Mark' occurs often in Acts and the epistles ('John' the Jewish name, 'Mark' the Latin). His mother had a house in Jerusalem where the early church met (Acts 12:12). And he was cousin to Paul's companion, Barnabas. Mark blotted his copybook with Paul by going home half-way through the first missionary tour. But Barnabas gave him a second chance, and he later won the love and respect of Paul and of Peter. He was a real comfort to Paul in prison (Colossians 4). And Peter, whose companion he became, loved him as his own son (1 Peter 5:13).

1:1-13 THE GOOD NEWS OF JESUS

1:1-8 John the Baptist
See also Matthew 3:1-12; Luke 3:2-22, and map. Mark passes over Jesus' birth. For him the good news begins with John, the voice Isaiah had predicted, crying out from the desert, urging the nation to make ready for God's coming. The rest of his account will show that Jesus is the Messiah – the one whose coming John announced – and Son of God.

Verses 2-3: Mark, like Matthew, combines Old Testament references: Exodus 23:20; Malachi 3:1; Isaiah 40:3.

Verse 8: water is a symbol. It can only clean the outside. The Holy Spirit can clean heart and mind and will.

The prophet from the desert: the 'wilderness' or desert-country around Jericho and south of Jerusalem is rough and uninviting. Scarcely anything grows: it is empty of human habitation, occupied only by wild animals. No doubt the very loneliness of the place, and the freedom from distraction, made it the ideal training-ground for John. Paul, too, was prepared for his mission during a time in the desert. There seems to be something in the stark simplicity of desert life which puts men – some men at least – in close touch with God. In the harsh sunlight there is only black or white, no shades of grey. It afforded John no other luxuries – only the simplest of food and rough clothing. His camel-hair tunic and leather belt may have been worn in conscious imitation of Elijah (see 2 Kings 1:8 and the prophecy in Malachi 4:5). He was certainly recognized instantly as a prophet. He not only looked the part, he possessed the prophet's cast-iron assurance that he had a God-given message to proclaim. The people flocked from far and wide to hear him, probably gathering beside the Jordan near Jericho, close to the place where Joshua had crossed into the promised land so many centuries before.

1:9-13 Jesus' baptism and temptation
See on Matthew 3 - 4; Luke 3:21;4:1-13. Mark gives only a brief résumé.

1:14 - 9:50 JESUS IN GALILEE

Galilee. The Roman province, under Herod's jurisdiction, lay to the west of the Sea of Galilee. We tend to think of it as a remote country district. But in Christ's day the region was prosperous and densely populated, criss-crossed by Roman military roads and ancient trade routes – north, south, east and west. The fresh-water Sea of Galilee – 13 miles long, 7 miles wide, sunk in the deep trough of the Jordan rift valley over 600 feet below sea-level – is the focal point in Jesus' travels. It divided Herod's territory from that of his half-brother Philip, to the east. Most of the apostles came from the towns around the lake-shore which enjoyed a sub-tropical climate. Capernaum was Jesus' base. Tiberias, 10 miles away, was a spa town famous for its hot baths. Many of the sick people Jesus healed must have come to the area for the mineral waters at Tiberias. On the hill behind the town was Herod's splendid summer palace. The lake is ringed round with hills – brown and barren on the east; in those days green, fertile, wooded on the west. Over the tops, and funnelling down through them, races the wind that can whip the lake into a sudden fury of storm. North, the snow-capped summit of Mt Hermon dominates the skyline – the mount of the transfiguration. In Jesus' day palms, olives, figs and vines grew on the hillsides round the lake. And the little towns and villages on its western shore were thriving centres of industry – fish pickled for export; boat-building; dyeworks; potteries. John the Baptist lived an ascetic life in the desert. By contrast, Jesus chose to be in the thick of things, in Galilee, one of the busiest, most cosmopolitan regions of Palestine.

1:14-20 Jesus calls his first disciples

John's voice is silenced. Jesus travels north again, and begins his own public proclamation of God's good news. By the Sea of Galilee he calls his first disciples – all of them fishermen. (John 1:35-42 fills in the background.)

Peter and Andrew probably used a cast net rather like this one. They also fished from their boats, using drag nets.

1:21-45 Jesus begins to teach and heal

From now on Capernaum is Jesus' headquarters. His teaching in the synagogue and his handling of the possessed man both convey an extraordinary *authority*.

Again and again, as in the case of the leper here, Mark stresses Jesus' insistence on *secrecy*. The people were expecting the Messiah to be a political leader. News of Jesus' amazing powers, which marked him out as the Messiah, could easily have sparked off a rising against the Roman occupation. It was imperative the miracles should be accompanied by teaching to explain the kind of 'kingdom' Jesus had come to inaugurate, and the Messiah's real mission.

Verse 32: at sunset the sabbath was

At Capernaum the local Roman centurion contributed to the building of the synagogue. The ruins of the Capernaum synagogue shown here probably date from the next century, but they show a combination of Roman and Jewish symbols.

over, and restrictions on movement no longer applied.

Verse 44: see Leviticus 14:1-32. In the Bible, the term 'leprosy' covers a variety of skin diseases.

2:1-12 The paralytic walks

It is easy enough simply to tell a man his sins are forgiven. But by healing him Jesus visibly demonstrates his power in both physical and spiritual realms. When he says the word, something really happens.

Verse 4: the house would have an outside staircase leading to a flat roof, giving extra living-space. The roof would be made of tiles or lath and plaster – not difficult to break through.

Verse 11: ordinary people slept on the floor on a mat or bedding which could be rolled up in the daytime.

2:13-22 Levi (Matthew) becomes a disciple; the question of fasting

See on Matthew 9:9-17; Luke 5:27-39.

Scribes, Pharisees (16): see article 'The Religious Background of the New Testament'.

2:23 - 3:6 The purpose of the sabbath; opposition

See also Matthew 12:1-14; Luke 6:1-11. Jewish interpretation of the fourth commandment (Exodus 20:8-11; 34:21) had hedged it about with so many petty rules and restrictions that its primary purpose was lost. The day of rest was intended for man's physical and spiritual good, not to deny him food and help. It is a day for doing good – and not only in an emergency.

Verses 25-26: see 1 Samuel 21:1-6. The loaves David took were those the priests placed each week on the altar.

Herodians (6): supporters of Herod Antipas. They collaborated with the Romans, and were therefore normally abhorrent to the scrupulous Pharisees.

3:7-19 The Twelve

Crowds flock to Jesus from the south (Judea, Jerusalem, Idumaea); from the east across the Jordan; and from Tyre and Sidon, the coastal towns in the north-west.

Jesus chose an inner circle of 12 disciples who became founder-members of the new kingdom – the counterparts of Jacob's 12 sons, who gave their names to the tribes of Israel. Three – Peter, James and John – were specially close to him. Four of the Twelve, all from Galilee, were partners in a fishing business (Peter

and his brother Andrew; James and his brother John). One (Matthew/Levi, who may have been the brother of James son of Alphaeus) was a tax collector, serving the Romans. Simon, at the other end of the scale, belonged to an extremist guerilla group (the Zealots) working to overthrow the occupation. We know little of the others. The full list also appears in Matthew 10:2-4 and Luke 6:12-16. The 'Thaddaeus' of Matthew and Mark seems to be the same as 'Judas son of James' (Luke, Acts 1:13). Bartholomew is often identified with the Nathanael of John 1. They were certainly a very mixed bunch of men.

Verse 12: see on 1:21-45.

3:20-35 Suspicion and accusation

See on Matthew 12:15-37 and 49.

4:1-34 Jesus teaches in parables

See on Matthew 13:1-52.

Verses 1-25: the seed and the soils.

Verses 26-29: the wheat and the weeds.

Verses 30-32: the mustard-seed.

Verse 12: in Jewish idiom, result is often expressed as if it were intention. This verse refers to the *consequence* not the *purpose* of Christ's teaching. It is clear from verses 22-23 that the reason for wrapping up the meaning is to encourage the listener to search it out for himself.

4:35-41 Jesus calms the great storm

Sudden storms sometimes whip the Sea of Galilee into fury. Jesus has power to control the elements.

5:1-20 Across the lake; the man possessed by demons

See also Matthew 8:28-34; Luke 8:26-39. The man is a pitiful sight – a fragmented personality at the mercy of a hundred conflicting impulses; totally incapable of a normal life. Is any greater contrast imaginable than the description of 2-5 and verse 15? Jesus had power not only over nature but also over human nature; and not only over human nature but over the spiritual forces of evil.

Country of the Gerasenes (1): the general area south-east of the lake. At only one point on the eastern bank is there a steep slope (13).

Decapolis (20): ten free Greek cities – see map.

5:21-43 Jairus' daughter restored to life; the woman with the haemorrhage

See also Matthew 9:18-26; Luke 8:40-56.

The woman tries not to advertise her

presence, because the haemorrhage makes her polluted and untouchable to her fellow Jews. There is no magic about Jesus' clothes. He knows the difference between the casual contact of the crowd and someone reaching out in need. The incident must have encouraged Jairus. The fact that he came to Jesus shows that not all religious leaders were against him.
Verse 39: this was not just a coma – the child really was dead. Everyone knew it (40). Jesus' words describe death as God sees it – a sleep from which we wake to a new day.
6:1-13 In and around Nazareth; the Twelve sent out
Verses 1-6: in Jesus' home town it is not a case of 'local boy makes good' but 'who does this jumped-up carpenter think he is?' It was not in line with Jesus' purpose to make a display of his powers in order to convince sceptics (see Matthew 4:6-7).
Verses 7-13: see on Matthew 9:35 10:42.
Verse 3: see on Matthew 12:49. James later became the leader of the church in Jerusalem (Acts 15:13). Judas wrote the Epistle of Jude.
6:14-29 Herod and John the Baptist
Guilt and superstition make Herod think Jesus is John come to life again. Herod had divorced his own wife to marry Herodias, wife of his half-brother Philip. John had denounced this as incest (Leviticus

Five loaves and two small fish, given to Jesus, fed 5,000 people. These fish from Lake Galilee are known as St Peter's fish, as their large mouths, in which they carry their eggs, could hold a coin (see Matthew 17:27).

18:16; 20:21), and been imprisoned for his pains. According to Josephus his prison was the fortress of Machaerus in the far south, east of the Dead Sea. But Herodias wanted to still the preacher's tongue permanently.
6:30-44 5,000 miraculously fed
See also Matthew 14:13-21; Luke 9:10b-17; John 6:5-14. John's death casts a shadow. Jesus is desperately tired and hard-pressed. Yet instead of being annoyed or irritable with the pursuing crowds, his heart goes out to them.
Verse 37: needless to say they did not have this kind of money: the denarius was a working man's wage for the day – this would be over six months' wages.
6:45-56 Jesus walks on the lake
It was some time between 3 a.m. and 6 a.m. Again it is the disciples' need that calls out Jesus' love. And again he demonstrates his supreme power over creation: he is Lord of wind and water.
Fringe (56): the blue-tasselled border of his cloak.
7:1-23 The Pharisees and their traditions
See on Matthew 15:1-20. Mark adds an explanatory note for non-Jewish readers (3-4). The Pharisees were concerned not with hygiene but with religious 'cleanness'. Man's real problem is not dirty hands but a polluted heart, which no amount of washing can clean. Jesus exposes their wrong thinking.
7:24-37 The Greek woman's daughter; the deaf mute
Verses 24-30: see on Matthew 15:21-28.
Verses 31-37: the man's speech defect, as so often, was the result of his deafness. Saliva was popularly thought to have healing power.
8:1-21 4,000 fed; the demand for a sign; the 'yeast' of the Pharisees
Verses 1-9; see on Matthew 15:29-39. Dalmanutha is not known.
Verses 11-21: see on Matthew 16:1-12. The disciples lack spiritual discernment. They are so taken up with the bread-supply that they cannot see that Jesus is warning them against the ever-present danger of religious hypocrisy (see Luke 12:1) and materialism (the prime concern of the pro-Herod faction).
8:22-26 A blind man regains his sight
Jesus once again guards against publicity – see on 1:21-45.

8:27 - 9:1 'Who do men say I am?';
Jesus predicts his death
See on Matthew 16:13-28. Here and
elsewhere Mark records in full
incidents which show Peter's failings,
but plays down the credit side –
understandable if the information
came from Peter himself. This
episode is a pivotal point in the story.
From now on, Jesus stresses the
suffering which lies ahead.
Caesarea Philippi (27): 25 miles north
of the Sea of Galilee.
9:1: see on Matthew 10:23.

JESUS IN GALILEE AND THE NORTH

- Zarephath/Sarepta
- △ Mt Hermon
- Tyre
- Caesarea Philippi
- Chorazin
- Capernaum • Bethsaida
- Gennesaret
- Magdala • Sea of Galilee
- Tiberias
- Cana
- Nazareth • **GALILEE**
- Gadara
- Nain

9:2-13 The disciples see Jesus
transfigured
See also Matthew 17:1-13; Luke 9:28-
36. The apostles are sure now that
Jesus is the Messiah. This special
glimpse of his glory, given to the
inner three, must have been tremen-
dously reassuring through all that lay
ahead. Moses (Israel's great law-
giver) and Elijah (the first great
prophet) converse with Jesus about
his coming death (Luke 9:31).
Verse 2: the mountain is believed to
be 9,000 foot Mt Hermon as it is only
12 miles north-east of Caesarea Philippi. The tradition that it was Mt
Tabor does not fit the geography so

well. Peter wants to prolong the present moment. Perhaps Moses and Elijah will stay if they make shelters for
them, like the tent (tabernacle) where
God was present in the old days,
before the temple was built. The
glory of all he saw that day imprinted
itself indelibly on Peter's memory
(2 Peter 1:16-18).
Verse 13: 'Elijah', i.e. John the
Baptist (see Matthew 17:13). Malachi
(4:5) had predicted a reappearance of
Elijah to announce the day of God's
coming.
9:14-29 The epileptic boy
See also Matthew 17:14-19; Luke
9:37-42. The disciples fail because of
their lack of faith (see Matthew
17:19-20). Yet Jesus will accept even
a grain of faith in him (24). He does
not wait to heal the child until the
father's faith is greater.
9:30-50 Status and Christian
responsibility
See on Matthew 18. No one who is
preoccupied with selfish ambition can
become a 'great' Christian. It has to
be other people first, self last. Today
we lay great stress on self-fulfilment
and the full development of personality. Jesus puts this in perspective. It
is better deliberately to limit that fulfilment, to handicap ourselves in this
life (44-45) than miss God's kingdom
altogether.
Verses 43-48: Jesus draws his terrible
picture of hell from Jerusalem's permanently smouldering refuse-tip in
the valley of Hinnom (Gehenna), and
the dead bodies gradually eaten away
by worms.
Verse 49: 'Salted with fire' – i.e.
purified in the 'refinery' of suffering.

10 ON THE WAY TO JERUSALEM
10:1-12 Divorce
See on Matthew 19:1-15.
10:13-16 Jesus blesses the children
To enter God's kingdom we must all
become, not childish, but childlike –
receiving him with humble, loving
trust (15).
10:17-31 The positive disadvantage
of wealth
See on Matthew 19:16-30; Luke
18:18-30. This incident does not
imply that all Christ's followers must
become penniless. He is speaking to
one man, not to all, and in this case
the man's possessions kept him from
becoming a disciple. Anything that
takes first place – God's place – in
our lives must go. So Jesus tells him,
'Go, sell' *and* 'Come, follow me'.

10:32-45 Jesus again predicts his death; the disciples bicker over their future status
See on Matthew 20:17-34.
10:46-52 Blind Bartimaeus
See also Matthew 20:29-34 (where there are two men); Luke 18:35-43. Only Mark tells us the beggar's name. As he afterwards joined the company of Jesus' followers, Peter presumably came to know him.

11 - 13 JESUS IN JERUSALEM

11:1-11 The triumphant entry
See introduction to Matthew 21; and see on Luke 19:28-44.
11:12-26 The fig-tree; the purging of the temple
See on Matthew 21:18-22 and 12-17.
11:27 - 12:12 The religious leaders question Jesus' authority; the parable of the vineyard
See on Matthew 21:23-46.
12:13-44 Test question; Jesus in the temple
See also Matthew 22:15-46; Luke 20:19 - 21:4. Luke 20:19-20 gives the background to these questions.

Verses 13-17: there was little love lost between the strictly religious Pharisees and the opportunist Herodians. But they join forces to try to trap Jesus into a treasonable statement.

Verses 18-27: the materialist Sadducees try to ridicule the idea of resurrection with an absurd case of Levirate marriage (see Ruth). But the laugh is on them, because there *is* a resurrection – to a life where there is no sexual union or procreation because there is no death.

Verses 28-34: the third question is a genuine one. With 613 commandments to choose from, Jesus replies in the words of Israel's creed (the Shema; Deuteronomy 6:4-5) and Leviticus 19:18. If the Pharisees hoped for an unorthodox reply (Matthew 22:34-35) they were disappointed. The astonishing wisdom of Jesus silences his opponents – but *he* has not finished with *them* (35-40).

In strong contrast to the self-advertisement of the men of religion comes the little incident in verses 41-44. What counts with God is not the size of the cheque, but the amount of love and self-sacrifice it represents.
13 Judgement on Jerusalem: Jesus speaks about his return
See on Matthew 24. See also Luke 21 and 17:22ff.

14 - 16 JESUS' DEATH AND RESURRECTION

14:1-11 The plot against his life; the costly flask of perfume; betrayal
See also Matthew 26:6-13; John 12:1-8. Jesus' public ministry is at an end. As the Passover festival approaches (see on Matthew 26) events move swiftly to a climax. Against a dark backcloth of hatred and treachery shines the story of one woman's love for the Lord (3-9). Perhaps intuitively sensing the tragedy ahead, Mary (see John 12:3) pours out the precious perfumed oil in a lavish, extravagant gesture of affection. (A working man earned one denarius a year. This luxury import was worth nearly a year's wages.) John (12:1-8) places the event some days earlier and tells us the unpleasant truth about Judas' embezzlement of the funds. In Luke 7:36-50 the occasion is similar, but the woman concerned different.
14:12-25 The Last Supper
See on Matthew 26:14-29.
14:26-52 Gethsemane; Jesus is arrested
See on Matthew 26:30-56. There seems little point in the mention of the young man (51-62) unless this is Mark himself.
14:53 - 15:15 The Jewish trial; Peter denies Jesus; the Roman trial
See on Luke 22:54-71.

The trials
The Jewish court which tried Jesus was the Sanhedrin, the supreme court at Jerusalem. Its 71 councillors came from influential families – elders, lawyers, Pharisees and Sadducees. The high priest for the year presided. The Sanhedrin had wide powers in civil and religious matters in Judea, but under Roman rule was not empowered to carry out the death sentence. So Jesus had also to appear before the Roman governor on a charge which would merit the death sentence under Roman law. Blasphemy was sufficient for the Jews. To be sure Pilate would ratify the sentence, the safest charge was treason. The Jewish trial was far from regular. It was held at night. There were no defence witnesses. The witnesses for the prosecution could not agree. And the death sentence, which should not have been pronounced till the day following the trial (the Jewish day ran from sunset to sunset), was immediate.

The sequence of events
1. The audience with Annas, father-

PILATE

Harold Rowdon

In 1961 a stone slab was discovered at Caesarea bearing the name Pontius Pilatus. This is one of the few pieces of evidence outside the Bible for the life and work of this unhappy man. Tacitus, the Roman writer, does refer to the execution of Jesus by Pilate, and two Jewish writers, Josephus and Philo, relate several incidents. Apart from this, we have only the biblical evidence. In addition to the accounts given by the writers of the Gospels, there are brief references to him in Acts 3:13; 4:27; 13:28; 1 Timothy 6:13.

Pilate was evidently a middle-class Roman with military and administrative experience who in AD 26 was appointed to the office of procurator of Judea. As procurator (or governor) he possessed very wide powers, especially in military and financial matters. He appointed the high priest and controlled the temple funds.

Philo describes Pilate as a harsh, spiteful and brutal man. According to Josephus, in one of his historical works, Pilate antagonized the Jews almost as soon as he was appointed. He allowed the Roman troops to bring their regimental standards into Jerusalem. These contained representations of the emperor, and the Jews were furious because they felt that the holy city had been desecrated by these idolatrous symbols. Pilate bowed to the storm and ordered the removal of the standards.

On another occasion, according to Philo, the Jews took violent objection to some golden shields which Pilate had dedicated in his residence in Jerusalem. This time Pilate refused to remove them, but the Jews appealed to the Emperor Tiberius, who ordered them to be removed to Caesarea, Pilate's headquarters.

Josephus records an incident arising from Pilate's plan to use money from the temple treasury to finance the building of an aqueduct to bring water from a spring 25 miles away into Jerusalem. Mass protests were met by force, and many Jews died. This may be the incident referred to in Luke 13:1.

Each of the Gospels records the trial of Jesus before Pilate (Matthew 27:1-26; Mark 15:1-15; Luke 23:1-25; John 18:28 - 19:16). Mark records the basic story. Luke adds the sending of Jesus to Herod (23:6-12) and Pilate's triple assertion that Jesus was innocent (23:4, 14, 22). Matthews relates the dream and message of Pilate's wife (27:19), how Pilate disclaimed responsibility for Jesus' death (27:24f.), and his setting a guard on the tomb (27:62-66). John, who had been present at the trial, supplics even fuller details.

Pilate's final blunder was to seize a number of Samaritans who had assembled on Mt Gerizim as a result of a rumour that sacred vessels from the tabernacle were hidden there. Some of the ringleaders were executed. In response to a Samaritan protest, Vitellius, governor of Syria and Pilate's superior, ordered the ham-fisted procurator to answer to the emperor for his handling of the affair. The reigning emperor, Tiberius, died before Pilate reached Rome. We do not know the outcome of the affair, but Eusebius, the 4th-century Christian historian, recorded a report that Pilate had committed suicide.

Several unreliable traditions regarding Pilate's body are in existence. A number of *Acts of Pilate*, alleged records of Pilate's rule, appeared during the early Christian centuries. They are forgeries, intended to discredit Christianity.

in-law of high priest Caiaphas (John 18:12-14).

2. The late-night session at Caiaphas' house before the Sanhedrin (Matthew 26:57-68; Mark 15:53-65; Luke 22:54-65; John 18:24).

3. The early morning ratification of the sentence by the Sanhedrin (Matthew 27:1; Mark 15:1; Luke 22:66-71).

4. Jesus before Pilate (Matthew 27:2, 11-14; Mark 15:2-5; Luke 23:1-5; John 18:28-38).

5. Since Jesus is a Galilean, Pilate refers him to Herod (Luke 23:6-12).

6. Jesus before Pilate again. He is scourged, sentenced and handed over to the soldiers (Matthew 27:15-26; Mark 15:6-15; Luke 23:13-25; John 18:29 - 19:16).

15:16-41 Mockery and crucifixion
Jesus is now utterly alone. The Gospel writers play down the physical horror of the six hours (9 a.m.-3 p.m.) on the cross when Jesus touched a depth of suffering in body, mind and spirit beyond the stretch of our imagination. But the whole New Testament declares that his suffering was 'for us'. By his death he paid in full the penalty for our sin. He saved us from the death sentence, making possible the free gift of eternal life.

Seven times in those six hours (the last three in darkness) those who watched heard him speak.

A first-century rock-cut tomb at Nazareth, seen from the inside, with the entrance stone rolled partway back.

The words from the cross

1. *'Father, forgive them; for they know not what they do'* (Luke 23:24) – a prayer for the Jewish people and the Roman soldiers.

2. *'Truly, I say to you, today you will be with me in Paradise'* (Luke 23:43) – his word to the repentant thief, crucified beside him.

3. *'Woman, behold your son!'* *'Behold your mother!'* (John 19:26-27) – commending his mother to John's care.

4. *'My God, my God, why hast thou forsaken me?'* (Matthew 27:46; Mark 15:34) – expressing in the words of Psalm 22:1 the agony of separation from God as the full weight of human sin pressed upon him.

5. *'I thirst'* (John 19:28).

6. *'It is finished'* (John 19:30).

7. *'Father, into thy hands I commit my spirit!'* (Luke 23:46).

Verse 21: Cyrene in north Africa had a strong Jewish colony. Alexander and Rufus evidently became Christians. This may be the same Rufus as the one mentioned in Romans 16:13.

Salome (40): Zebedee's wife; mother of James and John (Matthew 27:56).

15:42-47 Burial
Death by crucifixion was long drawn out. It often took two days or more. But Jesus was dead in six hours. Joseph saves him from the final indignity of a mass grave.

Day of preparation (42): i.e. the day before the sabbath, which began at 6 p.m.

16 The resurrection
See on Luke 24. For some unknown reason – most probably damage to very early copies of the Gospel – the best manuscripts we have of Mark end abruptly at 16:8. Verses 9-20 represent early attempts to round the Gospel off more satisfactorily.

LUKE

Luke gives us the fullest life-story of Jesus we possess. The Gospel is part one of a two-part history of Christian beginnings – Luke/Acts. Both parts are dedicated to the same man, the Roman Theophilus, and both are written with the same purpose. The Gospel is carefully compiled from reliable, first-hand sources. Luke is not simply a biographer. His over-riding concern is to get at the truth of what happened in Palestine in the critical years of Jesus' life-time. His Gospel shows Jesus as the Saviour of all men; his coming, a world-event. He lets us see Jesus the Man. And his selection of stories reflects his own warm interest in people, especially the sick and helpless, the poor, women, children, the social outcasts.

The writer. The Gospel does not mention the author's name, but all the evidence points to Luke the doctor, Paul's companion on his missionary journeys (see introduction to Acts). The precise way diseases are described in the Gospel fits in well with this. From the Gospel itself it is clear the writer is an educated man, with a wide vocabulary, and capable of marshalling and selecting material. He is an artist with words. And he is at home with both Greek and Jewish backgrounds – although he writes for non-Jews, using Greek titles and quoting from the Greek version of the Old Testament. Archaeology has proved him an accurate historian. Luke worked with Mark and knew him well (Colossians 4:10, 14; Philemon 24), and the Gospel Mark wrote is one of his main sources.

1:1-4 PREFACE

The church very soon realized the need to get down in writing the stories of Jesus and his teaching which were circulating by word of mouth. Luke – perhaps having time on his hands, and opportunity to check on the facts during Paul's imprisonment at Caesarea – sets himself the task of compiling an accurate record.

Theophilus (3): an otherwise unknown Roman, who had at least some interest in Christianity. 'Most excellent' may be his title as a high-ranking official.

1:5 - 2:52 THE BIRTH AND CHILDHOOD OF JOHN AND JESUS

Only Matthew and Luke take their accounts as far back as Jesus' birth. The two accounts supplement one another. Luke's is fuller. Much of his information must surely have come from Mary herself.

1:5-25 The angel's message to Zechariah

God was in the events which led up to the birth of Christ. John's conception is in itself inexplicable on a purely human level (as with Isaac, Jacob, Samuel, Samson). Zechariah was in Jerusalem for his annual two-week spell of duty as a priest. This year came the honour of a lifetime. He was chosen to offer the incense alone in the temple. And at that moment God sends to tell him that the long years of prayer for a son are over. He will remove the stigma of childlessness – but more than that. As he answers the deep inner longing of this couple God at the same time fulfils far wider purposes – for the nation, and for the world. John will be the link between the Old Testament and the New. He will be the new Elijah (17; Malachi 4:5), herald of the long-promised, long-awaited Messiah.

Verse 15: compare Samson's dedication to God, Judges 13:4-5; and the Nazirite rules, Numbers 6.

1:26-38 The angel's message to Mary

Six months later the Messiah's birth is announced – this time to the young woman chosen to be his mother, and without the agency of a human father. Mary's quiet acceptance of a situation bound to cause scandal, and possibly the breaking of her marriage contract, shows something of the kind of woman through whom God chose to fulfil his purposes.

1:39-56 Mary visits Elizabeth

Having heard the news, Mary sets straight out on the four- or five-day journey south. It is a meeting of special joy and significance for the two women who have much to share. Their thoughts and feelings are crystallized in Elizabeth's benediction and Mary's hymn of praise. The hymn is full of the Old Testament phrases which Mary must have known and loved from childhood (see especially Hannah's song, 1 Samuel 2:1-10). Matthew 1:18-25 tells us what happened after Mary went home.

1:57-80 The birth of John

The child's strange name, Zechariah's sudden recovery of speech and the outburst of prophecy as his pent-up thoughts find voice, make a deep impression on the people around. They expect great things of John.

In the desert (80): other people at the time also withdrew, world-weary, from ordinary life and people. For instance the Essene community at Qumran flourished in John's day in the same area. John, by contrast, had a message for his nation. See also the note under Mark 1:1-8.

2:1-20 The birth of Jesus

Bethlehem – 6 miles south of Jerusalem, 70 south of Nazareth – had a long history. It was the home of Ruth and Boaz, birthplace of King David. But for Jesus there was no room; just an outhouse, a cradle shared with the animals. And the only ones to be told that the King of glory has come are some humble shepherds. 'He became poor' – Paul's phrase was the literal truth.

Verse 2: we know Quirinius governed Syria-Cilicia AD 6-9, but Luke's census is at least nine years earlier. It may be that Quirinius served an earlier term as governor; or possibly the name should read Saturninus. Luke has been proved such a reliable historian elsewhere that it is difficult to think he would make such a factual blunder.

Verse 7: the 'inn' (Revised Standard Version) may equally well be the guest-room of a house (see New English Bible and Matthew 2:11). The animals were probably stabled in a cave beneath the house.

Verse 14: 'his peace for men on whom his favour rests'. God's peace does not come to men because they deserve it.

2:21-40 The presentation of Jesus in the temple; Simeon and Anna

Leviticus 12 gives the Jewish background. Forty days after Jesus' birth his parents present him to the priest in the temple. They are poor people who cannot afford to sacrifice a lamb. It is all routine procedure – until Simeon and Anna see the child, and recognize their Messiah.

Verse 39: Matthew 2 supplies the other events which took place before the family settled in Nazareth.

2:41-52 Jesus astonishes the teachers in the temple

When he was 12, a Jewish boy underwent preparation for adult status in the religious community. This visit to Jerusalem is therefore a special one

THE ROMAN EMPIRE

Rome

Black Sea

Athens

Carthage

Antioch

Mediterranean Sea

Jerusalem

Alexandria

THE VIRGIN BIRTH

John Simpson

Both Matthew (1:18-25) and Luke (1:30-35) state that Jesus Christ was conceived by an action of the Holy Spirit without the intervention of a human father, and thus born of a virgin, Mary. We call this event the virgin birth – or, more accurately, the virginal conception – of Jesus.

In both Matthew and Luke the emphasis lies on the power and activity of the Holy Spirit in the birth of Jesus. It is this, not the absence of a human father, nor even the co-operation of the virgin mother, which is the important point. From his mother, Jesus was born as a man, but by the creative act of the Spirit his is a new humanity, the starting-point of a new race.

It is arguable that this would have been possible apart from a virgin birth, but the biblical evidence points to this miracle as the means which God employed in order to bring his Son into the world. We are not told anything about the physiology of the incarnation, but simply that it was through the activity of the Spirit that Mary became pregnant.

That is indeed all that can be said, since we are concerned here with the entry of the infinite God into his own creation, and this is something that cannot be described, any more than the act of creation itself can be described. Nor can the virgin birth be rejected simply because it is a miracle. The supreme miracle is the incarnation itself, and if we can accept that miracle, there should be no difficulty about accepting the means by which God chose to effect it.

The virgin birth is seldom mentioned elsewhere in the New Testament. That is a warning to us not to get it out of proportion. The fact is stated, but Scripture nowhere makes the deity of Christ, nor his incarnation, nor his sinlessness stand or fall by the method of his birth. The prophecy of Isaiah 7:14 that a 'young woman' should conceive and bear a son called 'Immanuel' ('God with us') was seen to have a deeper meaning after the birth of Jesus (see Matthew 1:22-23). In Mark 6:3 the people of Nazareth call Jesus 'son of Mary', a phrase that may well have been an insult based on the rumour that Joseph was not his father. John 8:41 contains a similar slander. Some have found further references to the virgin birth in Galatians 4:4 where Paul says that God 'sent forth his Son, born of woman', and again when he spoke of Jesus as the 'second Adam', the first of the new race (1 Corinthians 15:45-47).

for Jesus. Visitors flocked into Jerusalem for Passover travelling in large parties for safety. Jesus' parents had no reason to suspect he was missing till the evening halt. Next day they retraced their steps, and on the following morning found him in the temple. This is the first indication we have that Jesus realized his special relationship with God. The next 18 years are passed over in total silence.

3 - 4:13 JOHN THE BAPTIST AND JESUS

3:1-20 The preaching of John
See also on Matthew 3; Mark 1:2-8. Luke's historical detail makes it possible to date John's ministry (and the beginning of Jesus' ministry a few months later) somewhere between AD 26 and 29. Verses 10-14 occur only in Luke. Genuine repentance shows itself in daily life – in kindness, generosity, honesty. The soldiers are told, 'No bullying; no blackmail; make do with your pay!' (New English Bible).
Verses 19-20: see on Mark 6:14-29.
3:21-22 Jesus' baptism
See on Matthew 3.
3:23-38 Jesus' family line
See on Matthew 1:1-17. Luke traces the line beyond Abraham to Adam, emphasizing Jesus' work for all mankind, as well as establishing his claim to be the Messiah descended from David.
4:1-13 The temptation
See on Matthew 4; Mark 1:9-13. Luke reverses the order of the second and third temptations. The real target of attack is Jesus' relationship as Son to his Father. Satan's attempts to undermine it and sow doubts are not so different from his methods in Genesis 3 – 'Did God say? ...' But this time he does not succeed.

4:14 - 9:50 TEACHING AND HEALING IN GALILEE

See note on Galilee, under Mark 1-9.
4:14-30 In Nazareth
Luke chooses to start here, although this was not the first event in Jesus' ministry. Astonishment at Jesus' teaching quickly changes to hostility. And at the implication that because of their disbelief the gospel will be offered to non-Jews, the people are all set to lynch him. See also Matthew 13:53-58; Mark 6:1-6.
The synagogue (16-17): anyone might be invited to take part in the service

of prayers, readings and sermon. The leader stood to pray and read from the scrolls, sat down to teach (20).
Verses 26-27: see 1 Kings 17:8-16; 2 Kings 5:1-14.
4:31-44 Capernaum
See on Mark 1:21-45.
Judea (44): the term is used here of Palestine generally, not the south in particular. Jesus went there later.
5:1-11 The catch of fish; Peter and his partners follow Jesus
Luke fills in detail omitted in Matthew (4:18-22) and Mark (1:16-20). The decision to follow Christ was based on more than casual contact.
Gennesaret (1): another name for Galilee.
5:12-16 Jesus heals a leper
See on Matthew 8:1-4.
5:17-26 The paralytic walks
See on Mark 2:1-12.
Pharisees (17): see 'The Religious Background of the New Testament'.
5:27-39 Levi (Matthew) becomes a disciple; questions about fasting
See on Matthew 9:9-17.
6:1-11 Controversy over the sabbath
See on Mark 2:23 - 3:6. 6:12-16 Jesus chooses the Twelve
See on Mark 3:7-19. Only Luke tells us of Jesus' night of prayer. He tells us more about Jesus as a man of prayer than any other Gospel writer.
6:17-49 Jesus teaches his disciples
This is most probably a shorter version of the sermon recorded in Matthew 5 - 7. Jesus must have taught these truths on many different occasions. Having chosen the Twelve, Jesus comes some distance down the mountainside to a level area. Here he sits down to teach, with the apostles, disciples and crowd gathered round him. His words are for his followers – those who realize their poverty in God's sight, who have an appetite for spiritual truth, who grieve at the evil they find in their own hearts. This is not a question of material poverty or riches.
Verses 20-23: a description of Jesus' disciples – men who seem pitiable now, but who have a great future.

Verses 24-26: the dreadful predicament of those who enjoy all life offers now, and fail to look beyond it. See on Matthew 5:1-16.

Verses 27-36: the command to treat others as God treats us – even in the face of injustice; even those who do us down. See on Matthew 5:17-48.

THE NEW TESTAMENT MIRACLES

Howard Marshall

The Gospels contain stories of about 35 different occasions when Jesus performed various kinds of deeds that seemed miraculous to those who saw them. In addition there are several passages where we are told in quite general terms that Jesus performed miracles.

More than half of these stories about Jesus tell how he healed the sick of various diseases including fever, leprosy (probably not the modern disease of that name), dropsy, paralysis, blindness, deafness, and dumbness.

In other cases he cast demons out of people who were suffering from physical or mental disorders.

Three times we hear that he raised people from the dead.

The remaining stories show his power over things – to feed a large multitude with very little food, to walk on the water and still a storm, to curse a fig-tree so that it withered away, to change water into wine, and to catch enormous quantities of fish.

Modern objections to miracles

These stories testify to the tremendous impression which the work of Jesus made on those who saw it. Even if the stories were legendary (which they are not), we should still want to know what it was about Jesus that made people tell such stories about him. One thing is certain at the outset, that we cannot dismiss the miracles to try to have a non-miraculous Jesus. They are an integral and central part of the story. Why, then, do people try to dismiss them?

First, it is argued that science rules out the possibility of miracles. In fact, however, this argument is nothing more than the statement of a presupposition, namely that in a purely material universe nothing can happen that cannot be accounted for in terms of natural causes. But that is purely an assumption about the nature of the universe which cannot be proved to be true. At most it could be

argued from it that normally miracles do not occur; but it is illegitimate to claim that therefore miracles can never occur. We ought at least to have open minds on the point.

Second, it is argued that we have no reliable historical evidence for miracles. We must have good evidence that the alleged miracle happened, and that it cannot be explained in a non-miraculous manner. Since we are dealing with something as unusual as a miracle, the evidence needs to be extremely strong, since (it is argued) it is more likely that the witnesses got it wrong than that a miracle actually happened.

The resurrection

If, however, only one miracle could be claimed as historical, this would be sufficient both to demonstrate that miracles are possible and to make further ones probable. Such an event is the resurrection. The evidence that reliable witnesses claimed to have seen Jesus alive after his death (1 Corinthians 15:3-8) is incontrovertible. The only explanation that makes sense of the evidence is that he was miraculously raised from the dead. If you want to disagree, then you must produce some convincing alternative explanation.

If the resurrection did take place, then it makes the fact of other miracles highly likely. For, first, it establishes the possibility of the miraculous taking place at all. It means that God can act in the natural order in an unusual manner. Second, the resurrection is God's 'Yes' to the life of Jesus – including Jesus' own claim to work miracles (Luke 7:21f.; 11:19).

This evidence is confirmed by the reliable historical tradition that Jesus did work miracles, which is found in the Gospels. To be sure, we cannot test and affirm on purely historical grounds the truth of every single miracle story. In some cases, what seemed miraculous to

1st-century people may be explicable in natural terms (e.g. in the psychological healing of a psychosomatic disease); in other cases there may not be enough evidence to confirm or disprove the Gospel story.

The purpose of the miracles
One important point often raised against the historicity of the New Testament miracles is that similar stories are told of other great men of the period. Hence it is likely that Christians, who shared the superstitions of their day, would invent similar stories about Jesus.

One could reply that if it was necessary for Jesus to be a miracle-worker in order to be seen to be 'the greatest' in 1st-century terms, then God could and would do mighty wonders through him. More important is the fact that the stories of Jesus display some important differences from those told about other men. The importance of Jesus' miracles lies not so much in the miraculous power which he displayed in them, as in the significance attached to them.

— In general they were effected by his simple word (Mark 1:27; 2:11) or touch (Mark 5:41) rather than by the use of magical devices.
— They did not bring glory to him, but were meant to bring glory to God (Luke 7:16).
— They testified to God's love for suffering humanity (Mark 1:41; 8:2).
— They fulfilled the Old Testament promises of the coming time of salvation when God would heal men's bodies as well as their souls (Luke 7:22; Isaiah 29:18-19; 35:5-6; 61:1).
— They were done in order to lead men to faith in the saving power of God at work in Jesus (Mark 9:23f.). They were not compelling signs of God's power: the Pharisees felt able to attribute them to the power of Satan (Mark 3:22). But to those with the eyes to see, they constituted the sign that God was at work in Jesus in fulfilment of his promises, and were meant to awaken and confirm faith in him.

All this applies to the miracles of Jesus himself. It also applies to the miracles in the early church. The early Christians displayed powers similar to those of Jesus. We hear of sick people being cured, the dead being raised, the miraculous release of prisoners and even the power to inflict physical judgement. These were signs that the same power of God which was at work in Jesus was still at work in his disciples, confirming their message of salvation, and also warning of the reality of God's judgement.

Verses 37-49: see on Matthew 7.
7:1-10 The centurion's slave
See on Matthew 8:5-13.
7:11-17 Jesus brings the widow's son back to life
We have no other record of this incident. It is a further example of Luke's concern for the under-privileged. The widow's son is her only means of support. Once again Jesus shows himself Lord of life and death.
Nain (11): a village south of Nazareth. See map.
Verse 13: Luke is the only Gospel writer to refer to Jesus as 'the Lord', a term probably not much used during his lifetime.
7:18-35 Messengers from John the Baptist
See on Matthew 11:1-19.
Verse 35: 'God's wisdom, however, is shown to be true by all who accept it'. People turned to God in response to the preaching of both John and Jesus.
7:36-50 In the Pharisee's house
This is a different incident from the one recorded in the other Gospels. Simon shows Jesus no special courtesy. But a common prostitute, to whom he has opened up the possibility of forgiveness, pours out her gratitude in lavish love – not caring what anyone thinks. Her love does not *earn* forgiveness (47), it follows it.
8:1-21 'If you have ears ... then hear'; Jesus teaches in parables
Verses 1-3: only Luke tells us the part the women played in Jesus' mission. Susanna is not mentioned again. Mary Magdalene stood watching at the crucifixion, and she and Joanna were at the tomb and saw the Lord on the resurrection morning. Their love, and that of many other women who followed him from Galilee, never wavered. Mary is not the woman of 7:36ff., but there was a real battle in her heart before she became a disciple.
Verses 4-15: see on Matthew 13:1-52. See also Mark 4:1-20.
Verse 19: see on Matthew 12:49.
8:22-39 The stormy crossing; the man possessed by demons
See on Mark 4:35-41; 5:1-20.
Verse 32: pork was forbidden food for Jews. But the country east of the lake was largely non-Jewish.
8:40-56 Jairus' daughter; the woman with a haemorrhage
See on Mark 5:21-43.

9:1-17 The Twelve sent out; Herod is puzzled; 5,000 fed
Verses 1-6: see on Matthew 9:35 - 10:42.
Verses 7-9: Luke seems to have a special source of information about Herod, perhaps through Joanna (8:3).
Verses 10-17: see also Matthew 14:13-21; Mark 6:30-44; John 6:1-14. This is yet another example of Jesus' power.
9:18-27 'Who do you say I am?'; Jesus speaks about his suffering
See the fuller version in Matthew 16:13-28, and Mark 8:27 - 9:1. Luke abridges at this point.
9:28-36 Jesus is transfigured
See on Mark 9:2-13.
9:37-50 The epileptic boy; 'Who is the greatest?'
Verses 37-43: see on Mark 9:14-29.
Verses 46-48: see on Matthew 18 and Mark 9:30-50.

9:51 - 19:27 ON THE MOVE TOWARDS JERUSALEM: TEACHING AND HEALING

In this section Luke groups incidents and teaching from various periods of Christ's ministry, on the general theme of discipleship. He may have had several journeys to Jerusalem in mind. Much of what is recorded in these chapters is unique to Luke.
9:51-56 The Samaritan village
Jesus' insistence on going to Jerusalem was red rag to a bull to the Samaritans (see article 'Religious Background' and on 10:29ff.).
Verse 54: no wonder Jesus nicknamed these two brothers 'sons of thunder'!
9:57-62 No turning back
See on Matthew 8:18-22.
10:1-24 Jesus sends out the seventy
Compare this with Jesus' instructions to the Twelve (Matthew 10:5-15). See also Matthew 11:20-27. Those entrusted with God's good news are entitled to support from the people they go to. But they are not to look for luxury (the 'going from house to house', 7, is with a view to a better living). Time is too precious to waste on endless social formalities (4). There is work to be done, a message to be made known. And God himself will judge those who reject it. The seventy are overjoyed at their new power. But greater cause for joy is the certainty of eternal life (20).
Son of peace (6): a peace-loving man.
Verses 13-17: for the places mentioned, see map. Tyre and Sidon: heath-

en cities denounced by the Old Testament prophets. 'Hades': the place of the dead – a metaphorical phrase, 'brought down to the depths' (New English Bible).

I saw Satan fall (18): their ability to exorcise evil spirits is a sign that Satan's power is broken. The preaching of the new age means that the power of evil is to be defeated at last. Jesus rejoices in this fulfilment of his ministry.

10:25-37 A test question; the good Samaritan
Only Luke tells this story. Jesus gives a textbook answer to the question. The lawyer, chagrined, in an attempt to save face asks another. Instead of answering directly, Jesus replies with a parable. There was a long history of hatred between Jew and Samaritan (see article 'Religious Background'). The Samaritans were regarded as scum – untouchables. Yet Jesus shows this one carrying out the law whereas the injured man's fellow Jews – even the religious leaders – fail. A real 'neighbour' is one who gives help wherever it is needed, even to someone who yesterday, so to speak, kicked him in the teeth.

A model of an eastern inn, built around a courtyard.

Verse 30: the road which winds its way down from Jerusalem to Jericho (dropping 3,300 feet in 17 miles) passes through lonely, desolate, rocky terrain – ideal brigand country.

10:38-42 Martha and Mary
The two sisters and their brother Lazarus lived at Bethany, near Jerusalem. Martha gets into a state slaving to prepare an elaborate meal. She would have done better to keep the menu simple and leave time to listen to Jesus.

11:1-13 Jesus teaches his disciples how to pray
Matthew (6:9-13) gives the longer form of the Lord's Prayer. Jesus is not supplying just a form of words. His prayer provides us with a pattern. It teaches us to come to God simply, talking to him as we would our own father, both sharing his concerns and confidently telling him of our own needs. And we are not to be discouraged if time goes by and we see no answer. Persistence will in the end win over even the most reluctant friend – and there is no reluctance to answer on God's part. See also Matthew 7:7-11.

Verse 7: a poor family slept all together on thin mattresses on a raised section of the one all-purpose room.

Verses 11-12: fish and serpents look alike, so do eggs and rolled-up scorpions.

11:14-36 Opposition; Jesus slates his contemporaries
Verses 14-23: see on Matthew 12:15-37. Verses 24-26: see on Matthew 12:43-45. Verses 29-32: see on Matthew 12:38-42. Verses 34-36: see on Matthew 6:22-23. Only Luke includes 27-28.

Verse 24: dry, desert places were thought to be the natural home of evil spirits.

11:37-54 Jesus' rebuke infuriates the Pharisees
Verses 37-41: see on Matthew 15:1-20. Verses 42-52: see on Matthew 23.

12 – 13:9 Warning and reassurance; be ready
A collection of Jesus' teaching about the future, and the way future events should affect life here and now. The consequences of following a short-sighted materialist philosophy will in the end prove disastrous. Much of this section is paralleled in Matthew.

Verses 1-12: see on Matthew 10:26ff.

Verses 13-21: the parable of the rich fool – unique to Luke.

Verses 22-34: see on Matthew 6:9-34.

Verses 35-48: see on Matthew 24:42-51.

13:1-9: Roman troops had slaughtered some Galilean pilgrims in the temple at Passover. People assumed that the victims of the two disasters must have been specially wicked – but that was not true. The whole nation is ripe for judgement and will meet an equally horrible fate if present opportunities for a change of heart are let slip.

Verse 10: see on Matthew 12:15-37.

Verse 35: for freedom of movement

at work the long tunic was drawn up through a belt.

Verses 49-50: the good news of the gospel will run through the earth like fire. But first Jesus must plumb the depths of suffering.

13:10-17 The woman with arthritis

Only Luke records this story. It is one of numerous clashes with the Pharisees over healing on the sabbath. See also Mark 3:1-6.

Verse 16: Satan bears ultimate responsibility for bringing suffering into the world along with sin.

13:18-21 Pictures of what God's kingdom is like

See on Matthew 13, and article 'The Kingdom of God and the Kingdom of Heaven'.

13:22-35 The narrow door

Verses 22-30: speculation over how many will be saved is futile. The important thing is for each individual to make sure of his own place. It is not enough merely to recognize Christ. He requires response – and there is a time limit.

Verses 31-35: Jesus is not bothered by Herod's threats. He knows what lies ahead, and grieves at the fate of the city that will destroy him.

14:1-24 Jesus dines out; two parables

Verses 1-6: another sabbath healing – see 13:10-17; Mark 3:1-6. Human life is cheap, livestock precious!

Verses 7-11: guests were carefully seated according to rank and status (as at a formal banquet today), but everyone wants a seat at the top table. Jesus is commending a genuinely humble spirit, not false modesty.

Verses 12-14: real generosity does not look for returns.

Verses 15-24: the story illustrates how people react to the invitation God makes through Jesus. Many reply with a snub. It is not really a case of 'I *cannot* come', but 'I *will* not come'. The 'reasons' are no more than excuses.

Dropsy (2): fluid collecting in parts of the body and causing swelling and pain.

14:25-35 Counting the cost of discipleship

The guests in the story had their priorities wrong. Jesus' claim must take precedence over all others. No one can follow him unless he is prepared for all that this means. Too many people start to build in fine style and then run out of funds (28-29).

Verse 26: Jesus teaches us to love even our enemies. He is not telling us to hate our family! He means we must love him more than anyone or anything else (33). The black-and-white contrast was a figure of speech.

15 The lost sheep; the lost coin; the drop-out son

These three stories contrast strongly with the severity of chapter 14. God cares for those who have gone wrong in life. He is always ready to forgive any who turn to him. The men of religion (1-2), like the elder son in the story, show neither love nor pity for those who fail to meet their standards. But God rejoices at their rescue.

Verse 8: the silver coins were probably the woman's dowry, worn round her neck or on her headdress.

16 The dishonest manager; the danger of being taken up with money

Verses 1-13: Jesus commends the manager's astuteness, not his dishonesty. He knows how to make money work for him.

Verses 16-17: compare Matthew 11:12-13. The emphasis here is different.

Verse 18: see on Matthew 19:1-15.

Verses 19-31: the rich man and Lazarus. Jesus uses popular picture language (Abraham's bosom, the great chasm, etc.). But the story makes it clear that if we will not respond to the message God has already clearly given in the Bible, we will not respond at all. No amount of miracle-working would make any difference. Our future is determined by our present response, or lack of it.

Verse 9: New English Bible gives a plausible rendering of a difficult verse. Friends bought by money *cannot* get us to heaven. But the way we use our money now may affect our eternal destiny. It is a test of how we could handle wealth of a different kind. Is God, or money, our master?

17:1-10 Forgiveness; faith; duty

17:11-19 The ten lepers

The men are sent to the priests in order to be declared fit to return to normal society. By going, they demonstrate their faith in Jesus' word. All are cured, but only one takes the trouble to say thank you.

Samaritan (16): see article 'Religious Background'.

17:20-37 Teaching about Jesus' return

See on Matthew 24. No amount of

calculation can fix the time (20-21) or place (37) of Christ's return in judgement. The world will be caught unprepared, as it was by the flood.

18:1-14 More about prayer

Two parables which appear only in Luke. Like all Jesus' parables, these are stories from life.

Verses 1-8: God is no unjust judge. If a woman could persist with her plea against such odds, surely we can pray on if the answer does not come at once.

Verses 9-14: the Pharisee 'prays' simply to give himself a pat on the back. It is the tax collector, who can find nothing in himself to be proud of, whom God hears.

18:15-17 Jesus and the children

See also Matthew 19:13-15; and on Mark 10:13-16. To the disciples, the children were a nuisance. But Jesus loved them. Verse 17 makes the same point as the story of the Pharisee and the tax collector. Admission to God's kingdom is never denied to those who come in humble trust.

18:18-34 The rich ruler's question; Jesus again predicts his death

See on Matthew 19:16-30; 20:17-19; see also Mark 10:17-34.

18:35 - 19:10 At Jericho: the blind beggar; Zacchaeus

18:35-43: see on Mark 10:46-52. 19:1-10: Zacchaeus, like Matthew, was a social outcast because of his job. He made himself a fat living by fleecing his own people of money to pay the Roman taxes. But when Jesus chose to stay at his home, Zacchaeus became a new man.

19:11-27 The parable of the pounds

This story is similar to the parable of the talents in Matthew. Verse 11 is the key. Herod's son, Archelaus, did just what the nobleman in Jesus' story did – went to Rome to be given his title to the kingdom of Judea. (He was followed by a delegation of Jews opposed to his rule.) Jesus is no despot, like Herod, but he too is about to leave his people for a time. In his absence they must faithfully carry out the work given them to do. For he will return with authority to judge every man.

The pound (13): the Greek mina.

19:28 - 21:38 JESUS IN JERUSALEM

19:28-48 The triumphal ride into the city; Jesus in the temple

See also Matthew 21:1-17; Mark 11:1-19. Jesus rode in on an ass (Zechariah 9:9), not a war-horse. He came on a peace mission. But Jerusalem would have none of it, choosing instead the violent course which led to total destruction at the hands of the Romans in AD 70.

Bethphage and Bethany (29): villages east of the Mount of Olives, two miles from Jerusalem.

Verse 38: Luke paraphrases for his non-Jewish readers.

Verse 45: see on Matthew 21:12-17. Luke, like Matthew, compresses the events; compare Mark 11:11 and 15ff.

20:1-18 On whose authority ... ? The parable of the vineyard

See on Matthew 21:23-46. See also Mark 11:27 - 12:12.

20:19 - 21:4 Jesus' enemies set traps

See on Mark 12:13-44. See also Matthew 22:15-46.

21:5-38 Jesus talks about the destruction of the temple and the end of the world

See on Matthew 24. See also Mark 13.

Verses 8-11: signs of the end.

Verses 12-19: suffering and witness of the disciples.

Verses 20-24: the fall of Jerusalem: phase 1 of the end.

Verses 25-28: cosmic upheaval and Jesus' return: phase 2 of the end.

Verses 29-33: the certainty of these events. 'All' (32) must refer to the warning signs, including the fall of Jerusalem. All the indications are that Christ's coming is near: yet God still delays, giving time for the good news to be made known throughout the world. The fig-tree is the first to come into leaf in Palestine.

Verses 34-36: the need to be ready.

22 - 24 JESUS' LAST HOURS: THE CROSS AND RESURRECTION

22:1-38 Judas turns traitor; the Last Supper

See on Matthew 26:14-29. See also Mark 14:12-25; John 13 - 14.

Verse 10: it was usually the woman's job to carry water, so this man would have been conspicuous.

22:39-53 On the Mount of Olives; the arrest

See on Matthew 26:30-56. See also Mark 14:26-52.

22:54-65 Peter denies Christ; the mockery of the soldiers

Only Peter and one other disciple had the courage to keep within sight of Jesus. But with nothing to do but wait, courage oozes away and fear

A model of the Fort of Antonia, in the Ecce Homo Convent, Jerusalem. Here Jesus was taken to be tried by Pontius Pilate, the Roman Governor.

takes control. Three times Peter says what he swore he would never say (22:33; Mark 14:29-31). Even Peter, leader of the disciples, denies him. Afterwards one look from Jesus is enough to break the big fisherman's heart.

22:66 - 23:12 Jesus before the Sanhedrin; before Pilate; before Herod
See also on Mark 14:53 - 15:15.
Blasphemy is a capital charge under Jewish law. But the accusation and charge is rephrased for Pilate in order to get Jesus convicted of treason. The Roman governor is not interested in offences against Jewish religious law.

Herod was in Jerusalem for the Passover. If Pilate was attempting to pass the buck by sending his prisoner to Herod, it did not work. It is strange that the exchange over Jesus should have brought these two old enemies together.

Verse 3: the answer is non-committal. What Jesus would mean by the title, and what Pilate would understand, are two very different things. See the fuller record in John 18:33-38.

23:13-31 Sentenced to death
Although acquitted by both Herod and Pilate, Jesus is condemned to death – because Pilate dare not risk another unfavourable report reaching the emperor (John 19:12). So a convicted murderer is freed, and an innocent man scourged and crucified.

23:32-49 On the cross; the two criminals; Jesus' last words
See on Mark 15:16-41. Only Luke tells us that one of the mocking robbers repented and was forgiven.

Verse 45: the curtain divided the sanctuary from the body of the temple. Only once a year could the high priest pass through and intercede for the people (Hebrews 9:7). Now no intermediary is needed – all may have access to God (Hebrews 10:19-22).

23:50-56 Joseph sees to the burial
See on Mark 15:42-47.

24 Christ is risen!
In the stillness of that Easter morning the extraordinary news gradually broke, the light dawned. The tomb was empty. Jesus was alive! The details given in the four accounts of what took place on that momentous morning are difficult to harmonize. The fact that it happened is clear, and has stood up to the most searching examination. Like reports of any major event, it is difficult to piece together the information of a number of independent witnesses. A rough sequence of events is set out in the article 'The Accounts of the Resurrection'.

No matter what the variation in detail, the main facts are absolutely clear. As day broke on that Sunday morning, Jesus' followers were shadow-men. When Jesus died the group became a body with the heart wrenched out. They were terribly afraid. They were without hope. They did not expect a sequel to the story. Peter, the natural leader, was crushed beyond bearing by the knowledge that he had denied Christ. The two on the Emmaus road were typical of the rest.

Yet within twelve hours everything is changed. Not only is the tomb empty – Jesus himself has been seen on at least five different occasions, by more than 16 of his followers. And it really was Jesus, not a ghost. They recognized him. They saw the crucifixion scars. And he ate with them. Peter is a new man. Despondency and mourning are things of the past. Fear is gone and in its place, indescribable joy. On the concrete certainty of the resurrection rests the whole of subsequent Christian history. Nothing else can account for the facts.

Verses 50-52: Luke compresses events. As he makes clear in Acts, his sequel, the ascension took place 40 days later.

THE ACCOUNTS OF THE RESURRECTION

David Wheaton

A superficial reading of the accounts of the resurrection in the four Gospels may suggest that there are many points of disagreement among them. Closer examination reveals a remarkable degree of unanimity, and suggests that in fact the apparent discrepancies provide evidence that although the Gospel writers obtained their information from different sources in the early Church, all four had the same basic tale to tell. Anyone who has heard evidence from different witnesses to an accident knows how in that situation people with different interests, backgrounds and emotional make-up tend to notice and remember different elements in a composite picture.

The main witnesses who first saw the empty tomb were a group of women who had recently been under severe emotional strain. Immediately after the momentous discovery they would appear to have scattered in order to take the news to different people. So it is not surprising that the accounts vary in detail. The variation suggests that the writers collected their evidence from more than one source, which makes the over-all agreement of the four accounts all the more impressive. The events in the records can be set out more or less as follows.

The Bible evidence

A group of women go to the tomb early on the first day of the week to embalm the body of Jesus (Matthew 28:1; Mark 16:1-2; Luke 24:1; 10; John 20:1a).

They discover that the stone has been rolled back (Matthew 28:2-4; Mark 16:3-4; Luke 24:2; John 20:1b).

The body of Jesus is no longer in the tomb; instead they see an angel who explains the situation and gives them a message (Matthew 28:5-7; Mark 16:5-7; Luke 24:3-7).

The women run back to Jerusalem to tell the other disciples, and are greeted in the main with disbelief (Matthew 28:8; Luke 24:8-11; 22-23; John 20:2).

Peter and the 'other disciple whom Jesus loved' go to the tomb and find it empty; they then return home (John 20:3-10; see Luke 24:24).

Mary Magdalene follows them back to the tomb, and remains there after they have left. Jesus then makes his first appearance to her (John 20:11-18; Matthew 28:9; Matthew names Mary Magdalene and the 'other Mary').

On that same day he appears to Peter (Luke 24:34; 1 Corinthians 15:5), to the two going to Emmaus (Luke 24:13-32; see Mark 16:12-13), and then to the rest of the disciples apart from Thomas back in Jerusalem (John 20:19-23; Luke 24:36-43; Mark 16:14). Other appearances, outside the scope of this article, are recorded in the four Gospels, Acts 1 and 1 Corinthians 15. What emerges from all the accounts is a remarkable consistency on two points – that Jesus could now reveal himself and disappear at will and that he only showed himself to his followers.

Apparent discrepancies

Which women went to the tomb? Apparently Mary Magdalene, Mary the mother of James, Salome, Joanna, and 'the other women from Galilee' (Luke 23:55). John singles out Mary Magdalene for mention (20:1) presumably because it was she who brought information back to Peter and the other disciples: she herself implies in 20:2 that there were others with her – we do not know. So the writers could each be mentioning by name those of the party whose behaviour made an impact on those from whom the writers gained their information.

When was the stone rolled back? Mark 16:3-4 and Luke 24:2 imply that it had been rolled back before they arrived on the spot. Then Matthew 28:2-4 could have happened before their arrival, and as a result the guards went off back to the city (in 28:11-15 the guards have presumably already reached the city and are busy spreading their tale by the time the women are on their way back from the tomb).

How many angels were there?
When the women arrive, the angel who descended to roll back the stone (Matthew 28:2) has moved inside the tomb and been joined by another (Luke 24:4 – Mary Magdalene also sees two, John 20:12). Matthew and Mark may refer only to the one who acted as spokesman, and therefore engaged the attention of their informants, and the plural in Luke 24:5 ('the men said') may refer loosely to the fact that while one spoke the other corroborated.

What did the angels say?
Again, the accounts can be put together to help us see the full picture:

> Do not be afraid: we know why you have come. Jesus is not here because he has risen. Look at the empty tomb. Tell his disciples; he is going to

meet you in Galilee. Remember how he foretold all this.

Who was the first to see Jesus?
Mark 16:9 says he first showed himself to Mary Magdalene, and this agrees with John's story. Luke has nothing to conflict with this. In Matthew 28:9 Jesus appears to Mary Magdalene (the key figure) and 'the other Mary'. It seems likely that this is the first appearance, and natural that when the story went round Mary Magdalene was named.

It has been pointed out that Matthew and Mark both record appearances of Jesus to the disciples in Galilee, and Luke and John in Jerusalem. In fact, of course, John 21 takes us back to Galilee, and Mark in his postscript refers to the Jerusalem appearances. In the case of Matthew and Luke, it accords with the purpose and structure of the writers for Luke to conclude his Gospel where he began – in Jerusalem – and for Matthew to conclude with the King's final proclamation on a mountain (28:16-20).

THE GOSPELS AND MODERN CRITICISM

Leon Morris

The Gospels are not biographies, though they contain much biographical information. They are books written by convinced Christians to commend and explain their faith to others (see Luke 1:3-4; John 20:31). They are quite unlike any other type of ancient literature. This means that they cannot be approached in quite the same way as other documents. We must bear in mind, first and foremost, that they are documents of faith; and second that they convey historical information.

The New Testament scholar comes to the Gospels with such questions as these: What purpose were these writings meant to serve? How accurate is the history recorded in them? What can we learn about their method of composition and what light does

this throw on their authors' intention and achievement?

Some scholars consider it possible that writers seeking to commend their faith may not be very interested in historical accuracy. They have sometimes concluded that there is very little history in the Gospels at all. They feel that theology is all-important to the Gospel writers, and that they never intended their history to be taken seriously.

Others think that this approach is too subjective. A more objective approach finds good evidence that the Gospel writers do take their facts with the utmost seriousness; Luke, for example, claims to have made a careful examination of the evidence before writing his Gospel (Luke 1:1-3).

Textual criticism

The scholar's first task is to establish the text. Textual criticism, as this is called, is a patient study of the manuscripts, the versions (that is, translations into languages other than the original), the quotations in early writings, the lectionaries used in worship and anything else that can help establish the text.

Behind all this is the fact that it is a trying process to copy out by hand a book as long as a Gospel, and mistakes are liable to creep in. But a careful comparison of the manuscripts, and a study of the methods of scribes, helps the textual critic to distinguish between early and later readings, and so to establish the text.

With thousands of manuscripts involved, textual criticism is an arduous business. But those engaged in it are agreed that the text of the New Testament is in surprisingly good shape (much better than the text of most of the classics). Although we may be uncertain of the original reading here and there, this rarely affects anything important. None of the basic Christian doctrines is in any doubt. And we may now be confident that we have the text of the New Testament substantially as it was written.

Source criticism

Having established the text, critics go on to observe that there are important similarities between the first three Gospels, over against the fourth. Matthew, Mark and Luke all describe a ministry of Jesus in Galilee, with a journey to Jerusalem at the end, at which time he is arrested and crucified. The passion story, with its sequel, the resurrection, occupies a large proportion of each account. But apart from this and the stories of Jesus' birth in Matthew and Luke there is not much that can be confidently located in Judea. John, on the other hand, speaks of a longer ministry (this is clear from his references to Passover feasts), and he describes many incidents which took place in Judea.

The resemblances between the first three Gospels led to their being given the name 'Synoptic Gospels': they can be set side by side and studied together. When this is done, however, differences as well as resemblances come to light, and the problem of the relationship between these Gospels (the 'Synoptic problem') has teased scholars for generations.

At one time it was commonly held that Matthew wrote first and that Mark has abbreviated him. A few still hold this view. But most scholars these days are impressed with the greater freshness of Mark, and by the fact that Mark's order seems always to be followed by either Matthew or Luke. They also point out that, although Mark is the shortest of all the Gospels, it is usually longer than Matthew in the narratives they have in common, which does not look like abbreviation. There is also very little indeed in Mark that is not contained in Matthew or Luke, so why should this Gospel have been written after the others? For these reasons it is now commonly held (though it has not been proved beyond doubt) that Mark was written first and that both Matthew and Luke made use of our second Gospel.

There is also a certain amount of material common to Matthew and Luke but absent from Mark. This is usually thought to represent another source, which has not survived, denoted by the symbol Q. Most see Q as a collection of sayings, with little narrative material. Many scholars think of it as a single document. Others point out that the amount of resemblance in the sections common to Matthew and Luke varies greatly. Sometimes the two are almost word for word (e.g. Matthew 3:7-10 = Luke 3:7-9), but in other places there are considerable differences (e.g. the Beatitudes). They therefore think in terms of several documents (see Luke 1:1), and use Q to denote the shared material in general, without committing themselves to any particular theory of documents.

Other material appears in only one Gospel, and clearly each of the Gospel writers had sources of his own. Symbols used for these are M for material that occurs only in Matthew, and L for material only in Luke. It has been suggested that in the case of Luke this is particularly important. Luke has his material from Mark in blocks, sometimes with long stretches in between. Some scholars hold that he first combined L and Q into a Gospel which has been called 'Proto-Luke'. Later he came across Mark's Gospel and incorporated a good deal of it to make up our present third Gospel. This view of Gospel origins takes the Lukan material very seriously and sees Proto-Luke as quite old and reliable.

Form criticism

That is about as far as source criticism has been taken, perhaps as far as it can go. In recent times attempts have been made to get behind the written sources to the time when the tradition was transmitted by word of mouth. The form critics pay attention to the form of the units which make up the Gospels and identify miracle stories, 'pronouncement stories' (i.e. stories leading up to some memorable saying) and so on. They point out that these units must have been passed on orally for many years.

Why were these particular stories preserved, out of the vast amount of material originally available? The answer, according to the form critics, is that they met the needs of the early Christians; it was the requirements of preaching that determined what would be preserved. Many form critics are rather radical and think that the preachers manufactured stories when they did not have suitable ones, under the belief that the Spirit of God was inspiring them to say what Jesus would have said in the circumstances confronting them. Usually they feel that the Gospels tell us more about the faith of the early church than they do about the teaching of Jesus. This is a highly subjective judgement, and form critics have often been criticized for propounding bold hypotheses on very little actual evidence.

Redaction criticism

The redaction critics take up where the form critics leave off, concentrating on the editorial framework which links together the various units of the Gospel story. Redaction critics find these links highly important, for they help us to see the evangelists' purpose as they wove the stories into their complete accounts. Thus the critics conclude that Matthew was interested in the church and provided a manual for teachers; that Mark used the 'messianic secret' to show that Jesus' true nature was not known until it was revealed by the cross and associated events; and that Luke was the theologian of 'salvation history'.

It is not easy to compare the fourth Gospel with the Synoptists and some feel that the Jesus of John's Gospel is so different from the Jesus of the other Gospels that we must reject one or the other. But Jesus must have been so great a figure that no one evangelist could be expected to capture his whole personality. It has been suggested that the Synoptists reflect the public teaching of Jesus, whereas John reflects Jesus' informal teaching of his disciples and his disputes with his enemies. The two portraits are not irreconcilable.

Probably no other documents in any language have been subjected to such detailed critical examination as the Gospels. The most minute details of vocabulary and syntax have been critically weighed for their bearing on the larger questions. That this searching examination has disclosed difficulties need not surprise us. It could scarcely have been otherwise. But in the judgement of many competent scholars the difficulties are by no means insuperable. They should certainly not deter us as we approach the Gospels. It requires no intellectual compromise, even today, for a humble man to read these books and find his Saviour there.

See further 'The Gospels and Jesus Christ'.

JOHN

John's Gospel is strikingly different from the other three. It was the last to be written – probably about AD 90 – and seems to assume that the readers already know the facts about Jesus' life. John supplements the other accounts, and concentrates on interpreting and bringing out the meaning of what took place. He selects from Jesus' many miracles certain 'signs' which show most clearly who he was. Everything he writes is subordinated to the main aim of bringing the reader to faith (20:30-31). He records mainly what Jesus said – especially about himself – in a style very different from Matthew, the other Gospel which concentrates on Jesus' sayings. There are no parables in John. Most of the events recorded take place in and around Jerusalem at the various festivals. And it may well be that Jesus adopted a different teaching method for the nation's capital city and theological centre. The keynote of John's Gospel is Jesus as Messiah and Son of God.

The author (who may, like Paul, have used a secretary) refers to himself simply as 'the disciple whom Jesus loved' (21:20, 24). He is one of the Twelve, and one of those closest to Jesus and also to Peter. These facts – and the fact that this Gospel makes no mention of the apostle John and describes the Baptist simply as 'John', make it likely that he is himself John, son of Zebedee, brother of James, and business partner of Peter and Andrew. The early church certainly thought so – and taught that the aged apostle wrote or dictated this 'spiritual' Gospel from Ephesus in present-day Turkey. John may have been Jesus' cousin (his mother, Salome, being Mary's sister: Matthew 27:56; Mark 15:40; John 19:25).

The Capernaum fishing business must have been a flourishing one, as the household had hired servants, and a house in Jerusalem. If the 'other disciple' of 18: 15-16 is John it may have been through the business that John was acquainted with the high priest (John 18:15-16). He may also be the unnamed disciple of John the Baptist referred to in John 1:35, 40.

John and James (nicknamed by Jesus 'sons of thunder') with Peter were the leaders of the Twelve disciples and later of the Jerusalem church. They were the inner circle of three who were allowed to see Jesus transfigured, who saw him restore Jairus' daughter to life, and who were near him in the garden of Gethsemane. Jesus committed his own mother to John's care as they stood near the cross. It was not given to many to know Jesus as closely as John did.

1:1-18 PROLOGUE

John begins his Gospel with a tremendous statement about Jesus Christ: on these truths his whole case rests. In him (the Word) God speaks to man. He is the most perfect and complete expression of the Person of God we can ever know. He is far and away above all humanity – God's executive in creation. When God spoke (see Genesis 1), his Word brought life itself into existence. And it was this Supreme Being who became man – the man we know as Jesus Christ. His life shone out – and still shines – against the darkness of a world which failed to recognize him. But to individuals who give him their allegiance he makes available all God's loving forgiveness (grace, 16). And he makes a new, transformed life possible (12).

John (6): John the Baptist (see on Luke 1, Matthew 3, Mark 1), the herald sent by God to tell people of the coming Christ and prepare for his arrival.

Verse 14: John may be thinking especially of the transfiguration – the time when he and Peter and James saw something of Jesus' supernatural splendour (Matthew 17:1-8).

1:19 - 2:12 EARLY DAYS

1:19-34 John the Baptist identifies Jesus as Messiah

John's dramatic preaching attracted

much attention. But he directs it away from himself. He is not Messiah. Nor will he admit to being the predicted second Elijah (Malachi 4:5; in contrast, Jesus leaves us in no doubt that this prediction was realized in John, Matthew 17:10-13). Nor is he the prophet like Moses (Deuteronomy 18:15). As soon as God has shown him the Messiah (32-34) he directs men to Jesus.

Pharisees (24): see article 'Religious Background'.

The Lamb of God (29): a phrase from the Old Testament sacrifices (Leviticus 4:32-35; see also Isaiah 53:4-12). Sin puts every individual under sentence of death – separation from God. But in Old Testament times God accepted the death of an animal as substitute for the death of a person. Further sin meant repeated sacrifices. Jesus was to die to give his life once and for all, sacrificed like a lamb for human sin throughout the ages.

1:35-51 Jesus' first followers

See also on 'The Twelve', Mark 3:7-19. At John's words, two of his followers leave him for Jesus – Andrew, the fisherman (see also 6:8-9; 12:22) and an unnamed follower, possibly the apostle John. The news is too good not to share; so first Andrew brings Peter, and then Philip (see also 6:5; 12:21; 14:8) brings the intellectual Nathanael.

Verse 39: it seems likely, judging by 19:14, that John uses the Roman (and modern) method of reckoning the hours, in which case the time here is 10 a.m.

Verse 42: 'Cephas' and 'Peter' both mean 'the rock-man'.

Verse 48: Nathanael was following the Jewish custom of meditating on the scriptures under his fig-tree. It seems likely, from Jesus' words in verse 51, that he was thinking about Jacob's dream of a stairway between heaven and earth (Genesis 28:12). Jesus is himself a 'ladder' giving man access to God.

The Son of man (51): Jesus' favourite description of himself. The title was also applied to the Messiah (Daniel 7:13-14).

2:1-12 Jesus at the wedding

Jesus' first miracle has a homely setting. The wedding festivities lasted several days, and when the wine ran out the bridegroom (who footed the bill) must have been highly embarrassed. This is the first of seven 'signs' selected by John. All

A large water-pot at the Rockefeller Museum, Jerusalem, of the type used for Jewish rites of purification.

have a purpose – they actively support the claims Jesus made, and are intended to lead to faith. Here the new wine of the Gospel is contrasted with the water of the old faith (see verse 6). Jesus had come to bring something really new.

Cana (1): Nathanael's home town (21:2); a few miles north-east of Nazareth.

Verse 4: no one, not even his mother, has the right to put pressure on Jesus. But his reply is not as harsh as some translations make it sound. New English Bible 'Your concern, mother, is not mine' is better.

Verse 6: the water-pots were there for the ritual washing of hands and utensils.

2:13 - 3:36 JESUS' PUBLIC MINISTRY BEGINS: JERUSALEM

2:13-25 Jesus ejects the traders from the temple

See on Matthew 21:12-17. John places this at the beginning of Jesus' ministry, the other Gospels at the end. Jesus may, of course, have turned the traders out of the temple on more than one occasion. But it seems more likely that John overrules strict chronology for more important considerations. The incident illustrates the dishonesty, hypocrisy and prejudice at the heart of Israel's religious life. It makes us see that a head-on clash between Jesus and the religious authorities is inevitable.

Passover (13): see on Matthew 26:14-29.

Verses 20-21: the temple was in a special sense the place of God's presence – the closest man could come to God himself. With the coming of Jesus that changed: he could accurately describe himself as the Temple of God.

3:1-21 The interview with Nicodemus

Nicodemus comes secretly; later he comes out openly on the side of Christ (7:50-51; 19:39). Men need an entirely new spiritual re-birth in order to enter God's kingdom. The new age Jesus was announcing was not to be bound by the old cycle of physical birth and death. It was to be a radical new beginning, a new quality of life – eternal life.

Verses 16-21 may be Jesus' words (New English Bible), or John's comment (Revised Standard Version). They contain the heart of the Gospel message. Jesus comes to save – but the consequence of his coming, for those who refuse him, is judgement.

Verse 14: see Numbers 21:4-9; Jesus is referring to his crucifixion.

3:22-36 John the Baptist steps down

For a while Jesus' ministry overlaps with John's and Jesus draws the bigger crowds. John's reaction, in a situation which goes very much against the human grain, is absolutely right. He allows no trace of bitterness or jealousy to sour his gladness at Jesus' God-given success.

Verses 31-36 may be the Baptist's words or the apostle's comment.

Verse 24: see Mark 6:17-29. The writer here as elsewhere assumes that his readers know the basic facts.

4:1-42 SAMARIA: THE WOMAN AT THE WELL

Jesus chooses the short route from Jerusalem to Galilee which takes him through Samaria – normally avoided by Jews, for over 700 years of religious and racial prejudice separated the Jew from the Samaritan (see article 'Religious Background'). Add to this the Jewish prayer, 'Blessed art thou O Lord ... who hast not made me a woman' and one can understand the Samaritan woman's surprise (9) when Jesus talks to her. Tired and thirsty though he is, he can never

ignore human need. As the conversation develops he makes it clear that the woman's need is spiritual rather than physical (7-15), moral rather than 'theological' (16-26). As a result of this seemingly insignificant encounter, many others believe – some through the woman's testimony, more through Jesus' own words.

Verse 20: for the Samaritan, Mt Gerizim was the centre of worship; for the Jew, Jerusalem. Jesus says that the place is unimportant. What matters is that worship should be genuine and spiritual.

4:43-54 GALILEE: HEALING OF THE OFFICIAL'S SON

This is the second of the signs recorded by John (see on 2:1-12 above). Jesus never performed miracles simply to impress. They were intended, as here (verse 53), to lead to faith. John's purpose in recording them is precisely the same.

Verse 44: Jesus was speaking about Nazareth (Mark 6:1-6). John may be giving the words a wider reference, to lack of response in Judea.

5 JERUSALEM AGAIN

5:1-18 Trouble over healing on the sabbath

This is the third sign (see above). Jesus clashed with the religious authorities a number of times over healing on the sabbath (Mark 3:1-6; Luke 13:10-17; 14:1-6; John 9). It was not the general principle of the sabbath that he disagreed with (he regularly attended the synagogue) but the petty restrictions imposed by the religious authorities, which often worked *against* God's purpose in giving man a weekly day of rest. Here the Jews attack him on two counts – sabbath-breaking and blasphemy – because he puts his own work on the same level as God's (17). God's activity in the world did not finish with the creation.

5:19-47 The claims of Jesus

The Jews were right. Jesus *was* making himself God's equal (18) – though this did not mean setting himself up as an independent authority (19). In this passage alone he claims to have:
— knowledge of God's plan (20)
— God's authorization for all he says and does (19, 30)
— power to give eternal life (21, 24, 40)
— the right and authority to judge all men, living and dead (25-29).

A man who makes these claims must be 'mad, bad, or God'. What support can he give them?

— the word God spoke at his baptism (37)
— the testimonial given by John the Baptist (33-35)
— the evidence of his own miracles (36)
— the words of Old Testament Scripture (39).

6 GALILEE

6:1-21 Food for 5,000; Jesus walks on the lake

See on Mark 6:30-56. See also Matthew 14:13-36; Luke 9:10b-17. These are the fourth and fifth signs. The events stand out clearly in John's mind. He remembers which disciples replied to Jesus' question; he recalls the lad; he remembers how far they had rowed from shore when they saw Jesus.

6:22-59 The crowd tracks Jesus down; Christ, the bread of life

The crowd is all in favour of a Messiah who can provide free meals for the asking (26, 34). No one can live without food. But life is more than physical existence (27). Jesus comes to provide bread for the spiritually starving. He is the giver *and* the gift itself. He is the bread of the new life; the one on whom we depend entirely for existence. And the bread we feed on – the source of life for us – is his death (51). Because sin has placed us under God's sentence of death, we live only because of Christ's death on our behalf. We know life only as we make his death and all it means our own. The forgiveness his death has bought is the meat and drink of Christian living. Each one of us must receive it for himself (52-58). The Lord's Supper proclaims this same fact in visual terms (Matthew 26:26-28).

Manna (31): see Exodus 16 and Deuteronomy 8:3.

6:60-71 Reaction

Those who put a crudely literal interpretation on Jesus' words were disgusted. The law forbade the drinking of blood. Meat had to be specially butchered to meet the law's requirements. Yet had they bothered to think back to the reason for the rule they would have understood. Leviticus 17:11 says, 'it is the blood that makes atonement, by reason of the life.' Jesus is saying, 'I am atoning for your sin; avail yourselves of my sacrifice.' The crowd turn away –

they do not want this sort of Messiah. But the Twelve remain, in growing faith.

7 - 10:21 TO JERUSALEM FOR THE FEAST OF TABERNACLES

7:1-13 Danger

Last time Jesus visited Jerusalem there was trouble, ending in a plot against his life (chapter 5). This time he avoids publicity.

Tabernacles (2): September/October – the 8-day Jewish harvest festival, commemorating the nation's desert wanderings. See 'Feasts and Festivals'.

Not going (8): some manuscripts add 'yet', showing that Jesus did not intend to mislead. He waited for the opportune moment and then seized it.

7:14-52 Jesus' message gets a mixed reception

As opposition mounts, individuals take sides. Jesus' teaching (40) and his miracles (31) convince some. Others raise difficulties (27, 41-42). But no one who genuinely wants to do God's will is left in doubt (17). Jesus draws his imagery from the ceremony appointed for each day of the festival, when water from the Pool of Siloam was offered to God. Jesus is a bubbling spring, reviving and transforming the thirsty human heart.

Dispersion (35): the Jewish communities abroad.

Verse 42: they cannot have heard the story of Jesus' birth. The Old Testament reference is Micah 5:2.

7:53 - 8:11 The woman guilty of adultery

Although this story is quite genuine, it is unlikely that it originally belonged here (some manuscripts place it at the end of John's Gospel, others insert it after Luke 21:38). The lawyers were trying to trap Jesus. They intended to push him either into contradicting the Mosaic law, or into falling foul of the Roman authorities, who did not allow Jews to carry out a death sentence. But Jesus did neither – nor did he condemn, or condone, the woman's conduct. He gave her a second chance.

8:12-59 Jesus, the light of the world

Jesus again uses one of the ceremonies of the feast to explain his own mission. At dusk they lit four great golden candelabra to symbolize the pillar of fire by which God guided his people through the desert by night (Exodus 13:21). Jesus lights the way

Jesus taught in the porticos of the temple area in Jerusalem.

through life for all who follow him. He strengthens his claim to be, in a unique sense, God's Son (see also on 5:19-47).

Verses 12-30: unlike the rest of us, he knows where he comes from and where he is going. He knows the future. The Jewish people have their origin and ancestry in this world, but not Jesus.

Verses 31-47: other men are held in the grip of sin. Jesus is free, and has the power to free others.

Verses 48-59: Jesus asserts his control over death and the eternal destinies of men. Only God has these powers.

9 The blind man sees; the sighted shut their eyes
Jesus really is the light of the world. This sixth sign makes that plain. It also gives us some insight into the problem of human suffering.
— Although there is a direct connection between human suffering and man's sin, the individual is not necessarily suffering because of his own or his parents' sin (3).
— There are times when God allows suffering for a purpose. And he brings good out of it, for the individual himself and all he comes into contact with.
Here the man's blindness leads to an encounter with Jesus. His eyes were opened and he saw (7). His mind was opened and he believed (35-37). By contrast, the sighted men allow prejudice and pride to blind them to the truth (40-41). Confronted by a miracle, all they can see is a broken rule (16). Their minds are closed. They will not listen to the simple

logic of the man in the street (30-34).
Verse 6: Jesus uses the methods of popular medicine (saliva was thought to have healing properties). But the method is not the important thing. What counts is the man's faith, demonstrated by his ready obedience (7).
Sent (7): because the water was channelled from another source.
Verse 22: anyone who followed Christ faced excommunication.

10:1-21 Jesus, the good shepherd
This passage follows straight on from chapter 9. The shepherd was a familiar figure in Palestine. He spent much of his life with his flock. His own sheep knew and responded to his voice. He led (not drove) them to fresh grazing, and guarded them from wild animals by lying across the entrance to the sheepfold at night, so becoming its 'door'. In the Old Testament God is often called the shepherd of Israel. And his chosen leaders are also the nation's 'shepherds'. Now Jesus chooses to describe himself as the *true* shepherd. The phrase sums up so much: the close, personal relationship between himself and each of his followers; the absolute security we have in him; his leadership and guidance; his constant company; his unfailing care; his sacrificial love.
Verse 16: Jesus' concern goes out beyond the Jewish nation to the waiting world. Jew and non-Jew, slave and free man, man and woman, all are one flock (see Galatians 3:28).

10:22-42 JERUSALEM: THE FEAST OF DEDICATION
This eight-day feast – the festival of lights – took place in December. It commemorated the great Jewish victory under the Maccabees and the rededication of the desecrated temple.

The Jews remain in suspense because they will not believe (24-26). They are ready to stone Jesus as a man making himself out to be God (33). But they have it back to front. Jesus is not man made God, but God made man (30).

11 LAZARUS RETURNS FROM THE DEAD; JESUS, THE RESURRECTION AND THE LIFE
This is the seventh sign. Lazarus' death is permitted for the same reason as the man's blindness (4 and 9:3). Time and again we see how

Jesus' miracles back up the claims he made. No wonder he so often referred his critics to the work he was doing. He claims he can give men new, spiritual life. What clearer assurance that this is so than Lazarus' return from the dead after four days in the grave? So we too can take him at his word. Neither the disciples nor the two sisters could understand Jesus' behaviour, but the result for all of them was renewed trust in him (15, 27, 42). The event is decisive – for faith and life on the one hand (45); for hatred and death on the other (53).

Thomas (16): see also 20:24-29.

Verse 50: the high priest's words took on a significance he never dreamed of.

12 FINAL DAYS OF PUBLIC TEACHING IN JERUSALEM

12:1-8 Mary's precious flask of perfume

See on Mark 14:1-11.

12:9-11 The plot to kill Lazarus

12:12-19 Jesus rides in triumph into Jerusalem

See on Luke 19:28-48 and introduction to Matthew 21. See also Mark 11:1-11.

Branches of palm (13): the symbol of victory.

12:20-36a The Greeks search Jesus out

The arrival of the Greek converts brings Jesus face to face with his destiny. The time has come for him to buy life for mankind with his own death. Verses 20-36 and 44-50 record his last public statement. It is full of paradox: life through death; glory through the ignominy of the cross; the world judged in the execution of judgement.

Verse 25: Jesus is not advocating a death-wish. But love for him and concern for eternal things must far outweigh all selfish, material concerns.

12:36b-50 Jesus steps out of the limelight

Verses 36b-43: at the end of Jesus' public ministry and despite all his miracles the Jews remained unconvinced. And many of those who did believe were too afraid to say so openly.

Verses 44-50: it matters how each of us reacts to Christ. Because he comes on God's authority, it is all-important whether we believe in him or not.

Verse 40: God never hardens the heart of someone willing to respond. But in the end, if we choose to be blind and persistently reject his truth, he lets us become immune to it.

13 - 17:26 JESUS' LAST WORDS TO THE TWELVE

13:1-20 Jesus washes the disciples' feet

The occasion is the Last Supper (see on Matthew 26:14-29). The disciples have been arguing over who is greatest (Luke 22:24). Jesus gives them the answer in this simple action. The Master, conscious of who he is and in his love for men, has willingly made himself their slave (Luke 22:27). His followers must do the same.

13:21-30 Judas, the traitor

Judas has already volunteered to help the priests make a secret arrest (Luke 22:3-6). Now the moment has come. The rest of the disciples have no idea of what is afoot. But Jesus knows. 'It was night' – quite literally. But light and darkness acquire a special meaning in this Gospel (1:4-9). These were Jesus' darkest hours, but nothing could extinguish the light of his life (1:5). Judas, by contrast, stepped from the light into darkness so intense it destroyed him (3:19-20; Matthew 27:3-5).

Verse 23: most probably John himself; see introduction.

13:31-38 The command to love one another; Jesus predicts Peter's fall

The prospect of death on the cross,

Pool of
Bethesda

Fort of Antonia

Temple

Herod's
Palace

House of Caiaphas

Kidron Valley

Valley of Hinnom

—— Present (Turkish) wall of old city

- - Probable location of walls

200 m

**JERUSALEM IN
NEW TESTAMENT TIMES**

cut off from his Father by the colossal burden of the world's sin, appalled Jesus (Luke 22:42-44). Yet because of all it would achieve, he could describe it in terms of triumph and glory. It was his love for others that took him there. And it is love of this same calibre he looks for in his followers.

14 Jesus reassures his disciples; 'I am the way, and the truth, and the life'

The disciples are worried and upset by the talk of betrayal and the thought of Jesus leaving them. Jesus himself is concerned at the effect his death will have on them all. And so he tries to get them to understand why it has to happen.

His death means his return to the Father (12, 28). He is making the approach-road for men to come to God (6). He is going to get a permanent home ready for his disciples, and in due course he will come for them (2-3). Meanwhile his return to God will be to their good: it will bring new power in action, new certainty in prayer (12, 14). Best of all, the Holy Spirit will come to be with them always and everywhere (not limited by a physical body as Jesus had been). He will teach and counsel and bring to mind all that Jesus has said (16-17, 26). And Jesus' own unshakable peace will be theirs (27).

For their part, the disciples must continue to love and trust him (1). And the way to show their love is to do all that he says (15, 21, 23).

15 - 16 Jesus, the true vine; opposition; the promise of the Holy Spirit

The conversation continues as they make their way to Gethsemane (14:31). There is not much time left.

15:1-17: in the Old Testament, Israel is the vine – so often failing to yield fruit (see Galatians 5:22-23). But Jesus was the true vine, the fulfilment of God's purpose where Israel had failed. Those who believe in him are branches. Every branch of a vine grows directly from the main 'stock'. When they are cut back, branches which have borne fruit are pruned to within an inch or two of the stock. They then 'abide' in the stock for most of the year as it grows round them. Then the branches grow out rapidly to bear fruit again. Branches which have not borne fruit at all are cut right back, and are fit only for burning.

15:18 - 16:4a: those who belong to

A vine, with the main 'stock', branches growing from it, bunches of grapes on the fruitful branches, and the unfruitful ones cut off to be burnt.

Christ will inevitably encounter the hatred of self-centred humanity, just as Christ himself did. They will even be hounded by men who (like Paul) consider themselves to be doing God a service.

16:4b-15: Jesus' going means the coming of the Holy Spirit to convict men of the truth and lead them into deeper understanding of it.

16:16-33: at Christ's death there will be grief, but only for a little. With the resurrection will come lasting joy.

16:25, 29: 'figures of speech', New English Bible.

17 Jesus' prayer; for himself and for his followers

Jesus has accomplished all he set out to do during his lifetime. He has passed God's message on. He has made God known. Now there remains only death, and beyond it the glory he renounced to become man. But his followers will be left bereft in a hostile world. So he prays that God will protect them; that their lives may be shaped by the truth of God's word; that they may display such unity among themselves that the world will be shaken out of its disbelief; and that they may, in the end, go to be with him and see his glory for themselves.

Verse 12: the reference is to Judas.

18 - 21 TRIAL, DEATH AND RESURRECTION

18:1-12 Betrayal and arrest
See on Matthew 26:30-56. See also

Mark 14:26-52; Luke 22:39-53. John omits Jesus' prayer in the garden. But he tells us the name of the slave, and that the swordsman was Peter.

18:13 - 19:16 Jesus before Annas and Caiaphas; Peter's denial; Jesus before Pilate

See on Mark 14:53 - 15:15; Luke 22: 54 - 23:31. See also Matthew 26:57 - 27: 26. The detail John fills in shows his close knowledge of what happened – the cold night; the charcoal fire (18:18); the blow to the prisoner (18:22); Jewish religious scruples over entering the Roman's house at such a time (18:28); the exchanges between Jesus and Pilate, and Pilate and the Jews; the terrible national apostasy as God's people declare they have no king but Caesar.

19:14: unlike the other Gospel writers, John probably uses Roman time, counting as we do from midnight. Unless, as some believe, John dates the Passover one day later than the other Gospel writers (see Mark 14:12), the reference here is to the preparation for the sabbath of Passover week (19:31).

19:17-37 The crucifixion

See on Mark 15:16-41; Luke 23:32-49. See also Matthew 27:27-56. Again John shows his vivid recollection of events – the details of the inscription (20-22); the seamless tunic (23-24); the moment when Jesus entrusted his mother to John's care (26-27); the incontrovertible evidence of Jesus' death (34).

Verse 31: Jewish law said that the bodies of criminals must not be left hanging after sunset (Deuteronomy 21:23).

Verse 34: John is implying more than that Jesus was without question dead. As a Jew, he could not help seeing special significance in the flow of blood (for sacrifice) and water (for cleansing). The blood atones for man's sin, the water gives him a clean, new start. Jesus' death brings us forgiveness and new life.

19:38-42 Burial

See on Mark 15:42-47. See also Matthew 27:57-66; Luke 23:50-56. The death of Jesus brings two secret disciples out into the open. Only John mentions the part played by Nicodemus (see 3:1-15).

20 The resurrection; Jesus appears to the disciples in Jerusalem

See on Luke 24. See also Matthew 28; Mark 16. John gives his own personal account of what happened – what he heard and saw for himself, and what he learnt from Mary Magdalene. Thomas the realist's momentous declaration of faith – 'My Lord and my God!' – is the climax of the whole Gospel. John's purpose in writing is to bring men to just such assured and clear-cut belief in Jesus (31).

Verse 7: John sees the grave-clothes and head-cloth lying undisturbed, still in place. But now an empty space separates the head-cloth from the rest. No one could steal a body and leave the grave-clothes like that. Jesus' body can only have passed through them. So John took note, and believed.

21 Jesus appears again in Galilee; the author's final word

Only John tells us how Jesus came to the seven of them as they were fishing, just as in the old days. John was there. He remembers how many fish they caught, and their surprise and relief at finding the net intact. He remembers how Jesus gave Peter the chance to cancel out his three-fold denial with the three-times-repeated question 'Do you love me?'; how he restored Peter to his old place as leader, and gave him the task of caring for his people. He remembers Peter's question about his own destiny – and sets the record straight.

And having remembered it all, he closes his Gospel with an affirmation of the truth of what he has written.

Verse 18: a prediction of Peter's death – stretched out on a cross, like his Master.

ACTS

The book of Acts covers a period of some 30 years, from the birth of the church on the Day of Pentecost to the close of Paul's imprisonment at Rome. It describes the spread of Christianity around the northern Mediterranean – through present-day Syria, Turkey and Greece, to the heart of the Roman Empire. The 'acts' related are mainly those of the apostles Peter and Paul, though the book might well be called 'the acts of the Holy Spirit'. It is under his direction that the new-born church bursts through the national frontiers of Israel to become an international, world-wide movement.

Who wrote it? All the evidence, from earliest times, points to Paul's 'dear friend Luke, the doctor'. He wrote Acts as a sequel to his earlier volume, the third Gospel. Luke is the only non-Jewish writer in the New Testament. He came from Antioch, or possibly Philippi. Although we have a few facts about his life, his writings prove him a fine and reliable historian. We know, from the way he changes from 'they' to 'we' in Acts (16:10; 20:5; 27:1), that he was present at many of the events he describes. He was with Paul at Philippi. He made the fateful journey with him to Jerusalem, stuck by him during the two years at Caesarea, and shared the voyage and shipwreck on the way to Rome. He had plenty of opportunity to obtain his other information first-hand – from Paul and Barnabas and others in the church at Antioch; from James, the Lord's brother, among others at Jerusalem; and from Philip and his daughters at Caesarea. And we know from Luke 1:1-4 just how concerned he was to get at the facts.

Why did he write? It was in order to give the Roman Theophilus an accurate record of the true facts about Christianity (Luke 1:1-4). There were plenty of strange and distorted rumours flying about. This explains Luke's emphasis on the spread of the gospel to the Gentiles, who, unlike many Jews, were eager

TIME-CHART

There are not enough fixed points to be exact, but the dates below are accurate within a year or two either way.

AD 30 The founding of the church in Jerusalem (Acts 1 - 2)
32/35 Paul's conversion (Acts 9)
34/37 Paul's first visit to Jerusalem (Acts 9:26ff.)
45 or 46 Famine relief sent to Jerusalem from Antioch (Acts 11:27ff.) Death of James
46 or 47 First missionary journey (Acts 13 - 14)
48 Apostolic Council at Jerusalem (Acts 15)
48-51 Second missionary journey (Acts 15:36 - 18:22)
50 Paul reaches Corinth (Acts 18)
53 Third missionary journey begins (Acts 18:23)
54-57 Paul's stay in Ephesus (Acts 19)
57-58 Paul in Greece (Acts 20)
58 (June) Paul reaches Jerusalem (Acts 21)
58-60 Imprisonment at Caesarea (Acts 24 - 26)
60-61 Appeal to Caesar and voyage to Rome (Acts 27)
61-63 Imprisonment in Rome (Acts 28:30)

to hear (28:28). He is also concerned to account for the disturbances which so often followed the preaching. In every place the troubles are fomented either by Jewish jealousy, or vested interest. Time and again he relates how the Roman authorities cleared the Christians of all charges of subversion and sometimes protected them from the fury of the mob.

When was Acts written? Most probably at the close of Paul's two-year imprisonment in Rome, in the early or mid-sixties. There is no hint of Nero's persecutions, or the Jewish revolt (AD 66-70), or Paul's death (about AD 67). On the contrary, the

EARLY CHRISTIAN PREACHING

Michael Green

The truly amazing thing about early Christian preaching is that it did not proclaim religious duties or moral standards, or even a reforming programme, but a person: one Jesus who was crucified and whom the Christians knew to be alive. They devoted their energies to understanding him better (from studying the Old Testament) and making him real to people who had never met him. Common belief and varied presentation are the keynotes of their achievement. Above all it is crucial to recognize that both the content and the dynamic of their preaching was the Risen One, whom many of them had known and followed for several years while he had been a carpenter and rabbi.

It has been shown that the early Christians had a broadly uniform pattern for preaching Jesus Christ. It ran something like this:

'The ancient prophecies have been fulfilled and the new age has been inaugurated by the coming of Christ. He was born of David's family, died according to the scriptures in order to deliver us from the present evil age. He was buried, rose again the third day as scripture foretold, and is now exalted at God's right hand as Son of God and Lord of the living and the dead. He has given his Holy Spirit to his followers as an assurance of his Lordship and as a foretaste of his return to be the Judge and Saviour of men at the Last Day.'

This pattern of teaching was already developed from an early date. This can be seen in the pieces of early preaching, or hymns, or creeds, incorporated into the Letters. For instance, Philippians 2:4-11 is very early, possibly coming from the Aramaic-speaking church; yet it is as doctrinally advanced as anything in the New Testament. Other fragmentary statements of belief from very early days have been preserved in such passages as 1 Corinthians 15:3-4; Romans 1:3-4 and 1 Timothy 3:16.

Slight variations in emphasis may also be detected. When speaking mainly to Jews, the deliverance Christ gives from the broken law of God is stressed. Forgiveness, justification, cleansing are the important things. When the readers are predominantly pagan in background, stress is laid on the deliverance Christ gives from the demonic powers of which men of the ancient world were so acutely aware.

So to the Jews Jesus was shown as Christ, the messianic Deliverer, the climax of the Old Testament revelation. To non-Jews, to the pagan world, he was presented as Lord and conqueror of all the forces of evil.

When preaching to the pagan world, without the background of the Old Testament revelation of God, the early missionaries also had to start further back in their teaching. Acts gives us two examples, one of preaching to unsophisticated people (14:15-17), the other the approach to the cultured (17:22-31). In both cases the Christians seek to establish the fact that there is one God, discredit idolatry and through the light of natural revelation (God the Creator and Sustainer) to prepare the way for the special revelation of God contained in Christ. This way of proceeding had been used by Jews in the previous century or so, when seeking to commend the ethical monotheism of Israel to an immoral and idolatrous but wistful pagan world. It formed a useful introduction to the specifically Christian proclamation, and it remained the staple approach for centuries.

Whether preaching to Jews or Gentiles, the early Christians emphasized not only what God had done for men through Christ, but what he offers (new life by the Holy Spirit, forgiveness of sins) and what he requires (repentance, faith and commitment). This commitment involved three strands which must be held onto together: baptism, faith and reception of the Holy Spirit. These three make a man a Christian.

Acts makes a point of the depth at which this early preaching was carried on. Words are used which indicate that the Christians acted like heralds, like teachers, like debaters. They discussed this good news, argued it, gave testimony to it, and showed how it fitted in with the Old Testament scriptures. It was the task of no single category of Christians; women chattered it at the laundry, philosophers argued it at the street corner, prisoners told their fellows. Men of every background and culture demonstrated its power by their transformed lives (see 1 Corinthians 6:9-11) and their willing acceptance of suffering and death (e.g. Acts 20:22-24).

It was these qualities which commended the new message, with the power of the Spirit in their social and personal lives which backed up their claims. There was also an intellectual characteristic which contributed largely to their success. They discovered how to interpret Jesus in varying ways to meet varying needs – they were not rigorously hidebound. Neither were they 'syncretists': they did not say that other religious insights were equally true and could be merged with the new faith. Christianity, like Judaism, would have nothing to do with the syncretism of the pagan world. But Christians succeeded, as Judaism never did, in giving great flexibility to the expression of their faith while retaining the main common pattern and content which we have seen.

For instance, Jesus' preaching of 'the kingdom of God' might be meaningful in a Jewish constituency but could be politically inflammable elsewhere. So the early preachers preferred to use Jesus' other expressions 'eternal life' or 'salvation'.

Again, 'Son of man' was a peculiar form of address with highly apocalyptic associations understood in some circles in Judaism but meaningless elsewhere. Words which rang a bell with pagans – such as 'Son of God' or 'Lord' – were used instead by these versatile early preachers.

When engaged in interpreting the person of their Master, they used the language and thought-forms familiar to those they sought to reach. Their aim was to make crystal clear the unique saving work of the divine, crucified and risen Jesus who was both the Lord they served and the message they proclaimed.

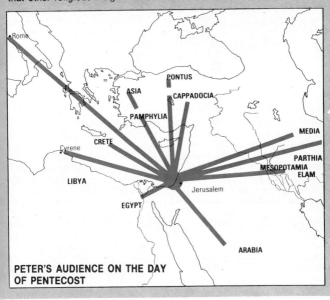

PETER'S AUDIENCE ON THE DAY OF PENTECOST

book ends on an optimistic note. It must have been written after the Gospel, which some date later than AD 70. But the evidence points to a date about AD 60, which makes 63 or thereabouts a likely date for Acts.

1 - 8:1a THE BIRTH OF THE CHURCH: JERUSALEM

1:1-14 Introduction; the 40 days from resurrection to ascension

Luke's 'first book' (his Gospel) is an account of all that Jesus 'began to do and teach' during his life on earth. Acts continues the story of his work after the ascension, by the power of the Holy Spirit in the lives of the apostles. It shows how the promise in verse 8 was fulfilled: in Jerusalem (2:1 - 8:1a), Judea and Samaria (8:1b - 11:18) and way beyond (11:19 to the end).

A cloud (9): all that human eyes could see of the glory of God's presence (compare also Exodus 40:34 and Luke 9:34-35).

Sabbath day's journey (12): the law limited travel on the sabbath to 2,000 cubits – about two thirds of a mile.

Mary ... and his brothers (14): this is the last time Jesus' mother is mentioned in the New Testament, and the first time his brothers are associated with the disciples. We know at least one of them – James – had seen the risen Jesus (1 Corinthians 15:7).

1:15-26 A twelfth apostle is chosen

As far as we know, this is the last time the apostles use the time-honoured method of casting lots. It is not just a 'lucky dip' – the decision is made after much prayer. The twelfth man had to have been with Christ throughout his earthly ministry, and to have seen him after the resurrection.

2:1-13 Pentecost: the coming of the Holy Spirit

With the coming of the Holy Spirit – made unmistakably evident by inward transformation and signs that all can see and hear – the waiting is over. The apostles and disciples become the new church, full of life and power, as different from their former fearful selves as can be imagined.

Pentecost (1): the old Jewish festival of firstfruits, which took place at the beginning of the wheat harvest. It was 50 days after the Passover, the time of Jesus' crucifixion.

Each heard in his own language (6): the audience of Jews and converts were from many countries, though all would speak either Greek or one of the Aramaic dialects. Normally the apostles' difficult Galilean speech would have been hard to follow. Now, to their astonishment, everyone in this mixed audience heard his own language being spoken. The curse of Babel (Genesis 11) is dramatically reversed.

2:14-47 Peter's sermon and what follows

The sermon evokes an immediate response. Baptism is followed by a new, joyous sense of community. And spiritual unity finds practical expression in readiness to share money and possessions.

The third hour (15): 9 a.m., and on that day there was fasting till mid-morning.

3-4:31 Healing of the lame man; Peter and John taken into custody

Healing and teaching, as in Jesus' ministry, go together, both made possible by the power of the Spirit of God. It is the teaching, centring as always on the risen Christ, which annoys the Sadducees – naturally enough, as they denied the possibility of resurrection. Paul, in his turn, divided the Pharisees and Sadducees over the very same question (23:6). The resurrection was the core of the Christian message from the very earliest days. Everywhere the apostles spoke about Jesus and the resurrection – so much so that the Athenians thought Paul was talking about *two* new deities (see on 17:18).

The ninth hour (3:1): 3 p.m. Prayer times were early morning, afternoon (as here) and sunset. The first two coincided with the morning and evening sacrifices.

Annas ... Caiaphas (4:6): Annas was senior ex-high priest, his son-in-law, Caiaphas, ruling high priest (AD 18-36).

This is the stone (11): a quotation from Psalm 118:22.

Uneducated, common men (13): 'untrained laymen', New English Bible.

4:32 - 5:11 Ananias and Sapphira

The pooling of property was quite voluntary, but some were prompted less by real generosity than by a desire to impress. In lying to the church, Ananias and Sapphira were practising deceit against God himself. The terrible consequences served as an example to the whole church.

Barnabas (4:36): later chapters show how aptly he was named. A leader in the church at Antioch, he and Paul were sent out together as

THE NAZARETH DECREE
This remarkable inscription most probably dates from the first century AD. It was sent to a French collector from Nazareth in 1878. Was it the rumour that Jesus of Nazareth had risen from the dead that made the decree necessary?

ORDINANCE OF CAESAR. It is my pleasure that graves and tombs remain undisturbed in perpetuity for those who have made them for the cult of their ancestors, or children, or members of their house. If, however, any man lay information that another has either demolished them, or has in any other way extracted the buried, or has maliciously transferred them to other places in order to wrong them, or has displaced the sealing or other stones, against such a one I order that a trial be instituted, as in respect of the gods, so in regard to the cult of mortals. For it shall be much more obligatory to honour the buried. Let it be absolutely forbidden for anyone to disturb them. In the case of contravention I desire that the offender be sentenced to capital punishment on charge of violation of sepulture.

missionaries. Paul benefited from Barnabas' encouragement – so too did his young cousin, John Mark.

5:12-42 The apostles before the council
It was like the days of Jesus in Galilee all over again, so many were being healed by the apostles. No wonder the Jewish authorities grew jealous of their enormous influence. But threats, imprisonment, even the lash are no weapons with which to resist the power of God.

Solomon's Portico (12): it was common practice for groups to meet for teaching and discussion in the courts of public buildings, and for disciples to listen to their teachers in the courts of the temple. The Christians met in Solomon's porch – but knowing the authorities' hostility towards them, the bystanders kept their distance.

This man's blood (28): the apostles openly held the council responsible for Jesus' death, and they fear reprisals.

Hanging him on a tree (30): the upright of the cross was a fixture, and might well be a sawn-off tree-trunk. See also Deuteronomy 21:22-23.

Gamaliel (34): leader of the Pharisees; Paul's teacher. His is wise advice.

6 Seven assistants appointed; Stephen arouses opposition
Complaints come from the Greek-speaking, non-Palestinian Jews of unfairness in the daily share-out. The apostles' answer is to let them choose seven of their own number – men of spiritual calibre – to oversee these practical matters. At least two left a permanent mark on the young church: Stephen, a powerful preacher, the first martyr, and Philip the evangelist.

The charge against Stephen is blasphemy – the very same charge that was brought against Jesus. Stephen seems to have been among the first to foresee the inevitable break with Jewish worship which the new teaching entailed.

The synagogue of the Freedmen (9): probably attended by freedmen from the places mentioned.

7 - 8:1a Stephen's defence and death
The defence takes the form of a review of the nation's history. The court knows the facts, but the interpretation is revolutionary. And the sting lies in the tail (51-53). Israel of old rejected the prophets from Joseph and Moses onwards. The present generation has rejected the Messiah himself. Verses 44-50 are Stephen's answer to the charges about the destruction of the temple. A permanent building to 'house' God was never more than second-best.

Delivered by angels (53): Galatians 3:19 and Hebrews 2:2 also connect angels with the giving of the law, but there is no mention of this in the Old Testament.

The witnesses ... Saul (58): the prosecuting witnesses, by law, had to cast the first stones – though in other respects this particular affair was little more than a lynching. The 'young man' Saul was probably in his thirties. He appears here for the first time. As the apostle Paul (the Roman version of his name) he is the central figure in the later chapters of Acts. Here he shares the responsibility for Stephen's death. ('Consenting' may mean that as a member of the Sanhedrin he cast his vote against Stephen.) But the scene at Stephen's death burnt into Saul's mind (22:20), and must have played its part in preparing him for the encounter on the Damascus road.

8:1b - 11:18 PERSECUTION: THE GOSPEL SPREADS TO JUDEA AND SAMARIA

8:1b-25 The response among the Samaritans

The persecution following Stephen's death led to the first broadening of the church's outreach. The attack seems to have concentrated on Stephen's fellow Hellenists (Greek-speaking Jews), leaving the apostles free to remain in Jerusalem. Wherever the scattered believers went they preached the good news – in Philip's case with such marked success that two of the apostles came down to see what was happening.

THE GOSPEL BEGINS TO SPREAD

Paul went to Damascus to persecute the church and returned a Christian

GALILEE

Caesarea home of Cornelius

Joppa where Peter had his vision

SAMARIA

• Lydda

• Azotus

• Jerusalem

On the road to Gaza Philip met the Ethiopian

Gaza

JUDEA

That power of God which is called Great (10): Simon saw himself as the sole agent of the supreme God.
That they might receive the Holy Spirit (15-17): every believer has the Spirit of God – see Romans 8:9; 1 Corinthians 12:13. But the visible sign of the coming of the Spirit – given when the apostles officially

recognized that these members of th[e] despised enemy nation had become God's children – underlines the spec[ial] significance of the Samaritans being welcomed into the church.

8:26-40 Philip and the Ethiopian treasurer

At the height of Philip's flourishing Samaritan campaign God calls him away to meet the need of an individ[ual].

An Ethiopian (27): the man, a Jewis[h] convert, was treasurer not of present day Ethiopia, but of the old kingdo[m] in northern Sudan.
Candace (27): the title of the queen mother who ruled the country on behalf of her son. The king himself, deified as the child of the sun-god, was considered too holy for such secular functions.
The scripture (32): Isaiah 53:7-8. The quotation is from the Greek (Septuagint) text which differs slightly from the Hebrew (massoretic) text on which our Old Testament is based.
Caesarea (40): Philip seems to have settled at this sea-port and brought up a family. See 21:8-9.

9:1-31 The Damascus road: Saul's conversion

Saul's conversion marks a turning-point in the history of the early church. The story is told three times in Acts, once, here, by Luke, and twice by Paul – 22:5-16; 26:12-18. Never has any conversion meant a more complete about-face and radical change of thinking. The encounter with Christ was followed by three sightless days: Saul was identified with Jesus in his death and three days in the grave, and identified with him too in baptism and newness of life. By the time Ananias reached him, Saul the persecutor had become 'Brother Saul' – a man to be hunted down, in his turn, by those whose cause he once led. With his conversion, the church for a while had peace.
The Way (2): the church was known by this name before the people of Antioch invented the new name 'Christian' (11:26).
Tarsus (11): a university city with a population of half a million; meeting-place of East and West, Greek and Oriental.

9:32-43 Peter at Lydda and Joppa: Tabitha raised from the dead

With peace at last, Peter is free to visit the Christian groups. He settles for a time at Joppa (the port from which Jonah, another reluctant

The first stop for Paul and his companions on their first mission was Salamis in Cyprus. Here they confronted the power of the contemporary Roman civilization.

missionary to the Gentiles, embarked). His host's job is the 'unclean' one of tanning – perhaps an indication that Peter is already to some extent emancipated from his religious taboos. But a far more radical challenge is to follow.

10 Peter and Cornelius

Up to this point the gospel has been preached only to Jews, converts to Judaism (proselytes) and Samaritans (who observed the law of Moses). Now God steps in to make it plain that the message is for all men (34-35). He prepares Cornelius, and he prepares Peter. Three times the vision and message come – apparently instructing Peter to break the Jewish food-laws (see Leviticus 11). But when the men from Cornelius arrive, he is quick to realize the far deeper, human implications of his dream (28). A second Pentecost – the coming of the Holy Spirit on the Gentiles – fol-

lows his teaching. No one could then deny baptism to those who had received such an obvious mark of God's favour.

Cornelius, a centurion (1): one of those who formed the back-bone of the Roman army. The centurions stationed in Palestine appear in a very favourable light in the New Testament. Cornelius was an adherent to Jewish faith and worship, but not a circumcised convert. (See article 'Roman Soldiers'.)

Peter's trance (9-16): it was midday when Peter fell into his waking dream – and Cornelius' men were already nearing Joppa. Peter's hunger, and perhaps the leather awning overhead, shape the images of a vision which God uses to convey his message.

11:1-18 The apostles approve Peter's action

This repetition of the events at Caesarea underlines their significance. The criticism Peter faces from a particularly narrow faction of Jewish Christians in Jerusalem is to dog every stage of Paul's missionary work. The admission of Gentiles to full membership of the church, without circumcision, is the most controversial question of the apostles' generation. But Luke makes it clear that the apostles and leaders had a full report from Peter and fully approved his action – the hand of God was so evident in it all.

11:19 - 16:5 ANTIOCH AND THE MISSIONARY EFFORT: ADVANCE INTO PRESENT-DAY SYRIA AND TURKEY

11:19-30 Antioch: the first Gentile church

At about the same time as the events in Caesarea, things are moving in the north, at Antioch, third largest city in the world (after Rome and Alexandria), busy commercial centre and

PAUL'S FIRST MISSIONARY TOUR

Antioch in Pisidia
Iconium
Perga
Attalia
Derbe
Tarsus
Lystra
Antioch
Seleucia
Salamis
CYPRUS Paphos

capital of the Roman province of Syria. The warm response of the Greeks to the Christian message brings Barnabas back from Jerusalem. He in turn tracks Saul down at his home city of Tarsus. And the stage is set for the next great advance, described from chapter 13 onwards.

A great famine ... in the days of Claudius (28): Claudius was emperor AD 41-54. The famine hit Palestine about AD 46.

12 Death of James; imprisonment of Peter

While Paul and Barnabas are in Jerusalem, handing over Antioch's donation for the famine relief, Herod (posing as a champion of the law) instigates a new wave of persecution. James, one of the three apostles closest to Jesus, dies. But God has other plans for Peter. Even a maximum security prison presents no problems to God.

Herod the king (1): Herod Agrippa 1, grandson of Herod the Great (Luke 1:5). The kingdom was given him by his friend, the Emperor Caligula, and extended by Claudius. His sudden death (23) in AD 44 is also described by the Jewish historian Josephus. See further 'The Herod Family'.

Unleavened Bread (3): the seven-day feast immediately following Passover, and regarded as part of that festival (4).

Four squads of soldiers (4): one squad of four soldiers for each watch of the night, two with Peter, two at the door.

13 - 14 Barnabas and Saul sent out: the first missionary journey

The church, directed by the Holy Spirit, selects its best men for pioneer work.

The tour begins with **Cyprus** (Barnabas' native island; 13:4-12) where they encounter Elymas, the magician, and make a notable convert, the proconsul Sergius Paulus. Saul adopts the Roman version of his name, Paul, and becomes the natural leader of the company.

At **Perga** (13:13) John Mark returns home – for what Paul considers insufficient reason (15:37ff.).

Pisidian Antioch (13:14-52): Paul's first reported sermon; opposition from the Jews.

Iconium (14:1-6): a mixed reception followed by attempted stoning.

Lystra (14:6-20): the cripple healed; Paul and Barnabas acclaimed as gods.

Derbe (14:20-21): a good reception

after Paul's narrow escape from death by stoning at Lystra. This does not deter him from a follow-up visit there and to each of the other towns on his way to the coast.

15:1-35 The Council at Jerusalem

Ten years or more have passed since the apostles approved the admission of Cornelius' gentile household to the church (chapters 10-11), and opposition has hardened. When reports of Paul's successes amongst the Gentiles reach the 'salvation by faith *and* circumcision party', they see the red light and openly oppose his teaching. On such a vital matter an authoritative decision by the apostles and elders is essential to avoid a complete split. Peter's reminder of the earlier events, and the account given by Paul and Barnabas of God's work among the Gentiles, carry the day. The final summing-up and verdict given by James, the Lord's brother and leader of the Jerusalem church, finds general acceptance. The Gentiles are asked only to accommodate the Jewish Christians in certain social matters, so that the church may meet together as one.

15:36 - 16:5 Paul and Barnabas separate; the second missionary journey begins; churches in present-day Turkey revisited

The dispute over Mark results in two missionary journeys instead of one. Barnabas' special gift of encouragement no doubt helped his young nephew to make the grade and win Paul's approval later (2 Timothy 4:11).

Silas (Silvanus) (15:40): representative of the Jerusalem church (15:22). Like Paul, he was a Roman citizen. He travelled with the apostle as far as Beroea (17:14) and rejoined him at Corinth. Silas was associated with Paul in the writing (from Corinth) of 1 and 2 Thessalonians; also with Peter in the writing of his first letter.

Timothy (16:3): the decision to circumcise Timothy was taken in order to regularize his position as a Jew, not in order to secure his salvation. Paul had a special affection for his loyal, though timid, companion and successor. He came to regard him almost as his own son.

16:6 - 19:41 PAUL TAKES THE GOSPEL TO EUROPE

16:6-40 At Philippi

At Troas, close to ancient Troy, Luke joins the party for the first time, and Paul receives his call to

PAUL'S SECOND MISSIONARY TOUR

cross to Europe. It is tempting to think that Luke himself was the man in Paul's dream.

The church at Philippi is born from a bunch of oddly assorted converts – a business woman and her household, a slave-girl and a gaoler. But the Philippian Christians brought Paul much joy down the years by their loving, faithful support and unfailing concern for him (Philippians 1:3ff.; 4:10ff.; 2 Corinthians 8). When Paul moves on, Luke the doctor remains behind. Philippi was a medical centre. See also on Philippians.

A place of prayer (13): small groups of Jews would often meet for prayer. A minimum of ten men was required to constitute a synagogue proper. The riverside at Philippi was a quiet place near the town.

Thyatira (14): a church was later formed in Lydia's home town (see Revelation 2:18ff.).

17:1-15 Thessalonica and Beroea
Thessalonica (1-9): the response to Paul in this sea-port and capital city of Macedonia was no mere flash in the pan (see 1 Thessalonians 1:2-10; 2 Thessalonians 1:3-4). The Jews were 'jealous' because here as elsewhere Paul won over the 'devout Greeks', those already attracted to Judaism – the very people they themselves hoped to win as converts.

Beroea (10-15): the Jewish group here were notable for their open-minded study of the scriptures.

Rutted by chariot wheels, the Via Egnatia is the road Paul and his companions trod on their journey from Philippi to Thessalonica.

The acropolis and Parthenon temple at Athens. Here, where countless gods were worshipped, Paul made known the one true God, the Creator.

17:16-34 Paul at Athens

The apostle Paul was a strategist. He campaigned in the great cities of the Roman world. He selected centres on trade-routes, sea-ports, places where there was much coming and going. From these centres the message would run like fire far and wide. He started with present-day Turkey, moved on to Greece and then set his sights on Rome, and beyond that, on Spain. So he came from Beroea to Athens, a city with 1,000 years of history, glorying in past greatness; Athens, the founder of democracy, home of Aeschylus, Sophocles, Euripides, Thucydides, Plato, Socrates; the greatest university of the world, centre of philosophy, literature, science and art – but hard ground for the gospel.

The Epicureans (18): materialists whose philosophy often amounted to little more than the pursuit of pleasure.

The Stoics (18): rationalists, propounding a philosophy of self-sufficiency and dogged endurance.

Foreign divinities (18): so inseparably did Paul speak of Jesus and the resurrection *(anastasis)* that the Athenians took these to be the names of two new-fangled deities. Several philosophical schools believed in the immortality of the soul, but the Greeks regarded the idea of *bodily* resurrection as completely ludicrous (32).

The Areopagus (19): an ancient court of great prestige, possibly responsible for licensing public lecturers.

In him we live and move ... (28): Paul quotes the Cretan poet Epimenides. According to legend, it was he who advised the Athenians to erect 'anonymous' altars.

18:1-17 Paul in Corinth

See on 1 Corinthians for background. Paul was there during Gallio's pro-consul-ship, probably arriving in AD 50. Gallio's decision was an important one for the Christian faith.

Aquila and Priscilla (2): tent-makers or leather-workers. They became staunch friends of Paul. Travel took them to Corinth, Ephesus and back to Rome. Everywhere this hospitable pair were a great support to the young churches.

Claudius' edict (2): issued about 49-50 against the Jews for 'constantly rioting at the instigation of Chrestus'. No doubt an allusion to disputes between Christian and non-Christian Jews in Rome.

18:18-28 Paul returns to Antioch; start of the third missionary journey; Apollos meets Aquila and Priscilla

Apollos (24): thanks to Aquila and Priscilla this eloquent Alexandrian became a man of great influence in the Corinthian church (see 1 Corinthians 1:12; 3:4ff.).

19 Paul at Ephesus

Ephesus was another great commercial centre, although its fine harbour was already beginning to silt up by Paul's day. Situated at the end of the Asiatic caravan-route, the city was a bridgehead between East and West. The tradition is that the apostle John made his home there. So effective was Paul's ministry that it actually affected the takings of the silversmiths. Probably all seven churches mentioned in Revelation 1:11, as well as those at Colossae and Hierapolis, were also founded during this period.

Hall of Tyrannus (9): a lecture-hall which Paul probably used during siesta-time, from 11 a.m. to 4 p.m. (See the Revised Standard Version footnote.)

Magic arts ... books (19): such was the city's name for magical papyrus scrolls of spells that these were known in the Roman world as 'Ephesian letters'.

Artemis (Diana) (24): the cult adopted the name of the Greek goddess, but continued to worship the many-breasted mother-goddess figure of the ancient religion of Asia Minor. The temple was one of the seven wonders of the world, four times the size of the Parthenon. The 'sacred stone' (35) was a meteorite, supposed to resemble the goddess, and kept in the temple.

The theatre (29): an ideal place for the crowd to gather, since it could hold 25,000 people.

The Asiarchs (31): important officials specially responsible for maintaining order at religious functions.

The town clerk (35): the leading civic official, answerable to the Romans for such an illegal assembly.

20 - 28 HOW PAUL EVENTUALLY REACHES ROME

20:1-16 Paul sets out for Jerusalem

2 Corinthians fills in some of the details for the period covered in 20:1-6. The apostle is preoccupied with the collection for the poverty-stricken Christians in Jerusalem (the men listed in verse 4 are delegates from the Gentile churches). His mission to the Gentiles has been much criticized by the Jews. This is his great gesture – a practical expression of the unity of Jew and Gentile in the church of

PAUL'S THIRD MISSIONARY TOUR

THE HOLY SPIRIT IN ACTS
G. W. Grogan

The Acts of the Apostles is a book in which the Holy Spirit is especially prominent. Indeed his activity dominates it. The book might well be called 'The acts of the risen Christ by the Holy Spirit through the apostles'.

A divine Person
It is quite clear from the book that the Spirit is personal, for he did what only a person can be said to do. He spoke (1:16; 8:29; 10:19; etc.), and caused others to speak (2:4; 4:8; 31; etc.). He bore witness (5:32), sent out Christian workers (13:4), forbade certain courses of action (16:6-7) and appointed men to office in the church (20:28). He is associated with other persons (15:28) and is clearly believed to be equal with God (5:3, 9).

The agent of Christ
Acts 1:1 may imply that Jesus continued his work after the ascension through the Holy Spirit. He is the gift of the ascended Christ to his disciples (2:33) and is called 'the Spirit of Jesus' (16:7). He is also described as 'the promise of the Father' (1:4).

The creator of the church
The church as we know it today was created at Pentecost. Wind and fire (2:2-3) are Old Testament symbols of deity (see Exodus 19:18; 1 Kings 19:11-12). The gift of tongues (2:4-13) may have been deliberately chosen by God to symbolize the ultimate universality of the church, its presence among men of every language. The Spirit created a fellowship of love and unity (2:43-46) and he was promised to those who responded to the Christian message (2:38; see also 5:32).

The uniting force of the expanding church
Luke is vitally interested in the progress of the gospel and the consequent expansion of the church through the activity of the Spirit. The church at Pentecost was composed of *Jews* and *proselytes*, Gentiles who were committed to Judaism and so reckoned as if they were Jews (2:10). Jews hated Samaritans, who were of mixed race and schismatic religion, but in Acts 8:14-17 the Spirit came upon *Samaritan believers*. It is significant that this happened only after the (Jewish) apostles had laid their hands on them, indicating an attitude of love and fellowship on their part as well as the fact that 'salvation is from the Jews' (John 4:22). The barrier between Jew and Gentile was broken down in Acts 10:44-48 (see also 11:1-18) when the phenomena of Pentecost were repeated by the Spirit as Peter preached the gospel to *Gentiles*. It was through John the Baptist that the promise of the Spirit had first been given (Matthew 3:11-12; see Acts 1:5; 11:16), so Luke records how a group of *John's disciples* also received the Spirit (19:1-7). These passages reveal how the Spirit bound these divergent groups together and prevented division.

The power behind the church's witness
The Holy Spirit was given to the church to enable it to witness for Christ (1:8; compare 4:33). The church was directed by the Spirit when they sent Barnabas and Saul to evangelize the Gentiles (13:1-4), just as he had earlier guided Peter to preach the gospel to Cornelius and his friends (10:19ff.; compare also 8:29; 16:6-7). Filled with the Spirit they spoke with power (4:8, 31; 6:10) and undertook the various aspects of the new church's life and witness (6:3, 5; 11:22-24). The Holy Spirit gave men power to reveal Christ both by their lips and by their lives.

The life of the church
The Spirit of God is concerned with the inner life of the church in every place (9:31). It was the Spirit who

appointed elders of the church as its guardians (20:28). The new age was to be one of prophecy (2:17-18), concerned with the instruction and upbuilding of the church itself (15:32) and prediction of things to come (11:28; 21:4). The church in council sought guidance and believed that this was given through the Holy Spirit (15:28). So Acts occupies a unique position in the revelation of the person and role of the Holy Spirit. It records a fulfilment which is also a new beginning. The prophecies of the Old Testament and the promises of the Lord Jesus about the Holy Spirit find their fulfilment at Pentecost. The new age, the age of the Spirit, preached by Jesus, so evident in the Letters, had begun.

Christ. It is supremely important to him – hence his determination to get to Jerusalem.

Before he left Ephesus, Paul wrote 1 Corinthians. From Macedonia (1) he wrote 2 Corinthians. From Corinth he wrote the letter to the Romans. It is likely he also visited present-day Albania and Yugoslavia ('Illyricum', Romans 15:19) at this time. Back in Philippi, Luke joins the party to Jerusalem.

A Roman legionary

Troas (7-12) provides an interesting glimpse of early church worship – the meeting on a Sunday evening for the Lord's Supper followed by a meal together (11); the length of time given to Paul's preaching (they had no New Testament); the private house, lit by torches; the effort to listen for so long, so late at night, which proved too much for the weary Eutychus.

20:17 - 21:14 Paul addresses the Ephesian elders; Miletus to Caesarea

This is the only address we have in Acts which was given to Christians – and the only recorded address by Paul which Luke actually heard him give. The apostle foresaw so clearly the troubles the church would face, from inside and out. Revelation 2:2 shows what notice the elders took of his warning.

Trials (20:19): there was serious trouble in Asia quite apart from the riot at Ephesus (see 2 Corinthians 1:8-11).

Philip ... one of the seven (21:8): see Acts 6:5; 8:4-40.

Agabus (21:10): acted prophecy of this kind is familiar from the Old Testament (e.g. Ezekiel).

21:15 - 23:35 Paul in Jerusalem: the arrest

Garbled tales have reached the Jewish Christians in Jerusalem that Paul has been teaching *Jews* to abandon circumcision and the law. The troubles loom so large that the relief fund on which Paul set such store is not so much as mentioned by Luke.

The vow (21:23): compare Numbers 6:13-21. By identifying with these men Paul openly shows his respect and conformity to the law.

Brought Greeks into the temple (21:28): anyone might go into the outer court, but notices in Greek and Latin forbade Gentiles, on pain of death, to enter the inner courts.

The barracks (21:34): the cohort was stationed in the fort Antonia. Two flights of steps led down from the

fort to the outer court of the temple.
The Egyptian (21:38): leader of the
'dagger-men' who specialized in
assassinating Romans and pro-Roman
Jews. They murdered Ananias the
high priest in AD 66.
Is it lawful ...? (22:25): the Roman
citizen had a right to a fair trial, and
even if guilty he was spared the
scourge. This horrible whip of several thongs armed with pieces of lead
or bone was a far more deadly instrument than the Philippian 'rods'.
Caesarea (23:23): headquarters of the
administration of the Roman province
of Judea. The size of the escort
provided for Paul and his friends –
heavy-armed infantry, cavalry, light-
armed troops – is an indication of the
restiveness in the province.
Felix (23:24): Pilate's successor;
governor of Judea AD 52-59. His
residence was the palace built by
Herod the Great (35).

24 - 26 In Caesarea: the defence
before Felix, Festus and Agrippa
Paul spends two years in custody in
Caesarea, probably AD 58-60. Three
times he is called before the authorities, and the skill with which he
conducts his case is some measure of
the apostle's ability. So effectively
does he answer the charges that his
hearers are compelled to admit there
is no case against him – no case, that
is, apart from the theological
question of the resurrection.
Before Felix (chapter 24). A violent
but ineffective governor, Felix was
eventually recalled (about AD 59) for
mishandling riots in Caesarea. Dru-
silla, a Jewess, daughter of Herod
(Acts 12:1), was his third wife. She

was presumably the source of Felix'
information about 'the Way'. Paul's
talk of 'justice and self-control and
future judgement' was too near the
bone for this pair, especially as Felix
was hoping for a fat bribe from his
prisoner (26).
Before Festus (25:1-12). Festus was
not governor for long: he died in AD
62. His attempt to curry favour with
the Jews compelled Paul to appeal to
Caesar. He had more hope of justice
from Nero than from the Sanhedrin!
Before Agrippa (25:13 - 26:32). This
is Agrippa II, son of the Herod of
Acts 12:1, great-grandson of Herod
the Great. Bernice, his sister and acting wife, went on to complete an
inglorious career by becoming
mistress to the emperors Titus and
Vespasian. The mention of resurrection strikes the pagan Festus as completely crazy. Agrippa laughs it off –
to avoid either losing face with
Festus or annoying the Jews by
denying the prophets.

Paul's conversion story in chapter
26 differs in emphasis from the
account in chapter 22. The 'goads'
are the pressures compelling Paul to
a complete change of direction in
life. Verses 16-18 summarize the
Lord's words on the Damascus road,
what Ananias said, and the message
which came to Paul in the temple
(22:17ff.).

27 - 28 Paul's journey to Rome:
shipwreck and house-arrest
The voyage is made in three ships: a
coaster from Caesarea to Myra; a
cargo vessel (carrying grain on the
regular run from Alexandria to
Rome) from Myra to Malta; and

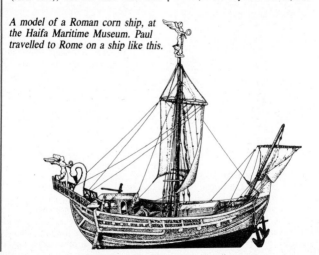

*A model of a Roman corn ship, at
the Haifa Maritime Museum. Paul
travelled to Rome on a ship like this.*

THE VOYAGE TO ROME

another from Malta to Puteoli in the Bay of Naples. Luke gives a superb account of the eventful passage, and a vivid impression of the outstanding courage and leadership of Paul under strain. So Paul reaches Rome at last, though hardly in the way he imagined.

The fast had already gone by (27:9): i.e. the Atonement, September/ October. These were dangerous months for sailing, which ceased for winter in mid-November.

Secure the boat (27:16): the dinghy had been towed behind – now they brought it on board.

Undergird the ship (27:17): by passing ropes round the hull.

The Syrtis (27:17): quicksands and whirlpool off the North African coast.

Neither sun nor stars (27:20): without which they were unable to set a course or calculate their position.

The Twin Brothers (28:11): Castor and Pollux, the sailors' patrons.

Two whole years (28:30): Paul made good use of his free custody. It is not known what happened after this time. Most probably he was released, went to Spain as planned, and then back east before further imprisonment and execution in about AD 67.

THE HISTORICAL AND POLITICAL BACKGROUND OF THE NEW TESTAMENT

Colin Hemer

The Persian Empire was overthrown by the spectacular conquests of Alexander the Great (336-323 BC). Alexander aimed to unite the cultures of Greece and the East, and from his time Greek influence spread in the eastern Mediterranean. After the conqueror's untimely death his enormous dominions were divided. His general Ptolemy took Egypt and also established control over Palestine. The country was of strategic importance to Ptolemy and his successors, but he allowed it a large measure of autonomy in religious affairs. Many Jews actually migrated to Alexandria, his new capital in Egypt, and their community received limited political rights in that brilliant and successful city.

Greek influence

The whole succeeding period is often called the Hellenistic age (*Hellen* = 'Greek'). The *Koine* ('common') dialect of Greek became an international language. The 'Dispersion' (expatriate) Jews, particularly in Alexandria, adopted it, and a Greek translation of the Old Testament, the Septuagint, was made there, commissioned originally, it is said, by King Ptolemy II himself, and completed by the middle of the 2nd century BC.

The Hellenizing movement was also strong among the Jews, though the Hasidim ('pious'), and later the Pharisees, resisted Greek influences in the name of devotion to the Jewish law.

When the power of the Ptolemies declined, Palestine finally fell in

The theatre at Ephesus was the scene of the demonstration against Paul and his companions described so dramatically in Acts 19.

200 BC to Antiochus III ('the Great'), one of the Seleucids, the rival Macedonian dynasty of Syria. The Seleucids at first treated Jewish institutions with respect. But Antiochus made a fatal error. His ambitions in Asia Minor and Greece provoked a clash with the rising power of Rome. He was decisively beaten in 190 at Magnesia in western Asia Minor, and forced to surrender large territories and to pay punitive reparations. So Rome became a force in the East.

Antiochus IV Epiphanes ('god manifest') (175-164 BC) tried to restore the fortunes of his kingdom. He profited from intrigues among the Jewish factions to force upon the Jews a Greek culture and then a pagan altar and cult actually in the temple in Jerusalem.

This act provoked a violent response. The Jewish patriots found a leader in the priest Mattathias and then among his five sons. The family are known collectively as the Maccabees, from Judas Maccabaeus, the third son, who first assumed the leadership upon his father's death.

After a long struggle the brothers achieved religious freedom for their people and eventually established a virtually independent Jewish state, ruled by a succession of high priests of the Maccabean family. These rulers are known by the dynastic name Hasmoneans, and they later took the title of 'kings'. They cultivated good relations with Rome, conquered Samaria and Galilee to the north, and remained in power until 63 BC. In that year Pompey, the Roman commander in the East, intervened in a dynastic dispute, occupied Jerusalem, and added Palestine to the Roman province of Syria, newly organized from the former Seleucid dominions.

Rome: from Republic to Empire

The Roman state itself was deeply divided by social and party strife. It had become evident that its municipal institutions were hopelessly unequal to the government of its huge conquests. A series of Roman civil wars had repercussions throughout the East. Julius Caesar defeated Pompey and became dictator until murdered by republicans in 44 BC. His faction, now led by Antony and Octavian, overthrew the republicans under Brutus and Cassius at Philippi in Macedonia in 42. Antony and Octavian in their turn fought for supremacy, and Octavian won the decisive victory at Actium in western Greece in 31.

The new master of the Roman world was still a young man, the great-nephew and adopted son of the great Julius Caesar. In 27 the Roman Senate conferred upon him the title 'Augustus'. He was careful to disguise the extent of his power by a scrupulous appearance of legality. He claimed to have restored the Republic, but in fact founded what we must call the 'Empire', though in theory the idea of hereditary monarchy was abhorrent to the Romans. He and his immediate successors gave a new peace and prosperity throughout the Mediterranean world. He died in AD 14.

Among the New Testament writers only Luke ever names a Roman emperor. His references give us in outline a framework for the events of the Gospels and Acts. Jesus was born in the time of Augustus (Luke 2:1). The preaching of John the Baptist (Luke 3:1-2) and the ministry, death, resurrection and ascension of Jesus happened under Tiberius (AD 14-37). Paul's journeys occupied much of the reigns of Claudius (AD 41-54; mentioned in Acts 11:28 and 18:2) and Nero (54-68), the Caesar to whom Paul appealed. Paul reached Rome about AD 60.

The fullness of time
The times were ripe for the coming of Jesus and the spread of the gospel. Augustus had given his world respite from war. A great network of new roads united the civilized world, with its focus in Rome. Communications became easier than ever before. Latin and Greek became official languages, with Greek spoken everywhere in the East. It was already the language of the Septuagint translation of the Old Testament, and now was to become the natural vehicle of the new scriptures.

Among the Jews there was fervent expectation of the prophesied Messiah (see 'The Religious Background of the New Testament'), and among the Gentiles a less articulate reaching after a personal 'salvation'. Meanwhile the communities of Dispersion Jews scattered in strategic centres throughout the Empire provided a ready-made audience for the future preaching of Paul and others.

Rulers of Palestine
The more immediate political background to the Gospels goes back to a dominant figure in Palestine before the Roman occupation, an unscrupulous, half-Jewish adventurer named Antipater. He and his son Herod courted the favour of successive Roman rulers, and Herod ('the Great') was made king of the Jews by them. He reigned 37-4 BC: Jesus was born just before he died (see Matthew 2; Luke 1:5).

At his death his kingdom was divided among three of his sons. Herod Archelaus, the ruler of Judea and Samaria (Matthew 2:22), was deposed in AD 6 and replaced by direct Roman rule under 'procurators', junior governors subject to the governors of Syria. Galilee and other territories continued for the most part to be ruled by the Herods. Herod Antipas, ruler of Galilee (4 BC-AD 39), was responsible for the death of John the Baptist (Matthew 14 and parallels). In the Acts we read of Herod Agrippa I (died AD 44; Acts 12), under whom all Palestine was

again briefly united, and his son Herod Agrippa II (Acts 25 - 26).

The best known of the procurators is Pilate (26 - 36), known from other sources as a tactless, violent offender of Jewish scruples. Paul later appeared before the procurators Felix and Festus (Acts 23 - 26).

Political tensions
Palestine was an occupied country, and a strong resistance movement emerged. Nationalists looked for a political Messiah who would liberate his people from the Romans. There were messianic pretenders, especially in turbulent Galilee. The Zealot party of extreme nationalists resisted payment of taxes to Rome.

Meanwhile the high priests and their Sadducee followers collaborated with the Romans. Annas and his family in particular had a vested interest in co-operating with the authorities to whom they owed their position. The Herods too were servile in their dependence on Rome. And the 'publicans' and their tools enriched themselves in the process of collecting taxes for the Romans.

There were evidently many who expected Jesus to fulfil the role of nationalist leader and who were alienated when he showed no intention of fitting in with their plans for him (see John 6:15, 66). But the tenseness of the whole political situation emerges in the manoeuvres at the time of his trial. Pilate was only impelled to action by the supposed political implication of the charge presented.

The gospel in the Roman world
The history of the times is too often viewed exclusively through the perspective of Roman imperial affairs. The Acts of the Apostles stands in its own right as a most important document of the neglected aspects of provincial life and administration. There we have vivid glimpses of provincial governors, client kings and Greek city magistrates. Asia Minor, the land where so much of the narrative is set, was the real centre of the Greek civilization of the period, and it became a strategic focus of Gentile Christianity. There Rome worked through the institutions of Greek

civic life, while also accepting and finally authorizing as a bond of loyalty the ruler-cult congenial to the oriental mind. In many of the strategic cities there were wealthy Jewish communities, with privileges guaranteed by the Romans.

Paul of Tarsus was at once Jew, Greek and Roman, a man singularly fitted to communicate the gospel across racial and cultural barriers. We may trace his route along the great roads, and see him adapting his approach to the individual character of each audience. The record of Acts notes the various local institutions with minute correctness: the 'town clerk' at Ephesus, the 'politarchs' (Authorized Version 'rulers of the city') at Thessalonica, the court of 'Areopagus' or 'Mars' Hill' at Athens. The pride of Philippi in its status as a 'colony' of Roman citizens comes over clearly and with an ironic humour (Acts 16:12, 20-21, 37-39; compare Philippians 3:20, Revised Version). The confirmation of many details of this kind is preserved for us on stone in contemporary inscriptions from these cities.

The cosmopolitan Paul found in Roman institutions a protection and aid for the gospel. Judaism was a legally recognized and licensed religion, and in Jesus was the messianic fulfilment of Judaism. At Corinth this view faced a severe challenge. It was a test case and a potential legal precedent. Paul was accused before Gallio, the new Roman governor, of teaching a religion contrary to the law (Acts 18:13). Gallio, brother of the famous philosopher Seneca, the tutor of the future Emperor Nero, was not impressed. In his view the whole thing was a matter of Jewish sectarian theology, in which he took no interest. But by dismissing the case he implicitly acknowledged that Paul's message was entitled to the same standing as other forms of Judaism. This event may probably be dated in 52: an inscription from Delphi in Greece mentions Gallio and gives a fixed point for the chronology of Paul's life.

Paul made full use of the advantages of being a Roman citizen, an unusual privilege at this period for a provincial Jew. At a time of increasing tension in Palestine he exercised his ultimate right of appeal to the emperor. He finally reached Rome as a prisoner, but apparently confident of gaining justice and a vindication of the gospel before the highest tribunal of Nero. The narrative of the Acts breaks off suddenly without telling us the outcome.

Crisis and persecution

The history of the following years was marked by events of far-reaching consequence. In 64 Nero made the Christians the scapegoats for the great fire which destroyed much of Rome. He killed a great number of them with every refinement of cruelty. This was, however, no part of a considered policy, but an irrational, and perhaps quite localized, outburst.

Meanwhile events were moving to a tragic climax in Palestine. The misdeeds of the later procurators and the defiance inspired by the Zealots culminated in a desperate rebellion and war against Rome (66-70). The Roman commander Vespasian was proclaimed emperor in 69 and left his son Titus to finish his campaign. In 70 Titus captured Jerusalem, utterly destroyed Herod's temple and laid waste the city.

The disaster was fraught with profound consequences for Jews and Christians alike. The two faiths became much more decisively separated. Judaism lost some of its privileges and Christianity was faced with new problems and the renewed peril of official persecution.

The relation of some of the later New Testament books to the fall of Jerusalem and the early persecutions is often debated. There are strong reasons for believing at least that Revelation belongs to the last years of the Emperor Domitian, Vespasian's younger son (81-96). Rome was not now a protector, but a mortal adversary. Domitian demanded as a test of loyalty the worship of himself as 'Lord' and 'God'. People were faced with a fundamental choice between Christ and Caesar.

THE LETTERS

The letters make up about a third of the New Testament. Their contents are varied, but all are important because they represent what the apostles and their associates taught. They combine teaching about God and the Christian gospel with instruction on life and behaviour. They also give an insight into the problems of the early church and how they were met.

As letters they were written by real people because of real situations or needs. So it will help to trace the story which lies behind them. It will also help us to understand them to know the ideas which were held at the time. Then we can gather together some of the main themes.

THE LETTERS IN GROUPS

The obvious way to group the letters is by author, and this is in fact already done for us in the New Testament. There are thirteen letters under Paul's name, one anonymous letter (Hebrews), one by James, two by Peter, three by John, one by Jude.

Paul's letters fall naturally into four groups:
— 1 and 2 Thessalonians are probably the earliest, and are particularly concerned about Christ's return.
— Romans, Galatians and 1 and 2 Corinthians share a common emphasis on the gospel which Paul preached.
— The 'captivity letters', in all of which Paul mentions that he is a prisoner, consist of Ephesians, Colossians, Philippians and Philemon. Some of his most profound teaching is included in these letters.
— The 'pastoral letters', 1 and 2 Timothy and Titus, are concerned with practical matters of church leadership and organization.

The other letters are often grouped under the title of 'General Epistles'. They are addressed to a more general, less precisely defined, readership than Paul's letters. Exceptions are Hebrews, which really stands on its own, and 2 and 3 John addressed to a specific individual or church.

THE SETTING OF THE LETTERS

It is not always easy to reconstruct the historical setting of the letters. They were the products of the life of the early church, not written systematically. They supply much basic Christian teaching, but not in a formal way as theological or ethical treatises. The fact that the letters grew out of the life of the church in this way is also their strength: Christian teaching was dynamic, not stereotyped.

The book of Acts is our only other source of historical information about the early church. But Acts was selective. It did not claim to be a complete record of the events, so there are many gaps in our knowledge.

This creates a problem when it comes to trying to decide the setting of the letters. There are many issues about which we cannot be dogmatic. But the following possible reconstruction may help by showing in outline the story behind the letters.

The first letters

We can be certain of the rough dates of the first letters at least.

1 and 2 Thessalonians were written during Paul's time at Corinth on his second missionary journey. An inscription at Delphi helps to fix this date at about AD 50-51.

After his remarkable conversion Paul had spent some years at Tarsus. He had had time to think over the implications of his new faith. He had also spent a year teaching at Antioch, and about two years in missionary work, when many churches were established in non-Jewish areas.

So Paul's first letters were from someone whose Christian thinking had already matured. They were also essentially practical, and did not call for the great assertions of Christian truths which are so characteristic of some of his later letters.

The 'gospel' letters

The next group may fairly confidently be placed during the third missionary tour, though there is a good case for assigning **Galatians** to the period between the first and second tours.

Paul had sailed from Corinth in Greece to Ephesus. He had spent some time there when he heard reports of difficulties in the church back at Corinth. He also received a letter from the church itself. **1 Corinthians** was his reply. Again this is essentially a practical letter which throws light on the many problems facing a newly established community in a pagan environment notorious for its immorality.

Paul's various contacts with the church at Corinth are not easy to unravel, though **2 Corinthians** provides some information. Paul may have visited Corinth after writing his first letter, and have written another letter which has not been preserved. At any rate, it is plain that he was not too happy about the Corinthians' attitude to him. Then Titus was sent to Corinth, and gave Paul better news of the situation. So in 2 Corinthians Paul expresses his relief, his anxiety to restore good relations, and warns and encourages the church.

Shortly afterwards Paul visited Corinth again himself. While there he wrote his famous letter to the **Romans,** the nearest of all his letters to a theological treatise. In it he works out in some detail the great theme of righteousness by faith and shows the practical outcome of the doctrine.

It is not certain why he wrote in this way to the Romans. He expected to be visiting them soon, so may have wanted them to know the basics of his thinking. He may also have wanted to lay the foundation of further outreach to Spain.

But it was not to work out as Paul had planned. Soon afterwards he travelled to Jerusalem, where he was arrested. He was held captive for some time at Caesarea. Then he claimed his right to be tried before the emperor. He arrived in Rome – as a prisoner.

The prison letters

Tradition favours Rome as the place from which Paul wrote a number of his letters. However some believe these 'captivity letters' were written at Caesarea. There is also growing support for Ephesus as the place of origin of the letter to the Philippians, if not of the others too. If it was in Rome, this would agree with what is said in Acts: Paul was allowed considerable freedom during his imprisonment there. This would also agree well with the allusions in these letters to frequent communication between himself and his associates.

Ephesians and **Colossians** are close in content. The former seems to deal in general terms with a situation seen more specifically in the latter. A heresy was threatening the churches in the Lycus Valley east of Ephesus, and Paul writes his letter to Colossae there to strengthen the Christians and give them positive teaching about the person and work of Christ to help them resist the error. Many of the same themes are echoed in Ephesians, often in similar words, but applied more to the doctrine of the church. In spite of its title, this letter may well have been a circular letter sent round to many churches in the province of Asia.

The little letter to **Philemon** belongs to the same period. Paul writes tactfully, pleading for leniency towards a runaway slave. Many of Paul's associates mentioned in Colossians are also mentioned in Philemon.

Philippians deals with a different situation. Paul wants to thank the Christians at Philippi for the concern they have shown in sending him gifts. The main reason for writing is because he wanted to return to Philippi. He also wanted to prepare the way for Timothy's coming visit.

The remarkable feature of these 'captivity letters' is the depth of Christian understanding Paul shows in them. Perhaps it was a by-product of a period when physical freedom was denied him.

The pastoral letters

If Paul wrote these letters in his old age, he must have been released from his captivity in Rome. **1 and 2 Timothy** and **Titus** show something of his care and concern for the churches and their organization. Some have queried whether in fact Paul was the author of the letters as stated, partly because they require a period of further activity in Ephesus and Crete of which there is no hint in Acts.

Hebrews

The letter to the **Hebrews** seems to have originated in, or been addressed to, Rome, although it is impossible to be certain about this. The letter is not addressed to a specific church, but to a group of Christian Jews who, it is generally supposed, were segregating themselves from the main church and were hankering after the glories of Judaism. The unnamed author shows the superiority of Christ to the old religion.

The general letters

It is difficult to be certain of the precise historical setting of the general letters.

1 Peter is the most specific, mentioning Christians in five provincial districts of Asia Minor who were threatened with persecution. The letter is intended to encourage those who are suffering for Christ's sake, and the basis of that encouragement is found in the sufferings of Christ himself.

2 Peter was presumably sent to the same general circle of readers. It warns against a particular heresy which encouraged immorality, and gives an idea of the influences which threatened the teaching and conduct of the early church.

1, 2 and 3 John are generally thought to be among the latest of the New Testament writings. They probably date from the last decade of the 1st century. According to tradition John lived in Asia Minor, so the background to the letters is probably the church life there. For instance 'Docetism', a heresy which regarded Christ as a heavenly being incapable of suffering, and so denied his incarnation, was beginning to take root and spread.

Of the remaining letters, **James** is almost wholly practical, concerned with encouragement and warning. There is some uncertainty about the setting of this letter, but there seems no reason to doubt that it reflects early conditions within the church. It could even belong to a period before the fall of Jerusalem in AD 70. It appears to come from the Jewish Christian section of the church. The brief letter of **Jude** is closely linked to 2 Peter since much of the material about the heresy occurs in both, often in similar language. Jude describes himself as James' brother. It is reasonable to suppose that both were brothers of Jesus.

THE BACKGROUND OF THE LETTERS

It seems clear, then, that all the letters belong to the second half of the 1st century, the formative period of early church development. They are therefore our only source of information on what the apostles taught.

To interpret them properly we need to understand their background. We have to know something of the thought and practice against which the letters were written for many of their ideas to be meaningful. The following paragraphs simply draw attention to the main areas, to indicate the methods by which light can be thrown on problems of interpretation.

The Old Testament

Although some letters make more direct use of the Old Testament than others, there is a basic assumption that Christianity is essentially a fulfilment of what the Jewish scriptures predicted. The writers therefore appeal to the Old Testament as their authority. Paul frequently uses it to support his arguments. Sometimes he strings quotations together as the rabbis did, with little consideration for the original context (for example in Romans 3), but more often he cites separate passages to lend authority to his argument.

Much of the imagery of the letters is drawn from Old Testament sources: for instance, the 'redemption' and 'priesthood' themes in 1 Peter and the allegory of Sarah and Isaac in Galatians. Many of the phrases in a letter such as James are echoes of Old Testament language. There can be no doubt that since the church took the Old Testament as their scriptures it played a dominant part in the thinking of those who wrote the New Testament letters. All these writers were Jews who had become Christians.

Hellenism

How far Greek thought influences the writers has long been a matter of debate. Certainly much of the earliest missionary activity took place in areas where Greek influence was very strong. When Paul discusses 'wisdom' it is not necessary to see this as evidence of Hellenistic influence. Even so, his Christian interpretation of wisdom cannot properly be understood except against the kind of debate common in his time. Similarly, his idea of 'fullness' must be understood against the Greek philosophical background.

The method of argument in Hebrews is in some respects similar to that of Philo of Alexandria (although there are even more striking differences). In 1 John some find echoes of Greek catchwords which have been taken up and used in a Christian sense. The ideas of light and life, for example, have parallels in contemporary thought.

Paganism

The New Testament church grew up in a pagan environment. Some of the problems discussed in the letters stem directly from this. The situation behind 1 Corinthians is a classic example of the practical difficulties which arose in the church as a result of the previous pagan background of the converts. Some Christians were taking legal action against each other before pagan judges, and Paul had to point out the incongruity of this. There was even a problem from the market-place: meat offered to idols was the only meat sold and this posed a dilemma for sensitive consciences.

The immorality of the Gentile world is vividly painted by Paul in the opening chapter of his letter to the Romans. When the developing church is set against its environment, the grace of God – such a dominant theme in the New Testament letters – is most triumphantly seen.

Judaism

In the ancient world, before the rise of the Christian church, the most ethical form of religious teaching was undoubtedly Judaism. It was because they were dissatisfied with pagan religions that many of the more thoughtful Gentiles became proselytes, adherents of the Jewish faith.

From this growing group of interested Gentiles Paul won many converts on his missionary journeys. The letter to the Hebrews points out Christ's superiority to Judaism by showing that the old system of worship has its spiritual fulfilment in Christianity.

THE MAIN THEMES OF THE LETTERS

It is not possible to summarize here all the themes of such a varied collection of letters. In some letters important doctrines are carefully discussed. In others they are merely stated, and in yet others no more than implied. Nevertheless, in spite of the variety, there is a basic uniformity in the teaching – explicit or implicit - which runs through them all

God

The letters teach that God is a holy God who expects holiness. He is himself the pattern for Christian behaviour. He is moreover sovereign. The Christians were in no doubt that he controls the world. But the most characteristic view is that which Jesus taught, echoed many times in the Epistles: that God is Father. The intensely personal view of God which the letter-writers all share springs from this conviction. God is both Creator and author of the new creation. Paul describes the cosmic reconciliation of the world to God through his action in sending Christ.

Christ

The early Christians expressed their view of Jesus in a variety of ways. This is reflected in the letters, and shows the impossibility of reducing the person of Christ to a single formula.

They use various titles to describe him. 'Jesus Christ' is used to show Jesus as the fulfilment of the promised Jewish Messiah (Christ). But the fuller title, 'Lord Jesus Christ', is also frequent, and shows that the Christians at once acknowledge his sovereignty.

The most characteristic passages of Paul's letters are those which show his exalted view of the person of Christ. He existed before the world was made. He set aside his riches to become poor for our sakes (2 Corinthians 8:9). He humbled himself to become a man in spite of his position of equality with God (Philippians 2:5-11). He was the exact 'image' of God (Colossians 1:15).

The other letters demonstrate a similar view of Christ. Hebrews shows him as fully God (chapter 1) and at the same time fully man (chapter 2), able to represent his people as their High Priest before God the Father. The letters of Peter and John show no essential difference. Through Christ God the Father brings salvation to men. He is the supreme expression of God's love.

Man and his salvation

The world is corrupt and evil. The completely new start, the new era brought in by Christ, is the only answer. The new creation, salvation, eternal life, this is the main theme of the Letters, expounded in them or simply reflected and expressed. Life in Christ demands a new morality, living not according to the old pagan ways but according to God's law of love, and this must be worked out not only in church life, in the new community, but in the world.

ROMANS

Paul, the traveller and Roman citizen, had still not been to Rome when this letter was written (about AD 57). He had made three prolonged and extensive journeys, pioneering the Christian message throughout the eastern provinces of the Empire and establishing churches. Now, probably in Corinth, about to take the relief fund to Jerusalem (see on Acts 20), Paul felt free at last to turn his eyes west – to Spain. And on the way he would fulfil the ambition of years and visit the Christians at Rome. He was not to know that three weary years would elapse between the letter and the visit, or that when he eventually entered Rome it would be as a prisoner (Acts 28).

The city and the church. Rome in Paul's day was the capital of an empire which stretched from Britain to Arabia. Wealthy and cosmopolitan, it was the diplomatic and trade centre of the then-known world. There was constant coming and going. The Roman Peace made travel safe; Roman roads made it relatively swift and easy. Visitors from Rome heard Peter's first sermon in Jerusalem on the Day of Pentecost. So it is not surprising that there was a large and flourishing Christian community there by the time Paul wrote. It was the usual mixture of Jews and Gentiles. There was no serious rift between the two sections, as there had been in the Galatian churches. But there was a tendency for each to criticize and look down on the other.

Some time earlier there had been trouble with the authorities. And although all was now quiet, the Christians were still suspect. Their Founder had, after all, faced a charge of treasonable activity against the emperor. And despite their efforts to live as loyal citizens of Rome, only a few years after this letter (in AD 64) Nero was able to make a scapegoat of the Christians, laying the blame on them when the city went up in flames. Tradition says that Paul – and Peter too – died in the ferocious persecution that followed.

The letter. Romans takes pride of place among the New Testament letters. In point of time, it follows the Thessalonian and Corinthian letters and Galatians, and precedes Colossians and Ephesians. Some of the themes of the earlier letters are taken up again in Romans, which is the fullest and most closely reasoned statement we have of the basic Christian truths. It is Paul's gospel manifesto. What impelled him to write this unique document we do not know. Perhaps he had already sensed he was risking his life by going to Jerusalem, and felt he might never give his message to the Roman Christians in person.

The great theme of Romans is faith in Christ as the only ground of man's acceptance by God, who treats all men alike, Jew and Gentile. Paul pulls no punches in describing the state the world is in (1:18-32). Every one of us stands condemned by God's standards. Even the Jew, who has the unique privilege of knowing God's law, cannot keep it (2 - 3:20). But God offers us free pardon and new life. Jesus has served our sentence for us (chapter 5). We are free to make a fresh start – this time with all the power of God at our disposal (chapters 6 - 8). Why, then, when the Gentiles respond to God's offer of salvation, do the Jews reject it? It is because they see salvation in terms of works. But in the end they too will come in (chapters 9 - 11). God's forgiveness and love spur us on to live up to our new calling – to reshape our whole way of thinking and manner of life. God's 'good news' is not an end in itself. It is meant to transform human relationships – making it possible for Jews and Gentiles to treat one another as equals in the church – and to permeate every aspect of daily living (chapters 12 - 15).

The impact and influence of Romans is immeasurable. It has fired great men – Augustine, Luther, Bunyan, Wesley – and through them shaped the history of the church. But

God has also touched the lives of countless individuals through this letter – ordinary men and women who have read and believed and acted on the apostle's teaching.

1:1-15 INTRODUCTION

The apostle's whole life-mission is captured in this first, typical, aside (1-6). Paul, Christ's slave and emissary, whose commission is to carry God's good news to the nations, writes to his fellow Christians in Rome. His 'grace' and 'peace' blend the traditional Greek and Jewish greetings into something uniquely Christian. Romans is the product of an intellectual, someone with a keen mind – but also a warm, human personality. That much is clear from verses 8-15. Paul is full of appreciation, longing to see and share with a group of Christians he has not yet met.

Saints (7): not a special, super-grade elite, but all who belong to Christ.

Barbarians (14): New English Bible, 'non-Greek' – and therefore uncivilized!

1:16 - 8:39 THE CHRISTIAN GOSPEL

1:16-17 The gospel in a nutshell
Paul glories in his message: that God is able to save – and will save – anyone prepared to rely completely on him.

Verse 17: the first part means that salvation is a matter of faith, from beginning to end. The quotation from Habakkuk is open to more than one interpretation. Here the meaning is: 'he who is put right with God through faith shall live' (Good News Bible).

1:18 - 3:20 The old humanity
Why should anyone need to be 'put right with God'? Paul begins his thesis with a penetrating analysis of the human situation.

The pagan world (1:18-32). Here man is caught in a downward spiral. Evidence of God is all around him, in the natural world that God has created. But man closes his mind to the truth. Because of this his whole mental process becomes warped. He is determined to go his own way, and in the end – since he has been given real freedom of choice – God lets him. So he sinks deeper and deeper into the morass of his own perverse and perverted behaviour. Wrong thinking (irrationality) and wrongdoing go hand in hand. The man who rejects reason (25) will not listen to conscience either (32).

The forum at Rome as it looks today. When Paul wrote his letters, Rome was the proud and glorious capital of a great empire.

Moralist and Jew (2 - 3:20). There were some high-principled individuals, even among pagans. And there were the Jews, who prided themselves in possessing and knowing God's law. Both would be quick to condemn the vices of the pagan world. But are they in any better position? Does the moralist actually live up to his high standards? Is his conscience clear? Does the Jew actually keep the law he is so proud of? If not, he is as morally bankrupt as the pagan. God judges with strict impartiality.

Paul can imagine the questions the hecklers will fling at him. He meets their points one by one:

— Has the Jew any advantage, then? Yes, the fact that God has entrusted him with his revelation (3:1-2).

— If the Jews have failed in their trust and will be judged, what about all God's promises to them? God still keeps his word (3:3-4).

— It seems human sin serves a good end, then, by throwing God's goodness into relief. So why should it be punished? Why not go on sinning so that people can see God's goodness all the better? Because God is a just Judge – and the end does not justify the means (3:5-8).

— Are the Jews any better off than other people? No. Everyone is in the grip of sin. And the law makes man accountable – it is powerless to put anyone in the right with God (3:9-20).

2:6-10: the point is God's impartiality, not that salvation can ever be earned, as 3:20 makes clear.

Circumcision (2:25): see on Genesis 17.

2:29: there is a play on words here. 'Jew' is derived from 'Judah', which means praise.

Justified (3:20): Paul often uses this legal term. It means acquittal or free pardon. See 4:25.

3:21 - 5:21 Acquittal

Free pardon on the ground of faith (3:21-31). Since God is just, the man who infringes his law must be punished. The whole human race stands under sentence of death unless the demands of justice can be met some other way. Jesus has provided that other way by standing in for us at the cost of his own life (chapter 5 explains how this was possible). God will now forgive and receive *anyone* who comes to him trusting in Jesus. This opens up a new life. It is the essence of the good news Paul was commissioned to preach, and the heart of the Christian message still.

The case of Abraham (chapter 4). Paul picks up on his statement in 3:21-22 that this same faith-principle is inherent in the Old Testament scriptures. If he can prove his point in the case of Abraham – father of the Jewish nation, and the prime example of an upright man – surely the Jewish objectors will be convinced. And God accepted Abraham not because of his good life, but because of his faith (4:3; Genesis 15:6) – because against all the odds Abraham stuck to his conviction that God would do what he promised (21). The covenant-agreement, of which circumcision was the outward sign, came later (Genesis 17). So it is to those who share Abraham's faith, not simply his national identity, that God extends his friendship still.

Christ and Adam (chapter 5). The death and resurrection of Jesus has given us a new standing before God. We have life. We have peace. We have hope. We have the presence of the Holy Spirit. There is point and meaning now to the rough and tumble of life (1-5). But how can one man's death result in pardon for millions of others? The key lies in the solidarity of the human race. Sin, disobedience, began with one man (Adam) and spread to all his descendants. We all share the 'disease' and its inevitable consequence, death – being cut off from God. On the same principle, Jesus has made acquittal and life available to all. Adam was the head of the old humanity; Jesus is the head of the new, reborn humanity. We were 'in' Adam when he sinned. We are 'in Christ' when we put our trust in him.

Grace (5:2): another of Paul's favourite words. It means the (wholly undeserved) favour of God.

5:20: we all have an innate tendency to feel that laws were made to be broken. The fact that something is forbidden actually makes us want to do it more (see 7:8).

6 - 8 The new humanity

The old life and the new (chapter 6). God's forgiveness is 'big' enough to deal with any amount of human sin. Does that mean Christians have an insurance policy to go on as before? What an absurd idea! Becoming a Christian means identifying ourselves with Christ – becoming one with him – and so sharing in his death and resurrection. Baptism – going down into the water and coming up again – gives us a living picture of what has actually happened. there is as complete a break between the old life and the new as if we had actually died and been reborn. We were dead to God before – now we are alive to him (11). We have been given a new inclination to obey, with which to fight the old tug of sin (17). And we must act on it. Sin is not our master any longer. We are in the service of God. The result of serving sin is death (21), but the result of serving God is life – God's life at work in us, transforming us (22).

The law and its limitations (7 - 8:4). In order to counteract the widespread belief that men can 'work their passage' to heaven, Paul has said some harsh things about the law. Now he stops to set the record straight. For Jews like himself, who took the matter seriously, the law could be a real tyrant. Christ sets us free from the killing struggle to get right with God by keeping the law to the letter – but not free to do as we please. There is nothing wrong with God's law in itself. It is wholly good. And the Christian, with the new power at his disposal (6, and 8:4) has the potential to keep it. The root of the trouble, as Paul shows from his own experience, is not the law but our own bias to sin (7:14). And conversion does not end the tension (22-23). Left to ourselves we are still helpless to obey. But we are not now left to ourselves. The law serves its purpose when it makes us despair of our own efforts. Only at this point are we ready to ask Christ to do for us what we cannot do for ourselves.

The Holy Spirit – and God's eternal purpose (8:5-39). The Holy Spirit of God is alive and actively at work in everyone who belongs to Christ (9). He helps us to keep God's law. It is his presence that convinces us we really are God's children (16). He is our foretaste (first instalment, 23) of glory to come – a living spring of hope within us. And he turns our inarticulate longings into prayer (26-27).

It is God's intention that every one of us should be like Christ (29). Like him in character now. Like him in glory eventually. In other words, God is recreating us 'in his own image' (Genesis 1:27). And every little circumstance of life is worked into this great overall purpose (28). Nothing can shake it. No one can ever make him write us off – we have Christ in heaven to plead our cause. And there is no power in heaven or earth that can cut us off from his love. So whatever life may bring, we can win through. These are the great certainties of the Christian life.

Sinful body (6:6): not the human body, but the 'sinful self' (New English Bible).

Verse 11: this is not a matter of playing games, pretending to be what we are not – but of being what we are. 'Dead to sin': in the sense that the score for the old life has been settled, not that we no longer feel its pull.

Flesh (7:5, etc.): Paul often uses this word, in distinction from the 'spirit'. He means 'self' – the old, sinful nature.

Body of death (7:24): human nature, subject to the laws of sin and death.

Likeness of sinful flesh (8:3): Paul chooses his words with care. Jesus was a real man, but in one respect he was not identical to other men. He did not share the sinfulness that ordinarily goes with human nature.

Your bodies are dead (8:10): i.e. we still die physically.

8:11: Christians are promised a resurrection like Christ's.

Abba (8:15): the ordinary word a Hebrew-speaking child still uses for his 'daddy'.

Creation (19ff.): because man is part of nature, when he sinned he brought pain and death not only on himself but on the whole created world. So in the day man is transformed, the crea-

tion will share his transformation. There will be 'a new heaven and a new earth' (Revelation 21:1).

Predestined (8:29): see the note on Election.

9 - 11 THE NATION OF ISRAEL

As Paul dwells on God's glorious provision for all who are 'in Christ', he is filled with distress for Israel, God's own specially chosen and

---

ELECTION

In Romans 9 and 11 we have perhaps the most forthright treatment of this subject in the whole Bible. Paul's starting-point is that no one has any claim to God's mercy. He shows how God in his love has chosen certain individuals down the ages to play a special role in his purpose for the world (9:6-13). And he emphasizes the wideness of God's mercy (11:28-32). God the Creator has the right to choose, and we have no right at all to question his choice or doubt his justice.

If God selects some men for forgiveness, does he select others for destruction? Paul is much more cautious about this ('What if ... ?'). He contents himself with asserting God's right to do so – but at the same time stresses God's patience (9:22). He talks about God hardening men's hearts (9:18; and see 1:28), but in every instance these are people who have deliberately refused to listen to him. God never hardens someone's heart against his will.

Human beings are not helpless pawns in the hands of a capricious god. The Bible teaches God's election. It also teaches man's responsibility: his freedom to choose. It may be beyond our understanding how both can operate simultaneously (just as it is hard to understand how scientists can describe light in terms of both waves and particles – two ideas which seem mutually contradictory). God is outside time: we cannot imagine anything beyond our limited range of understanding. So we can only take God's word for it, and hold on to both God's sovereignty and man's freedom to choose – not try to find a compromise between them.

privileged people. How could they refuse to believe in their own, promised Messiah? The Gentiles responded eagerly to the gospel – but not the Jews. And Paul would have sold his own soul to have had it otherwise.

How can he account for this strange anomaly? God has not broken his word (9:6). All along he exercised his sovereign right of choice (9:6-13). And we can hardly call him to task for it. The Maker has an indisputable right to do as he pleases with what he makes (9:14-21). It is only by virtue of his patience and mercy that even a remnant of stubborn, rebellious Israel survived his judgement (9:22-29). People of other nations, knowing their failure, welcomed God's offer of acceptance through faith. The Jews, thinking they could earn salvation by keeping the law, refused to consider it (9:30-33).

Paul himself once shared this misplaced zeal. Now he longs for the Jews to share his faith (10:1-4). God offers salvation – life – to men and women on only one condition: an open declaration of belief in the risen Christ as Lord (10:5-13; and see Philippians 2:11). It is the preacher's task to see that everyone hears about it. And Israel *has* heard, and understood – yet still refused to believe (10:14-21).

Is this the end for Israel, then (11:1)? No. The very fact that Paul and some of his fellow Jews had become Christians is living proof God has not given Israel up. The nation's blindness is partial and temporary. And it has given the Gentiles their opportunity all the sooner. They owe the Jews a great debt; they should never disparage them. And in due course their own faith will lead to a great turning to God among the Jews. God's ways are beyond us, but his purpose is forgiveness through Christ for Jew and Gentile alike.

9:12-13: the quotations are from Genesis 25:23 and Malachi 1:2-3. Both refer to nations – Israel, descended from Jacob; Edom, descended from Esau – rather than individuals. See on Obadiah.
9:18, 22: see the note on Election.
Like Sodom ... like Gomorrah (9:29): i.e. utterly obliterated. See Genesis 19:24ff.
10:6-10: in the style of a rabbi of his day, Paul gives a running commentary on Moses' words in Deuteronomy 30:11-14.

11:7: see the note on Election.
11:17: it was the ancient practice, when a cultivated olive failed to yield, to graft in a slip of wild olive to give the tree new vigour.
All Israel (11:26): the phrase means Israel as a whole, rather than every Jew without exception.
Mercy upon all (11:32): without distinction, rather than without exception.

12 - 15:13 THE CHRISTIAN LIFE

Out of sheer love, and at great cost, God has saved our lives. What stronger motive could we have for turning them over to him from now on? This means complete mental re-orientation affecting our whole character, our motives and our behaviour (12:1-2).

12 Human relationships

This is where the transformation begins, as every individual takes his place in the new 'family' of Christ. His own stock goes down. His opinion of others goes up. And individual gifts are pooled for the good of the whole Christian community. We put ourselves at God's disposal, and we don't pull out when the going gets hard. Old attitudes change – not only towards fellow Christians but towards the outside world. Instead of giving tit-for-tat when we are wronged, we treat the enemy as if he were our best friend, and leave God to do the judging.
Burning coals (20): in Egypt people went through the ritual of carrying a pan of burning charcoal on their heads as a token of their penitence.

The Colosseum at Rome was built in AD 80. Here spectators could watch fights between gladiators – and Christians were thrown to the lions.

13 The powers that be

God delegates his power to the authorities for the public good. Christians must therefore respect them. Taxes are to be paid, and laws observed. The Christian has a duty to meet all 'Caesar's' authorized demands. Only when these demands directly conflict with the commands of God is it right to say 'No' (Acts 5:29).

We must incur no debt, other than our permanent obligation to love – and not to wrong – our fellow men. The time we have left is short, and we must live accordingly (11-12 – Paul is alluding to Christ's return).

14 Freedom and responsibility

There are some matters of conscience over which Christians disagree. (Paul instances the eating of meat, 2-3 – see on 1 Corinthians 8 – and observance of Jewish feast-days, 5.) We should not try to force agreement, and so create division. We ourselves may feel free to do things that would give a weaker Christian a bad conscience. That is no reason to despise him. We are answerable, not to one another, but to Christ. It is better to limit our own freedom than exercise it at a fellow Christian's expense.

14:2, 14: there was the problem that meat sold in the market had been sacrificed to pagan gods; and there were also the Jewish food-laws about 'clean' and 'unclean' animals and the method of slaughter. If Jewish Christians insisted on the letter of the law, and Gentile Christians stuck out for freedom, the two sections would never share a meal together.

15:1-13 The example of Christ

There is nothing Christian about pleasing ourselves. Good relations between Christians are far more important than 'my rights'. We must do all we can to promote real oneness, regardless of former background.

15:14 - 16:27 EPILOGUE

15:14-33 Personal

In more than 20 years as apostle to the non-Jewish world, Paul has seen churches established all over the countries we now call Cyprus, Syria, Turkey and Greece. Now he has discharged his responsibilities. And once the Jerusalem trip (about which he

has real misgivings) is over, he can look west.

Illyricum (19): present-day Yugoslavia.

Macedonia and Achaia (26): northern and southern Greece.

16 Greetings to friends

It is in one way surprising to find such a long list of friends in a church which Paul had never visited. (For this reason some believe this chapter originally belonged to a copy of Romans which was sent to Ephesus.) Yet all roads led to Rome, and many Christians from the eastern provinces must have passed through the capital at one time or another. It is obvious that despite his busy life Paul did not lose interest in people or lose touch with them.

His last word is one of warning against a set of troublemakers whose disruptive influence on the churches he knew all too well (17ff.). But, as always, at the close his thought returns to the wisdom and glory of the eternal God.

Phoebe (1): it was probably Phoebe – travelling from Cenchreae, the port of Corinth – who carried Paul's letter to Rome.

Prisca and Aquila (3): a couple whose home was in Rome, but who travelled extensively in the course of their leatherworking business. They did sterling Christian work at Corinth and Ephesus (Acts 18:2-3; 18-28).

Rufus (13): may be the son of Simon of Cyrene (Mark 15:21).

Verse 21: Timothy is well known in the letters. He was like a son to the ageing Paul. Jason may be Paul's host from Thessalonica (Acts 17:5-8). Sosipater may be Sopater from Beroea (Acts 20:4).

Tertius (22): the Christian who acted as Paul's secretary in writing this letter.

Erastus (23): this may be the same public official whose name has been found inscribed on a marble paving-block at Corinth, dating from this time.

1 CORINTHIANS

Paul probably wrote this letter from Ephesus, about AD 54. Acts 18 recounts Paul's 18-month stay at Corinth on his second missionary journey – and describes the founding of the church.

The city. The old Greek city of Corinth was destroyed and rebuilt by the Romans. It stood in a strategic position to control trade across the narrow neck of land between Aegean and Adriatic. A thriving centre of commerce and a cosmopolitan city where Greeks, Latins, Syrians, Asiatics, Egyptians and Jews rubbed shoulders, it was an obvious target for Paul. Establish a church here, and the Christian message would quickly spread far and wide.

Yet in other ways it is hard to imagine a less likely place for Christianity to take root. The town was dominated by the temple of Aphrodite (goddess of love; what a contrast to 1 Corinthians 13!), built on the heights of the acropolis. Thousands of temple prostitutes, a large floating population, and the general racial hotch-potch, all contributed to Corinth's unsavoury name. The city was a by-word for excess and sexual licence. There was even a word for it: to 'Corinthianize'.

The church. The Christian church, like the city, was a racial and social mixture. There were a few Jews, but more Gentiles: some men of wealth and position, but most from the lower classes. Many were converts from a permissive pagan background. They had little to boast of – yet, in Greek fashion, they prided themselves in their intellectual prowess. They bandied about such slogans as 'Liberty' and 'Knowledge'. It was a group which had little cohesion.

The letter. Two factors lie behind the writing of 1 Corinthians.

1. Paul had received reports of the church which made him very uneasy (1:11;5:1).

2. A delegation arrived from Corinth, and (or with) a letter seeking his advice on various questions (7:1;16:17).

The great Temple of Apollo at Corinth. The fact that meat on sale in the markets had been offered to idols in the temples was a real problem of conscience for the Corinthian Christians.

In the letter, Paul takes up five of the matters reported to him:
— divisions in the church;
— a case of incest;
— court-cases between members;
— the abuse of Christian 'freedom';
— the general chaos reigning in church services, even in the Lord's Supper.

He also answers questions the Corinthians have written about:
— questions about marriage and single life;
— problems over food consecrated to idols and social functions held in the temples;
— whether or not women should be veiled, and their place in public meetings;
— the matter of spiritual gifts; the meaning of the resurrection of the dead.

His reply takes the lid off one of the early churches, and gives us a fascinating glimpse of the none too edifying contents.

1:1-9 Greeting and prayer

Opening and thanksgiving (1:4-9) are characteristic. Paul believes in

Paul's letters played a key role in his relations with the churches. This papyrus letter from the 1st century AD begins, 'Prokleios to his good friend Pekysis, greetings...'

encouragement. Only Galatians, of all the letters to churches, lacks this note of praise.

Sosthenes (1): possibly the synagogue leader mentioned in Acts 18:17. He may be acting as Paul's secretary.

1:10 - 4:21 Rival cliques

In a day before church buildings, when Christians met in houses or halls, and a large group might well have to split up, it is easy to see how divisions could arise.

Paul mentions three sects centred on rival 'leaders': Paul (their founder), Apollos and Cephas (Peter). A fourth sect, in their pride, claimed exclusive rights to the label 'Christian'.

Apollos (1:12) was a Jewish Christian from Alexandria (Egypt). When he arrived in Ephesus, Aquila and Priscilla took him home for fuller instruction (Acts 18:24ff.). He travelled to the province of Achaia (of which Corinth was capital), where he proved a powerful and eloquent teacher.

The mention of Peter (Cephas, 1:12) does not necessarily mean he visited Corinth. As leader of the twelve apostles it would be natural for him to have a following, particularly among Jewish Christians.

It is clear from these chapters that the groups were making invidious comparisons between Paul and the more eloquent Apollos. Paul, although a trained scholar, had had

his troubles at Corinth (Acts 18:9-10; 1 Corinthians 2:3). God's message, not polished speech, was his main concern.

But the Corinthians were infected with something of the spirit of nearby Athens. They fancied themselves as thinkers and took a pride in their supposed intellectual superiority. In fact, as Paul points out (3:1-4), their argumentative, judgemental attitude shows they are still bound by the world's way of thinking. They stand in need of teaching. They have to be reminded that human cleverness is a far cry from God's wisdom (1:18 - 2:16). It is not proud and clever people who appreciate the wisdom of God's plan of salvation through Christ's death on the cross, but those who are spiritually wise. This kind of wisdom, and with it true values and real judgement, is God's gift to man through his Holy Spirit. A man must become a fool in the world's eyes in order to be really wise (3:18).

So Paul and Apollos are not rivals but partners, sharing the work of building God's church (3:5-9). Once the basic foundation of faith in Christ is laid, every Christian is responsible for what he does with the new life he has been given. We must see to it that we build to last (3:10-17).

There should be no place for pride among Christians and no looking down on others. The greatest Christians regard themselves as no more than God's slaves. We are to follow their example (chapter 4).

Chloe's people (1:11): presumably members of Chloe's household.

Stephanas (1:16): a founder-member of the church at Corinth, and one of the delegation sent by the church to Paul at Ephesus (16:15ff.).

Jews and Greeks (1:22): national characteristics show through. The Jews always wanted miracles as concrete evidence. The Greeks saw salvation in terms of wisdom.

The Day (3:13): when Christ returns; the day of judgement.

5 Incest

In the name of their boasted 'liberty' the church is condoning incest. It is a case which would shock even the pagans in that notorious city. The old immorality – and worse – has gained a foothold and the whole church is endangered (as Paul had warned in a previous letter, 5:9).

His father's wife (5:1): presumably his step-mother, or Paul would have said 'mother'.

Deliver ... to Satan (5:5): Paul is expressing God's judgement on the man for abusing his body through gross sexual immorality. Short-term discipline is to be exercised for long-term good. Such discipline would certainly include expulsion from the church.

Leaven (5:6-8): yeast – often (though not always) used as a picture of the corrupting power of evil. Bread for the Passover was made without leaven, as a reminder of the Israelites' hasty departure from Egypt. Christ has become our Passover sacrifice, says Paul; it is time we got rid of the old yeast of evil in our lives.

6:1-11 Lawsuits

Even Jews would not take cases before Gentile courts – not because the courts were corrupt, but because it would be an admission of Jewish inability to operate their own laws. Surely the Christian community – these 'wise' Corinthians – should be capable of settling internal disputes. Better to be wronged than drag one another to court.

The saints will judge the world (6:2): a development from Christ's teaching in Matthew 19:28. The angels are mentioned as the highest order in the created universe.

6:12-20 Freedom or licence?

The Corinthians claim they are free to do anything. 'No doubt,' says Paul, 'but I for one will not let anything make free with me' (6:12). Sexual needs, they argue, are like hunger: they must be satisfied. The body is not important anyway. But this is wrong thinking, a carry-over of the old Greek ideas. For the Christian the body is part of the whole personality. Body *and* soul are the Lord's. You cannot sin with the body and keep the 'soul' untarnished: man is a unity.

7 Questions about marriage

The Corinthians have raised six questions about single and married life. Several reflect the Greek tendency to regard the physical side of existence as evil.

— Are married couples to continue normal sexual relations after conversion? Yes (7:1-7).

— Should single people marry? Paul prefers the single life – but only for those with the gift of self-control (8-9).

— Is divorce between Christians permissible? No (10-11).

— What about the unconverted husband or wife? The Christian is to stick to his pagan partner unless that partner wants a separation (12-16).

— This question is not so clear. Most likely it is: 'Should engaged couples marry?' This must be a matter for personal decision, but in the very troubled times Paul sees ahead, single people will find it easier to work out their Christian priorities (25-38).

— May widows remarry? Yes, but Paul qualifies this (39-40).

8 Food offered to idols: problems over social customs

It was hard in Corinth to make a clean break with paganism. Trade groups and clubs held their social functions at the temples. Most of the meat sold in the shops had first been offered to idols. Some Christians maintained that 'idols were nothing'. They were free to eat meat and attend club dinners. But others were worried. Freedom is right, says Paul. But no one should exercise personal freedom at the expense of another man's conscience.

9 Forgoing rights

Paul takes examples from his own life to push this lesson home. If anyone has rights, surely it is the apostle. Yet he has gladly given up his right to take a wife with him on his trips and expect the church to provide for her keep. There are more important things than rights. He willingly restricts his freedom to help him win men for Christ.

In a race ... (24-27): the Isthmian Games (second only to the Olympics) were held every three years at Corinth. Each competitor underwent 10 months' stiff training, hoping to be crowned with the victor's pine wreath. Paul was afraid, not of losing his salvation, but of forfeiting his 'crown'.

10:1-13 A warning from history

It is easy to be over-confident, especially when life is smooth (10:12-13). The fate of many of the children of Israel during the wilderness wanderings stands as a solemn warning. (Hebrews 3:7ff. draws similar lessons from the same events.)

10:14 - 11:1 Paul's appeal and summary

Christians must choose between the Lord and idols (empty in themselves, but behind them, real demonic powers). There can be no compromise. It is playing with fire to have any part in pagan sacrifices. As far as meat is concerned, the rule is unselfish concern for the good of others.

The cup of blessing (10:16): the name given to the third cup in the Passover feast, over which a prayer of thanksgiving was said. This may well have been the cup with which Jesus instituted his memorial Supper – hence the thought here.

11:2-16 Women and the veil

No decent woman would appear unveiled in public at this time. The veil guaranteed safety and respect in the streets. But there were differences in Greek and Hebrew custom when it came to prayer. Greek women, as well as men, prayed bare-headed. Roman and Jewish men and women prayed with their heads covered. The church needed a ruling.

The ruling Paul gave rested on the relative roles of men and women in the created order. He was also concerned not to flout current social convention and so bring the Christians into disrepute. Men, because they are the 'head' of creation, are under no authority but Christ's. They were therefore to pray bareheaded. Women were to pray veiled, the veil being a token both of their acceptance of their husband's authority and of the current standards of decency.

Dishonours his head (4-5): i.e. Christ (3). The veil was a token of submission to another person; he should submit only to Christ. *Dishonours her head:* i.e. her husband (3). By discarding the veil she discarded her husband's authority, as if she were a prostitute.

Shorn or shaven (6): the punishment for a prostitute at that time.

The image and glory of God (7): Genesis 1:26-27 includes both sexes in God's 'image', but does not mention 'glory'.

Because of the angels (10): the angels, representatives of order, would not want to look on immorality, or even the appearance of it.

11:17-34 Disorder at the Lord's Supper

In the early days the Lord's Supper took place in the course of a communal meal. All brought what food they could, and it was shared together. Not so in Corinth. There they could not even wait for everyone to arrive before they began eating. And some got drunk while others went hungry. It is not surprising that Paul could not 'commend'

them – it was a disgrace. He pulls them up short with a reminder of the circumstances in which the first Lord's Supper took place. Their offence is serious.

This is my body (24-25): this is the earliest record we have of Jesus' words.

Unworthy (27-30): no Christian is ever 'worthy' to come into God's presence, but that is not the point here. Judgement has overtaken the Corinthians not for insufficient self-examination, but for stuffing themselves at the meal as if it had no connection with the Lord's death.

12 - 14 Spiritual gifts

In contemporary religions trances or strange, ecstatic speech showed a man's spiritual status. It was therefore not surprising that the Christian church at Corinth, to whom God gave a variety of gifts by his Holy Spirit, should have been specially taken up with the more spectacular ones, among which was the ability to speak in unknown 'tongues'.

Paul does not underestimate these gifts. He would have them all speak in tongues, he says (14:5); and he himself excels in this gift (14:18). But it does not top the list on his scale of values. Those seeking experiences for themselves needed to be reminded that the life of the church was more important. There are other gifts Christians should seek even more strenuously.

Christian unity does not imply uniformity. The gifts come from a single Source, and are given for the good of the whole church. Every individual has an indispensable part to play in the life of the one body. This should prevent a universal scramble for the same gifts. The important thing is not which gifts are most impressive, but which best serve to build up the church. This means that prophecy – a message from God which everyone can understand – is of more value than tongues.

Yet there are things more important still. Three qualities of life – faith, hope, love – will outlive all the gifts. And these are for everyone. Without them no one is anything. And Christian love outshines all. This is the best way of all; this is what we should really set our hearts on. Paul bursts into a great hymn on the theme (chapter 13), one of the most glorious passages in the whole Bible. And as he paints his picture of what love is, he consciously or unconsciously draws us a portrait of a person – Jesus himself. He is the living embodiment of this outgoing, long-suffering, self-giving, self-effacing love. Without it – without him – there would be no church.

14:26-33 provides a glimpse into an early-church service. Again Paul stresses the need for order. Paul forbids the women to disturb the service by talking (34-35). From verse 35 it seems that some were calling out questions and comments (they sat apart from the men). Their new liberty was not to be abused. But it is clear from 11:5 that he did not condemn the women to absolute silence: the gift of prophecy was exercised in public.

12:8 'One man ... has the gift of wise speech, while another ... can put the deepest knowledge into words' (New English Bible).

Faith (12:9): not saving faith, but faith in special measure.

Prophecy (12:10): inspired speech, conveying the message of God to the hearers. *Tongues:* inspired speech to express the praise of God or other deeply-felt emotion; the person uttering it did not know its meaning, hence the need for interpretation.

15 The resurrection

This chapter is the classic Bible passage on the subject. Most of the Jews believed in the resurrection of the body (the same body that had died). To the Greeks it was the soul that was immortal. The very idea of resurrection seemed ridiculous to them (see Acts 17:32).

Paul declares that Christ's resurrection is of the first importance: it is no optional extra. On it the Christian faith stands or falls. What is more, it is a fact and a well-attested one. Most of those who saw the risen

Lord are still alive (about 25 years after the event). Christ's resurrection implies resurrection for the Christian. But the body which is raised will be better than the body which is buried. The old was physical, the new will be spiritual and immortal – but still a body. It will as far outshine the old body as a full-grown plant outshines the shrivelled seed from which it grows.

Baptized on behalf of (or for) the dead (29): possibly by proxy for those who died unbaptized. But the meaning may be that people became baptized in order to be reunited with Christian friends and relatives who had died.

Beasts at Ephesus (32): one of the spectacles at the arena was to watch men fighting savage wild animals. But Paul is probably speaking metaphorically about what he went through there. Ephesus had a magnificent theatre but no arena as such.

16 Practical matters

Paul gives directions for collecting money for the poor at Jerusalem (the Gentile churches were contributing). He looks forward to an extended visit to Corinth. And he gives news and instructions about various individuals. The letter closes with greetings from the Asian churches (Ephesus was the provincial capital), especially from Aquila and Priscilla, the leatherworkers in whose house Paul lived during his stay in Corinth. The final greeting he writes himself (the rest presumably having been dictated to a secretary).

Macedonia (5): Philippi and Thessalonica were both in this province.

Apollos (12) is probably reluctant to return because of the split (3:4).

2 CORINTHIANS

An interval of not much more than a year separates Paul's two letters to Corinth. The second letter was probably written about AD 56, from a town in Macedonia (the Roman province in northern Greece whose capital was Philippi).

After 1 Corinthians was written, affairs seem to have come to a head, and Paul paid a swift unscheduled visit (his second; on his first visit to Corinth the church was founded) which proved unpleasant both for him and for the church (2:1). He promised to return (1:16). But instead, to avoid an even more painful visit (1:23), he returned to Asia (where he ran into grave danger, 1:8ff.) and wrote them a sharp letter which caused him a great deal of anguish (2:4). He could enjoy no peace of mind until he heard their reaction, so he left for Troas, on the coast, hoping for news. Although things were going well there, he could not bear to wait, and crossed the Aegean into Macedonia (2:12-13) where at last Titus reached him with the news that the letter had brought the Corinthians to their senses (7:6ff.). His relief knew no bounds.

Now, as he writes again, the worst is over. He looks forward to a third visit, which he hopes will be a happier one. So the final part of the letter is specifically intended to clear the air (13:10). (He did pay his visit, and wrote to the Romans during his stay at Corinth. So there was presumably a happy ending to the troubles.)

2 Corinthians is perhaps the most intensely personal of all Paul's letters. We feel for ourselves the weight of his burden of care for all the churches (11:28): the depth of his love for them and his anguished concern for their spiritual progress. We see in personal terms the cost of his missionary programme: hardship, suffering, deprivation, humiliation, almost beyond human endurance. And we see unshakable faith shining through it all, transforming every circumstance.

The personal nature of the letter makes it difficult to analyse. Paul's thought flows on, almost unbroken (apart from the break before chapter 8, when Paul turns to the matter of the relief fund for Jerusalem; and again before chapter 10, when he takes up the accusations made by his critics), and themes are often recurring. In the main, Paul writes in defence of his ministry and his God-given authority as an apostle.

1:1-7 Greeting and thanksgiving

Paul's associate in this letter is Timothy. His readers are the Christians at Corinth and the surrounding province of Achaia, which would include the groups at Athens and Cenchreae.

His prayer strikes a more personal note than usual. Instead of praise for the church, Paul thanks God for his special goodness during recent trials. His suffering has had two wholly good side-effects:
— the experience of God's comfort in it all;
— a new ability to help and comfort those in similar circumstances.

1:8 - 2:17 News and explanations

Facing death (1:8-14). The reason for Paul's prayer is now explained. While in the province of Asia (capital city, Ephesus) Paul ran into trouble so serious it seemed likely to cost him his life. At first sight this looks like a reference to the uproar at Ephesus recounted in Acts 19:23-41. But there Paul's life was not in danger. It is perhaps more likely he was either seriously ill, or in danger from mob violence somewhere in Asia Minor.

Paul accounts for his changes of plan (1:15 - 2:11). In his first letter (1 Corinthians 16:5) Paul promised to come to Corinth via Macedonia. Later he decided to make two visits, on the way to and from Macedonia (1:16). In the event he has done neither, and the Corinthians have criticized him for shilly-shallying. But this is not the reason for the changes of plan. He took his decision because of the state of affairs in the church.

The road leading down from Corinth to its port. Behind the ruins of the ancient city is the fortified acropolis.

Having had one head-on clash, he wanted to delay visiting them again until relations were happier. So he tried to sort things out by letter – a letter he feared would hurt them, and which cost him a great deal to write.

The trouble seems to have been personal antagonism to Paul on the part of one man (2:5-11; not the man guilty of incest, 1 Corinthians 5:1). Now that the church has dealt with him, Paul urges his forgiveness.

Paul's recent travels (2:12-17). After writing the letter, Paul could not rest. He went to Troas hoping to meet Titus on his way back from Corinth with news of the church's reaction. Not finding him there he crossed the Aegean to Macedonia. The reason for the thanksgiving of verses 14-17 becomes clear in chapter 7. In Macedonia he met Titus, and the news from Corinth was good.

Leads in triumph (14): Paul takes this picture from the triumphal procession accorded to a victorious Roman general. He headed a parade through the streets of Rome, accompanied by incense-bearers and followed by his captives and the spoils of war.

3 - 6:10 Paul's ministry
Past, present and future interweave in these chapters. As for the past, the old covenant has been replaced by a new life-giving one (3:6-18). The present is an anomaly: on the one hand the apostle is appointed ambassador of God himself, charged with his amazing message to mankind (3:4-6; 4:1ff.; 5:16 - 6:2); on the other, he is subjected to every kind of human weakness, persecution and suffering (4:7-12; 6:3-10). But the future, in all its glorious certainty, eclipses any suffering the present can hold (4:13 - 5:10). Weigh the cost of discipleship, incredible though it seems, against the 'eternal weight of glory' being made ready for the Christian and you have the true balance of things.

Letters of recommendation (3:1): in the early days, Christians moving to a new town often took with them such letters from the old church to the new. Paul has no need of such a letter – the very existence of the Corinthian church is sufficient testimony.

Moses' face (3:7ff.): when Moses came down from Mt Sinai with the tablets of the law, his face dazzled the Israelites, so close had he been to God. In order to overcome their fear he veiled his face (Exodus 34:29ff.).

Reflecting the glory (3:18): the 'glass' or 'mirror', being made of polished metal, gave only an imperfect reflection.

In Paul's day mirrors were made of polished metal (like the bronze mirror pictured here) and gave only a dim and imperfect image (3:18).

Earthenware vessels (4:7): cheap pottery lamps (see verse 6), or, if Paul is picturing the Roman triumphal procession, earthenware pots deliberately chosen as a foil to the magnificent treasures inside.

The earthly tent (5:1): our physical body. Paul uses an ordinary Greek expression, which at the same time reminds us of the body's impermanence.

Found naked (5:3): as a disembodied spirit.

6:11 - 7:1 The need for a clean break

Paul's feelings are deeply stirred (6:11-13). He longs for the Corinthians to match his own complete open-heartedness towards them.

The change of tone at 6:14 is abrupt – but there is no evidence that this section has been misplaced, as some argue. Paul's love for his churches always holds them to the highest standards. He has warned them before of the dangers of compromise with the pagan world (1 Corinthians 8:10). Now he stresses the utter incongruity of permanent relationships between Christians and heathen.

7:2-16 Paul's joy at the good news from Corinth

He had reached this point in the story at 2:13. Now he takes it up again. At last Titus is able to set Paul's mind at rest. The Corinthians' reaction to his letter is all he could have hoped. The result has been entirely good. The apostle's relief and joy are overwhelming. His faith in them has been completely vindicated.

Not on account of ... (12): a Jewish idiom meaning 'Not so much on account of'.

8 - 9 Money matters

Now that confidence is restored, it is possible to raise the matter of the relief fund for the poor in Jerusalem. Titus had helped the Corinthians make a start, following Paul's instructions in his earlier letter (1 Corinthians 16). Now he is to return and supervise the completion of the collection, accompanied by delegates from the Macedonian churches (8:18, 22) as a safeguard against any charge that Paul was embezzling the fund (8:20-21; 12:16-17).

The Jerusalem church seems to have been in financial trouble almost from the start, probably because the break with Judaism cut the convert off from his family and often cost him his job. Converts from Islam face the same problems today. Paul was quick to encourage the Gentile churches in Galatia, Macedonia and Corinth to help their Jewish fellow Christians. By doing so they would learn the duty and blessing of systematic Christian giving, and at the same time show their appreciation of what they owed the Jewish parent-church.

Practical instructions rub shoulders with spiritual principles in these chapters. Christian giving is a loving response to the self-giving of the Lord Jesus. Christians should need no urging to give cheerfully and generously. Those with more than they need will make up the incomes of those with too little, so that all have enough.

The churches of Macedonia (8:1) included Philippi (see Philippians 4:15ff.), Thessalonica and Beroea. Harsh treatment from the Romans and a succession of civil wars had impoverished the province, and the persecuted Christians must have been worse off than most.

10 - 12:13 Paul answers his critics

Paul now turns his attention to the hostile minority at Corinth who have challenged his authority and criticized his behaviour. This sounds very like a continuation of the old rival cliques of 1 Corinthians 1 - 4, particularly the pro-Jewish faction. They show the same conceit, the same old mistaken standards of judgement. They have attacked Paul on a number of counts:

— He may be a brave letter-writer, but meet him face to face and he's a coward (10:1, 9-11).
— He is no speaker (10:10; 11:6).
— He is a second-rate apostle (11:5; 12:11) – his insistence on earning his own living underlines this (11:7ff.).

Paul answers every charge, showing the hollowness of their standards of judgement.

— When he comes, they will discover he is as ready to act as he is to write: but he would much rather use his authority to build up the church (10:1-11).
— Their boasting counts for nothing: it is God's commendation which is all-important (10:12-18). Yet he can surpass them all in boasting, though he will make suffering and weakness his boast, and the vision and revelation God has given him (11:16 - 12:10).
— Apostleship does not consist in

oratory and lording it over the church (11:6, 13-15, 19-20). Paul is not lacking in any of the qualities of true apostleship (11:6; 12:12). As for earning his own living, he was concerned that no one should think him a sponger, and anxious not to burden them (11:7ff.).

King Aretas (11:32): Aretas IV ruled the Nabataean kingdom (stretching from the Euphrates to the Red Sea) from his capital, Petra, from 9 BC to AD 40. The Jews were behind the governor's action – see Acts 9:22-25.

Visions and revelations (12:1): we know of three early visions from Acts: on the Damascus road (9:4ff.); at the house of Judas (9:12); and in the temple at Jerusalem (22:17ff.).

A man in Christ (12:2-3): i.e. a Christian. Paul is speaking of himself. *Fourteen years ago:* AD 41-42, six or seven years after Paul's conversion, but before the great Gentile missions. The *third heaven* is a Jewish expression meaning to be actually in the presence of God. Paul is describing the most sublime experience imaginable.

A thorn ... in the flesh (12:7): this may be some physical illness (a painful eye disease, or malaria) or a reference to the unremitting opposition he encountered. Either way it was a constant source of pain and depression – Satan's work – yet the means God used to keep Paul humble and to demonstrate his power.

12:14 - 13:10 The coming visit

Paul looks forward to his third visit to Corinth. And the reason for the tone of these last chapters becomes clear. He is afraid he will find the same bickering splinter-groups, the same cockiness and general disorder that made him write the first letter. He is afraid his pride in them will take a knock, in the face of typical 'Corinthian' sins: sexual promiscuity, bitter quarrels and disorder (12:20-21). And so he calls them to put things right before he comes, so that he may not have to discipline the church severely.

Two or three witnesses (13:1): the procedure laid down under Jewish law (see Deuteronomy 19:15).

13:11-14 Conclusion

After last-minute instructions, and farewell, Paul closes with the lovely words of 'the grace'.

A holy kiss (12): a kiss on the cheek had become the customary Christian greeting, expressing a loving family relationship.

Galatia was a huge Roman province extending almost from coast to coast through the mountain and plain of central Turkey. How much of it Paul evangelized we do not know. But Acts 13 and 14 record how he founded churches in the southern cities of Antioch, Iconium, Lystra (Timothy's home town) and Derbe on his first missionary journey. And we know of two follow-up visits made later on (Acts 16:6; 18:23).

Not long after Paul's first visit, other Jewish teachers arrived in Galatia. Whereas Paul had taught that repentance and faith were all that was needed in order to receive God's forgiveness and the gift of new life, these men insisted that non-Jewish converts must also be circumcised and observe the Jewish law – virtually become Jews – in order to be saved. (The same thing happened at Syrian Antioch, Acts 15:1.) When Paul heard this he was distraught (Galatians 4:20). He saw that it struck at the roots of the Christian message. Salvation – new life – is God's gift to all who believe. No man can earn it by living the perfect life God's standards demand. But these men were saying that faith is not enough; there are things we must do to merit salvation. And the Gentiles in Galatia were being taken in. It was a desperate situation, requiring the most strongly worded of all Paul's letters.

The date is probably about AD 47, shortly before the committee of enquiry met in Jerusalem to resolve this very issue (Acts 15). Paul raises many of the same points nine or ten years later, in the letter to the Romans, when less extreme circumstances allowed a more dispassionate consideration of the issues. But the letter to the Galatians stands out, none the less, as the great charter of Christian freedom.

1 The God-given gospel

We can sense Paul's urgency right from the start. The abrupt assertion of authority (1) and lack of any word of praise are most unlike him. He gets straight to the point (6) – and he does not mince his words. The matter is serious. The whole fabric of the Christian gospel is threatened. As if this were not enough, the Jewish troublemakers have tried to undermine confidence in Paul himself. They have accused him of currying favour (10). They have called him a bogus apostle, and he is forced to defend himself (1, 11ff.). In flat contradiction of the charges, Paul asserts his God-given commission and authority. The very gospel he preaches was revealed to him, not by man – not even the other apostles – but by God. This is the point of his brief autobiography (13-24).

Verses 4-5: Paul stresses the fact that the initiative was God's.

My former life ... (13): see Acts 8:1; 9.

Arabia (17): probably the Nabataean kingdom whose capital was Petra in present-day Jordan. Acts 9:22-23 does not mention this. This 'three years' may have been one full year and part of two others. Paul does not say why he went. Perhaps after the dramatic about-turn of his conversion, he needed a time away on his own to reorientate his thinking.

Cephas (18): Peter. This seems to be the visit of Acts 9:26ff.

Syria and Cilicia (21): Antioch was in Syria, Tarsus (Paul's home town; Acts 9:30) in Cilicia – the south-east corner of the coast of modern Turkey.

2 The apostles sanction Paul's mission

Paul's next visit to Jerusalem seems to be the one mentioned in Acts 11:30. He took the opportunity to raise the matter of his own position with the other apostles. This attack of self-doubt seems rather out of character but Paul had, after all, been working very much on his own. And he was under attack (4). The apostles had no hesitation in approving his work among the Gentiles – God's hand was so clearly in it (7-9). But Peter later failed to practise what he preached, and had to be called to

A sundial inscribed with Greek symbols at Ephesus. Paul was concerned that the Galatians, delivered from being slaves of the 'elemental spirits of the universe', should not fall into the new bondage of observing 'days, months and years'.

task over his inconsistency (11ff.). As Jews, Peter and Paul both knew that it was hopeless for any man to try to earn acceptance with God (15-16). Having once gained their freedom through faith in Christ, how could they put their heads back in the noose of the law? If good deeds had been enough to save a man, Christ need never have died.

From James (12): James did not share their view, see Acts 15:13-21.
Ate with the Gentiles (12): see on Romans 14:2, 14.
Verses 17-18: Paul is saying that the real sin lies not in breaking Jewish food-laws, but in turning back to the law for salvation.
Verses 19-20: see on Romans 6-7.

3 - 4 Slavery under the law
Anyone willing to exchange Christian freedom for the Jewish law is a fool. The Jews talk about making the Gentiles sons of Abraham through the rite of circumcision. But Gentile Christians are already Abraham's sons and heirs – because they share his faith (3:7, 29). God accepted Abraham centuries before the law was given through Moses. So how can the law win man free pardon (3:15-18)? The law operated as a temporary restraint until the promise made to Abraham was fulfilled in the coming of Christ (3:19-24). Now, by

faith in him, we are all God's children – regardless of race or status or sex.

The Galatians had responded eagerly to Paul's preaching. What happened to make them change (4:12-20)? Can they really want to throw their freedom away (4:8-9)? Those under the law are like the son Abraham had by his slave-woman, Hagar. But Christians are free-born – heirs, like Isaac, to all God's promises.

Elemental spirits (4:3, 9): the forces that controlled them; the pagan no-gods they once served.
Days ... (4:10): Jewish feast-days.
Bodily ailment (4:13): see on 2 Corinthians 12:7.
Mt Sinai (4:24): where the law was given to Moses.

5 - 6 Freedom in Christ
It is not circumcision that matters, but what it stands for. Paul is so incensed by those who have unsettled his young converts that he could wish they would go the whole hog and castrate themselves (5:12)! Christ has saved us to set us free – free, not to live permissive, self-indulgent lives, but to put ourselves at God's disposal. We harvest what we sow in life (6:7-9). When we live to please ourselves it shows in the way we behave (5:19-21). When we live to please God we harvest a life and character produced in us by the Holy Spirit (5:22-24). And there is no mistaking the two. Christ has dealt with the old life (24) and made us new. Now we have to act accordingly, letting his Spirit control our everyday life and transform our relationships (5:25 - 6:10).

At this point (6:11) Paul takes over from his secretary to pen the last lines himself. For him there is only one thing worth glorying in: the power of the cross of Christ to re-create and transform human lives.

The marks of Jesus (6:17): the scars Paul's Christian service has earned him (see 2 Corinthians 4:7-12; 6:4-10; 11:23-29); living proof, if proof is still needed, that he is Christ's true apostle.

EPHESIANS

Paul's letter to the Ephesians differs considerably from his other letters. There are none of the usual personal greetings, although Paul had spent some years in Ephesus and had many friends there (see on Acts 19). Nor does Ephesians deal with particular problems or news. Even the words 'at Ephesus' (1:1) are missing from some of the early manuscripts. So it seems likely that Ephesians began as a circular letter written to a group of churches in what is now western Turkey – of which Ephesus itself was the most important. John's 'seven churches' (Revelation 1:11) were in this general area, as was the church at Colossae.

The fact that Paul wrote from prison (probably in Rome in the early 60s) links this letter with Philippians, Colossians and Philemon – the other 'letters from prison'. Of the three, Ephesians is closest in thought to Colossians. Because of its general nature the letter provides few clues to the situation in the churches. But it is clear that the Gentile Christians predominated, and that they tended to look down on their Jewish fellow Christians. Paul had been specially commissioned to work among the Gentiles, but he held no brief for a divided church. And so his great theme in this letter is God's glorious plan to bring men of every nation and background together in Christ (1:10). As Christians, all are on equal terms. We are one. And we must see that we express that oneness in personal relationships and the way we behave.

1 - 3 GOD'S GREAT PLAN

1:1-14 The eternal purpose of God

Paul catches his breath in wonder at the very thought of it. God has poured out his love on us. From the very beginning he determined to share his spiritual riches and glory with us – 'in Christ' (the key phrase of Ephesians). Christ stands at the very heart of God's plan. As we believe in him, his death sets us free: we can be forgiven. We can also share his new, risen life. We are

Temple dedicated to the Roman Emperor Hadrian at Ephesus.

made one with him, part of him. And in him we too are caught up in God's great world-plan as we live to his glory.

Saints (1); grace and peace (2): see on Romans 1.

Mystery (9): no human mind could have guessed God's intention. Paul usually uses this word to mean the 'open secret' of the gospel.

1:15-23 Paul's prayer

It warms Paul's heart to hear of the faith and love of these Christians. He prays that they may have greater understanding, a surer grasp of their glorious destiny, and increased awareness of the power at their disposal. The power God exercised in raising Christ from the dead and setting him in supreme control of the universe is at work in us, too!

2:1-10 From death to life

Because of our sinful nature we could not have fellowship with God: and to be cut off from him means death. But Christ has taken our death himself. God in his goodness – through no effort of our own – has given us new life in Christ. He has made us part of his new creation, set us off on a new life with power to carry out what he intends.

Prince of the power of the air (2): Satan, whose rebellious spirit is actively at work in the world of men.

2:11-22 Broken barriers

In the ancient world the Jew was separated from the Gentile by racial, religious, cultural and social barriers. If Christ could bring these two together, there was, and is, no human gulf too great for him to bridge. And he did. His death on the cross is the one means of peace with God for all men, without distinction. And all who belong to him have a common bond which is deeper and stronger than any of their former differences – of race or colour or status or sex or background. Jew and Gentile are one in Christ.

The circumcision (11): i.e. the Jews. See on Genesis 17.

Verse 12: the Gentile Christians have no cause to give themselves airs. Up till now they have been outsiders. The Jews, as God's people, were the only ones for whom there was hope.

3:1-13 Paul's mission to the Gentiles

Before Christ came, God's promises had been largely confined to the Jews. His purpose for the world at large had remained a secret (4-6, 8-9). When Paul was commissioned to take the message of salvation to the Gentiles, a new phase in God's plan was opened up. As men of all nations are brought together in Christ they demonstrate God's power and wisdom, not just to the watching world (see John 17:21), but to the cosmic powers beyond and behind it (10). The scope of God's purpose is breathtaking. In the light of it, Paul could keep his own troubles in perspective – and so can we.

Verse 3: not necessarily a separate letter – Paul had just told them how God had revealed his 'secret plan' to him (1:9, etc.).

3:14-21 Paul prays again

Paul has prayed that the church might have understanding (1:15-23). Now he prays more urgently than ever that they may have love; that they may be strong; that Christ may make his home in their hearts; that God may fill them completely. He can do all this and more.

4 - 6 CHRISTIANS IN ACTION

4:1-16 Unity – in practice

Christian unity is a fact. We are bound together by a common faith, a common life, common loyalty, common purpose. We serve one Master. He is the head, we are the limbs of a single body (see also 1 Corinthians 12 - 13). But we are not identical in temperament, personality or gifts. We must constantly cement the bond by a loving, forbearing attitude to one another, and by using our different gifts for the common good. We have to grow up together until we are all Christ wants us to be – until we are really like him.

Verse 8: following his ascension Christ gave gifts to men (see verse 11).

4:17 - 5:20 The new life

Salvation is God's free gift, but it carries with it the obligation to live and behave from that point on as God wants (4:1). This means deliberately discarding the old, selfish way of life, shedding former habits – and letting the new life change our thinking and remould our pattern of behaviour. This calls for truth and honesty; no harboured grudges, no spite and bitterness – instead kindness and a new readiness to forgive. In a word, we are to copy God's character. All that we think and do and say must be able to stand his searchlight.

5:21 - 6:9 Christian relationships: family and household

If everyone subordinates his own interests (21), no one can lord it. The Christian wife gives her husband complete respect and loyalty. The Christian husband cares for his wife with unselfish, undemanding love. Each depends on the other, and both model themselves on Christ. Their relationship, in turn, reflects the relationship between Christ and the church. In the family, children owe their parents respect and obedience. Parents must exercise discipline – not behave like petty tyrants; Christian slaves (and, presumably, employees) serve their masters as willingly and well as they serve Christ. Christian masters (and employers) will not bludgeon or bully, knowing that they must answer to a Master themselves.

5:32: the close physical bond between husband and wife is an illustration of Christ's spiritual oneness with his church.

6:10-24 The armour of God

Paul does not pretend it will be easy to maintain these standards – to keep our feet in the Christian life. The fight is on. And we are up against powerful external forces. It is a spiritual struggle for which we need spiritual weapons. But we are not left helpless. The whole armoury of God is at our disposal – and with this defence we can stand.

PHILIPPIANS

Philippi was a Roman colony, on the Egnatian Way – the great northern east-west highway. It was occupied by Italian settlers following Octavian's great battles, first against Brutus and Cassius, then against his former ally Antony. The colonists were proud of their special rights and privileges, and intensely loyal to Rome. In Philippi, as in the province of Macedonia as a whole, women enjoyed high status. They took active part in public and business life – a situation which is reflected in the church.

The church was founded about AD 50, during Paul's second missionary journey (see Acts 16:12-40). When Paul, Silas and Timothy left, Luke, the doctor, stayed on. Philippi was a medical centre, and may possibly have been Luke's home town. He no doubt did much to put the group on its feet and continue the evangelistic outreach. The letter reveals a church taking its share of suffering (1:29), and in some danger of division (1:27; 2:2). There may have been some leaning to a doctrine of perfectionism (3:12-13). And the arrival of the Judaizers (see on 3:2ff.) introduced a new threat. But Paul loved this church and rejoiced over its progress.

The letter. Paul wrote from prison (1:12). If this was in Rome (Acts 28:16, 30-31), the date was about AD 61-63. But conditions were harsher than they appear in Acts; judgement is imminent, and there is a real possibility of death. Timothy, but not Luke (to judge by 2:20-21), is with him. It may therefore be that the imprisonment is an earlier one not recorded in Acts. A good case has been made out for Ephesus, which would make the date of writing about AD 54. We cannot be certain either way.

There are several reasons for writing. Paul wanted to explain why he was sending Epaphroditus back. He wanted to thank the Philippians for their gift. He had news for them. And what he had heard about them made him long to encourage and advise. Further news reached him while he was writing that made it imperative to add a word of warning (3:1b).

1:1-2 Opening greetings
The letter comes from Paul 'and Timothy' – the young man who was with Paul when the church was founded, and who would shortly be coming to Philippi again (2:19). The 'slaves of Christ Jesus' write to the 'saints': not an elite, but all the Christians, as men and women set apart for God's service. The 'bishops' (overseers) and 'deacons' (administrators) receive special mention.

1:3-11 Paul's prayer for the church
Paul's prayer is full of love, joy (a keynote of the whole letter) and thankfulness. He longs for them to enjoy progressively richer and deeper spiritual knowledge which will mould their lives to God's pattern.

The first day (5): see Acts 16:12-40.
My imprisonment (7): see introduction above.

1:12-26 Personal news
Paul speaks of the past (12), present (13-18) and future (19-26), weighing the alternatives of life and death.

What has happened to me (12): if Paul writes from Rome, this includes mob violence, injustice, plots, prison, shipwreck and long detention under constant guard.

The whole praetorian guard (13): the crack imperial force from which Paul's warders were drawn.

Deliverance (19): if the judgement goes against him, death will deliver him into Christ's presence; if it goes for him, his captors will release him to serve the church.

To live is Christ ... (21): possessing more and more of him, becoming more and more like him, until on his death the process is completed in one glorious moment.

1:27 - 2:18 A plea for a united stand
There is more than a hint of division in the church (see for example 4:2). Paul urges them all to pocket their pride, and to live and work and think

as one. Anything less lets down the gospel and the Lord, whose life on earth is the supreme example of humility. It is because Jesus gave up all that was his by right – even his life – that God has given him the highest place of all. (2:5-11 is probably a quotation from an early hymn in praise of Christ.)

Have this mind ... (2:5): 'The attitude you should have is the one that Christ Jesus had' (Good News Bible).

The form of God (6): the actual nature, not just the appearance (as also in verse 7).

Emptied himself (7): New English Bible, 'made himself nothing'. In becoming man the Lord stripped himself of his glory: he lived a life of humble obedience. But he cast off none of his essential deity.

Day of Christ (16): the day of his return.

A libation (17): Paul's death adds only the finishing touch to the real offering, the faith and life of the church.

2:19-30 Paul commends his fellow workers

Verses 19-23: Timothy (see on 1:1-2). Verses 25-30: Epaphroditus. The Philippians had sent him to help Paul. In sending him home, Paul is anxious to make it clear he has not fallen down on his job. Far from it.

3 Warning and example

Paul had been rounding off his letter (3:1a), but fresh and alarming news compelled him to take up his pen again. He does not mind repeating former advice, as a safeguard (3:1b). They must beware of those 'dogs' the Judaizers – that group of Jewish Christians who followed Paul everywhere, insisting that Gentile converts must be circumcised and keep the law (despite the official edict of Acts 15:19ff.). They are in fact altering the whole basis of salvation, making it 'by faith *and* ...', instead of 'by faith only': hence Paul's anger.

The true circumcision (3): the true Israel, the true people of God.

Gain ... loss (7-8): God does not operate a credit and debit account. The finest human achievement is garbage compared with the standard of life he demands, and provides for us, in Christ.

I press on ... (12ff.): like the athlete or charioteer, who does not waste time looking back, but strains every nerve and concentrates every effort

'I press towards the goal to win the prize': whether Paul is thinking of the athlete, or of the Roman chariot race, pictured here, the point is the same.

to cross the line or pass the post. Paul counters the idea that perfection can be reached here and now.

Their god is the belly (19): i.e. appetite; whatever they want; revelling in things they should be ashamed of.

Our commonwealth (20): 'state' or citizenship. They are to regard themselves as a colony of heaven. The Philippians, being intensely proud of their status as a Roman colony, would be quick to grasp all that that meant.

4 Advice and encouragement: grateful thanks

Verse 1: a general appeal. Verses 2-3: personal appeals. Euodia and Syntyche are two women who have quarrelled.

Verses 4-9: rejoice, rejoice. The advice comes from a man in prison, facing death; a man who had been stoned and beaten and hounded by the mob. Yet experiences which leave others sour and bitter leave Paul overflowing with joy! The secret is in verses 6-7: learning how to off-load all our cares on the One who cares for us (1 Peter 5:7). Nothing is beyond him. Having emptied our minds of worry, the next step is to fill them with the sort of things that will shape a truly Christian character (8).

Verses 10-20: the apostle's appreciation of the church's gifts. From the very first they have supported him (15), with a generosity that extends to all in need (2 Corinthians 8:1-5). At real cost they have given themselves and all they possess. No wonder Paul loves these Christians: a group of faithful, loyal, thoughtful, generous, outgoing men and women.

Caesar's household (21): Christian members of the imperial staff (the palace staff, if Paul is at Rome).

COLOSSIANS

Colossae was a small town in the beautiful Lycus Valley, about 100 miles east of Ephesus, near Denizli in modern Turkey. Its near neighbours were the more prosperous Laodicea (Colossians 4:16; see on Revelation 3:14ff.) and Hierapolis. There were Christian groups in all three towns.

The church. We have no record of how it began. But it was probably during Paul's three years in Ephesus (Acts 19) that two prominent men from Colossae – Epaphras and Philemon – became Christians. And they were active in spreading the Christian message in their home area (Colossians 1:6-7; 4:12-13; Philemon 1-2, 5).

The letter. Although Paul had never visited the group at Colossae, he had heard all about it from Epaphras. There was much to be thankful for, but some of the news was worrying. So he wrote to them from prison – probably in Rome, about AD 61. He had a ready-made opportunity to send the letter with Tychicus (who may well have carried the letter to the Ephesians at the same time) and Philemon's runaway slave Onesimus, whom he was sending home (see on Philemon).

The problem. The trouble at Colossae was 'syncretism' – that tendency to introduce ideas from other philosophies and religions on a level with Christian truth, which is also perhaps our greatest temptation today. It was understandable. There were Greeks and Jews in the Colossian church, as well as 'native' Phrygians. It was natural that they should cling to their own ideas and want to incorporate them into Christianity. It seemed harmless enough. But Paul knew that it struck at the heart of the Christian faith. By trying to retain circumcision, their food-laws and festivals (2:11, 16), the Jewish Christians brought the whole basis of man's acceptance with God into question (see on Galatians). The idea of angel intermediaries (2:18) was a direct challenge to the supremacy of Christ. And the introduction of asceticism and high-flown philosophy threw man back on himself and on human wisdom (2:18-23) – which had already been proved a failure. Although Paul does not deal with these issues point by point these are the thoughts that lie behind his letter. The Colossians needed to take fresh hold on Christ, on his complete supremacy and utter sufficiency. This is Paul's theme.

1:1-14 Opening greetings and prayer

It is characteristic of Paul to begin with thanksgiving. He has his Christian priorities – and his psychology! – right. But his warm-hearted praise is genuine, not just sugar to coat the pill of the lecture to follow. His loving care (and his prayer-list) extended beyond the churches he himself had brought into being, to groups of Christians he had never even met (2:1). It cheered him immensely to hear of their faith and love and hope. And he longed for God to give them fuller understanding and spiritual maturity.

1:15-23 Jesus Christ the Lord

Jesus is the living expression of God himself – active in the creation and holding together of all that exists. He was first, he is first – in existence, in power, in position. He has first place in God's new creation and his new people, the church. He brought it into being. He is its Head. Through his death it is possible for us to become God's friends – this is the good news of the gospel.

Firstborn (15): not first to be created, but the heir whose position is unique.

Thrones ... (16): unseen beings and powers outside our visible world.

1:24 - 2:5 Paul's own task

The apostle's job is to make God's message known. The philosophers hint at secrets, at deep things known only to the initiated. This is God's open secret: Jesus Christ – at home in every Christian, preparing him for a glorious future. And Jesus really is a 'secret' worth knowing. This makes all Paul's efforts worthwhile.

What is lacking ... (1:24): Paul is not

implying that Christ's suffering was not enough for our salvation. But the church – Christians – cannot be perfected without suffering too.

2:6 - 3:4 Wrong teaching and right attitudes

False argument was filtering into the Colossian church from various quarters (see introduction above). It was misleading and dangerous. The Christian cannot afford to compromise either with philosophy or with legalism. Both of these are man-centred. Christianity is Christ-centred – or it is nothing at all. We have all we need in him. We do not need to invoke other spiritual powers or intermediaries (2:8, 23), because Christ is infinitely greater. No religi-

Paul warned his readers against those bringing false teaching and writing letters which claimed apostolic authority. 'Embroidered' stories of the life of Jesus have survived. These fragments of an unknown 'Gospel' date from the first half of the 2nd century.

ous rite (2:11) can give us more than we already have. Old Testament practices are no more than a shadow of the reality – which is Christ (16ff.). He is our life. He is the One we must hold on to. We depend on him, not on ourselves, our spirituality, our asceticism.

2:12: see Romans 6.

Food and drink ... (2:16): despite all

that the Jews said, salvation does not depend on things like these.

Elemental spirits (2:20): Christians must throw off the old pagan superstitious idea that spirits control the world.

3:5 - 4:6 The old life and the new

Becoming a Christian means a definite break with the old selfish way of life. It means determination to let the new life which is in us govern all we think and say and do. It means a permanent resolve to become like Christ, to take on his character (3:10). His life – his love and forgiveness – is our model (3:12ff.). His word (3:16) shapes our thinking. The hallmark of the Christian life is prayer and thanksgiving to God, and outgoing unselfish love in all our human relationships. Our concern is no longer to get, but to give.

3:18 - 4:1: see on Ephesians 5-6, where Paul treats the same subject more fully.

4:7-18 Personal news

The reference to Tychicus and Onesimus links this letter with Ephesians (see 6:21-22) and Philemon. All three letters would seem to have been sent at the same time by the same messenger. (The letter from Laodicea, 16, may be Ephesians.) It is good to find Mark reinstated after the trouble he once caused between Paul and Barnabas (Acts 13:13; 15:36-40). Aristarchus, who though a Jew came from Greece, was another long-standing companion of Paul's and had been involved in the riot at Ephesus (Acts 19:29). Luke stayed with Paul to the end, but Demas defected (2 Timothy 4:10-11). Epaphras, the Colossian, has been mentioned already (1:7, and see introduction). Archippus may be Philemon's son (Philemon 2). Nympha, in Laodicea, is only one of those who opened their homes to the local Christian group long before there were church buildings. Aquila and Priscilla at Ephesus (1 Corinthians 16:19) and later at Rome (Romans 16:5), Philemon at Colossae and Gaius at Corinth (Romans 16:23) all did the same. The whole church is deeply in their debt.

1 AND 2 THESSALONIANS

Thessalonica was a free city, capital of the Roman province of Macedonia (northern Greece). It was a prosperous port on the Aegean Sea, across the bay from Mt Olympus. It also stood on the Egnatian Way, the land trade-route from Dyrrachium on the Adriatic to Byzantium (Istanbul). Thessaloniki is today a flourishing modern city, centre of government for northern Greece, and second only to Athens.

The church was founded about AD 50, after Paul (with Silas and Timothy) left Philippi on the second missionary journey. See Acts 17:1-9. Paul did not stay in Thessalonica long: three successive sabbaths preaching in the synagogue, followed by a short time based at Jason's house. Then the Jews stirred up trouble. Jason and the other Christians were hauled before the magistrates and bound over to keep the peace. For safety's sake the newly-formed church sent the missionaries away. But persecution continued, from Jews and others.

The letters. From Thessalonica, Paul and his party went to Beroea, then Paul continued alone to Athens. It seems Timothy joined him there (1 Thessalonians 3:1-2), but was almost immediately sent back to Thessalonica for news. Paul was acutely anxious to know what had become of the Christians. He was in Corinth by the time Timothy returned with good news. 1 Thessalonians, written at this point, is full of relief and joy. Paul answers questions that had arisen, and repeats his teaching on matters where the church was weak. The second letter followed a few months later, reinforcing the teaching and clearing up misunderstandings, particularly over Christ's return. These two letters are the earliest of Paul's surviving writings (with the possible exception of Galatians). They were written only 20 years after the crucifixion of Jesus.

1:1 Opening greetings

Paul is the author of the letter. But he writes in association with Silvanus (=Silas, see on Acts 15:40) and Timothy, his companions on the mission to Thessalonica, and now in Corinth.

1:2-10 Paul thanks God for good news of the church

What happened at Thessalonica was the work of God. What else could account for the way this little group – persecuted, deprived of their teachers from the word go – stood firm? More than that, within months they have become an example of unwavering faith to the rest of Greece (7), spreading the good news far and wide by word and life. No wonder Paul has cause for thanks.

They themselves (9): the people of Macedonia, Achaia, etc.

Verses 9-10: the gospel in a nutshell. Paul had preached the character of God; Jesus, his Son, who died to deliver man from judgement; the resurrection; and the return of Christ from heaven. The promise of the Lord's return is specially precious to all who suffer. These letters are shot through with it.

2:1-16 Paul recalls his visit

It is clear that Paul's enemies have been pursuing a campaign of vilification. The apostle clears himself of their charges by reminding the Christians of what actually happened when he was with them. He did not come as an itinerant quack teacher peddling dubious wares, and out to deceive (3). Nor was he on the make, in any sense (5). He came to give, not get (8), willing to face more trouble while still smarting from the wounds of Philippi (2; see Acts 16:22ff.). He even refused financial support (9).

Each one of you (11): Paul counselled enquirers personally, individually.

Verses 15-16: nowhere does Paul speak so harshly of his own people. His tone is prophetic. There is a point of no return for those who implacably oppose God. Judgement is as certain as if it had come already (16b).

2:17 - 3:10 Subsequent events

Paul is as close to his converts as

parent to child. No matter how far away, they are deep in his heart and thoughts. The knowledge that they are in trouble fills him with unbearable anxiety. Paul's happiness – his life, even – depends on their continuance and progress in the faith. So he longs to see them and hear from them. He is even prepared to face Athens alone, rather than do without news. So Timothy's welcome report brings the apostle an influx of joy, a new lease of life.

Little remains of ancient Thessalonica today. As Thessaloniki, it is the second largest city in Greece. In later Roman times the Via Egnatia passed under the Arch of Galerius, pictured here. The street is still called by the same name.

Satan hindered us (2:18): it is in his interest so to engineer circumstances that the missionary and his converts are kept apart.
We told you beforehand ... (3:4): 1st-century Christians were taught from the outset to expect trouble and suffering.
3:11-13 Paul's prayer
Paul prays for reunion, and for love and holiness in the church.
4 - 5:22 Specific teaching
On sexual matters (4:1-8). Pagan standards of sexual behaviour fell far short of Jewish and Christian ones. The pull of the old ways was strong for the young converts.

On Christian love and right living (4:9-12). Even where love already exists there is always room for more. The Greeks despised manual labour. And there were idlers in the church quite happy to sponge on the generosity of fellow Christians. But Paul worked with his hands and encouraged others to do the same. The prospect of Jesus' return was a great temptation to opt out of hum-drum

daily work (see also 2 Thessalonians 3:11-12).

On the Lord's return (4:13 - 5:11). Two problems have arisen out of Paul's teaching on the subject:
1. Some had died in the months between Paul's departure and the writing of this letter. So will Christians who die before Christ comes lose out (13-18)? Far from it, says Paul. They will be raised first when Christ comes. And dead and living together will join in the Lord's triumph and enjoy his presence.
2. When will the Lord come (5:1-11)? No one knows. But he will come suddenly and unexpectedly – and we need to be ready.

On general matters (5:12-22). Time, or space, is running out. But Paul manages to pack seventeen practical and characteristic commands into these few verses.
Wrong his brother (4:6): the same principle applies before and after marriage – sexual promiscuity deprives a fellow man of what is rightly his.
Asleep (13) ... fallen asleep (14): for the Christian, death is merely a sleep from which he awakes to the presence of Christ.
The breastplate (5:8): faith, love and the certainty of future salvation are the Christian's defences against all attack. Compare Ephesians 6:14ff.
5:23-28 Conclusion
Paul's prayer is comprehensive: for the whole man in every aspect ('spirit, soul, body'). Authority (the stern command to read the letter to the whole church) sits beside humility. The apostle, who never ceases to pray for his readers, knows how much he needs their prayers.
A holy kiss (26): see on 2 Corinthians 13:12.
2 THESSALONIANS
1:1-2 Opening greetings
1:3-12 Praise and encouragement
Verses 3-4: the Thessalonians seem to have protested against the extravagant praise of Paul's first letter (chapter 1). He replies that it is only right to thank God for their growing faith and love, and their firm stand in face of persecution.
Verses 5-12: the universe is a moral universe; God is a just God. It is therefore certain that those who make his people suffer, and reject his truth, will themselves be eternally, irrevocably punished at his coming. This is a fact no Christian gloats over.

2:1-12 The events leading up to Christ's return

This passage is one of the most difficult in all Paul's letter; and even Peter found Paul hard to understand (2 Peter 3:16)! He alludes to teaching of which we have no surviving record, so that much which was clear to his first readers is now obscure. It is better, in some cases, to admit we do not know the meaning, than to speculate.

Some of the Thessalonian Christians thought the day of the Lord had already begun. But Paul has never said (or written, 2) so. Before this happens, he explains, there will be a great, final rebellion against God, headed by an individual utterly opposed to him. (Compare Revelation 13, and 1 John 2:18-25.) At present there are forces at work restraining evil – but in the end these will be swept away. Victory will come only through Christ, at his coming.

Man of lawlessness (3): not Satan himself, but the leader of the anti-God forces, who sets himself up as God. ('Son of perdition' is Hebrew idiom, meaning 'the one who is doomed to destruction'.)

He who now restrains it (7): perhaps Paul personalizes the principle of law and government which holds evil in check; perhaps he means an angelic being. We really do not know.

Those who are to perish (10): because they do not welcome the gospel. They turn their backs on the truth which offers salvation. In effect, like Satan, they say 'Evil be thou my Good' (12).

2:13 - 3:5 Thanksgiving and prayer

Paul turns, with tremendous contrast, to the Thessalonians. They responded gladly to the truth. And now all the glory of the Lord awaits them.

From the beginning (13): from eternity (see Ephesians 1:4).

The traditions (15): not customs, but the truth about Jesus and his teaching, faithfully handed down by the apostles: the same truth that we possess in written form in the New Testament.

Comfort (17): in the old sense of strengthen.

3:6-15 The need to work for a living

Paul stressed this in his first letter (4:11). But excitement about Christ's coming seems to have made the situation worse, not better. So Paul speaks out in strong terms against those who idle their life away and sponge on others. They can find no warrant for this in his own behaviour.

3:16-18 Conclusion

The present is tough, the future will be tougher (2:3-12). But no matter what times may be like, no matter what may be going on around, the Christian has an inexhaustible, unfailing source of peace.

At verse 17 Paul takes over from his secretary. His own signature authenticates this letter (see 2:2). He added his personal signature to each of his letters in the same way.

1 AND 2 TIMOTHY

Timothy was the child of a mixed marriage – his mother being Jewish, his father Greek. His home was at Lystra in the Roman province of Galatia (not far from Konya in present-day Turkey). Paul came to Lystra on his first missionary journey, and it must have been then that Timothy was converted. He made such strides as a Christian that when Paul called again he decided to take Timothy with him on his travels. The local church leaders formally commissioned the young man and gave him their blessing. And from then on he became Paul's constant, loyal, trusted and greatly loved companion.

Timothy was not naturally brave, and he was often unwell. He needed a good deal of encouragement. But Paul's confidence was not misplaced. In the letters to the different churches he speaks most warmly of this 'son in the faith'. Timothy not only travelled with Paul and was associated with him in many of his letters, he frequently acted as Paul's envoy to the churches. Very early on he was left behind in Beroea to consolidate and follow up Paul's work there and at Thessalonica. He was sent to Corinth when Paul heard of the troubles in the church there – no easy assignment. And at the time Paul wrote to him he was in Ephesus,

supervising the local Christian groups and responsible for choosing and training church leaders.

The letters. 1 and 2 Timothy and Titus belong to the end of Paul's life. Paul was free when he wrote 1 Timothy and Titus, and had recently been engaged in further evangelism in Greece and what is now Turkey. This does not tally with anything we know from Acts, and it may be assumed that Paul was released from the imprisonment described in Acts 28, resumed his preaching for some time, and was then re-arrested and taken to Rome for trial. In 2 Timothy he is in prison and expecting to be executed.

In these 'pastoral letters' – the general title for the three letters – we have a directive from Paul on the way Timothy and Titus should handle the various problems they encountered in the oversight of the churches in their charge. Paul sets out the qualities to look for in appointing church leaders. He gives advice on personal conduct. And in the face of much false and misleading teaching he urges them to concentrate on essentials and not be side-tracked. The best way to counter wrong ideas is to teach the truth.

The early church had no doubt that these letters were genuinely written by Paul to the two men named. Mod-

THE SETTING OF
THE PASTORAL EPISTLES

ern scholars have questioned this on the grounds that they differ in language and content from Paul's other letters, and that they counter 2nd-century heresies. Some suggest they are the work of a later writer who incorporated some genuine Pauline material. This raises fresh problems, however, and there may be a simpler explanation.

Paul signed the letters he dictated, adding a greeting. The wooden pencase containing reed pens, with an ink-well half-filled with black ink, dates from the 1st century.

We know that Paul often used a secretary, for instance, and if he was given a good deal of freedom this would make arguments based on vocabulary very uncertain (even with computer analysis!). The problem over content is that Paul tells Timothy and Titus things they must surely have known already. The reason may be that the instructions were meant to be read to the churches over which the two men ministered. Even the point about heresies is by no means certain. There is nothing in the letters that we can categorically say Paul could not have written.

1 The trouble at Ephesus; Paul and Timothy

There had been a tremendous respon-se to Paul's preaching in and around Ephesus (Acts 19). A great many Christian groups had sprung up almost overnight. And Paul was quick to realize how vulnerable they were to wrong teaching (Acts 20: 29-30). Ten years later his fears had materialized. Apocryphal Jewish legends and family-trees (4) were being made the basis of strange teaching. This was a wrong approach to the Old Testament law, and Timothy must stop it spreading. The Christian message should result in faith and love and a clear conscience – not idle speculation. It has always seemed more exciting to argue over abstruse topics than to live the Christian life.

Paul had been a Christian for over 30 years. He had been on the road with the gospel message for 20. Yet he never forgot that he had once gone all out to destroy this sect (13; Acts 8:1-3; 9). He never ceased to be amazed that God should have taken a man like him into his service. Paul's directive is a good one: 'hold to your faith; obey your Christian conscience'.

Prophetic utterances (18): the indication (given either to Paul, or at Timothy's commissioning) that God had chosen Timothy for this work.

Delivered to Satan (20): we do not know exactly what this means – but see on 1 Corinthians 5:5.

2 Prayer; the place of women

The first duty of the Christian church is prayer. It is in answer to prayer that God gives conditions in which Christians can lead peaceable lives and put all their energy into making his good news known to the whole world (4).

The Christian message upgraded the status of women (see e.g. Galatians 3:28). But God did not intend them to take over. Men and women are equal in his sight, but their roles in life are not identical. So Paul's word to Christian women is to be conduct-conscious, not clothes-mad, and not to lord it over the men.

Verse 15: Paul could never have meant that women win eternal salvation through childbirth (compare verse 5)! The thought may follow on from verses 13-14 – i.e. though woman was the first to sin, it was through woman that the Saviour was born (Revised Standard Version margin). Or he means that women will be 'brought safely through' childbirth ... (New English Bible margin).

3 Church leaders

It was Paul's practice to appoint several elders (the same thing as bishops, 1) to take charge of each church (Acts 14:23). These in turn were assisted by 'helpers' (deacons, 8). His list of qualifications for these leaders makes sound sense. They must be men (and women, 11, unless these are deacons' wives) who can control themselves and their families, who have proved to be stable Christians, and who have the respect of the outside world. Timothy was not a naturally forceful character. To have Paul's written authority was the next best thing to having the apostle with him (14ff.).

Mystery (9): God's revealed secret in Jesus Christ; the Christian faith is God-given, not man-made.

Verse 16: Paul seems to be quoting a Christian hymn.

4 False teachers – and true

The ultimate source of false teaching is the devil himself. It is promoted by men who are dead to conscience. They ban marriage and lay down rigid rules about diet – things God has designed for man's good. They claim that their thinking is super-Christian. In fact it is sub-Christian. Timothy, as a true teacher, has to make this clear. And this does not stop at words. His whole life must bear out what he teaches others. So he has to let the truth mould his own life (6); he has to keep spiritually fit (7, 8). He has always to watch himself, and watch his teaching.

5 - 6:2 Dealing with people; widows; elders

To treat other people as we would our own family (1-2) is sound advice. There was no welfare state in Paul's day and the widow's lot was unenviable. The church was quick to realize and accept its responsibility to help (Acts 6:1). It soon had a sizeable problem, and not all of the cases were equally deserving. Paul's rule is that the church should reserve its help for those who are really destitute. It should take on to its books only older widows of good Christian character, and committed to Christian work. The younger ones should remarry. And wherever possible widows should be cared for by their own relatives. In the city where the goddess Diana was served by a host of prostitutes, the reputation of those who serve Christ must be beyond reproach.

Elders must be carefully chosen, treated with respect, and paid for their work.

As Christians, slaves are free men – but they are not to drag Christ's name in the mud by turning on their masters (see also on Ephesians 6:5ff.; Philemon).

5:9: not 'only married once', but 'faithful in marriage to one man' (New English Bible).

5:22: 'lay hands on': i.e. commission men for Christian service.

5:23: sound medical advice at the time; wine counteracted some of the harmful impurities in the water.

6:3-21 Real wealth; personal instructions

The subject of false teaching comes up yet again. The superior 'knowledge' (*gnosis*, 20) claimed by these men soon grew into the full-scale heresy of 'Gnosticism', whose initiates felt free to discard some of the cardinal Christian truths, including the fact that Christ was a real man.

Some men see Christianity as a road to riches. And Christians *are* rich – though not in money. Not that money is wrong in itself. It can and should be put to good and generous use. It is the *craving* for money that leads to all kinds of evil. The 'man of God' (11) craves for a truly Christian character, and all his effort is directed to this end. He knows that Jesus will one day return in glory, and he lives in the light of that fact. **The root (10):** more accurately, 'a root'.

2 TIMOTHY

This is Paul's last and most moving letter. After a lifetime of service and suffering for Christ he is in prison again, and death is imminent. He is alone except for Luke, and longs to see Timothy again. Yet there is no hint of self-pity; there are no regrets. His last word is one of encouragement to all who follow after. He can face death without fear and without doubt. The race is over – ahead is his reward.

1 'I thank God'

Gratitude was the habit of Paul's Christian life. He had long since ceased to grumble about his own discomforts. Deep thankfulness fills his heart now as he thinks of Timothy. And he longs for this man of many fears, as well as real faith, to share his own confidence. The secret is simply to *know* Christ (12; and see Philippians 3:10). We have good news for the world – a gospel that brings men life. We need neither apologize for it, nor try to improve on it.

Tears (4): shed when they parted.

That day (12): the day of the Lord's return; the day of judgement.

All ... in Asia (15): false teaching took such a hold in Ephesus (see on 1 Timothy 1) that Christians rejected the very man to whom they owed their faith. It must have been a bitter moment for Paul.

2 On active service

It costs something to be a Christian – no man knew this better than Paul. Timothy will need single-minded determination not to get sucked in by the demands of life (4) or side-tracked by fruitless, divisive argument (16, 23). Not everyone who makes a good beginning stays the course. The way we live must demonstrate the truth of what we say. We are not to bicker and fight over words, but hold to the truth with gentleness and love.

Verses 11-13: Paul is probably quoting a hymn.

The resurrection (18): they 'spiritualized' the teaching and denied any future bodily resurrection.

3 Troubled times ahead

Paul warns that as the time for Christ's return draws near evil will intensify – even within the church (5-6). Those who are true to Christ will go through persecution – as Jesus himself predicted (John 15:20). Timothy must stand firm in the truths taught him from the scriptures. They contain all that is necessary for salvation and for right living.

Jannes and Jambres (8): in Jewish tradition, the names of Pharaoh's magicians (Exodus 7).

Verse 11: see Acts 13-14. Timothy would vividly recall these events since they took place near his home. Paul was stoned and left for dead at Lystra, Timothy's home town.

4 Final instructions

Paul may be put to death any time

'I have finished the course, the victor's wreath awaits me' – Paul uses the vivid picture of the athlete's crown. This gold wreath was found at Pergamum.

now. The prospect does not ruffle him. But he has a last charge for Timothy: to go on declaring God's message, come what may; though, sadly, this is not what men are itching to hear.

Personal news is left till last. Paul's fellow missionaries – Titus, Tychicus, Trophimus – are all away. One is ill, and one (Demas) has defected. At the first stage of his trial (16) Paul, like the Lord, stood alone. All his friends deserted him, and his enemies were not slow to make capital. Now winter is coming and he wants his books and papers, and his thick cloak. He has only Luke's presence, and the faithful Christians in Rome (21) to warm his heart – and the hope that Timothy and Mark will reach him in time.

Endure suffering (5): despite his fears, Timothy did just that (see Hebrews 13:23).

Books and parchments (13): possibly copies of Old Testament books, Paul's own notebooks, or personal papers.

Alexander (14): see 1 Timothy 1:20.

The lion's mouth (17): this may just be a manner of speaking; or it may refer to the lions in the arena, to Nero, or to the devil.

TITUS

See introduction to 1 and 2 Timothy. **Titus** is not mentioned in Acts, but it is clear from the letters that he was one of Paul's trusted inner circle. As a Greek he was made a test case on the visit to Jerusalem, to clarify the position of non-Jewish converts (Galatians 2:1-4). Later when, despite Timothy's work, trouble flared up in Corinth Paul chose Titus as the man for the job. He not only sorted things out, but established really good relations with the church – no small tribute to his tact and strength of character (2 Corinthians 2; 7; 8; 12). Some years later again, when Paul wrote this letter, Titus had been left to consolidate the apostle's work in Crete. He faced a situation very similar to Timothy's at Ephesus (see 1 Timothy). The last mention of Titus is in 2 Timothy 4:10, when he was away (presumably still furthering the Christian cause) in Dalmatia (Yugoslavia).

Crete was probably one of the first places to hear the Christian gospel. There were Jews from Crete in the crowd that listened to Peter on the Day of Pentecost (Acts 2:11). But the message fell on rough ground. The Cretans were such habitual liars (1:12) that the Greeks coined a special verb for lying – 'to Cretize'. And it is plain from Paul's letter that even the Christians were an unruly, hot-headed, volatile bunch who needed firm handling.

1 Elders – and trouble-makers

It is the thought of the Cretans and their lies (12) that makes Paul dwell on the dependability of God's word. When he holds out the promise of eternal life, we can rely on it. He tells us the truth – we can pass it on with absolute confidence.

For the qualifications of church leaders (5-9) see on 1 Timothy 3.

False teachers have produced a situation so bad it calls for a really strong line. Physical force is never justified, but there are times when forceful words certainly are. The worst heretics were Jewish – but there were others too (10, 14; and see on 1 Timothy 1).

Verse 12: a quotation from the poet Epimenides.

Verse 16: the acid test of faith is how we live. It is not enough simply to call ourselves Christians.

2 - 3:11 Christian conduct

By the way we behave we can discredit, or reinforce, the Christian message. Paul's instructions throw no flattering light on the Cretan temperament. They were a naturally belligerent, argumentative people, uncontrolled, resentful of authority and partial to the bottle! But the Christian life calls for discipline, obedience and respect for others – within the family and household, within the church, and in relation to the authorities. Jesus gave his life to buy us back from our old sinful ways and make us into people whose consuming passion is to do good (2:14). The Christian teacher must use his authority to insist on Christian standards – and he must set a good example. Doing good results *from* (not *in*) salvation (3:3-7).

Washing (3:5): a picture of the cleansing, renewing work of the Holy Spirit which is symbolized in Christian baptism.

Genealogies (3:9): see on 1 Timothy 1.

3:12-15 In closing

When his 'relief' arrives, Titus is to join Paul at Nicopolis on the west coast of Greece. Tychicus is another member of Paul's inner circle of partners in the gospel (Ephesians 6:21, etc.). Zenas and Apollos (see Acts 18:24-28) may have been the ones who brought Paul's letter to Titus.

PHILEMON

This is a private letter from Paul to Philemon, one of his converts and a good friend. Philemon was a man of some standing. A group of local Christians regularly met in his home at Colossae. One of his slaves, Onesimus, had stolen some money (18) and run away to the big city (probably Rome) where he could easily escape detection. There he somehow came into contact with the imprisoned apostle, and through him became a Christian. Paul loved this young man like a son, but he was Philemon's legal property. It was hard for Paul, and hard for Onesimus – who was liable to terrible punishment for what he had done – but he must go back and make amends. Paul could not keep him without Philemon's willing consent. So he wrote this 'covering note' for Onesimus. And Tychicus went with him for company and moral support, taking the latest news and a letter from Paul to the Colossian church (Colossians 4:7-9).

Paul's intention in writing is to ask Philemon to be lenient. A very different Onesimus is returning from the one who ran away. He is not just a slave now, but a brother-Christian. And Paul wants Philemon to welcome him as such. He could have insisted. He had the authority – and Philemon was deeply indebted to him. But instead his letter is loving and tactful, considerate and full of warm praise. He knows this man. He knows his faith and his Christian love. There is no need to make demands. Philemon will do all that he asks – and more.

Apphia (2): probably Philemon's wife. Archippus may be their son.

No use ... (11): Paul plays on Onesimus' name, which means 'useful'.

Verses 15-16: it is not clear whether Paul has any thought of Onesimus being set free. But the ideas expressed here are radical enough to have a far-reaching effect. Slavery was such an integral part of the social structure of the day that to preach freedom would have been tantamount to revolution. Paul's brief was not not to engage in political campaigning but preach a gospel capable of transforming human life from within.

Verses 18-19: Paul's 'IOU' recalls the Samaritan's good neighbourliness (Luke 10:35).

Epaphras, Mark ... (23-24): see on Colossians 4.

HEBREWS

Who wrote the letter? The origin of Hebrews is something of a mystery. The oldest manuscripts are anonymous, and there are none of the conventional greetings with which a 1st-century letter usually began. In fact it is more a treatise than a letter. Even in the first few centuries AD no one knew for certain who the author was, though many people attributed it to Paul. Today this is considered very unlikely. Hebrews reflects neither Paul's style nor his thought. But having said that, we are no nearer to solving the puzzle. From the letter, we know that the author knew Timothy (13:23). He writes extremely polished Greek. And he is plainly an able teacher. He knows the Old Testament inside out. And the version he quotes is the Greek Septuagint – which means he is probably a Greek-speaking (Hellenistic) Jew, writing to fellow Greek-speaking Jews. He is a Christian who has thoroughly thought through the relation of his faith to Judaism.

To whom was it sent? The title 'To the Hebrews' is very old, but may not be original. It is a fair inference from the letter – with its discussion of priests and sacrifice and its many Old Testament quotations – that it was written to a group of Jewish Christians. They were men of some intellectual ability. The group had been established a good many years (2:3; 13:7), and had a history of persecution. They should have been mature Christians by this time, capable of teaching others (5:11 - 6:2). Instead they are withdrawn and inward-looking. And they seem to have half a mind to turn back to Judaism. They need a forceful reminder that what they possess in Christ is far better.

When was it written? The most likely date is the late 60s. If Jerusalem and the temple had already fallen to the Romans the author would have been almost bound to mention it when he referred to the priests and sacrifices. So it is fairly certain it was written before AD 70. If the letter was written to Rome (see on 13:24) and alludes to Nero's persecution this places it sometime between AD 64 and AD 70.

What is it about? Hebrews was written for a group of Christian Jews wavering between Christianity and Judaism. It is in a sense the counterpart to Paul's letter to the Romans, this time directed to a Jewish audience and explaining Christ's relationship to all that had gone before in the religious history of Israel. So the writer compares and contrasts the person and the achievements of Jesus with the Old Testament priesthood and sacrificial system. He is not only incomparably greater and better than these, he is the ultimate realization of all they stand for. He is the perfect priest, offering the perfect sacrifice. He has finally removed the barrier of sin and given men access to God in a way the sacrificial system could never do. That was the copy: he is the original pattern. That was the shadow: he is the reality men have always been searching for. If we turn away from him – back to an inferior substitute, back to a proven failure – we lose everything.

1 Jesus Christ – the Son of God

The letter begins with a tremendous affirmation of the deity of Christ (1-4). Through Jesus, God has made his supreme and final revelation of himself to man. Jesus is the living embodiment of the character and majesty of God. He has dealt with the problem of human sin, once and for all. He is now at God's side, in the position of supreme power.

The angels – whom the Jews came near to worshipping – themselves worship Christ (6). They are spiritual beings, but no more than God's servants (14). The Son is far and away above them – as the scriptures prove.

The writer's use of the Old Testament. The quotations in Hebrews are from the Greek Septuagint version, which differs in some respects from our own Old Testament. And the writer is in any case more taken up with the meaning than with the precise words used. Comment and quotation are often merged, as was then quite customary. And if we look the references up, we find that the writer – like other New Testament writers – exercises a surprising freedom of interpretation. Some verses are filled with meaning far beyond their original context. See 'New Testament Quotations from the Old Testament'.

The quotations in this chapter are from Psalm 2:7; 2 Samuel 7:14; Psalm 97:7 or Deuteronomy 32:43; Psalm 104:4; Psalm 45:6-7; Psalm 102:25-27; Psalm 110:1.

2 Jesus Christ – the Son of man

If the message of the angels – that is the law of Moses, Acts 7:53 – proved true, how much more important is the Son's message of salvation (1-4).

We are not to underestimate Christ because he shared our human nature. God created man for a great destiny (7-8) – a destiny we can now realize, because Christ has suffered and died for all men (9-10). He became man to win forgiveness for us. He became man to help us.

Verses 6-8, 12, 13: the texts quoted are Psalm 8:4-6; Psalm 22:22; Isaiah 8:17-18.

Perfect (10): the idea is not moral improvement, but that through suffering Jesus was perfectly able to do the task God gave him. Only by this means could he make man's salvation possible.

Verse 17: this idea is more fully explained in chapter 5.

3 Jesus Christ – greater than Moses

Moses made Israel into a nation. He led them out of slavery in Egypt and through the desert. He gave them God's law and their forms of worship. No man was more revered by the Jews, and rightly so. But he could never be more than God's faithful servant. Jesus is God's Son (1-6).

The readers are in a very similar position to Israel at the time of the exodus. Both have seen God at work in an amazing way. But despite this the Israelites rebelled against God in the desert – and never entered the promised land (11). What happened to them can happen to us if we now turn our backs on God.

Verse 8: see Exodus 17:1-7; Numbers 20:1-13.

4:1-13 God's rest

The parallel is made more explicit. The 'rest' God spoke of was more

than just a stable and secure life in the land he had promised. Through the psalmist (Psalm 95), hundreds of years after Joshua's day, God was still appealing to people to enter his rest. There is a spiritual counterpart to the promised land, and the passport to it is faith. We enter into God's eternal rest, his peace, as we trust him and take him at his word (3). Salvation is his gift, not a reward for our own hard work (10). And we cannot hope to conceal our real attitude from him.

4:14 - 5:10 Jesus – our great high priest

Aaron (5:4) was the first high priest of Israel appointed by God. He was the intermediary between a holy God and a sinful people, the go-between who represented each to the other. The Jewish religion – the system these Jewish Christians were tempted to return to – still had its high priest. But in Christ we have a high priest who fulfils all the statutory requirements, and far more, because he has no need to atone for his own sins. He is the perfect high priest appointed by God as mediator for all time.

Under the Jewish law the same sacrifices were offered year after year. Jesus' sacrifice of himself was made once and for all.

Melchizedek (5:6, 10): the king/priest of Salem to whom Abraham gave a tenth of his possessions (Genesis 14:18-20). Chapter 7 develops the thought of these verses.

5:8: not learning to obey, but learning the full cost and meaning of obedience through suffering.

5:9: see on 2:10.

5:11 - 6:20 Warning – and encouragement

The writer breaks off to do some plain speaking. His readers have got stuck at the ABC of Christianity (5:11 - 6:3). Their lack of progress is bad enough in itself. But it is symptomatic of something much more serious. They are in danger of throwing the whole faith overboard. The situation calls for shock tactics. So the writer spells it out. If, despite all their Christian knowledge and experience, they deliberately reject Christ there is no hope for them. It is not that God refuses to forgive, but that they refuse the one available means of forgiveness. And their thinking is leading them in this direction, though they have not yet reached the point of no return.

But he is quick to comfort. He cannot believe they will go so far – or that God will allow it. Faith and perseverance will lead to the realization of all God has promised. The presence of Jesus in heaven guarantees that hope (6:19-20).

6:2: 'baptisms' – not the usual word for Christian baptism. The teaching may be on the difference between Christian baptism and Jewish ritual washings. 'Laying on of hands', at baptism and commissioning for special service, symbolized the empowering of the Holy Spirit.

7 A new high priest

6:20 brings us neatly back to the point made in 5:10 – this chapter carries it forward. Jesus has superseded the Levitical priesthood by becoming high priest for all time. This fact is anticipated in Psalm 110, where the Messiah is described as priest of a different order. The shadowy figure of Melchizedek (Genesis 14:18-20) reflects something of the nature of Christ's priesthood – the dual role of king *and* priest; the timelessness of it; its superiority to the old order. Levi in a sense acknowledged this by paying Melchizedek tithes through his ancestor Abraham! If the priesthood of Aaron and his fellow Levites had been good enough, no change would have been needed. Neither these men nor their work was perfect. Jesus is. They were not able to meet our needs. Jesus can and does.

8 A new covenant

The Old Testament is constantly pointing forward. David anticipated a new priesthood. Jeremiah (31:31-34) spoke of a new covenant – because the old agreement God had made with his people (Exodus 34:10-28; 20) had already broken down. The system of sacrifices instituted by Moses, and the tabernacle he had built, are only copies. In Jesus we have the original – the pattern – the reality. When Jesus offered up himself as the one final sacrifice (7:27) he arranged

a new and better covenant between God and men – the one Jeremiah looked forward to. And the new supersedes the old.

9 - 10:18 Shadow and reality; the perfect sacrifice

The writer's thoughts are again back in the time of the exodus, when God made his covenant with Israel through Moses and gave them the pattern on which to construct the tabernacle. (The temple was later modelled on it – but it is not the temple he has in mind here.) Although God had chosen to live with his people, in a tent like their own, they had no right of access to him. The layout of the tabernacle and the whole system of animal sacrifice emphasized God's apartness and the people's sin. Only one man (the high priest) once a year (on the Day of Atonement) was allowed to enter the inner sanctuary (9:7). And the very repetition of the sacrifice made its ineffectiveness all too clear (9:25).

These things are the shadow. They point forward and prepare men for Christ, who is the reality. When Christ came, the whole system was reformed (9:10). As perfect high priest he offered himself as the perfect sacrifice (9:14) – a single offering for sin, valid for all time. He has dealt with human sin once and for all, removing the stain completely – something the Old Testament animal sacrifices lacked the power to do (10:10-12). And his death brought the terms of his will (the new covenant) into effect (9:16ff.). We are forgiven. We can come to God. No further sacrifice is needed (10:9).

10:19-39 No turning back

The way is open. We can come right into God's presence – if only we will. Christ's death has made it possible (19-22).

If we reject that sacrifice there is no other. We condemn ourselves to God's judgement. He holds us accountable for our actions (26-31).

No one pretends the Christian life is easy (32ff.). It calls for courage and perseverance. But it is infinitely worth while. If we turn back, we are lost – eternally. If we hold on, and keep trusting, God will give us all he has promised.

Through the curtain (20): see Mark 15:38.

11 Faith

The faith under discussion here – following directly on from 10:38-39 – is not man's first unsteady step towards

God. It is a life-long attitude of confident reliance on God's word. To have faith is to be certain – not of the here and now, the tangible things – but about things future, the unseen realities (1). The Old Testament abounds in examples of men who possessed a faith like this, and who lived and died accordingly. God has given us their record – he is proud to own them and be known as their God (16). They all looked forward to the time when God would fulfil his promises, but none of them lived to see it (13). Because God planned to include us too – to save and perfect every one of his people through Christ (39-40).

Abel demonstrated his faith – and was killed (Genesis 4). Enoch walked by faith – and lived (Genesis 5:21-24). Noah's faith saved his whole family (Genesis 6-8). Abraham's took him away from his settled life at home (Genesis 12:1-7) and made him an alien and refugee. Faith made him willing to offer up his only son, trusting that God would bring him back to life (Genesis 22). Isaac, Jacob and Joseph in turn all demonstrated their belief in God's promise (Genesis 27; 48; 50:24-25). Faith overcomes fear (23). It determined Moses' choice to leave court and throw in his lot with a nation of slaves (Exodus 2; 12; 14). Jericho was taken by faith, not superior force (Joshua 2 and 6). And so on through the Judges – Gideon (Judges 6 - 7); Barak (Judges 4); Samson (Judges 15 - 16); Jephthah (Judges 11 - 12) – through King David and the prophets. Daniel's faith saved him from the lions (33; Daniel 6). Elijah and Elisha brought the dead back to life (35; 1 Kings 17; 2 Kings 4). In answer to faith, God has given men remarkable triumphs and victories. But not always. Faith is demonstrated – equally – through those who have endured imprisonment, torture and death. Jeremiah was beaten and imprisoned (36; Jeremiah 38); Isaiah, it is said, was sawn in half (37); Zechariah was stoned (37; 2 Chronicles 24). And there were many more.

12 The incentive to go on

We are being watched by these great heroes of faith. They are crowding round the track to see us run. Let us strip off everything that hinders, and run the Christian race with all we have. Christ did not give up when the going got hard; neither must we. When we suffer, it is not because God does not care – but because he

The people of Israel came to Mt Sinai in fear, to the blast of the trumpet. The Christian, by contrast, comes to 'Mt Zion, the city of the living God'.

cares enough to discipline us for our own good. We must not be discouraged and give up.

We have come to God by a better way than the terrors of Sinai (18-21; Exodus 19) – through Christ himself. But we must not forget who God is. We do well to listen carefully to what he says (25) and take his warnings to heart (15-17), because our life depends on it. One day the world as we know it will cease to exist. We need to be sure we have put first things first.

Esau (16-17): see Genesis 25:29-34; 27:34-40.

13:1-17 Pleasing God

God is concerned with the whole of life – with how we use our homes; how we respond to the need of others; with marriage; with our use of money. We grow strong as Christians, not by a code of religious observance, but by obeying God. Those who depend on the Jewish sacrifices cannot benefit from Christ's sacrifice. It is a straight choice – and the principle still holds good. Christ offers salvation to all, but there is an exclusiveness at the heart of Christianity which men have always found hard: one, and only one, sacrifice for sin; one, and only one, way of coming to God. He calls us to identify ourselves unashamedly with him (13).

13:18-25 Personal messages

The writer closes with a deeply moving prayer and blessing (20-21). He has intended his letter to be one of encouragement, not censure. He hopes to see the readers soon.

Verse 24: this may mean the letter was sent to Italy; equally it may mean from Italy.

JAMES

James is the first of a group of letters addressed to Christians in general (see on 1:1), rather than to a particular church. It is an extremely practical letter about the Christian life. Christian freedom can be a heady thing to people previously bound by a strict legal code of conduct. If salvation is God's free gift, what does it matter how we live? There is no question in James' mind – it matters immensely. In fact we can tell whether someone's faith is real by how they behave. Genuine faith in Christ *always* spills over into the rest of life. It affects our basic attitude to ourselves, to other people, and to life in general. There should be no discrepancy between belief and action. James reminds us of the need for genuinely Christian standards and values in every area of life. It is so easy to let things slip; so easy for the world around to squeeze us into its own mould, to convince us that there are no absolutes, no black and white, only grey. The early Christians needed the letter of James – and so do we.

We know little or nothing of how the letter came to be written, or who it was sent to. We are not even sure who the author was. But the most likely candidate is the James who was Jesus' brother. He became a Christian when he saw the risen Jesus (1 Corinthians 15:7) and went on to become a leader in the church at Jerusalem (Acts 12:17; 15:13ff.; 21:18). The letter was written early, but the exact date is unknown.

1 Deeds not words

This somewhat staccato chapter mentions almost all the topics dealt with more fully later: testing (2, 12-15), endurance (3; 5:7-11), wisdom (5; 3:13-18), prayer (5-8; 4:2-3; 5:13-18), faith (6; 2:14-26), riches (9-11; 2:1-13; 5:1-6), the tongue (19, 26; 3:1-12; 4:11), Christianity in action (22-25; 2:14-26). The crisp, succinct style and some of the themes remind us of Proverbs in the Old Testament and the Sermon on the Mount in the New (Matthew 5 - 7).

James' comments in this chapter provide us with a fair idea of what a Christian should be like. He has a positive attitude to the difficulties of life, knowing their value. He does not blame God when things go wrong. He knows where to turn for help and guidance. His values are right. He has control of his tongue and his temper. He sets himself to discover God's standards and to live them out. He puts faith into practice – and it shows.

Twelve tribes in the dispersion (1): the Dispersion was a technical term for the Jews scattered abroad. Here the phrase symbolizes all God's people.

Verse 27: real religion shows itself in care for the needy and in an exem-

Two superior Greeks are pictured on these coins: James criticized his readers for snobbery, paying more attention to the rich than the poor.

plary life. But James is not saying that these things are all God looks for.

2:1-13 Social distinctions

We all have a natural tendency to play up to social superiors and despise those below us on the social scale. But Christians must not make these distinctions. We are to treat everyone with equal respect – regardless of status, intellectual ability, race or colour. When we fail to do so we are breaking one of God's greatest commandments (8; Mark 12:28-31).

Law of liberty (12): the law of Christ, under which we are forgiven and set free from sin – something the law of Moses could not do.

2:14-26 Faith and actions

Faith that stops at words is not faith at all. Even the devil believes in God in that way, but it won't save him from God's judgement. Faith is proved – and develops – as we act on it. God accepted Abraham (Genesis 15:1-6; 22) and Rahab (Joshua 2) not because they *said* they believed him, but because they proved it by what they did. It is a good test.

Verse 24: only by taking this right out of context can James be made to contradict Paul (Romans 4). James is discussing the difference between real faith and mere words; he is not saying we can earn salvation.

3:1-12 The ambition to teach – and controlling our tongues

The man who wants to be a teacher in the church must first learn to control his tongue. A wrong word in public can have serious repercussions. James' terrible description is no exaggeration. Words can be so destructive – wrecking character, reputation, relationships, undoing years of good work. By one careless, venomous, inflammatory remark we can unleash forces we are powerless to stop. What is said can never be unsaid. If we can iron out the contradictions here, we have our whole personality under control.

Cycle ... (6) 'the entire course of our existence' (Good News Bible).

3:13-18 True wisdom

Christian wisdom is a very different thing from being worldly-wise. The worldly-wise are full of selfish ambition, eager to get on, asserting their own rights. God reckons a man wise when he puts selfishness aside and shows disinterested concern for others. This kind of wisdom is seen in a man's personality and behaviour – not in mere intellectual ability.

4 - 5:6 God's way – or the world's?

Christians can sell out to the world – the hostile, unchristian, anti-God world – and not even realize it. It happens every time we let the things we want from life overpower our judgement and Christian principles. This is the stuff wars are made of. It happens when we try to use prayer to further our own ends. It happens when we set ourselves up as judges of other people. It happens when we plan our lives without reference to God. It happens when wealth and pleasure become an end in themselves and justice flies out of the window.

How can we avoid it? By prayer – the right kind of prayer. By continually resisting the things we know are wrong. By seeking God out; by seeing ourselves as we really are and submitting whole-heartedly to him. By realizing we can count on nothing in this life – not even tomorrow – and depending on him. 4:15 expresses our whole attitude to life – not just tacking an automatic 'God willing' on to our own plans.

There is a special danger in affluence (5:1-6; 2:6-7). It cocoons people in false security. They are so well-insulated that they cease to feel for those who are cold and hungry. And values become warped. This life is so pleasant they lose sight of eternity. But God sees it all – and judges. Compare this with Jesus' parable of the rich fool (Luke 12:16-21).

5:7-20 Patience and prayer

Job is our model of patient endurance of suffering, and its reward; Elijah our example of the power of prayer (1 Kings 17:1; 18:1, 4). The Christian life is God-centred. In trouble we pray; in joy we praise. Believing prayer is a force to be reckoned with. God heals the sick and forgives sin in response to it. It is the prayer, not the oil, that is important. And there is nothing more worth while than bringing a man back to Christ, who can cover all his sin. Heaven itself rejoices (Luke 15:7).

1 AND 2 PETER

Peter met Jesus first of all through his brother Andrew (John 1:40-42). The two brothers came from the fishing-village of Bethsaida. But they were living at Capernaum, at the northern end of the Lake of Galilee, when Jesus called them to leave their fishing business and become his disciples. Peter quickly became the leader and spokesman of the group of twelve men who were with Jesus right through his ministry. He was one of the inner three who saw some of Jesus' greatest miracles and who were allowed to see him in his true glory (Mark 9; 2 Peter 1:16-18). But when Jesus stood trial, Peter, for all his fine words, denied all knowledge of him – a fact he never forgot. Knowing his remorse, Jesus appeared to Peter before any of the other apostles after the resurrection. And he became the leader of the new-born church, as Jesus had predicted (Matthew 16:13-20) – the very first to preach the gospel (Acts 2). After a lifetime of preaching and teaching (accompanied in his travels by his wife), tradition has it that Peter was crucified head downwards in Rome during the Emperor Nero's terrible persecution which began in AD 64.

The letters. The first letter was sent to scattered groups of Christians in the five Roman provinces which covered the greater part of modern Turkey, north of the Taurus mountains. Peter most probably wrote from Rome (see on 5:13), at the outbreak of Nero's persecutions. He had John Mark with him, and Paul's companion Silvanus (Silas) to help him write. Christians in other parts of the Empire would soon be suffering as they were in Rome. Peter's message is one of comfort, hope and encouragement to stand firm.

The second letter mentions neither place of writing nor destination. Scholars have very great doubts whether the letter is really Peter's. It certainly differs in language and subject from 1 Peter – and some scholars point out anachronisms and believe the writer 'borrowed' from Jude. It is possible that a disciple of Peter wrote in his name, incorporating his teaching, but there is no conclusive proof. Longstanding tradition, and the care taken by the early Councils to exclude documents they regarded as forgeries incline us to assume the letter is Peter's. He is facing death as he writes (1:14). The church is beset and confused by false teaching – about Christian behaviour, and about Christ's return. His theme, therefore, is true knowledge.

1 Faith and hope
Christians can be glad, even in times of suffering. This is the way faith is tested and proved genuine. The dark days are short in comparison with the joy that lies ahead, when hope will be realized and we shall come into our promised inheritance. These are the realities nothing can change. One day soon we shall see the Lord we love and trust – and then what inexpressible joy and blessing. What greater impetus could there be to live as we should, modelling our behaviour on what we know of God's own character?

Dispersion (1:1): see on James 1:1.
Verses 10ff.: the Old Testament prophets had a message for their own generation – but they also looked to the future, when Christ would come. The author of Hebrews writes in very much the same vein (11:39-40).

2 - 3 Instructions for living
Remember who you are (2:1-10) – God's own people, chosen to make known the wonderful things he has done and still does. We are all being built into the fabric of a living temple which rests on the work of Christ. The world sees God in the lives of his people, individually and collectively.

The world at large and the powers that be (2:11-17). The Christian will always be suspect because he is a 'foreigner' in the world – but he must ensure that the accusations are groundless. Civil authorities must be obeyed – even if Nero is emperor! (See also Mark 12:17; Romans 13:1-7.) Christians in Peter's day had to live down unsavoury rumours that they practised incest, held sexual orgies and even indulged in cannibalism.

Slaves (2:18-25). The emphasis all through this section is on accepting authority and giving respect and loyal service where it is due, no matter what the other man is like. If we suffer unjustly, we have Christ's example before us.

Wives and husbands (3:1-7). In every case Christians are to do what is right, not insist on their own rights. Love and respect – sheer quality of life – is the surest way to win over a non-Christian partner. Christian character is more important in a woman than the latest fashion. The Christian husband, for his part, will be considerate. Prayer withers in an atmosphere of friction.

First-century ornament from a necklace; Peter exhorts his readers to avoid ostentatious dress.

In summary (3:8-22). Be at one. Be loving. Be humble. If suffering comes, let it be undeserved, let it be for doing good.
Living stone (2:4): a favourite New Testament metaphor for Christ (see Mark 12). The quotations are from Isaiah 28:16; Psalm 118:22; Isaiah 8:14-15.
Spiritual sacrifices (2:5): see, e.g., Romans 12:1; Hebrews 13:15-16.
Spirits in prison ... (3:19-22): Peter seems to say that between his death and resurrection Jesus preached (or proclaimed his triumph) to the spirits of the disobedient men (or fallen angels – see 2 Peter 2:4-5; Genesis 6:1-8) of Noah's day. The flood-water which destroyed the world saved Noah and his family by floating the ark. Similarly, Peter sees the water of baptism as a symbol of rescue from death. Of course it was the ark, not the water, which really saved Noah. So it is the risen Christ, not baptism in itself, who saves those

who trust him and are cleansed from sin.

4 - 5 When suffering comes
Peter anticipates a time of suffering and persecution for his readers. When it comes, they must be ready – level-headed, alert, prayerful and unfailingly loving to others. It should come as no surprise to Christians to suffer for Christ's sake. It is a cause for joy, not discouragement! Christ's suffering was the prelude to glory. So it is for the Christian. God always keeps his promises.

As a leader himself – and a witness of the crucifixion – Peter appeals for a real 'shepherd spirit' in all church leaders (5;1-4; and see John 10 and 21:15ff.). And the younger people must respect their authority. Every Christian needs to acquire a genuinely humble spirit, like Christ's. He also needs a stout heart to face formidable and unrelenting opposition (8-9). But God cares for us. He perfects our Christian character through the things we suffer. He is in control!

Head of Nero, the Roman Emperor behind the persecution which was the subject of Peter's first letter.

4:1-2: the reference may be to the Christian's identification with Christ in his death, and the freedom from sin – the new life – that follows.
To the dead ... (4:6): i.e. Christians who are now dead. They suffered the judgement of death, like other men, but they will live.
Love covers ... (4:8): a proverb also quoted in James 5:20.
Judgement (4:17): the thought may link with 4:6, see above.

5:5ff.: these verses echo the thought in James 4:6ff. The 'roar' is intended to frighten, but Satan no longer has the power to destroy the Christian.

Silvanus (12): Silas, companion to Paul on his second missionary journey (Acts 15:22, 32ff.), and his associate in writing to the Thessalonians.

Babylon (13): probably a code-name for Rome (see on Revelation 17).

Mark (13): see introduction to Mark's Gospel.

2 PETER
1 Knowing God and his message
The purpose of our salvation is that we should become like Christ (4). And Christian growth depends on knowledge (2-3) – the kind of knowledge which gets translated into action (8). Peter shares Paul's determination to know Christ, and to put every effort into growing like him (see Philippians 3:10-16). Like James, he stresses the fact that real faith shows itself in the quality of life, in love and goodness (5:11; see James 1:26-27; 2:14-17).

The Christian message does not rest on myth and legend, but on the evidence of eye-witnesses (16). Peter actually saw Jesus in all his glory – transformed (see Mark 9:2-8). We have in addition the written testimony of the prophets – not simply human opinion, but a word from God himself.

Verse 14: Peter, facing death, recalls the Lord's words: John 21:18-19.

Verse 19: the scriptures light our path through life until the dawning day of Christ's return. Psalm 119:105; Revelation 22:16.

Verse 20: this may mean either 'it is not the interpretation that authenticates the prophet's message', or 'the true interpretation, like the message itself, is God-given'.

2 False teachers
The argument of this chapter is closely paralleled in Jude 4-16. To be forewarned is to be forearmed – so Peter warns his readers against the false teachers who have already disrupted other Christian groups. They are anti-authority. They respect no one. They teach self-gratification, and their dissolute lives deny the Lord and shame his church. They are out to exploit others for profit. And they are merchants of false hope, like a dried-up spring in the desert, or clouds that promise rain but blow over (17). Their punishment is certain. The Old Testament affords plenty of examples of God's punishment of wicked men, and his ability to rescue those who are his: the flood, and the saving of Noah (Genesis 6-8); the destruction of Sodom and Gomorrah, and the rescue of Lot (Genesis 19).

Angels (4,10-11): see on Jude.

Balaam (15): it seems this true prophet turned traitor when the price was high enough (Numbers 31:16).

Verses 19-22: for all they had learned of Christ, their conduct makes it clear that their basic nature remained unchanged.

3 The certainty of Christ's return
There will always be men who scoff at the idea of Christ's return – the more so as time passes. But Peter and Paul are unanimous on the subject (15-16; see e.g. 1 Thessalonians 4:13 - 5:11; 2 Thesalonians 2). We have God's word that it *will* happen; a word of such power that it brought our whole world into being (5; Genesis 1:3). If God 'delays' it is out of mercy, not weakness. The certainty that Jesus will come, and that it could happen any day, is our strongest incentive to Christian living. We want to be ready. We want him to be pleased with what he finds – and we may have only today.

Second letter (1): the first may be 1 Peter, or some other letter now lost.

Follow their own passions (3): 'live self-indulgent lives', New English Bible.

The fathers (4): either the Old Testament fathers, or the first Christians. *Fell asleep:* this is the way Jesus talked of death.

Verse 16: it is a comfort to know that Peter sometimes found Paul hard to understand! But he had a high regard for Paul's writings – placing them alongside the other scriptures. Romans 3 shows how people twisted Paul's words – they took his teaching on freedom, for example, as carte-blanche for licence.

1, 2 AND 3 JOHN

John's Gospel was written to bring men to faith. 1 John, clearly by the same person, is intended to re-assure Christians about their faith – to renew confidence shaken by false teaching. Both Gospel and letter belong to the close of the 1st century. The Christian faith was 50 or 60 years old by this time and had spread throughout the Roman Empire. John, living out his last years at Ephesus in modern Turkey – a strategic centre of the Christian church – was probably the only apostle still alive. There was pressure on many Christian groups to incorporate ideas from other philosophies as part of the faith.

John's letter was written to counter some early form of 'Gnosticism' being propounded by men who were once church members but had now withdrawn from the group. They liked to think of themselves as intellectuals – possessing a superior knowledge of God. They made a complete distinction between the spiritual (which was pure) and the material (which was evil). In practice this often led to immorality – because nothing the body did could tarnish the purity of the spirit. It also led to a denial of Christ's human nature – which was either 'make-believe' or only temporary. The Christ – being spirit – could not have died.

In this strong but tender appeal to his 'little children' in the faith, John makes it plain that these ideas cut the heart out of Christianity. If Christ did not become man and die for human sin there is no Christian faith. If any man sins deliberately and habitually he is not a Christian. God is light, and he calls men to walk in the light of his commands. He is love, and he requires his people to love one another.

1 JOHN
1 God is light
John writes as one who knew Jesus, the life-giving Word of God (see John 1:1-5), personally. He knew that Jesus was both Son of God and real man: no apparition but a person you could see and touch.

Jesus, the 'light of the world' (John 8:12), shows us that God is light. By 'light', John means not just the blinding radiance of his presence, but truth, purity, moral perfection. No one who has access to him can live in 'the dark' – dealing in sin and evil and lies, qualities opposed to his very nature. This is not to say that Christians are perfect. The searchlight of God's presence shows us up. Friendship with him involves seeing ourselves as we really are, and constantly asking his forgiveness.

2 To know God is to obey him
We are not perfect, but that is our constant aim: to become, to behave just like Christ (6). And when we fail, he has provided the remedy (1-2). Being a Christian means obeying God; doing what is right; loving, not hating, our fellow men. This is the real test of any man's claim to know God. To know is to obey.

The early Christians were taught that an arch-enemy of Christ – the embodiment of evil – would come on the scene when the Lord's return was imminent (18; the actual word 'antichrist' occurs only in John's letters, but 2 Thessalonians 2 makes the same point). John sees the 'explosion' of false teachers – who deny that the man Jesus was the Messiah and Son of God – as a sign that the time is near.

Abiding (6, 28): see on John 15.
Children ... fathers ... young men (12-14): the threefold address is probably used for emphasis. Forgiveness, knowledge of God and victory over evil are things all Christians possess.
The world (15): man organized for some end of his own without thought of God, or in open hostility to him. God, of course, loves the world of mankind (see John 3:16), despite its rebellion.
Anointing (27): John refers to the discernment the Holy Spirit gives to Christians. See also 4:4-6. He is talking about false teachers, not saying that Christians have no need of teaching.

3 Right living; true love

For the Christian – the child of God – sin is no longer inevitable. On the contrary, it is a denial of his new nature. Christ has really given us the freedom not to sin, and we are to live in the light of that fact. It is not possible for anyone born into God's family to go on breaking his law deliberately and habitually (the Greek John uses conveys the sense more clearly than our English translations: verses 6 and 9, in the light of 1:8 - 2:2). A man who behaves like this cannot be a Christian, no matter what he may say.

The Christian life-style can be summed up in the one word 'love'. The command to love one another rolls up into one all God's instructions about human relationships. But Christian love – Christ's love – is more than just words or feelings. It will inevitably touch our pocket and possessions – it may cost us life itself. We can measure the reality of our love for God by our determination to do as he says and love our fellow men. If our conscience is clear on this score, we can be confident that God will answer our prayers.

4 Distinguishing false from true; God is love

There is one basic test by which to judge any teacher – his recognition of Jesus Christ as man (emphasized here because this was the particular heresy of the day) and God. No man who denies this can possibly come with a message from God. The Holy Spirit enables the Christian to recognize truth when he hears it.

God is love. In the death of Christ for human sin he has shown us what love is (10). And if we really share his life – his nature – that love must flow through us to all around. Genuine love for God is bound to show itself in action towards others. This is John's favourite theme. But love is not trite or sentimental, nor inconsistent with plain speaking (of which verse 20 is a sample!). Love and obedience are bound up together (21). If we love and obey God we need not dread the day of judgement (17-18).

5 We can be sure

To know God is to love God. To love God is to obey God. To be his child is to love his children. Eternal life (the life of God), and the ability to defeat the anti-God forces of the world we live in, are ours as we believe in Jesus Christ as God's Messiah. God himself stands witness that Jesus is his Son. 'To believe is life, to disbelieve is death' (12). We can be sure of these things. We know he hears all we ask. We know he always answers.

The false teachers loved to talk about 'knowledge'. John makes his own list of things Christians know for a certainty. We know the gravity of sin. We know it is no longer the norm for Christians. We know we are absolutely secure in Christ. We know we belong to God in an alien world. We know that through the Son of God we know God himself, and real life.

Verses 6-8: the Authorized Version incorporates words that do not form part of the original letter, but are a late addition. These are omitted in all modern versions.

Three witnesses (8): the Holy Spirit, the baptism of Christ and the death of Christ – of which Christian baptism and the Lord's Supper stand as permanent reminders.

Verse 16: John does not say what this deadly sin is. The New Testament knows only one 'unforgivable' sin – that which attributes the Holy Spirit's work to the devil, and persistently rejects the One who makes forgiveness possible (see Matthew 12:31-32; Hebrews 6:4-6; 10:26).

2 JOHN

There is little doubt that all three letters are the work of one author – traditionally the apostle John since we know of no other apostle still alive at this time. As an apostle and senior elder of the church at Ephesus John's choice of the term 'Elder' is appropriate enough. The 'lady' is most probably a local church, rather than an individual. The 'children' would then be church members (as in 1 John); the lady's 'sister', John's own church.

Here again we have John's favourite theme: Jesus' command that those who follow him should love one another (5; John 15:12-17). To love others as Jesus loves us means keeping all God's commands. 'Love' which breaks any of the basic rules God has set to govern human relationships is not love at all. The love of Jesus is self-giving, not self-seeking.

For the Christian, love and truth go hand in hand. But he should content himself with what Christ taught. Only the false teachers are compelled to eliminate or elaborate (9-10). John is combatting the same sort of trouble here (7) as in his first letter. There had been travelling evangelists and teachers from the very start of the Christian mission, usually responsible to one of the apostles. The time had come to tighten up and refuse hospitality to anyone whose teaching contradicted the fundamental truth about Jesus Christ. It was essential for survival.

3 JOHN

See on 2 John above. This is a personal letter to an individual. **Gaius** was a common name, and it is not likely that this Gaius is the same as any of the others mentioned in the New Testament. If tradition is anything to go by, he may have been a leader of the church at Pergamum. What matters more, Gaius was a man who 'lived in (and therefore lived out) the truth'. His words, his deeds, his character were all of a piece. His life and conduct are in striking contrast to that of another local leader, **Diotrephes**. Gaius, a man of integrity, is doing all in his power to help his fellow Christians, especially the travelling evangelists and teachers who depended on Christian hospitality and support. Diotrephes is damaging John's own character, suppressing his letter, spreading lies, hugging his own position as leader and hindering missionary outreach. It seems the church has always had its petty dictators, men like Diotrephes who consider themselves indispensable. The third character in the letter, **Demetrius,** may have been John's messenger (there was no postal service!). This man's life speaks for itself. He richly deserves the high regard in which John holds him.

JUDE

The author is Jude, the younger brother of Jesus and James, now an old man (the date is uncertain, but may be around AD 80). He was already thinking of writing, when alarming news of false teaching (see below) made him pen this short, vigorous letter with all speed. The letter is obviously Jewish – full of Old Testament references and allusions, and drawing its illustrations from at least two Jewish apocryphal writings (see below). Jude is dealing with a situation very like that dealt with in 2 Peter. And in fact the bulk of Jude's letter is paralleled in 2 Peter 2. The two are so similar that either one made use of the other, or both drew on an existing tract which countered false teaching.

Jude writes to a group of Christians threatened from within by men who have 'slipped in' and are now creating division by their false teaching. These men are characterized by arrogance and immorality, and their claim to superior knowledge. They are anti-authority. They are out for what they can get. And they are self-indulgent to a degree. They will argue black is white if it suits them.

But they are marked out for destruction – as Sodom and Gomorrah were for their sexual immorality and perversion (Genesis 19); as Cain was for murdering the brother whose life showed up his own (Genesis 4); as Balaam was for betraying his position as a prophet (Numbers 31: 8, 16 – see on 2 Peter 2:15); and as Korah was for his rebellion against God-given authority (Numbers 16). The examples are carefully chosen. These are the very things of which these teachers are guilty.

Jude's intention is to stiffen the resistance to such teachers. The Christians are not defenceless, but they must make full use of their defences. They must build on 'the faith' – that definite body of truth they have been given. They must pray and use the power of the Holy Spirit. They must live in the light of Christ's coming again. There is no need to be afraid or despair, for God is indeed able to keep them from falling.

The angels (6): the statement about the 'sons of God' in Genesis 6:1-2 led to a belief in an earlier war in heaven between good and evil angels whose pride and ambition led to their downfall. It was an apt illustration for Jude's argument.

Verse 9: the story comes from the apocryphal *Assumption of Moses.* Michael was sent to bury Moses, but the devil challenged his right to the body, on the ground that Moses had murdered an Egyptian. Jude uses Michael's circumspect reply as a lesson to men to watch their words, and not to treat the devil lightly.

Verses 14-15: a quotation from the apocryphal *Book of Enoch.* Jude takes his illustrations from books he and his readers know and respect, as well as from the scriptures themselves.

REVELATION

Revelation was written about AD 90-95, though some say earlier. The author is named as John. The style and language of Revelation is so different from John's Gospel that many have concluded this writer must be a different John. But we do not know of anyone apart from the apostle so well known that he could simply describe himself as 'John'. And tradition says that the apostle left Israel to make his home in Ephesus – capital city of the Roman province of Asia, in which the seven churches of Revelation 2 - 3 are located, and itself the recipient of one of the letters.

The book was written during a time of persecution. John's own exile on Patmos (1:9) probably entailed hard labour in the island's quarries. Some Christians had been killed (2:13) and others imprisoned for their faith. And there was worse to come (2:10), as worship of the Roman emperor became obligatory. The early Christians lived in eager expectation of Christ's return. But 60 years after his death this hope was still unrealized. It was only human for some to waver. So the letters to the churches, and the book as a whole, were needed to encourage them to stand firm. God is in control, no matter how things may look. Christ, not the emperor, is lord of history. He has the key of destiny itself. And he *is* coming again to execute justice. There is a glorious, wonderful future for every faithful believer – and especially those who lay down their lives for Christ. This world and all that happens in it is in God's hands. His love and care for his people is unfailing.

John's message was conveyed in a form designed to inspire as well as instruct. The vivid symbols, only too clear to those who first heard his circular letter to the churches, would have meant little to the authorities (who were always ready to pounce with a charge of sedition). More important, they would be equally vivid to Christians of every age. Christians are still enduring the pressures of totalitarian regimes. The victory of Christ and his people is vitally relevant today, when the machine, or the state, so often takes the place of God.

In our own materialistic age it has been only too easy to miss the spirit of the book. On the one hand, instead of seeing it as something to catch the imagination, we reduce it to a timetable of events. On the other, reacting against the rational, we reduce it to fantasy and mysticism. But to understand Revelation we must see it both as a book of vision and imagination *and* as a book firmly rooted in history, proclaiming Christ as Lord of history. Today – perhaps more than ever – we need its eternal, timeless realities. And we need its perspective.

A few basic pointers to the interpretation of the book may help those coming fresh to it:

1. The first thing to establish about any Bible passage is what it meant to the original readers; to see it in the light of contemporary history.

2. Revelation belongs to a particular type of literature – apocalyptic (see note). It is poetic and visionary, expressing its meaning through symbols and imagery. To take this picture-language literally, or treat the book as a logical treatise or timetable, is to go against the whole spirit of it.

3. Revelation is rooted in the Old Testament. This is where we find the clues to the meaning of the various symbols – comparing scripture with scripture.

4. Obscure passages must always be understood in the light of passages that are clear – never the other way round.

5. This is a book of visions. The fact that John is not over-concerned about harmonizing details makes it clear that it is the main thrust of each picture which is important. We should treat visions as we do parables, looking first at the whole picture and trying to discover the main idea.

6. We are not necessarily meant to

THE SEVEN CHURCHES

ASIA

Pergamum
Thyatira
Sardis
Smyrna
Philadelphia
Ephesus
Laodicea

take John's visions as a sequence of events which follow on one after the other. The eastern mind is not so preoccupied with chronology as we tend to be.

1 INTRODUCTION: JOHN'S VISION OF CHRIST

In more than one sense this book is 'the revelation of Jesus Christ' (1). He is John's source *and* his subject. Jesus draws back the veil on future events for John to make them known. There is nothing speculative about it. These are certainties, things that will take place 'soon'. The vision of Christ is at one and the same time for John's immediate audience – the seven churches in the Roman province of Asia (western Turkey) – and for Christians down the ages. No true Christian group is ever alone and abandoned. Jesus stands among his people (12-13, 20): the living Christ in all his power and glory; the Master of life and death and human destiny.

Soon (1): we do not know God's time-scale, and the prophets tend to foreshorten the future. The word serves to remind us to be ready.

Reads aloud (3): this was how the scriptures were made known in John's day.

Seven churches (4, 11): John makes great use of the number seven (seven seals, seven trumpets, seven bowls, etc.), which usually in this book stands for completeness, perfection. Here the number is also literal. Of the seven churches only Ephesus is well known (Acts 19). Acts 16:14 mentions Thyatira as Lydia's home town. The church at Laodicea is mentioned in Colossians 4:15-16. The rest occur nowhere else in the New Testament.

Alpha and Omega (8): the first and last letters of the Greek alphabet.

Patmos (9): a small Greek island off the west coast of Turkey (see also introduction).

Lord's day (10): usually taken to mean Sunday.

Sword (16): see Hebrews 4:12. Jesus' words are double-edged. They can cut a man free, or administer judgement.

Hades (18): the place where the dead await resurrection and judgement.

Angels (20): some see this as a reference to pastors, some to guardian angels, some to the essential spirit of each church. Elsewhere in Revelation angels are always heavenly beings.

2 - 3 SPECIAL MESSAGES TO THE SEVEN CHURCHES

The letters are addressed to particular churches, but the message is for the whole church. It is worth noting that – with the exception of Smyrna and Philadelphia – the danger from within each church is more destructive than the danger from without. Jesus knows the strength and weakness of each one. The opening description reminds each church of some specially relevant aspect of his person and work.

2:1-7 Ephesus

See on Acts 19. The church at Ephesus was firmly established and possessed spiritual discrimination. There was sound teaching but an absence of the love – for Christ and one another – which had been their hallmark to begin with.

Nicolaitans (6): unknown outside this book. Their abhorrent behaviour sprang from false teaching (15), which had infiltrated the church at Pergamum.

Tree of life (7): the ban of Genesis 3:22-24 is lifted for all who are faithful to Christ. Eternal life is his to give.

2:8-11 Smyrna

The little church at Smyrna was poverty-stricken – but rich in all that mattered. Jesus' word to them is all encouragement. He has set a definite limit to their suffering – and he holds out to them the gift of life beyond the grave.

Synagogue of Satan (9): those Jews who harass the church are not God's people. See John 8:39-44.

Second death (11): explained in 20:14-15.

2:12-17 Pergamum

At Pergamum the church had made a brave stand despite external pressure, but some members had become addicted to false teaching. As a result, old pagan practices were creeping in.

Satan's throne (13): Pergamum was the principal centre of emperor-worship in the region. An immense altar to Zeus dominated the town from its acropolis. And people flocked to be healed at the Temple of Asclepius. One or all of these may be referred to.

Balaam, Balak (14): see Numbers 31:16; 25.

Food sacrificed to idols (14): see on 1 Corinthians 8.

Verse 17: *manna* (Exodus 16) – i.e. food which God supplies. The meaning of the *white stone* is unknown. The *name* stands for the whole character. In the ancient world, to know a man's name was to possess power over him.

2:18-29 Thyatira

This was another very mixed church.

'Smyrna' is modern Izmir, main city and port on the west coast of Turkey. The most important remains from Roman times is the Forum, pictured here. It was at Smyrna, in about AD 155, that the aged bishop Polycarp refused to renounce Christ and was martyred.

In many ways it was healthy. But within the fellowship there was an influential woman advocating easy compromise with the immoral, idolatrous pagan world. And many fell in with her way of thinking. There were 'Christians' who plunged deep into evil – perhaps to demonstrate their moral superiority; perhaps because they drew a false (Greek) distinction between soul and body. Those who remain faithful are promised Christ's power and his presence (the morning star – see 22:16).

Jezebel (20): King Ahab's evil wife; see 1 Kings 21:25-26.

3:1-6 Sardis

For all its reputation, the church at Sardis was dying on its feet. It was not opposition this church had to overcome but apathy, indifference and self-satisfaction.

Verse 2: it is by his life that a man demonstrates the reality of his faith. A formula of words will not save him – see Matthew 7:21.

3:7-13 Philadelphia

This letter, like the letter to Smyrna, contains no word of blame. To judge by these letters, it is not the biggest, most impressive-looking churches, or those with most prestige, which are necessarily in best spiritual shape. Christ opens the door for effective work (8 and 1 Corinthians 16:9), not to those who are strong, but to those who are faithful.

Verse 9: see on 2:9.

3:14-22 Laodicea

The worst case of all seven is a church so self-satisfied as to be totally blind to its true condition. It is so far from what it should be that Jesus stands *outside*, knocking for admittance to the lives of individuals who call themselves Christians (20). This letter is full of local colour. Banking and the manufacture of black woollen clothing made Laodicea affluent (17-18). The town was proud of its medical school, and renowned for a special ointment for sore eyes (18). Laodicea's water-supply was channelled from hot springs some distance away, reaching the town tepid (16). The church was like its water – lukewarm. There was nothing to commend it.

Beginning (14): 'the origin' (Good News Bible) or 'prime source' (New English Bible).

4 JOHN'S VISION OF HEAVEN

The scene shifts, characteristically, from what is happening on earth to what is happening in heaven. John is constantly getting this life into perspective by turning to the eternal realities. So the picture of the struggling churches fades before this sublime vision of the throne: God in control of all that goes on. Everything speaks of his power and glory, his utter faithfulness (3, and see Genesis 9:12-17), and purity (the white garments, the shining, transparent 'sea'). The 'elders', who represent all his faithful people, join with the 'living creatures', who represent the whole creation, to honour him.

Seven spirits (5): the Holy Spirit. See on 1:4 for the meaning of seven.

Four living creatures (6): similar, but not identical, to Ezekiel's 'cherubim' (Ezekiel 1 and 10).

5 - 8:1 THE SEVEN SEALS
5 The sealed scroll

At this point John begins to see the things which must take place (4:1). The scroll contains the world's destiny, revealed to John in a series of pictures (6:1 - 8:1). Only Christ has the right to set these things in motion – not by virtue of his power (the Lion) but through his sacrificial death (the slain Lamb). Chapter 4 pictured God the Creator. This chapter pictures God the Redeemer. The response to both is universal praise and worship (4:8-11; 5:8-14, and see Philippians 2:8-11).

Seven horns, seven eyes (6): i.e. all-powerful, all-seeing.

6 The breaking of the seals

The breaking of the seals sets in train a series of disasters. On the heels of conquest (2) come slaughter, famine and disease (4-8) – the classic judgements of God so often predicted by the prophets (see on Jeremiah 14:12; Ezekiel 14:21; the riders come from Zechariah 1:8). But no matter what the disaster, God is in control. His love and care for his people never fails (9-11). Verses 12-17 picture the cataclysmic events which usher in God's great day of reckoning. In apocalyptic language John depicts the disintegration of the fixed and stable world we know. See also Matthew 24:29; Joel 2; Zephaniah 1.

Verse 2: not the same figure as in 19:11.

Verse 6: the price of basic essentials is so inflated that ordinary people must give their day's wage for bread.

7 - 8:1 The people of God; the seventh seal

The four winds may be the same as the four horsemen of chapter 6 (see Zechariah 6:5). If so, John sees the forces of destruction held back while God sets his mark of ownership on everyone who belongs to him. The Christian is not promised a trouble-free life on earth. But he will come through it to the permanently trouble-free life of heaven (14-17). Solemn silence follows the breaking of the last seal. We are brought to the time of the end.

After this (1,9): indicates a new vision, not time in relation to the events of chapter 6.

144,000 (4): this number has been much debated, but it seems best to take it symbolically, as the complete total of all God's people (12 x 12 x 1000), identical with the 'great multitude' (9). We take Israel to mean, not the nation, but God's people – Old Testament believers and New Testament Christians alike.

8:2 - 11:19 THE SEVEN TRUMPETS
8:2-13 The first four trumpets are blown

The trumpets follow the pattern of the seven seals, but the judgements are intensified. The prayers of God's people play a significant part in all this (5:8; 8:3-4). The trumpets sound a note of warning. The judgements, though severe, are not total. They are intended to bring men to their senses (9:20-21). In symbolic picture-language John describes four calamities affecting the natural world – earth, sea, water and the heavens. The 'woes' of the lone eagle imply that there is worse to come. The remaining judgements directly affect mankind.

9 The fifth and sixth trumpets

Demonic forces (monstrous locusts-cum-scorpions), servants of 'the Destroyer' (Apollyon/Abaddon, 11), are next unleashed. But God sets them a time-limit (five months is the approximate life-span of the real locust). Though men are their target they have no power to touch those who belong to God (4).

The 'locusts' torture; the angel army has power to kill – within limits. Yet even in the face of the most fearsome warnings men stubbornly refuse to change their ways (20-21). This is the world we live in: a world that resists God to the bitter end; a world that prefers to make its own 'gods', to choose its own standards of behaviour.

200,000,000 (16): there were so many, John had to be told the number. He could not count them. God has colossal powers at his disposal.

10 - 11:13 Interlude; the little scroll and the two witnesses

There is a break between the sixth and seventh trumpets, as there was between sixth and seventh seals. God delays his final judgement, but not for ever (6-7). The glorious angel brings John a message for the world – a message which is 'sweet' to him as a Christian (9; and see Jeremiah 15:16; Ezekiel 3:1-3). But he derives no joy from the bitter message he must make known to those who refuse God.

Chapter 11 is difficult. John draws his symbols from Ezekiel 40-41 (the measuring of the temple) and Zechariah 4 (the olive-trees). The measuring indicates God's protection and care for his people. The two olives represent the church, faithful to the death. (The Old Testament law required that evidence must be attested by at least two witnesses – Deuteronomy 19:15.) Warring against them are the anti-God forces of the Satanic 'beast', with power to kill and dishonour, but not destroy or prevent their triumph.

10:4: John is under orders about what he writes. Not all he sees is for public knowledge.

Forty-two months (11:2): equal to 1,260 days (3), and 'a time (1 year), times (2 years) and half a time (6 months)' (12:14). This may be derived from the length of Antiochus Epiphanes' tyranny in Jerusalem, or from Israel's 42 encampments in the desert. But the precise length of the trial is less important than the fact that God has set a definite limit to it.

Sodom and Egypt (11:8): bywords for evil and oppression. The final phrase suggests Jerusalem, but it is more likely that the 'great city', stands for the city of rebel man.

11:14-19 The seventh trumpet

The seventh trumpet announces the end. Jesus reigns: the world is his kingdom. Praise God! The ark, once hidden away in the most sacred and inaccessible part of the temple, is now visible to all (19). The way into God's presence is wide open.

12 - 14 VISIONS CONNECTED WITH THE TROUBLES OF THE CHURCH

12 The woman and the dragon

John was writing for a persecuted church, and these chapters are full of encouragement to take heart. The woman (1, and contrast 17:3ff.) stands for God's chosen people, from whom first the Messiah (5), and through him the church (17), was born. The dragon bent on destruction is Satan himself (9). Verses 7-12 are a reminder that the struggle Christians are caught up in is part of a much greater conflict (Ephesians 6:11-12).

The main message is clear. Although Satan is strong and powerful – his attack fierce – his time is short. He has been overpowered by Christ: he can be overcome by Christians. He is destined for destruction, the church for triumph. God's people are at all times and everywhere under his protection.

13 The two beasts

The beast from the sea (an evil place in Jewish thinking) is a composite creature drawn from the four beasts which represent successive world empires in Daniel 7. With its crowns and horns (sovereignty and power) and its open defiance of God, it stands for the authoritarian anti-God state. It derives its power from the evil one (2, 4) and is it seemingly indestructible (3). It dupes the world, but not the Christian (8).

The second beast – the pseudo-lamb which speaks with Satan's voice (11) – is state-sanctioned, state-dominated religion. 16:13; 19:20 identify it as the 'false prophet'. It apes the real thing, and misdirects men's worship. Refusal to worship cost some their lives (15), others their livelihood (17). For John, the two beasts were the Roman Empire and emperor-worship. But every age – our own included – has its equivalents.

Forty-two months (5): see on 11:2.

The mark (17): indicating ownership, and acceptance of the beast's authority. Men bear either the 'mark' of the world or the 'seal' of God – and it shows (16; 7:3).

The number (17-18): many have tried to identify an individual (e.g. Nero Caesar), since the letters of the alphabet doubled as numbers in ancient times. But the key may lie in the symbolism of the numbers, 6 being 'a human number', the number of man. No matter how many times repeated, it always falls short of 7, God's number. No matter how powerful the 'beast', it is not God.

14 The joy of the redeemed; the harvest

This chapter stands in dramatic con-

trast to chapters 12-13. In the world
God's people can expect implacable
hostility. In God's kingdom the tables
are turned (compare 9-11 with 13:15-
17). The world sets its face against
God; God sets his face against evil.
He offers men a gospel which is
timeless (6); the greatest of world-
powers is temporary (8). In the end
there will be absolute justice. All that
is good will be lovingly harvested; all
that is evil, totally crushed (13-20).
Verses 3-4: see on 7:4. The Bible
nowhere implies that sexual intercourse is in itself defiling, or that it is
more godly to be celibate than married. Verse 4 must therefore refer to
those who are faithful to God. The
prophets frequently use the same fig-
urative language: idolatrous Israel is
a 'prostitute', an 'adulteress'. The
'first-fruits' are that part of the world
harvest which belongs to God.
Babylon (8): see on chapter 17.
One like a son of man (14): since he
is under orders (15) this must be an
angel, not Christ himself.
1600 stadia (20): the *stadion* was
about 202 yards. But *1600 stadia* is
clearly another symbolical number –
4 (which stands for the earth) x 4
x 10 x 10 = the complete destruction
of the wicked throughout the earth.

15 - 16 THE SEVEN LAST PLAGUES
The great disasters of human history
are warnings of the final, total calamities which will overtake those who
refuse to listen. The plagues John
describes were vividly recall those
which fell on Egypt at the time of the
exodus. But first we see the joy and
security of God's people. They are
not subjected to the final terrors,
which are specifically directed
against evil (16:2, 9, 11). Again and
again in Revelation heaven is seen as
a place of song – not everlasting,
lugubrious, dutiful hymn-singing, but
spontaneous song. In heaven life is
so good, people so utterly happy and
carefree that they just cannot help
singing. Praise, at last, comes
naturally.
Song of Moses (15:3): the great
rejoicing after the crossing of the
Red Sea (Exodus 15). Both songs are
songs of deliverance and freedom.
16:12: the Euphrates separated the
civilized world from the barbarian
hordes beyond.
Armageddon (16): the hill (mound) of
Megiddo, the famous fortress on the
edge of the plain of Jezreel which

guarded the pass through the Carmel
range. The scene of so many battles,
it came to stand for battle itself.
The great city ... great Babylon (19):
see on chapter 17.

17 - 20 GOD'S FINAL TRIUMPH
17 - 19:5 The fall of Babylon
So often and so vigorously did the
Old Testament prophets denounce
the literal Babylon (see references
below) that it became a byword for
human pride and vainglory. For John
and his readers, Babylon, the luxury-
loving prostitute, was Rome, city of
the seven hills (see verse 9) – pamp-
ered, decadent Rome; Rome, where
Christians were thrown to the lions
and burnt alive as public entertainment; Rome, the cess-pit of the
Empire. But every age has its 'Babylon', the personification of all the
greed and luxury and pleasure which
entice men away from God; the
things that promise so much and give
so little. And Babylon, the epitome
of all that cheats, is doomed!
   Chapter 18, describing Babylon's
fall, echoes the spirit and language of
all the great 'downfall' prophecies of
the Old Testament. (Isaiah 13-14, 24;
Jeremiah 50-51; Ezekiel 26-28.) It is
one final, comprehensive pronouncement of doom on every power in
every age that grows fat on evil and
treats men as mere commodities to
be bought and sold (13). God's
people are tempted to come to terms
with the world. But they are called to
take an uncompromising stand (4).
They will be vindicated. Justice will
be done. It is so certain, it can even
be said to have happened already.
Babylon *has* fallen!
Was and is not (17:8): at times evil
powers rampage through human history; at times they go underground –
but they always return.
Seven kings (17:10): these may be
emperors, or empires.
Ten kings (17:12): sometimes taken
to mean Roman emperors, but John
is describing a future coalition.
19:2-3: this is not sheer vindictiveness, or gloating over the fate of
others. God's people stake their lives
on his truth and justice. They rejoice
to see militant, unrepentant evil
overthrown.
**19:6-10 The wedding-feast of Christ
and his bride, the church**
John paints a lovely picture. The
bride's wedding-dress has been
woven out of all those truly Christian

acts in which the Lord himself takes pleasure.

Verse 10: John would hardly need to be told to worship only God (here and again at 22:9). But presumably some in the church needed this lesson (compare Hebrews 1).

19:11-21 Christ victorious

Satan's two henchmen and their allies are now seized and destroyed – in a 'war' without weapons, armour, or battle, so great is the power of Christ.

A name (12): see on 2:17.

20 Evil eradicated; the overthrow of Satan; the last judgement

There has been a great deal of argument over the meaning of this chapter – which contains the Bible's only mention of a 'millennium'. But first the things that are clear.

John sees Satan under God's firm control (1-3). He sees the souls of the martyrs, not every Christian (and this is important for the persecuted early church), resurrected to reign with Christ 1,000 years (4-6). At the end of it the forces of evil muster to attack God's people, but are utterly destroyed – even Satan and his henchmen (7-10). There is a general resurrection, when all men stand before God and each is judged on his own record. The verdict is life or death. And for those who live there will be no more death (11-15).

With regard to detail it pays to be cautious. The same rules of interpretation apply here as for the rest of the book (see Introduction). To ask 'where' the reign takes place, and work out a time-table of events, is to miss the spirit of the book. The idea of an earthly millennium belongs to the Old Testament, not the New. Peter simply speaks of 'new heavens and a new earth'. John himself gives no location (elsewhere in Revelation thrones, 4, are in heaven). Nor does he mention timing, or the relation of all this to Christ's return.

1,000 years (2): other numbers in Revelation are symbolic figures. 1,000 years is long enough to show God's complete authority over Satan, and to far outweigh the earthly sufferings of the martyrs.

Gog and Magog (8): see on Ezekiel 38.

Beloved city (9): the community of God's people in contrast to the 'great city' of Babylon.

21 - 22:5 GOD'S NEW WORLD

With everything evil gone, and death destroyed, what is the new age like? What John describes is a heaven-on-earth. The new life is one long unclouded wedding-day for all God's people – the happiest, most joyful time imaginable. And there is never anything to spoil it: no sorrow; no pain; no parting with loved-ones; no night even. For God is always there. He is *near*. There is no sin, outside or in, to drag us down, to spoil the perfect relationship, to leave us groping for God or to fill us with shame. The cities of the world have their riches and beauty, but they are nothing to the glorious splendour, the shining radiance, of the city of God's people. There is peace there, too, and freedom and security. It is all infinitely precious, infinitely worth while.

12,000 stadia (21:16): 1,500 miles. But this is not intended to be taken literally. It is 12x1000 (see on 7:4 and 14:20). On earth God's people seem few and scattered. But they are part of a vast community – a great heavenly city.

21:19-20: the list of jewels echoes those which were set into the high priest's breast-piece, to represent Israel.

22:2: fallen man was denied access to the 'tree of life' (Genesis 3:22-24). Now the edict is reversed. Redeemed man will never again abuse his freedom.

22:6-21 EPILOGUE

The final statements may be somewhat disjointed, but they lack nothing in vigour. John affirms the truth of what he has written. In the sternest terms of his day, he warns against tampering with it. His closing words are full of urgency. The things he has described will happen soon. Christ's coming is imminent. And men will then be fixed in their attitudes. It will not be possible to change. In the end, those who are not saved will be lost; those who do not enter into eternal life and the presence of God will be shut out for ever. So 'let him who is thirsty come'. Let him 'take the water of life' which is 'without price'.